D1566543

CONCERT LIFE
IN HAYDN'S VIENNA:

Aspects of a Developing Musical and Social Institution

CONCERT LIFE IN HAYDN'S VIENNA:
Aspects of a Developing Musical and Social Institution

by
Mary Sue Morrow

SOCIOLOGY OF MUSIC NO. 7

PENDRAGON PRESS
STUYVESANT, NY

To my parents

THE SOCIOLOGY OF MUSIC SERIES

No. 1   *The Social Status of the Professional Musician from the Middle Ages to the 19th Century,* Walter Salmen, General Editor (1983) ISBN 0-918728-16-9

No. 2   *Big Sounds from Small Peoples: The music industry in small countries* by Roger Wallis and Krister Malm (1984) ISBN 0-918728-39-8

No. 3   *A Music for the Millions: Antibellum democratic attitudes and the birth of American popular music* by Nicholas Tawa (1984) ISBN 0-918720-38-Y

No. 4   *Music in Society: A guide to the sociology of music* by Ivo Supič ić (1987) ISBN 0-918728-35-5

No. 5   *Excelsior: Journals of the Hutchinson Family Singers, 1842–1846* edited and annotated by Dale Cockrell (1989) ISBN 0-918728-65-7

No. 6   *Music for Hire: A study of professional musicians in Washington, 1877–1900* by Katherine K. Preston (1989) ISBN 0-918728-66-5

Library of Congress Cataloging-in-Publication Data

Morrow, Mary Sue, 1953-
  Concert life in Haydn's Vienna: aspects of a developing musical and social institution by Mary Sue Morrow.

  p. cm. — (Sociology of music: no. 7)
Bibliography: p.
Includes index.
ISBN 0-918728-83-5: $47.00
1. Concerts—Austria—Vienna. 2. Music—Austria—Vienna—18th century—History and criticism. 3. Music—Austria—Vienna—19th century—History and criticism. 4. Haydn, Joseph, 1732-1809. 5. Music and society. 6. Music—Economic aspects. I. Title. II. Series.
ML246.8.V6M87 1988
780'.7'30943613—dc19   88-23385

Contents

List of Tables   ix

List of Illustrations   xi

Acknowledgements   xiii

Preface   xv

Chapter One   Private Concerts   1

Chapter Two   Public Concerts   35

Chapter Three   Public Concert Locations   65

Chapter Four   Business and Financial Aspects of Concert Giving   109

Chapter Five   Public Concert Programs   141

Chapter Six   Performers and Performance Practice   165

Chapter Seven   The Treatment of Viennese Concerts in Periodicals   191

Chapter Eight   The Cultural Context of Viennese Concerts   223

Appendix One   Public Concert Calendar   237

Appendix Two   Private Concert Calendar   365

Appendix Three   Concert Calendar Index   413

CONTENTS

Appendix Four   Private Concert Patrons   463

Appendix Five   Foreign Language Quotations   473

Bibliography   523

Index   543

List of Tables

Table 1.	Oratorios Given by the Gesellschaft der Associierten Cavaliere, 1786-1792	11
Table 2.	Private Oratorio Performances, 1793-1797	12
Table 3.	Private Concert Patrons	16
Table 4.	Oratorios Presented in the 1750s	40
Table 5.	Concert Participants, 1754-1764	42
Table 6.	Court Theater Officials, 1776-1810	67
Table 7.	Burgtheater Dimensions, 1788 (Floorplan)	75
Table 8.	Dimensions of the Viennese Theaters	90
Table 9.	Exchange Rates. Cost of 100 Gulden (Silver Coins) in Paper Money	110
Table 10.	Yearly Incomes	112
Table 11.	Salaries—Court Actors, Musicians, and Dancers (Highest and Lowest Given)	113

Table 12.   Food Prices (in Kreutzer) for   115
             Vienna in 1787.

Table 13.   Living Expenses (Gulden per   116
             Year)

Table 14.   Lighting Expenses at the   130
             Court-Controlled Theaters

Table 15.   Theater Prices   131

Table 16.   Concert Prices   133

Table 17.   Proceeds for Virtuoso   136
             Concerts

Table 18.   Proceeds for Benefit Concerts   138

Table 19.   Battle Pieces   157

Table 20.   Chamber Music on Public   161
             Concert Programs

Table 21.   Court Theater Orchestras   175

Table 22.   Private Theater Orchestras   176

Table 23.   Private Theater Orchestra   176
             Totals

Table 24.   Orchestra at *Die Schöpfung*   177
             (March, 1808)

Table 25.   Orchestra at *Il ritorno di Tobia*   179
             (1784)

Table 26.   Private Concert Orchestras   180

Table 27.   German-Language Periodicals   193
             with Viennese Concert
             Information

List of Illustrations

Plate 1.   Festsaal of the Lobkowitz   21
           Palace. Photograph, ca. 1930.

Plate 2.   Altes Burgtheater. Pen draw-   72
           ing, before 1800.

Plate 3.   Altes Burgtheater.   72
           Anonymous print, ca. 1800

Plate 4.   Altes Burgtheater. Seating   74
           plan, 1782.

Plate 5.   Altes Burgtheater. Floorplan,   74
           1779.

Plate 6.   Altes Burgtheater. Seating   76
           plan, ca. 1820.

Plate 7.   Altes Burgtheater, interior.   77
           Print, early 19th century.

Plate 8.   Altes Burgtheater, interior.   77
           Print, early 19th century.

Plate 9.   Kärntnerthortheater. Print by   79
           Johann Ernst Mansfeld, before
           1796.

Plate 10. Kärntnerthortheater.   80
           Floorplan, 1784.

Plate 11. Kärntnerthortheater. Seating   82
           plan, ca. 1820.

Plate 12.   Kärntnerthortheater, interior.   83
              Early 19th-century print.

Plate 13.   Theater in der Leopoldstadt.   86
              Print by F. Sager.

Plate 14.   Theater in der Leopoldstadt.   87
              Seating plan, ca. 1820.

Plate 15.   Theater in der Leopoldstadt,   88
              interior. Early 19th-century
              print.

Plate 16.   Theater an der Wien. Water   91
              color, ca. 1800

Plate 17.   Theater an der Wien, interior.   92
              Print, ca. 1830.

Plate 18.   Augarten. Print by Joseph   94
              Ziegler, 1780.

Plate 19.   Augarten. Print by Joseph   94
              Ziegler, 1782.

Plate 20.   Augarten Gartengebäude.   95
              Print by Leopold Porasseky.

Plate 21.   Mehlgrube. Heliogravure after   99
              the Canaletto painting of ca.
              1760.

Plate 22.   Grosser Redoutensaal. Early   105
              19th-century print.

Plate 23.   Concert Zettel.   119

Plate 24.   Concert Zettel.   145

Acknowledgements

One of the pleasures of finishing a book is taking the time to recognize all the people who have helped to make it possible. I would like first of all to thank Dr. A. Peter Brown for his help and encouragement at all stages of the project. In addition, Dr. Austin B. Caswell, Dr. Hans Tischler, Dr. Mary Wennerstrom, and Dr. Mark McKnight also read the manuscript and provided valuable comments and suggestions. The assistance and cooperation of librarians and archivists is of course essential to the successful completion of any research project; I would like to express special appreciation to Dr. Otto Biba of the Gesellschaft der Musikfreunde Archives in Vienna, and to Dr. Dirnberger and the other archivists at the Haus- H of- und Staatsarchiv. Other libraries also provided me with material and assistance, including the Vienna Stadt- und Landesbibliothek, the Musik Sammlung, Theater Sammlung, Handschriften Sammlung, and Bild Archiv of the Oesterreichische Nationalbibliothek, the Vienna Hof-Kammer Archiv, and the Theatre Collection of the Harvard University Library.

Funds for the initial research were provided by the Fulbright Commission, and a grant from Loyola University of New Orleans aided in the final preparations for publication.

A note of thanks also goes to the people who helped in the proof reading and final preparation of the manuscript, among them Mr. Lars Larson, who also did the translation of the excerpts from the Zinzendorf diaries, Mr. Ted Hall, Ms. Melissa Shelby, Mr. Ronald Aucoin, and especially my assistants, Ms. Elizabeth Miller, Ms. Lisa Wilkinson and Ms. Lorayne Kircher.

I would also like to thank Mr. Ted Hall for his support and en-

ACKNOWLEDGEMENTS

couragement during the writing and revisions. Above all, I would like to thank my parents. Without their unfailing encouragement, assistance and financial support, this project could never have been completed.

Preface

The institution of the concert occupies a central position in the musical world of the twentieth century. There is scarcely a major city which does not support at least one orchestra and several societies devoted to the organization and presentation of musical performances, and most smaller cities and towns usually boast of some sort of concert or recital series. The concert has, in fact, become such an essential part of our musical lives that we tend not only to take its existence for granted but also to assume that it has always had the form it does today. However, even a superficial glance at the history of musical performance will show that music has been written for and performed in many different environments and has served many different purposes, all influencing the style of the composer and the perceptions of the audience. To understand fully the music of any historical period then, we must understand the context in which it was heard.

Concert life in Vienna during the late eighteenth and early nineteenth centuries has not always enjoyed the best of reputations. Especially in comparison with the German capitals and London, where professional and amateur subscription series dominated the musical scene and provided a steady supply of performances, Vienna's concert structure seemed inadequate and haphazard at best to many early commentators:

> Public concerts, as the term is now understood, may be said not to have existed, and regular subscription concerts were few. Mozart gave a few series of them, but after his death there appears to have been no one of sufficient note in the musical world to make such

a speculation remunerative. Single subscription concerts given by virtuosos, and annual ones by some of the leading resident musicians, of course, took place then as before and since. The only real and regular concerts were the four annual performances in the Burgtheater, two at Christmas and two at Easter, for the benefit of the musicians' widows and orphans. These concerts, established mainly by Gassmann and Salieri, were never exclusive in their programmes—oratorio, symphony, cantata, concerto, whatever would add to their attraction, found place. The stage was filled with the best musicians and vocalists of the capital and the superb orchestra was equally ready to accompany the playing of a Mozart or of an ephemeral *Wunderkind*. Riesbeck was told ten years before that the number taking part in orchestra and chorus had even then on some occasions reached 400—a statement, however, which looks much like exaggeration.

Very uncommon semi-private concerts were still kept up in 1793. The reader of Mozart's biography will remember that in 1782 this great composer joined a certain Martin in giving a series of concerts during the morning hours in the Augarten Hall, most of the performers being dilettanti and the music being furnished from the library of von Kees. These concerts found such favor that they were renewed for several years and generally were twelve in number. According to the *Allgemeine Musikalische Zeitung*: "Ladies of even the highest nobility permitted themselves to be heard. The auditorium was extremely brilliant and everything was conducted in so orderly and decent a fashion that everybody was glad to support the institute to the best of his energies. The receipts from the chief subscription were expended entirely on the cost of the concerts. Later Herr Rudolph assumed the direction."

This man, still young, and a fine violin player, was the director when Beethoven came to Vienna, and the extraordinary spectacle was still to be seen of princes and nobles following his lead in the performance of orchestral music to an audience of their own class at the strange hours of from 6 to 8 in the morning![1]

Though many of the statements made here by Thayer—and echoed and repeated by successive generations of writers—contain

[1]Forbes/BEETHOVEN, pp. 152-53.

a certain amount of truth, his perspective actually distorts the form and significance of Viennese concerts. Problems there were, but the variety and level of performances to be heard in the Viennese Classic period certainly surpassed his meager description. Like many nineteenth-century authors, he did not acknowledge that the eighteenth century might have had a different attitude and approach to music, and like many non-Viennese, he failed to appreciate the features that made the city an attractive place for musicians, despite the frustrations they invariably encountered.

Many aspects of Viennese concert life during the late eighteenth century are indeed puzzling and problematic, most of all the apparent absence of regular concert series and concert societies. Although the city could boast of an usually large number of fine amateur musicians and many generous patrons, the first permanent society devoted to the cultivation of music and the presentations of concerts (the Gesellschaft der Musikfreunde) was not formed until 1812, very late in comparison with other European cities. That tardiness would seem to imply that the Viennese did not consider concerts to be an essential part of the city's cultural activities, an assumption strengthened by the fact that Vienna had no specially designated music room or concert hall before 1831, a century and a half after that type of facility was found in London. If indeed those two facts do indicate a subordinate role for public concerts, we might well ask why that type of attitude prevailed, and why Vienna nonetheless was able to assume the role of musical capital of Europe.

The place of private concerts or salons in the city's musical life cannot be ignored, both in their relationship to the public realm and in their function as a social institution. Long a feature of aristocratic circles all over Europe, musical salons assumed particular importance in the Imperial city, where noble families from the far corners of the Austrian empire's extensive domains gathered to spend the winter season. The wealth and splendor of these families often matched (and sometimes exceeded) that of the court itself, and their presence in the capital insured a brilliant array of musical performances. Though the very abundance of the musical salons may well have stunted the development of a complete public concert roster, the relationship between the two spheres involves more than a simple competition for audiences. Private concerts were inevitably tied to the city's class structure, so that their role cannot be evaluated without examining them from a social as well as a musical perspective.

Another issue that always arises in the discussion of Viennese concerts concerns the treatment accorded Haydn, Mozart, and Beethoven. The citizens of the Imperial city have been censured time and again for their scandalous and callous disregard for these three geniuses and have been accused of preferring instead any trivial charletan that came along. To anyone with even a slight acquaintance with the literature, the accusations are familiar: Haydn went unrecognized by the Viennese until after his triumphant return from London; Mozart was quickly spurned and forgotten by an uncaring and frivolous public; Beethoven had to fight against intrigue and public indifference to gain a hearing for his masterpieces. Like the Thayer quotation above, these oft-repeated charges and accusations contain perhaps a kernel of truth, but they reflect nearly two centuries of idolization of the classic masters, selective reading of some of the available sources, and a lack of knowledge about the cultural and musical world in which the three lived and composed. If we are to place their achievements in perspective, an objective study of their environment is essential.

Until recently, the only work to cover the subject at all was Eduard Hanslick's *Geschichte des Concertwesens in Wien*, written 1869.[2] Though an admirable study of an enormous subject, its treatment of the pre-Gesellschaft der Musikfreunde period is inadequate. Hanslick relies heavily on the *Allgemeine Musikalische Zeitung* (Leipzig) and other nineteenth-century periodicals for information and frequently generalizes from circumstances in the 1820s back forty or fifty years to a completely different era. In addition, he takes a "virtuoso" approach, devoting much of his discussion to a chronicle of performers (an incomplete one, at that), whose potential usefulness is destroyed by the absence of an index or list of sources. Otto Biba's excellent article "Grundzüge des Konzertwesens in

[2]Hanslick/CONCERTWESEN.

Wien zu Mozarts Zeit" provides the only modern comprehensive discussion of the institution, but its necessarily limited scope raises as many questions as it answers.[3]

Other studies of concerts and musical life have concentrated on the period after the founding of the Gesellschaft der Musikfreunde in 1812, in part because the existence of a central organization facilitates the location of sources. In fact, the only studies dealing with the earlier period at all focus on the short-lived predecessor of the Gesellschaft—the "Liebhaber Concerte" at the University in 1807-08. Theophil Antonicek includes them in his monograph on music in the University Festsaal, simply drawing on the account in the periodicals *Allgemeine Musikalische Zeitung* and *Vaterländische Blätter*.[4] Otto Biba's article on "Beethoven und die Liebhaber-Concerte,"[5] based on documents in the Gesellschaft der Musikfreunde archives, delves a little deeper into the society's organization and musical presentations. His and Antonicek's forthcoming collaboration on a history of the Gesellschaft should bring to light much unknown material, but still leaves the great majority of Viennese concerts uninvestigated.

The greatest problem in writing a history of Viennese concerts has always been locating and collecting the relevant source material. Because most of the pre-Gesellschaft der Musikfreunde concerts were not given under the auspices of any organization, no centralized source of information exists. Documentation is instead scattered throughout diaries, memoirs, reviews, and various archives, making it virtually inaccessible. Haydn, Mozart, and Beethoven scholars have uncovered and published many items, but references to the remainder of the Viennese musical world remain buried in archives, so that an evaluation of the classic masters in context and wider understanding of the period in general has been impossible.

The most obvious source of information—actual concert programs—are quite rare; not more than 150 survive for the period before 1810, the boundary of this survey. This low number can partially be explained by the fact that individual hand-held programs

[3]Biba/KONZERTWESEN.
[4]Antonicek/FESTSAAL.
[5]Biba/LIEBHABER.

did not become common until well into the nineteenth century. For eighteenth-century concerts, the order of pieces was announced on a program placard ("Zettel") placed outside the theater or hall and on kiosks around the city. In the absence of a bureaucracy governing the structure of concerts, the placards survived totally by chance. Those for performances in the court theaters had a better chance of survival, since the announcements for all plays and operas were saved and bound after 1776, but even here the distribution is random. For example, we have an almost complete run of concert announcements for the 1787 and 1788 Lenten seasons, but almost none for the remaining years of the decade, though other sources tell us concerts did take place.

Published descriptions of Vienna and the Viennese, written by visitors and by natives of the city, furnish a more subjective but still valuable perspective on musical life. If used with care, they can illuminate social and musical customs otherwise lost to history. Many such books appeared in the eighteenth and nineteenth centuries, all written from different viewpoints and emphasizing different aspects of the city's culture. For music, two of the most important are the observations of Charles Burney from the early 1770s[6] and those of the Berlin Kapellmeister Johann Friedrich Reichardt, whose *Vertraute Briefe* describe his visit during the winter season of 1808-09.[7] Reichardt recorded many of his experiences in the private musical salons, allowing us a glimpse into a world that left few traces of its activities. Visitors with a less musical orientation, such as Carl Gottlob Küttner,[8] Ernst Moritz Arndt,[9] or the writer of the anonymous *Vertraute Briefe zur Characteristik Wiens*[10] may have paid less attention to musical events, but nonetheless give us additional perspectives on Vienna's cultural and social ambience. No less enlightening are the comments of the Viennese about themselves. In his *Neue Skizze von Wien* for example, Johann Pezzl penned

---

[6]Burney/PRESENT STATE.
[7]Reichardt/VERTRAUTE.
[8]Küttner/REISE and Küttner/WANDERUNGEN.
[9]Arndt/BRUCKSTUECKE.
[10]CHARACTERISTIK.

a series of vignettes about many of the city's customs and institutions.[11] Joseph Richter set out to do the same with a satirical slant in his sketches known as the *Eipeldauer Briefe*.[12] Written in broad Austrian dialect, they purport to be letters of a country bumpkin living in Vienna to his cousin back in the provinces; these epistles give Richter the opportunity to lampoon all things Viennese. While this type of literature does not contribute many facts and figures, it does round out our knowledge of Viennese society as a whole.

Diaries can provide a more personal, and a more consistent viewpoint of musical and cultural activities. Two in particular, long known for their importance to music but never published in their entirety, are of significance here, especially since they provide insight into the different levels of society—aristocratic and bourgeois. The first was kept by Count Karl von Zinzendorf, a Dresden aristocrat who came to Vienna in 1761 and immediately entered the social world of the Viennese upper crust. He served in various court positions, including a tenure as Governor of Trieste (1776-82), and remained in Vienna until his death in 1813. Though he cannot be counted among the city's leading patrons of music, his social calendar took him to many important musical functions. The other diary stems from the pen of Joseph Carl Rosenbaum, a middle-class accountant who served for a time as Controller of the Stabling Accounts for Prince Nikolaus von Esterházy but left his position to marry the court opera singer Therese Gassmann. His connection with the musical world make his observations especially pertinent.

Such sources, plus archival material, court records, and a variety of studies from the fields of architectural and theater history have provided the basis for this study. I have begun with the ascension of Maria Theresia to the throne in 1740; however, few documents pertaining to concerts survive from the early years of her reign, so that the chronicle of the 1740s-60s is necessarily brief. The founding of the Gesellschaft der Musikfreunde in 1812 (and the preliminary movements toward it the previous year) marked the

---

[11]Pezzl/SKIZZE.
[12]Richter/EIPELDAUER.

beginning of a new era in Viennese concert life, so that 1810 seemed a natural ending point. Within this time span, I have tried to consider Viennese concerts from various perspectives—their organization and relation to the city's social and cultural world, the locations and environment in which they were heard, their business and financial structure, the programs, the performers, composers and critics, and finally the relationship of Haydn, Mozart and Beethoven to the overall structure.

CHAPTER ONE

Private Concerts

Musical salons in late eighteenth-century Vienna derived from the tradition of private concerts in the residences of the nobility. Many aristocratic music lovers maintained an orchestra and expected their musicians to provide whatever type of entertainment was required, be it dinner music or a full-scale concert.[1] By the end of the century (1796), however, the number of noble patrons who supported music on such a grand scale had dwindled to a handful:

> Whether it is a cooling of the love of music [Kunst], or a lack of taste, or frugality, or other causes, in short, to the detriment of art, this praiseworthy custom has been lost, and one orchestra [Kapelle] after another is disappearing until, except for that of Prince Schwarzenberg, almost none are in existence. Prince Grassalkowitz has reduced his orchestra to a wind band with the great clarinettist Griessbacher as director. Baron von Braun keeps his own wind band for table music.[2]

But the change did not signify the end of aristocratic patronage of music or the disappearance of music-making in the home. Prince

---

[1]Haydn's earliest contracts typify this type of arrangement.

[2]Schönfeld/JTWP, pp. 77-78. (I/1) The numbers in parentheses at the end of some of the notes refer to the place in Appendix 5 where the original language of the quotation cited is given. For example, (I/5) indicates the fifth quotation under chapter 1.

Hildburgshausen, for example, dismissed his orchestra in 1759,[3] but continued to give concerts in his Viennese palace the following decade, using musicians hired for the occasion.[4] The custom remained the same; only the arrangement was different. At the same time, the practice of giving formal private concerts in the home began to trickle down the social scale, with the lower nobility and the wealthy middle class assuming an increasingly active role. By the end of the century, the musical salon had become firmly entrenched in the Viennese cultural world, so that all segments of the population who had the means to participate in the city's cultural life at all could have had access to at least one or two musical coteries.[5]

The audience and participants in these salons were drawn from a populace well educated in music and eager to display the fruits of their studies, for in aristocratic circles (and hence in the middle class households that emulated them), musical talent was considered a definite social asset. Girls especially were encouraged to learn to sing or play the keyboard, since a modicum of success in those areas might help to attract a suitable husband, but a certain application to the art was also expected of boys. Although many dilettantes (the word, incidentally, did not carry the negative connotation then that it does today) probably never rose above the ranks of the mediocre, many did attain a level of excellence which rivaled—or even surpassed—that of their professional counterparts. In fact, judging from the frequent words of praise bestowed by visitors to the city, Vienna had an unusually high number of very

---

[3]Dittersdorf/AUTOBIOGRAPHY, p. 102.

[4]Count Zinzendorf attended concerts there on December 21, 1763, January 11, 1764, January 18, 1764, February 1, 1764, and March 19, 1764. See VIENNA-ZINZENDORF.

[5]It should be pointed out that the majority of the Viennese middle and lower classes simply did not earn enough money to attend public concerts or have enough social standing to attend private ones. Though they may have been able to afford the cheaper tickets at the theaters occasionally (see chapter 4), in general they do not figure in the discussion here at all. The division into "high" and "low" status concerts William Weber sees in the later nineteenth century certainly did not exist at this time. See Weber/SOCIAL.

competent amateur performers. Largely through their efforts, private concerts came into prominence.

While defining what is meant by a public concert is a fairly straight-forward matter; private concerts present more of a problem. Many types of music-making occurred in the home, making it difficult to state categorically what constituted a "concert." But a careful reading of the sources discloses patterns of social and musical purpose that allows us to group the various private performances described into no fewer than six categories, ranging from 1) spontaneous social music, 2) the more formalized after-dinner entertainment, 3) special parties and celebrations including musical performances, 4) participatory chamber music, 5) gala occasions with elaborate productions, to the 6) musical salons, or regular formal concerts.

SOCIAL MUSIC

Undoubtedly, the most prevalent type of private music-making involved spontaneous and informal performances for the family or a group of friends at a social gathering. During the course of an evening the host or hostess, or perhaps one of the guests, would be persuaded to play or sing something for the entertainment of those present:

> At Prince Galizin's where we dined with the Woynas, the Jublonowskys, Mme de Durrazzo and de Brenner, M. de St. Sarphoun, Renuer, Mme de Bassewitz and Lalotte. Afterwards we played whist, Lalotte played the keyboard [*clavecin*] and Mme de Woyna sang like an angel.[6]

The image evoked by this description, and by countless others in the Zinzendorf diaries, is one of elegant, gracious living, but the

---

[6]VIENNA-ZINZENDORF, July 13, 1790. The phrase "like an angel" was Zinzendorf's stock description of most female performers, so it can hardly be accepted as a critical evaluation. (I/2)

ever-observant Eipeldauer tells the other side of the story, when the charming lady did not sing quite "like an angel."

> She's already taken me with her to an assembly a couple of times. Oh my, cousin, it looks strange there! The ladies and gentlemen sit around in a circle and look at each other, or they chat at great length about the bad weather or about fashion, or what they've eaten or drunk. (The women usually keep everyone informed.)
>
> This lasts a little while, and then they start gaping like they haven't slept in twenty-four hours. But as soon as the lady of the house notices that the company's started to yawn, out come the cards.
>
> Or if there's a young lady in the house, she has to bang out something on the keyboard and sing, so that the ladies and gentlemen don't fall asleep.
>
> Then you have to stand around the keyboard and cry bravo, even when the young lady howls like a little dog.
>
> Finally the card games start and everyone gets lively again.[7]

The repertoire at these mini-performances was probably more prone than any other to follow the fads and fashions of the musical world and particularly favored the lighter, easier, and innocuous pieces of composers like Leopold Koželuch and Ignaz Pleyel:

> Among lady dilettantes, Kozeluch still ranks first [as a composer] for their favorite instrument, the pianoforte. But recently he is being given a run for his money by Pleyel, whose symphonies and string quartets have been generally sought after for two winters now, and who has specially transcribed some of the latter for keyboard.[8]

Though a higher level of taste certainly reigned among more accomplished dilettantes and—one would hope—among professional musicians, in general Social Music did not stand at the forefront of musical development.

[7]Richter/EIPELDAUER 1, pp. 65-66. (I/3)
[8]JOURNAL DER MODEN, June 1788:230. (I/4)

AFTER-DINNER ENTERTAINMENT

Closely allied in function to Social Music, though of a more formal nature, was After-Dinner Entertainment. Following a dinner party, a host would frequently arrange a small concert usually performed by professionals, either invited virtuosos or the host's house musicians. For such occasions, instrumental arrangements of popular operas were very popular; Zinzendorf recounts several performances, all at the palace of Prince Schwarzenberg:

> Dined at Prince S[chwarzenberg's]. The Prince's musicians played *L'arbore di Diana* [by Vincent Martin y Soler].

> Dined at Prince Schwarzenberg's with the Fürstenbergs, the Jean Liechtensteins, Caroline Fürstenberg. There were 13 of us. After dinner charming music of Mozart, *Die Zauberflöte*.

> Dined at Princess S[chwarzenberg's] with 2 Lobkowitzes, 2 Ferraris, 2 Wilzeks and the Princess Oettingen, Chaminesse de Thoren, and Mme de Wilzek. After dinner, music from *Il matrimonio segreto* [by Cimarosa] was played.[9]

These performances illustrate the difficulty of maintaining hard and fast categories for private events. Zinzendorf never refers to them as concerts, but they were formal, planned musical performances.

PARTIES AND CELEBRATIONS

Special occasions, such as birthdays or name days, also called for the presentation of some type of music. Generally the festivities included a skit, occasional poems and songs, a cantata with appropriate text composed for the event, and perhaps other musical pieces according to the talents of those involved. Rosenbaum describes a birthday party for Franz Nitschner:

[9]VIENNA-ZINZENDORF, February 11, 1788, February 19, 1793, December 25, 1793. (I/5)

Garden party at Nitschner's. . . . After dinner immediately to the garden. . . . We worked until nine o'clock. The wind hindered us a lot and spoiled much. . . . The company began to slip out into the garden before we were ready. Then the wind kept putting out what we had lit. The symphony from *Die Zauberflöte* was done first, then Nitschner sang the aria "In diesen heil. Hallen," with words befitting his father. At the end Roman candles were set off and "To the Biedermann Franz Nitschener," appeared in lights. Thereafter Therese sang the cantata by Tribensee-excellently, then "To Thalien's Priest Franz Nitschner from his brothers" appeared. A trio sung by Joseph Goldman, Therese and Weilen brought [the program] to a close. Finally comic duets were sung. In the garden supper was served. Before 12 o'clock we began to extinguish [the candles].[10]

Although on such occasions the music had a function secondary to the celebration, it was considered essential.

The amount of time, planning and money involved in arranging such events insured their relative infrequency among middle class families, particularly if there was no army of servants to assist. In 1803, Joseph Carl and Therese Rosenbaum planned and gave a big concert celebration for Therese's name day; the preparations took weeks, and it was such an event that Rosenbaum even mentioned it several years later. We can follow the entire process through its lively musical culmination in Rosenbaum's diary entries:

November 30, 1803. At dinner we agreed upon the big musicale that we are planning to give a week from tomorrow. Umlauf's sister will sing the first aria that Umlauf wrote for his sister Pepi three years ago for Th[erese's] name day, and Therese herself will sing the new grand aria that he wrote for her. [Mlle] Gyulas will play a sonata with violin accompaniment played by Mme Pepi Ringbauer. We decided already on the orchestra that we want to get in order to get a full one.

December 1, 1803. At 11 Salieri came and Therese did the Umlauf aria he likes so well with him. Th. and I discussed the arrangements for the musicale on Thursday. The fun is a lot of work.

[10]VIENNA-ROSENBAUM, June 4, 1808. (I/6)

6

December 2, 1803. Th. and I discussed what was necessary for Thursday and wrote everything down.

December 5, 1803. To the Schreyer's to invite them for Thursday. I ran into Moreau and Schmidt and invited them, and they suggested I make a quodlibit from various pieces, to which I gladly agreed. I asked Schmidt to take care of the orchestra with Umlauf. After dinner, we started arranging and organizing things for Thursday. I went to the glass shop for glasses and bottles, to Schardlager, Grandel and Nilschner for poultry.

December 6, 1803. Umlauf was here before noon. He brought us the music Dönst had written, along with the opinion that it is badly written and that much of it has to be re-written—"Fatal"—then that the two Weidingers can't come until five o'clock, and perhaps not at all. . . . In the afternoon I trimmed and readied the lamps. Therese stayed at home in the evening and cleaned the porcelain.

December 7, 1803. After dinner Umlauf came to correct the mistakes in the aria. I was mostly at the theater arranging for the orchestra and the instruments with Umlauf, Schmidt and Kothel.

December 8, 1803. Eckhart, whom I invited yesterday in doggerel, accepted in doggerel. Th. invited Babet Tepfer and her brother. Schmidt and Moreau came over and helped me carry out the beds and some other things and clean up and put things in order. I sent Moreau to the Sattmans to see if she could sing the little cantata instead of Liese Umlauf who is sick. . . . At 10:30 we met together at home. There were originally 11 people, but Kärner couldn't come because of the prince, so there were only 10 of us. Woller and his wife, Lisette, Kühnel and his wife, Umlauf, Mayer with Pepi, Th. and I. I got 3 bottles of champagne and 2 of Tokay from the Count [Esterházy] which we opened at noon. At 3:00 the orchestra arrived. We were still sitting there. They were served cold cuts, white and red wine, beer at once. At 4:00 Bernardi started playing variations with the accompaniment of the whole orchestra. He played very beautifully. Then Mme Sattman sang Umlauf's little cantata that Lippert wrote 3 years ago for Th. name day. . . . Schmidt handed out printed copies to everyone there. Afterwards Th. sang Umlauf's new aria, which was encored. Together with the orchestra of 28 there were 101 of us. . . . This number was entertained without servants and were adequately served. After the first piece, everyone was

7

served coffee. The orchestra dispersed, satisfactorily refreshed (whereby many indiscretions happened). By 6:30, excluding the white wine and beer, 40 bottles were emptied. We danced for an hour. [Pepi] Ringbauer played the violin and Sattman the piano alternating with Tandler, Schmidt, Lieber, Stegmayer on the violin, Scholl (flutist), . . . Umlauf played too, but was so inspired [begeistert] that he could barely sit up straight. Rotlauf, Sattman, Tandler, Latzl, Schmidt and Th. sang canons in alternation. Sturioni sang several arias and accompanied himself on the guitar. Later he parodied in voice and demeanor Simoni and Holleschek [Viennese opera singers]. At 9:00 Moreau and Korn started their Intermezzo "A rogue does more than he can" by Franzky. Moreau played 9 characters in 9 costumes— many were really excellent. Everyone particularly liked "handsome Carl" the coachman, (Jesas! Jesas!), the Frenchman, the quick-talking servant. Afterwards we danced again and cold cuts, coffee and other drinks were served. At 1:00 the entertainment ended with unanimous assurances that it had been a lot of fun for all. My wish that everyone leave our house satisfied appears to have been fulfilled. Rosalin sang a few little arias very artistically. She slept at our apartment—Schmidt and Tandler helped us carry in the beds, re-hang the doors, and so on. At 2:00 we went to bed. Th. and I were irritated because the coffee wasn't ready for so long. Therese distributed with me the flower bouquets among the lunch company. We slept little, were very tired and exhausted.[11]

PARTICIPATORY CHAMBER MUSIC

In some cases, the situation was reversed, and socializing took a back seat to music-making, e.g. when a small group of music lovers gathered for the express purpose of playing together. These gatherings normally took place during the day and included both professionals and amateurs. At such events, string quartets and similar chamber music were favored. Perhaps the most famous took place at Baron Gottfried van Swieten's residence on Sundays in the early 1780s. There Mozart was introduced to the works of J.S. Bach and introduced his own piano and chamber pieces to an ad-

[11]VIENNA-ROSENBAUM. (I/7)

miring audience. Some twenty years later, Beethoven participated in regular chamber gatherings at Emanuel Försters on Thursday evenings and Sundays at noon, along with Nikolaus Zmeskall and the professional musicians Franz Weiss, J. Linke, Heinrich Eppinger, Joseph Mayseder, and Johann Nepomuk Hummel.[12] Participatory Chamber Music could also assume a more social character, as implied by one of Beethoven's friends and patrons, the Countess Josephine Deym von Stritetz, in reporting a "concert" at her house, where Punto (Johann Wenzel Stich), Beethoven, Ignaz Schuppanzigh, and Nikolaus Zmeskall played Beethoven's Horn Sonata (Op. 17) and Piano Quintet (Op. 16):

> They all lunched with us and then we made music all the afternoon.[13]

By the turn of the century, chamber music mornings had become a regular part of the Viennese musical world:

> Sunday mornings, and perhaps also Fridays, are usually devoted to true music, which one never loses sight of here. The string quartets of Haydn, Mozart, Beethoven or Romberg, occasionally of Wranitzky, are usually played. The easier keyboard music of a Pleyel, Wanhall, Kozeluch is entirely out of style. Compositions of Clementi, Cramer, Beethoven and Dussek have taken its place.[14]

From this institution, the first professional string quartet developed. Around 1795, Ignaz Schuppanzigh and several other Viennese musicians began giving regular Friday morning performances at the residence of the Prince Lichnowsky, and later at Prince Rasumofsky's as well.[15] The group, known both as the Schuppan-

---

[12]Forbes/BEETHOVEN, p. 262.
[13]Landon/BEETHOVEN, p. 134.
[14]ZEW, February 2, 1805, p. 120. (I/8)
[15]Wegeler & Ries/NOTIZEN, pp. 34-36. According to Wegeler, the other three members were Franz Weiss, Kraft and Linke. Schindler omits Linke and lists both Anton and Nikolas Kraft, while Thayer adds second violinist Louis Sina. Kalischer postulates the later group included Weiss, Linke and the cellist Karl Holz.

zigh and the Rasumofsky quartet, established a name for itself, and in the following decade, Schuppanzigh organized formal subscription concerts, still in the mornings, given at the Rasumofsky palace. Reichardt reported attending several of the performances during his visit in 1808-09.

However frequent or musically significant all of these types of music-making may have been, none are really concerts in a formal sense, focusing as they did on socializing and musical participation. The final two categories, on the other hand, while certainly including both those elements, centered around a planned, rehearsed presentation of a musical program of a scope and size equaling that of a public concert. With them we reach the core of Vienna's private musical world.[16]

GALA OCCASIONS

Gala Occasions resembled events in the Parties and Celebrations category by virtue of their festive atmosphere, but their main purpose was the presentation of some large work, usually an oratorio. For many years, Baron Gottfried van Swieten, prefect of the court library, was the guiding spirit in this area:

> Every year he gives very large and splendid musical presentations where only pieces from the old masters are performed. Above all he loves the style of Händel, in which he mostly has grand choruses performed. Just this past Christmas he held such a concert at Prince Paar's, where an oratorio by this master was performed.[17]

Van Swieten's productions were supported by a group of noblemen known as the "Gesellschaft der Associierten Cavaliere," whose original members included the Princes Schwarzenberg, Lobkowitz, and Dietrichstein, and the Counts Apponyi, Batthyana, and Johann Esterházy. During the years 1786-1792, the society presented an

---

[16]The Private Concert Calendar in appendix 2 includes events from categories 1-4 only if the name of a professional performer or composer was mentioned.
[17]Schönfeld/JTWP, p. 73 (I/9)

TABLE 1. Oratorios Given by the Gesellschaft der Associierten Cavaliere, 1786-1792

1786	Handel	Judas Maccabäus
1787	Hasse	La conversione di S. Agostino
1788	C.P.E. Bach	Die Auferstehung und Himmelfahrt Christi
1789	Handel	Der Messias
1790	Handel	Der Messias
1791	Handel	Alexandersfest and Ode auf den Tag der heiligen Cäcilia
1792	Mozart	Requiem

For sources, see appendix 2. I have retained the German spelling for the Handel pieces, as they appear in nearly all the sources.

oratorio each winter, utilizing the orchestra and chorus of the court (table 1). Joseph Starzer directed the concerts until his death in 1787; at that time Mozart assumed the responsibility. The performances took place in the late afternoon (3:00 P.M.) in the court library, then were repeated in the Schwarzenberg or Esterházy palace. If the piece met with approval, van Swieten arranged a public performance at the Burgtheater or at the hall of Ignaz Jahn.[18] One of the productions was described as follows:

> Vienna, February 1788. On this day and on March 4, Rammler's cantata *Die Auferstehung und Himmelfahrt Jesu Cristo* in the excellent composition of the incomparable Hamburg Bach was performed at Count Esterhazy's by an orchestra of 86 people in the presence and under the direction of that great connoisseur of music, Baron van Swieten, with the general approbation of all the distinguished personages present. The Imperial Royal Kapellmeister Hr. Mozart directed [was

[18]Bernhardt/VAN SWIETEN, pp. 148-150. He gives the reason for the 3:00 P.M. time as lighting, but in the winter, dusk begins to fall by 4:00 P.M., so not much time would have been gained. For a discussion of the two public locations, see chapter 3.

11

concert master] and had the score, and the Imperial Royal Capellmeister Hr. Umlauf played the harpsichord. Among the singers were Mme Lang, the tenor Adamberger, the bass Saal, [and] 30 choristers. On the 7th the same piece was performed in the Imperial Royal Court Theater.[19]

The activities of the society from 1793 to 1797 are unclear, but several performances from those years could have been under its auspices (table 2). In 1798 the society surfaced again, this time in connection with the premiere of Haydn's oratorio *Die Schöpfung*. According to records in the Schwarzenberg family archives, there were ten active members at that time,[20] but other sources report as many as twenty-four:

There is a musical society here whose members are 24 of the most esteemed and richest local noblemen, i.e., the Princes Lichtenstein, Esterhazy, Schwarzenberg, Kinsky, Lobkowitz, the Counts Traut-

TABLE 2. Private Oratorio Performances, 1793-1797

Mar	93	Handel	*Alexandersfest*
24 Dec	93	Handel	*Ode auf den Tag der heiligen Cäcilia*
			Die Wahl Herkules
28 Dec	93	Handel	*Alexandersfest*
		Haydn	*Der Sturm*
15 Apr	94	Handel	*Judas Maccabäus*
31 Dec	94	Handel	*Athalie*
5 Apr	95	Handel	*Der Messias*
26 Mar	96	Haydn	*Die sieben Worte*
27 Mar	96	Haydn	*Die sieben Worte*
24 Mar	97	Handel	*Acis et Galathea*

For sources, see appendix 2.

[19]Forkel/ALMANACH 1789, pp. 121-22. (I/10)
[20]Croll/SCHWARZENBERG, p. 86.

mansdorf, Harrach, Fries, Esterhazy, among others. Baron Swieten is the founder and actual director of the society. . . . The concerts that the society gives are not limited to any one time; normally, however, they are performed during Lent in Prince Schwarzenberg's palace.[21]

Prince Schwarzenberg bore the extra expenses of lighting and security; the cost to the society ranged from 800-1000 Gulden each year, or about twice the annual salary of a theater orchestra musician.[22] Naturally the city's elite received invitations to these special occasions, but middle-class music lovers were not slighted. Rosenbaum reports that his future mother-in-law, the widow of the composer Florian Gassmann, attended the repeat performances of *Die Schöpfung* in May of 1798,[23] and the visitor Karl Gottlob Küttner was accorded the same honor in the following year.[24]

MUSICAL SALONS OR REGULAR CONCERTS

The Gala Occasions have captured the attention of historians, but the less elaborate regular Musical Salons actually formed the core of the private concert world in the winter season. During the summers, the nobility retired to their country estates to escape the heat and dust of the city, and the less fortunate who were obliged to remain turned to diversions offered by the outdoors. But the colder months witnessed a flurry of concert activity, particularly during Advent and Lent when the theaters were closed and balls were prohibited. Friedrich Nicolai noted this when he visited the city in 1780:

Whoever wishes to travel for [the purpose of hearing] music, must travel in the winter, not in the summer. One hears the best concerts and musical plays in the winter. In summer, the great

---

[21]Küttner/REISE, 3:295. (I/11)
[22]See chapter 4 for an explanation of Austrian currency and finances.
[23]VIENNA-ROSENBAUM, May 10, 1798.
[24]Küttner/REISE, 3:296. For the soloists and other details, see appendix 2.

gentlemen who maintain orchestras enjoy the pleasures of the country and do nothing with their music. The virtuosos are travelling
then, etc.[25]

In the winter season, interested music lovers would organize and
give regular private concerts in their residence, sometimes weekly, sometimes twice a week, sometimes twice a month. Table 3 lists
the significant patrons and the years of their salons, beginning with
the 1760s.

Because the sources of information about private concerts are so
spotty and incomplete, it is difficult to draw firm conclusions about
their scope and nature. On the surface, there seems to have been
a great burst of activity in the middle class and lower aristocracy
in the 1790s, a circumstance that would fit nicely with the theory
of the growing democratization of music in the late eighteenth century. However, the increase may simply be due to the fact that the
only significant source before Schönfeld's *Jahrbuch der Tonkunst von
Wien und Prag* (where the bourgeois concerts are reported) is the
diary of a nobleman who would not have moved in those social
circles and hence would not have reported on the concerts that may
very well have taken place.

The participation of individual patrons cannot be traced with
much certainty either. Some prominent families, like the Schwar-
zenbergs, the Buquoys, the Paars, the Auerspergs, are mentioned
consistently, but nothing more than occasional concerts can be
documented. In other cases, names appear for a short, intense
period, then disappear, perhaps because of the actual cessation of
the activities, perhaps only because of the inadequacy of our information. For example, Rosenbaum mentions a series of concerts
at the Schmierer residence in 1801 and 1803. The absence of reports
in the surrounding years could mean the concerts were not given,
but could also indicate the Rosenbaums simply did not attend them
because their interests were focused elsewhere. Along the same
lines, the tremendous variation in the number of private concerts
Zinzendorf heard (some years are packed with reports, others have

[25]Nicolai/BESCHREIBUNG, 4:524. (I/12)

no mention of any) probably only reflects his erratic attendance, not an erratic fluctuation in concerts. About the only thing that can be reliably deduced from table 3 is that there was never a gap in the activity; when one salon ceased, another sprang up to take its place.

Before taking a look at some of the individual salons, we should discuss a few general characteristics—programs, performers, rooms, audience, and atmosphere. Only a bare handful of facts about private concert programs has been preserved, but enough has survived to say with certainty that they differed very little in content and scope from public ones. They featured a mixture of instrumental and vocal music,[26] the only variation being that solo keyboard music was played and that string quartets sometimes replaced the symphonies always found on public performances.

The performers at the Musical Salons included both dilettante and professional musicians. The few patrons who still maintained an orchestra or a wind band naturally used them for their performances; Prince Lobkowitz even loaned out his personnel to Mme de Rittersburg for her concerts in 1809.[27] However, most orchestras consisted of amateurs, except for the wind instruments, which were not popular among dilettantes:

> They perform large musical works, such as symphonies, concertos, and overtures with a precision and accuracy that is even more worthy of admiration since these orchestras, which are for the most part fully staffed, consist almost completely of dilettantes, if you except a few wind instruments that do not often attract afficionados here.[28]

Frequently, a patron would insure a firm guiding hand by hiring a professional violinist as concert master; Franz Clement, the concert master at the Theater an der Wien, served in this capacity for the Würth concerts in 1804.

Wealthier salon patrons also hired as soloists the more famous foreign virtuosos who passed through the city as well as the latest

[26]See the full discussion of programs in chapter 6.
[27]Reichardt/VERTRAUTE, 1:466-67.
[28]FM, December 5, 1803, p. 770. (1/13)

15

TABLE 3. Private Concert Patrons

Name	Frequency	Years	Source
1760s			
Prince v. Colalto	3/week	61-64	Z
Prince v. Hildburgshausen	regular	61-64	Z
M. de Thauernathy	regular	61-64	Z
Mme de Thurn	regular	61-64	Z
1770s			
Prince Adam v. Auersperg	occasional	74-79	Z
Mme de Wallenstein	occasional	74-79	Z
Prince Paar	occasional	74-79	Z
1780s			
Prince Dimitry v. Golitzin	weekly	81-89	Z,M
French Ambassador	regular	81-83	Z
Count Johann v. Esterházy	2/week	84	Z,M
	occasional	88-89	Z
Hofrath v. Kees	2/week	85	G
Gottfried Ignaz v. Ployer	regular	85	Z,M
Madame de Buquoy	occasional	85-88	Z
Prince Paar	occasional	86-87	Z
Prince Joseph v. Schwarzenberg	occasional	87	Z
Venetian Ambassador	occasional	87-88	Z
1790s			
Prince Dimitry v. Golitzen	weekly	90-93	Z
Prince Joseph Maria v. Lobkowitz	regular	93-99	Z
Prince Franz Maximilian v. Lobkowitz	regular	93-99	Z
Franz Georg Ritter v. Kees	2/week	90s	Z,F,G
Count v. Appony	frequent	ca. 97	J
Count v. Ballassa	weekly	ca. 97	J
Baronness v. Buffendorf	weekly	ca. 97	J
Count Franz v. Esterházy	occasional	ca. 97	J
Hofrath Franz Ritter v. Greiner	weekly	ca. 97	J
Baron Joseph v. Henikstein	daily	ca. 97	J

PRIVATE CONCERTS

Name	Frequency	Years	Source
Mlle Marianna v. Martines	weekly	ca. 97	J
Hofrath Baron v. Mayern	occasional	ca. 97	J
Hofrath v. Meyer	occasional	ca. 97	J
Regierungsrath v. Paradies	weekly	ca. 97	J
Baron Gottfried van Swieten	occasional	ca. 97	J
Baroness v. Zois	weekly	ca. 97	J
Count Moritz v. Fries	regular	99	Z
Mme de Buquoy	occasional	90s	Z
Prince v. Paar	occasional	90s	Z
Prince Joseph v. Schwarzenberg	occasional	90s	Z

1800s

Name	Frequency	Years	Source
Baron Nathan Adam v. Arnstein	regular	00	MR
Prince Franz Maximilian v. Lobkowitz	regular	00-09	Z,R
Count Moritz v. Fries	weekly	00-02	Z,A
Herr Schmierer	regular	01,03	Ros
Baron Peter v. Braun	weekly	02-05	Z,A
Count v. Haugwitz	regular	02,07,08	Z
Hofrath Schubb	regular	02-03	Ros
Baron Anton v. Spielmann	weekly	02	Z,A
Herr v. Würth	regular	04-05	FM
Countess Josephine v. Deym	2/month	04	F
Mlle Marie Therese v. Paradies	weekly	09	A
Mme de Rittersburg	weekly	09	R
Princess Luise v. Starhemberg	regular	08-09	Z
Prince Joseph v. Schwarzenberg	occasional	00s	Z
Mme de Buquoy	occasional	00s	Z
Herr Quarin	occasional	00s	Ros

A = AMZ
F = Forbes/BEETHOVEN
FM = FM
G = GYROWETZ
J = Schönfeld/JTWP

M = Mozart/LETTERS
MR = Mörner/SILVERSTOLPE
R = Reichardt/VERTRAUTE
Ros = VIENNA-ROSENBAUM
Z = VIENNA-ZINZENDORF

local sensations. Mozart, for example, maintained a dizzying schedule of private appearances at his zenith in the mid-1780s. Less well-known artists might even offer their services gratis in the hopes of building up a following among the local music lovers. In many cases, though, these soloists shared the stage with amateurs just as the orchestral players did. At a performance in 1810 of Joseph Weigl's oratorio *La Passione di Gesu Cristo* at the Lobkowitz palace, the singers included Princess Therese v. Fürstenberg, Madame d'Appony, and the Prince Lobkowitz, as well as the professional singers Mlle Wranitzky, Herr Vogel, and Herr Simoni.[29] Therese Gassmann-Rosenbaum often performed alongside her dilettante acquaintances in the private concerts at the Schubb's and the Schmierer's. Unfortunately, we have no record of professional musicians voicing their feelings about the musical quality of such performances or the problems they encountered, but critics continually attacked dilettante performances as detrimental to the art of music. One column was occasioned by the appearance of a new Mozart work, which, according to the commentator, could never be sufficiently interpreted by amateurs:

Mozart has now gone to Vienna as Imperial Royal Kapellmeister (*sic*). He is a remarkable man for every philosophical *Liebhaber* of music. He was a very young genius and was playing and composing as a true virtuoso by the age of nine (or even earlier) to everyone's amazement. The unusual thing is that not only was he an accomplished musician unusually early, but traveled on successfully and still showed himself in enduring growth as a man. We all know from our own experiences about the quick geniuses that flash by. Where are the fruits in good time? And the permanence in solidity? Not the case with Mozart! But now a few words about a bizarre phenomenon that he (or his fame) has caused. A little while ago a quartet of his (for keyboard, violin, viola and cello) came out in print. It is very artistically arranged and demands the utmost precision from all four voices, but even with a successful performance, as it appears, can delight only connoisseurs of music in a chamber [atmosphere]. The call, "Mozart has written a new, really special

---

[29]VIENNA-ZINZENDORF, April 21, 1810.

quartet, and this and that Princess and Countess have it and are playing it,'' gets around quickly,, arouses curiosity and leads to the foolishness of producing this original composition in grand noisy concerts and therewith to be heard, *invita Minerva*, in splendor. Many other pieces can survive even a mediocre performance; but this product of Mozart can hardly be listened to when it falls into the hands of mediocre dilettantes and is carelessly performed. This happened countless times last winter; almost everywhere I visited on my trip and was taken to several concerts, a young lady or a proud bourgeois Demoiselle or some other young whipper-snapper of a dilettante stalked into a noisy company with this quartet and pretended that it was fashionable. It could not meet with favor: everyone yawned out of boredom over the unintelligible muddle of 4 instruments that were never together [for] even four beats, and with whose inconsistent *Concentu* there could be no thought of unity of feeling; but it *had* to meet with favor; it had to be praised. Chiding this foolishness as an ephemeral *Manie du jour* says too little, . . . The fact is this unseemly forwardness is not only improper, not only useless and to no advantage, it also harms art and the spread of true taste. ''Is that all there is?'' (thinks the listener who knows a little about music). This is supposed to border on the extremes of excellence in the art? And nonetheless I quite often feel the urge to shut my ears? How does it all fit in? Do I really know what I may rightly praise or fault in music?'' So one renders true music—*Liebhaberey*—disagreeable, confuses healthy human reason and healthy natural feeling and hinders that exactness and solidity of culture, without which no art ever rises to a level that can be maintained. What a difference it makes when this much-mentioned work of art is presented by 4 talented musicians, who have probably studied it, in a quiet room where not even the suspension of each note escapes the ear, in the presence of 2 or 3 attentive people.[30]

This attitude became increasingly prevalent in the nineteenth century as dilettantes began to surrender their role as participants to professional musicians, but it had very little actual impact on the period under discussion. The guiding philosophy of all of the types of music discussed here—from Social Music to Regular Concerts

[30]JOURNAL DER MODEN, June 1788: 230-33. (I/14)

assumed both performing and listening to be integral parts of the appreciation of music.

The perception of the music by performer and listener alike was definitely affected by the ambience of the salons and the elegance of the surroundings. Unfortunately, detailed descriptions of the rooms in which concerts took place did not figure into the reports of contemporary observers, who took their surroundings for granted. But many eighteenth-century residences are still standing today, so that a general description is possible. Most palaces and upper-class residences had three stories, the second containing the rooms where entertaining was done. At the top of a spacious central staircase was the ballroom, flanked by other large rooms directly connected without hallways. The ceilings were very high, the equivalent of two modern stories, or about fifteen to twenty feet, as seen in plate 1, which depicts the main ballroom of the Lobkowitz palace. Normal apartments, in which middle class patrons would have lived, would have had three or four main rooms (also directly connected without hallways) with relatively high (ten to twelve foot) ceilings, as found in Mozart's apartment on the Schulerstrasse. One can assume that the concert was held in the room most appropriate for the number of guests invited, with the other social activities taking place (perhaps even simultaneously) in the adjoining rooms.

Zinzendorf has left us a few hints about the arrangements at some of the events he attended. At one on April 5, 1799, at the Fries residence, at least three rooms were involved:

> At 6:30 passed into the home of Fries, which has no ante chamber. You enter directly into a room with a fireplace. . . . In another room, Mme de Fries occupied the sofa surrounded by the ladies. . . . The concert in a very resonant, pretty room.[31]

Sometimes some of the listeners were placed in an adjoining room, for Zinzendorf twice mentions being in a "seconde chambre," probably the second room of a double parlor:

[31]VIENNA-ZINZENDORF, April 5, 1799. (I/15)

20

Plate 1. Festsaal of the Lobkowitz Palace. Photograph, ca. 1930.
(Courtesy of the Oesterreichische Nationalbibliothek – Bild-Archiv.)

> The evening at 7:00 to the concert of M. de Braun, where I sat down in the second room for fear of dying from the heat.

> At 7:00 went to the Ambassador of France's. . . . went with Dietrichstein to the second room.[32]

Especially in smaller apartments, where the rooms were not as large, space limitations undoubtedly necessitated such an arrangement.

In such rooms, the audience and performers assembled for an evening of musical entertainment and social enjoyment. In some circles, card playing found a place, though most serious patrons did not tolerate it, but conversation, refreshments, and socializing were common to all. The latter inevitably brings up the question of how the Musical Salons affected and were affected by the class structure that divided Viennese society. The part of that society associated with the salons fell into several levels: 1) the high nobility, including the princes and counts whose titles dated back several centuries and who derived their income and power from their landed estates, as well as barons with more recent patents of nobility;[33] 2) the lower nobility, families recently ennobled, usually for service to the state—the simple "Edler von" or "Ritter von"; 3) the wealthy middle class, composed of businessmen and lower court officials. The salons had the potential at least of bringing together the various classes of patrons and middle-class musicians at a level of social equality unknown elsewhere; whether or not they actually did so requires closer examination. In 1808, the *Vaterländische Blätter* rhapsodized:

> Music works the miracle here that is normally ascribed only to love: it makes all classes equal. Aristocrats, bourgeois, princes and their vassals, superiors and their subordinates sit beside each other at one desk and forget the disharmony of their class in the harmony of the tones. All palaces and exchanges are open to the practicing artist,

---

[32]VIENNA-ZINZENDORF, April 10, 1803; April 1, 1810. (I/16)
[33]In the Vienna of 1809, there were 21 families holding the rank of prince, ca. 70 at the rank of count and ca. 50 at the level of baron. See Pezzl/BESCHREIBUNG, p. 354.

22

and the composer of any significance will be handled with all the distinction he could ever wish, which says a lot in the case of many of these gentlemen.[34]

Eduard Hanslick seized upon this idea in his book on Viennese concert life and, supporting his arguments with the experiences described by J.F. Reichardt, asserts that a democratic attitude reigned among those in attendance:

> Music effected this free coming together to a degree of which our democratic, so progressive society has no idea. Just the way in which Reichardt, a simple Kapellmeister, and in no way celebrity of the first degree, was invited to and feted in the most distinguished circles speaks for their interest in art and their amiability.[35]

He further buttresses his assertion by quoting Caroline Pichler's description of her social contacts with the Lobkowitz family:

> I was never reminded of the differences in our classes in society by any rudeness or disdain on the part of the ladies.[36]

According to Hanslick, then, the atmosphere of the salons was remarkably free: "Everyone associating with each other without any restrictive etiquette."[37]

Hanslick's views on the socially progressive nature of private concerts in eighteenth and early nineteenth-century Vienna have crept into the literature as facts and indeed do fit nicely with the popular view of the concurrent rise in the status of musicians from servants to independent artists. But his opinions should not be accepted uncritically. First of all, his statements are part of a longer diatribe berating the nobility of his own era for their lack of interest in and support for the arts. By emphasizing the "democracy" of the earlier period, he could demonstrate that association with the ever-more-powerful middle class was not necessarily demeaning and thereby

[34]VB, 1808, p. 39. (I/17)
[35]Hanslick/CONCERTWESEN, p. 50. (I/18)
[36]Hanslick/CONCERTWESEN, p. 51. (I/19)
[37]Hanslick/CONCERTWESEN, p. 50.

exhort the aristocracy to greater participation. Secondly, foreign visitors like Reichardt always attracted attention and allowed the aristocracy to demonstrate Viennese hospitality and their own largesse. Especially if they came armed with letters of introduction from their own noble patrons, they could count on a certain number of invitations. The same type of hospitality might not have been extended to Reichardt the resident as it was to Reichardt the visitor.

Finally, Hanslick does not distinguish between the association of bourgeois and aristocrat as performers and their relationship as members of the audience or as a social group. Musicians had been playing alongside their noble employers for centuries without doing any damage to the class system, so that collaboration in performance does not necessarily signal social change. A mixing of classes on the side of the audience would be a much better indication that a process of democratization was occurring, for though aristocrats necessarily had to associate with middle-class musicians in performance (on whatever basis), they were in no way obliged to fraternize with bourgeois music lovers by inviting them to concerts or by attending concerts in humbler homes. Whether or not they chose to do so is a difficult question to answer, but the diaries of two people who consistently attended concerts—the nobleman and socialite Count Karl von Zinzendorf and the middle-class accountant Joseph Carl Rosenbaum—indicate that social boundaries were maintained in the various salons.

In their descriptions of the private concerts they attended, both men mention the names of other guests. Zinzendorf was fairly particular about giving titles, so that the majority of names can be identified by social rank; not surprisingly, prince and princess, count and countess, baron and baroness appear most frequently. Of course, he may simply have ignored the non-nobles present, but the sheer number of names he does list make the case for social exclusiveness compelling. Moreover, Rosenbaum's guest lists, while rarely as extensive, are solidly middle class, with only an occasional ''Edler von'' or baron. One might expect he would have mentioned a prince or countess in attendance.

The salons frequented by Zinzendorf and Rosenbaum prove to

be equally revealing. A tally of the Zinzendorf entries over the years 1760-1813 yields about fifty names of hosts for private concerts he attended. For two he gives no title, nine are families belonging to the lowest class of nobility, the "Edler vons." In each of these eleven cases, however, he made only a single appearance. The remaining names can be identified as having the rank of Baron or Baroness or above, and those concerts he attended regularly (sometimes weekly) were those of the Princes Golitzin, Lobkowitz, Schwarzenberg, Starhemberg, and the Counts Windischgrätz and Haugwitz, all families of the Viennese upper crust. Though he occasionally deigned to descend in social rank for a concert, for the most part he remained with his own class. For Rosenbaum we have only thirteen names (for the period 1799-1810): two barons and eleven without title, including several actors and musicians. The absence of illustrious names like Lobkowitz and Schwarzenberg is particularly telling here because Therese Rosenbaum's position as a court theater opera singer might well have opened a few aristocratic doors for them. It would seem then, that the institution of the Musical Salon tended to reflect the conservative nature of the Viennese cultural world.[38]

Whether or not the salons were an instrument of social change, their contribution to Vienna's music cannot be questioned and deserves further investigation. From the many possiblities, I have selected a representative sampling, ranging from the brilliant gatherings at the palace of Prince Golitzin[39] to the modest entertainments given by the Schmierer family. The Russian Prince Dimitry Michajlowitsch Golitzin served as special ambassador to the Hapsburg court from 1761 to 1792, and hosted (as did other ambassadors) a glittering calendar of social functions that included weekly concerts in the winter season. Though Zinzendorf attended them regularly, he rarely mentions any performers or pieces. His entries

---

[38]For additional evidence supporting this contention, see the quotation from Pezzl/BESCHREIBUNG on p. 228.

[39]I am using the modern transliteration of the Russian. Most Viennese spelled his name "Galitzin," a usage I have retained in direct quotations. I have followed this procedure for all names, keeping the spelling found in the quotation but using the form found in NEW GROVE for my own discussion.

usually read: "To a concert at Prince Galitzin's," brief even for him. The Golitzin concerts were probably professional rather than dilettante (Mozart was engaged for the 1784 season), resembling in atmosphere and structure those of families with private orchestras. Separate entrances were arranged for the musicians, who were obviously not expected to mingle with the guests, though the brash young Mozart made a point of doing so:

> Moreover, when we are summoned to a house where there is a concert, Herr Angerbauer [one of the Archbishop's private valets] has to watch outside until the Salzburg gentlemen arrive, when he sends a lackey to show them the way in. On hearing Brunetti tell this in the course of a conversation, I thought to myself, "Just wait till I come along!" So, the other day when we were to go to Prince Galitzin's Brunetti said to me in his usual polite manner, "Tu, bisogna che sii qui stasera alle sette per andare insieme dal Principe Galitzin. L'Angerbauer ci condurra." Ho risposto: "Va bene—ma—se in caso mai non fossi qui alle sette in punto, ci andate pure, non serve aspettarmi—so bene dove sta, e ci verro sicuro." I went there alone on purpose, because I really feel ashamed to go anywhere with them. When I got upstairs, I found Angerbauer standing there to direct the lackey to show me in. But I took no notice, either of the valet or the lackey, but walked straight on through the rooms into the music room, for all the doors were open, and went straight up to the Prince, paid him my respects and stood there talking to him. I had completely forgotten my friends Ceccarelli and Brunetti, for they were not to be seen. They were leaning against the wall behind the orchestra, not daring to come forward a single step.[40]

From the tone of the Mozart quote and the off-hand nature of Zinzendorf's entries, we might assume that the Golitzin concerts were mainly an opportunity for the Russian ambassador to demonstrate the culture and generosity of his country.

In the palace of the young Prince Lobkowitz, amateur participation assumed special importance, undoubtedly because the Prince himself played the violin and cello and reportedly had a fine bass

[40]ML 2:717.

voice.[41] There has been some confusion as to the exact identity of the "Prince Lobkowitz," for the family had two lines, both headed by music-loving princes who supported the arts in a grand style. Prince Joseph Maria Carl hosted the concert at which Beethoven made his Viennese debut (March 1, 1795). The other Lobkowitz, Prince Joseph Franz Maximilian (later Beethoven's patron), began giving concerts as early as 1793, and from then until 1802, when Joseph Maria Carl died, it is not always possible to separate their activities.[42] For the younger prince, music proved to be his downfall (his eventual bankruptcy was due in large part to his extravagance in the arts), but until financial troubles set in, he entertained his friends and acquaintances with lavish opera productions, oratorios, and concerts. In his love of music, he did perhaps extend a welcome to a wider range of people than usual, considering his own high rank:

> Then I go to the Lobkowitz concerts, that are really more like general "Assemblies."[43]

Nonetheless, more exclusive performances did take place. The Viennese magazine *Der Sammler* reports that Joseph Weigl's *La Passione di N. S. Gesu Cristo*:

> was presented on the evening of Holy Saturday in Prince Lobkowitz's theater in the presence of the all-highest court and the first nobility.[44]

Lobkowitz's salons often stretched out for longer than the relatively brief time society was accustomed to. (Judging from Zinzendorf's other activities, the affairs at Prince Golitzin's could not have lasted more than an hour and a half.) Reichardt comments:

[41]Zinzendorf did once refer to it as disagreeable. See VIENNA-ZINZENDORF, January 6, 1811.
[42]Landon maintains that Zinzendorf distinguishes between the two by referring to Josef Franz Maximilian and his wife as "les jeunes Lobkowitz," but he does not consistently do so.
[43]Bauer,W/BRIEFE, p. 25. An "Assembly" resembled an open house. See the discussion in chapter 8. (I/20)
[44]SAMMLER, April 28, 1810, p. 206. (I/21)

Once again at this Prince's, who cannot have enough of music, there was singing straight through from eight until midnight.[45]

Though the emphasis seems to have been on vocal music, instrumental virtuosos were not neglected:

From there to the Lobkowitz's, from whence I did not exit until the hours past midnight. There were almost 40 ladies of which the Stembergs and the Buquoys went from there to the assembly. First a sextet by Wransky [Wranitzky], then Madame de Schönfeld sang with Pär, then Madame Frank sang like an angel. Punto made his solo hunting horn heard. Stäbel played the keyboard [Zinzendorf says *clavecin* but undoubtedly means fortepiano] with volubility that was not very interesting. Mme de Schönfeld, Therese de Schwarzenberg, Mlle Francoise Zichy, Mme Frank, Prince Lobkowitz and two men did the finale of *Griselda* marvelously. Then the suppers (*sic*). After the suppers, Madame Steubel played a children's game with a sort of tambourine that probably makes her fingers hurt.[46]

Symphonies and overtures with full orchestra and in piano reductions also found their way onto the programs:

At 6:45 to the Prince Lobkowitz, Mlle Goubaud sang a piece from Corolian; the Archduke [Rudolph] played a Hummel symphony that was very pretty.The Baroness Kraft accompanied on the other keyboard.

I went to the concert at Lobkowitz's overture from a comic opera entitled *Joanna* by Méhul. . . . quintet by Prince Louis of Prussia. . . . duet of Weinmüller, . . . bassoon by Börmann from Berlin. . . . a quartet from *Axur* [by Salieri]. . . . Casimer played the harp.[47]

In 1807-08 the Count Haugwitz initiated a series of "Concerts Spirituels" in addition to his usual salon. They attracted an elite audience and featured sacred cantatas and other choral works:

[45]Reichardt/VERTRAUTE, 1:267. (I/22)
[46]VIENNA-ZINZENDORF, April 16, 1800. (I/23)
[47]VIENNA-ZINZENDORF, January 6, 1811; January 27, 1811. (I/24)

Before 7:00 to the concert spirituel at Count Haugwitz's. Lots of ladies and the Duke Albert. I sat behind Mme de Bisringen, between Princess Clari and Nani Dietrichstein, behind the Princess Lobkowitz and Mme de Schönborn. "Zeit und Ewigkeit," music by Nauman was given, beautiful, touching, perfectly executed. . . . The second [piece was] "Das Lob Gottes," music of Schutz (sic).[48]

These concerts represent one of the few attempts to present sacred works on a regular basis, but they lasted only two seasons.

Count Moritz von Fries belonged to one of Vienna's recently ennobled families, his father having been raised to a Baron in 1762 then to a 'Reichsgraf" or "Imperial Count" in 1783. Because of his talents and influence (he headed the banking firm of Fries & Co.) and his exceptional patronage of the arts, he had risen to an eminent social position. His salon reflected his wide-ranging interests:

At 7:00 at a concert at young Fries's. In the billiard room two beautiful Hakerts and one Kouchich representing the Vestales fleeing Rome set aflame by Brenus and his warriors (?). . . . In the concert chamber three Watki. . . . After a nice symphony, Madame de Schonfeld sang a duo by Paisiello with Pär: "Nei giorni tuoi felici." Stich Punto, Bohemian in spirit, played the furious cor de chasse with admirable delicacy and accuracy.[49]

Another of the lower nobility who entertained lavishly, Baron Peter von Braun, made his name in the silk industry, secured the lease on the two court theaters in 1794, and was made a Baron in 1795. As theater director, he exerted an enormous influence on Viennese musical life (see chapter 3), and the professional nature of his salons reflected his status: many of the performers were court employees:

---

[48]VIENNA-ZINZENDORF, March 15, 1808. There is no work by Heinrich Schütz with exactly that title, but there are several that closely approximate it. Since Zinzendorf did not always get his information entirely correct, the piece may indeed have been by the Baroque composer and would have been an unusually early performance for one of his works. (I/25)
[49]VIENNA-ZINZENDORF, March 31, 1800. (I/26)

At 7:00 passed by the concert of Baron Braun. . . . The heat was intense. I sat down at the front next to Hardegkh and Spielmann. Czervenka played the oboe well, but his concerto put Swieten to sleep. In the second half Madame Muller's harp, Paisiello's duo Wranski's [Wranitzki's] wind band [piece], Nasolini's aria and the finale from *Horace* by Cimarosa. The good Wrbna was there at the beginning and returned for the end. Princess Auersberg was sad.

The evening at 7:00 at the concert of Monsieur de Braun, where I instantly placed myself, out of fear of dying of the heat, in the second room. *Gli Orazzi ed i Eriazi (sic)* was the opera that was given. Madame Mara sang there with her most touching voice and Sarut (?) screamed like he did 20 years ago. I was beside Madame de Metternich for a long time. Madame de Revaj nice.[50]

One member of the lower nobility achieved almost legendary status as a patron of music, but practically all traces of his activity have disappeared. Franz Georg Ritter von Kees (1747-1799) held the important court rank of "Hofrath" and supposedly helped organize Vienna's first public dilettante concerts (see chapter 2). Apparently, he came from a musical family, for in 1761 Zinzendorf noted that a M. de Kees was the "director" of the concerts of a "very rich young man," M. de Thauernathy.[51] The only other mention of the name in the diaries occurs in 1793, when Zinzendorf attended a concert given by "the old Kees" (probably Franz Bernhard von Kees), on March 21, 1793. According to several reports that appeared after his death, the younger Kees's salon cultivated the symphonic genre in particular. His position in this respect was assumed by the Banker Würth, who had assembled an amateur orchestra that gave outstanding performances to a select and attentive audience:

The musicales at Herr von Würth's are drawing to a close. This attractive institution, in which the organizer has collected connoisseurs and music lovers of all educated classes, presented again this year almost exclusively the greatest musical masterpieces of Mozart,

[50]VIENNA-ZINZENDORF, April 3, 1802; April 10, 1803. (I/27)
[51]VIENNA-ZINZENDORF, December 22, 1761.

Haydn, Eberl, Beethoven, etc. in the full splendor of a beautiful and successful execution.[52]

The artistic enjoyment is increased there through the officious demeanor of the master of the house and through a very select company.[53]

Since neither Zinzendorf nor Rosenbaum frequented the salon, we have no information on who might have made up the "select company."[54] Würth's concerts were among the few private ones to receive continuing attention from reviewers, an indication of their musical significance.

The two salons regularly attended by the Rosenbaums offered a more intimate, social atmosphere than the serious Würth presentations. At the home of the Schmierers and at Hofrath Schubb's, Joseph and Therese enjoyed and participated in performances that featured both amateur and professional musicians, like the Schuster family from the Theater in der Leopoldstadt. Though Rosenbaum does not regale us with guest lists the way Zinzendorf does, many of the names he does mention surface elsewhere in the diaries, suggesting that those in attendance were part of a larger social circle.

With a few exceptions, the repertoire of these two salons seems to have tended more toward chamber music and arias with keyboard accompaniment than symphonies and overtures, probably a result of the more limited financial means of the patrons:

At 7:00 Kühlbach came over and [we] drove to the musicale at Hofrath Schubb's. Keller played in a quartet. Fräu[lein] Gilberg pounded out a sonata which a Russian officer accompanied on the clarinet, and Tomasini played a quartet [on the violin]. Th. sang the aria by Cimarosa "A torna la belle aurora." We came home at 10:30.

After 7:00 went with Th. to Hofrath Schubb. She sang the aria "Parto" from [Mozart's] *Clemenza di Tito*, accompanied by [Baron] Gruft with obbligato clarinet by Pär.

[52]FM, April 19, 1805, p. 212. (I/28)
[53]AMZ, January 9, 1805, p. 242. (I/29)
[54]The men of the aristocracy mixed downward in society to a certain extent, so that the guests may well have included music lovers of high rank.

In the evening Th., Naumann, Moreau and I went to Schubb's. The Serenate of Fuchs was done first, then the introduction to Don Juan, a concerto by Mme Jacobi and a trio from [Pär's] *Achille*.[55]

Among the exceptions were performances at the Schmierer's of Haydn's *Die Schöpfung* (November 16, 1801) and *Die Jahreszeiten* (May 13, 1803). For the latter Rosenbaum imparts a little information on the size of the forces:

> This evening we have been invited to the Schmierer's (since the theaters are closed in mourning for the Empress Louisa). Die 4 Jahreszeiten will be given. Th. and I went . . . at 7:00. Jeanette and both Schusters sang. Liparsky directed at the pianoforte. . . . The violins were doubled, cello and bass. With the boys, there must have been 16 in the chorus, which included Pfeifer. The performance was a success. The company was numerous. Lang, . . . the poet Weissenbach, the 2 Straks. We had a pleasant time and stayed until 11:30.[56]

As can be seen from this discussion, private music-making in Vienna encompassed a wide variety of activities and purposes. No matter what the level of musical sophistication or taste, all involved a certain amount of socializing, something that was not considered necessarily antithetical to the true appreciation of music. In an intimate setting, before a select group of listeners who most likely knew each other, a performance could exact an amount of involvement not possible in the cold, impersonal atmosphere of a concert hall. The two functions—social and musical—combined to provide a type of experience peculiar to the private concert world.

Given the strong social component, it is not surprising that the Musical Salons mirrored the class structure of Viennese society. While some patrons may have cultivated a more democratic atmosphere, the majority of patrons and guests alike simply felt more comfortable among people of their own rank and background. The middle class was gaining ground in all spheres of influence, the status of musicians and other artists was improving, but very little

[55]VIENNA-ROSENBAUM, March 10, 1802; March 17, 1802, March 31, 1802. (I/30)
[56]VIENNA-ROSENBAUM, May 13, 1803. (I/31)

of that progress can be directly attributed to the institution of the Musical Salon.

Viewed from a strictly musical standpoint, all the categories of performance in the private world embody one of the quintessential attitudes of the late eighteenth century: that the appreciation of music involved both listening and participation. Though, as we shall see, amateur performance did extend to the public realm, private soirées provided the perfect setting for the realization of this ideal. Its gradual abandonment in the nineteenth century marked a profound change in the perception of music.

We have seen that during the winter season, the Musical Salons presented a fairly continual array of concerts in such numbers as to raise the question of competition with public ventures. On the surface, at least, it would seem that the plethora of private offerings could well have contributed to Vienna's supposedly tardy development in the public concert realm, but to sufficiently address that question, we must first examine the public concert structure and the attitudes of the Viennese audiences.

CHAPTER TWO

Public Concerts

The institution of the public concert began to emerge at different times and in different forms at the musical centers on the European continent and in England. Particularly in Germany, public concerts developed from the originally private performances of societies known as *Collegium Musicum* or *Akademie*, which were associations of amateurs and professionals devoted to the cultivation of music. Their legacy can be seen in the use of the term "musical academy" to designate a concert, a practice that continued into the nineteenth century. Similar groups, known as *Liebhaber Gesellschaft* (Friends of Music Societies), non-profit organizations that produced public concerts for their town or city, became the mainstay of concert music in Germany during the eighteenth century. The Gewandhaus Concerts in Leipzig, which began in 1761, are perhaps the most famous, but scores of similar undertakings can be found in other parts of Europe. In Munich, the "Dilettanten Unterhaltung" (Dilettantes' Entertainment) was founded in 1789 and was still active four years later.[1] The smaller towns of Gotha, Halle, Schweignitz in Schlesien, all had concert associations, particularly important in their case since traveling virtuosos might ordinarily be tempted to bypass them for the perhaps greater profits to be made in the larger cities.[2]

[1]BMZ SPAZIER, November 2, 1793, p. 163.
[2]MW, December 1792, p. 160; BMZ SPAZIER, December 7, 1793, p. 185, and June 1, 1793, p. 65.

By the late eighteenth century, the city of Berlin supported at least three separate concert series: 1) the "Liebhaber Concerte" (founded in 1773), 2) the performances at the home of Herr Fliess (to which subscription tickets were sold), and 3) the "Konzerte in der Stadt Paris," held in a locale known as the "Stadt Paris."[3] The English, however, seem to have outdone the Germans in organizing series of performances. In 1790, the *Morning Chronicle* of London listed the following series for the London winter season: the Salomon concerts, the Cramer concerts, the "Antient" Concerts (led by Cramer), the Lady's Subscription Concerts, and twice-weekly oratorios during Lent at the Drury Lane and Covent Garden theaters, plus the Academy of Antient Music.[4] In most cases, a flourishing concert series soon demanded a location of its own, so that music rooms and concert halls began to be built accordingly.

The state of concert life in Vienna in the last half of the eighteenth century seems relatively quiet in contrast to the flurry of activity that characterized most other European cities. Periodicals that reported on concerts elsewhere turned to opera when the discussion moved to Vienna. One of the few exceptions to this rule, a report in Hiller's *Wöchentliche Nachrichten* in 1766, mentions only private events, and then very briefly:

> Every week, in addition to other established [ones], concerts are held at Count Collaldo's, Herr Land owner von Kees's, Herr von Örtel's, and at least once at His Excellency the Prince von Sachsen Hildburgshausen's, the latter under the direction of Herr Joseph Bono.[5]

Why was there such a dearth of information about concerts in Vienna? First, much of the activity did take place in private salons,

[3]BMZ SPAZIER. March 9, 1793, pp. 16-18.
[4]Landon/C & W, 3:31.
[5]Hiller/NACHRICHTEN, September 23, 1766, p. 100. (II/1) Count Collaldo (Colalto) and Prince Hildburgshausen (Karl Ditters von Dittersdorf's employer) were two of Vienna's more prominent aristocratic music patrons. For von Kees, see the discussion in chapter 1. Joseph Bono (Giuseppe Bonno 1711-1788) served as Kapellmeister to Prince Hildburgshausen for nearly twenty years and later became Court Kapellmeister in Vienna.

generally not a concern of newspapers and periodicals. Second, theater and opera dominated the Viennese cultural scene, so that attention was naturally focused on them:

> It is apparent from some recently received news about the state of theater in Vienna how much the taste there is for musical, and particularly Italian musical plays. Within a year (from November 1791, till December 1792), Italian opera was given 180 times. A single opera seria was performed 24 times. Ballets were seen 163 times.[6]

> Vienna. That the public's well known love for the enjoyments of the stage has not decreased even during the horrors of war, but has probably risen still more, can be seen daily in the crowd at the entrances to the three favorite theaters.[7]

Finally, the Viennese had a somewhat exasperating tendency to experience an event but not to write about it, a trait that resulted in an almost total absence of Viennese periodicals dealing in any way with music until the nineteenth century.

Public concerts did indeed exist in Vienna, and in fairly respectable numbers, but they arose at a later date (1740s) and developed on a different pattern than elsewhere in Europe. In contrast to other Germanic cities, no strong "Friends of Music" society emerged to take control of the concert organization, surprising in view of the great number of excellent dilettantes to be found there. Isolated, short-lived appearances of such societies did occur (and will be discussed later), but they came into existence after public concerts began and never exercised the guiding influence they did elsewhere. The impetus came from a different direction: the court theaters.

CONCERT HISTORY TO 1776

The beginnings and subsequent development of public concerts in Vienna are closely connected with the history of the city's

[6]BMZ SPAZIER, May 4, 1793, p. 51. (II/2)
[7]MUENCHNER, April 11, 1801, cols. 243-44. (II/3)

theaters. For the first three quarters of the eighteenth century, Vienna had only two public theaters, the Burgtheater and the Kärntner-thortheater, both under the jurisdiction, at least theoretically, of the Emperor. Their connection with concert history derives from the fact that religious practice dictated that no staged drama, spoken or sung, be presented during Advent and Lent. The entertainment-hungry public, forced to turn elsewhere for amusement, found concerts to be an acceptable substitute. Glad of the extra revenue, the theater management obliged and began to present concerts during these enforced periods of inactivity. Of course, Vienna was not unique in this response to such restrictions—the "Concerts Spirituels" in Paris in 1725 were prompted by a similar closing of the theaters. In that case, however, a private individual provided the impetus, and the institution then rapidly grew beyond the bounds governed by religious matters. With Vienna, on the other hand, concerts remained in the theaters and under the control of the court theater management for more than a quarter of a century, lending them an air of "substitute" entertainment. They were presented only when other cultural diversions were not allowed and tended to fluctuate with the ever-changing theater management.

One of the earliest notices of a public concert in the theaters occurs in the *Wienerisches Diarium* on March 6, 1745, but the wording makes it difficult to ascertain whether it was the first such concert ever, or merely the first of that year:

> It is herewith brought to the attention of the public that next Sunday, the 7th of this month in the afternoon at 6:30, the concerts of various vocal and instrumental pieces will be held for the first time in the Royal Burgtheater. The other days will be announced later at the appropriate time.[8]

At that time, both theaters were under the direction of the former ballet master Joseph Selliers. In December of 1747, he relinquished

[8]WZ, March 6, 1745, n.p. (II/4) The name *Wienerisches Diarium* was changed to *Wiener Zeitung* in 1780. I have used the appropriate name in the text, but all footnotes give WZ.

control of the Burgtheater to Baron Rochus de la Presti,[9] who continued the Lenten performances on a regular schedule of three per week:

> Since all drama and comedy is suspended for the holy period of Lent, three concerts a week (Sunday, Tuesday, and Thursday) will be held in the Imperial Burgtheater for the enjoyment of the high nobility and the public.[10]

After la Presti's bankruptcy in 1752, the theater management was brought under more direct court control (both la Presti and Selliers had operated under a lease-type arrangement), with the directors Franz Esterházy and Giacomo Durazzo reporting to a court official with the title "Directorial Präsident."[11] Count Esterházy resigned after a year, but Count Durazzo served for more than a decade.

The new management was immediately faced with the restrictions imposed that year by the Empress Maria Theresia's "Norma" edict, a document formally declaring the days on which theater productions were forbidden.[12] In addition to the customary Lent and Advent, the "Norma" days initially comprised other church holidays such as Corpus Christi and Pentecost, the birth and death days of various members of the royal family, and Fridays throughout the year. From the viewpoint of theater history, the effect was catastrophic, since the already short theater year was reduced even further from 260 to 210 days, but the abbreviated schedule afforded increased opportunities for concerts.

Count Durazzo energetically continued the practices of his predecessors and also made the best of the "Norma" days by expanding concert activity to other times of the year. From this period comes the first actual description of one of the Lenten concerts, which must have had some of the characteristics of an amateur night, although professional musicians also performed:

[9]He retained the Kärntnerthortheater until April of 1751. Zechmeister/THEATER, pp. 23-24.
[10]WZ, February 18, 1750, n.p. (II/5)
[11]Probably Prince Kaunitz or Count Dietrichstein.
[12]I was not able to discover why the term "Norma" was used.

Their Imperial Highnesses appeared this evening at the concert—
or so-called musical academy—held for the first time today. They
will be continued each Sunday, Tuesday and Thursday. These
Lenten spectacles last from 6:00 to 9:00; you pay the admission fee,
anyone can play in it. The theater was beautifully arranged and well
lighted. In order to [attract] people, Count Durazzo, who has charge
of this department, decided to present in part foreign voices, among
whom surely Signorina [Katharina] Gabriel: *detta la cochetta*, beautiful
soprano voice, in part to produce different variations of choruses,
oratorios, psalms, arias, duets, and has always found a numerous
public.[13]

The three hour length and the mixed format of vocal and instrumental music approximate the features of programs from later in the
century. Oratorios and sacred works were also given; works
featured in the 1750s included those in table 4. By the 1760s, the
Lenten concerts had become such an institution that it was possible to buy subscription tickets:

On Sunday the 28th of the current month of February in the Imperial Royal Burgtheater, the concerts will begin and will be held

TABLE 4. Oratorios Presented in the 1750s

Bernasconi, Andrea	*La Betulia Liberata*
Wagenseil, Georg C.	*La Redenzione*
Jomelli, Niccolo	*Il Sacrificio d'Abramo*
Wagenseil, Georg C.	*Gioas*
Adolfati-Wagenseil	*Il rovetto di Mose*
Adolfati	Psalm #6
Gluck, Christoph W.	Psalm #8
Wagenseil, Georg C.	Psalm #40
Porpora, Niccolo	2 choruses
Sammartini	chorus

Information taken from Zechmeister/THEATER, p. 234.

[13]Böck/KHEVENHUELLER, p. 18. (II/6)

three times a week, namely, Sunday, Tuesday, and Thursday, throughout Lent. Prices will be as they have been in other years. There will also be places at the usual price of the 2nd Parquet. Inquire about series tickets for both boxes and gallery at the Keeper of the Boxes.[14]

Further information on these performances can be found in court theater records preserved in the Hofkammer Archiv in Vienna. Among other things, they show that the receipts from the concerts amounted to only five percent of the total income for the theater year 1754-55. The records also contain a roster of musicians employed by the theater during the decade 1754-64, including those hired for concerts.[15] Only rarely are actual salaries given, and the dates reflect only the quarter-year in which the person was paid,[16] but the list does at least give us an idea of the major professional performers (table 5).

More information on concert activity during these years is found in the chronicle of court theater activities kept by Philipp Gumpenhüber, Count Durazzo's secretary, for the calendar year 1758.[17] He describes, albeit not in the greatest detail, the series of fifteen Lenten concerts beginning of February 12, 1758, and continuing three times per week through March 14. In an obvious attempt to preserve as close a resemblance to actual theater as possible, the management provided elaborate sets as a backdrop for the performances, the aspect that Gumpenhüber found most worthy of comment:

[14]WZ, February 27, 1762, n.p. (II/7)
[15]Four of the forty account books are missing (55/56 I, 57/58 I, 59/60 I, 62/63 II), and the years 54/55, 58/59, and 63/64 have no names listed for concerts, though, as the description quoted above shows, concerts were given in at least one of those years (1755). See Hadamowsky/AKADEMIEN, p. 115.
[16]Most were paid for the fourth quarter, which included Lent, though concerts took place throughout the year. Zechmeister gives the following figures for the year 55/56: May 31 to August 29, 1755—16 concerts; August 30 to November 28—12 concerts; November 29 to March 5, 1756—25 concerts; March 6 to April 9, 1756—15 concerts. Zechmeister/ THEATER, p. 234.
[17]Four volumes of the diaries are housed in the Harvard University Theater Collection, but only the 1758 volume contains any mention of concerts.

TABLE 5. Concert Participants, 1754-1764

Name	Capacity	Dates—year and quarter
Aprile, Hr.	Concerts	57/58 IV
Baglioni, Clementina	Concerts	61/62 IV
		62/63
		500 Dukaten
Bareggi, Paolo	Soprano Concerts	56/57
Belli, Giuseppe	Soprano Concerts	56/57 I-III
Beneventi, Maria	Concerts	55/56 IV
		57/58 IV
Boccherini and son	Concerts	57/58 IV
Bon-Ruvinetti, Rosa	Concerts	61/62 IV
Bortoletti	Tenor Concerts	56/57 I-II
Carlani, Carlo	Concerts	55/56 III-IV
Collona, Sgra.	Concerts	Jan-April 58
Dimezzo, Pietro	Tenor Concerts	56/57 II-IV
Ditters, Karl	Concerts	61/62 III
Farinelli, Maria	Concerts	55/56 II-III
Gabrielli, Catharina	Concerts	May 55-Dec 57
		60/61 IV
Gabrielli, Franzisca	Concerts	55/56 IV
		56/57
Gallieni, Gius.	Concerts	61/62 IV
Giacommazzi, Antonia	Concerts	59/60 IV
		62/63 III
Giacomazzi, Theresia	Concerts	59/60 III-IV
		61/62 IV
Giardini, Giov. Dom.	Concerts	61/62 IV
Gluck, Christoph Willibald Ritter v.	Director	Nov 61-Lent 62
	Concerts	206 fl 15x
		412 fl 30x

42

PUBLIC CONCERTS

Name	Capacity	Dates—year and quarter
Grüch, Felice	Concerts	57/58 IV
		59/60 III-IV
Guarducci, Tommaso	Concerts	55/56 IV
Kellerin, Carolina	Concerts	55/56 IV
Lucchi, Tommaso	Concerts	55/56 II
Masi, Violante	Opera	Sept 62-end
	Concerts	Carnival 63
Mazzanti, Ferdinando	Concerts	56/57 III-IV
Pilaja, Catharina	Concerts	61/62 IV
Porpora	Concerts	55/56 IV
Pugnani	Concerts	55/56 IV
Rhem, Barbara	Concerts	61/62 IV
Roselli, Franc.	Concerts	61/62 IV
Saiz, Sigra.	Concerts	57/58 IV
Tibaldi, Pietro	Concerts	61/62 IV
Torre, Teresa	Concerts	Oct 62-Mar 63
		230 Dukaten
Torti	Concerts	55/56 II

The theater year began after Easter, so that the four quarters correspond roughly to these months: 1: April-June, II: July-September, III: October-December, IV: January-March. The information in this table is taken from Hadamowsky/ AKADEMIEN.

The first academy. The theater was ornamented with transparent scenery, depicting the protection the august house of Austria has given the fine arts at all times. Five people sang, and there was a Pantaleon concerto by Herr Helman, with a chorus composed by Gluck.

The seventh academy. With a new decoration that depicted a temple adorned with "Dornres" and transparent. In the middle of which, amid the exclamations of the people, the famous celebrity and crown, the name of our sovereign. Several new arias were sung, and a chorus composed by Herr Porpora. And a concerto for several solo instruments composed by Herr Wagenseil.

The thirteenth academy. Today the scenery depicted a new transparent grand Tableau depicting Telemachus led by Minerva and covered by his shield moving along a steep path toward the Tem-

43

ple of Immortality. From a distance the mark of Honor and Glory, who are waiting for them. One sees the hurling in[to] the abyss of Orgenil, Envy and the other vices or monsters that were standing in the way of his passage. Through this symbol if recognized, the intention was to recall the idea of that which has to be in store for a young hero when he is lead by Largess. In this scenery an oratorio for four voices composed by Sr. Balthasar Galuppi (called Boranello) was given. And the title was Adam et Eva.[18]

Though he waxes most enthusiastic about the scenery, he does manage to note the names of a few composers and performers. Three of the singers he mentions, Herr Aprile, Herr Grück (Grüch), and Mlle Sais, appear on the court theater payroll for that year (see table 5).[19] Apparently these singers functioned as "staff," appearing on more than one program:

> The fourth academy. The concert had ordinary scenery. Among others that sang, there was the Herr Joseph Aprile—called Sciroletto. The Herren Francois and Grück, a tenor, for the first time. All the arias were mixed with symphonies, and there was a concerto for several solo instruments composed by Herr San Martino.

> The fifth academy. The concert was again adorned in an ordinary way. The same people sang, and there was an oboe concerto played by Herr Jauzer.[20]

None of the various instrumentalists, though they also performed several times, are listed on the payroll. However, three of them (Jauzer, Hirsch, and Woscicka) were members of one of the court theater orchestras and were perhaps paid from a different fund.

---

[18]HARVARD-GUMPENHUEBER, February 12, 1758; February 26, 1758; March 12, 1758. (II/8) The pantaleon was a large dulcimer invented by Pantaleon Hebenstreit (1667-1750); though late eighteenth-century writers sometimes used the term to refer to a small square piano, that meaning seems unlikely in this instance.

[19]His descriptions are so incomplete that he did not record the performance of Maria Beneventi or Boccherini and son, also on the payroll for Lent of 1758.

[20]HARVARD-GUMPENHUEBER, February 19, 1758; February 21, 1758. (II/9)

In any case, most, if not all, of the performers appear to have been theater employees.

The programs presented at these Lenten concerts included both oratorios (Wagenseil's *Il roveto di Mose* and Balthasar Galuppi's *Adamo et Eve*) and the mixed format type of presentation described by Khevenhüller-Metsch in 1755, in which the singers were apparently expected to satisfy the wishes of the audience:

> The sixth academy. Among others that sang, Herr Sciroletto didn't sing the arias that were demanded. Herr Helman played a concerto on the Pantaleon, and he also played divers caprices.[21]

At the final concert, the performers presented new pieces and encored earlier favorites:

> The fifteenth and final academy. Decorated as it was two days before. N.B. The different singers who sang during the course of Lent were heard with new arias. They repeated those which had proved to be most to the taste of the audience. Sieur Helman played a concerto on the Pantaleon. Several symphonies in a new style were played. And at the end the new grand chorus of Sieur Wagenseil was repeated for the second time. It began at six o'clock.[22]

From Gumpenhüber's descriptions, which imply a consistent audience familiar with the arias sung and fond of scenery and spectacle, it seems that the main purpose of these Lenten concerts was to allow regular theater patrons to continue their entertainment unabated, even during the solemn period of Lent.

In 1764, Count Wenzel Spork was appointed general director of both theaters; under his authority they were leased first to Franz Hilverding van Wewens and then to Giuseppe d'Affliso, who went bankrupt in 1770.[23] Count Johann Kohary took over the d'Affliso lease but also went bankrupt two years later, leaving the theaters

[21]HARVARD-GUMPENHUEBER, February 23, 1758. (II/10)
[22]HARVARD-GUMPENHUEBER, March 14, 1758. (II/11)
[23]Zechmeister/THEATER, p. 68.

in the hands of a committee of his creditors.[24] Under d'Afflisio, the three-per-week schedule of Lenten concerts had continued:

> 20 February [1765]. The concerts at the theater don't start until next week, and then will continue *al solito* every Sunday, Tuesday and Thursday.[25]

> In 1769, the management again received permission to give concerts on Fridays as well as during the periods of Advent and Lent, except for the last days of Advent and the last 14 days of Lent.[26]

Also during d'Afflisio's term we find the first report of a virtuoso concert not given under the auspices of the theater administration but as a private undertaking of the musician:

> Next Monday, the 29th of December, the young Dutchman, known here by the name of Franz la Motte, 13 years old, will have the honor of giving a concert in the Imperial Burgtheater. It will begin at 6:00 sharp, and the prices will be as usual in the theater.[27]

After Kohary's creditors took over the management, they curtailed performances to about half of the former Lenten schedule and, if the sources are complete in their account, almost completely did away with performances during the rest of the year:

> During Lent [of 1773] 6 concerts were given in the Burgtheater and 3 in the Kärntnerthortheater. The receipts of one and half the receipts of 2 others were designated for the benefit of the widows and orphans of local musicians [i.e., the concerts of the Tonkünstler Societät].[28]

> There were 6 musical academies during Lent in the month of April, one on May 6, and 3 in the last 9 days of Advent.[29]

---

[24]Zechmeister/THEATER, pp. 70-71.
[25]Böck/KHEVENHUELLER, p. 36. (II/12)
[26]Müller/NACHRICHTEN, p. 95. (II/13)
[27]WZ, December 27, 1766, n.p. (II/14)
[28]ALMANACH 1774, n.p. (II/15)
[29]TASCHENBUCH 1777, p. 171. (II/16)

However, reports in the *Wienerisches Diarium* (WZ) and the *Realzeitung* indicate continuing activity, some possibly sponsored by individual and not the theater direction (also see appendix 1):

> Next Friday, the 30th of November [1770], a musical academy will be held in the Burgtheater in which the two Colla brothers, famous musicians on the unusual instrument known as the Calassioncino (a species like the familiar mandolin) will perform various concertos. Herr Joseph Milliko, like the rest of the local Italian opera company, will perform, and in particular, the above-mentioned Herr Milliko will sing an aria with obbligato Calassioncino. These will be mixed with duets, concertos and symphonies. No one will be allowed into the parquet or boxes free of charge.[30]

> The 30th [of October, 1772] musical academy. The music began with a grand symphony by Hr. Ditters. Madames Weiglin, Weisen and Kurzen, Mlle Rosina Baglioni and Herr Poggi sang assorted arias. Mme Weisin and Hr. Poggi also repeated some from the opera Armida. Hr. Pichl played a new concerto on the violin, as did Hr. Krumpholz on the harp. All these pieces were mixed with symphonies, including one with the English horn by Chevalier Gluck, and another by Hr. Bach, with which the academy concluded.[31]

> The 8th [of January, 1773] musical academy. Herr Drechsler performed for the first time and sang several arias, one of which was accompanied by an oboe solo. Hr. Ulrich played for the first time a concerto and solo on that same instrument. Both great virtuosos are employed at Anspach. Mlle Rosa Baglioni, Mmes Weisin and Kurzin sang several arias. All of these pieces were mixed with several grand symphonies, of which the first was by Hr. Piccini and the second by Hr. Gassmann.[32]

In 1775, the Kärntnerthortheater was leased to a troop of French actors who had permission to present plays three days a week. Occasional concerts still occurred, apparently organized privately by individual virtuosos:

[30]WZ, November 28, 1770, n.p. (II/17)
[31]RZ, November 7, 1772, pp. 709-10. (II/18)
[32]RZ, January 23, 1773, p. 47. (II/19)

Monday, the 16th of this month [March] there was a grand concert for music lovers in the Kärntnerthortheater. On this occasion, two virtuosos in the employ of Prince Öttingen-Wallenstein, who have just arrived, namely Herr Janisch on the violin and Herr Reicha on the cello, played masterfully with their own strength and charm, concertos and duets composed according to the latest fashion. Mademoiselle Cavallieri, a native Viennese, also sang two arias in their full setting. The audience—as numerous as it was brilliant—rewarded the efforts of these incomparable musicians with well-earned general approbation.[33]

This arrangement remained in effect until the 1780s, when the Kärntnerthortheater again came under direct court control.

It is obvious from the foregoing discussion that running the two theaters was fraught with financial risk. From an artistic standpoint, the ever-changing business arrangements created an unstable atmosphere unsuitable for creative activity. As a result, in 1776, a contingent of actors went to Joseph II to request that he take the Burgtheater under the protection of the court and elevate it to the status of national theater.[34] The proclamation was issued on April 2, 1776, and a new era began in Viennese theater and concert history.[35]

Only one reference to concert activity outside the two court theaters during the pre-1776 period was found: a Signora Fumagalli placed an advertisement in the *Wienerisches Diarium* announcing she would perform on July 8, 1752, in the Gasthaus and dance hall known as the Mehlgrube.[36] Although the Mehlgrube very probably witnessed other musical presentations during this period, it is not mentioned again until the 1780s. It would have been one of the very few locations where traveling virtuosos could have presented their own concerts, since the court theaters were not let for that purpose until the late 1760s, and then only rarely.

Other traceable public concerts began in 1772 under the auspices of the Tonkünstler Societät. Founded a year earlier by the Court

[33]WZ, March 18, 1778, n.p. (II/20)
[34]Zechmeister/THEATER, p. 100.
[35]The theater administration's impact on concert life is discussed in chapter 3.
[36]WZ, July 8, 1752, n.p.

48

Kapellmeister Florian Gassmann, the society had as its main purpose the establishment of a retirement fund and pensions for deceased members' widows and orphans. To raise money, the members gave four concerts a year (on December 22 and 23, and on two days at the end of Lent) in the Kärntnerthortheater (later in the Burgtheater). Most of the programs centered around an oratorio written for the occasion, but some featured a mixture of vocal, instrumental and choral music. The concerts soon became a tradition and were among the first Viennese non-operatic performances to receive critical attention in newspapers.[37]

Vienna did indeed have a continuous and fairly active concert life beginning at about the middle of the century, but it remained dependent on the court theaters and their performance calendar for many years. That dependence insured its secondary status in the city's cultural world. Moreover, since the theater management exercised such strong control in providing public concerts, there was not much impetus for forming a "Friends of Music Society" along the lines of the German model. When the theater management abdicated its responsibility in 1776, no organization was there to take up the slack and provide a regular calendar of performances. In that void, the rich and colorful array of concerts characteristic of the Viennese High Classic period began to emerge.

PUBLIC CONCERTS FROM 1776-1810

The variety found in the public concert arena equals that of the private sphere. But while for private concerts the purpose of the event proved to be the significant identifying factor, for public ones, the sponsorship is the key. Their organizers ranged from individual concertizing virtuosos and entrepreneurs to charitable organizations, each type with its own particular problems and characteristics.

---

[37]These concerts have been discussed in C. F. Pohl's history of the society (Pohl/TS). Because of their high visibility and the availability of records on them, they have been accorded a position in Viennese concert history that overstates their actual significance.

Virtuoso Benefits

Virtuoso Benefits were set up independently by the individual performer, who made all the arrangements, assumed all the expenses, and received all the profits. Especially in the 1780s and early 1790s, benefits were by far the most frequent type of public concert activity. No one guiding hand is apparent—whoever wished simply applied to the appropriate authorities for permission to use the theater or hall. In 1794, when Baron Braun took over the court theaters, independent virtuoso concerts were dealt a blow, because he simply quit leasing the theaters to private artists. Only Josefa Auernhammer—apparently a favorite of his—and a few other musicians, mostly associated with the court, were allowed to use the Burgtheater. He let the Kärntnerthortheater occasionally, but generally to already established musicians. Other locations gradually absorbed the overflow, but the absence of a concert hall was sorely felt.

The list of names of independent concert givers includes both foreign and resident instrumental virtuosos, singers, members of the local theater orchestras, and composers. Only those musicians holding the higher court positions (such as *Kapellmeister*) never gave their own concerts, although they frequently assisted at charity fundraisers (see page 178). Probably their secure positions and higher salaries obviated the necessity for such enterprises.

Another possibility open to the virtuoso involved organizing a series of three or four concerts and selling subscriptions rather than individual tickets. Since the theaters were not available on such a regular basis, the artist had to depend on other locations, such as the dance hall of the Mehlgrube or specially rented rooms, which of course had a limited capacity. Most of what we know about this type of concert has been uncovered by Mozart scholars, since he is known to have given two such series. In 1784, Mozart and Georg Friedrich Richter rented Room 9 of the Trattnerhof together, each intending to give several performances there. Mozart planned three concerts, for which he managed to assemble 174 subscribers, thirty more, he boasted, than Richter and [John Abraham] Fischer

50

together.[38] Richter apparently intended to give six, but there are no documents to prove that either his or Fischer's plans ever came to fruition.

During Lent of the following year, Mozart gave a famous series of six concerts in the Mehlgrube, to which over 150 of Vienna's aristocratic and bourgeois music lovers subscribed. One can imagine the difficulties in arranging such concerts; not only did the orchestra and soloists have to be engaged, but the hall itself had to be outfitted each time. Leopold Mozart, who fortunately was visiting Vienna, wrote detailed letters back to Mozart's sister and reported that Mozart's piano had to be transported to the Mehlgrube for each performance. The toll exacted in time alone must have been enormous. Apparently he repeated his efforts the next winter, for Leopold informed Nannerl: "He wrote me that he hurriedly gave three subscription concerts for 120 subscribers."[39] That no notice of the concerts appeared in the local papers should be taken neither as a slight to Mozart nor as an indication the performances never took place. Such private undertakings were of no interest to the *Wiener Zeitung,* (a court newspaper) and since subscription tickets were sold in advance with targeted appeals to patrons and music lovers, advertising probably realized little.[40] We know of Mozart's endeavors largely because his fame led to the preservation of his letters; undoubtedly other musicians undertook similar enterprises, though no trace of them remains.

Charity Fundraisers

Following the precedent set by the Tonkünstler Societät, other organizations and sometimes private individuals began to organize concerts to raise money for a charity or other worthy cause. Musicians often donated their services; other expenses were sometimes

[38]ML 2:872. Fischer apparently was organizing a series too.
[39]MB, 3:484. (II/21)
[40]Only one ad mentioning a subscription concert appeared in the WZ before 1810—for Bernhard Romberg's series in March of 1808. See WZ, March 5, 1808, p. 1100.

paid by a noble patron. In most cases, the court and the high nobility could be counted on for donations well above the price of admission, so that huge sums were often realized (see chapter 4). In some cases, profits were enhanced by the added attraction of a masked ball:

> Upon highest command, after Easter a masked ball as well as a musical academy for dilettantes will be given each month. The latter will be open to anyone who participates in the rehearsal. Proceeds of this entertainment will go to the Institute for the Poor.[41]

Nothing more was heard of this laudable effort, though it may well have continued. By the end of the century, a variety of causes began to tap this source of revenue. In 1796, the actors of the court theaters gave the first of their annual concerts to raise money for poor families connected with the theater. The St. Marx Bürgerspital, an organization that cared for indigent citizens of Vienna, soon followed suit. Though the record of the concerts is irregular, they seem to have begun in 1801 and continued through 1810 twice a year, on Christmas day and once in the spring. In 1804, the newly founded "Wohlthätigkeitsanstalten" (Charity Organization) began its semi-annual concerts, which generally took place on St. Leopold's Day (November 15) and on Pentecost.

Apart from these regular events, special fundraisers were organized from time to time to meet some particular need. The earliest uncovered was given by the court musician Leopold Koželuch on March 25 and 27, 1793, with the proceeds going to the "Taubstummeninstitut," a school for deaf and dumb children.

Given the proclivity of the Austrian monarchy to constant warfare, appeals for aid for wounded soldiers or for war widows occurred constantly. Often the program consisted of a cantata on a topical patriotic theme, which, if it proved successful, might be repeated several times. Herr Lizentiat v. Rautenstrauch organized one of the most successful ones to benefit the "Korps der Wiener Freywilligen" (Viennese Volunteer Army). Franz X. Süssmayer's

[41]PZ, April 13, 1791, p. 288. (II/22)

cantata for the occasion, entitled "Der Retter in Gefahr," was produced in the Grosser Redoutensaal four times.[42] The court newspaper, the *Wiener Zeitung,*reported every detail of the proceedings, including a performance given by the citizens of nearby Wienerneustadt. Others also rallied to the cause, with other fundraisers in the Kärntnerthortheater[43] and in the Theater in der Leopoldstadt.[44]

Entrepreneur Subscription Series

The history of long-term concert series in Vienna is dominated by two names: Philipp Jacques Martin and Ignaz Schuppanzigh. P. J. Martin is a shadowy figure who surfaced several times in connection with public concerts during the period 1781 to 1791, then dropped out of sight completely. He appears first as the organizer of dilettante concerts at the Mehlgrube in 1781:

> Herr P. J. Martin has undertaken a grand dilettante concert, which will be held, summer and winter, in the grand hall of the Mehlgrube from 6:30 until 9:00 P. M. Any dilettante of either sex can practice or perform on his instrument. A contribution of 2 Gulden 10 Kr. will be given monthly. In the adjoining rooms gaming tables for all types of games will be held in readiness, and each person will be served with refreshments upon demand.[45]

According to Friedrich Nicolai, who visited Vienna that year, the concerts actually did take place. The atmosphere of the location—a dance hall offering several kinds of pleasantries—has already been encountered in the private concerts discussed and obviously did not please Nicolai. These comments by a North German tourist on a South German custom indicate a difference in mentality and perspective on musical enjoyment and appreciation. Austrian

[42]September 19 and 21, 1796, October 4, 1796, and November 15, 1796.
[43]September 27, 1796.
[44]October 14, 15, and 16, 1796.
[45]RZ, July 10, 1781, p. 446. (II/23)

writers reacted with righteous indignation to his frequently acid remarks on Viennese people and society, and indeed he does seem quite pompous occasionally, but his opinions were often echoed by other visitors from North German states.

There aren't any public concerts in summer, but many in winter. Particularly during Lent, when the theaters are closed and therefore there is a scarcity of diversions, many so called academies are held in public and private houses, where during the music-making, people play cards and eat refreshments. When I was in Vienna, someone by the name of Philipp Jacques Martin announced—as entrepreneur "the organization of a grand dilettante concert [series] in which many local dilettante gentlemen are pleased to practice with a full orchestra; our fine company assembles, sees each other and converses, which could become one of the most wonderful sights for a foreign observer of national entertainments." . . . These "Liebhaber Concerte" were to be held on Fridays from 6:30 to 8:30, summer and winter, in the Mehlgrube. They really did take place, but ended the following summer. Paragraph 6 of the announcement read: "In the adjoining rooms gaming tables for all types of games will be held in readiness, for which *à Discretion* money for playing will be laid out, and the company will be served with refreshments upon demand." This is at the least not arranged after the example of the Music Lovers' Concerts in Berlin. There they are content with the pure enjoyment of the music, without wishing to have the pleasures of card playing, eating and drinking in addition. There you would think you showed both the music lovers and professional musicians a discourtesy and dishonored the music, if you rattled playing chips and hot chocolate cups throughout.

There are many ardent lovers of music in Vienna and not a few who are connoisseurs and could more or less pass for virtuosos. These certainly do not approve of hindering the enjoyment of the music, which can completely fill the spirit of someone capable of being sensitive to it, by card playing and eating. In the private concerts of true music lovers that I attended in Vienna, it was not so.[46]

The programs themselves seem to have been, at least from this

[46]Nicolai/BESCHREIBUNG, 4:552-53. (II/24)

description, similar to the theater-sponsored Lenten concerts in the 1750s, a type of amateur pot-luck.

The following summer, Martin moved his enterprise to the Augarten, a pleasure garden on the edge of the city:

> Not long ago, Herr Martin moved his Dilettante concerts (original-
> ly in the city at the Mehlgrube) to the Augarten for the summer,
> where you can now, at very cheap prices, have the pleasure every
> Sunday of admiring many virtuosos of both sexes, and enjoy
> yourself most pleasantly in the beautiful company.[47]

In the process, he enlisted the support of at least one professional musician, W. A. Mozart, who wrote to his father:

> May 8, 1782. This summer there is to be a concert every Sunday
> in the Augarten. A certain Martin organized last winter a series of
> amateur concerts, which took place every Friday in the Mehlgrube.
> You know that there are a great many amateurs in Vienna, and some
> very good ones too, both men and women. But so far these con-
> certs have not been properly arranged. Well, this Martin has now
> got permission from the Emperor under charter (with the promise
> too of his gracious patronage) to give twelve concerts in the Augarten
> and four grand serenades in the finest open places of the city. The
> subscription for the whole summer is two ducats. . . . The orchestra
> consists entirely of amateurs, with the exception of the bassoon
> players, the trumpeters and drummers.[48]

In his next letter, he describes the first concert, which took place on May 26 at about nine o'clock in the morning:

> For tomorrow our first concert takes place in the Augarten and at
> half past eight Martin is fetching me in a carriage. . . . [Tonight]
> we are having the rehearsal of the concert. A symphony by Van
> Swieten and one of mine are being performed; an amateur singer,
> Mlle Berger, is going to sing; a boy of the name of Türk is playing
> a violin concerto; and Fräulein Auernhammer and I are playing my
> E-flat concerto for two pianos.[49]

[47]WZ, June 1, 1782, n.p. (II/25)
[48]ML 2:804-05.
[49]ML 2:805.

Mozart never mentioned the series again. It was discontinued some-
time during that summer (see the Nicolai quote above), and the
next sign of a similar undertaking does not occur until 1791, with
Martin's announcement of a series of open-air concerts at various
times and at various places around the city. It is impossible to ascertain whether they simply continued the previous year's activities,
or whether they were being presented again after a pause of several
years:

> The undersigned has the honor—after receiving the highest
> permission—of most respectfully notifying the high and most
> gracious nobility and the most estimable public that upon the
> repeated requests of the patrons and lovers of the noble art, he will
> have the most flattering pleasure of renewing his much-loved and
> very pleasant grand musicales in the Augarten. They will be free
> to everyone, but in the following manner: 1) His wind band music,
> some fully orchestrated, some in select arrangements, will be held
> from 5 to 8 every Monday morning in the Augarten in the open air,
> but the best precautions will be taken against the intense heat of
> the sun. 2) On Tuesdays, however, it will be held next to the
> Lusthaus Avenue, where the last cafe is, from 5 to 7 in the after-
> noon. 3) Thursdays it will always be in the city at the square "Am
> Hof" after the theaters are out, from 10 until midnight (like a
> serenade). These arrangements will continue all summer. 4) Only
> those with series tickets will be allowed in the circle; anyone who
> wishes can listen to the music outside of the circle free of charge.[50]

Martin had cleverly chosen the locations to coincide with the daily
patterns of fashionable Viennese society. The Augarten was the
favored spot for breakfast and a promenade, but the shady paths
of the Prater, with its many cafes, were more alluring during the
heat of the afternoon. Any music earlier in the evening would have
had to compete with the theaters, but a serenade under the stars
after the stuffy buildings would have provided a delightful end to
the day. However, the success of this rather ambitious scheme
depended upon finding enough patrons to buy a subscription seat

[50]WZ, May 14, 1791, p. 1294. (II/26)

in the circle of chairs arranged around the musicians, and here Martin ran into problems. Most of the Viennese nobility retired to their country estates during the summer and were not particularly interested in supporting a series they would not hear. Not surprisingly, several weeks later he was forced to announce that the first concert would have to be postponed because he had not raised enough money to cover his expenses. In the hopes of doing so, he introduced the possibility of buying individual tickets to attract more listeners, leaving the price of the ticket up to their generosity (not an unusual practice at that time):

> The undersigned has herewith the honor of announcing most respectfully that he will have the honor of providing individual tickets to his musical performances—for a voluntary contribution, as a convenience for those who do not plan to buy a series ticket but who only wish to attend a few of his performances now and then, either because of an upcoming trip to the country or because of other business. . . . The undersigned has been forced, due to insufficient series ticket sales, (because many of the ladies and gentlemen who would normally have supported him, as they always do, have either already departed or are leaving every day for the country) to postpone the opening concert to the 14th of June in the Prater instead of the 6th of June in the Augarten.[51]

We can assume the concerts finally did get underway—no notice to the contrary appeared, but no further trace of either Martin or his open-air concerts could be found.

The history of public concerts in the Augarten would then appear to start with Martin's enterprise in 1782, but a brief history of public concerts given in the *Allgemeine Musikalische Zeitung* in 1800 discusses an entirely different series and does not even mention Martin's name:

> Then there are generally 12 musical performances in the Augarten in the morning, under the name Dilettante Musicales. These were organized by Herr Vice President von Kees. After the time when

[51]WZ, June 4, 1791, p. 1505-06. (II/27)

57

the Emperor Joseph, to his eternal glory, dedicated the Augarten to the public's enjoyment, the personnel consisted mostly of dilettantes, except for the wind instruments and the double basses. Even ladies of the highest nobility played. The audience was very brilliant and everything proceeded with such order and respectability that everyone gladly contributed all their energy to its support. The proceeds of the low-cost subscription were used entirely for expenses. Afterwards Hr. Rudolph took over as director. Things still were going well, but not as brilliantly; the nobility withdrew, since most of them had only come to please the Emperor Joseph; nonetheless, the performances were still very pleasant. Now Hr. Schuppanzigh has them, and that rousing audience is entirely gone. No true music lover wants to play any more, even the professional musicians only rarely play concertos. In general, the fire of the institution has entirely gone out. The concertos are seldom accompanied well; the symphonies go a little better. Since the purpose of the entrepreneur now is not so much love of art or pleasure as his own profit, it is simply not possible with the low subscription price to have something renowned in the music.[52]

This paragraph has been the basis for most subsequent references to the "Augarten concerts," but upon closer observation, it contains some puzzling statements and has an unwarranted negative slant. In fact, the article from which it comes was written by a North German visitor to the city, who had little regard for Viennese concert organization, and who may not have had all his facts straight.[53] The correspondent implies a continuous non-profit series beginning after 1775, when Joseph II opened the Augarten to the general public, up to 1799, when Herr Schuppanzigh took over and turned it into a crude and crass money-making operation.[54] It does seem unlikely, however, given the difficulties involved in securing an audience in the summer, that there would have been two competing series—Martin's and Hofrath von Kees's—in the same place. Actually, the organization described sounds more like the "Friends

[52]AMZ, October 15, 1800, cols. 45-47. (II/28)
[53]See chapter 7 for a discussion of the article.
[54]The disparaging mention of a low subscription price might also imply the disparagement of an audience unable to afford anything higher.

of Music'' who presented the Belvedere concerts in 1785-87 (see page 62); perhaps the writer confused the two. In any case, Martin's efforts and the legendary von Kees concerts are not the same.

During the 1790s, concerts which could be those under Herr Rudolph's direction did take place, although the local press took no notice of them. The visiting composer Friedrich Witt wrote to a friend about the Augarten performances in 1796, which he says occurred every day at 7:00 A.M.:

> The day before yesterday I gave one of my symphonies there and Bär (Beer) played one of my [clarinet] concertos. Presumably the director trumpeted the news about, for Wranizci [Wranizky], Girowez [Gyrowetz] and our Papa Haydn were present.[55]

Two years later, another visitor to the city, Ernst Moritz Arndt, reported that concerts were often given there as well as music by dilettantes, which could be heard every Thursday.[56] Thus it would seem that both series and individually organized performances were presented.

In 1799, Ignaz Schuppanzigh, a violinist and leader of the string quartet founded by Prince Rasumofsky, took charge of what he called the ''Liebhaber-Concerte,'' featuring both amateur and professional soloists in series of four concerts:

> On the 30th of May the ''Liebhaber Concerte'' in the Augarten will begin and will continue through the next three Thursdays. The gentlemen subscribers may at their pleasure send for their series tickets at the undersigned's [apartment] on Obere Bäckerstrasse #813, the third floor. The price of each series ticket is 4 fl 30 x, and includes 6 tickets for each concert.[57]

They began at the somewhat early hour of 7:00 A.M. and lasted approximately two hours, with the mixed type of program found everywhere at this time.[58] The orchestra was praised for the preci-

---

[55]Landon/C & W, 4:34.
[56]Arndt/BRUCKSTUECKE, p. 219.
[57]WZ, May 22, 1799, p. 1636. (II/29)
[58]AMZ, May 22, 1799, col. 543.

sion of its playing and the concerts in general received favorable reviews:

> The usual academies are continuing. One almost always gets to hear good symphonies. Otherwise it is mostly dilettantes of both sexes, many of whom are just beginning to think about studying, who make an appearance playing or singing. For many listeners, this holds an interest that is not at all to be censured, but, for musicians, little or none.[59]

> This park has often given me the greatest pleasure, particularly lively, when, on a cool, clear morning, Herr Schuppanzigh gives his concerts in the park hall. The pieces, which are almost entirely given by dilettantes, were limited to grand symphonies, overtures, vocal pieces and concertos. The former are presented here (especially Cherubini's wonderful overtures from *Die Tage der Gefahr*, *Medea*, and *Lodoiska*), according to the unanimous opinion of all connoisseurs, with an exactness, precision, and strength, that is seldom attained by our court theater, whose orchestra is certainly good.[60]

> The pieces performed were mostly very select and were presented with industry, precision, and fire, although the company consisted almost exclusively of dilettantes.[61]

Only two series of four concerts each took place in 1804, instead of the normal three or four, perhaps because of lack of interest on the part of the audience. Next year things appeared to get even worse; the *Allgemeine Musikalische Zeitung* reported that attendance was dropping, then that the series had been canceled, "presumably because it found too little support,"[62] though the *Zeitung für die elegante Welt* mentioned cool and rainy weather as the reason. Finally in September, Schuppanzigh collected enough subscribers for another series.[63] The concerts continued in 1806, but in the following years, no mention is made of them. In 1808, the *Allgemeine Musikalische Zeitung* reported:

[59]AMZ, August 26, 1801, col. 800. (II/30)
[60]FM, August 1, 1803, p. 483. (II/31)
[61]AMZ, September 5, 1804, cols. 823-24. (II/32)
[62]AMZ, June 26, 1805, col. 630; July 24, 1805, col. 689.
[63]AMZ, September 18, 1805, col. 810.

Although the old Augarten concerts under Schuppanzigh's direction appear not to be coming up this summer again; nonetheless, since the first of May we have heard several concerts that have been given there by other local artists.[64]

Schuppanzigh resumed his activities as concert organizer in 1810, this time with a series of six concerts in what appeared to be only one series:

After so many friends of music have fervently expressed the wish that the Music Lovers' Morning Concerts in the Imperial Royal Augarten Hall would start up once again, Schuppanzigh intends to undertake the enterprise. Any friend of music of either sex whom it would give pleasure to perform or play in the orchestra and who at the same time has the requisite talents is herewith publicly invited. Each of these dilettantes must register at Herr Schuppanzigh's apartment on Landstrasse in Prince Rasumovsky's residence (first side building, second floor) and also must promise to appear without fail at all 6 of the concerts. The necessary instruments will always be available. Since this enterprise always entails many expenses, it is necessary that Schuppanzigh be covered in advance against losses. . . . Each subscriber will receive a refund in the event that no concerts are given due to lack of subscribers.[65]

Clearly, Schuppanzigh, like other series organizers, attempted to present his concerts at times when they did not conflict with other events, i.e., the theater and salons, a tacit acknowledgment of the public concert's less than primary status in the Viennese cultural world. That status is confirmed by the small number of performances in the final category of public concerts.

Series Organized by a Friends of Music Society

The typical pattern of concert organization in most European cities included at least one or two standing series provided by a group

[64]AMZ, June 23, 1808, col. 623. (II/33)
[65]WZ, May 30, 1810, p. 1006. (II/34)

of music lovers using a core of dilettante performers and occasional professional soloists. In Vienna, however, such "Friends of Music" concerts are quite rare. Before the founding of the Gesellschaft der Musikfreunde, only two such groups appeared on the scene, both for very brief periods, exercising very little influence on the city's musical structure.

We know nothing about the organization sponsoring the first series. The concerts, which took place during three successive summers (1785-87) in the gardens of the Belvedere palace, did attract the attention of the *Wiener Zeitung*:

> For several weeks now, a society of eminent musicians and friends of music has been giving public musical academies for the enjoyment of local audiences every Monday, weather permitting, in the gardens of the Belvedere palace. A pleasant company of local residents has been there each time. Last Monday, the 8th of this month [August] Hr. Mestrino, musician with Count Ladislaus Erdödi, played an excellent concerto on the violin there, for the enjoyment of all.

> A society of music lovers entertained the local public this year, as last, with excellent music every Thursday or Monday at the Belvedere palace, with a considerable number of listeners there each time. This musical entertainment will be given for the last time this year on Thursday the 24th of this month [August].

> Several friends of music are once again giving weekly concerts at the Belvedere palace for the entertainment of the public. They have been every Thursday, but from now on, Wednesdays are designated for them.[66]

Aside from these three notices, nothing about the performances has survived, and nothing suggests the activity might have been continued indoors during the winter months.

A more famous concert organization presented a series of performances twenty years later, in the 1807-08 season. Known to its members as "Musikalisches Institut," "Liebhaber Concerte,"

[66]WZ, August 10,1785, p. 1874; August 23, 1786, pp. 2006-07; July 14, 1787, p. 1685. (II/35)

"Musikfreunde," or the "Gesellschaft der Musikfreunde," this society presented twenty performances to a carefully chosen audience of subscribers. Each of the 70 members had a certain number of tickets that could be distributed to friends and acquaintances. None were sold to the general public, however, so that technically the concerts were semi-private, although most music lovers could secure a ticket to at least one or two performances. Altogether, 1309 places were available;[67] originally the concerts took place in the dance hall known as the Mehlgrube, but when that proved inadequate, the noblemen who acted as "protectors" helped to secure permission to use the grand hall (the Aula) at the University. There the season ended with the famous performance of Haydn's *Die Schöpfung* in Carpani's Italian translation, attended by the aging composer. Despite the triumphant finish and the general success of the series, it was not resumed the following year due to the increasingly difficult political and economic situation.

Short-lived as they were, the concerts marked the first appearance in Vienna of a philosophy of concert-giving that recognized as its main purpose the support and furtherance of the art of music:

> The productions of native and foreign masterpieces will purify taste and give it a secure, lasting direction; it will encourage native artists to compete with each other, secure the genius from the oppression of intrigue, bring young talent to perfection, and of itself educate, through continuing common practice in the orchestra, finished masters on the various instruments, masters who will then spread a good method through their students. . . . Each concert must distinguish itself by the performance of significant and undeniably excellent musical works, because only in such a manner is the Institute in the position to maintain its position and reach an ever-higher perfection.[68]

This quotation from the society's statutes embodies an attitude more typical of the nineteenth-century "romantic" conception of music,

---

[67]The information is taken from Biba/LIEBHABER and VB.
[68]Regulations of the "Liebhaber Concerte," quoted in Biba/LIEBHABER, p. 84. (II/36)

one which raised the entire process of performance to a loftier plane than just entertainment. The appearance of that attitude signaled the dawn of a new era, when the structure and function of Viennese public concerts began to take on the characteristics we recognize as appropriate today.

Thus there appears to have been no lack of public concerts in late eighteenth-century Vienna, though they did not assume a primary role in the city's musical world. Before 1776, they were controlled by the management of the court theaters, for whom they were of minor importance. Even when freed of that association, concerts still had to fit into the existing entertainment schedule dominated by the theater and private salons. (Thus the most popular times for performances remained the summer season and theater holidays.) The absence of a sponsoring organization further insured that they would not be able to effectively compete with other cultural offerings.

This ad hoc nature affected not only the frequency and consistency of concert offerings, it also made life difficult for concertizing artists. Having no central agency to assist them, they were forced to undertake all practical matters involved, including finding a suitable place to perform and making all the business arrangements. It is to those aspects that we now turn.

CHAPTER THREE

Public Concert Locations

In 1831, nearly a century after the earliest signs of concert activity, Vienna's first public building devoted specifically to the presentation of concerts opened its doors. In other European centers, e.g. London, Berlin, Leipzig, the development of public concerts had necessitated the building, or at least the designation of, a concert hall or music room within a few short decades. But the structure of Viennese concerts, as discussed in the previous chapter, did not demand, and perhaps would not have supported, any such facility. Indeed, the Viennese did not appear to be overly disturbed by this quirk in their musical life. Occasional comments about the drawbacks of various locations appeared from time to time in reviews and other commentaries, but only rarely was the suggestion made that the situation might be helped by the construction of a building designated as a concert hall.[1] In its absence, a colorful array of places served as concert locations. Performances were held in parks, in pubs, in dance halls, restaurants, theaters, hotels, elegant ballrooms—anywhere, in fact, that offered enough space for musicians and audience. Each of these places brought a different atmosphere, different traditions and a different clientele to the music presented, and each posed its own particular problems for the performer. By far the most desirable locations were the

[1]AMZ, May 15, 1805, col. 534.

theaters, both in terms of comfort and acoustics, so we shall consider them first.

COURT-CONTROLLED THEATERS

The availability of the two court-controlled theaters, the Burgtheater and the Kärntnerthortheater, decreased as the century drew to a close, partly because the easing of the "Norma" regulations allowed more dramatic productions and partly because of the theater bureaucracy's changing attitudes toward concerts. With the elevation of the Burgtheater to the status of National Theater in 1776,[2] a three-tiered hierarchy of administrative and artistic direction was established. At the top was the *Oberstkämmerer*,[3] an official with control over a wide variety of court affairs, who functioned in this instance mainly as an intermediary between the Emperor and the lower theater administration in matters of general theater policy. The second level, also a court position, dealt with the day-to-day business of running the theater, and the third level, filled by representatives of the actors, assumed the artistic direction. Table 6 lists the office holders in the top two levels from 1776 to 1810. A musician wishing to give a concert at the Burgtheater would have applied to the person in the second level of administration, as did Franz Thurner in1783:[4]

[2]According to tradition, Joseph II proposed the founding of a theater devoted to the German-language tradition under the artistic control of the actors themselves, to which the latter responded gratefully. Zechmeister has uncovered documents which indicate that the suggestion came from the actors and was agreed to by Joseph II after he had decided to assume control of the theaters again. See Zechmeister/THEATERS, p. 100.

[3]The court administration was divided into several main sections, each run by a member of the high nobility, the three most important being the Oberstkämmerer, the Obersthofmeister and the Oberststallmeister.

[4]See chapter 4. Mozart first approached the Inspector of the Properties about giving a concert "since most matters of this kind depend on him and because he has much influence with Count Rosenberg and Baron Kienmayr" (the theater directors, see table 6). ML 2:792.

TABLE 6. Court Theater Officials, 1776-1810

Official Head Court Department	Administration
1776 Prince Johann Josef Khevenhüller (Obersthofmeister)	1776 Baron Johann Michael Kienmayer
	1783 Count Franz Xaver Orsini-Rosenberg
1791 Count Franz Xaver Orsini-Rosenberg (Oberstkämmerer)	1791 Count Johann Wenzel Ugarte
	1792 Count Johann Ferdinand Küfstein
	1793 Count Küfstein Count Vinzenz Strassoldo

From 1794 until 1817 the Burgtheater was leased.

1796 Count Franz Colloredo (Oberstkämmerer) 1806 Count Rudolf Wrbna- Freudenthal (Oberstkämmerer)	1794 Baron Peter von Braun
	1807 Prince Nikolaus Esterházy Prince Josef zu Schwarzenberg Count Ferdinand Palffy Prince Josef Lobkowitz Count Stephan Zichy Count Franz Esterházy Count Franz Nikolaus Esterházy Count Hieronymus Lodron
	1810 Count Palffy Prince Lobkowitz Prince Schwarzenberg

Information taken from Obzyna/BURGTHEATER.

67

No. 18. Thurner, Franz asks permission to give an academy on the flute in the National Theater.[5]

A note appended to the request (which was granted) indicates that the matter was taken care of orally. Only one or two other requests are preserved in the theater records, so apparently no consistent record was kept of them.

Though court documents may be silent on this point, concert activity was noted in various journals:

> Mixed with the plays are musical academies which different virtuosos give on their own responsibility and for their own benefit.[6]

Both the *Wiener Zeitung* and *Das Wienerblättchen* ran notices of concerts during the 1780s, but not consistently.[7] Nonetheless, they record the presentation of three concerts per week in Lent of 1784, and show an increase in activity in Lent of the following year, with a total of thirty-four performances. In 1786, however, Joseph II began to gradually lift the restrictions imposed by the "Norma" edict, thus reducing the number of days the court theaters were available for concerts. The Burgtheater remained closed during Lent, but four plays (or operas) per week were allowed in the Kärntnerthortheater:

> Since during this Lenten period plays are to be given by the Court theater actors in the Kärntnerthortheater for five weeks on Sundays, Mondays, Tuesdays and Thursdays, [they] began on March 2. . . . On the remaining days each week, musical academies will be given in the same theater; the first was to benefit Sig. Coltellini, and the second for Herr Calvesi, both members of the I.R. Italian opera troupe.[8]

[5]VIENNA-INTENDENZ, Verzeichniss und Index über die Theater-Acten, February 8, 1793. (III/1)
[6]PFEFFER, p. 15. (III/2)
[7]For example, only a few of the 1787 concerts documented by placards in the Theater Archives of the Oesterreichische Nationalbibliothek were advertised in the WZ.
[8]WZ, March 8, 1786, p. 510. (III/3)

Even given the full availability of the Burgtheater, competition with the plays at the Kärntnerthortheater would have limited the feasibility of giving concerts. The arrangement with alternating plays and concerts continued in the Kärntnerthortheater during Lent of 1787, with only a few concerts announced during the rest of the year. In 1788, the theater closed and remained closed until late 1791, so that the main concert location shifted back to the Burgtheater. Ten Lenten concerts could be identified there during that year, with similar numbers in 1791, 1793, and 1794.

On August 1, 1794, the Burg and the Kärntnerthortheater were leased to Baron Peter von Braun. Nominal court control was maintained through the office of the *Oberstkämmerer*, and the Emperor continued to grant a subsidy, but administrative, artistic, and financial matters were handled solely by the Baron. With regard to concerts, his contract specified:

> The Vice Director is also free to organize unmasked balls, concerts spirituels or similar entertainments as he wishes.[9]

His responsibility to the court involved submitting yearly financial statements, which are preserved in the Hofkammerarchiv in Vienna. However, his private dealings with individual artists were his own matter and are thus not documented in court records, so that his negotiations with musicians about giving concerts have been lost.

After Baron Braun assumed control in the fall of 1794, the number of concerts dropped sharply.[10] Aside from the four annual presentations of the Tonkünstler Societät and one or two for the poor of the theater, only a few took place each year. The reasons for Braun's hesitancy to grant the theater are unknown; perhaps he saw no financial advantage in doing so, since he would have been creating competition for himself.

[9]VIENNA-CAMERALE, folio 87r. (III/4)
[10]Although his contract permitted him to produce plays during Lent (with the exception of Holy Week), he continued to maintain partial schedules during that time, with each theater closed two to three days per week. See VIENNA-CAMERALE.

His policies were censured by his contemporaries, and later by music historians, especially by those who deplored his unwillingness or inability to recognize the genius of Beethoven. That charge stems in part from a letter written by Beethoven's brother Carl:

> My brother would have written to you himself, but he is ill-disposed towards everything because the Director of the Theatre, Baron von Braun, who, as is known, is a stupid and rude fellow, refused him the use of the Theatre for his concert and gave it to other really mediocre artists.[11]

The "mediocre artist" undoubtedly refers to Josefa Auernhammer, a pianist of less than first rank who nonetheless gave a concert in the Burgtheater on March 25th each year. A review of one of her performances occasioned comment on the theater's use:

> At this opportunity, one might reasonably ask why the theater is not lent to our great masters, for example Beethoven, Eberl, etc., and instead it is preferred to leave it unused and closed? Why should the fate of so many excellent artists in many fields be dependent on the moods of a single person?[12]

These remarks echoed a complaint made two years earlier in the *Allgemeine Musikalische Zeitung*:

> The first two locations [the court-controlled theaters and the Redoutensaal] are very difficult (and without a special recommendation from high up) impossible to secure from Hr. Baron Braun. I do not know the reason for this; for the worn-out Redoutensaal can scarcely get any shabbier than it already is, and a theater often stands entirely empty, namely when only the other one is open, or when there is no rehearsal.[13]

Thus, Braun's policies had a negative effect on all concertizing musicians, not just Beethoven. In any case, beginning with 1805, the

[11]Forbes/BEETHOVEN, p. 300.
[12]ZEW, May 3, 1806, col. 432. (III/5)
[13]AMZ, April 11, 1804, col. 470. (III/6)

theaters closed only during Holy Week and on other isolated church and state holidays, so that for all practical purposes, their significance as concert halls ended.

Baron Braun's lease was taken over on January 1, 1807, by a group of noblemen called the "Gesellschaft von Kavaliere," made up of the Princes Nikolaus Esterházy, Joseph Schwarzenberg, and Joseph Lobkowitz, and the Counts Ferdinand Palffy, Stephan Zichy, Franz Esterházy, Franz Nikolaus Esterházy, and Hieronymus Lodron. One by one, the members resigned, until by November of 1810 only Palffy, Lobkowitz, and Schwarzenberg remained. The society had the same responsibilities and duties as Baron Braun.[14] Under their administration, permission for the few available days, which generally went to charity fundraisers, was dispensed by Court Councilor Joseph Hartl, who frequently bargained with musicians— their services at the fundraisers for the poor of the theater in return for a concert of their own.

Burgtheater and Kärntnerthortheater—Physical Description

The Burgtheater and the Kärntnerthortheater were situated only a few hundred yards apart, both in close proximity to the Imperial palace. The Burgtheater, on the Michaelerplatz, was built in 1741 on the site of the Imperial Tennis Courts according to plans drawn by Friedrich Wilhelm Weiskerns. It underwent significant renovations in 1743, 1748 (when the building itself was enlarged), 1759, 1779, and 1794 and then remained essentially unchanged until its demolition in 1889.[15] Plate 2, a print done before 1800, shows the arrangement of buildings on the square. The end of the building facing the Michaelerplatz had no doorway and was actually the back of the stage; the main entrance led from the palace, emphasizing the theater's original role as court theater. A later view, from around 1820 (plate 3), depicts an improved rear facade. A public

---

[14]Some, though not all, of their correspondence with musicians concerning concerts is preserved in the theater records at the Haus- Hof- und Staatsarchiv in Vienna.
[15]Zechmeister/THEATER, p. 21.

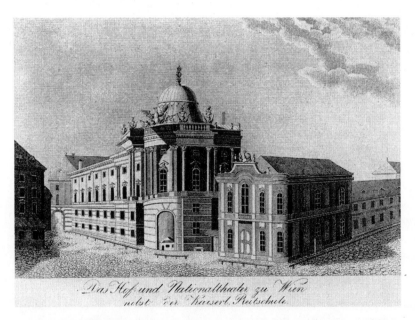

Das Hof und Nationaltheater zu Wien nebst der kaiserl. Reitschule

Plate 2. Altes Burgtheater. Pen drawing, before 1800 (above). Plate 3. Altes Burgtheater. Anonymous print, ca. 1800 (below). (Courtesy of the Oesterreichische Nationalbibliothek – Bild- Archiv.)

entrance from the Bibliotheksplatz was probably constructed during the 1779 renovations.[16] Judging from a plan of the ground floor dating from 1778, the entryway was quite cramped, a situation made worse by the fact that it was often used for storing sets. Two winding staircases, wide enough for two people, led to the upper floors; after a performance it sometimes took an hour to clear a full house.[17]

A seating plan from 1782 (plate 4) shows the oval-shaped house with boxes on the upper floors, typical of Viennese theaters of the time. The parquet was divided into two sections;[18] in the front (Noble Parquet) there were eight rows of covered seats with backs that could be folded down and locked and were opened only upon payment of a small charge above and beyond the price of admission (the so-called "Gesperrter Sitz"). Behind and slightly higher than the Noble Parquet was the Second Parquet, with backless benches and a space about ten feet deep for standing room.[19] The first and second balconies were taken up by boxes which the nobility rented on a yearly basis; approximately five feet deep, they were capable of holding six people, though it is doubtful that they were ever that full.[20] The upper two levels held galleries with benches and standing room. The whole interior was decorated in red, white, and gold.[21]

The exact dimensions of the Burgtheater and the alterations made during the various renovations have been discussed at length by various scholars of theater history, without any firm agreement being reached.[22] One of Konrad Zobel and Friedrich Warner's

---

[16]Schindler/BURGTHEATER, p. 44.

[17]Hennings/BURGTHEATER, p. 12.

[18]This division was created in 1748 as a special place for the nobility and other "distinguished persons" who did not have boxes. See Zechmeister/THEATER, pp. 26-27.

[19]Schindler/BURGTHEATER, pp. 42-43.

[20]Schindler/BURGTHEATER, pp. 42-43.

[21]Schindler/BURGTHEATER, p. 48.

[22]See Schindler/BURGTHEATER (perhaps the most authoritative), Zobel & Warner/STRUCTURAL and Heartz/JADOT. Heartz incorrectly gives the length of the 1748 theater as 38 meters, but that figure actually refers to the total length of the building, including the stage.

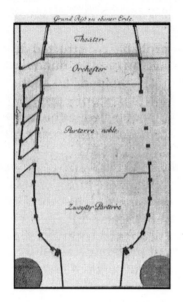
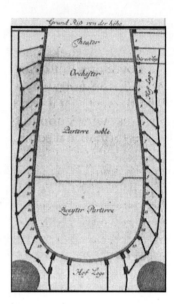

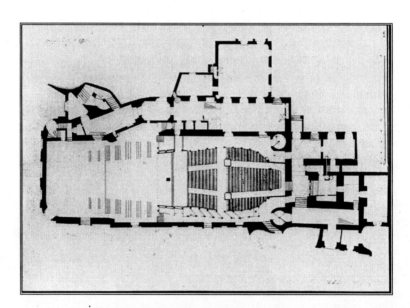

Plate 4. Altes Burgtheater. Seating plan, 1782 (above). Plate 5. Altes Burgtheater. Floorplan, 1779 (below). (Courtesy of the Oesterreich- ische Nationalbibliothek – Bild- Archiv.)

reconstructions, based partially on a 1778 floor plan (plate 5), yielded the figures found in table 7,[23] though calculations using the scale given on the plan itself (presumably representing the *Claster*, the normal measure of the time) indicate a total interior length of 42 rather than 38 meters. Estimates of audience capacity during the 1770s (which was not greatly affected by the 1779 renovation) vary from around 1000 to about 1350, quite small in comparison to other European theaters.[24] Visitors to the city commented on the theater's inadequacy:

> Here I must also mention the Burgtheater, which doesn't look like anything from the outside, but on the inside is decorated almost too elegantly and with almost too much gilt—and is not large enough for Vienna.[25]

Nonetheless, a concertizing musician who managed a full house would have realized a tidy profit. Plates 7 and 8, both dating from the early nineteenth century, give a more precise view of the interior.

The Burgtheater was attended by both the middle and upper classes,[26] but subtle distinctions of class did exist. The boxes were

TABLE 7. Burgtheater Dimensions 1778 (Floorplan)

Wall to wall	ca. 39'
Interior width	ca. 49'
Length of auditorium	ca. 74'
Depth of stage	ca. 49'

[23]Zobel & Warner/STRUCTURAL, p. 24.
[24]The Comédie Française in Paris had a capacity of 2000, while Haydn reported that the Haymarket Theater in London held about 4000. See Landon/CCLN, p. 274.
[25]Arndt/BRUCKSTUECKE, p. 250. (III/7)
[26]The cheapest gallery tickets about equalled a day's wage of a common laborer. The proportion of the same—15 Kreutzer—ticket to a respectable income of 480 Gulden a year is approximately equal to a 6.00 ticket to a person with a net income of 12,000 dollars a year.

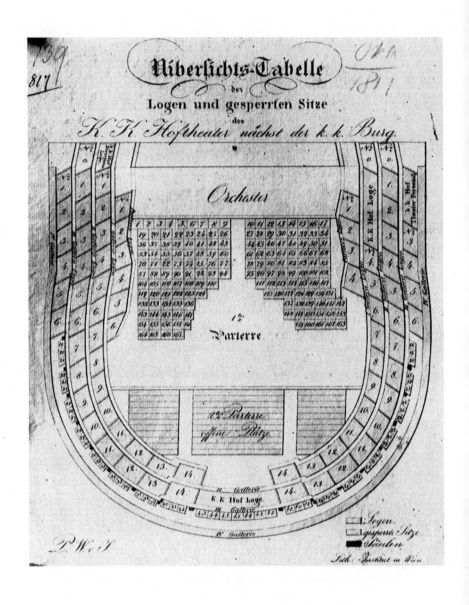

Plate 6. Altes Burgtheater. Seating plan, ca. 1820. (Courtesy of the
Oesterreichische Nationalbibliothek – Bild- Archiv.)

Plates 7 and 8. Altes Burgtheater, interior. Prints, early 19th century.
(Courtesy of the Oesterreichische Nationalbibliothek – Bild-Archiv.)

rented by the nobility, who frequently used them as places for socializing; the less wealthy were relegated by financial necessity to the upper floors. Even the division of the parquet into two parts kept some of its original air of separating the upper crust from the masses:

> In both [Burg- and Kärntnerthortheater] there are seats in the parquet. It is divided into the common and noble parquet. . . . Both are frequented by women and men, and no man need to be ashamed to go to the latter, no matter what his rank.[27]

This implies, of course, that a person of rank would not be seen in the second parquet, let alone in one of the galleries. Nor would the common folk have been likely to frequent the noble parquet:

> Parquet. The Noble Parquet, the showplace, so to speak of the aristocracy. The common people, however, who hate the French term, call it the cattle pen because of a similar crush of cattle in front of the Stubenthor.[28]

Much less information was available on the physical facilities of the Kärntnerthortheater, which was located next to the city wall near the south gate which led toward the province of Kärnten.[29] The original building, dating from 1709, burned in 1761 but was rebuilt immediately on an almost identical plan. Plate 9 shows the exterior of the new building after 1766, when the covered entry way was added to the front. The structure was demolished in the late nineteenth century during the construction of the Ringstrasse.

From a floor plan dated 1784 (plate 10), we can determine the approximate size of the house. Assuming that the scale given represents the *Claster*, the distance from the back of the boxes to the curtain is just under 10 *Claster* or 18.4 meters (ca. 60'). At the widest point, measuring from the fronts of the side boxes (taking

[27]Küttner/REISE, 3:274. (III/8)
[28]Zechmeister/THEATER, p. 27. (III/9)
[29]The noise of the traffic through the gate frequently covered the softer passages, especially during the summer months. See Pezzl/SKIZZE, p. 283.

78

Plate 9. Kärntnerthortheater. Print by Johann Ernst Mansfeld, before 1796. (Courtesy of the Oesterreichische Nationalbibliothek – Bild-Archiv.)

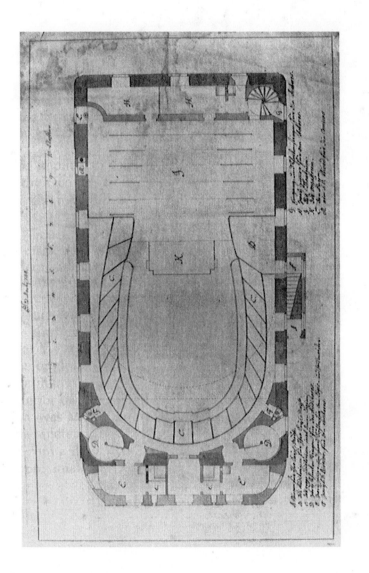

Plate 10. Kärntnerthortheater. Floorplan, 1784. (Courtesy of the Oesterreichische Nationalbibliothek – Bild- Archiv.)

the heavier line), the distance is 5 *Claster,* or 9.5 meters (31'), making the house shorter and wider than the Burgtheater. Like it, the Kärntnerthortheater had two circular staircases leading to the upper floors.

Plate 11 is a companion piece to plate 6 and reveals the same interior arrangement, although the Kärntnerthor had an additional floor: a parquet divided into two sections, floors 1-3 with boxes, and the top two with benches and standing room. The extra width is demonstrated by the rows of 25 seats, as opposed to rows of 17 in the Burgtheater. A seat count done from this chart indicates that approximately 670 were available, about a hundred less than the Burgtheater. With standing room, the total capacity could probably have been pushed to about a thousand people. The interior view given in plate 12, obviously by the same artist as the interior of the Burgtheater in plate 7, points up the similarities in structure.

PRIVATE THEATERS

During the last quarter of the eighteenth century, three private theater companies were founded in Vienna. The oldest (1776), the Theater in der Josephstadt, has no significance for the early history of Viennese concerts. No record of any non-operatic musical performances there exists, except for occasional reports of virtuosos playing as entertainment during the intermissions of the plays.[30]

A few years after the founding of the Theater in der Josephstadt, Carl Marinelli, an actor and a dramatist, received permission to open a theater in the suburb of Leopoldstadt, now Vienna's Second District. Construction began in March of 1781, and on October 20th of the same year, the theater opened. Marinelli ruled the company with a firm, fatherly hand until his death in 1803, standing up for

---

[30]This custom of *Zwischenakte,* as they were called, can be found in all of the Viennese theaters. (Charles Burney recounts how the audiences totally ignored the intermission symphonies he heard in the theaters during his visit to Vienna in the early 1770s.) Child prodigies frequently performed, but older musicians sometimes used these intermission features as a means of gaining a little publicity, hence their link to the overall concert structure.

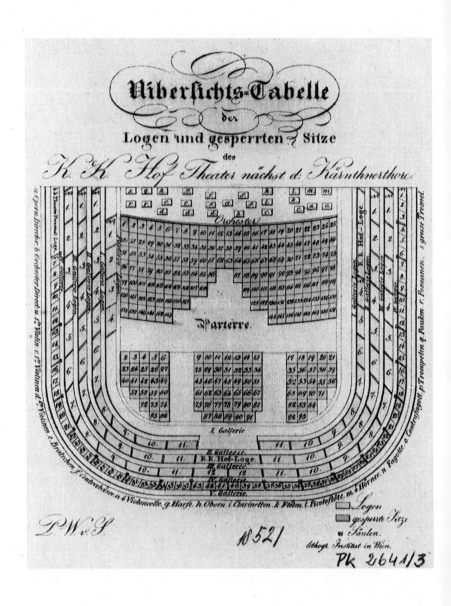

Plate 11. Kärntnerthortheater. Seating plan, ca. 1820. (Courtesy of the Oesterreichische Nationalbibliothek – Bild- Archiv.)

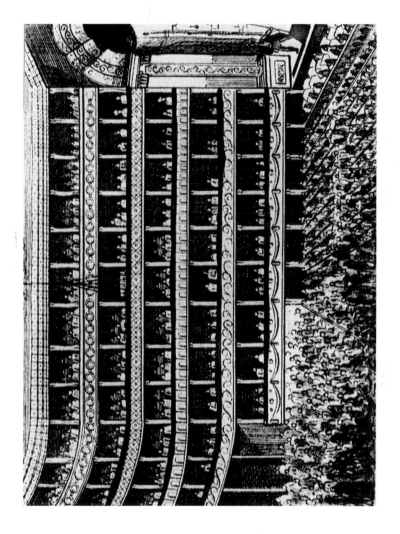

Plate 12. Kärntnerthortheater, interior. Early 19th-century print. (Courtesy of the Oesterreichische Nationalbibliothek – Bild-Archiv.)

his actors in disputes with the government, paying them extra when he was pleased with a performance, and providing them with free lodgings in the building in which the theater was housed.[31] After his death the theater was leased to the dramatist Karl Friedrich Hensler.[32]

Concerts at the theater seem to have been limited to those given by members of the company, although an occasional intermission feature by outside artists can be found. Information comes from program announcements preserved in the Vienna Stadtbibliothek and from the performance diary of Wenzel Müller, the *Kapellmeister* from 1786 to 1812. The first documented concert dates from 1785, with several occurring in 1787 and 1788 (also active years in the court-controlled theaters). Very few were found for the rest of the period, except on either March 25, September 8 (Mary's Ascension) or November 15 (St. Leopold's Day). These three holidays, some of the few survivors of the "Norma" edict, were popular concert dates in all of the theaters, but especially so in the Theater in der Leopoldstadt.

The Theater in der Leopoldstadt catered to less elevated tastes than did the court theaters:

> The Theater in der Leopoldstadt's attraction is in its farces, travesties, magic pieces, and low comedy presentations, in which it competes with the Theater an der Wien and—in the opinion of some suburban friends of art—occasionally wins out.[33]

Its musical repertoire tended to light opera and *Singspiel*, the latter particularly cultivated after the dismissal of the *Singspiel* troupe at the Kärntnerthortheater in 1787 halted the productions there. In general, Leopoldstadt concerts had a limited musical significance and were either ignored or panned by reviewers, especially the dramatic oratorios and huge descriptive orchestral pieces of the music director Ferdinand Kauer. The theater's other claim to notoriety was Bazyli Bohdanowicz, a violinist in the orchestra whose

[31]Hadamowsky/LEOPOLDSTADT, p. 50.
[32]Hadamowsky/LEOPOLDSTADT, p. 53.
[33]PARIS, p. 157. (III/10)

bizarre musical academies featuring his "unusual" family form an interesting footnote to musical performance (see chapter 5).

The theater was located at what is today 31 Praterstrasse and continued to operate until 1929.[34] (It was destroyed during World War II.) Plate 13 depicts a modest building which housed the theater and the apartments of the actors. The audience entered through a passageway that led by the apartments to the box office and then up a stairway to the building's second floor, which was the parquet of the theater. Six smaller passageways led from the box office to the upper three floors. The house was 17 meters (56') long and 15 meters (49') wide, with the parquet divided into two sections, 5 and 10 meters (16' and 33') deep.[35] Boxes were located only on the first balcony, the smaller number perhaps reflecting the more bourgeois character of the theater.

Plate 14 shows a plan which must be dated after 1817, when Franz Marinelli took over the theater management. Note the absence of a royal box, another indication of the theater's non-aristocratic atmosphere. With a seating capacity of approximately 385, it was considerably smaller than either of the two court-controlled theaters, although standing room was available. The interior is shown in plate 15.

The Theater an der Wien actually began its existence in 1787 as the Theater auf der Wieden under the direction of Christian Rossbach. Johann Friedl took over in March of the following year, but the real force behind the company was Friedl's companion, Elenore Schikaneder. Upon his death, she inherited the theater and turned it over to her husband Emanuel, who moved the company to a new building on the other side of the Wien River. Renamed the Theater an der Wien, the new house opened on June 13, 1801. In 1806, Schikaneder left, turning the company over to the "Gesellschaft von Kavaliere" who had just replaced Baron Braun as directors of the Burg- and Kärntnerthortheater.[36]

---

[34]Previously numbered Leopoldstadt 324, 452, then 511.
[35]Hadamowsky/LEOPOLDSTADT, p. 46. The stage was 16 meters wide and 10 meters deep.
[36]Bauer, A./WIEN. The Theater auf der Wieden continued operating until 1809.

Plate 13. Theater in der Leopoldstadt. Print by F. Sager. (Courtesy of the Oesterreichische Nationalbibliothek – Bild-Archiv.)

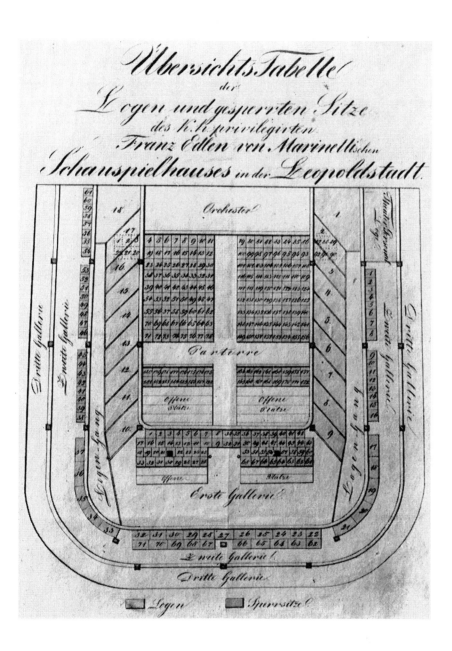

Plate 14. Theater in der Leopoldstadt. Seating plan, ca. 1820. (Courtesy of the Oesterreichische Nationalbibliothek – Bild-Archiv.)

87

Plate 15. Theater in der Leopoldstadt, interior. Early 19th-century print. (Courtesy of the Oesterreichische Nationalbibliothek – Bild-Archiv.)

The company specialized in theater pieces featuring much pomp and spectacle as well as the burlesques that placed it in competition with the Theater in der Leopoldstadt,[37] though after the turn of the century it began to compete with the court theaters.[38] Its concerts achieved considerable musical significance because of the quality of musicians employed there. (As was the case with the Theater in der Leopoldstadt, performances were generally limited to members of the company.) Franz Clement, a child prodigy on the violin, who took the position of "Music Director" (concert master) in 1805, gave yearly concerts best remembered for the premieres of some of Beethoven's works, e.g. the Third Symphony and the Violin Concerto, Op. 61. Beethoven himself, who along with the Abbé Vogler served briefly as resident composer, gave several concerts of his own music.

The original Theater auf der Wieden was located in the enormous building owned by Prince Adam Georg Starhemberg. It occupied a triangle of land in the area of the present-day Operngasse.[39] Karl Hofbauer gave this description in 1864:

> His [Christian Rossbach's] temple of art rose in the back courtyard lying next to the Schliefmühlgasse, and looked (according to Castelli's description) not unlike a big, long, rectangular box. The theater was, incidentally, the size of the Theater in der Josephstadt and had only two floors. The house was simply painted; to the side of the portals, in front of the stage, stood the life-sized figures of a knight with a dagger and a half-masked lady.[40]

According to one estimate, it was 30 meters long (98') (with a 12 meter (39) stage), 15 meters wide (49') and arranged along the lines of the other theaters—a divided parquet, two balconies with boxes, and two galleries, with a capacity of 1000.[41]

---

[37]PARIS, pp. 155-56.
[38]Pezzl/SKIZZE, p. 126.
[39]Most of the building was taken up by apartments; at one time over a thousand people lived there. It was torn down in the early twentieth century. See Czerke/WIEDEN, p. 41.
[40]Hofbauer/WIEDEN, p. 258. (III/11)
[41]Komorzynski/FREIHAUSTHEATER, p. 138.

The Theater an der Wien was, and still is, located on the Linke Wienzeile, as seen in plate 16, a print made shortly after its construction in 1801. The original design had a parquet with side boxes and four additional floors (each with boxes):

> The amphitheater has a pleasant appearance; it is sky blue with silver. It has eighteen boxes, 2 Parquets and four galleries, one above the other. In order to make room for more people, the seats have been squeezed together on all sides more than is comfortable. In general, this theater is better built than the others here.[42]

Although the seating capacity of 700 approximately equaled that of the Burgtheater, its larger standing room areas raised the total figure to ca. 2200.[43] For a comparison of the sizes of the Viennese theaters, see table 8.

TABLE 8. Dimensions of the Viennese Theaters

Theater	Total Length	House Length	Stage Length	House Width
Burg	125'	74'	49'	49'
Kärntner		60'		31'
Leopold	95'	56'	33'	49'
Wieden	98'	44'	39'	49'
Wien	148'	62'	43'	69'

GARDEN CONCERTS

Early morning concerts in the cool and shady surroundings of a formal pleasure garden were a tradition dear to the hearts of the Viennese. Although Belvedere, the palace and gardens that had

[42]Pezzl/SKIZZE, p. 124. (III/12)
[43]Bauer,A./WIEN, p. 47. This seems a little exaggerated, but since Bauer does not give the sources for his figures, it cannot be disproved. Both Bauer and Fred Hennings, who has also written on the Burgtheater, seem eager to prove that their theater was the biggest and the best.

Plate 16. Theater an der Wien. Water color, ca. 1800. (Courtesy of the Oesterreichische Nationalbibliothek – Bild- Archiv.)

Plate 17. Theater an der Wien, interior. Print, ca. 1830. (Courtesy of the Oesterreichische Nationalbibliothek – Bild-Archiv.)

belonged to Prince Eugene of Savoy, served as a setting for such events in the mid-1780s, as had other locations around the city, the Augarten remained the focal point of outdoor concert activity.[44] The Augarten (plates 18 and 19), a walled park located in the suburb of Leopoldstadt, originally served as a retreat for the aristocracy who wanted to escape the heat and dust of the summer without having to leave the city. In 1775, Joseph II opened the park to the general public; his intentions as an "enlightened monarch" still stand engraved in stone over the entrance: "Allen Menschen gewidmeter-Belustigungsort von ihrem Schützer." He had a modest summer residence there and, legend has it, liked to mix unnoticed with his subjects by walking along the shady paths in ordinary clothes.

The Augarten became a favored spot for early morning walks; fanning out from the central green meadow, its wide pathways laid out between rows of elegantly trimmed trees offered an ordered nature so dear to the eighteenth-century mind. Facing the main entrance at the end of a broad boulevard was the "Gartengebäude," (plate 20) a large one-story building that housed the establishment run by Ignaz Jahn, who provided the visitors to the park with a wide variety of services:

> Yesterday, May 1, Herr Jahn, Restaurateur at Schönbrunn, began serving the local public in the Augarten too. . . . [There are] 13 rooms with tables (10 are provided with their own entrance) and a grand hall in which customers can be served not only with a midday meal, but also with breakfast, an afternoon snack evening meal, mineral waters [Gesundheitswässern], and, during this month, with herb soup. Academies, dances, weddings, picnics, legal gaming and other diversions can also be held.[45]

Music of all types—wind bands, dance music and organized concerts—could be heard both in the building and outside in the park, even before Jahn's establishment opened:

[44]The history of concerts there has already been discussed extensively in the previous chapter, so that remarks here will be limited to a physical description.
[45]WB May 2, 1784, pp. 23-24. (III/13)

Plates 18 and 19. Augarten. Prints by Joseph Ziegler, 1780 (above) and 1782 (below). (Courtesy of the Oesterreichische National-bibliothek – Bild- Archiv.)

Plate 20. Augarten Gartengebäude. Print by Leopold Porasseky.
(Courtesy of the Oesterreichische Nationalbibliothek – Bild-Archiv.)

Places for walks and diversions: Augarten. Two dance halls are provided with pretty music, that can often be heard at various places in the park itself.[46]

A large shady half circle ringed with tables, green chairs, and benches makes up the entrance into the Augarten itself. At the front is the perspective Seufzerallee (Avenue of Sighs) which is lined with benches. To the right is the very simple summer residence of the monarch and to the left the Side Avenue, which divides the Augarten, and a small enclosed garden. In this green amphitheater, music is often made in the morning.[47]

At 6:00 [A.M.] I went to the Augarten. There were a lot of people and a wind band on the oval place.[48]

Opening of the Augarten and the new concert hall that has been very tastefully decorated. . . . With real pleasure we saw the newly furnished hall.[49]

The atmosphere of the park and its many entertainments were described by Ernst Moritz Arndt, who visited Vienna in the summer of 1798:

At its entrance are several large buildings in a square, all built by the Emperor Joseph. . . . These rooms have been leased by a certain Jahn, from whom every possible article of luxury or mere necessity for the stomach is to be had—both cheap and expensive. Here there is a crowd mostly in the mornings, taking coffee or [hot] chocolate, often wandering around the beautiful walks till midday, and finally having a hearty meal under the chestnuts and poplars. There are also often people here in the evening. In the largest halls, academies are frequently given, or music performed by dilettantes, as happens now every Thursday. Frequently people will have a complete party here, and Jahn caters according to whether they want to feast frugally or sumptuously. . . . At midday one usually finds music there, often the orchestra of the Leopoldstadt Theater. . . . It is [the favorite

[46]KOMMERZIALSCHEMA 1780, p. 75. (III/14)
[47]REISEN, 1:405-06. (III/15)
[48]VIENNA-ROSENBAUM, May 1, 1800. (III/16)
[49]VIENNA-ROSENBAUM, May 4, 1809. (III/17)

spot] of the Viennese beautiful ladies, who are seen here in the morning especially on concert days—wandering up and down in great numbers in the lovely and flattering paleness of the morning (that isn't true, most of them smear themselves up to the ears with rouge as soon as they get out of bed) and in the graceful négligé in which Amor hatches his greatest cunning and upon which should be written in big letters for all imprudent eyes and inconstant hearts: Beware. In other words, the grand play of a long and onerous day begins here.[50]

Although the Augarten attracted attention as a place where all social classes supposedly mingled in common enjoyment of the beauty of nature, it increasingly became the domain of the bourgeois:

During the reign of Theresia, the Augarten was intended only for the high nobility, excluding the other classes, but the Emperor Joseph opened it according to his philosophical basic beliefs about all people. . . . Since the Emperor Joseph had a very simple dwelling here in the Augarten, and often mingled with the strollers, the spot was much frequented, but since his death the company has decreased. On Sundays it is still rather numerous, but during the week it is often empty; the eminent nobility organize fêtes here and give grand dinners, but otherwise it is fashionable to go to the Prater.[51]

Count Zinzendorf dryly remarked after one of his rare visits to the park about the number of middle-class patrons:

After 9:00 [A.M.] to the music in the Augarten. Lots of bourgeois.[52]

The middle-class orientation is further confirmed by a report appearing in *Der Freimüthige*:

This park has often afforded me. . . great pleasure, particularly lively when Herr Schuppanzigh gives his concerts in the park hall on a

[50]Arndt/BRUCKSTUECKE, pp. 219-20. (III/18)
[51]CHARACTERISTIK, p. 84-85. (III/19)
[52]VIENNA-ZINZENDORF, May 3, 1801. (III/20)

cool, clear morning. . . . Everyone from the middle class assembles who wants to unite the enjoyment of a beautiful morning with music, which for the most part is well chosen and performed.[53]

Of course, all of the nobility did not simply stop coming to the Augarten, but it did cease to be "the place to be seen," a trend that must have affected to a certain degree the audiences that heard the regular concerts there. This link to the social world, along with the mixing of the pleasures of fresh air, refreshments, and music, must be considered an intrinsic part of the character of Viennese concert life.

DANCE HALLS AND BALLROOMS

Though a dance hall or restaurant may seem to be an inappropriate place for a serious concert to a twentieth-century music lover, both were quite frequently used for that purpose all over eighteenth-century Europe. In Vienna, the Mehlgrube and Ignaz Jahn's restaurant on Himmelpfortgasse, and the ballrooms of the Imperial palace were all very popular. *Der kaiser.- königlichen Residenzstadt Wien Kommerzialschema* of 1780 listed the Mehlgrube (plate 21) as a *Gasthof* and place where music and dancing were held during the Carnival season (the period before Lent).[54] It had a hall for dancing and music flanked by several rooms where food was served.[55] Except for one comment that the ceiling "was too low for the effect of the music," and the hall "too small for the number of the audience,"[56] no description of the rooms survives.

As discussed in chapter 2, concerts had been held at the Mehlgrube as far back as the 1740s, and it continued to be used sporadically through 1810 for both individual and series concerts. Philipp Jacques Martin rented the hall for his winter concerts in 1781, Mozart for his subscription series in 1785. Even as late as 1808,

[53]FM, August 1, 1803, p. 483. (III/21)
[54]KOMMERZIALSCHEMA 1780, pp. 23-24.
[55]SITTENGEMAEHLDE, p. 104.
[56]VB, 1808, p. 40.

Plate 21. Mehlgrube. Heliogravure after the Canaletto painting of ca. 1760. (Courtesy of the Oesterreichische Nationalbibliothek – Bild-Archiv.)

it was the first location found for the midday "Liebhaber Concerte," which had to be moved because of the inadequacy of the facilities.

The Mehlgrube had a reputation as a place where the lower and middle classes went, although that did not preclude members of the nobility from attending concerts there. Küttner described the clientele as follows:

> The Mehlgrube is a large building on the Neuer Markt . . . where the greatest number of those present are well and stylishly dressed. . . . It is the particular place of amusement for the good bourgeois class, the well-to-do shopkeeper, some artists, government workers, rich artisans and the like. . . . However, even the very lowest classes are not excluded, especially during Carnival, provided they are at least dressed in a certain fashion. Livery and the uniform of the serving girl are not admitted, nor is a woman who comes alone.[57]

Nicolai may have turned up his North German nose at the atmosphere, which he considered inappropriate for the appreciation of serious music (see page 54), but as we have seen, the mixture of gambling, eating, socializing, and concertizing was a fairly standard feature of Viennese concert life. However, one would hope that the situation rarely deteriorated to the point that it did in this amusing account from 1789:

> Yesterday we had a scene á la Paris *in miniature.* There was music at the so-called Mehlgrube. One of the customers didn't like the music: he complained [in an insulting fashion]. A virtuoso from the full orchestra that was firmly holding the beat gave him a sturdy box on the ears, almost like Achilles did to Thersites in Homer. Thereby the *point d'honneur* of the nobility present was attacked. Our Herculean Youth, together with many young ladies, cried: Allons! Storm the Bastille! The uncouth Orpheus was pounced upon. He was encircled. He had to kneel down and beg pardon. The remaining chorus of the sons of Apollo found that ignominious for their noble art. They armed themselves to avenge the disgrace of their colleague. The waiters and busboys hurried to bring them rein-

---

[57]Küttner, REISE, 3:265-66. (III/22)

100

forcements. Now the skirmish became universal. All sounding instruments were squashed and smashed. The silver spoons of the waiters and bottles, glasses, and chairs flew everywhere. Finally this comical barricade was overcome by the superior strength of the enemy. The conquered inhabitants tried to save themselves by fleeing, and the victors too parted laughing, after they had admired the wreckage their bravery had caused.[58]

The restaurant run by Ignaz Jahn on Himmelpfortgasse aimed at a somewhat higher class of patrons. Jahn bought the building in 1785 and opened the restaurant three years later.[59] He offered a midday meal for a fixed price, but food service during the evening was available only upon special request.[60] The first record of a concert given there dates from March 4, 1791, with Joseph Bähr (Bär) on clarinet and Mozart on the piano. The last documented performance was given by Joseph Mayseder on March 28, 1806. Very few program announcements survive, and only occasionally are its concerts mentioned in the *Wiener Zeitung*, but the hall must have been much more frequently used than the extant data indicates. The *Allgemeine Musikalische Zeitung* reported that Jahn's was the place used by musicians for performances if they were not granted use of one of the court-controlled theaters.[61] Moreover, Rosenbaum attended quite a few concerts there that are not known from any other source. Beginning on January 1, 1807, Ignaz's son Franz announced that the restaurant would be open to the general public during the evenings, thus limiting, if not ending, its usefulness as a concert hall.

The arrangement of the rooms was similar to that of the Mehlgrube—a hall used for dancing and concerts with smaller rooms to the side:

[58]RAPPORT 1789, pp. 33-34. (III/23)
[59]Pemmer/ALT-WIENER, 3:6.
[60]BESCHREIBUNG 1808, p. 125. Traiteurs like Jahn could be found all over the city. Prices for a midday meal ranged from 20 kr. in the cheapest suburban establishments up to a Ducat in the most expensive. See Pezzl/BESCHREIBUNG, p. 127.
[61]AMZ, October 15, 1800, col. 48.

Now I want to take you to the Restaurateur Jahn, who has, on the street known as the Himmelpfortgasse, his own rather pretty building, whose second floor is entirely devoted to the serving of his customers. It is a long but very narrow hall that actually had been made out of three earlier rooms. The arches that still stretch across where the dividing walls once stood make the room—which is already narrow—even more so for the dancers. . . . As for the rest, the hall is very finely furnished and lighted with cut-glass chandeliers that have a much better effect than the former gilded wooden chandeliers. (I was always afraid that their heavy weight might fall down one time from the rather low ceiling onto the dancers and kill several pairs.) Adjoining the hall on both sides are very nicely furnished gaming and supper rooms. In this hall and the adjoining rooms the Court Restaurateur serves his customers at noon and in the evening throughout the year; dinners and suppers in all price ranges can be ordered and had.[62]

Despite its attractions, the hall did not provide the optimum musical environment:

Jahn's hall. . . isn't high enough [i.e., the ceiling is too low] and is also too narrow, so that it restricts the effect of the music; in addition it holds at most 400 listeners.[63]

Given the undoubtedly better acoustics of the theaters and their greater seating capacity, one can see why artists went to Jahn as a last resort.[64]

In 1747-52, the two rooms in the Imperial palace known as the large and the small Comödien Säle were redone by the architect Antonio Galli Bibiena into the Grosser and Kleiner Redoutensaal.[65] They were used for private court functions, but also for the beloved public balls during the Carnival season. Until 1794, the administrative control of the halls came under the jurisdiction of the *Obersthofmeisteramt*, the department that also had charge of the

[62]SITTENGEMAEHLDE, pp. 95-96. (III/24)
[63]AMZ, April 11, 1804, cols. 470-71. (III/25)
[64]By way of comparison, the Hannover Square concert hall in London held an audience of 800. See Landon/C & W, 3:29.
[65]Zechmeister/THEATER, p. 19.

Hofkapelle. When Baron Braun leased the court theaters in August of 1794, he also gained control over the use of the two Redouten-säle, a policy that continued during the administration of the "Gesellschaft von Kavaliere."

The two halls were not commonly used for public concerts until the last decade of the century (the availability of the theaters until then precluded the necessity of their use). Count Zinzendorf attended a performance there on March 15, 1793, but it was probably a private, not a public function. The first assuredly public presentation occurred on January 21, 1794, with a performance of Marie Therese von Paradies's cantata, "Ein deutsches Monument: Ludwig der Unglückliche" to benefit war widows and orphans. Encouraged by the success of this venture, others with similar charitable intentions attempted to organize their concerts, but the court was not prepared to grant permission to just anyone.

Toward the end of March 1794, the Countess Hatzfeld[66] applied to the *Obersthofmeisteramt* for permission to use the Redoutensaal for her own concert, likewise benefiting the war widows and orphans, in which she proposed to use a group of musical dilettantes. Her request for the use of the hall was denied, and it was suggested she apply to the court theater management for the use of the Burgtheater instead. Not willing to give up, she appealed the decision to the Emperor. Acting for the monarch in his absence, Prince Leopold dumped the matter back into the lap of Prince Starhemberg, the director of court music, in a directive dated April 10. Starhemberg replied with an explanation of his decision the following day, and his words reveal two crucial aspects of the use of the Redoutensaal: 1) their use as a public concert facility had probably not been restricted to the one performance on January 21 of that year; and 2) they still retained an aristocratic atmosphere, at least in the minds of the upper nobility:

> It is strange [auffallend] how she [the Countess Hatzfeld] as a foreigner gives herself airs and wants to lay claim to privileges that would hardly be granted to native ladies of higher rank.

[66]Probably Countess Hortense Hatzfeld, née Countess Zierotin, an amateur singer. See Deutsch/DOKUMENTE, p. 487.

> Nor can I understand how Countess Hatzfeld and her dilettantes can be demeaned in any way by singing or performing on instruments in the Court Theater. This condescension would be more likely to receive general approbation.

> The receipts would also be much more considerable than in the Redoutensaal, most of all because all classes of local inhabitants could contribute; contrary wise, it is known that diverse people hesitate to appear at a musical academy in the Redoutensaal.[67]

The matter was finally resolved to the satisfaction of Starhemberg, and the concert was given on April 6 in the Kärntnerthortheater.

In 1796, the smaller of the two halls began to be used occasionally for midday concerts given by individual virtuosos (the first found was on April 8, 1796). The great upswing in activity came after the "Gesellschaft von Kavaliere" took charge in 1807 and began using the promise of a yearly concert there as "contract sweeteners" for their opera stars:

> December 28, 1806. To Mlle Fischer in Berlin: With regard to your letter of the 29th of November, the theater management has decided [to offer] you a yearly salary of 4000 Gulden and the benefit of a musical academy in the Grosser Redoutensaal with the agreement that you are required to sing as Prima Donna in German and Italian opera, alternating among the three theaters under the direction of the society.[68]

This new policy caused a sudden increase in the number of concerts given in the two halls (at least fifteen during the first four months of 1809, for example).

The only extant illustrations depict the Grosser Redoutensaal in its main function as a ballroom (plate 22). For concerts, a special platform was constructed, with the audience seated on the main floor and on the small balconies to the side.[69] The large hall was

[67]VIENNA-PROTOKOL, April 11, 1794. (III/26)
[68]VIENNA INTENDENZ, Korrespondenz und Briefprotokoll, Dez. 1806-Dez. 1808. (III/27)
[69]VIENNA-ROSENBAUM, April 27, 1803. "It was empty. There weren't more than 650 people in the Parquet and Gallery."

Plate 22. Grosser Redoutensaal. Early 19th-century print. (Courtesy of the Oesterreichische Nationalbibliothek – Bild-Archiv.)

considered too big for concerts. (The small hall is actually almost the same size.):

> The performance [Cherubini's *Anacréon* as oratorio] was not excellent. . . . It must be admitted, however, that the vast Redoutensaal is unfavorable for music; those in the back of the hall can neither understand the singers nor hear the music in the softer places. In general an appropriate concert hall for Vienna will remain a pious wish for a long time.[70]

> Nevertheless, the Grosser Redoutensaal with its far-flung corners is not favorable to the music, and the impression that this splendid masterpiece [Handel's *Messiah*] produced in the Theater an der Wien was incomparably greater.[71]

Its size even prompted one composer to re-orchestrate an accompaniment:

> 4-part vocal nocturne, which—though actually written with only a piano accompaniment—will be accompanied by a wind band because of the size of the room.[72]

According to contemporary reports, the capacity of the large hall exceeded a thousand. Rosenbaum reported that 1200 attended a performance of Haydn's *Die Schöpfung* in January 1801, and on several occasions mentioned that the hall was almost empty, with an audience of only 600 or 700.[73]

One senses a certain contradiction, however, on reading all these reports. On the one hand, Jahn's Restaurant and the Mehlgrube were too small for the effect of the music and could hold only a small audience. On the other, the Grosser Redoutensaal had a capacity equaling that of the theaters, but was too large for the music

[70]AMZ, May 15, 1805, col. 534. (III/28)
[71]AMZ, February 18, 1807, col. 336. (III/29)
[72]VIENNA-ONB-MS, June 5, 1806. (III/30)
[73]VIENNA-ROSENBAUM, May 4, 1798, April 5, 1801, May 29, 1801, April 27, 1803. The AMZ reported for December 25, 1810 that the hall could barely hold all the crowd, and there may well have been over 3000 listeners there. See AMZ, January 30, 1811, col. 87.

to be heard properly. The hall at the University, where the last 1807-08 "Liebhaber Concerte" were given, was itself two stories high, of approximately the same proportions as the Redoutensaal, and subject to the same criticism:

> However, one notices that many-voiced pieces, i.e. concertos and symphonies, come off better than single voices, which dissipate in the large hall.[74]

What we are dealing with here, however, is not only a variety of opinions about acoustical properties, but the increasing recognition of the need for an actual concert hall.

The absence of a concert hall affected the character and structure of Viennese concert life in two major ways. First, the association of concerts with establishments like Jahn's Restaurant, the Mehlgrube, and the Augarten served to reinforce the "entertainment" aspect of performances. In a sense, this carried the atmosphere of private concerts over into the public realm and blurred the distinction between the two. Second, and more importantly, the situation forced an over-reliance on the theaters as performance locations, and the theater directors, whose main concern was after all the production of plays and operas, not of concerts, did not always feel called upon to assume the additional responsibility. Though their attitudes often caused hardships for the musicians wanting to perform, they should not be too severely censured for not providing a service that properly should have devolved on someone else. Even with a supportive management, the fact that concerts were of a necessity dependent on the theater schedule made it difficult for them to develop into a force that might have shaped rather than merely reflected the Viennese musical world.

[74]ZEW, December 25, 1807, col. 1645. (III/31)

CHAPTER FOUR

Business and Financial Aspects of Concert Giving

After the performance location had been selected, a whole host of other business and procedural matters remained before the concert could be given. In most cases, the performing musicians themselves handled all the arrangements, for the concept of a manager or agent was foreign to the eighteenth-century world. Details such as publicity and the hiring of an orchestra demanded attention, and the harried performer could only hope that the concert's receipts would at least cover expenses. As the entire procedure was vastly complicated by Vienna's lack of a concert superstructure, it bears close consideration, but any discussion of finances first requires a brief detour into the Viennese monetary system.

AUSTRIAN CURRENCY

A bewildering variety of gold and silver coins circulated in Europe during the eighteenth and nineteenth centuries. Although visitors occasionally referred to other types, the four main coin values in Vienna were the Kreutzer (abbreviated ''x''), the Gulden (abbreviated ''fl''), the Thaler, and the Ducat. The silver Konventionsthaler was established in a contract with Bavaria in 1753 and remained in use for over a hundred years. It equalled 2 Gulden or

120 Kreutzer. The gold Austrian Ducat originally was worth 250 Kreutzer, but its value steadily increased to 270 Kreutzer (4 1/2 Gulden) by 1786, when it ceased to fluctuate. Most figures from the period quote the Gulden, or the Florin, as it was sometimes called, as the monetary unit.[1]

In addition to the gold and silver coins, paper bank notes (Bankozettel) circulated in steadily increasing numbers, until by 1810 the amount reached a value of two billion Gulden.[2] This increase in paper currency contributed to the rampant inflation of the first decade of the nineteenth century, a trend halted only with the currency reforms of 1811. Table 9 details the decreasing value

TABLE 9. Exchange Rates. Cost of 100 Gulden (Silver Coins in Paper Money

1796	100.13
1797	101.61
1798	101.06
1799	107.83
1800	114.91
1801	115.75
1802	121.67
1803	130.75
1804	134.25
1805	134.75
1806	173.01
1807	209.43
1808	228.15
1809	296.03
1810	492.12
1811	1,093.75

Information taken from Pribram/PREISE, p. 78.

[1]There is some confusion about the relative value of Thalers and Ducats, even during the eighteenth century. For example, the AMZ reported that the price of a concert was seldom under a ''Speciesthaler'' or ''Ducat.'' (AMZ, June 10, 1801, col. 626) The former would have equalled 2 Gulden (which was in fact the standard price for concert tickets), the latter 4 1/2 Gulden.
[2]HAYDN ZEIT, p. 571.

of paper money from 1796 to 1811. Before then, prices and wages had remained fairly stable, so that a figure quoted for 1780 could still be valid fifteen years later. After 1800, however, care must be taken in assessing real profits and expenses in view of the inflation.

Table 10 lists the incomes of various classes of Viennese society, from the Esterházys, the wealthiest of the Austrian nobility, down to a serving girl. At that time, skilled workers, such as a brick layers, could expect to earn at the most only 75 to 135 Gulden per year, low enough to exclude them from any thought of participation in concert or cultural life.[3] Only when we reach the lower level bureaucrat, with a salary in the 400-1000 Gulden per year range, do we begin to encounter the concert public. Top positions at the court paid around 5000 Gulden per year but were generally held by members of the aristocracy, whose estates provided the bulk of their considerable income. Figures on small businessmen were not available. Table 11 gives the salaries of the court-controlled theater employees for the 1784-85 and 1792-93 seasons. The *Kapellmeister* and orchestra members rank approximately with lower level bureaucrats, while the top-paid singers could compete with the highest court positions.[4]

This information on typical salaries must be balanced with some on living expenses. Prices for food remained fairly stable before 1800, fluctuating according to the harvest, but increased in keeping with inflation after that date (table 12). Prices for accommodations varied widely, depending on the size and location of the apartment or room, as well as the length of time it was rented. Travel-

---

[3]Comparisons with today's prices can be misleading, but these percentages may help. The cheapest ticket in the Burgtheater (7 Kreutzer) to a person earning 100 Gulden per year (incidentally, those tickets were not always available for concerts) would approximately equal a 12.00 ticket to a person with a net income of 10,000 dollars per year. The normal 2 Gulden ticket would have been 2% of the year's salary, or the equivalent of 200.00 with an income of 10,000 dollars.
[4]The scarcity of good wind players is perhaps reflected in their increased salaries at the expense of the strings in the later season. Moreover, wind players could sometimes find double employment. A directive from Joseph II in 1782 states his wish to hire a certain eight wind players for his own private wind music at 400 fl per year as well as for the court orchestra at 350 fl per year, for a total of 750 fl per year. See Payer/BURGTHEATER, p. 31.

TABLE 10. Yearly Incomes

Class	Position	Gulden/Year
Aristocrats	Esterházy	ca. 700,000
	Middle aristocracy	50,000-100,000
Court Positions	President of a Court Dept.	4000-6000
	Secretary of a Court Dept.	1500-2000
	Chancery Clerk	400-900
Administrative	Hospital Director	1000
Positions	Superintendent	350
Bürgerspital	Accountant	500
1779	Doctor	400
	Pastor	300
Day Labor	Carpenter & roofer	27x/day
Bürgerspital	(Journeymen)	300 days = 135 fl
1779	Roofer (Assistant)	18x/day 300 days = 90 fl
	Mason (Assistant)	15x/day 300 days = 75 fl
Household Help	Serving girl	16-20 + room & board
	Coachman	20 fl + room & board
	Tutor	50 fl + room & board
Military 1769-1800		
Infantry	Captain	852
	Soldier	42
Calvary	Captain	900
	Soldier	48

Information taken from Pribram/PREISE, pp. 339-50, 564, and HAYDN ZEIT, p. 80-81.

TABLE 11. Salaries—Court Actors, Musicians, and Dancers (Highest and Lowest Given)

1784-85 season

Actors	Hr. Stephanie d.A.	1736 fl
	Fr. Adamberger	1600 fl
	Hr. Distler	200 fl
	Fr. Dauer	200 fl
Singers	Hr. Benucci	4061 fl
	Fr. Storace	4061 fl
	Hr. Bussani	2445 fl 12x
	Hr. Adamberger	2133 fl 12x
	Fr. Lang	1706 fl 36x
	Fr. Cavalieri	1333 fl 20x
	Frl. Prener	400 fl
Kapellmeister	Hr. Salieri	853 fl 28x
	Hr. Umlauf	850 fl
Orchestra	Concert master	450 fl
	First cellist	450 fl
	Violinists	400 fl
	Wind players	350 fl

1792-93 season

Actors	Hr. Lang	2300 fl
	Hr. Brockmann	1900 fl
	Hr. Stephanie d.A.	1600 fl
	Fr. Adamberger	1600 fl
	Fr. Hantz	100 fl
Singers	Hr. Benucci	4500 fl
	Hr. Maffoli	4500 fl
	Hr. Calvesi	3600 fl
	Hr. Bussani	2250 fl
	Hr. Saal	1200 fl
	Fr. Tomeoni	4500 fl
	Fr. Sessi	2250 fl
	Frl. Gassmann d.A.	487 fl 30x
	Frl. Gassmann d.J.	487 fl 30x

113

Dancers	Hr. Vulcani	4905 fl
	Hr. & Fr. Muzzarelli	7740 fl
Kapellmeister	Hr. Salieri	853 fl 20x
	Hr. Weigl	1000 fl

Orchestra	
Burgtheater	
Concert Master	500 fl
First Cellist	450 fl
Strings	350 fl
Flutes	350 fl
Other winds	
& horns	400 fl
First Clarini	300 fl
First Timpani	300 fl
Kärntnerthortheater	
Strings	125 fl
Flutes	125 fl
Other winds	
& horns	166 fl 40x

Information taken from VIENNA-INTENDENZ, Halbjahresrechnungen Bd. 21, Bd. 27.

ing virtuosos who needed lodgings for only short periods could naturally expect to pay more for the same arrangements than residents remaining for longer periods.[5] Joseph Martin Kraus paid 6 Ducats (27 Gulden) per month for lodgings in 1783,[6] a price that seems a little high, since the *Vertraute Briefe zur Charakteristik Wiens* indicated that a room in the city could be had for 12 Gulden a month in 1793.[7] The latter price is confirmed by Ernst Moritz Arndt, who reported prices ranging from 8 to 24 Gulden a month and went on to state that the suburbs offered rooms for 3 to 4 Gulden that

[5]According to the reports of most travelers, rooms at the city's inns were rarely tolerable, so that most visitors were forced to seek accommodations in private buildings.
[6]Leux-Henschen/KRAUS, p. 250.
[7]CHARACTERISTIK, p. 114.

TABLE 12. Food Prices (in Kreutzer) for Vienna in 1787

Beef (2.2 pounds)	10.7
Pork (2.2 pounds)	12.5
Butter (2.2 pounds)	30.4
Sugar (2.2 pounds)	64-75.0
Wine (Quart)	5.7-25.5
Beer (Quart)	6.0
Coffee (cup)	10.0

Bread Prices per Pound in Kreutzer.

1780....2.	1790....3.97	1800....2.46
1781....2.21	1791....3.37	1801....3.62
1782....2.11	1792....2.42	1802....3.62
1783....2.11	1793....1.86	1803....4.68
1784....1.86	1794....1.56	1804....4.57
1785....1.81	1795....2.11	1805....6.19
1786....2.01	1796....2.46	1806....7.84
1787....2.01	1797....2.21	1807....5.82
1788....3.12	1798....2.56	1808....4.83
1789....3.70	1799....1.96	1809....7.46
		1810....9.60

As a reference: An income of 100 Gulden per year divided into 16.4 Kreutzer per day, 500 Gulden per year into 82 Kreutzer (1 Gulden, 22 Kreutzer) per day. Two pounds of beef was three quarters of a day's wages for a mason's assistant. Information in this table taken from Pribram/PREISE, p. 439 and HAYDN ZEIT, pp. 575-76.

would be 12 to 16 in the city.[8] More spacious apartments, such as the one Mozart lived in during 1784-85 (460 Gulden a year)[9] or the one taken by Küttner in 1798 (30 Ducats or 135 Gulden per month),[10] were probably out of the question for most musicians, resident or foreign. Rent prices rose along with everything else in the first decade of the nineteenth century, with Pezzl complaining that

[8]Arndt/REISEN, 1:197.
[9]ML 2:885.
[10]Küttner/REISE, 3:112.

landlords were asking for three times as much in 1804 as they had twelve years earlier.[11] By 1810, quarters consisting of four rooms could run as high as 300 Gulden per month.[12]

Estimates of total living expenses (always given for a single man) also varied widely according to expectations about standard of living (table 13). Using the expenditures given by Pezzl and the *Vertraute Briefe zur Characteristik Wiens*, we come up with a bare minimum figure of 40 to 50 Gulden per month. The figures given by Küttner can be applied only in the case of a person wishing to enter society at the level of the lower aristocracy and must not be

TABLE 13. Living Expenses (Gulden per Year)

1785—Pezzl (middle-class man)

Apartment	60
Wood and candles	24
Clothing	170
Meals	180
Servant and Hairdresser	30
TOTAL	464
TOTAL with entertainment	500-550

1792—*Vertraute Briefe* (single man)

2 room apartment in the city	144
Servant and linens	30
Wood and candles	30
Hairdresser	36
Shoes	10
Clothing	160
Meals	365
Total essentials	775
Drinking and gambling money, entertainments, theater, transportation, lectures, etc.	ca. 225
TOTAL (You can't make a big splash with 1000 Gulden)	1000

[11]Pezzl/SKIZZE, p. 37.
[12]PARIS, p. 149.

1804—Pezzl (middle-class man)

Apartment	128
Wood and candles	40
Clothing	255
Meals	500
Servant and Hairdresser	44
TOTAL	967
TOTAL with entertainment	1200

1799—Küttner (single man of society)	3000

1802—Küttner (single man of society)

3 furnished rooms with servant's room (third floor)	600
1 servant	230
Coach for evenings (5 months)	450
Breakfast, lunch and dinner plus ice cream, lemonade, etc. (from time to time you have to have a bottle of Tokay, champagne or the like) (4 Gulden/day)	1460
Theater and concerts	200
Wood and candles	70
Clothing	300
Linens	100
Hairdresser	50
	3460
Tips, riding, parties, books, etc.	1040
TOTAL	4500

Information taken from Pezzl/SKIZZE, p. 161-62 (Pezzl incorrectly gives his 1804 total as 923); CHARACTERISTIK, p. 114, and Küttner/REISE, pp. 322-23.

viewed as typical for a musician. The Rosenbaums, for example, had total expenditures of 3219 Gulden for the year 1801, a sum which he considered outrageously high.[13] Nonetheless, that works out to well over 100 Gulden per month per person, substantially more than the estimates given by either Pezzl or the *Vertraute Briefe*. While the ordinary court orchestra member, on a salary of 350 to 400 Gulden per year, certainly must have lived more cheaply, the star performers, who would have been the ones giving concerts,

[13]VIENNA-ROSENBAUM, December 31, 1801.

may very well have required at least the above figures since they, to a certain extent, had to move in the higher circles of society. If they were not able to appear before that society in proper form and fashion, they could not hope to even take the first step toward a successful concert: creating an audience.

ORGANIZATIONAL MATTERS

The first task of the performing artist was to set the publicity process in motion. Relatively little advertising was done by way of newspapers. For several years, *Das Wienerblättchen* ran notices about all upcoming plays, operas, and concerts at the theaters, but as a type of public service feature rather than as true advertisements. Occasionally artists would buy a spot in the *Anhang* of the *Wiener Zeitung*, but this never became general practice. After 1800, the *Wiener Zeitung* ran a few full-page ads for concerts, but again, these were exceptions.[14] Advertising was done much as it is today in Vienna, with notices placed on walls and Kiosks around the city (plate 23).

Public advertising must have had some effect in reminding patrons of the concert date, but the most effective method of creating an audience, especially for travelling virtuosos who might not be well known in Vienna, involved personal contact with the aristocracy:

> Herr and Madame Benda from Ludwigslust arrived in Vienna not long ago and are finding many supporters and friends. They performed at Prince von Kaunitz's and Countess von Bassewitz's to much applause and will be giving a public concert shortly.[15]

Rarely did any performing artist dare to travel without letters of

[14]Anton Eberl—January 4, 1804, p. 44; Anton Eberl—January 19, 1805, p. 280, Marie Bigot de Morogues—April 27, 1805, p. 1936; Josepha Auernhammer—March 19, 1806, p. 1106; Franz Clement—December 10, 1806, p. 6064; Louis Wolf—February 28, 1807, p. 871; Bernhard Romberg—March 5, 1808, p. 1100.
[15]Cramer/MAGAZIN, 1783, p. 172. (IV/1)

Plate 23. Concert Zettel. (Courtesy of the Oesterreichische Nationalbibliothek – Theater Sammlung.)

introduction from patrons at home that provided entrance to the circles of the local nobility. Michael Kelly recounts that his patron in Venice gave him:

> a letter to her noble relative, the Grand Chamberlain; one to Prince Charles of Lichtenstein (*sic*), Governor of Vienna, and one to Sir Robert Keith, His Britannic Majesty's Minister at Vienna. From Count Durazzo I had one for Grand Marshal Lacy, one for Marshal Laudon, and a third for. . . Prince de Ligne.[16]

One such letter, written on behalf of a certain Anton Griesbacher by a Count Starhemberg in Vienna to relatives and acquaintances in Munich, Dresden, and London, reads as follows:

> The bearer of this letter is the Imperial Royal subject Anton Griesbacher, who is taking a trip through Germany to London in order to polish his musical talent. He plays the so-called Paridon [baryton] with much facility and wishes to perform at public as well as private academies. Therefore I beg you to be of the best possible assistance to him in reaching his goal.[17]

Only the boldest or the most famous could afford to flout this procedural rule of conduct. The critic for the *Allgemeine Musikalische Zeitung* marveled that Bernhard Romberg managed to clear a respectable 600 Gulden at his concert, even though he had arrived without a single letter of introduction.[18]

Only rarely did a performer actually advertise his availability for private concerts in the newspapers, and then in the humblest of terms:

> The little Pohl, who is recognized for his special ability in playing the violoncello, has the honor of notifying the high nobility of his

[16]Kelly/REMINISCENCES, p. 98.
[17]VIENNA-KABINETT, Karton 11, April 21, 1804. (IV/2)
[18]AMZ, June 10, 1801, col. 626. Haydn arrived for his first visit to London with letters from King Ferdinand IV (of Naples) to the Neapolitan ambassador, and with one from the Austrian Chancellor Prince Kaunitz to the Austrian ambassador in London, Count Stadion. See Landon/C & W, 3:35.

arrival here again. On his trips through France, Holland, and the Holy Roman Empire he has become much more secure in his art than [he was] when last here and thus hopes to enjoy the favor of being allowed to perform for a noble audience. In this case, one need only contact him in his apartment "Im goldenen Ochsen" on the Neuer Markt no. 8 and determine the place and time where he is to be in attendance.[19]

Of course, by creating an audience in such a manner, performers ran the risk of "wearing out their welcome" in the musical community before they actually gave their concert. So they had to tred the fine line between appearing too little and therefore having a small following, and appearing too much and becoming passé. If, however, they managed to find the right balance between familiarity and newness, they could count on sizable profits at their public concerts, and perhaps even renewed invitations to private soirées afterwards. Local virtuosos also performed at private performances, but the time span during which a particular artist was in demand was relatively short, since the semi-social private world thrived on the newest and the most sensational. Thus, even though the young Mozart declared a musician could easily earn a living giving lessons and playing at private concerts, it—as Mozart himself was to learn— definitely did not provide long-term security.

Payment the artist might have received for performances in private homes could vary widely, but in general depended on the generosity of the patron and on the type of occasion. Ordinary musicians did not set the fee themselves:

> A company of musicians consisting of 3 women and 4 men has just arrived here and has received gracious permission to perform different kinds of music and instrumental art, i.e. buffo arias, duets, trios and finales, in private homes. They herewith offer their most respectful services to the high nobility and a most honored public, with the assurance and in the most flattering hope of receiving general approbation. Their apartment is by the Rother Thurm 674 on the second floor. Upon receiving a gracious notice, they will ap-

---

[19]WZ, March 22, 1780, n.p. (IV/3)

pear immediately upon demand. It will be left entirely to the judgment of the *Herrn Liebhaber* to determine the remuneration according to the service.[20]

For the star singers at a gala oratorio, the honorarium sometimes reached 50 Ducats or 230 Gulden, quite a tidy sum. That was standard for the singers at the court's public New Year's celebration; Rosenbaum reported that Therese received the same amount for singing in a performance of Haydn's *Die sieben Worte* at Prince Esterházy's. Mozart quoted the identical figure for Joseph Adamberger and Madame Weigl at Countess Thun's in 1781,[21] but for an ordinary concert at the home of one of the less wealthy aristocratic families, the sum seems greatly exaggerated. Since in that letter Mozart was complaining about the paltry sum his employer had given him on the same evening, he may have misrepresented what he "could have had" or perhaps repeated a rumor he had heard. Singers however, definitely occupied the top position on any pay scale; the ordinary instrumentalist, even as soloist, might have expected to receive perhaps a tenth of that sum. For example, Prince Colloredo tipped each of the Archbishop of Salzburg's musicians 5 Ducats (23 Gulden) after a performance at his home.[22] An entire company, in fact, might be allotted the same amount as a star singer:

> On the 27th we presented singing and dance music at Prince Auersperg's in the presence of the all highest Imperial Royal [Crown Prince]. . . . Prince Auersperg gave the company 50 Ducats to divide among themselves.[23]

Musical efforts could even go unrewarded: in one case the transgressor was Vienna's unwelcome guest, Napoleon, who, after a concert at Schönbrunn, let the orchestra go without praise or payment. [24] Although one must make allowances for a certain lack of

[20]WB, September 9, 1783, p. 32. (IV/4)
[21]ML, 2:723.
[22]ML, 2:720.
[23]VIENNA-MUELLER, fol. 57v. (IV/5)
[24]VIENNA-ROSENBAUM, December 14, 1805.

good will toward the French general, the anecdote does emphasize the dependency of the musicians on the whim of the patron.

After the publicity process had been set in motion, the concertizing musician could devote time and attention to the more concrete details of organizing a performance, including choosing and obtaining a location, if that had not already been settled. Because of their greater seating capacity and undoubtedly better acoustics, the theaters were the first choice of most, but were not always available. Musicians in the theater's company would have received preferential treatment and free use of the theater, but outside artists probably either paid a fee or turned over a certain percentage of their profits to the management, but practically no information was found on that point.

Financial arrangements from the 1820s and later have been documented, but earlier practices remain obscure. None of the court theater records before then preserve any mention of income generated by renting the building to individual artists. Such fees would have probably been lumped together under the rubric "Extra ordinari" ("Additional Income") in the yearly financial report, but some years itemize the extra sources and do not list anything that could be construed as a rental fee.[25] In the case of the suburban theaters, financial records do not appear to have survived.

Rental of smaller halls could be accomplished fairly cheaply. According to tax records uncovered by Hermine Cloeter (which have since disappeared), Mozart was able to rent one of the rooms in the Trattnerhof in 1784 at the rate of 38 Gulden, 42 Kreutzer for three evenings (or 12 fl, 54x per evening).[26] The following year, he paid 1/2 Souverain d'or (ca. 9 Gulden) per evening for his concerts in the Mehlgrube.[27] No figures were available on the rental fee charged by Jahn, either in the Augarten or on Himmelpfortgasse, but since the latter was frequented by a higher class clientele than was the Mehlgrube, one might suppose it was also more expensive. Whatever the case, it appears that the rental of the hall did not constitute a major expense.

---

[25]Items listed included the sale of old costumes, librettos at opera performances, etc.
[26]Cloeter/TRATTNER, p. 101.
[27]ML, 2:886.

Another detail that demanded attention involved obtaining permission from the police, who had to be notified about any public assembly:

> Permission to hold musical academies in public places will be given only by the police.[28]

Though police records were destroyed in the 1927 Justizpalast fire, a few glimpses into the bureaucracy survive. For example, early in 1797, Constanze Mozart sought permission from the Niederösterreichische Landesregierung to hold a concert in the Burgtheater. She was referred to the Emperor by the police on April 6 and eventually gave a performance on April 11 in the Theater an der Wien.[29] The extra paper work for the police only increased Beethoven's frustrations about his inability to get a concert date:

> I have three documents about a day in the theatre last year; and if I include the police documents, I have altogether five written statements about a day which has never been allotted to me.[30]

To add to the problem, matters of jurisdiction also arose. In December of 1802, the Police Department refused to allow Ferdinand Franzl to give a concert in the Redoutensaal on the grounds that such performances were not allowed during Advent. Baron Braun protested the action, saying that his contract allowed him to decide when concerts could be given. The case was brought before the Emperor, who ruled that in the future Baron Braun must notify the police of all such applications but said that the concert could take place. Judging from the wording of the report, the basic question of authority remained unresolved:

> The Chief of Police (December 9, 1802) reports that the musician Ferdinand Franzl was refused permission to give a musical academy in the Redoutensaal on the grounds that such [events] may not take

---

[28]Biba/KONZERTWESEN, p. 133-34. (IV/6)
[29]Eibl/DOCUMENTA, p. 87.
[30]BL 1:186.

place during Advent; that Baron Braun declared that type of permission was assured him contractually and not deferred to the police. Finally, instructions for Baron Braun were requested.

Expedited—answered (December 10) the Police Department that this matter was brought to the attention of His Majesty and that Baron Braun is instructed in the future to bring all such petitions to the attention of the police. The. . . academy may take place, but must start after 1:00 P.M.[31]

No record could be found showing whether or not the poor musician caught in the struggle actually succeeded in giving his concert.

After the necessary permission had been obtained, tickets could be sold. If the performer ran an ad in the newspaper, it usually included a line or two stating that the tickets were available at his or her apartment during certain hours. Sometimes they were even distributed personally:

Mme Mozart came by to invite me to come to her concert next week.[32]

The Bohdanoviczes brought tickets to their academy at Jahn's on Monday.[33]

Had the artist done the right amount of public relations with the nobility, they might be persuaded to buy a whole block of tickets, even if they never used them.[34]

Aside from these major tasks, a number of minor details remained, such as printing up the program notices and seeing that they were posted, possibly moving a piano if a good one was not available, etc. At least by this time the custom of providing free refreshments at intermission had died out, but the number of arrangements to be made was still formidable.[35]

[31]VIENNA-INTENDENZ, Theater-Acten, No. 218. (IV/7)
[32]VIENNA-ZINZENDORF, March 30, 1795. (IV/8)
[33]VIENNA-ROSENBAUM, October 13, 1802. (IV/9)
[34]Reichardt/VERTRAUTE, 1:339.
[35]VB, 1808, p. 41.

In general, preparations for concerts seem to have been done at the last minute. Rosenbaum noted that the flutist Bayr asked Therese on the afternoon of April 9, 1802, to sing in his concert on April 12. Even for annual benefit performances, which would have involved learning the part in an oratorio (not just brushing off a favorite piece) the performers had little time for preparation:

> March 24, 1804. Karl brought her [Therese] a part for the academy for the poor on Tuesday [April 1] and asked her, in the name of the Baron, to sing.[36]

Court theater records reveal that the organizers of a benefit concert held on April 12, 1808, asked Beethoven as late as April 8 if he had any vocal pieces he was willing to contribute.[37] In the case of traveling virtuosos, who often stayed in the city less than a month, such hurried preparations would have been expected, but they were apparently the general rule with local endeavors as well.

PREPARATIONS AND EXPENSES

Since eighteenth-century protocol required that the musician giving the concert be assisted by other virtuosos and a full orchestra for the symphonies and concertos,[38] the concertizing artist had to hire a number of other musicians. For local virtuosos, who could count on friends and acquaintances, this task would have not been unduly difficult, but for foreigners only in the city for a few weeks, it must have been a major headache. The theater orchestras had the best players (and, one supposes, the most expensive), and were apparently utilized, especially for concerts given in the theaters. Mozart complained in 1784 that:

> My first concert in the theatre was to have been tomorrow. But Prince Louis Liechtenstein is producing an opera in his own house, and

[36]VIENNA-ROSENBAUM, March 24, 1804. (IV/10)
[37]VIENNA-INTENDENZ, Korrespondenz und Briefprotokoll, April 8, 1808.
[38]See chapter 5.

has not only run off with the cream of the nobility, but has bribed and seduced the best players in the orchestra. So I have postponed my concert until April 1st.[39]

The court-controlled theater orchestras even provided players for concerts in other theaters. Rosenbaum recounts a conversation about the performance of Beethoven's *Christus am Oelberge* in the Theater an der Wien:

To Fuchs's, where we talked about today's performance of Beethoven's cantata *Christus am Oelberge*, which will certainly be deficient because Braun is giving *Die Schöpfung* in the B[urgtheater] with both orchestras for the poor of the theater.[40]

We also know that the orchestra from the Theater in der Leopoldstadt frequently played in the Augarten,[41] but aside from these few references, few other comments or information on concert orchestras could be found.

In lieu of the theater musicians, who in any case would have been available only on days when the theater was dark, an orchestra might have been assembled by using such books as the *Kommerzialschema* that listed the professional musicians living in Vienna. Reichardt commented that Beethoven's orchestra and chorus for his concert on December 22, 1808, were "put together from very heterogeneous parts,"[42] undoubtedly true since the Tonkünstler Societät performance on the same day would have occupied most of the city's professional musicians. Though dilettantes may very well have filled out the string section in such cases, their presence is documented only in the Augarten and in the 1807-08 "Liebhaber Concerte."

The only mention of the cost of hiring an orchestra was found in a letter from Johann Thomas Kleinhardt to Count Franz Sternberg dated April 1786 concerning a concert given by Josefa Dušek, who was accompanied by Mozart and a Herr Eck:

[39]ML, 2:872.
[40]VIENNA-ROSENBAUM, April 5, 1803. (IV/11)
[41]Arndt/BRUCKSTUECKE, p. 220.
[42]Reichardt/VERTRAUTE, 1:255.

The accompaniment of the remaining musicians cost Mme Duschek 100 Thaler. Expensive Austrian musicians! It would have cost 12 Ducats with our countrymen, who certainly are truly courteous.[43]

Assuming an orchestra of 35,[44] the 100 Thalers (or 200 Gulden) comes to ca. 6 Gulden for each musician, a sum that seems a little high. A third to a sixth of that would be more in line with other evidence. The Tonkünstler Societät, for example, charged members who lived outside Vienna and were unable to participate in its four annual concerts 6 Gulden per year in lieu of their appearance, implying their value was set at 1 fl 30x a concert.[45] In 1799, uncomfortable with the society's plan to double admission prices for their presentation of *Die Schöpfung*, Haydn requested each performer be reimbursed 2 Gulden.[46] Substituting musicians at the court theaters, regardless of their instrument, received anywhere from 2 to 6 Gulden for their services.[47] Unfortunately, the number of performances is never specified, but the basic fee was no more than 2 Gulden.[48] Thus, a more realistic top figure for the cost of the orchestra would be around 70 Gulden.

Assisting virtuosos frequently performed without remuneration, either as a personal favor or in return for the main artist's guest appearance at their own concert. Mozart wrote his father that he would let Ceccarelli (a castrato in the service of Mozart's employer, the Archbishop of Salzburg) sing at his concert, then would play *gratis* at Ceccarelli's.[49] A few years later Leopold reported that "as a favour he has been playing frequently at other concerts in the theatre."[50] Though it seems unlikely that assisting musicians never

[43]Deutsch/DOKUMENTE, p. 237. (IV/12)
[44]This was the number of the court controlled orchestras, though a lower figure of 25—30 would have been adequate. See chapter 6.
[45]Pohl/TS, p. 38.
[46]Pohl/TS, p. 51.
[47]VIENNA-INTENDENZ.
[48]In Salzburg, at the Cassin Concerts, Heinrich Marchand (as first violinist) received 2 Gulden, as did other section leaders, the rank and file musicians 1 Gulden each, and anyone performing a concerto 1 Ducat (4 1/2 Gulden). See MB 3:513. See MB 3:513.
[49]ML, 2:780.
[50]ML, 2:888.

received a fee, no specific reference to such a payment was found. Therese Gassmann-Rosenbaum often sang in concerts at Jahn's restaurant, but Rosenbaum never once indicated she received an honorarium.[51] He did, however, mention having tickets to distribute, so that finances may have been settled in that manner:

> Soon afterwards Therese got ready [to go to] Jahn's where she sang an aria at the concert of the flutist Bayr. . . . I gave tickets to Rotruff, Korn, Weibe, Gridl.[52]

Additional expenses would have included the cost of advertising, the printing of program announcements, and candles for lighting the hall. No record of the cost for an advertisement in the *Wiener Zeitung* was found. Printing and distribution of program announcements probably did not exceed 4 or 5 Gulden,[53] but lighting expenses could be considerable, especially for one of the theaters. Although no figures for individual performances were available, working from the total cost of lighting given in the yearly reports of the court-controlled theaters, an approximation can be reached. Of course, rehearsal time inflates the figures somewhat, but since a limited amount of rehearsal also applied to concerts, the sums can at least be taken as an outside possibility. The costs for the smaller halls would have been much less, perhaps half as expensive,[54] and would not have applied for the morning concerts in the Augarten or the midday ones in the Kleiner Redoutensaal (table 14).

Two pieces of evidence set the total expenses for an individual virtuoso concert at 100-120 Gulden. Leopold Mozart reported in 1785 that the violinist Heinrich Marchand had accumulated ex-

[51]He did when she sang at court, but that may have been because a considerable sum was involved.
[52]VIENNA-ROSENBAUM, April 12, 1802. (IV/13)
[53]The cost of the librettos donated by Schönfeld & Co. for a benefit concert in 1794 amounted to 55 fl 40x (PZ, January 31, 1794, p. 90), but announcements involved much less printing and many fewer copies.
[54]In 1800 and 1801, Prince Schwarzenberg paid 61 fl 3x and 58 fl 49x respectively for three evenings of oratorio performances in his private theater. See Croll/SCHWARZENBERG, pp. 89-90.

TABLE 14. Lighting Expenses at the Court-Controlled Theaters

Year	Total Cost	No. of performances	Cost per performance
1783-84	6,094 fl 42x	289	ca. 21 fl
1796-97	10,571 fl 59x	321 (B)	ca. 22 fl
		152 (K)	
1803-04	22,128 fl 18x	309 (B)	ca. 35 fl
		321 (K)	

B = Burgtheater, K = Kärntnerthortheater
Figures taken from VIENNA-INTENDENZ, VIENNA-CAMERALE, and Hada-movsky/HOFTHEATER

penses of 115 Gulden.[55] Nearly two decades later, in 1802, Therese and Joseph Rosenbaum were trying to pay off an unexpected 830 Gulden debt. They considered the possibility of Therese giving a concert to raise money but dismissed the idea as too risky. Their friend Karner, an official with the theater, advised them that the average outlay ran to around 100 Gulden, a sum which they felt was too much of a gamble.[56] This figure is in line with other estimates and suggests the expenses of Josefa Dušek may not be typical:

Orchestra of 35 at 2 Gulden each	70
Hall rental	15
Lighting	20
Program announcements and incidentals	10

Even assuming the concert giver paid two assisting musicians 10 Gulden each (remembering that amount would have equalled 2.2% of a concert master's yearly income), the total comes to 135 Gulden, still considerably under the 200 Gulden Dušek sum.[57] Keeping these estimates in mind, we can now turn to the kind of profits to be made.

[55]He netted 18 ducats, which Leopold Mozart considered to be a poor profit. See MB 3:378.
[56]VIENNA-ROSENBAUM, June 28, 1802.
[57]Expenses at charity fundraisers could vary widely since performers sometimes donated their time and various benefactors often assumed part of the costs. They have therefore not been considered here.

RECEIPTS AND PROFITS

The first item to be considered in assessing receipts is the price of the tickets. For theater concerts, the program announcements generally gave the same prices charged for dramas or operas. As can be seen in table 15, these prices remained stable until around 1804, when they began a steady rise. The Tonkünstler Societät always charged prices above the norm, but individual artists did so only occasionally.[58] Tickets for the Redoutensäle and Jahn's

TABLE 15. Theater Prices

Burgtheater

	1776	1805	1809	1810
Box	3 fl	5 fl	7 fl	12 fl
1st Parquet	1 fl	1 fl 14x	2 fl	2 fl 30x
Locked seat		1 fl 36x	2 fl 30x	3 fl 30x
2nd Parquet	20x	30x	40x	1 fl 20x
3rd Floor	30x	36x	50x	1 fl 40x
Locked seat		50x	1 fl 10x	2 fl 40x
4th Floor	7x	24x	30x	40x

Kärntnerthortheater

	1785	1805	1809	1810
Box	4 fl 20x	5 fl	7 fl	15 fl
1st Parquet	1 fl	1 fl 14x	2 fl	2 fl 30x
Locked seat	1 fl 20x	1 fl 36x	2 fl 30x	3 fl 30x
2nd Parquet	24x	30x	40x	1 fl 20x
3rd Floor	30x	36x	50x	1 fl 40x
Locked seat		50x	1 fl 10x	2 fl 40x
4th Floor	24x	30x	40x	1 fl
5th Floor	10x	14x	20x	30x

[58]Musicians giving concerts in the theaters also had to contend with the problem of free admission, particularly in regard to the nobility who rented their boxes by the year. Such patrons of the theater could theoretically attend concerts there without paying the entrance fee. Advertisements in the papers frequently appealed to those holding boxes to relinquish them for an evening, if they themselves did not plan to attend.

Theater an der Wien

	1801	1804	1809
Box	4 fl	4 fl 30x	7 fl
1st Parquet & Gallery	36x	42x	1 fl
Locked Seat	48x	56x	10 fl 20x
2nd Gallery	30x	30x	40x
Locked Seat	36x	42x	1 fl
3rd Gallery	20x	24x	30x
2nd Parquet		24x	
4th Gallery	9x	12x	15x

Theater in der Leopoldstadt

	1791	1804	1809	1810
Box	2 fl 30x	3 fl	4fl	5fl
1st Parquet & Gallery	34x	36x	45x	51x
Locked seat		48x	1 fl	1 fl 15x
2nd Parquet & Gallery	17x	20x	24x	30x
3rd Floor	7x	10x	12x	15

Information taken from Program Announcements.

restaurant remained at around 2 Gulden for most of the period; Rosenbaum was enraged that Herr Galiani had the audacity to charge 3 Gulden for his concert at Jahn's in 1799.[59] The quoted prices (table 16) can only be used as a guideline, however, since a generous patron might contribute more than the ticket actually cost. The Romberg brothers reportedly received 50 Gulden for one ticket at one of their concerts.[60]

Nonetheless, we can estimate possible receipts based on the size of the halls. With the theaters, it is difficult since ticket prices varied, but with a capacity of over 1000, sums of 2000 Gulden were theoretically possible. Since the Grosser Redoutensaal could com-

[59]VIENNA-ROSENBAUM, March 6, 1799.
[60]AMZ June 10, 1801, col. 626.

TABLE 16. Concert Prices.

Burgtheater	23 Jan 1780	22 Sep 1780
1st Parquet	1 fl	1 fl
2nd Parquet	36x	1 fl
3rd Floor	24x	
4th Floor	12x	

Burgtheater	23 Dec 1784	15 Apr 1810
Box	4 fl 20x	10fl
1st Parquet	1 fl 25x	3 fl
Locked Seat	1 fl 42x	4 fl
2nd Parquet	24x	1 fl
3rd Floor	40x	1 fl 20x
Locked seat	50x	2 fl
4th Floor	20x	40x

Theater in der Leopoldstadt		12 Mar 1808
Box		4 fl 30x
1st Parquet & Gallery		1 fl
Locked seat		1 fl 12x
2nd Parquet & Gallery		30x
3rd Gallery		15x

Jahn's Restaurant		
23 May 95	Lusini	2 fl
6 Apr 97	I. Schuppanzigh	2 fl
29 Mar 98	J. Dušek	1 fl
13 Apr 98	L. Caldarini	2 fl
6 Mar 99	A. Galliani	3 fl
3 May 99	F. Berwald	2 fl
3 Jan 00	Local musicians	1 fl
8 Apr 02	B. Bohdanowicz	2 & 5 fl
19 Apr 05	C. Kreutzer	2 fl

Redoutensaal		
8 Sep 99	Benefit	1 & 2 fl
8 Dec 00	Benefit	1 fl

16 Jan	01	Benefit	2 fl
30 Jan	01	Benefit	2 fl
27 Apr	03	G. E. Mara	2 & 4 fl
1 Apr	04	Benefit	2 fl
20 May	04	Benefit	2 & 5 fl
14 Apr	05	Benefit	1 & 3 fl
12 Jun	05	M. Sessi	1 & 2 fl; 36x
24 Dec	05	Benefit	1 & 2 fl; 2 fl 10x
21 Apr	06	F. Bernardi	2 fl
26 Oct	06	Benefit	1, 2 & 3 fl
23 Jan	07	Pixis brothers	2 fl
25 Jan	07	F. A. Seidler	2 fl
6 Mar	07	Louis Wolf	2 fl
28 Jan	08	F. A. Seidler	2 f1
12 Apr	08	A. Scaramelli	2 fl
18 Dec	08	C. Longhi	3 fl
2 Apr	09	Benefit	2 fl
11 Apr	09	I. Müller	2 fl
15 Mar	10	L. Wolf	3 fl
25 Nov	10	A. Heberle	
		V. Schuster	1 fl 30x

Augarten

16 Jun	99	Benefit	1 fl
30 Sep	02	I. Schuppanzigh	2 fl
1 May	05	M. Bigot de Morogues	2 fl
9 May	05	K. Zeuner	2 fl
28 May	05	J. Posch	1 fl
6 May	10	I. Schuppanzigh	3 fl
5 Jun	10	F. Leppich & C. Kreutzer	3 fl

Augarten Subscription Series Prices

Year	Number	Tickets/subscriber	Price
1799	4	6 each = 24 tickets	4 fl 30x
1800	4	6 each = 24 tickets	4 fl 30x
1801	4	4 each = 16 tickets	4 fl 30x

1802	4	4 each = 16 tickets	5 fl
1804	4	4 each = 16 tickets	5 fl
1805	5	2 each = 10 tickets	5 fl
1810	6	2 each = 12 tickets	10 fl

fortably hold at least 1200, it could have brought ca. 2500 Gulden. By way of contrast, Jahn's restaurant filled with 400 patrons would have realized only 800 Gulden, yet another reason for virtuosos to apply elsewhere first.

The actual intake from Mozart's subscription series in 1784 and 1785 can be calculated to give a more definite idea of the amounts of money involved. For the 1784 season, he reported having 174 subscribers who paid 6 Gulden each for three concerts, a total of 1044 Gulden. Estimating 210 Gulden total expenses for the orchestra, 40 for renting the hall, and another 50 for printing, lighting, and miscellaneous and subtracting that total from the ticket sales, Mozart could have made over 700 Gulden (which would have at least covered his rent for the year!). The following year, with over 150 subscribers at 3 Ducats each (13 1/2 gulden) (for 6 concerts) he would have taken in at least 450 Ducats, or 2025 Gulden, easily clearing 1400 Gulden.

Receipts of single virtuoso concerts were sometimes reported in newspaper articles and reviews, (see table 17) but it is rarely clear whether the figures quoted represent gross or net profits. In addition, the sums could easily have been exaggerated, particularly in the case of the foreign newspapers that depended on a correspondent for their information. The *Wiener Zeitung,* on the other hand, reported exact numbers down to the last Kreutzer, lending their figures a greater credibility. Reliability aside, however, such accounts can result in an unrealistically high level by which to judge profits, for journals naturally considered large profits the most news worthy. Such was the case with the 4088 Gulden, 30 Kreutzer Haydn made with the performance of *Die Schöpfung* at the Burgtheater (clear profit since the nobility assumed all the expenses), according to the *Allgemeine Musikalische Zeitung* "a sum never before taken in by a Viennese theater."[61] Of course, Haydn

[61]AMZ, April 10, 1799, col. 446.

TABLE 17. Proceeds for Virtuoso Concerts

Date	Musician	Amount	Source
23 Mar 83	Mozart	1600 fl	Cramer
2 Mar 85	Marchand	81 fl net	MB
23 Feb 85	Lebruns	1100 fl	Eibl
28 Feb 85	Lebruns	900 fl	Eibl
7 Mar 85	Lebruns	500 fl	Eibl
11 Mar 85	Mozart	559 fl	ML
23 Feb 88	Storace	4000 fl	Deutsch/ DOKUMENTA
23 Dec 91	C. Mozart	1500 fl	PZ
29 Jan 98	Eck	400 Ducats	AMZ
19 Mar 99	Haydn	4088 fl 30x	AMZ
b6 Oct 01	Rombergs	600 fl net	AMZ
29 May 01	Haydn	3209 fl	Pohl
5 Apr 03	Beethoven	1800 fl	FM
27 Apr 03	Mara	2000 fl	FM
9 May 05	Zeuner	2500 fl	BMZ

For exact citations, see concert date in Appendix 1.

was by that time a national treasure; the average musician could never have hoped to earn that much. Even a sixth of that sum was considered respectable, judging from a remark of Leopold Mozart about his son's concert in the theater in 1785:

> Your brother made 550 Gulden at his concert, which we never expected, as he is giving six subscription concerts at the Mehlgrube.[62]

After the turn of the century, the inflation rate must be taken into consideration, but the 1800 Gulden made by Beethoven and the 2000 by Mara in 1803 represent decent profits.[63] That those figures were indeed quite acceptable is confirmed by the cor-

[62]ML, 2:888.
[63]*Der Freimüthige* implied that Mara's profits were quite low, since concerts in the Redoutensaal often realized two or three times that amount. However, such large profits came from charity fundraisers. It is unfair to compare their results with that of a private virtuoso.

respondence of the court theater management with musicians they were trying to tempt to come to Vienna. In 1808 the gentlemen assured Herr and Frau Fischer that their benefit concert in the Kleiner Redoutensaal at noon could be counted on to bring in at least 500 Gulden, and that they doubtless would make three or four times that amount.[64]

But these were all success stories; other musicians did not always break even, although that supposedly occurred rarely in Vienna:

> Although H[eberle] is a good flutist, it was his misfortune that he didn't even cover his costs, which hasn't happened to an artist here in Vienna for many years.[65]

Even sadder was the case of Diego Somoriva (Sommariva):

> Today, after his midday concert in the Kleiner Redoutensaal, Diego Somoriva went to prison because of his debts.[66]

Profits at charity fundraisers greatly exceeded the normal intake at individual virtuoso concerts, since the court and members of the nobility frequently used the opportunity to demonstrate their largesse by donating large sums of money. Although the asking price for the tickets usually remained around 1 to 2 Gulden, those attending were often encouraged to give more:

> December 8, 1800. Benefit for the Niederösterreichischer Scharf-schützencorps. The set entrance price is 1 Gulden; generosity cannot be limited.[67]

Of course the amount of money raised depended on the popularity of the cause and of the work on the program, and could range from the paltry 270 Gulden at the Tonkünstler Societät concerts on December 22 and 23, 1792, to the 9400 Gulden Madame Frank

---

[64]VIENNA-INTENDENZ, Korrespondenz und Briefprotokoll, March 26, 1808.
[65]AMZ, July 12, 1809, col. 650-51. (IV/14)
[66]VIENNA-ROSENBAUM, June 12, 1807. (IV/15)
[67]VIENNA-GDMF. (IV/16)

raised to support wounded soldiers on January 30, 1801. As might be expected, special causes often managed greater sums than the charities that put on annual events, and war-related causes seem to have been especially lucrative (table 18).

TABLE 18. Proceeds for Benefit Concerts

Date		Beneficiary	Amount	Source
21 Jan	94	War widows & orphans	2076 fl 50x	PZ
24 Jan	94	War widows & orphans	625 fl 4x	PZ
19 Sep	96	Viennese Vol. Army	5805 fl 18 x	WZ
21 Sep	96	"		
4 Oct	96	"		
23 May	99	Tyroleans	2596 fl	Ros
9 Aug	99	War widows & orphans	660 fl 50x	WZ
8 Apr	00	Theater poor	516 fl	Ros
16 Jan	01	Wounded soldiers	7183 fl	Ros
30 Jan	01	Wounded soldiers	9463 fl 11x	WZ
5 Apr	01	?	3390 fl	Ros
29 Jun	03	Business Institute	2500 fl	Ros
26 Dec	03	Bürgerspital	4000 fl	AMZ
1 Apr	04	Charity Organization	9071 fl 1x net	WZ
15 Nov	04	Charity Organization	4621 fl 28x	WZ

For exact citations, see Appendix 1.

Tonkünstler Societät Proceeds

Spring 1781	2394 fl
Spring 1782	512 fl
Spring 1789	436 fl
Winter 1789	270 fl
Winter 1790	2007 fl
Winter 1792	232 fl
Winter 1793	1629 fl
Spring 1796	2243 fl
Spring 1798	2367 fl
Winter 1799	4162 fl
Winter 1801	3209 fl

Information taken from Pohl/TS, pp. 42, 49, 51, 52.

Generalizing from this assortment of data is impossible, because the financial gain to be made in concerts depended on many variables, from the performer's flair for public relations to competition from other performances.[68] If the circumstances were right, one performance could bring in 1000-1500 Gulden or more (two to three times the court orchestra concert master's annual salary). Even a half-empty hall at Jahn's would have brought in 400 Gulden and left ca. 250 Gulden after expenses. The situation in Vienna offered musicians a good chance to make money, if they had the business sense and the talent to take advantage of it.

[68]For example, traveling expenses of foreign virtuosos would have taken up a large portion of their budget, so that while a small profit of 100 to 200 Gulden might have sufficed for a local musician, they would have needed more to cover their greater expenses.

CHAPTER FIVE

Public Concert Programs

The most striking difference between eighteenth-century and modern concerts is without a doubt the content of the programs. A twentieth-century audience expects to hear a voice recital, a symphony concert, a piano recital, an evening of string quartets, i.e. a selection of pieces in one medium. To eighteenth-century listeners, such a mono-chromatic program would have seemed not only strange but possibly a little dull. One reviewer remarked about a concert given by Marianna Sessi:

> She gave exclusively vocal pieces by Pär, Farinelli and Mayr. The absence of instrumental pieces alone made the concert become monotonous.[1]

An audience then expected to be entertained with variety, to be dazzled by an instrumentalist's virtuosity, to applaud a favorite opera aria, to hear the latest symphony, all in one evening. Even cantatas and oratorios, varied genres in and of themselves, were often preceded by unrelated symphonies or overtures and almost invariably featured a concerto during the intermission. The single-medium concert actually originated during the nineteenth century, when the contemplation of music became a much more sober affair, and when admiration of virtuosos intensified into the form of personality cults.

[1]AMZ, June 26, 1805, col. 629. (V/1)

While the eighteenth century certainly appreciated and applauded its virtuosos, not even the most famous of them thought of performing entirely alone: if a single-medium concert could be criticized as monotonous, a single-performer evening would have been even more so. No musician ever concertized without the backing of an orchestra and the assistance of other soloists who played numbers of their own choosing. This system insured a varied program, but also meant that the actual concert giver did not appear in every piece, in some cases performing only two or three of the eight or ten listed. Though the main performer did run the risk of being upstaged, assisting musicians would have also attracted their own fans, thus increasing the concert receipts. Singers assisting other singers appeared quite frequently, perhaps because ensemble numbers from operas enjoyed great popularity as concert pieces, instrumentalists assisting other instrumentalists less often.

The extant program announcements reveal a more or less standard order that changed very little during the period under discussion. Almost invariably, the program opened with a symphony or overture (in private concerts a quartet might be substituted), which signaled that the concert had actually begun and gave the audience a chance to quiet down. While it is easy to criticize this "noise-killer" function from a twentieth-century point of view, we should remember that eighteenth-century audiences did not have the two cues that alert us to a concert's beginning: the dimming of the lights (how do you dim candles?) and the dramatic entrance of a baton-carrying conductor. The music itself had to provide the signal.

The symphony's function as a concert-opener naturally influenced style to a certain extent—loud opening chords get attention better than a quiet melody. Not taking this into account was even grounds for criticism as late as 1806:

My curiosity about the first piece, namely about the symphony by Rösner . . . was, so to speak, satisfied quite imperceptibly. The symphony has a very unusual beginning that isn't, however, striking at all; what kind of an effect is it supposed to make when the entire house is engaged in a comfortable murmuring, and after the customary signal to begin (I mean from the director) the beginning itself consists of a soft violin unison. You couldn't really tell if they were tuning again, playing a prelude or actually starting. The composer will know what idea he was thinking of with this prelude. The following thoughts occurred to me: The violins (viola, cello, and bass included) are actually in symphonies the general, most characterless element. They are the building blocks that carry and connect everything. The variety and embellishment of the intended characters is produced above all by the proper use and distribution of the wind instruments. Now, since the symphony here already has a certain form and a certain character, it is unsatisfying when it announces itself with a characterless beginning. To my knowledge, no composer has ever let his symphony start with a violin unison alone, and in Adagio to boot. The beginning should invite and challenge you to listen. This happens either with a full chord, or through a rich unison, or through an interesting but somewhat faster melody. Hr. Rösner could remedy the whole situation just by putting a note with a fermata, either a chord with any kind of instruments or a unison with all of them, before his symphony.[2]

Even loud chords, however, did not assure that the audience would pay attention, as critics continually complained:

First a quartet or a symphony, which basically is viewed as a necessary evil (you do have to start with something!) and therefore to be talked through.[3]

The concert opened with a Haydn symphony which, as is usual with the opening pieces of concerts, was only half heard.[4]

Part of this attitude stemmed from the association of symphonies with opera and the theater. Opera overtures were routinely ignored, and the symphonies used as fillers during the intermissions of plays were generally regarded as background music, a fact which the ever-critical Nicolai observed in 1781:

I have already mentioned the orchestra in the Kärntnerthortheater. The one in the Burgtheater seems to me to be almost more

[2]WJ, April 15, 1806, pp. 241-43. (V/2)
[3]AMZ, October 22, 1800, col. 65. (V/3)
[4]AMZ, May 29, 1805, col. 570. (V/4)

preferable. I was very attentive, not only in the *Singspiele*, but also to the symphonies between the acts, which the audience normally pays so little attention to.[5]

This disregard for symphonic works would have easily transferred from the theater to the concert hall. Nonetheless, the custom of opening every type of musical performance with a symphony or an overture continued into the nineteenth century.

In programs not featuring an oratorio or cantata, the opening symphony was nearly always followed by an opera aria, even in concerts given by instrumental virtuosos,[6] and then by an instrumental concerto. After these three fairly standard numbers, the program would consist of alternating vocal and instrumental pieces, for a total of seven to nine selections, with another symphony opening the second half. Instrumental virtuosos giving concerts would often program variations or a fantasy as the penultimate number, (assisting instrumentalists generally played only concertos and did not improvise), and both vocalists and instrumentalists would conclude with a symphony or large vocal ensemble. The resulting mixture incorporated two to three symphonic, two to four vocal and two to three solo instrumental works. Plate 24 shows a typical program.

When considering such eighteenth-century concert programs, the question of length naturally arises. Typical wisdom has always held that they lasted an eternity, usually three to four hours, citing the Beethoven concert on December 22, 1808, which, according to Reichardt, began at 6:30 P.M. and ended at 10:30 P.M.[7] That program included both the fifth and the sixth symphonies, an aria, a piano concerto, the choral fantasy, and two movements from his C Major Mass. But the bulk of the evidence suggests that such a lengthy program was not typical.

For the early-morning Augarten concerts, two hours, with an intermission, was the norm.[8] Rosenbaum confirms this with his

---

[5]Nicolai/BESCHREIBUNG, 4:541. (V/5)
[6]In the extant program announcements we find only five instances of instrumental artists appearing second, i.e., for the "real" opening number.
[7]Reichardt/VERTRAUTE, 1:254-55.
[8]AMZ, May 22, 1799, col. 543.

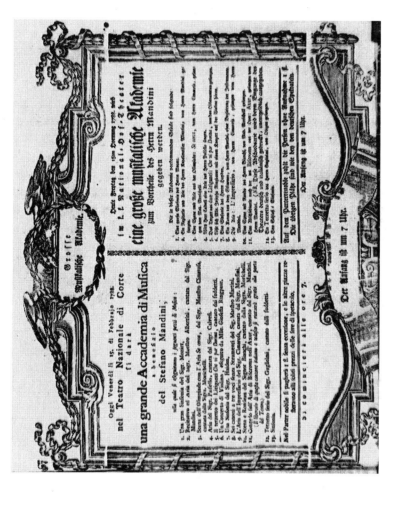

Plate 24. Concert Zettel. (Courtesy of the Oesterreichische National-bibliothek – Theater Sammlung.)

complaint about the concert given by Marie Bigot de Morogues, which began at 8:00 A.M.[9]

> The concert of Mme Margot (*sic*) lasted forever. We left for home at 10:45 and it still wasn't over.[10]

Although the complete program for that concert is not extant, various reports indicate that the works included two overtures, one new symphony, one aria, one piano fantasy, and two concertos. Hers was a private concert occurring at the official spring opening of the Augarten (a beloved Viennese gala event) and not a part of the Schuppanzigh concert series, perhaps explaining its greater length.

Midday concerts given in the Kleiner Redoutensaal were sometimes advertised as lasting from 1 1/2 to 2 hours:[11]

12 Dec 02—12:00 to 2:00 Ignaz & Anton Bök		WZ
31 Mar 05—12:30 to 2:00 Anton Weidinger		WZ
23 Feb 06—1:00 to 2:30 M. Kirchgessner		ONB-MS
11 May 06—12:30 to 2:00 M. Kirchgessner		ONB-MS
23 Jan 07—12:00 to 2:00 Pixis brothers		WZ

But perhaps a conscious effort was made to keep these programs short, since they did occur during the work day. The wording of the announcement of the Kirchgessner concert of May 11, 1806, even suggests that the 1 1/2 hour length was a selling point:

> Incidentally, the order [of the program] is such that the entire concert will be over by 2:00.[12]

The selection of pieces does show an attempt at brevity—it opened with an opera overture rather than a symphony, the fifth number consisted only of an "Allegro" rather than an entire symphony,

[9]WZ, April 27, 1805, p. 1936.
[10]VIENNA-ROSENBAUM, May 1, 1805. (V/6)
[11]For exact citations see appendix 1.
[12]VIENNA-ONB-MS, May 11, 1806. (V/7)

and the concluding symphony was omitted entirely. Programs for the other concerts are unfortunately not extant, but the handful of announcements for other noon virtuoso performances list only six or seven selections instead than the eight or nine common at evening performances. The time limitation even applied to some oratorio performances held at midday; both Süssmayer's "Der Retter in Gefahr" on September 19, 1796, and Haydn's *Die Schöpfung* on December 26, 1802, were advertised as lasting from 12:00 to 2:00 P.M.[13]

Though evening performances probably lasted a little longer than those given in the morning, the relative brevity of eighteenth-century instrumental pieces and arias would have kept the duration of a typical concert to well under three hours. In fact, we have an eyewitness report that one of Abbé Vogler's programs did not exceed two—from 6:30 to 8:30 P.M.[14] Estimation from other programs can be only tentative, because of inexact titles, but using *outside* time limits, we can arrive at a probable *greatest* length:

3 symphonies at 25 minutes each	75 minutes
3 vocal works at 15 minutes each	45 minutes
2 instrumental works at 20 minutes each	40 minutes
	160 minutes
	or 2 hours and 40 minutes

As a norm, this would be a little longer than the typical twentieth-century concert, but one should keep in mind that the variety of the format would have been less tiring to the listener. A number of short cuts—the use of overtures instead of symphonies, partial performance of symphonies could also have been used to keep the entire production within reasonable lengths. Thus it appears that a normal performance might have lasted about 2 to 2 1/2 hours and would not have had the marathon length that has sometimes been suggested.

[13]WZ, September 14, 1796, p. 2647, and December 18, 1802, p. 4557.
[14]VIENNA-ROSENBAUM, March 26, 1804.

INDIVIDUAL GENRES AND COMPOSERS

Even though the overall format of concert programs did not change over the thirty-year period, some trends in preference for certain types of works can be seen. These changes can most easily be identified by examining the individual genres of choral, solo vocal, symphonic, solo instrumental with orchestra, and small ensemble. Since the source material is incomplete and uneven (the program information for the period 1760-1800 about equals the information for the following ten years), a strict statistical study of frequency of type or genre or of the popularity of composers is not possible. However, the preservation of the source material seems to have been largely random, so that, except for a few cases that have been noted,[15] the resulting data is not obviously weighted toward any one composer or genre. In view of that fact, a few observations about Viennese musical taste can be made.

Choral

Oratorios, the most frequent type of choral works, were presented almost exclusively at charity fundraisers. Frequently topical, especially those given for war-related causes, they received a few performances—sometimes only one—on the occasion for which they were written, then disappeared. Haydn's *Die Schöpfung,* and to a lesser extent *Die Jahreszeiten,* were the only real exceptions to this high mortality rate, receiving many performances in the decade after they were composed. Handel's oratorios appeared regularly on public (and private) programs, but their popularity never approached that of the Haydn works. There would have been occasion for only six or seven oratorios during the course of the year, and given the interest in new music, once a work had been performed, it was not likely to be revived later. Thus, for example,

---

[15]For example, a composer who gave two concerts of his own music but was never heard on another program could statistically be on the same plane as one who had a single work performed on fifteen different programs, but the latter obviously enjoyed a much greater popularity.

the fact that Beethoven's *Christus am Oelberge* only had a few performances should be considered normal, not as evidence of the public's misunderstanding of a great composer.

Performances of operas as oratorios occurred only sporadically before 1800; Haydn's *L'Isola desabitata* (March 19, 1785), Cimarosa's *Heimliche Heirat* (*Il matrimonio segreto*, March 9, 1793), and Constanze Mozart's almost yearly productions of her late husband's *La Clemenza di Tito* are the only ones that can be documented. Even after 1800 they are relatively infrequent and were usually given by an opera composer.

Small solo or ensemble vocal cantatas replaced the usual opera arias on solo virtuoso concerts only rarely, and then before 1800. In such cases, they constituted the first half of the program; the final half contained instrumental works. After 1800, pieces billed as cantatas generally resembled secular oratorios and appeared on fundraisers. Although masses and similar liturgical compositions were almost never programmed on secular concerts, their occasional occurrence does not appear to have been plagued by problems with the censors of the type Beethoven had in presenting his *Missa Solemnis* in the 1820s. He did disguise the "Gloria" and the "Sanctus" of the C Major Mass on his concert of December 22, 1808, by calling them a "Hymne" and a "Heilig" respectively, but four years earlier, Abbé Vogler had simply designated a "Benedictus" as such (March 26, 1804). Moreover, there had been two complete performances of the Mozart *Requiem,* one on January 2, 1793, under Baron van Swieten's direction and the second on April 9, 1805, at the Theater an der Wien as a fundraiser for the poor of the theater. None of these performances occasioned any comment from critics or observers about the suitability of sacred works in concert.

Solo and Ensemble Vocal Works

Italian opera arias and concert arias written in an operatic style, e.g. Mozart's concert arias, dominated the solo and ensemble vocal repertory. Naturally, the selections tended to reflect both the particular singer's repertoire and the current popular operas. For example, in 1787 almost every program listed at least one aria from that year's big hit, Vincent Martin y Soler's *Una cosa rara;* in 1788 his *L'arbore di Diana* took its place.

A substantial percentage of the arias listed on program announcements do not name a composer, a frequent occurrence with the numbers of an assisting singer. The concert-giver very likely did not know when the announcements were printed exactly what the vocalist would select, but one could hazard a guess that it would be from whatever opera role he or she might currently be playing. Even when the composer was acknowledged, the name of the piece or the opera from which it came did not always appear, making exact identification of many of the works impossible.

Of the arias identified by composer, the overwhelming majority were written by Italians, indicative of Italian opera's hold on the Viennese musical world. No one composer stood out dramatically during the 1780s and 1790s, but Sarti and Paisiello appeared frequently. Cimarosa arias began to be programmed in the 1790s and remained popular through 1810. During the period 1800-1810, the names Ferdinando Pär, Simon Mayer, and Sebastiano Nasolini (the first two lived for a time in the city) predominated. Pär, in fact, appears at first glance to have been an overwhelming favorite in those years: of the nearly 200 identified arias and other operatic excerpts on public concerts from 1800-1810, 41 are by Pär, with Mayer (18), Cimarosa (16), and Nasolini (11) far behind. Even if the data were complete, however (and it is not), the numbers could not be taken to mean that Pär was twice as popular as anyone else, for 17 of those excerpts were performed at concerts he gave or were sung by his wife, Francesca Ricardi Pär. His arias were chosen for performance by other artists 24 times, still more than the other composers, but not overwhelmingly so. Other composers worthy of note include Cherubini and Mozart. Considering the popularity of the former's overtures (see page 156), his arias seem to have been neglected on concert programs.Mozart's arias, on the other hand, especially ones from *Die Zauberflöte*, continued to be performed consistently even in the decade after his death, a significant fact considering the rapidity with which musical fashions changed.

Non-operatic solo and ensemble vocal works were so scarce as to almost be non-existent. Only a handful of *Lieder* can be found, all in the last ten years of the period. Of these, the Zumsteeg Ballade sung on May 11, 1806, should be mentioned. Two programs from the same decade featured a collection of non-operatic vocal works. On March 25, 1805, in the Theater in der Leopoldstadt, some of Haydn's vocal trios and quartets with piano accompaniment were performed on an extremely unusual program that also included "Frühling," "Sommer," and 'Herbst" from *Die Jahreszeiten*. The only other documented program in any way similar to this one contained popular patriotic songs composed by various musicians to texts by Heinrich von Collin (March 25, 1809, March 28, 1809, April 2, 1809, April 16, 1809).[16]

Instrumental Music—Symphonic

Symphonies were very much in demand since each virtuoso concert included two or three and every oratorio generally opened with one, not to mention the countless works that served as intermission fillers in the theaters. Unfortunately, as was the case with opera arias, printed program announcements were frustratingly imprecise about designating specific works. Anonymous pieces were probably simply selected from the repertoire of the orchestra (if a theater orchestra was used), or perhaps left to the discretion of the Concert Master, and very likely did not represent the most recent compositions. Even when the composer was given credit, the occasional identification of a work by key began only after 1800. A typical entry might read: "Eine grosse Symphonie vom Herrn Joseph Haydn," or "Eine neue grosse Symphonie,'or "Eine ganz neue grosse Symphonie" (the last can roughly be translated as "the very latest symphony'). Even though the addition of the adjective "new"

---

[16]Declamatory concerts enjoyed a brief popularity in the period from 1800 to 1810. In them, an actor would do dramatic readings of a poetic or dramatic text against an appropriate musical background. Since their main purpose was not the concert presentation of music, they have not been considered here, but the occasional declamatory pieces or melodramas that appeared on concert programs have been listed in the appendix.

does help narrow the possibilities, you can never be sure if it means that the work was recently composed or simply that it had never been heard in Vienna. On rare occasions, other details were given, such as on the program listing a Haydn symphony "written for the *Concerts Spirituels* in Paris," (October 13, 1787) but such specificity occurred only rarely. Only overtures received exact designations, since the opera was inevitably mentioned.

The number of opera overtures actually appearing on concerts increased dramatically after the turn of the century, from ca. 5% of the identified symphonic works before 1800 to ca. 50% afterwards. Of course, part of the increase may be illusionary; some of the earlier works listed as symphonies could have actually been overtures, especially the unidentified pieces, so that the sudden explosion after 1800 may simply be a result of more precise terminology. More likely, however, it represents an attempt to keep program length under control as the dimensions of the individual works expanded.

The problem of concert length became more critical as the longer symphonies of the early nineteenth century gradually began to overwhelm other works on the program. Instead of changing the entire program concept and structure, however, concert organizers resorted to performing single movements rather than entire works. Many of the Gesellschaft der Musik concerts in the 1820s and 1830s reveal this type of compromise. But to assume that a practice from the 1830s was in force fifty years earlier, as has often been done, errs in historical logic. No evidence exists to support such an assumption for the late eighteenth century.

First of all, in the 1780s and 1790s, the total length of a symphony would rarely have exceeded 20 to 25 minutes, and many were even shorter, so that even the inclusion of three on a program would not have made it inordinately long. However, if audiences couldn't manage to keep quiet and pay attention to the opening symphony, would they have been willing to sit through an entire three to four movement work after the conclusion of what they had really come to see—the virtuoso "fireworks"? It does seem unlikely, although no one remarked about audiences leaving during the final work. If the program announcements are carefully scrutinized, however, they reveal that the final symphonic work was frequently listed as "Schluss-Symphonie" (Concluding Symphony), without a composer. (Most of the anonymous symphonies occupied the final rather than the opening or midway slot.) Perhaps the final movement of the opening symphony could have been encored there. Support for this supposition comes from a letter written by Mozart to his father describing his concert at the Burgtheater on March 23, 1783 (unfortunately no program announcement is extant). Symphonic works appeared as numbers 1, 5, and 10:

(1)The new Haffner symphony
(5) The short concertante symphony from my last Finalmusik
(10) The last movement of the first symphony.[17]

Therefore, when the final symphony has no named composer, one might suspect it actually consisted of a single movement.[18]

A scant handful of program announcements actually specify single movements, for example:

15 April 1791. Herr Dulon (flute)
(1) The newest symphony by Joseph Haydn
(7) Two movements from the latest symphony by Herr Pleyel
(9) Concluding movement from the above symphony by Herr Pichel
   (Pichel is a misprint)

24 March 1787. Joseph Christian Smrezka
(1) The latest symphony by Herr Koželuch
(4) A movement from a symphony by Joseph Haydn
(7) A movement from a symphony by Herr Wranitzky
(9) Concluding symphony.

Although one might argue that these performers were simply more meticulous than normal in their listing of exactly what was to be played, it seems more likely they were notifying their audience to expect a single movement rather than the complete work.

[17]ML 2:843.
[18]Incidentally, this example offers another solution to the question of excessive length, or about programs too heavily weighted with symphonic works.

Only once, in 1810, did a reviewer remark that only a first movement was heard when the entire work was listed on the program, although the tone does not suggest something greatly out of the ordinary:

> First part: Symphony by Capellmeister Rössler [Rosetti?]—only the first movement was performed, performed well, to be sure, but not well received. Only the first movement from a symphony by Ludwig van Beethoven (B flat major, No. 4) was performed, and that poorly.[19]

In conclusion, one should probably suspect incomplete performances after 1800, when the length of symphonies began to increase radically, especially on programs given by virtuoso vocalists or instrumentalists. After all, composers giving concerts would probably have programmed complete works, especially where new ones were involved. Before 1800, however, only anonymous concluding symphonies are good candidates for partial performance.

If Italians dominated the field of opera arias, Austrian empire composers certainly edged them out with symphonic works, Italian opera overtures excepted. Their dominance becomes even greater when one considers that anonymous symphonies probably came from the repertoire of the players and orchestra, which would have been heavily stocked with the pieces of local musicians.

Of all composers of symphonic works, one in particular stands head and shoulders above the rest as far as frequency of performance is concerned—Haydn. Especially in the case of a famous composer, however, one must be very cautious in assessing popularity, since his very name may have contributed to a selective preservation of sources and anecdotes. In Haydn's case, however, the preservation of the main primary source material cannot be explained by a special interest in him as a composer. For example, two important sources frequently listing his name from the 1780s are the *Wiener Zeitung* and a group of program announcements from 1787-1788. In the case of the former, every issue from the period is available, making Haydn's mention totally incidental in their

---

[19]AMZ, April 25, 1810, col. 477. See ROESSLER-ROSETTI for the identification of Capellmeister Rössler. (V/8)

preservation. The survival of the program announcements appears to have been pure chance, perhaps a result of some theater bureaucrat's interest in concerts (since no such run exists for the surrounding years). Haydn's name cannot have been the reason for their preservation, for many of the programs do not contain any of his works.

Thus, with reasonable assurance, we can accept the fact of Haydn's steady popularity throughout the entire period 1780-1810 in the symphonic genre. Many scholars, including C. F. Pohl and H. C. Robbins Landon, have maintained that Haydn remained unrecognized in his own country until his triumphant return from London in the late 1790s. Of course, before 1800, he had little to offer at public concerts except his symphonies. His operas were not published or (with the exception of *Orlando Paladino*) sung on the Viennese stage; he wrote few instrumental concertos and was not himself a virtuoso performer; solo instrumental sonatas and chamber music were not considered concert material then, so that his many contributions to those genres went without public performance. Not until he wrote his two secular oratorios did he have anything to offer the concert public besides symphonies. Those large works naturally attracted much more attention than the performance of a symphony, perhaps explaining the origins of the myth of non-recognition.

A survey of concert programs from the 1780s reveals just how popular Haydn was. Of the approximately 70 public performances on which we have relatively complete information, more than one-fourth (19) featured at least one Haydn symphony, for a total of 23. Considering the diversity of composers found, that number represents a remarkably high profile, one which he maintained through the next two decades.[20] His closest competitor in the 1780s

[20]In fact, his symphonies were so often performed during the intermissions of plays that one critic found cause to complain: "I close this overview . . . with the pious wish that we might get to hear something besides the oldest Haydn symphonies, in plays too. To be sure, this might become difficult with certain ones of Mozart, Beethoven, and Eberl, because they demand a very exact and studied execution, but more rehearsals would certainly do the trick. In addition, the newer Haydn works, the easier ones by Mozart, Romberg, etc., could perhaps be presented more often." See BMZ-REICHARDT, 1:246. (V/9)

was Mozart, with a total of 8 symphonies on 5 concerts, plus 5 other symphonies whose performance is documented only in his letters.[21] After 1800, Cherubini and Beethoven, whose symphonies account for nearly one quarter of the identified symphonic works then, began to dominate the concert programs. No other composer ever approached any of these four in terms of frequency of performance. Anton Eberl and Franz Clement presented their own overtures and symphonies on their own concerts, but although usually well received, they were not widely played elsewhere. Only one French composer, Méhul, ever made his way onto the concert programs.

Programmatic Works

Programmatic pieces span the symphonic instrumental and smaller ensemble genres; they actually make up a very small percentage of the works performed but are nonetheless interesting for their colorfulness. Battle pieces come to mind instantly, but only four (one was presented twice) examples could be found, three of which were presented in the Theater in der Leopoldstadt (table 19). All but the first refer to specific military engagements, making them too topical to survive very long, even if their musical content had merited it. According to the very detailed contents given in the program announcements, they all contained the requisite roaring canons, galloping horses, and crying wounded.

Aside from the composers of battle pieces, the only real proponent of programmatic music was Abbé Vogler. Some serious critical attention was given to his concert at the Theater an der Wien on March 26, 1804, which included an instrumental piece entitled "Die Anrufung der Sonne um Mitternacht in Lappland." It received the approbation of the general public, especially since Vogler had seen that a four-hand piano arrangement was published well before the concert, so that the audience already had a certain familiarity with it.[22] Less well known were gems that appeared on a concert he gave

---

[21]As equivalent letters for the other composers are not extant, including the five in the final tally would unfairly prejudice the data.
[22]ZEW, April 5, 1804, cols. 325-26.

TABLE 19. Battle Pieces

Date		Composer	Place	Title
24 Feb	87	Kloffter (Klöffler)	Burg	Untitled
25 Mar	98	Kauer	Leo	*Die Begebenheiten des Wiener Aufgeboths*
25 Mar	03	Kauer	Leo	*Die Geschichte des Wiener Aufgeboths* =3/25/98
8 Sep	98	Heidenreich	Leo	*Das Kriegslager*
23 Dec	98	Kauer	Leo	*Nelson's Schlacht*

on January 18, 1806, such as "Terassenlied der Afrikaner," "Die Hirtenwonne vom Donnerwetter unterbrochen," "Gesang der Hottentotten, der aus 3 Takten und 3 Worten besteht, 'Mayema, Mayema, Mayema, Huh, Huh, Huh'," and "Die Belagerung von Jericho."[23] These somewhat bizarre pieces seem even more so when one considers they appeared on an organ concert given in the Evangelisches Bethaus. But for the truly bizarre, no one could top the antics of the Bohdanowicz family, whose concerts featured everything from standard pieces to outlandish programmatic works. Bazyli Bohdanowicz, a member of the orchestra of the Theater in der Leopoldstadt, organized elaborate concerts as a showcase for his own compositions as well as for the musical talents of his many children. The programs generally opened fairly normally with his daughters singing several popular opera arias but then would inevitably deteriorate to selections for one violin played with four bows and sixteen fingers and similar nonsense. Programmatic pieces, often nature descriptions, frequently occurred as intermission or concluding numbers. One example, from the concert of April 8, 1802, should suffice:

[23]"Invocation to the Sun at Midnight in Lappland," "Terrace Song of the Africans," "Song of the Hottentots, consisting of 3 beats and 3 words, 'Mayema Mayema, Mayema, Huh, Huh, Huh'," and "The Siege of Jericho."

(a-cappella vocal symphony in 9 parts)—"The Hunt"—besides a beautiful melody, this part portrays the bellowing and howling of the hunting hounds, the medium and strongest murmur of the bears. After the cry of the hunters, however, the shooting of the latter to the ground brings the work to a close.[24]

None of Bohdanowicz's contemporaries took him very seriously; the concerts aroused more pity than anything else. Some effort has been made recently to repair his reputation by emphasizing his more normal compositions.[25] While they do exist, they were not the ones he presented on his concerts.

Concertos

Concertos were to instrumentalists what opera arias were to singers—the central showcase for their talents. Even though improvised variations became increasingly popular for displaying virtuosic tricks, the concerto still served as the instrumentalist's opening number and as the only genre used by assisting instrumentalists. As with symphonies, some have questioned whether they were played in their entirety. Eduard Hanslick, again basing his opinions on sources from the 1820s and 1830s, even maintained that many of the concertos probably did not even have second and third movements.[26] While possibly valid for the period Hanslick was discussing, the partial performance theory cannot be applied unequivocally any earlier. In the 1780s and into the 1790s a complete concerto would rarely have lasted more than twenty minutes and could even have been as short as ten. If only the first movement had been performed, the virtuoso would hardly have been on stage at all. Mozart certainly played his own concertos in their entirety (even composing new movements for them, e.g. K. 175 with the Rondo K. 382), so there is no reason to assume that less well-known virtuosos did not.

[24]VIENNA-GDMF, April 8, 1802. (V/10)
[25]The article in NEW GROVE, for example.
[26]Hanslick/CONCERTWESEN, p. 90.

Another assumption in general circulation maintains that instrumentalists played and were expected to play their own compositions, but extant program announcements show this not to have been the case. In the 1780s and 1790s, just under half of the concertos listed were written by a composer other than the performer. (Students playing their teachers' works account for a small percentage of these.) The remaining works are split about evenly between those without an identified composer and those specifically naming the performer as the composer: "Herr X performed a concerto of his own composition." Interestingly, female instrumentalists almost never advertised themselves as playing their own works.

After 1800, over half of the concertos were played by someone other than the composer. Significantly, reviewers began to criticize performers who thought it necessary to play their own, often second-rate, compositions instead of drawing on the repertoire of fine music by other genuinely talented musicians. The critic for the *Allgemeine Musikalische Zeitung*, for example, praised the wind players Went and Foita for programming works of accepted masters rather than their own, undoubtedly trivial pieces,[27] and lambasted Franz Clement for doing the opposite, asking "Why does every practicing musician want to be a composer as well?"[28] These comments probably reflect a change in attitude rather than a change in practice, though, since the situation had not altered much from the past twenty years. Unfortunately, too little criticism exists from the earlier period to deduce what the attitude might have been at that time.

Mozart and Beethoven stand out most prominently among the composers of concertos. In the 1780s, Mozart quite naturally performed his own works, but other artists also presented them occasionally. Josefa Auernhammer, who had been one of his students, continued to play his concertos into the 1790s, but after the turn of the century she turned mainly to the more recent compositions of Beethoven and Anton Eberl. Even after 1800, when the style of music had begun to change markedly, Mozart's concertos received

[27]AMZ, July 19, 1809, col. 668.
[28]AMZ, February 7, 1810, col. 296. (V/11)

frequent performances; he is found more than twice as often as any other composer except Beethoven during that period. Of course, by that time, critical acclaim for his compositions had placed him on the list of revered composers, so his name was even more likely to be mentioned in reviews, a major source of information about program contents in the first decade of the nineteenth century. Beethoven appeared during the 1790s playing his own works, and rapidly came to dominate the field, a remarkable feat considering the fact that only five piano concertos and one violin concerto could be drawn upon by other artists.

Other composers who deserve mention include Franz Anton Hoffmeister, who was popular in the 1780s and 1790s but disappeared from programs after the turn of the century. Anton Eberl's piano concertos were heard quite frequently in the 1800s, mostly as played by him or by his talented student, Fräulein Hohenadel. Rode and Viotti led the list of the most popular violin concerto composers after 1800.

Other Instrumental Music

Other types of instrumental music occasionally found on concert programs include arrangements for wind band, solo instrumental and small ensemble pieces. Arrangements for wind band, typically of popular opera numbers, enjoyed great popularity as After Dinner Entertainment (see chapter 1) and briefly invaded the public repertoire in the 1780s and 1790s, yet another manifestation of the enormous popularity of opera with the concert public.

Solo and Small Ensemble Instrumental Works

For instrumentalists giving concerts, the solo fantasy and/or variations, usually on a popular opera aria, formed the other essential part of their virtuoso offerings. Pianists and harpists especially took advantage of their instruments' self sufficiency and used the chance to be heard without the orchestra quite frequently. Other instruments, including the violin, cello, clarinet, and flute, performed sometimes with the orchestra and sometimes unaccompanied, as on March 26, 1791, when Herr Dulon announced he would "improvise alone for over a quarter of an hour."[29] Towards the end of the period, the term "potpourri" began to appear.[30] Non-improvisational solo material occurred only rarely, and only after the turn of the century, as in Herr Bayr's Polonaise and Andante for solo flute on December 30, 1810. No solo keyboard sonatas were found at all.

Works which can be considered chamber music—for piano and solo instrument, for two solo instruments, or for small instrumental ensemble—increased dramatically after 1800, as seen in table 20. The term sonata made its appearance in 1780, with the sonata played by Regina Heiss on the salterio and the pieces on Michael Esser's program. Both concerts can be considered somewhat outside the mainstream, and considering the nature of the instruments involved, the works very likely were in a Baroque style with continuo. Not until 1800 does the designation "sonata" begin to be used with any frequency, but no one commented on the new genre suddenly surfacing on concert programs. Small ensemble works were mostly for winds or mixed winds, strings, and/or keyboard. No public performance of a string quartet was uncovered.[31]

TABLE 20. Chamber Music on Public Concert Programs

Date	Composer	Work
23 Mar 84	Mozart	Wind music
1 Apr 84	Mozart	Wind quintet (K. 452)
29 Apr 84	Mozart	Violin Sonata (K. 454)
19 Aug 91	Mozart	Quintet for winds and glass harmonica (K. 617)

[29]VIENNA-ONB-TS, March 26, 1791.

[30]In general such fantasies were improvisations by the musician, the only exception found being when Iwan Müller played Ignaz Moscheles's Clarinet Variations to demonstrate a new clarinet on October 22, 1809.

[31]This contrasts with London, where string quartets on public concerts were quite common.

PUBLIC CONCERT PROGRAMS

Date	Composer	Work
28 Feb 92		Quintet on viola d'amour
6 Apr 97	Beethoven	Piano quintet (Op. 16)
29 Mar 98	Beethoven	Violin sonata (Op. 12?)
28 Mar 00	Kauer	Wind sextet
2 Apr 00	Beethoven	Septet (Op. 20)
4 Apr 00	Mozart	Wind quintet (K. 452)
18 Apr 00	Beethoven	Horn sonata (Op. 17)
25 Mar 01		Waldhorn quintet
25 Mar 03	Eberl	Caprice for 2 pianos
6 Jan 04	Pleyel	Cello duet
2 Mar 04	Gyrowetz	Sonata for fortepiano, clarinet and cello
Sep 04	Kannabich	Violin duet
Lent 05	Hummel	Trio in E flat
25 Mar 05	Steibelt	Duet for harp and fortepiano
25 Mar 05	Mozart	Four hand piano sonata
Summer 05	Kreutzer	Piano sonata with violin accompaniment
23 Feb 06	Mozart	Quintet for winds and glass harmonica (K. 617)
25 Mar 06	Steibelt	Piano duet
25 Mar 06	Pfeiffer	Instrumental quartet
11 May 06	Reicha	Quintet for harmonica with strings
20 May 06		Potpourri for 2 cellos
22 Feb 07	Romberg	Duet for 2 cellos
6 Mar 07	Hummel	Sonata for 2 fortepianos
1 May 07	Röth	Variations for cello with fortepiano accompaniment
25 Mar 09	Gebel	Piano quintet with flute, clarinet, horn and bassoon
30 Apr 09	Beethoven	Horn sonata (Op. 17)
8 Aug 09	Boieldieu	Duet for harp and fortepiano
18 Mar 10	Schneider	Quartet for 4 bassoons

For exact citations see Appendix 1.

CONCLUSIONS

It should be reiterated here that the incomplete state of the data prevents any completely irrefutable conclusions about Viennese musical taste as revealed by concert programs, but certain trends and tendencies can be noted. Viennese preferences tended to be rather provincial and chauvinistic, with, of course, the exception of Italian opera. While oratorios and cantatas were usually written by resident composers, both Austrian and Italian, Italians held almost complete sway over the remainder of the vocal concert repertoire. Instrumental music, on the other hand, with the exception of violin concertos, was the domain of Austrian empire musicians, especially those associated with the local court or theater. French and even North German music had practically no hearing unless brought in by a traveling virtuoso.

Despite the dangers inherent in popularity comparisons, the spread of sources is wide enough to confirm the solid reputation of Haydn, Mozart, and Beethoven over all other local composers. Haydn enjoyed a steady popularity throughout the period because of his symphonies; the big oratorios of the first decade of the nineteenth century only added to his already secure reputation. Mozart's works never appeared as frequently on programs, but one must remember that he had fewer mature symphonies to offer the concert public. His piano concertos and opera arias did, however, continue to receive performances after his death, a particularly significant fact since their style had become outmoded in a world concerned with new music, and since a composer's work did tend to die with him. No other non-living composer, with the possible exception of Cimarosa, was so frequently represented on concert programs of the time, a tribute to Mozart's mark on the Viennese musical world. These facts should help to further dispel the myth of the misunderstood genius and to exonerate the musical perceptions of Viennese audiences.

CHAPTER SIX

Performers and Performance Practice

In our study of performances in earlier historical periods, we tend to focus on composers and compositions as being the most significant, but for audiences of the time, the performers were frequently the main attraction. For the most part, orchestra members remained anonymous. Frustratingly little information survives on them, either individually or as a group. Soloists, on the other hand, are easier to track down and will be discussed first.

Singers made up a substantial percentage of concert-giving virtuosos. Local artists were especially popular and undoubtedly had the easiest time in attracting an audience since appearance in an operatic role guaranteed a degree of public exposure unavailable to instrumentalists. Sopranos, tenors, and basses all appeared regularly, but the lower female voices were not well represented, perhaps in part a result of the secondary role they played in operas. Marianna Marconi, for example, an alto who frequently sang in oratorios to consistent critical acclaim, apparently never gave a concert of her own. Only a few castrati can be found among the list of performers, a reflection not only of Viennese taste but also of changing musical fashion; operas required fewer and fewer male sopranos and altos and more and more tenors.

KEYBOARD INSTRUMENTS

Of the instruments featured as solo, the keyboard was certainly

165

one of the most frequent. Even as late as the 1780s, we must deal with the issue of fortepiano versus harpsichord, first considering the function—solo, accompaniment, or continuo. As a solo instrument on public concerts, the fortepiano appears to have completely replaced the harpsichord by the 1780s, for all but one of the extant sources specify "auf dem Fortepiano" when a keyboard concerto or fantasy appeared on the program.[1] By 1797, the *Jahrbuch der Tonkunst von Wien und Prag* could remark that "the harpsichord is never heard in concerts any more."[2] In some reviews from the *Allgemeine Musikalische Zeitung* and *Der Freimüthige*, references were sometimes made to a *Klavierkonzert* or to *Klavierspieler*, but by that time (after 1799), the fortepiano is almost certainly indicated.

Vienna possessed a large number of excellent pianists, both dilettante and professional, so that performance standards and expectations tended to be very high. Critics remarked time and again on the difficulties in reception faced by foreign artists on that account. Mozart ranked at the very top of the local performers during the 1780s. In the following decade and into the next century his student Josefa Auernhammer assumed a leading position, but her playing increasingly came under attack for its sloppiness, weakness of execution and general lack of musicality. Beethoven made his name in the late 1790s, and after the turn of the century, the rising stars included Anton Eberl and Eberl's student Fräulein Hohenadel, who received consistent praise for her clarity and strength.[3] Foreign musicians included representatives of the new nineteenth-century virtuosic school of playing, e.g., Ignaz Moscheles, Frédéric Kalkbrenner, and Johann Peter Pixis, none of whom caused much of a sensation. Also appearing during the very last years of the period in question were Beethoven's students Ferdinand Ries and Karl Czerny.

During this period, the placement of the solo fortepiano relative to the audience underwent a change. Tradition has always held

---

[1]An announcement in the WZ for Beethoven's 1808 concert, when a fortepiano was unquestionably meant.

[2]Schönfeld/JTWP, p. 184.

[3]Though Joseph Wölfl and Joseph Gelinek were both prominent pianists, their names appear only a few times. See appendix 3.

that Franz Liszt first thought of turning the piano sideways and playing with his profile toward the audience. However, the Abbé Vogler, surely as great a showman as Liszt, had discovered that trick before the Hungarian artist was even born.[4] Rosenbaum described with great disdain Vogler's concert at the Theater an der Wien on March 26, 1804, and in doing so commented on the somewhat unusual arrangement of the fortepiano:

> In general, both the [music] and the set-up were forced, since the orchestra was at its usual spot, but he placed the pianoforte sideways to the stage and sat *en profil* with his back to the court box. The singers and choir sat to the right and left.[5]

As an accompanying instrument for vocal works, the keyboard simply did not come into question at public concerts since the singer had an orchestra at his or her disposal. Michael Kelly did mention that he accompanied a song on the fortepiano at a concert in the 1780s, but that piece was an encore and non-operatic, making orchestral participation improbable or even impossible. As an accompanying instrument or equal partner in instrumental chamber music, the fortepiano began to be heard after the turn of the century; the harpsichord was never mentioned in that role.

Private concerts are, of course, a different matter. The harpsichord's continued use there remains a controversy which this study cannot clarify. We do know that Mozart had his own fortepiano transported to private concerts, which could reflect either the absence or inadequacy of fortepianos at his patrons' homes or his own particular fussiness.[6] Zinzendorf, who would have been able to illuminate the question beautifully, since his diaries run in

---

[4] J. W. Tomášek reported that Johann Ladislaw Dussek did the same at a performance in Prague in 1804. See Landon/C & W, 3:62.

[5] VIENNA-ROSENBAUM, March 26, 1804. (VI/1)

[6] Faced with an inadequate fortepiano, Mozart took the Countess Thun's instrument with him for his competition with Clementi at court rather than play on the Emperor's: "The funny thing was that although I had borrowed Countess Thun's pianoforte, I only played on it when I played alone, such was the Emperor's desire—and, by the way, the instrument was out of tune and three of the keys were stuck." See ML 2:793.

an unbroken span from 1760 to 1813, on all but a few occasions referred to keyboards with the indistinct *clavecin* or *clavessin*, whether it be Fräulein von X or Ludwig van Beethoven who was playing.

Quite naturally, the more intimate nature of a private concert would have made keyboard accompaniment of vocal and instrumental works much more appropriate, and although the wealthier patrons did hire orchestras, some evidence suggests that keyboard accompaniment was also used. Mozart, for example, wrote to his father that the Archduke Maximilian "suggested that I should play and accompany the arias."[7] For patrons of lesser means, such an arrangement occurred even more frequently: Rosenbaum often reported that Therese sang arias with the accompaniment of a fortepiano. Undoubtedly, harpsichords also still fulfilled this function, but they were definitely dated. Zinzendorf went to great lengths to borrow a fortepiano to accompany the singer who was entertaining at one of his dinner parties. Obviously, if one had to borrow, one borrowed the latest thing, and given the strong social element in private concerts, very few of the nobility would probably have wished to appear old-fashioned enough to feature only a harpsichord.

If the fortepiano had assumed the lead in solo and accompaniment roles, the harpsichord remained the keyboard of choice as a continuo member:

> The harpsichord serves mainly for vocal accompanying, for holding together and leading an entire piece of music, especially in operas, and for setting the actual tempo.[8]

The same sources that carefully specify "auf dem fortepiano" when referring to a concerto read "auf dem Claviere" or "auf dem Flügel" when continuo is involved. For example, a program announcement from November 15, 1808, listed as the third number "Ein Concert auf dem Pianoforte," while the end recognized Herr Gyrowetz for having had "die Direktion am Klavier." All of the public program

---

[7]ML 2:779.
[8]Schönfeld/JTWP, p. 184. (VI/2)

168

announcements observed this distinction, but nonetheless performances did utilize a fortepiano for the continuo, as did the 1807-08
"Liebhaber Concerte":

> Whenever there is to be singing, a square fortepiano should be
> placed in the front by the orchestra. (It will be tuned two hours
> before the beginning of the concert.)[9]

At the performance of *Die Jahreszeiten* at the Schmierers' on May
13, 1803, Herr Liparsky directed at the "pianoforte." The 1799
public performance of *Die Schöpfung* also featured a fortepiano, according to the report of Franz Berwald.[10] Of course, the similarity
of sound between the harpsichord and the early fortepianos would
have made either acceptable.[11]

The final question to be answered with regard to keyboard instruments concerns the status of the continuo in general orchestra
concerts. It certainly remained in use in oratorios because of the
requirements of the recitatives, but its presence in other concerts
cannot be completely proved or disproved. In the earlier part of
the period, the continuo player functioned partially as conductor,[12]
and as such constituted an essential part of the ensemble. This arrangement was noted by Joseph Martin Kraus, who attended a concert at the Burgtheater on April 1, 1783:

> On the same day there was an academy in the Burgtheater. The sym-
> phony in D major by Rosetti was an imitation of Haydn's symphony
> that I heard in Regensburg. Herr Umlauf directed from the Clavier.[13]

Later sources remain frustratingly silent on the subject, but certain evidence does point to the inclusion of the continuo into the
nineteenth century. Writing in 1802, the theorist Heinrich Christoph
Koch stated that "one still uses the harpsichord in the majority

---

[9]Biba/HAYDN ORATORIEN, p. 104. (VI/3)
[10]See the quotation on page 186.
[11]In London Haydn sometimes directed from a fortepiano. See Landon/C & W,
3:131.
[12]See the discussion on pages 180-81.
[13]Leux-Henschen/KRAUS, p. 105. (VI/4)

of large orchestras, partly for the support of the singers in the recitative, partly (and also chiefly) for the filling out of the harmony by means of the thorough bass.''[14] Moreover, non-oratorio concerts such as the one on November 15, 1808, cited above did acknowledge a director at the keyboard. Although his main role might have been leading the vocal numbers, it seems unlikely he would have sat idly by during the rest of the performance.

STRINGED INSTRUMENTS

As a solo instrument, the violin rivaled the fortepiano and dominated the other strings. Schönfeld considered it to be the ''most complete'' instrument after the keyboard and thought that, in places where the keyboard could only speak, it could sing.[15] Among the local performers, Ignaz Schuppanzigh and Franz Clement were the most prominent. Schuppanzigh made some solo appearances but is best known for his role in organizing and directing the Augarten concerts and for his quartet concerts held at Prince Rasumofsky's.[16] Franz Clement, a child prodigy, achieved his fame as a soloist even though he was concert master at the Theater an der Wien, the 1807-08 ''Liebhaber Concerte,'' and the private performances given by Herr Würth. After 1800, one of Schuppanzigh's students, Joseph Mayseder, began to make a name for himself, both as a soloist and as a member of Schuppanzigh's string quartet. The list of other violinists includes, interestingly enough, quite a few women: Ringbauer, Lausch, Blangini, Regina Strinasacchi, and Gerbini. Although the traditional view has held that women in the eighteenth century were not supposed to play the violin (only the keyboard), no commentator ever remarked on the impropriety, or even the unusualness, of a female violin virtuoso.

The cello ranked second in popularity among the string in-

[14]Zaslaw/ORCHESTRA, p. 179.
[15]Schönfeld/JTWP, pp. 185-86.
[16]Although widely respected as a player, he was criticized for his annoying habit of tapping his foot to maintain the beat, a sign of inadequate directing ability according to some commentators.

struments, and it *was* an exclusively male domain. All of the cellists who performed in Vienna were measured (and usually found wanting) against the two local virtuosos, Nicolas and Anton Kraft, both in the employ of Prince Lobkowitz during the period under discussion. The foreign cellist Bernhard Romberg also achieved a large following among critics and public alike and had the honor of being one of the very few instrumentalists invited by the court theater management to Vienna for the purpose of giving a concert.

As might be expected, the viola, the step-child of the orchestra during the eighteenth century, had the fewest proponents of any of the strings, largely because it was usually played by the least capable violinists. Only a few solo performances are recorded, two by Carl Stamitz in the 1770s and one by a Herr Fayard from France on June 2, 1787, and the possibility of the latter being a misprint cannot even be excluded. The remaining member of the string family, the bass, did not fare much better, with one performance of a concerto by Joseph Sperger on March 3, 1787. A Herr Häckel had played an instrument called a "contra violon" (double double bass?) on a concert given on April 25, 1784, which also included pieces on the viola da gamba. A similar hold-over from the Baroque occurred a few years earlier on November 17, 1780, when Michael Esser played on a "Violin d'Amour."

Both the mandolin and the guitar had a few soloists who appeared in the first decade of the nineteenth century: Herr Bartelozzi, who played a mandolin concerto with guitar accompaniment, Louis Wolf, and Mauro Giuliani being the most famous. Despite the guitar's popularity, however, it was not considered entirely appropriate for the concert hall. The *Zeitung für die elegante Welt* commented on a concert given by Herr Mitsch:

> He also plays the guitar quite agreeably—to be sure, it is not an instrument that belongs in a big concert hall—it must be regarded as a respite from the big music pieces.[17]

The critic from the *Allgemeine Musikalische Zeitung* voiced a similar opinion and intimated that its high visibility in the concert hall stemmed mostly from its position as "the latest rage":

[17]ZEW, January 26, 1804, col. 86. (VI/5)

PERFORMERS AND PERFORMANCE PRACTICE

Only fashion can justify and find it pretty as a solo, and particularly as a concert, instrument.[18]

Interestingly enough, the guitar was rarely mentioned in connection with private music making, although the considerable amount of guitar music being printed indicates a market somewhere.

The harp was heard quite frequently at both public and private concerts, mainly because of the extensive concertizing of the court harpist Josefa Müllner, who had captured the market almost to the exclusion of all other harpists. In the 1780s Madame Varenne and in 1803 the French virtuoso François Joseph Naderman offered a little variety, but no other names stand out.

WIND INSTRUMENTS

Woodwinds featured as solo instruments included the transverse flute, oboe, English horn, bassoon, and clarinet. Most of the local musicians belonged to one of the theater orchestras, but with the exception of Anton Stadler on the clarinet, none appear to have dominated the scene the way the Krafts did on the cello.[19] Stadler's only real local competition was an elusive figure by the name of Josef Bähr (or Bär or Pär), a student of the German clarinet virtuoso Josef Beer.[20] Other wind instruments, such as the contrabassoon (Theodor Lotz, probably on March 12, 1785), the bass clarinet (Stadler d.A. on February 20, 1788), and the basset horn (Iwan Müller on April 11, 1809) can also be found on concert programs.

With the exception of waldhorn players, brass players rarely made concert appearances during this period. The most famous of the horn players was Punto (Johann Wenzel Stich). Anton and Ignaz Bök count as the most significant foreign virtuosos on the instru-

---

[18]AMZ May 18, 1808, col. 539. (VI/6)

[19]Attributions to Stadler, however, cannot always be made with certainty, since his younger brother also played the clarinet.

[20]See Pisarowitz/BAER for a discussion of the problems of distinguishing the two men.

ment, with concerts given on trips through the city in 1787 and 1802. Excepting the concerts on the automated trumpet presented by Johann Nepomuk Mälzel in 1809, the only instance of a trumpet as a solo instrument occurred on March 31, 1805, when Anton Weidinger, court trumpeter, gave a concert on a keyed trumpet of his own invention. Even more unusual was the performance by the timpanist Johann Georg Roth on April 28, 1798, with a program that included a timpani concerto and various marches. In contrast to the pianists and string players, woodwind and brass players enjoyed a field relatively uncluttered by dilettantes. One does read of the occasional dilettante on the flute, more rarely on the clarinet, but never on the double reeds or brass. Thus, though amateurs did appear on public programs as soloists, it is safe to assume wind players, unless otherwise specified, were professionals.

MISCELLANEOUS INSTRUMENTS

Among the many instruments encountered in the eighteenth century, the glass harmonica certainly counts as one of the most interesting. In a form invented by Benjamin Franklin, it consisted of cylinders, partly submerged in water, that were rotated and played by applying the fingertips to the rotating disks. The eerie, ethereal sound that resulted both enchanted and entranced audiences, but the performers' constant exposure to the tone-producing vibrations could lead to nerve disorders that tended to shorten their life expectancy. Marianne Kirchgessner, one of the most famous, succumbed to the affliction at the age of thirty-nine. In an attempt to overcome this slight disadvantage, the Viennese bureaucrat Karl Leopold Röllig invented a keyed version of the instrument, which he demonstrated at a concert on April 2, 1791. Although his improvements brought advantages to the performer, they proved detrimental to the tone quality, which was after all the main attraction of the instrument in the first place, and it fell into a gradual decline in the course of the nineteenth century. Röllig, a tireless inventor of musical gadgets, produced another curiosity, a piano with bows instead of hammers called the Xänorphika, which enjoyed a brief popularity in 1805-06, then disappeared entirely. Other instruments, such as the Panmelodicon, occasionally surfaced, enlivened the musical scene, and then fell into a probably well-deserved oblivion. In general, critical opinion of the time recognized such inventions as insignificant to the larger musical world and passed on to more important matters.

Upon occasion, a truly bizarre performance on an invented instrument would take place. Perhaps the most ambitious one occurred on January 14, 1792, at the concert given by the blind flutist Francesco Vicaro von Navara. After serenading his audience with numbers on various types of flutes, he treated them to the undoubtedly dulcet tones of a flat moss pipe (whatever that might be) and a small pumpkin rind. A slightly less botanical, but equally intriguing *tour de force* was presented by a certain Herr Mayer from Mannheim, in which he imitated—using only his mouth— the bassoon, waldhorn, serpent, and trumpet, to the accompaniment of a full orchestra. It is somewhat comforting to note that both these performances were not full scale concerts but were used to fill out the rest of the evening after the presentation of a small play in one of the theaters.

ORCHESTRAS

Vienna had no official standing orchestra during the eighteenth century except for those associated with the theaters. Since they may have provided the players for concerts given in the theaters, their size and composition can give us an idea of the strength of the average concert ensemble.[21] The orchestras at the two court theaters remained essentially unchanged during this period, with a total of 35 members (table 21). The orchestras at the two important private theaters, the Theater in der Leopoldstadt and the Theater an der Wien, employed the same number and composition of winds, but fewer strings. By 1808, however, the Theater an der Wien had reached the level of the court theaters, a reflec-

---

[21]The court orchestra, or *Hofkapelle*, participated as a group only rarely in public concerts and has thus not been included here.

TABLE 21. Court Theater Orchestras

	1781 Burg	1796 Ital	1796 Germ	1808 Ital	1808 Germ
Violin 1	6	6	6	6	6
Violin 2	6	6	6	6	6
Viola	4	4	3	4	4
Cello	3	3	3	3	3
Bass	3	4	3	3	3
Flute	2	2	2	2	2
Oboe	2	2	2	2	2
Clarinet	2	2	2	2	2
Bassoon	2	2	2	2	2
Waldhorn	2	2	2	2	2
Trumpet	2	2	2	2	2
Timpani	1	1	1	1	1
Total	35	36	34	35	35

"Ital" and "Germ" refer to the separate ensembles that played for Italian operas and German Singspiele. Information taken from ALMANACH 1782, pp. 130-34; Schönfeld/JTWP, pp. 92-94; Gleich/WTA 1809, pp. 99-102.

tion of its increasing importance as an opera house (table 22). The *Wiener Theater Almanach* fills in some of the gaps for the private theaters with overall numbers, but their totals usually included any composers associated with the theater and show a resultant higher figure (table 23).

A musician giving a concert would have encountered difficulties in presenting pieces without a full complement of winds, although with judicious selection trumpets and timpani would not have been necessary. We can expect the minimum number of players necessary to have been around 22 or 23. A "vollbesetztes Orchester" probably meant a number more like 35.

More precise numbers for specific performances are rare in published sources; they tend to be buried in letters and memoirs of people who attended or had a hand in organizing them. Then, too, the occasions that called for comment were the big productions with the unusually large number of performers. Herr Klöf-

TABLE 22. Private Theater Orchestras

	1796 Leop	1796 Wien	1796 Wien	1808 Wien
Violin 1	4	3	5	6
Violin 2	3	3	4	6
Viola	2	2	4	4
Cello	1	1	3	3
Bass	2	2	3	3
Flute	2	2	2	2
Oboe	2	2	2	2
Clarinet	2	2	2	2
Bassoon	2	2	2	2
Waldhorn	2	2	2	2
Trumpet	2	2	2	2
Timpani	1	1	1	1
Trombone	-	-	3	2
Kapellmeister	1	1	1	-
	26	25	38	35

Information taken from Schönfeld/JTWP, pp. 95-96. The third column, which represents the Theater an der Wien orchestra until 1796 was taken from Komorzynski/FREIHAUSTHEATER, p. 138. No explanation for the conflicting figures was found. The final column was taken from TJ 1808, p. 7.

TABLE 23. Private Theater Orchestra Totals

Leopoldstadt		*Wien*	
1795	30		
1802	26		
		1802	32
		1803	40
1805	30	1805	37
		1806	39
1808	34	1808	44

Information taken from WTA.

fler (Kloffter), for example, announced in the *Wiener Zeitung* that his battle symphony would be performed with an orchestra of 60.[22] The papers of Moritz Dietrichstein in the archives of the Gesellschaft der Musikfreunde in Vienna contain the orchestra list for another, more important, large performance, that of Haydn's *Die Schöpfung* in the University Aula on March 27, 1808 (table 24). To this orchestra of 55 was added a chorus of 32. An additional comment, preserved in the directives of the society states:

> The orchestra may not exceed the members it had at that time, for its strength and excellence does not depend on bigger numbers, but on the ability of its members.[23]

The double bass players, the oboists, bassoonists, horn players, trumpeters, timpanist, and one clarinettist as well as the first chair players of the string sections were professional, paid musicians; the rest were dilettantes.[24] This mix of professional and amateur

TABLE 24. Orchestra at *Die Schöpfung* (March1808)

Violin 1	13
Violin 2	12
Viola	7
Cello	6
Bass	4
Flute	2
Clarinet	2
Oboe	2
Bassoon	2
Waldhorn	2
Trumpet	2
Timpani	1
Total	55

Information taken from Biba/HAYDN ORATORIEN, pp. 103-04.

[22]WZ, February 17, 1787, p. 378.
[23]Biba/HAYDN ORATORIEN, p. 103-04. (VI/7)
[24]Biba/HAYDN ORATORIEN, pp. 103.

clues us in as to a possible reason for the directive given above: Vienna had any number of amateur string players who would have loved to have played with the orchestra. Even though many of them were probably quite capable of enhancing rather than detracting from the quality of the orchestra, increasing the strings any more would have necessitated doubling the woodwinds and brass, and they did not exist in abundance and would have had to be paid as professionals.

The directive may also have resulted from a negative reaction to the monster forces featured each year at the benefit concerts sponsored by the Tonkünstler Societät. For these bi-annual extravaganzas, the program announcements proclaimed "an orchestra of 180," which by 1799 had increased to 200, but before conjuring up an image of a filled stage worthy of a Berlioz work, the twentieth-century reader should be aware of two things: 1) The numbers given were sometimes slightly exaggerated; 2) the word orchestra actually signified "performers" since the chorus and soloists were also included in the tally. Both these points are confirmed by the list of participants for the 1784 performance of Haydn's *Il ritorno di Tobia*, which was announced as being performed by an orchestra of 180. According to the records of the society, the "orchestra" consisted of about half that figure (table 25). Thus what we would consider to be the orchestra actually comprised only 85 players, far above the normal ensemble of the time, but much more suitable for the sizes of the halls available. According to Biba, the number of violins remained standard for the period under consideration, the lower strings increased slightly in strength (to 8 or 9 each) and the wind instruments varied in proportion to each other according to the requirements of the piece, and most probably to the availability of the players.

For other benefits, in particular those given for the "Wohlthätigkeitsanstalten," which had official court support, both theater orchestras and the Hofkapelle generally participated, so that the number of participants approximated the forces at the Tonkünstler Societät concerts. Although "the bigger the better" seems to have held true for major fund-raising events, the numbers never ap-

TABLE 25. Orchestra at *Il ritorno di Tobia* (1784)

Violin 1	20	Altos	2
Violin 2	20	Tenors	15
Viola	6	Basses	15
Cello	5	Boy choristers ca.	28
Bass	6	Soloists	5
Flute	2	"Battutist" (Haydn)	1
Oboe	7	Keyboardist	1
English horn	2	Solo instrumentalists	2
Bassoon	6		
Waldhorn	6		
Trombone	2		69
Trumpet	2		
Timpani	1		
	85		

Total: 154 participants.

Information taken from Biba/HAYDN ORATORIEN.

proached the multitudes assembled for performances of Handel oratorios in London.[25]

The strength of the orchestra in private concerts depended naturally on the financial resources of the patron, the nature of the occasion, as well as the size of the room in which the performance took place. It should not be assumed, however, that performing forces were necessarily smaller because the concerts were private. Undoubtedly much Social Music was performed with no more than a keyboard, string quartet, and maybe a few winds, but full-strength orchestras with string sections composed mainly of dilettantes could be found at the regular concerts of patrons such as Kees, Würth, and Lobkowitz.[26] Again, most of the information available refers to special oratorio performances, which were on a smaller scale than their public counterparts but nonetheless respectable, as seen in

[25]According to some reports, those productions could involve 800 to 1000 people.
[26]FM, December 5, 1803, p. 770.

table 26. Here too, the figures cited include the members of the chorus.

The direction of the orchestra in a concert with normal-sized forces was shared by the first violinist, called the *Musik Direktor*, or sometimes simply the Director of the violins, and the *Kapellmeister*, who presided at the keyboard. Although the exact division of duties undoubtedly depended upon the abilities and preferences of and the relationship between the two musicians involved, theoretically the violinist set the tempo and the interpretation, while the *Kapellmeister* maintained the tempo and beat, made sure that the

TABLE 26. Private Concert Orchestras

Date	Patron	Work	Forces
26 Feb 88	J. Esterházy	C.P.E.Bach	Orch = 86
4 Mar 88		*Auferstehung*	including
		und Himmelfahrt	chorus = 30
		Christi	
6 Mar 89	J. Esterházy	G.F. Handel	chorus = 12
		Der Messias	
23 Mar 99	Schwarzenberg	G.F. Handel	ca. 150
24 Mar 99		*Der Messias*	
13 May 03	Schmierer	F.J. Haydn	Doubled
		Jahreszeiten	strings
			chorus = 16
8 Dec 03	Rosenbaum	Mixed concert	Orch = 28
		& dancing	no chorus
Lent 10	Sala	F.J. Haydn	Orch = 60
		Schöpfung	

For the Lenten performance of *Die Schöpfung*, the exact description of the personnel reads: ''by an orchestra of 60, . . . whose members, with the exception of the first tenor, the waldhorn, trumpet and timpani players, were amateurs.'' Information taken (in order) from: Forkel/Almanach 1789, p. 121-22; Deutsch/DOKUMENTE, p. 294; Küttner/REISE 3:297; VIENNA-ROSENBAUM, May 13, 1803 and December 8, 1803; SAMMLER, April 21, 1810, p. 192.

vocalists entered correctly, and in general held the entire production together. Personality differences or professional jealousies must have created difficulties that were reflected in the music at times, and Schönfeld even went so far as to suggest that it would be good if the two in charge would go over a piece together beforehand to settle on a common tempo. The advantages to such an approach are immediately obvious. He then observed that if all members of the orchestra could rely on the *Musik Direktor* (i.e., the concert master) for the proper tempo, things would improve even more.[27] Even harmony between the two directors did not always insure harmony among all involved and in the music. When Beethoven insisted that Paul Wranitzky direct the orchestra instead of the *Musik Direktor* Conti at his concert on April 2, 1800, the orchestra members rebelled and played carelessly and poorly.[28]

Since both the *Musik Direktor* and the *Kapellmeister* were occupied with their respective instruments, their directing had to be done with whatever part of the body was free at the time. Particularly the *Kapellmeister* had to be bold in his movements:

> His movements must be even more vigorous, so that he often has to work with his head, his hands, and his feet on account of the tempo and beat. In fact, he is not infrequently forced to leave the direction at the harpsichord entirely in order to slash through the air with both arms. Certainly you could consider the fact that a *Kapellmeister* has to work in such a wood-chopper fashion to be an abuse; however, now it has already been established here, and we are used to it.[29]

The *Musik Direktor* was supposed to indicate "tempo, movement, fire, shadow, and light" by the direction of his bow, with his head, and in part with his entire body, but a certain amount of subtlety was expected.[30] Ignaz Schuppanzigh was in fact criticized because he frequently had to resort to foot tapping (or foot stamping, de-

[27]Schönfeld/JTWP, p. 175.
[28]AMZ, October 15, 1800, col. 49.
[29]Schönfeld/JTWP, p. 174. (VI/8)
[30]Schönfeld/JTWP, p. 174.

pending on your perspective) to keep his ensembles together, but in this regard, he probably was not alone. Nonetheless, some considered it a lack of sensitivity and musicianship on his part.[31]

The qualities expected of a good director were outlined in the *Berlinische Musikalische Zeitung* published by Carl Spazier in 1793. Entitled "Hints and Rules for Leaders of Music in Concerts," it declares as basic that the director must have the "right feeling" and the "thought" and "experience" to determine the nature of the piece. In addition, he should to be aware of the significance of each voice:

> For this purpose, however, the simple first violin part is not enough; he must make use of the score, particularly when it is a vocal piece.[32]

After discussing the general requirements in theoretical knowledge, the article goes on to give some practical tips:

> First of all he must be secure on his instrument; he must be sure that it exceeds the others in strength. Just being able to scream over 18 other violins and so many other parts is still not enough, he also must have an arm that has more influence than the others. That is, with a clear and powerful execution of all the advantages of his instrument and himself, he must observe and learn how he can strengthen and make his tone as penetrating as possible. In order to make the movement [i.e., tempo] clear to the others at the beginning of a piece, Pisendel was in the habit of giving the [tempo] with the head of the violin during the first few beats of play. If it was 4/4 time, he first moved the violin downwards, then up, to the side and up again. If it was 3/4 time he moved it downwards, then to the side, then up. If he wanted to slow the orchestra down in the middle of a piece, he played only the first note of each measure, in order to be able to give them more strength and expression, and thus he held [the orchestra] back, etc. Every attentive leader must always be on the lookout for such advantages. If he will only pay attention, many circumstances will give him the opportunity to do so.[33]

[31]AMZ, October 15, 1800, col. 47.
[32]BMZ-SPAZIER, p. 160. (VI/9)
[33]BMZ-SPAZIER, p. 162. (VI/10)

While such a method of directing sufficed for the music of the Baroque and the Early Classic periods, the increasing complexity and length of the pieces put an increasing strain on the system. Very possibly it was the inadequacy of the system rather than a lack of musicality that resulted in such things as foot tapping and *Kapellmeister* waving their hands wildly in the air.

For concerts involving large forces, the two director system simply would not work, if only because not all of the people would have been able to see either one of the leaders clearly. Such performances then added a general director to oversee the entire production. Many of the descriptions of the concerts given for the "Wohlthätigkeitsanstalten," for example, state that Herr Wranitzky directed the violins, Herr Umlauf sat at the keyboard, and Herr Salieri had charge of the whole. The Tonkünstler Societät presentation of *Il ritorno di Tobia* (see table 25) lists Haydn as "Battutist" or beatkeeper. It is not clear whether this position involved simply making a visible beat for the instrumentalists and vocalists, or whether the person was also seated at a keyboard. Even concerts with large forces not featuring an oratorio depended upon a general director, presumably because of the logistics of making sure everyone could see.

The placement of the orchestra and soloists in relation to each other as well as in relation to the audience has also occasioned considerable discussion. In concerts given in one of the theaters, the musicians could have performed either from the place immediately in front of the stage—their usual location for operas and *Singspiele*—or from the stage itself. As might be expected, contradictory evidence exists, but the weight of it seems to fall in favor of the stage. Daniel Heartz doubts that this was the case for ordinary concerts, citing the conflicts with rehearsals and the difficulties involved in moving the stage sets.[34] However, neither of these actually presented any real problems with locating the musicians on stage. In the first place, rehearsals for the operas were frequently held in the Redoutensaal; the minutes of court proceedings are filled with references to the wear and tear inflicted on it as a result. More-

---

[34]Heartz/JADOT.

over, they were generally held in the morning, as is evident from the notations in Rosenbaum's diaries about Therese's activities. Nor would the concert rehearsals have conflicted with the theater rehearsals, since concerts generally fell on holidays when the stage troupe would not have been rehearsing.[35] Finally, stage sets had to be broken down after a performance anyway, because all of the theaters operated on a repertoire system, offering different productions on successive evenings.

Even though nothing may have stood in the way of performances on the stage, that does not necessarily indicate it was customary. Heartz correctly notes that Johann Streicher's instructions about putting the piano several feet closer to the audience than normal when a concerto was being performed would not have been possible in the space allotted to the theater orchestra. The Rosenbaum quotation cited above (page 167), however, implies that the orchestra, at least, normally remained below the stage. However, he could also have meant that all performers were on stage, the instrumentalists simply being further upstage than was normal, with the piano out in front where one might have expected the singers. The latter interpretation receives support from several other sources. An article in the *Allgemeine Musikalische Zeitung* (which does not specifically refer to Vienna, but the conditions described could easily apply) decried the custom of singing opera arias on concerts because the different positions of the singers in relation to the orchestra distorted the sound:

> In concerts, however, singers and instrumentalists stand on an equal level, and if the orchestra is also raised a little to the rear, and the singers stand in front closer to the audience, they are even *lower* than the instrumentalists. . . . You hear arias without melody, at the most melody without words.[36]

Acoustics also proved to be a problem for the large forces of the Tonkünstler Societät, since sheer numbers forced the placement

---

[35]Rehearsals were almost invariably held the day of the concert. See the discussion on pages 186-88.
[36]AMZ, May 1, 1799, col. 482. (VI/11)

of the orchestra so far back upstage that the sound dissipated into the wings. Paul Wranitzky discovered this problem after he listened to one of the society's concerts in the ''Noble Parquet'':

> "To my astonishment," (said Wranitzky), "I heard one of my own symphonies and thought that the music wasn't even in the theater, or that it was very lightly orchestrated. I looked, and saw a number of people working. Why was that? The broad area where the orchestra usually is (the best because it is closer to the audience and is more in the theater) was entirely empty. The remaining apparatus [Maschine] was located too far upstage, where everything dissipates, and too high, where the sound rises above the whole parquet. I also discovered that the violins could not penetrate the basses standing in front at all." Wranitzky recommended changes be made, among them that a platform be built over the theater orchestra's normal place, on which the fortepiano should be placed up front, with the singers and Choristers (8 to a part) on both sides.[37]

Wranitzky presented these recommendations to the society in 1796, but the situation had more to do with the faulty acoustics of the Burgtheater than the placement of the orchestra.[38] Pohl goes on to mention that Antonio Salieri surprisingly preferred to position the chorus towards the back rather than in front, and that Wranitzky often had to protest against that placement, which implies that Wranitzky's view was the more common.[39]

Concerts given in halls like the Augarten or Redoutensaal generally placed the orchestra (including the singers) on a temporary stage, as Rosenbaum indicates in his description of a brief comic moment before a performance in the Grosser Redoutensaal:

> Later there was quite a press in the hall and the gallery. Before the concert began, a lamp trimmer provided involuntary entertainment by falling from the orchestra and pulling music stands and the barrier down with him.[40]

[37]Pohl/TS, pp. 34-35. (VI/12)
[38]A resonating dome was constructed there in the early nineteenth century, but it did little to help the matter.
[39]Pohl/TS, p. 35.
[40]VIENNA-ROSENBAUM, January 30, 1801. (VI/13)

The practice of raising the orchestra above the listeners became so ingrained that its absence occasioned complaints:[41]

> The hall [the Augarten] is very good, but the orchestra placed poorly (right in the middle without the slightest elevation).[42]

The arrangement of the performers cannot be documented with certainty, for seating charts of concert orchestras did not become common until the nineteenth century. If the orchestra was located in front of the stage, space limitations would have forced the positioning at long desks, as was customary for opera orchestras. Ensembles playing from the theater stage or on a specially constructed platform in one of the other halls may very well have used the amphitheater plan described by Johann Berwald, who attended the performance of Haydn's *Die Schöpfung* at the Burgtheater on March 19, 1799:

> When we entered, we saw that the stage proper was set up in the form of an ampitheatre. Down below at the fortepiano sat Kapellmeister Weigl, surrounded by the vocal soloists the chorus, a violoncello and a double bass [as continuo]. At one level higher stood Haydn himself with his conductor's baton. Still a level higher on one side were the first violins, led by Paul Wranitzky and on the other the second violins, led by his brother Anton Wranitzky. In the centre: violas and double basses. In the wings, more double basses; on higher levels the wind instruments, and at the very top: trumpets, kettledrums and trombones. That was the disposition of the orchestra which, together with the chorus, consisted of some 400 persons.[43]

REHEARSAL AND PERFORMANCE CUSTOMS

Given the short notice on which most public concerts were prepared, one would expect a minimum of rehearsals, and this in

---

[41]Even private concerts adopted the arrangement, often unnecessarily. Herr Schwarz, writing in the early 1780s, found it necessary to protest that such a platform really was not essential. See Schwarz/DILEKTANTEN.

[42]AMZ, October 15, 1800, col. 47. (VI/14)

[43]Landon/C & W, 4:455.

fact was the case. Oratorios usually had two on the days immediately preceding the performance. Since many of the oratorios were completely new works, the rehearsals must have been both crucial and hectic. Augarten concerts had one on the preceding day, with the singers often receiving extra coaching:

> September 2, 1801. At 11:00 A.M. Therese had a rehearsal of the two arias she is to sing tomorrow in the Augarten. . . . At 5:00 P.M. Salieri came over; she sang both arias.
>
> September 3, 1801. At 7:00 A.M. Therese sang, or rehearsed her arias a little, then we drove to the Augarten. It was a pretty concert. Therese sang with much art and to even greater approval.
>
> September 1, 1802. At 10:00 A.M. Therese had a rehearsal of the two arias; Salieri and Umlauf accompanied.
>
> September 2, 1802. Therese and I drove to the Augarten concert.[44]

Virtuoso concerts in particular tended to have rehearsals in the morning on the day of the concert, with sometimes an informal atmosphere reigning:

> Madame Mara's concert in the Redoutensaal. . . . At 11:30 A.M. we went together to Mara's rehearsal. She sang in her dressing gown, but masterfully as always. However, her years remind us clearly of the past. . . . At 6:30 P.M. went to the concert.[45]

When the program included several new works, however, an informal atmosphere could easily turn into pure chaos, a term that could be applied to Beethoven productions. Reichardt noted that for his 1808 concert, it had not even been possible to rehearse all of the pieces in their entirety.[46] A closer description of the conditions that prevailed at a Beethoven rehearsal is provided by Ferdinand Ries. One wonders that the concert came off at all—not only

[44]VIENNA-ROSENBAUM, September 2, 1801, September 3, 1801, September 1, 1802, September 2, 1802. (VI/15)
[45]VIENNA-ROSENBAUM, April 27, 1803. (VI/16)
[46]Reichardt/VERTRAUTE, 1:255.

because of the paucity of rehearsal time, but also because of sheer exhaustion on the part of the performers:

> The rehearsal started at 8:00 A.M., and of new works, besides the oratorio, the second symphony in D major, the piano concerto in C minor and another piece that I can't remember were played for the first time. It was an awful rehearsal and by 2:30 everyone was exhausted and more or less unsatisfied.

> Prince Karl Lichnowsky, who had been at the rehearsal from the beginning had sandwiches, cold cuts, and wine brought in big baskets. . . . The rehearsal got started again. The concert began at 6:00 P.M., but was so long that a couple of pieces weren't given.[47]

Rehearsals for private concerts were undoubtedly even more problematic, since many of the performers were dilettantes and not obligated to attend. At least one patron—Prince Lobkowitz—solved the problem by holding a practice session on the evening of the concert itself:

> The music wasn't rehearsed until right before and while the remaining guests assembled.[48]

Even this minimal rehearsal time was probably not always possible. Rosenbaum, for example, in his detailed description of his and Therese's musical party (see page 7), never mentions the orchestra practicing together. But the results need not have been disastrous for musicians accustomed to those conditions.

If indeed the performance—private or public—went well, the audience could show its approval by applause, not only for entire works, but also for individual passages:

> After Klement had been applauded at almost every passage, he brought in the melody from *Faniska* at the fermata of the last movement: ''On earth is no man as happy as I'' an original, witty musical way of thanking the audience.[49]

[47]Wegeler & Ries/NOTIZEN, pp. 91-92. (VI/17)
[48]Reichardt/VERTRAUTE, 1:185. (VI/18)
[49]WJ, April 15, 1806, p. 244. (VI/19)

If the approval went even further, an encore was called for, and the piece or the movement was repeated, or a new selection was played:

> In one movement of the first symphony, a *da capo* was called for, so it was repeated by the orchestra. After the variations with the pedal fugue the audience kept on clapping so long, that the Abt Vogler sat down at the fortepiano once more. He chose the current favorite from his opera *Kastor und Pollux*.[50]

Encoring eventually ran so rampant that a court order was issued forbidding it in the court theaters, but to no avail:

> A sonata for fortepiano and waldhorn, composed by Beethoven and played by him and Punto, distinguished itself so and was so well received that, in spite of the new theater ordinance that forbids *da capo* and loud applause in the court theater, the virtuosos were nonetheless moved by the very loud applause at the end to begin again and play it through one more time.[51]

Both the applauding of passages and the repetition of numbers and movements have fallen out of favor today but were still very much alive in the late eighteenth and early nineteenth centuries. Those were the ways in which the audiences expressed their opinions on performers and works. In order to have a broader view of the reception of music in concerts, we must now turn to the critical commentary that appeared in print.

[50]ZEW, April 5, 1804, col. 326. (VI/20)
[51]AMZ, July 2, 1800, col. 704. As early as 1786, Joseph II had forbidden encores during operas of any number for more than one voice in an attempt to keep the length of opera productions from becoming excessive. See Deutsch/DOKUMENTE, p. 275. (VI/21)

CHAPTER SEVEN

The Treatment of Viennese Concerts in Periodicals

Reviews and critiques appearing in the periodical literature of any historical period can serve as an important source of information for a phenomenon as ephemeral as musical performance. But criticism can prove to be as misleading as it is helpful if we unquestioningly accept as universal what can only be considered personal. In order to evaluate fairly a single critical opinion, therefore, we must examine it not only in the light of other opinions by the same author, but also in the larger context of other writers and other journalistic forums. For this chapter, I surveyed all concert notices and reviews in a wide variety of German-language journals and newspapers, encompassing many types of publications and many styles of criticism.

TYPES OF PUBLICATION AND COVERAGE

Politically oriented and/or court-controlled newspapers tended to focus on local and foreign political events—wars, diplomatic endeavors, treaties, etc., and on the activities of the monarch and high nobility. In Vienna, the *Wiener Zeitung* fulfilled this function. Its news section contained current events and the schedule of the court in almost painful detail; each issue concluded with a rather lengthy *Anhang* that contained various kinds of advertisements and notices.[1] Similar publications in the Imperial domains of Prague (*Prager Neue Zeitung*) and Pressburg (*Pressburger Zeitung*) have a certain significance here since they occasionally reported on noteworthy concerts, especially if they were related to court-sponsored causes. Most such publications, however, e.g., the *Brünner Zeitung*, restricted their coverage of musical events to local performances.

Literary/intellectual publications devoted their space to articles on scientific advancements, literary achievements, theater productions, and/or musical events, with the emphasis varying according to the tastes and preferences of the editor.[2] Many of the earlier columns treated only major oratorio productions, but after 1800 the coverage broadened, making them a significant source of information.

Musical magazines featured articles on music theory, music history, composers, new compositions, etc. and almost invariably devoted a page or so to local and foreign musical performances. Although they provide a greater concentration of material than do the literary/intellectual periodicals, their reviews should not be assumed to be more telling or more significant. Table 27 provides an overview of the periodicals with significant concert coverage to 1810, according to the types just discussed.

Table 27 reveals a concentration of literary/intellectual and musical journals after 1800; both types certainly existed before this time (Cramer's *Magazin der Musik*, for example) but carried virtually nothing about Viennese concerts, though often treating performances elsewhere in great detail. As we have seen, this does not mean that Vienna had no concerts, but does perhaps indicate that correspondents did not consider them as important as operas, which *were* covered in the same periodicals. In addition, most of the articles focused on series rather than individual virtuoso undertakings, and Vienna could not compete in this respect.

---

[1]Music publishers frequently advertised their new offerings in it.

[2]Many short-lived efforts appeared in the eighteenth century, often more collections of essays than actual periodicals, e.g. *Der Wienerische Zuschauer*, (1785) and *Der Freund* (Vienna, 1787), and generally can be discounted as a source of information for concerts.

TABLE 27. German-Language Periodicals with Viennese Concert Information

Viennese and Austrian Empire

Political/Court

Wiener Zeitung (1740-1810)
Provinzialnachrichten (1782-1789)
Pressburger Zeitung (1790-1810)
Prager Neue Zeitung (1802)

Literary/intellectual

Realzeitung (1771-1786)
Das Wienerblättchen (1783-1791)
Oesterreichische Monatsschrift (January 1793-June 1794)
Intelligenzblatt der Annalen der Literatur und Kunst in den österreichischen Staaten (1803-1805, 1807-1810)
Wiener Theater Zeitung (1806-1808)
Vaterländischen Blätter für den österreichischen Kaiserstaat (1808-1810)
Der Sammler (1808-1810)
Thalia (1810)

Music

Wiener Journal für Theater, Musik und Mode (1806)

Foreign

Literary/intellectual

Zeitung für die elegante Welt (Leipzig, 1802-1810)
Der Freimüthige (Berlin, 1803-1810)

Music

Allgemeine Musikalische Zeitung (Leipzig, 1798-1810)
Musikalisches Taschenbuch (1805)
Berlinische Musikalische Zeitung (1805-06)

The dates given represent the issues that were available for inspection.

Vienna itself had no magazine devoted exclusively to music before 1810. Only the short-lived *Wiener Journal für Theater, Musik und Mode* and the *Wiener Theater Zeitung* even came close. Tantalizing hints about planned musical journals appeared from time to time in other periodicals, but if the plans ever became reality, all traces have disappeared. For example, in 1785 the *Realzeitung* announced a forthcoming weekly Artaria publication called *Fragmente über die Musik, ihren Geschmak und ihre Künstler,* that was supposed to include reviews of Lenten concerts, but no copy has survived.[3] That same year brought mention of a similarly mysterious monthly magazine, the *Musikalische Monatsschrift,* (published by Toricelli's Kunst und Musikalien-Handlung) which was to cover operas and other musical events, provide information on foreign virtuosos, and contain announcements for concerts.[4]

There were several reasons for the absence of music periodicals in Vienna. First of all, we must remember that in general, the German-speaking countries lagged behind the rest of Europe in the development of independent, non-political publications. However, the telling factor seems to have been the character and attitudes of the Viennese themselves; they were too busy with new experiences to bother about writing down things past. As late as 1799, Georg August Griesinger, Breitkopf & Härtel's representative in Vienna, had trouble locating a suitable Viennese correspondent for the firm's musical magazine, the *Allgemeine Musikalische Zeitung.* He discussed the matter with the Baron Gottfried van Swieten, who certainly would have been in a position to help him, and received the following reply, which he communicated to his employers:

> He [Baron Swieten] confessed that he didn't know of anyone who could write a good essay; he himself had the policy of doing as much as he could and not talking about it.[5]

Thus the Viennese are in part responsible for the lack of informa-

---

[3]RZ, March 1, 1785, p. 142.
[4]WB, February 21, 1785.
[5]Olleson/GRIESINGER, p. 19. (VII/1).

tion that has contributed to the inaccurate depiction of Viennese concert life.

Mention of concerts in all of the publications discussed above falls into three categories, each providing different types of information:

(1) Reports and announcements
a) Announcements of upcoming concerts
b) Reporting of events without comment on the performance
c) "General Approbation Reviews" (often quite lengthy and detailed, but everything reported in glowing terms and standard phrases; no negative criticism)

(2) State-of-music articles (describe the overall musical situation of a particular city)

(3) Genuine reviews (both positive and negative comments)

Keeping these three categories in mind, we will now turn to a discussion of each of the important periodicals, with a view to what the reader can expect from them, beginning with those that mainly ran reports and announcements and progressing to those with genuine reviews.

REPORTS AND ANNOUNCEMENTS

Despite its somewhat erratic reporting and an absence of genuine reviews, the *Wiener Zeitung* counts as an important source because it covers the entire period under consideration. Most useful for our purposes are the announcements of upcoming concerts that appeared in the *Anhang*, a multi-purpose section that included a weather report, obituaries, current grain prices, real estate notices and advertisements for everything from pianos to jelly doughnuts. Concert announcements usually appeared after the obituaries and were characterized by a standardized format. They begin by telling where the virtuoso in question had performed, the name of his or her employer (generally a member of the nobility),[6] and sometimes give a hint about the program and the assisting artists before concluding with standard phrases flattering the nobility and the general public:

> On Thursday the 20th of March, Herr Schindlöker will have the honor of giving a concert in the Imperial Royal National Theater. In it he will play, with a former student of his, a dilettante, an entirely new cello concerto written especially for the occasion. He flatters himself that he will not only receive the approbation of the high nobility and the honorable public, with which he has already occasionally been favored, but will probably (thus encouraged and with talent and continued industry) even increase it two-fold.[7]

In the early 1780s, a few announcements listed the entire concert program, but this was clearly exceptional. Prices were first mentioned in an advertisement for Kapellmeister Johann Friedrich Kloffter's (Klöffler) battle symphony on February 17, 1787, and appeared sporadically in the succeeding years, presumably at the whim of the person giving the concert. Likewise, an address (usually the apartment of the virtuoso) where the tickets and reserved seats could be procured was also occasionally included. Full-page, large-print ads at the very end of the *Anhang* began to appear after 1800:

> Herr Anton Eberl will give a concert on Friday evening the 6th of January in the hall of the Imperial Royal Restaurateur Jahn, in which he has the honor of presenting a variety of his very latest compositions.

> For the enjoyment of the audience, Herr Calmus will assist with his celebrated well-known talent, and Fräulein Hohenadel, Herr Eberl's student, will play an entirely new double concerto for two fortepianos [with Eberl]. Details will be given on the program announcement on the day of the concert.

---

[6]Hanslick made a great deal out of this fact, saying that the musicians who did so flaunted their "distinguished collar" as proof of their superiority over their free-lance collegues, giving it as proof of the pre-Beethoven subservience of musicians. (Hanslick/CONCERTWESEN, p. 42) A more likely explanation would be that it simply makes good financial sense to list your credentials.
[7]WZ, March 15, 1783, n.p. (VII/2)

The tickets can be had from 8:00 to 11:00 A.M. at Herr Eberl's apartment on the Eisgrübel next to Petersplatz (No. 645 on the 4th floor).[8]

Though important, the announcements do not provide a complete picture of Viennese concert life. The amount of advertising fluctuated from year to year and did not always reflect the actual number of performances.

Another type of coverage provided by the *Wiener Zeitung* was the reporting of Lenten concerts in a brief section entitled "Theater News." Sandwiched in between the death listings and the beginning of the ads, the items rarely ran to more than a few sentences and did not comment on the performance:

The following concerts were given in the National Theater [Burgtheater]: Hr. Mozart on the first of this month [April] and Hr. Ludwig Fischer, formerly a singer with the German Singspiel of the National Theater on the fourth.[9]

This feature, however, appeared only in the years 1784, 1786, 1787, 1789, 1791, 1793, 1794, and 1799, though we know from other sources that the same types of concerts were held in the other years.

All of the *Wiener Zeitung*'s reviews belong to the "General Approbation" class and are to be found in the part of the domestic news section describing the activities of the court. Since the articles often ran a month or more after the event, they probably were saved for a slow news day. Nearly every performance covered was a charity fundraiser, and the reports generally devote more than half of the space to describing the purposes of the charity and enumerating the nobility who attended and gave generously. The musicians and pieces, when mentioned at all, are praised in lofty and glowing terms; no discordant note is ever allowed to creep in. The following report is atypical in the amount of time it devoted to the music, but does capture the normal tone:

The recently announced concert for the benefit of wounded soldiers was presented on January 30th of this year to the greatest enjoy-

[8]WZ, January 4, 1804, p. 44. (VII/3)
[9]WZ, April 7, 1784, p. 738. (VII/4)

ment of all the listeners; it was distinguished as much by the tasteful choice of works as by the most accomplished skill of their execution. The noble organizer, Frau Christina v. Frank née Gerhardi, reaped general admiration for the unusual superiority of her singing. Hr. v. Beethoven played one of his own sonatas on the Piano Forte, accompanied by Herr Punto on Waldhorn. Both completely met the expectations which the public entertains about these two masters of their arts. Frau Galvani and Herr Simoni with their singing and Kapellmeister Pär and Herr Conti, in their direction of the orchestra, likewise contributed to the glorification of this concert. Finally the great Haydn took over the direction of two of his own symphonies. The approbation was universal. The receipts amounted to the considerable sum of 9463 Gulden, 11 Kreutzer, in which the Emperor and Empress, the Queen of Naples, the Grand Dukes and the Duke Albert repeated the accustomed proof of their generosity.[10]

The rare, non-charity concerts mentioned include the summer concerts in the Belvedere gardens in the 1780s, the famous production of Haydn's *Die Schöpfung* on March 27, 1808, and the private virtuoso concerts given by Michael Esser in 1780 and Bernhard Romberg and Charles Philippe Lafont in 1808.

Two other Viennese periodicals covered the 1770s and 1780s, the *Realzeitung*, which introduced limited concert news in 1772, and *Das Wienerblättchen*, which followed suit in 1784. The latter simply ran notices about upcoming concerts, mostly during Lent, giving the performer, place, and date. Two listings, however, one for Nancy Storace and one for Mozart, gave the complete programs. The Lent issues for the years 1786 and 1787 are missing, and when *Das neue Wienerblättchen* appeared in June of 1787, the concert notices had been discontinued.

The *Realzeitung* included straight reporting of musical events in its theater section, usually listing some of the pieces that were played. It too avoided negative criticism, but did not favor the high-blown, poetic style of the *Wiener Zeitung*:

> Especially the bassoonist is an extraordinary man, at least he entranced me, and I will gladly admit, I have never heard anything comparable on the bassoon.[11]

[10]WZ, February 7, 1801, p. 398. (VII/5)
[11]RZ, April 30, 1776, p. 286. (VII/6)

The *Realzeitung* constitutes an important (indeed almost the only) source for the 1770s, but the coverage gradually decreased. In 1785, it began a feature called *Kunstanzeiger* (Art Notices), which included announcements for upcoming concerts and might have proved useful had the paper not ceased publication shortly thereafter. Occasionally, interesting tidbits about Viennese concerts found their way into other Austrian empire journals. The *Pressburger Zeitung*, the *Provinzialnachrichten*, and the *Prager Neue Zeitung* all emulated the non-reviewing reviews of the *Wiener Zeitung* in their occasional reports on special events. In a similar fashion, the *Oester-reichische Monatsschrift* and *Der Sammler*, both literary/intellectual publications, ran only laudatory pieces on concerts, especially disappointing in their case since they both contained genuine criticism of plays and operas.

For whatever reasons, none of the above provided continuous, consistent reports of concert activity that could give us a clue to the reception accorded both works and composers. It would therefore be false to assume that Composer A's genius was not recognized or that Composer B enjoyed little popularity because the local press took no notice of them. That type of reporting simply did not exist then in Vienna. (One wonders how much we would know about the popularity of Haydn in London if newspapers like the *Morning Chronicle* had not existed to tell us so.) The Viennese can be censured for this omission in their journalistic endeavors, but their silence had nothing to do with recognizing or not recognizing the talent in their midst.

STATE-OF-MUSIC ARTICLES

State-of-music articles were one of the most common ways of bringing a magazine's readership up-to-date on musical events in other cities and countries. Although they described the overall picture and rarely focused on a single performance, they often provide valuable information about the structure of musical life. Most of the early musical magazines, such as Hiller's *Wöchentliche Nachrichten die Musik betreffend*, Spazier's *Berlinische Musikalische*

Zeitung, and Reichardt's *Musikalisches Wochenblatt* regularly included such articles, but discussions of Vienna centered on opera. Others, like the *Musikalisches Taschenbuch,* relied on second-hand information for Vienna (in this case, essays in other periodicals), although they had their own correspondents for Berlin and Leipzig.[12] While this situation might be attributed to the lesser importance attached to concerts in Vienna, these North German publications would naturally have concentrated more on cities in their own realm.

In any case, one should always take the North German's viewpoint of Vienna with considerable caution because of the cultural and mentality differences that separated the Austrian empire from Prussia and the North German states. We have already seen Nicolai's disapproval of certain Viennese attitudes; the gulf between the two perspectives is articulated again in two articles published in the *Allgemeine Musikalische Zeitung* in 1800 and 1801. Both, but especially the negative first one, have been cited frequently without reference to their prejudiced viewpoints or to the fact that they contrast markedly from other, fairly well-balanced comments and reviews in the same periodical. If one accepts the first writer's opinion, musical, and especially concert, life in Vienna was moribund—no established concert series, no private concerts of any significance, inadequate performances, etc.:

> There are no regular concerts except for the four which are designated each year for the Widows' Fund [i.e., the Tonkünstler Societät fundraisers]. Earlier these were often very bad; however, now that P. Wranitzky is Secretary, one hears Haydn's *Sieben Worte* and *Schöpfung,* for example. . . .
>
> Then there are usually 12 musicales in the Augarten in the morning under the name Dilettante Musicales. . . . Now Hr. Schuppanzigh has them, and that rousing audience is entirely gone. No true music lover wants to play any more, even the professional musicians only rarely play concertos. In general, the fire of the institution has entirely gone out. The concertos are seldom accompanied well; the symphonies go a little better. . . .

[12]Leipzig received 63 pages, Berlin 47, and Vienna 10.

There are relatively few free-lance academies given by traveling artists, because the theater management rarely (and never without great intervention) rents out the theaters. There's not much to be gained there anyway. . . .

In general [people] don't like academies very much here, because they have been disappointed by foreign and local speculators too often; many a good artist must suffer because of that, if he does not have a lot of protection. [Getting] permission is made hard enough for him, and in addition, costs are very considerable.

There aren't any private academies of significance any more. . . .

The fortunes of traveling artists lie in the hands of . . . dilettantes, who in truth have too little knowledge, but often are very partisan. If the visitor doesn't appear at every invitation, doesn't flatter [everyone], doesn't find . . . talent everywhere, etc., then he must be a man of the greatest reputation in order to win acceptance, if worse comes to worst. If it should occur to him to remain here, then the entire *Corpus musicum* is his enemy.[13]

The angry retort came the following year from a Viennese reader and opened with some comments on the relationship between the two Germanic attitudes:

I do not know if there is any other country where the opinions of the inhabitants of one part about the inhabitants of another are as different as the opinions of Northern and Southern Germans about each other. This is not the place to pursue these opinions, which so often do an injustice, in detail; but unless I am mistaken, the North German assumes that the basis of all his Southern brother's actions is, as a rule: he wants to enjoy things in comfort; and the Southern German assumes about the Northern: he wants to be out of humor—tediously. Concerning music, the common prejudice of the Southern German concedes [the faculty of] criticism to the Northerner, but denies him everything else that might be decisive. The common prejudice of the Northern German, on the other hand, concedes to the Southerner a quicker feeling for music and a not undelicate skill, particularly in singing, but denies him anything else that might be decisive. That these opinions, like all things national,

[13]AMZ, October 15, 1800, cols. 45-50; October 22, 1800, cols. 65-69. (VII/7)

have *some* basis in truth is probably as illuminating as the fact that when both carry these opinions into particulars or want to make them into the principle of deeper judgments, both very often do each other an injustice. Both are cliches, and cliches are never more than half true. But if I am not mistaken, these accepted cliches have not a little influence on the opinions of even educated Northern and Southern Germans. The Northern Germans are already taking care of their business themselves; I will at least begin to make an attempt to take care of the business of the Southern Germans, and especially of the Viennese (since they have the say in matters of art and taste in Southern Germany). Others may then want to continue.[14]

Following these observations, the writer launched into a point-by-point refutation of the charges made in the earlier article, concluding that Vienna was a thriving, vibrant city with much to offer. The truth undoubtedly lies somewhere in between the two, but because of their rhetorical stance, both essays should be viewed with caution.

However unjust the first writer's observation may have been, he at least moved someone from the city to comment on the musical activities there. The next such effort came seven years later, this time in a Viennese publication, the *Vaterlandische Blätter für den österreichischen Kaiserstaat*. Though somewhat infused with a rosy glow, it does contain a detailed description of the organization of the 1807-08 "Liebhaber Concerte" and gives an idea of the pervasiveness of music in Viennese society. Also worthy of note is the writer's perception of the difference between concerts devoted to the serious cultivation of music and those with a lighter orientation:

Overview of the Current State of Music in Vienna

If one could assume that the cultivation of music kept pace with the cultivation of the mind, then one would have reason to congratulate the inhabitants of this capital; for there is probably no other place where this heavenly art is so commonly pursued, so much loved, so industriously practiced as it is here. Nowhere else will you find so many accomplished performers on almost all instruments among amateurs. Many might stand alongside (and some even surpass) the

[14]AMZ, June 10, 1801, cols. 622-27; June 17, 1801, cols. 638-43. (VII/8)

professors of the art. Music works the miracle here that is normally ascribed only to love; it makes all classes equal. Aristocrats and bourgeois, princes and their vassals, superiors and their subordinates sit beside each other at one desk and forget the disharmony of their class in the harmony of the tones. All palaces and exchanges are open to the practicing artist, and the composer of any significance will be handled with all the distinction he could ever wish, which says a lot in the case of many of these gentlemen. The practice of music has become a standard and necessary article in the list of accomplishments that parents of any means at all have taught to their children. The opposite would be at the least considered an unforgivable negligence in the education of their family, and indeed it has become rare to see a boy or girl from an educated middle-class home who has remained a stranger to the art.

The parents' birthdays are celebrated with music, and if they want to plan a pleasant evening for their children, it happens with music. No festive occasion passes without being glorified by this art; and it is believed only through it can one honor and delight one's friends and relatives.

In this large city you will find few houses in which on any given evening this or that family isn't entertaining itself with a string quartet or keyboard sonata and (thanks be to Apollo) has laid down the playing cards that once ruled so despotically.

However much is being done in the way of this so called chamber music, very little opportunity offers itself for [hearing] a full orchestra—for symphonies, concertos, oratorios. Since the death of Vice President von Kees, who served this last kind of music so, nothing solid, or at least lasting, has stabilized in this area. To be sure, last year the businessman Würth gave big concerts that showed themselves to great advantage with respect to the choice [of works] as well as their execution. But, for reasons unknown, they have not been continued. A few Concerts Spirituels, with which Count Haugwitz prepared a wonderful fete for a select group of music lovers and connoisseurs, were likewise only a meteor that quickly passed. The grand concerts under the direction of and benefiting Herr Schuppanzigh that are presented in the Augarten Hall every week in the morning throughout the summer months, cannot be compared to those of the late Herr v. Kees and of Count v. Haugwitz since they appear to consider mere pleasure more than the advancement of taste. Finally, there was hope that the symphony might be coming into favor again, as a company of esteemed and wealthy music lovers formed, at the beginning of this winter, an organization under the modest title "Liebhaber Concerte" that allows hope that each wish that could be entertained about the matter might be seen fulfilled. . . . In addition to these possibilities of hearing the larger genres of music, a similar opportunity often occurs because the lease holders of the Imperial Royal Court Theaters, with the humanity and respect toward foreign travelling virtuosos that is the common rule here, grant them the Imperial Royal Kleiner Redoutensaal so that they may delight the public with their talents. Finally each year the Pension Society of the Musicians Widows [Tonkünstler Societät] gives, with the permission of His Majesty, two concerts during Advent and two in Lent to raise money for their fund. These concerts are performed by an orchestra of over 200 musicians, whose effect has been considerably strengthened by a recently installed, costly resonance dome, although—incidentally—these musical presentations appear to have been decreasing in worth for several years due to a less than happy choice of compositions for performance.[15]

GENUINE REVIEWS

Eight of the periodicals surveyed contained genuine, critical concert reviews—four Viennese, all short-lived and four North German. Since the correspondents for the latter resided in the Imperial city and were very likely native Viennese, there is no difference in perspective. Therefore, I have considered them together, in order of increasing coverage. The least was found in the latest, *Thalia,* actually a theater magazine. It treated only oratorios and cantatas in fairly general terms without any technical discussion of either performance or music, but offered negative comments when appropriate.

For most of its existence, the *Intelligenzblatt der Annalen der Literatur und Kunst* simply listed concerts held in the theaters in its section on theater news, but one issue in 1807 featured an article entitled

[15]VB, 1808, pp. 39-41. (VII/9)

"Concert Music in Vienna." It begins with a section on two recently premiered works, the Beethoven Violin Concerto (Op. 61) and a double piano concerto by Anton Eberl, then moves to an enumeration of the main virtuoso concerts during the first part of the year, criticizing the performance techniques in fairly close detail. Couched in a slightly poetic, flowery style, it notes the virtuoso's good points before adding what might be improved:

> His brother the pianist (Johann Peter Pixis) has speed and strength in both hands, but he still lacks that certainty and precision upon which perfect beauty can only then rest and which is its [beauty's] essential fundamental requirement in any art.[16]

With only one example, it was not possible to draw any conclusions about the reviewer's slant.

The *Berlinische Musikalische Zeitung* followed the same approach in mentioning the main performers and the quality and reception of their performance, with no hint about the program or assisting musicians. An exception was made, however, for the Berlin pianist, Karl Zeuner—the critic gave his concert a very long, laudatory review that contrasted rather markedly with the slightly deprecating treatment he received from other critics.

The *Wiener Theater Zeitung* devoted its pages to articles on opera, drama, literary works, and important concerts:

> It would give the public little pleasure if we were to review every insignificant screech of many imagined virtuosos. We are therefore limiting ourselves to superior productions, in order not to deprive better things of space.[17]

It is difficult to generalize about this periodical, because it has relatively few reviews, all written by different people and, contrary to the normal practice, either signed or initialed by the author.[18]

---

[16]IB, April 1807, p. 176. (VII/10)
[17]WTZ, February 16, 1807, p. 102. (VII/11) The publication's name was changed to the *Zeitung für Theater, Musik und Poesie* in 1807, but I have used the original title throughout.
[18]Some were taken from other sources. See Note 21.

The writing style tends to be flowery, and the essays usually start with philosophical musings about such things as the value of music before getting down to the mundane details of the actual performance. Once the critic got going, however, he did not hold back: "The chorus, among other things, screamed horribly."[19]

The first Viennese periodical to regularly review concerts was the *Wiener Journal für Theater, Musik und Mode.* Appearing twice a month, it featured articles and miscellaneous items, including news of foreign concerts, particularly those given by Viennese artists. Most of the local concert reviews were written and signed by K. Jacob, who presented balanced criticism in a conversational tone without mincing words:

> Madame Auernhammer played the Beethoven concerto on the whole not badly. More precision here and there, and more expression and sensitivity, especially in the Adagio, would have been desirable. Particular delight was found in the Steibelt duo that she played with Demoiselle Auernhammer. In her variations on a theme from Prometheus by Beethoven, it was regrettable that, since the theme isn't very melodic, the whole thing, from a lack of clear unity, resembled more of a fantasy. This piece wasn't found to be interesting at all. Herr Verri, the bass, didn't enchant me in the least. His characteristics include rough low notes, forced high ones, and few graces. Perhaps he comes off better *alla camera.*[20]

In contrast to most of the other commentators, Jacob commented on each piece, its content, and execution. At the beginning of the season, he reviewed almost every concert, but the coverage tapered off in the later issues, and the journal ceased publication entirely after only one year.

Der Freimüthige, a literary/intellectual journal founded by August von Kotzebue and Gottlieb Merkel in 1803 featured, in its early issues, lengthy articles on musical life in Vienna. Probably stemming from the pen of Kotzebue himself, who was in Vienna at the time, they are among the first to relate significant information about

[19]WTZ, January 8, 1807, p. 24. (VII/12)
[20]WJ, April 15, 1806, pp. 245-46. (VII/13)

Vienna's private musical salons, particularly the one of the banker Würth. No programs are given, but the reports do give us a clear picture of the type of music heard there. Concert reviews also appeared in the "Theater" or "Correspondent" columns until 1805, when they were transferred to a small print section at the end of each issue entitled the "Nonpolitische Zeitung." Though somewhat reduced in size and scope, they were still substantial. After a brief suspension of publication in 1806-1807, the magazine returned to print with drastically reduced Viennese concert news.

Although unsigned, all the reviews (the feature length articles excepted) could very well stem from the same pen; their style and slant does not change. The writer granted the most space to performances by the best known Viennese musicians—Auernhammer, Beethoven, Eberl, Clement, etc.— with other virtuosos getting a one or two-line summary in a general run-down of concerts given. This tendency is related to his habit of spending more time discussing the merits of new works heard than the technical aspects of the performance itself; major premieres occurred more often on the programs of local artists than they did on those of the average traveling virtuoso.

Normally, performances received only mild criticism, couched in polite language; he saved his worst invective for Beethoven:

> Some, Beethoven's particular friends, assert that it is just this symphony [No.3] which is his masterpiece, that this is the true style for high class music, and that if it does not please now, it is because the public is not cultured enough, artistically, to grasp all these lofty beauties; after a few thousand years have passed it will not fail of its effect. Another faction denies that the work has any artistic value and professes to see in it an untamed striving for singularity which had failed, however, to achieve in any of its parts beauty or true sublimity and power. By means of strange modulations and violent transitions, by combining the most heterogeneous elements, as for instance when a pastoral in the largest style is ripped up by the basses, by three horns, etc., a certain undesirable originality may be achieved without much trouble; but genius proclaims itself not in the unusual and the fantastic, but in the beautiful and the sublime. Beethoven himself proved the correctness of this axiom in his earlier

works. The third party, a very small one, stands midway between the others—it admits that the symphony contains many beauties, but concedes that the connection is often disrupted entirely, and that the inordinate length of this longest, and perhaps most difficult of all symphonies, wearies even the cognoscenti, and is unendurable to the mere music-lover; it wishes that H. v. B. would employ his acknowledgedly great talents in giving us works like his symphonies in C and D, his ingratiating Septet in E-flat, the intellectual Quintet in D [C major?] and others of his early compositions which have placed B. forever in the ranks of the foremost instrumental composers. It fears, however, that if Beethoven continues on his present path both he and the public will be the sufferers. His music could soon reach the point where one would derive no pleasure from it, unless well trained in the rules and difficulties of the art, but rather would leave the concert hall with an unpleasant feeling of fatigue from having been crushed by a mass of unconnected and overloaded ideas and a continuing tumult by all the instruments. The public and Herr van Beethoven, who conducted, were not satisfied with each other on this evening; the public thought the symphony too heavy, too long, and himself too discourteous, because he did not nod his head in recognition of the applause which came from a portion of the audience. On the contrary, Beethoven found that the applause was not strong enough.[21]

[21]Forbes/BEETHOVEN, p. 376. In a review of Franz Clement's performance of Beethoven's Violin Concerto, a reviewer named Möser, writing for the WTZ, used almost identical language in a manner too close to be coincidental: FM, April 26, 1805: "Sie wünscht dass Hr. v. B. seine anerkannten grossen Talente verwenden möge uns Werke zu schenken, die seinen beiden ersten Symphonien aus C und D gleichen, seinem anmuthigen Septette aus Es, dem geistreichen Quintette aus D dur und andern seiner frühern Compositionen, die B. immer in die Reihe der ersten Instrumentalcomponisten stellen werden. Sie fürchtet aber, wenn Beethoven auf diesen Wegen fortwandelt, so werde er und das Publikum übel dabei fahren. Die Musik könne so bald dahin kommen dass jeder, der nicht genau mit den Regeln und Schwierigkeiten der Kunst vertraut ist, schlechterdings gar keinen Genuss bei ihr finde, sondern durch eine Menge unzusammenhängender und überhäufter Ideen und einer fortwahrenden Tumult aller Instrumente zu Boden gedrückt, nur mit einem unangenehmen Gefühle der Ermattung den Konzertsaal verlasse." WTZ, January 8, 1807: "Es sagt, dass Beethhofen (sic) seine anerkannten grossen Talente, gehöriger verwenden, und uns Werke schenken möge, die seinen ersten Symphonien aus C und D gleichen, seinen anmuthigen

His full scorn was unleashed on the overture to Fidelio:

> All impartial music *Kenner* and friends of music were in complete
> agreement that something so disconnected, shrill, confused and
> revolting to the ear had absolutely never been written before in the
> history of music.[22]

The *Freimüthige* critic's views were forcefully expressed and have
been quoted often enough to achieve a certain credibility, so that
they have sometimes been taken to represent the norm. However,
other critics and journals expressed equally pungent, though quite
different, ideas.

Founded by Karl Spazier and Aug. Mahlman in 1801, the *Zeitung
für die elegante Welt* is perhaps the least stodgy of the periodicals
under consideration here. In its third year of existence (1803), a
Viennese reader wrote to complain about the neglect of concerts
in his city and promised to remedy the situation "as a mere spec-
tator."[23] The reviews that followed differed considerably from the
others discussed here by virtue of their lively, often caustic tone:

> Once again, as she does every year, Mme Auernhammer obtained
> the Imperial Royal Court Theater for the production of her concert
> from the theater director, who especially favors her. Unfortunate-
> ly, she chose van Beethoven's grand C minor concerto. She hewed
> down the right-hand part fairly easily, but glided mutely up and

---

Septette aus Es, dem geistreichen Quintette aus D dur, und mehreren seiner
frühern Compositionen, die ihn immer in die Reihe der ersten Componisten stellen
werden. Man fürchtet aber zugleich, wenn Beethhofen auf diesen Weg fortwandelt, so werde er und das Publikum übel dabey fahren. Die Musik könne
sobald dahin kommen, dass jeder, der nicht genau mit den Regeln und
Schwierigkeiten der Kunst vertraut ist, schlechterdings gar keinen Genuss bey
ihr finde, sondern durch eine Menge zusammenhängender und überhäufter Ideen
und einen fortwährenden Tumult einiger Instrumente, die den Eingang
charakterisiren sollten, zu Boden gedrückt, nur mit einem unangenehmen Gefühl
der Ermattung das Koncert verlasse." Either the two reviewers are identical, or
Möser lifted his comments from the earlier FM article.

[22]FM, September 11, 1806, p. 212. (VII/14)
[23]ZEW, April 16, 1803, col. 362.

down the keys without touching them with her left, so that we heard for the first time a one-handed concerto on the Pianoforte.[24]

The reviewer repeated his anti-Auernhammer campaign at every opportunity (and there were plenty) but otherwise had no philosophical or musical ax to grind. He did, however, seem to be more receptive to newer styles of composition than did some of his colleagues. Although for some reason he did not write about the concert where Beethoven's Symphony No. 3 had its premiere, his views on Beethoven can be gleaned from his comments on *Christus am Oelberge* and stand in contrast to the more conservative stance of those in *Der Freimüthige*:

> *Der Freimüthige.* Isolated parts [of the oratorio] were found to be beautiful, but the whole was thought too extended, too artificial in composition and without the appropriate expression, particularly in the vocal parts. F. X. Huber's libretto appears to have been as hastily executed as the music.[25]

> *Zeitung für die elegante Welt.* Beethoven's music was in general good and has several excellent spots; the aria of the Seraphs with the trombone accompaniment was particularly effective, and in the . . . chorus (der Kriegsknechte) Herr v. B. proved that a composer of genius is capable of making something great even out of the worst material.[26]

This is not to say that he was an enthusiastic supporter of everything Beethoven wrote; the review cited also contained some biting words on the second symphony,[27] but he was definitely free of the prejudices of the *Freimüthige* correspondent. He also ventured, in contrast to the other reviewers, a few criticisms of the immensely popular and universally well received compositions of Anton Eberl, who wrote in a comparatively conservative vein more in the line of Mozart than Beethoven.

[24]ZEW, May 3, 1806, col. 431-32. (VII/15)
[25]FM, May 17, 1803, p. 310. (VII/16)
[26]ZEW, April 16, 1803, col. 364. (VII/17)
[27]See page 219.

In his choice of concerts, the *Zeitung für die elegante Welt* correspondent showed no particular preference for the big oratorio productions, but did tend to emphasize those by well known Viennese artists, e.g. Beethoven, Anton Eberl, Ferdinand Pär, and Abbé Vogler. Moreover, he usually treated only certain pieces or performers within a concert and rarely covered each selection. The coverage continued steadily through 1806, but began to taper off, until by 1809, Vienna had all but disappeared from the pages of the journal.

The last periodical to be considered here, the *Allgemeine Musikalische Zeitung*, had the longest, most continuous coverage in genuine reviews. The first articles to appear were written by a newcomer to the Imperial city, probably Georg August Griesinger, Breitkopf & Härtel's representative, who, as we have already seen (page 194), had some difficulty in finding a suitable correspondent. Either he did indeed locate someone, or he continued to write the reviews himself, for relatively brief, almost gossipy columns continued to run under the heading "Kurze Nachrichten" (News in Brief). After the two state-of-music articles already discussed, the magazine instituted an entire section on Vienna in October of 1801; appearing every several issues, it included reports on theater, opera, concerts, and related news.

The depth and range of coverage varied widely, although, to judge from the style, the same person did the writing, with again a natural emphasis on Viennese musicians. The critic also regularly included both private salons and the Augarten concerts in the columns, especially important for the latter, since program announcements, if they ever existed, have long since disappeared. In general, he focused on new events:

> I will note only those pieces which have not yet been presented [i.e., written about in the AMZ] or where progress in talent is noticeable.[28]

His observations were penned in a straight-forward, slightly humorless style using a plethora of descriptive nouns:

[28]AMZ, July 30, 1806, col. 701. (VII/18)

Fräulein Kurzböck played a Mozart piano concerto in C major with the delicacy, grace and elegance which are so well liked in her execution. Only a little more shadow, certainty and strength could raise it to excellence.[29]

A change in the correspondent very likely accompanied the change in format in 1809, since a slightly more sarcastic note crept into the essays. Headed "Overview of the months. . .," the articles tended to itemize and discuss the complete program rather than one or two pieces or performers. None took a strongly partisan stance; most are characterized by a balanced presentation.

The concert calendar in appendix 1 includes citations of articles and notices of many of the performances listed, but since some may contain much material and others comparatively little, it seems advisable to summarize here what can be expected from the most important ones. Notices of upcoming concerts in the *Wiener Zeitung*, while rarely supplying the program, do sometimes convey other significant information, such as prices, the employer of a virtuoso, etc. The reports of concerts in the "Theater News" section, on the other hand, only confirm that a concert took place; most of the post-concert references in the *Wiener Zeitung* for virtuoso concerts fall into this category. If a fundraiser was significant enough to attract the attention of the press, the article will usually—though not always—give the names of the main performers, occasionally indicate the amount of the receipts, and invariably state that the performance was excellent. Thus, the *Wiener Zeitung* can impart facts about concerts, but should never be used as a measure of audience reception or musical taste.

A similar caveat holds for the remaining periodicals providing mainly reports and announcements. The notices in *Das Wienerblättchen* (with the two exceptions noted above, page 198) give only the name, performing medium of the artist, and the date and place of the concert—nothing more. Although the reports in the *Realzeitung* rarely run to more than a few lines, they do provide the content of some concerts whose traces have otherwise vanished. Likewise, the scattered brief articles in the *Pressburger Zeitung* and

[29]AMZ, April 17, 1805, cols. 469-70. (VII/19)

the *Oesterreichische Monatsschrift* can fill in some holes since they too cover the pre-1800 years when press coverage of Viennese concerts was sparse. *Der Sammler,* however, only rarely offers information not found elsewhere.

Coverage in periodicals with genuine reviews also varies widely in slant and specificity. In general, private salons and Augarten concerts are discussed as series, not as individual concerts. Concerts by foreign virtuosos usually receive only a few lines commenting on the performer's talents and technique. Since the performances of prominent Viennese musicians and composers were most likely to include significant new compositions, they attracted the most attention from the reviewers. Only the *Wiener Journal für Theater, Musik und Mode* can be counted on for a fairly complete account of a concert, the other writers commented mostly on the high points.

Finally, with regard to general attitude, the columns in *Der Freimüthige* should be read with caution because of the reviewer's strong conservative musical taste. At the opposite end of the pole, K. Jacob from the *Wiener Journal für Theater, Musik und Mode* was the least likely to launch into a diatribe about a particular composition. He also frequently commented on pieces and performers that other reviewers ignored. The correspondent(s) for the *Allgemeine Musikalische Zeitung* generally penned carefully balanced reviews that betray a slightly conservative nature, but did not go to the extremes of *Der Freimüthige.* In contrast, the reviewer from the *Zeitung für die elegante Welt* voiced opinions that indicate a more progressive outlook.

POINTS OF AGREEMENT AMONG THE REVIEWERS

Despite the differences of style and viewpoint, however, some strikingly similar judgments about performers and aspects of musical practice emerged in the course of this survey. In reference to performance practice, we find continual complaints about over-ornamentation, particularly by singers,[30] with the expected snide remarks about the Italian style:

> Taste in music here is ruled by the Italians. . . So, with his eternal trills and flourishes, Marchesi was able to erase the memory of the heart-rending execution of his great predecessor Crescentini. If possible, Brizzi even does Marchesi one better with unnecessary flourishes; he leaves no note untormented, and that is true singing![31]

The critics seemed most disturbed by the use of such excesses in older music, i.e., the music of Handel, though the general public did not find such a distinction necessary:

> Madame Campi, who sang the soprano part in the *Messiah*, betrayed little taste and understanding in wanting to improve Handel's sublime simplicity and his noble, serious expression by unnecessary flourishes and roulades. It was not good that she was applauded for it; she should have been shown disapproval instead.[32]

Even when the music of Mozart, written in an Italianate style, was ornamented elaborately, disapproval was voiced:

> A Mozart aria was to have been sung by Mme Campi, but because of a sudden indisposition, Dem. Fischer took over. It was the beautiful aria from [Mozart's] *La Clemenza di Tito*: 'Parto!'' with obbligato clarinet. That one cannot keep from edging a gown of gold cloth with tinsel! Dem. Fischer, that rightly prized, excellent artist, should never reach for the usual Italian flourishes in this type of Mozart aria, because it is unpleasant for the connoisseur not to be able to enjoy such a work of art in its pure clarity.[33]

When the singers did conform to a sparser, more sober rendition, the results were not always successful:

[30]That composers were not entirely guiltless on this score can be seen from the fact that Salieri ornamented arias for Therese Gassmann-Rosenbaum. See VIENNA-ROSENBAUM, September 2, 1800.
[31]FM, June 16, 1803, p. 380. (VII/20)
[32]WTZ, January 8, 1807, p. 24. (VII/21)
[33]AMZ, April 25, 1810, col. 477. (VII/22)

The alto [Marianna Marconi] sang indisputably with good taste and understanding that was suitable to the sublime object. The other three probably felt that this was not the place for theatrical cadences and arabesques; this sensible forbearance, however, perhaps caused them to neglect the remaining means of expression, i.e., the shading of forte and piano, the clear enunciation of the words, etc.[34]

This last quotation in particular could apply to many performances heard today.

Critical opinion also reached a consensus about the low quality of concert performances at the popular Theater in der Leopoldstadt, which had a musical tradition of light opera and *Singspiel*. Notable musicians associated with the theater included Bazyli Bohdanowicz, whose contributions to the art have already been discussed, Ferdinand Kauer and Wenzel Müller. Only rarely were any concerts there treated seriously (if they were mentioned at all), either for the music or the performance. Some examples:

Leopoldstadt. Here Herr Wenzel Müller is making a nuisance of himself just as he always does. New operas spring up from him like mushrooms. If there has ever been an inexhaustible composer, it is he; for each new Ländler offers him the theme for a new aria. He gives the matter the proper water; then—some tired figurations and the like; now add trumpets and timpani, and the piece is finished, whether the hero or the blackguard gets to deliver it.[35]

[Review of *Die Sündfluth* by Ferdinand Kauer] Never has such sublime and poetic material come off so common and prosaic in an oratorio as is the case here.[36]

Haydn's *Die Schöpfung* was also given in the Leopoldstadt for the benefit of the chorus. Dem. Eigenwahl, Herr Pfeiffer and Herr Blacho (!) took the main roles and sang very vulgarly [gemein].[37]

While some of the programs at the theater featured interesting pieces, and while famous virtuosos occasionally appeared there (e.g.

[34]WJ, May 1, 1806, p. 284. (VII/23)
[35]AMZ, August 26, 1801, col. 800. (VII/24)
[36]WJ, October 1, 1806, p. 593. (VII/25)
[37]WTZ, March 31, 1807, pp. 189-90. (VII/26)

Conradin Kreutzer), in general the caliber of musicians associated
with the company did not compare with that of the court theaters
and the Theater an der Wien. Thus there is some basis for the critical
opinion, although reviewers often have a tendency to look down
on institutions of a more popular nature.

Negative criticism was also heaped upon the pianist Josefa Auernhammer. Reviewers faulted her both for her lack of precision and
especially for the absence of sensitivity and expression in her
playing:

> Mme Auernhammer was not master of the concerto; she played with
> too little certainty and precision.[38]

> Here too one missed the expression, certainty and principally that
> spirit in execution that is not indicated by any written-out forte and
> piano and which can come to the virtuoso only through a clear and
> deeply felt insight into the work of art to be played.[39]

> Madame Auernhammer had a full house even though her piano
> playing is very much behind the current state of the art.[40]

> Madame Auernhammer played a Mozart piano concerto in her usual
> manner—not without speed, but without expression or precision.[41]

> Madame Auernhammer gave a concert in the Court Theater to a
> full house. She played the Mozart Piano Concerto in D Minor, but
> whoever knows the spirit of this composition (the reviewer heard
> it executed by Mozart himself) could not possibly be satisfied with
> Mme Auernhammer's performance. She took all the tempos too
> slowly or made a ritard just at the brilliant and fiery places, because
> she did not have enough precision and certainty. All virtuosos who
> wish to perform should think over Goethe's adage first: Elegance
> radiates only from complete strength.[42]

At the opposite end of the pianistic scale was the almost universal
praise bestowed on Fräulein Hohenadel, one of Anton Eberl's
students:

[38]ZEW, April 16, 1803, col. 363. (VII/27)
[39]AMZ, April 11, 1804, col. 471.(VII/28)
[40]FM, April 19, 1805, p. 212. (VII/29)
[41]AMZ, April 17, 1805, col. 469. (VII/30)
[42]BMZ-REICHARDT, 1805, p. 128. (VII/31)

I was . . . witness to the extraordinary effect created by Eberl's piano quartet. . . . which is now being studied by all of our good female pianists [*Klavierspielerinnen*], among whom Fräulein Hohenadel maintains one of the first places by virtue of her strength, precision, fire, and accuracy.[43]

Fräulein Hohenadel. . . now indisputably belongs to our best female pianists [*Klavierspielerinnen*] and will find very few [female] rivals in speed, ease of execution, strength and delicacy even in Vienna, where a Beethoven, Eberl, Hummel and a Kurzböck and Spielmann live and certainly have attained a very high level of art.[44]

These last two citations bring up the question of the treatment of female instrumentalists in comparison to their male colleagues. Since the German language allows for a feminine plural (masculine: *Klavierspieler—Klavierspieler*; feminine: *Klavierspielerin—Klavierspielerinnen*), a reviewer could say ''one of our best pianists,'' (''eine unserer besten Klavierspieler*innen*'') and technically mean ''one of our best female pianists. Conversely, of course, the masculine plural could encompass both sexes, so the same statement about a male performer would indicate that he reigned supreme.

That comparisons using the feminine plural did indeed refer only to women is confirmed by a review of a concert by the violinist Mlle Gerbini. The critic used the masculine plural *Violinisten*, not *Violinistinnen*, and then made a special point of including men:

She can be counted among the strongest violinists [*Violinisten*] (men included) and has a power in her bow and certainty and strength even in the highest notes, and a precision of execution that make her completely worthy of the general approbation.[45]

In another periodical, her talents were praised in slightly more patronizing tones:

Madame Gerbini, . . . whose extraordinary power in her bow and

[43]FM, December 5, 1803, p. 770. (VII/32)
[44]AMZ, April 11, 1804, col. 470. (VII/33)
[45]IB, April 1807, p. 177. (VII/34)

217

strength in passages and difficult places reaches almost to the unbelievable for a woman.[46]

Though female performers were accepted as professionals, their sex relegated them to a separate, but not equal, class.

Much has been written about the conservative views of the eighteenth and early nineteenth-century Viennese critics, of their failure to recognize the genius of Mozart and their inability to understand the compositions of Beethoven. History has at least given them credit for venerating Haydn after his return from London, but faults them for not doing so earlier. Most of these accusations, however, are not justified if all the facts are considered. As has been pointed out, the absence of concert criticism before 1800 is responsible for part of the silence about Mozart and Haydn, for since both were frequently performed, they would have been written about had there been anyone writing. C. F. Becker undertook to investigate the actual status of Mozart during his lifetime by examining periodicals for any mention of his name in reviews of concerts, operas, and new publications.[47] To his amazement (he says), he found almost nothing and asks indignantly how an editor could grant space to this and that second-rate composer while ignoring a *Mozart* (Mozart always italicized). His assertions are only justifiable to a point. For example, according to his survey, Cramer's *Magazin der Musik* barely mentions Mozart's name. Cramer, though, included almost nothing about Vienna in his (short-lived) publication, but of the two mentions of concerts there, one is about Mozart:

> Today the famous Herr Chevalier Mozart gave a concert in the National Theater [Burgtheater]. In it were pieces of his compositions that are much loved anyway. The concert was honored by an extraordinarily strong demand [for tickets] and the two new concertos and the other fantasies that Herr Mozart played on the fortepiano were greeted with loud applause. Our Monarch, who graced the entire concert with his presence (against his usual custom) and the

[46]AMZ, March 18, 1807, p. 399. (VII/35) Three of the five women violinists in this study were Italian. One might speculate they had their training at institutions like the Ospitale della Pièta in Venice.
[47]Becker/KRITIKER.

entire audience shared the same unanimous approval as no one has ever known before. The receipts are estimated to be around 1600 Gulden.[48]

And while the (North-German) periodicals may not have given him his due honors, at least one Viennese publication did:

> The most note-worthy thing that has happened in the theater is the court appointment of the greatest genius that our century has to show, Herr Wolfgang Mozart.[49]

Part of the problem is our own perception of where priorities in musical journalism should be placed. The eighteenth century was flooded with new music, and editors would have been doing their readers a disservice if they had only paid attention to one or two names.

It seems, however, to make much better press to have a misunderstood genius, even if some information has to be left out. In discussing the reception of the concert where Beethoven's *Christus am Oelberge* and the first and second symphonies were heard, for example, Rudolph Klein asserts that the critics failed to appreciate the master's genius. As proof, he cites the article in *Der Freimüthige* (see page 210) and the *first part* of the review in the *Zeitung für die elegante Welt*:

> Of the two symphonies, the first is of greater value because it is executed with unforced ease, while in the second the striving for the new and the striking is more obvious. Of course, it is obvious that neither are lacking in noticeable and brilliant places. Less successful was the ensuing Concerto in C minor, that Hr. v. B., usually recognized as an excellent fortepianist, presented, not entirely to the satisfaction of the audience.[50]

He conveniently omitted the final paragraph where Beethoven's music is praised (see page 210). Only thus can the legend be maintained.

[48]Cramer/MAGAZIN, pp. 578-79. (VII/36)
[49]RAPPORT, December 20, 1788, p. 383. (VII/37)
[50]Klein/BEETHOVEN, pp. 35-36. (VII/38)

The press *did* greet the Symphony No. 3 with cries of bewilderment and entreaties for Beethoven to continue on his earlier paths instead of experimenting with such shrill, unpleasant, and lengthy music, and many reviews did remark on his "oddities" and compositional lapses. But no one has ever commented on the rapidity with which his music was accepted, as a quotation from 1810 shows:

> The first part [of the concert] opened with the great heroic Symphony No. 3 in E-flat by L. van Beethoven. Saying something about the worth of this artful and colossal work would be superfluous here.[51]

Moreover, it was recognized that his works' complexity required more than a superficial acquaintance to determine their merits and weak points:

> However, as is well known, one can rarely form a definite opinion about a Beethoven composition upon first hearing. Therefore I will defer saying anything further about the Concertino [Op. 56] until we have heard it several times.[52]

Beethoven was also included in the trilogy constantly cited as paragons of compositional excellence—Haydn, Mozart, and Beethoven. Usually the three were accompanied by one or two other names, depending on the critic, the occasion, and the genre, but their names appeared together again and again:

> [Speaking of Sunday morning private quartets]. The string quartets of Haydn, Mozart, Beethoven or Romberg, and occasionally Wranitzky are usually played.[53]

> [In reference to a piano concerto by Kalkbrenner and Klengel]. [It]

---

[51]AMZ, February 7, 1810, col. 295. (VII/39)
[52]AMZ, June 23, 1808, cols. 623-24. (VII/40) Robin Wallace finds a similar appreciation in his study of reviews of Beethoven's printed music. See Wallace/ BEETHOVEN.
[53]ZEW, February 2, 1805, col. 120. (VII/41)

was all in all insignificant. It must especially seem so here, where we are accustomed to Mozart, Eberl, and Beethoven piano concertos.[54]

[Summer Augarten concerts]. The symphonies were by Haydn, Mozart, Beethoven, and Eberl.[55]

[In reference to an Eberl symphony]. Nothing has appeared in the genre since the Mozart, Haydn, and Beethoven symphonies that could stand beside them so honorably.[56]

[At Schuppanzigh's quartet concerts]. So far, quartets by Mozart, Haydn, Beethoven, Eberl, and Romberg have been performed.[57]

[In reference to private concerts]. Besides these compositions [Eberl's] and several of Beethoven, the masterworks of Mozart, Haydn, and Clementi still maintain their rights.[58]

[In reference to a symphony by Tomášek]. It stood there in the company of the masterpieces of Mozart, Haydn, Eberl, Beethoven, Righini, Cherubini, etc., that you hear otherwise here, like a crow among peacocks.[59]

[At the 1807-08 ''Liebhaber Concerte'']. One hears the most famous masterpieces of the great masters, of Haydn, Mozart, Beethoven, Righini, Cherubini, etc., performed very well.[60]

The concerts at Herr von Würth's presented almost exclusively the greatest musical masterpieces of Mozart, Haydn, Eberl, Beethoven in the full splendor of a beautiful and successful performance.[61]

[In reference to Handel's *Alexander's Feast*]. The immortal Mozart, Haydn, Beethoven, Cherubini—all of these men pondered his [i.e., Handel's] works, and created energy and life out of them.[62]

No other name ever appeared so consistently as did those in this

[54]AMZ, June 13, 1804, col. 621. (VII/42)
[55]AMZ, September 5, 1804, col. 824. (VII/43)
[56]AMZ, May 15, 1805, col. 536. (VII/44)
[57]AMZ, May 15, 1805, col. 535. (VII/45)
[58]FM, December 5, 1803, p. 770. (VII/46)
[59]FM, August 4, 1806, p. 104. (VII/47)
[60]FM, January 14, 1808, p. 40. (VII/48)
[61]FM, April 19, 1805, p. 212. (VII/49)
[62]WTZ, March 31, 1807. p. 187. (VII/50)

trilogy. Thus we should forever lay to rest the myth of the genius unrecognized in his own country and time and properly credit the Viennese with the ability to absorb an enormous amount of new music while still recognizing superior talent. The Italian style may have ruled musical taste, but Germanic genius certainly did not go unrecognized.

CHAPTER EIGHT

The Cultural Context
of Viennese Concerts

Having investigated the history, sources, and musical characteristics of concerts in the Viennese High Classic period, we can now turn to a final aspect of interest: their relationship to the city's cultural life. Only then can we begin to address some of the questions posed at the outset of this study. Many of the answers to those questions are closely related to the attitudes of the Viennese—on how important they considered concerts to be in comparison to other activities and to what extent music-making permeated the lives of cultured people, even those not particularly interested in music.

An understanding of Vienna's cultural and social life requires a knowledge of how its citizens lived, how they worked, and how they filled their leisure hours. We have already encountered the different social classes, but they bear mentioning again, for in the eighteenth century, social rank largely dictated the daily routine. The men of the upper aristocracy—the princes, counts, and sometimes the barons—cultivated a life of leisure. Although custom allowed them to manage their own estates, serve at court or in the military, or enter the clergy, none could have conceived of ever entering business or a profession. The lesser nobility either served in the lower court positions or continued to be active in the business world. In both, the women devoted their time to entertaining or furthering the arts. For the lower classes, from the shopkeepers and artisans down to the unskilled laborers, life granted little but hard work to both sexes, and as a result, they had no part in the city's cultural life. The interaction of the various classes is vividly depicted in an anonymous observer's description found in the *Vertraute Briefe zur Charakteristik Wiens*:

The daily routine is curious—how the various classes go about their business, indulge in laziness, and kill time, from early morning till late at night. From six to seven A.M. you see the male and female domestics wandering into the churches for mass and then taking their breakfast in a café. . . . Around seven or eight the country people come with their products, and the herb, poultry, fruit, and milk women spread their wares out at the market place, where there are multitudes of shoppers, cooks, and the wives of the common citizens and lower officials. Here you hear, like in The Hall in Paris, the screeching repugnant accent of the market women, who swear out a whole scale of curse words in the coarse Austrian dialect. At this time the streets are full of wagons from the country or suburbs loaded with corn, wood, meat, and other things to provide for the needs of the townsman (who is still sleeping). After eight o'clock they come in from the suburbs—some merchants, manufacturers, artists and artisans who have shops and warehouses in the city, some the lower government workers. The great army of the assistants, recorders, registrars, draftsmen, and young lawyers first wander in passing into the cafés and wine cellars, and then to the offices at city hall and the customs house. After nine o'clock the coaches with the presidents and councilors roll towards the offices, courts, and other academies. The bourgeois pious matron walks or drives with her daughters to mass at Stephansdom, the Peterskirche, or the Schottenkirche; instead [of this] the ladies of quality begin gradually to arise from their beds around ten and eleven o'clock. At this time the cafés are filled with people of all classes reading the papers, doing business. From half past eleven to twelve o'clock, the beautiful people go to mass at the Michaelerkirche, Stephansdom, or elsewhere; the dandies stop their parade along the Graben and Michaelerplatz, attend to their toilette, and hold furtive rendezvous in the holy halls. Between twelve and one the high nobility, along with everything that belongs to them, including lap dogs and dandies, take a walk in the Prater. Part of the middle class strolls along the city wall in spring and fall if it's pretty weather; a larger part hurry to the cooks' shops that are steaming so delightfully.

The citizen and artisan eat at twelve o'clock, the middle class and businessman at one, the aristocracy at two, the highest of them not until three, and the Chancellor Prince Kaunitz not until five o'clock. Therefore it never gets completely quiet on the street, for if a large group is exercising to try and work up the appetite they have just satisfied with a good breakfast, yet another group is trying to aid the digestion with a cup of black coffee. Many, who have a bottomless pit for a stomach, hurry to different restaurants, trying one dish after another, and it is not at all unusual for someone to have the first meal in a cook's shop at twelve o'clock and the second at two with just as big an appetite. At three o'clock the "Discasterianten inferioris Ordinis" go about their business, for the gentlemen of the upper order are resting from the burdens of the day at a full table. After four o'clock in the summer, the carriages roll towards Baden, Schönbrunn, etc. At five o'clock the grand avenue in the Prater is filled with the coaches of the aristocracy arrogantly proceeding to the Lusthaus. Pedestrians from all classes sit in the booths and tents, which are found in great numbers in the Prater, and enjoy roast chicken, sausages, wine, beer, coffee, punch, lemonade, ice cream, etc. Between six and seven o'clock the din in the streets is the greatest. Some of the people of rank are coming back from their walks, some are hurrying to the theater, to concerts, open houses, and balls. The office workers are looking for refreshment, the business people, shop keepers, and artisans are closing their shops; a large part of them, like the working class, hurry home to their apartments in the suburbs. One group—the pious—with many meanings, receive the blessing that is conferred between four and six o'clock in all the churches. Another group—the pleasure seekers—look for excitement, station themselves on the Graben and sneak after the "nymphs," who know how to ply the tricks of their trade.

After seven o'clock until about nine it is the quietest in the streets. The lone carriage drives by; the theaters are full; the wine and beer halls and the cafés hold the multitude of the thirsty, the gamblers and the idle; lovers wander in the moonlight in the lonely alley ways instead of on the squares where the familiar god does his mischief theoretically and practically in the company of fauns and female revelers. At nine o'clock the din of carriages and pedestrians arises anew; the theaters are closing; the audiences hurry to the restaurants and public houses. In winter everything closes at ten o'clock; an exception is made in the summer, but still the streets are deserted by eleven and quiet reigns in this little world—except during Carnival. Then the coming and going lasts all night and the pedestrians do not leave the balls and dance halls until dawn, and one sees sleeping groups in the cafés.

This would be a portrait of the daily routine, and what material it provides the observer of mankind, who judges things, not according to their outward appearance but according to their true form. The Englishman was probably right. Amusement—mankind's highest wish—reigns everywhere. Life is but a play, and is then death a plaything?[1]

One upper class visitor to the city further explained how a gentleman of leisure might while away the hours—indeed a picture of the archetypical dilettante:

The man of this description [single with an income of 4500 Gulden per year] and in this situation will spend part of the morning reading in his rooms. He then amuses himself by viewing a free and cheerful scene outside his house, breathes the fresh air on the city walls, or occasionally takes a long walk in the Prater or the Augarten or in the open beautiful outdoors that surrounds Vienna. The beautiful view and dry gravel paths of the Belvedere are always there for him, as is the painting collection which offers an endless trove of entertainment. For a change he strolls through several parks or takes a trip to a near-by town. Now the ships on the Danube, now a busy army of men on the loading dock will attract him. Here he lingers at some new construction, there at the laying out of a garden that is open to the public. If he is a lover of literature and art, he will be entertained by a new product in the book shops, then by one of the various artist's works that he sees appearing under his hands. Here an art collection that has just arrived is being exhibited; there someone has recently acquired some paintings. This person invites

[1]CHARACTERISTIK, pp. 128-33. (VIII/1)

him to see a beautiful edition he has just received from London, that person notifies him that he has increased his print [collection]. For a change he occasionally goes to the Imperial Library, reads some work that he cannot find anywhere else for an hour; or he has a rarity that he has not seen in a long time brought to him. He also has to visit some friend, to chat for a half-hour with this or that female acquaintance. Already mealtime is approaching; he hurries home to dress, and still is held up in the alley ways, attracted by this or that new discovery—something especially well made, or a tasteful trifle in the shop windows.

In his restaurant he finds a well prepared meal and company, some of whom have become his close acquaintances through long association. He hears the news of the day; nearby, for a change, some newspapers are lying around. Or he has an invitation from a family, where a richly laid table and the friendly faces of the owners always invite joy and pleasure.

Gradually the evening arrives. But he still has to visit a few families, whose feminine side is always "at home" at this hour. Now he has the choice of seeing the new play at the theater, hearing a new opera, or going to one of the concerts that are given so often in so many houses and where gaining admittance is so easy. Or should he spend the whole evening at a tea party or gaming party, or first go to an assembly for an hour, where people gather early and where you do not have to stay? Occasionally he goes to a house where there is little or no gambling and finds pleasant entertainment that is amusing because it is carried on without pretensions, and because you leave as soon as you feel tired.[2]

Especially during the evening hours, which began around six or seven o'clock, Viennese society offered a myriad of diversions and entertainments, among which the theater ranked first and foremost. Competing with the two court institutions, which offered French and German plays and German and Italian opera, were the popular suburban companies that branched out into lighter drama and operetta. In addition, many of the nobility staged their own private amateur opera and drama productions.

Another possibility was offered by the various private salons:

[2]Küttner/REISE, 3:324-25. (VIII/2)

Among the most gratifying enjoyments of this city are the private salons (Abendgesellschaften). They are given by all classes from the highest nobility down to the well-to-do citizen. They are normally held mainly in the winter months, from November until the end of Lent. . . . In the winter they start at 7:00 P.M., in the summer at 8:00 and last until around 10:00.

In some homes they are given three times a week, in others twice, and sometimes only every two weeks; in a very few—every day. The entertainment at them is different: in some, everyone has to play cards, in others only if one wants to; some have music, others dancing; and again in others the evening is spent in friendly conversation. All of these gatherings are mixed; widows, women and girls attend, along with men of all classes: civil servants, clergy, scholars, military men, artists, citizens, etc., except for the gatherings of the high nobility, who only associate with their own kind.[3]

Other social events were of a less exclusive nature. Many of the nobility held open houses at which anyone who had already been "introduced" could appear without invitation. Zinzendorf attended many of these "assemblies," as they were called, but they were also frequented by many of lesser rank and by foreign visitors, for whom they provided an entrée to the city's social world:

Several families of the lower aristocracy in Vienna live on a level not much under many of the upper and exceeding others. Many of them, much like those [i.e., of the highest aristocracy], have open houses at which everyone who has been introduced once can appear uninvited. Indeed it is a courtesy and a sign of respect not to let too many of these open evenings go by without at least showing up. They also occasionally have lunches to which they also invite foreigners that have either been introduced to them or who have been especially recommended.[4]

Finally, during the Carnival season, which began after Christmas and continued at a frenetic pace until Lent, these activities were

---

[3]Pezzl/BESCHREIBUNG, 333-34. (VIII/3)
[4]Küttner/REISE, 3:346. (VIII/4) By the end of the decade (1810) the nobility had begun to retreat into social isolation, and such assemblies became much more infrequent. See PARIS, p. 235.

228

augmented by the balls that began at nine or ten o'clock in the evening and lasted until morning. They were held everywhere, in the Imperial ballrooms (Redoutensäle), in private clubs, in *Gasthäuser* and dance halls with increasing frequency, so that the weeks immediately preceding Ash Wednesday had at least one every night.

The degree to which music pervaded a person's life did vary somewhat according to both class and interest. For aristocratic music lovers (like the Prince Lobkowitz), music consumed a large part of their time and fortune. Their passionate devotion to the art even caused them to associate frequently with musicians far below them in rank and social class. Middle class music lovers obviously had less leisure time and money at their disposal, but frequently made a musical or theatrical event the focus of an evening's entertainment.

But we would expect music lovers to surround themselves with music as much as possible; greater significance lies in the fact that—at least for people of the upper class—music and concerts constituted an inescapable part of their social schedule, even if they did not show any marked interest in or talent for music. An evening for a member of the aristocracy was likely to include several activities, if the detailed diaries of Count Zinzendorf are representative. He maintained a dizzying social calendar seven nights a week, fifty-two weeks a year (except for an occasional flight to the country) up until the very last year of his life. On a normal evening he would pay two or three calls, one of which might entail a concert, attend the theater, and a late "assembly" and supper, ending at midnight or one o'clock, or, in the appropriate season, a ball.

The degree to which concerts and more informal musical performances filled his social life can be seen in the following excerpts from his entries for 1787.[5]

January 27. To Mme de Buquoy's concert. It was warm there. I took a chill when going upstairs, and I was coughing horribly.

February 22. Then at the concert of Prince Galazin, where I saw Mme du Buquoy.

February 23. This evening at [Nancy] Storace's concert at 7:00. No.

[5]I have not included any opera performances he attended, so his actual involvement with music was even greater than seen here.

229

11 of the Kärntnerthortheater, first floor on the left. A good box—
my carpets looked nice. Prince Lobkowitz was there. . . . The duet
from *La cosa rara* [Martin y Soler's *Una cosa rara*] was repeated three
times, a virtuosic aria that she sang was a bit boring. Her German
complement sang a pretty aria.

March 2. This evening at a concert where the Emperor's musicians
played all of *La cosa rara*, the music of which had a charming effect.

March 5. Dined at the Fürstenburg's with Prince Weilburg, Baron
Dunger, Prince Oettingen, Countess Oettingen and Sekendorf. Little
concert after dinner. Mme Fürst[enburg] played the keyboard [clave-
cin] and B. D. and the two Oettingens, violin.

March 10. The evening at the Kärntnerthortheater, where I heard
Conciolone sing and the young Schudel play the keyboard [clavecin].

March 14. The evening at the Kärntnerthortheater. Concert of Raum
[Ramm]. His oboe pleased me. In one piece he imitated the chalu-
meau. Neither Mlle Nani's voice nor that of Mme Lang scarcely
pleased me.

March 16. The evening at the concert of Christian Fischer, composer
of the famous minuet, his oboe at the service of the King of England.
He draws sounds that are quite sweet, quite pure, quite subterra-
nean, quite difficult from this instrument, but the choice of music—all
English and French—did not please. Mme de la Lippe seemed ill
to me. Mme A. was there with Prince Lobkowitz.

March 26. The evening at Prince Auersperg's at the concert by
Haydn on the *Seven Words of Our Lord on the Cross*. The second part
of paradise, the last of the Last Supper seemed well expressed to
me. I was in the box with Mme Kinsky, Rothenhahn, and Buquoy
and did not see my pretty one, who was in the parquet, at all.

March 29. Dined at Prince Schwarzenberg's with the Choteks, the
Clarys, Mme de Hoyas, Mme de Trautmannsdorf and her daughter,
Cobenzl. Nice dinner, Mme de Clary, nice music from *La cosa rara*,
divinely rendered by the wind instruments.

April 5. Dined at Prince Paar's with Mme de la Lippe and her brother
and the Count Auersberg. . . After dinner Callenberg played the
keyboard and sang some French songs like an angel.

April 10. Mme de Hoyo was generous enough to send me her

230

pianoforte so that M de Callenberg can play after dinner. The Clarys, the Hoyos, Mme de Buquoy, the Lippes, my sister-in-law, Marschall and Callenberg dined with me. After dinner Callenberg, who was suffering from his migraine, . . . asked for some salts and sang us the song of Hortense, "Ma paisible indifference est elle un mal, est elle un bien. *Elle est un bien!*" And then from "Zelie amour je ne veux plus." Then a German song "Die Schüm welch gleichgültig blieb.'

April 11. Dined at the Manzi's with the Lippes, Callenberg and the Khevenhullers. Callenberg played the keyboard and sang a German song "Hilf mir geliebt zu werden, die leichte Kunst zu linden weis ich schon." Then to the theater [Spectacle].

April 12. Dined at Prince Galizin's with the Hoyos, the Clarys, Mme de Thun and Caroline, the Baron Pellegrini, Lamberg, Comaschini, chamber singer of the Russian emperor, and Righini, the Kapellmeister. Comaschini sang right after dinner.

April 15. Dined at the Schwarzenberg's with the Lippes, Callenberg, the Kalbs. The music of *Cosa Rara* was played.

April 28. Then to the German Theater. Finished the evening at the Venetian Ambassador's, where there were pretty ladies and some music. Mlle Schewel played the harp. Morichelli sang alone, then Mlle Victoire Fries. Then they sang the nice duet from *La Sarola de Galou* together.

May 5. Dined at Princess Schwarzenberg's with the Marchessa and Joseph Colloredo. *La cosa rara* was played.

May 7. The evening at Mme Starhemberg's. She sang some nice French songs to me. "La bonne foi est me chimere" with music by Callenberg. "Plaisirs d'amour" did not last but an instant. "Chagrins d'amour" lasted a life time with music by Mme Ursel.

September 8. From there to the concert of a young lady Catoni who is pretty and sang very poorly. Morichelli sang an aria from *Olympiade*, "Piangendo parti" to perfection. Ended the evening at Prince Kaunitz's.

December 23. This evening at the widows' concert [Tonkünstler Societät].[6]

6VIENNA-ZINZENDORF. (VIII/5)

Judging from the tone of many of his remarks, concerts were simply a part of his social obligations, a part of the round of entertainment he made every evening. They had permeated the structure of society to the extent they touched all those who belonged to that structure in a degree not found in the modern world.

The attitude implied in the quotations above and in the Zinzendorf diary entries is one that regards music and specifically concerts primarily as a form of social entertainment, an attitude widespread in the eighteenth century but particularly strong in Vienna.[7] As entertainment, concerts would have needed to fit into the existing social/cultural framework in order to survive. That attitude coincides with much of Viennese concert history as we have discussed it.

It has already been pointed out that public concerts began as a substitute entertainment during Lent when the theaters were closed, and for a long time, musicians and entrepreneurs avoided direct competition with stage events. Instead, they arranged their ventures to coincide with the habits of the Viennese. Schuppanzigh's early morning Augarten concerts fit easily into the routine of the upper middle class. (His prices also fit easily into their budgets.) Since they arose more or less with the sun during the summer, they could comfortably enjoy breakfast, a stroll and the concert, and still make it to the office by nine or ten o'clock. The nobility, who had kept much later hours, did not find the prospect as tempting, hence the several remarks about its general bourgeois nature (see pages 97-98).

By way of contrast, the midday hours would have drawn a more aristocratic audience. Ardent music lovers of the upper classes were accustomed to use that time for music-making within a small circle, so that Schuppanzigh's quartet series capitalized on that tradition. In a similar fashion, the noon concerts in the Kleiner Redoutensaal were probably mostly attended by the nobility or by the women of the middle class, for a lower-level bureaucrat tied to an office would have had to leave work or give up his main meal of the day

---

[7]William Weber discusses the idea of music as primarily entertainment as contributing to the obsession with newness that pervaded most of eighteenth-century musical culture. See Weber/CONTEMPORANEITY.

in order to go. All classes, however, could be found in the Prater on a summer afternoon, so that Philipp Jacques Martin had a ready audience for his venture in 1791.

In a sense, then, the mountain was moved to Mohammed. Public concerts fit into the existing routine; they did not help determine it. Given this situation, it does not seem puzzling that Vienna had no "Friends of Music" society to organize a concert series. Such an enterprise would have demanded a place of its own in the city's cultural roster and would not have catered so conveniently to the habits of the public. Had an organization of this nature existed, it would have necessitated a concert hall that stood available at all times. As it was, the rather erratic scheduling meant that some type of location could usually be found, even if it proved less than satisfactory. Only with the first emergence of a "Friends of Music" society (the 1807-1808 "Liebhaber Concerte") do we find the first calls for a true public concert hall.

This attitude also explains the importance of private concerts, for though they featured essentially the same type of musical presentations found in public ones, they provided a very different type of entertainment and allowed an even closer blend of the social and musical worlds. But, their close dependence on the social calendar meant they were more likely to mirror social and class values than to change them.

In this context then, we can attempt to evaluate and understand the contributions and the reception of Haydn, Mozart and Beethoven. For Haydn and Mozart especially, any evaluation must take into account the availability of sources. Haydn's career before he left for London coincidentally took place in a journalistic vacuum that effectively draws a curtain across much of the musical life of the time. Nor do his letters help to fill in any information, for they are mostly concerned with business dealings. His music was even less likely to be noted by the few people writing than might be supposed because he did not offer the public any operas or concertos; his symphonies appear to have been extraordinarily popular, but the genre itself tended to be ignored in favor of works allowing virtuosic display. Thus, even though Haydn himself remarked that he was not valued by the Viennese public, from a larger historical perspective, we can see that other factors not specifically directed toward him were influencing his perceptions.

Mozart, of course, has been subjected to a great deal of romanticized biography. There is a general perception that after giving him an enthusiastic reception in the early 1780s, the fickle Viennese turned elsewhere for their amusement, leaving him without income or appreciation. This assumption permeates not only nineteenth-century accounts of Mozart's life, but recent scholarship as well:

> That this year [1786] he gave only a single concert in Lent . . . must be a commentary on the fickle taste of the Viennese public. Yet this is to ignore the catastrophic decline in Mozart's popularity in the second half of the decade. The change is documented most precisely in the tally of public appearances in Vienna each year. . . . The demand for his playing increased steadily over the first years of his residence in the capital. 1785 was the high point, with six Friday evening subscription concerts in Lent, three further subscriptions in December, and several appearances in benefits for other instrumentalists and singers. But interest waned rapidly; the following year Mozart was not invited to participate in any benefit for a Viennese artist. Not a single appearance as a soloist is documented between 1788 and 1790. Mozart's attempt to mount a series of concerts in 1789 failed miserably.[8]

Mozart's documented public appearances did indeed drop off dramatically after 1785, so on the surface, the evidence does seem damning and does not credit the audiences of the musical capital of Europe with much taste, discernment or even much character and integrity. A closer examination, however, reveals once again that an absence of sources is the root of the problem. 1786 seems to be the critical year, so let us examine the source situation for it. The only extant programs for the year are those for the Tonkünstler Societät concerts; we know nothing about the content of the many virtuoso benefits that took place. The Lent issues of the *Wienerblättchen* are missing, and the *Wiener Zeitung* ran only three concert notices, one of which reported on Mozart's own concert

[8]Steptoe/MOZART, p. 196.

of 7 April.[9] Furthermore, only one letter from Wolfgang to his father—previously the most significant source for information on Mozart's activities—survives for that year. Thus, the supposed sudden drop off in Mozart's concert activity in 1786 coincides with a sudden drop off in available sources. For 1787 to 1791, the final year of his life, approximately 50 programs survive. Mozart participated in or had at least one piece performed on 10 of those; only Haydn's name appears more frequently (17 times). Other significant composers include Dittersdorf and Koželuch (7 each), Righini (6), and Wranitzky and Paisiello with 5 each. Granted, his appearances as a soloist were infrequent, but he was also occupied with other trips and commissions then and may have been less interested in solo performance. Even so, he may well have appeared on any one of the concerts for which no program survives.

As for other sources for the last years of his life, the extant journals provide practically no information, and the importance of his own letters in that regard also decreases dramatically. In the early 1780s, Wolfgang was obviously playing the dutiful son, reporting every movement he made to his father in an attempt to prove to Leopold how well he was doing. In 1785, Leopold himself visited Vienna during the Lenten concert season and wrote equally informative letters to Mozart's sister. The absence of extant letters in 1786 has already been noted, and in 1787, Leopold Mozart died. After his death, Mozart wrote only cursory notes to his sister; there simply are no letters that chronicle his daily undertakings to any great extent. Thus, for Mozart as well as Haydn, the source situation must be considered in any evaluation of success and popularity. There is simply no basis in fact for the assumption that they were shunned by the Viennese public, though we will probably never know for certain. From the extant evidence, however, it appears that their talents were recognized and appreciated by their contemporaries.

Beethoven poses different problems of evaluation and interpretation. His popularity and the recognition of his genius have never been in question, but he supposedly suffered greatly from cabals

[9]WZ April 8, 1786, p. 785.

and intrigues perpetrated by jealous members of the Viennese musical establishment. Many of his "problems" came toward the end of his life and cannot be addressed from a source perspective here, but a few observations can be made. The stories of his frustrations about obtaining the theater for his concerts, for example, are very true, but do not indicate any special plot against him; those frustrations were felt by all musicians trying to work within the city's inadequate concert structure. With regard to the acceptance of his works, he enjoyed an immediate and steady popularity on concert programs from the time of his arrival through 1810. Part of any problems faced by works like his Symphony No. 3 had to do with the fact that they did not fit into the existing concert format: Their length and difficulty were at odds with the time allotted to them by custom on both the programs and in rehearsals. They simply demanded a structure that was not yet in existence; that they were nonetheless popular points to the willingness of the Viennese to accept and assimilate new ideas and styles.

Thus, in light of the re-evaluation of the sources, many of the notions about Haydn, Mozart, and Beethoven's problems with the Viennese concert public cannot be documented. Much of what has previously been interpreted as evidence of neglect can now be shown to be a problem of sources; in fact, a good percentage of the extant evidence indicates that the three Classic masters were indeed appreciated by their Viennese contemporaries. But as this study has tried to show, their position and accomplishments can never be accurately interpreted in a cultural and historical vacuum. Only after we have begun to fully explore the many-faceted and complex Viennese High Classic concert world on its own terms, will we be able to reach a true appreciation of the music it bequeathed to us.

Public Concert Calendar

This calendar contains information on all of the Viennese public performances I was able to locate and confirm for the years 1761-1810. As a general
rule I have not included reports of performances known only from secondary literature. For all entries I have followed a standard format: The first
line gives the date (as exact as possible), location (see abbreviations key)
and the name of the person or organization giving the concert. Following lines list the program (if it was available) in the format "composer-
work-performer" or "work-performer" in the case of anonymous pieces.
Each entry concludes with a citation of the sources providing the
information.

Most program designations of the time were not specific, so in the interests of clarity I have shortened the verbose but mostly useless descriptions of pieces to "sym" or "con" or the like. (For a sample of the
language of a typical program, see Appendix 5, IX/1.) Any descriptions
that actually help to identify the piece have of course been included in
quotation marks. When possible I have given K. numbers or opus
numbers in parenthesis.

The spelling of names proved to be a lexicographer's nightmare, as three
sources for a particular concert might spell a name three different ways.
For well-known people where no confusion about identity exists, I have
simply ignored the variants and given the spelling as it appears in NEW
GROVE. For lesser figures, or where any mis-identification would be
possible, I have retained the spelling of the most significant source, then
indicated in parenthesis the probable correct version. Only the latter is
indexed. Both German and French honorifics were used in the original

sources. Again in the interests of clarity and simplicity, I have standard-ized the terminology to Kapellmeister, Herr, Madame and Mademoiselle as appropriate, as they were the most widespread.

Opera and oratorio titles also created some confusion, both because of spelling and because of language. For works where the identification is certain, I have standardized the title for all entries. Sometimes foreign titles were given in German. In those cases, unless the translation is ob-vious, e.g. Handel's *Der Messias*, I have provided the original language in parenthesis.

ABBREVIATIONS KEY

con = concerto	A = Augarten
recit = recitative	B = Burgtheater
son = sonata	Bl = Belvedere gardens
sym = symphony	GR = Grosser Redoutensaal
var = variations	J = Jahn's restaurant
clar = clarinet	K = Kärntnerthortheater
fl = transverse flute	KR = Kleiner Redoutensaal
fp = fortepiano	L = Theater in der Leopoldstadt
horn = waldhorn	TR = Trattnerhof
kybd = keyboard	M = Mehlgrube
vlc = violoncello	O = Other
vln = violin	R = Redoutensaal
	U = Universitätssaal
	W = Theater an der Wien

1761

12 Feb	B?	Lenten concert
		Herr Mansoli sang
		VIENNA-ZINZENDORF

15 Feb	B?	Lenten concert
		Alcide al bivio
		VIENNA-ZINZENDORF

22 Feb	B?	Lenten concert
		Il ritorno di Tobia
		VIENNA-ZINZENDORF

24 Feb	B?	Lenten concert
		Herr Mansoli sang
		VIENNA-ZINZENDORF

1 Mar	B?	Lenten concert
		Alcide
		VIENNA-ZINZENDORF

10 Mar	B?	Final Lenten concert
		Herr Mansoli sang
		VIENNA-ZINZENDORF

1762

27 Aug	?	Concert
		VIENNA-ZINZENDORF

1763

27 Feb	B?	Lenten concert
		Holzbauer-*La Betulia liberata*
		VIENNA-ZINZENDORF

3 Mar	B?	Lenten concert
		aria with obbligato oboe-Nicolini
		Compassi sang
		Guadagni refused to sing
		VIENNA-ZINZENDORF

6 Mar	B?	Lenten concert
		aria-Compassi
		VIENNA-ZINZENDORF

10 Mar	B?	Lenten concert
		VIENNA-ZINZENDORF

APPENDIX ONE

22 Apr B? Concert
VIENNA-ZINZENDORF

1764

20 Mar B? Concert
Tretter played harp
VIENNA-ZINZENDORF

1766

29 Dec B Franz la Motte
WZ 27 Dec 66: n.p.

1770

30 Nov B Colla brothers—performers on the Calassioncine
arias-Joseph Milliko and Italian opera company
duets
con
sym
WZ 28 Nov 70: n.p.

1772

29 Mar K Tonkünstler Societät
Jos. Starzer-sym
Gassmann-*La Betulia liberata*-singers
from the Italian opera buffa
vln con-La Motte
Francois Asplmayr-sym
Pohl/TS, 57

240

1 Apr K   Tonkünstler Societät
              sym and oratorio as on 29 Mar
              fl con-Anton Schulz
              Pohl/TS, 57

5 Apr K   Tonkünstler Societät
              program as on 29 Mar
              Pohl/TS, 57

1 May B?   Concert
              baryton con-Herr Fauner
              glass harmonica pieces-Herr Frick
              RZ 9 May 72: 281-82

5 May B?   Herr Frick—glass harmonica
              vln con-Herr Zistler
              aria from *Der venetianische Jahrmarkt*
              RZ 23 May 72: 313

16 Oct B? Concert
              Venturini-ob con-Venturini
              RZ 24 Oct 72: 675

30 Oct B? Concert
              Ditters (von Dittersdorf)-sym
              arias-Mme Weiglin, Mme Weisen, Mme
                 Kurzen, Mlle Rosina Baglioni, Herr Poggi
              arias from *Armida*-Poggi
              vln con-Herr Pichl
               harp con-Herr Krumpholz
              Gluck-sym with English horn
              Bach-sym
              RZ 7 Nov 72: 709-10

17 Dec K   Tonkünstler Societät
              Hasse-*Santa Elena al Calvario*-Clementine Poggi,
                 Costanza Baglioni, Anna Maria Weiss,
                 Domenico Poggi, Dom. Guardasoni
              vlc con-Ignaz Küffel
              clar con- Herr Lotz
              Pohl/TS, 57

20 Dec K   Tonkünstler Societät
               oratorio as on 17 Dec
               viola con-Carl Stamitz
               Pohl/TS, 57

1773

8 Jan B? Concert
               Piccini-sym
               arias-Herr Drechsler
               ob con-Herr Ulrich
               ob solo-Ulrich
               arias-Mlle Rosa Baglioni, Mme Weisin, Mme
                   Kurzin
               Gassmann-sym
               RZ 23 Jan 73: 47

21 Mar K   Tonkünstler Societät
               Hasse-*Santa Elena al Calvario*-soloists as
                   on 17 Dec 1772
               clar con-Anton and Johann Stadler
               Pohl/TS, 57

25 Mar K   Tonkünstler Societät
               oratorio as on 21 Mar
               oboe con-Vittorino Colombazzo
               Pohl/TS, 57

19 Dec K   Tonkünstler Societät
               Dittersdorf-*Ester*-soloists from the Italian opera
                   buffa
               vln con-Dittersdorf
               Pohl/TS, 57

21 Dec K   Tonkünstler Societät
               oratorio as on 19 Dec
               fl con-Anton Schulz
               Pohl/TS, 58

1774

20 Mar K Tonkünstler Societät
Giuseppi Bonno-*Il Giuseppe ricognosciuto*-
soloists from the Italian opera buffa
viola con-Carl Stamitz
Pohl/TS, 58

18 Dec K Tonkünstler Societät
Hasse-*Il cantico dei tre fanciulli*-Costanza
Baglioni, Rosa Baglioni, Margaretha Spangler,
Anna Maria Weiss, Dom. Poggi
vln and vlc con-Anton and Johann Hoffmann
Pohl/TS, 58

21 Dec K Tonkünstler Societät
oratorio as on 18 Dec
vlc con-Joseph Weigl
Pohl/TS, 58

1775

2 Apr K Tonkünstler Societät
Haydn-*Il ritorno di Tobia*-Magdalena Friberth,
Margaretha Spangler, Barbara Teyber, Chris-
tian Specht, Karl Friberth; Haydn directed
vln con-Aloysio (Alois) Tomasini
Pohl/TS, 58

4 Apr K Tonkünstler Societät
oratorio as on 2 Apr
vlc con-Xaverio Marteau
Pohl/TS, 58

17 Dec K Tonkünstler Societät
Ferdinand Bertoni-*Davidde il penitente*-soloists as
on 2 Apr
Martini-sym from *Henri IV*
Pohl/TS, 58

19 Dec   K   Tonkünstler Societät
          oratorio as on 17 Dec
          clar con-Anton and Johann Stadler
          Pohl/TS, 58

1776

3 Mar   ?   Concert
          Traetta-*Iphigenie en Tauride*
          VIENNA-ZINZENDORF

17 Mar   K   Tonkünstler Societät
          Dittersdorf-*Isacco figura del Redentore*-Caterina
            Cavalieri, Margarethe Morigi, Marianne
            Vitadeo, Karl Friberth, Adalbert Brichta
          fl con-Johann Baptist Wendling
          Pohl/TS, 58

20 Mar   K   Tonkünstler Societät
          oratorio as on 17 Mar
          Martini-sym from *Henri IV*
          Pohl/TS, 58

12 Apr   B?   Former opera orchestra
          RZ 30 Apr 76: 286

19 Apr   B?   Former opera orchestra
          bassoon piece-Herr Schwarz
          RZ 30 Apr 76: 286

26 Apr   B   Concert
          chalmaux piece-Herr Mayer
          trombone piece-Herr Messerer
          RZ 7 May 76: 302

18 Dec   K   Tonkünstler Societät
          Gassmann-*La Betulia liberata*
          oboe con-Friedrich Ramm
          Pohl/TS, 58

1777

17 Mar   K   Tonkünstler Societät
Ordonez-sym
Haydn-chorus from *Il ritorno di Tobia*
Traetta recit and cavatina from *Armida*-Mlle
  Cavalieri
Paisible-vln con-Paisible
Carl v. Kohaut-sym
aria-Christof Arnobaldi
Kohaut-con for several instruments-Paisible
Wagenseil-cantata-Mlle Cavalieri, Mme Vitadeo,
  Herr Ponschab
Pohl/TS, 58

18 Dec   K   Tonkünstler Societät
Salieri-*La Passione di Giesu Cristo*-Mlle Cavalieri,
  (Herr?) Spangler, Vincenz Righini, Antonio
  Pesci
Ordonez-sym
Pohl/TS, 58

21 Dec   K   Tonkünstler Societät
oratorio as on 18 Dec
vln con-Anna Payer
Pohl/TS, 58

1778

16 Mar   K   Concert for music lovers
vln con-Herr Janisch
cello con-Herr Reicha
duets-Janisch and Reicha
2 arias-Mlle Cavallieri (Cavalieri)
WZ 18 Mar 78: n.p.; VIENNA-ZINZENDORF

245

23 Mar K   Tonkünstler Societät
Joseph Starzer-*La passione del Redentore*-Maria
Anna Tauber, Maria Anna Weiss, Mlle
Cavalieri, Josef Hoffmann
vln con-Janitsch
Pohl/TS, 58

27 Mar K   Tonkünstler Societät
oratorio as on 23 Mar
vlc con-Josef Reicha
Pohl/TS, 58

20 Dec K   Tonkünstler Societät
Johann Sperger-sym
Dittersdorf-aria-Matthäus Souter
Handel-grand chorus
Sperger-contrabass con-Sperger
Franz Teyber-aria-Therese Teyber
Sacchini-grand chorus
van Swieten?-sym
Giordani-aria-Mlle Cavalieri
Handel-grand chorus
vln con-Joseph Zistler
Sarti-trio-Cavalieri, Teyber, Souter
Handel-grand chorus
Pohl/TS, 59

1779

21 Mar K   Tonkünstler Societät
Handel-*Judas Maccabäus*-Anna Maria Vittadeo,
Matthäus Souter, Josef Hoffmann, Georg
Spangler
oboe con-Friedrich Ramm
Pohl/TS, 59

23 Mar K   Tonkünstler Societät
oratorio as on 21 Mar
Josef Starzer-con for 2 orch with trumpets and
drums—J. B. Wendling and Papendik
Pohl/TS, 59

19 Dec K   Tonkünstler Societät
              Maximilian Ulbrich-*Die Israeliten in der Wüste*-
              Mlle Cavalieri, Therese Teyber, Matthäus
              Souter, Josef Hoffmann
              vln con-Ludwig Schmid
              Pohl/TS, 59

21 Dec K   Tonkünstler Societät
              oratorio as on 19 Dec
              vlc con-Charles Janson
              Pohl/TS, 59

1780

23 Jan B   Regina Heiss
              sym
              Perotti-salterio con-Heiss
              solo-Heiss
              salterio son with bassettel-Heiss
              sym
              salterio solo—Heiss
              pastoral with bassettel-Heiss
              con
              sym "in the current style"
              "Gallanteriestück"-Heiss
              Bertoni-con
              VIENNA-GDMF

  Lent B   Herr Eck (12 years—violinist)
              Herr Sigmuntowsky (9 years—cellist)
              GM 21 Mar 80

12 Mar K   Tonkünstler Societät
              Bach-new sym
              Monza-aria-Mlle Cavalieri
              Handel-grand chorus
              Joseph Starzer-con for 5 wind instruments-
                 Anton and Johann Stadler, Herr Nagel, Herr
                 Zwirzina, Jacob Griesbacher

Tomasso Giordani-aria with fl-Cavalieri and
  Herr Gehring
Handel-grand chorus
vln con-Johann Toeschi
Friedrich Hartmann Graf-''Der verlorne Sohn''-
  Aloysia Weber, Therese Teyber, Matthäus
  Souter, Joseph Hofmann
Pohl/TS, 59

14 Mar K   Tonkünstler Societät
      Joseph Haydn-new sym
      Insanguine-aria-Mlle Cavalieri
      Handel-grand chorus
      vln con-Friedrich Eck
      Ig. Holzbauer-aria-(Johann Ignaz) Ludwig
        Fischer
      Anton (Antonio) Sacchini-chorus
      Cantata as on 12 Mar
      Pohl/TS, 59

22 Sep B   Mme Mara
      Haydn-sym
      Pugnani-aria-Mme Mara
      Herr Mara-vlc con-Herr Mara
      Raumann-varia-Mme Mara
      Koželuch-new sym
      Herr Mara-vlc solo-Herr Mara
      Francesco Majo-aria-Mme Mara
      Herr Mara-vlc con-Herr Mara
      sym
      VIENNA-ONB-TS; VIENNA-ZINZENDORF

13 Oct M   Chevalier Michael Esser
      WZ 18 Oct 80

17 Nov B   Chevalier Esser-violin
      Joseph Haydn-sym
      Esser-vln con-Esser
      Italian aria-Mlle Cavalieri
      Esser-vln d'amore solo-Esser
      Bach-sym
      Italian aria-Mlle Cavalieri

Esser-"Gallanteriestuecke"-vln d'amore-Esser
Vln son on the G string-Esser
Esser-flagiolette aria on vln-Esser
Esser-aria on vln d'amore-Esser
Haydn-sym
WZ 15 Nov 80; WZ 25 Nov 80

There were no Tonkünstler Societät concerts in Advent because of the death of the Empress Maria Theresia.

1781

26 Jan B Concert
           Bartta-oratorio
           VIENNA-ONB-TS

11 Mar K Tonkünstler Societät
           Thaddäus Huber-sym
           vlc con-Joseph Weigl
           Hasse-*Alcide am Scheideweg* (*Alcide al bivio*)-Mlle
             Cavalieri, Therese Teyber, Valentin
             Adamberger, Herr Ponschab
           Pohl/TS, 60

13 Mar K Tonkünstler Societät
           Thaddäus Huber-sym
           oboe con-Herr Ramm
           oratorio as on 11 Mar
           Pohl/TS, 60

15 Mar B Concert
           Guitar player
           aria-Herr Adamberger
           VIENNA-ZINZENDORF

20 Mar B Mme Mara
           ML 2:719

29 Mar B Mme Varenne—harpist
           VIENNA-ZINZENDORF

1 Apr K Tonkünstler Societät
          Georg Albrechtsberger-*Die Pilgrime auf*
          Golgatha-Mlle Cavalieri, Mlle Teyber, Herr
          Adamberger, Herr Fischer
          Pohl/TS, 60

3 Apr K Tonkünstler Societät
          Wolfgang Amadeus Mozart-svm
          fp solo-Mozart
          oratorio as on 1 Apr
          Pohl/TS, 60

9 May K Brigida Georgi Banti—singer
          VIENNA-ZINZENDORF

16 Nov ? Mlle Hauck (giantess)
          Haydn-sym
          Anfossi-aria-Hauck
          oboe con-Herr Ventovini
          Bologna-aria-Hauck
          vlc con-Herr Schindlöcker
          Sacchini-aria-Hauck
          Wranitzky-horn con-student of Stamitz
          sym
          WZ 14 Nov 81

22 Dec K Tonkünstler Societät
          Hasse-*Santa Elena al Calvario*
          Pohl/TS, 60

23 Dec K Tonkünstler Societät
          oratorio as on 22 Dec
          Pohl/TS, 60

28 Dec K Mme Tody (Todi)—singer
          aria-Adamberger
          WZ 26 Dec 81

1782

18 Jan K Mlle Tody (Todi)—singer
          aria-Mlle Cavalieri
          WZ 12 Jan 82

3 Mar B? Mozart
           Mozart-*Idomeneo*
           Mozart-fp con in D (K. 175) with a new Rondo
           (K. 382)-Mozart
           Deutsch/DOKUMENTA, 176

17 Mar K Tonkünstler Societät
           Marianne Martines-*Isacco figura del Redentore*-
           Mlle Cavalieri, Mlle Teyber, Mme Fischer,
           Herr Ponschab, Herr Fischer
           oboe and bassoon duo-Wenzel Kauzner (Kautz-
           ner) and Herr Triebensee
           Pohl/TS, 60

19 Mar K Tonkünstler Societät
           oratorio as on 17 Mar
           vln con-Josef Hofmann
           Pohl/TS, 60

2 May K Herr Kueffl—cellist
           aria-Herr Lippert
           WZ 1 May 82

26 May A Philipp Jakob Martin—organizer
           van Swieten-sym
           Mozart-sym
           aria-Mlle Berger
           vln con-Tuerk (boy)
           Mozart-double fp con (K. 365)-Mozart and
              Josepha Auernhammer
           WZ 1 Jun 82; ML 2:805

11 Aug M Philipp Jakob Martin—organizer
           music-Philipp Jakob Martin
           WZ 7 Aug 82

18 Aug M Philipp Jakob Martin—organizer
           Mozart-*Die Entführung aus dem Serail* arranged
              for wind band
           WZ 7 Aug 82

3 Nov B Josepha Auernhammer—fortepianist
           Mozart-fp con-Mozart
           ML 2:829

Nov	?	Regina de Luka—salterio player ML 2:831
22 Dec	B	Tonkünstler Societät Gluck-sym Gluck-2 choruses Naumann-aria-Herr Adamberger Handel-chorus Naumann-aria-Herr Ponschab Cambini-vln con-Herr Zistler Wagenseil-cantata-Mlle Cavalieri, Adamberger, Ponschab Sacchini-chorus Salieri-aria-Cavalieri Handel-chorus Pohl/TS, 60
23 Dec	B	Tonkünstler Societät Program as on 22 Dec Pohl/TS, 60

1783

11 Jan	M	Concert Mozart-vocal rondo (K. 416)-Aloysia Lange ML 2:863
11 Mar	B	Aloysia Lange—soprano Mozart-sym (K.297) Mozart-"Non so d'onde viene" (K. 294)-Lange Mozart-fp con (K. 415?)-Mozart ML 2:841-42
18 Mar	B	Mme Nicolosi née Cesarini—singer "a musical academy in 4 voices with the title Angelicke, und Medor in the latest style"— music by Minito and Cimarosa WZ 12 Mar 83
20 Mar	B	Herr Schindlöcker—cellist WZ 15 Mar 83

23 Mar	B	Wolfgang Amadeus Mozart

Mozart-sym (K. 385)
Mozart-"Se il padre perdei" from *Idomeneo*-
Aloysia Lange
Mozart-fp con (K. 387b)-Mozart
Mozart-aria (K. 369)-Joseph Adamberger
Mozart-sym (K. 320 mvts. 3 and 4)
Mozart-fp con (K. 175) with rondo
(K. 382)-Mozart
Mozart-"Parto, m'afretto" from *Lucio Silla*-Mlle
Teiber (Teyber)
Mozart-short fugue and var on themes from
Paisiello's *I filosofi imaginarii* (K.416e) and on
"Unser dummer Pöbel" from Gluck's *Pilger
von Mekka* (K. 455)
Mozart-aria (K. 416)-Lange
Mozart-sym (K. 385 last mvt.)
Cramer/MAGAZIN 1783, 578-791; ML 2:843

30 Mar	B	Mlle Teiber (Teyber)—singer

Mozart-fp con (K. 415)-Mozart
ML 2:843, 845

1 Apr	B	Concert

Franz Anton Rosetti-sym
Salieri-aria
Herr Umlauf directed at the keyboard
Mme N, Mme B, Mlle Cavalieri sang
Leux-Henschen/KRAUS, 105-06

6 Apr	B	Tonkünstler Societät

Ulbrich-*Die Israeliten in der Wueste*-Mlle Cavalieri,
Mlle Teyber, Herr Ponschab, Herr Hofmann
Went-wind band music-court wind band
Pohl/TS, 60

8 Apr	B	Tonkünstler Societät

oratorio as on 6 Apr
Graf-fl con-Herr Gehring
Pohl/TS, 60

8 Jul	K	Herr Muschietti—soprano

WZ 5 Jul 83

1 Sep	O	Christoph Torricella—organizer 6 Hoffmeister string quartets WB 31 Aug 83:11
22 Dec	B	Tonkünstler Societät Haydn-sym Haydn-chorus Sacchini-aria-Herr Mandini and Mlle Cavalieri Mozart-fp con-Mozart Koželuch-sym Mozart-vocal rondo (K.431?)-Herr Adamberger Sarti-vocal trio-Cavalieri, Adamberger, Mandini Hasse-chorus Sacchini-chorus Dittersdorf-chorus Director-Joseph Starzer Pohl/TS, 60-61
23 Dec	B	Tonkünstler Societät Program of 22 Dec substituting a vln con played by Herr Schlesinger for the Mozart concerto Pohl/TS, 60-61

1784

10 Jan	M	Herr Fischer—violinist WZ 14 Jan 84:71
29 Feb	B	Herr and Mme Mandini—singers WB 27 Feb 84:144; WZ 6 Mar 84:473
2 Mar	B	Herr Neukomm—harpist WZ 6 Mar 84:473
4 Mar	B	Mlle Dermer—harpist, flutist, fortepianist WZ 6 Mar 84:473
7 Mar	B	Vittorino Colombazzo arias-Mlle Cavalieri arias-Herr Mandini arias-Herr Adamberger WB 6 Mar 84:76; WZ 6 Mar 84:473

9 Mar	B	Anton Eberl—fortepianist WB 3 Mar 84:40
11 Mar	B	Mme Schindler—singer and flutist Schindler-aria-Schindler fl con-Schindler WB 10 Mar 84:120; WZ 20 Mar 84:585
14 Mar	B	Mlle Müllner—harpist WB 14 Mar 84:4; WZ 20 Mar 84: 585
16 Mar	B	Willmann family aria-Mlle Willmann d.J. fp piece-Mlle Willmann d.A. vlc piece-Willmann (boy) vln piece-Mlle Ringbauer WZ 20 Mar 84: 585-86
17 Mar	TR	Mozart Mozart-fp con (K. 449?)-Mozart ML 2:872
18 Mar	B	Mlle Storace Fischer-sym Holzbauer-German aria-Storace fp con-Sardi (Sarti) Sardi (Sarti)-aria-Herr O'Kelly (Kelly) Fischer-vln con-Fischer Fischer-sym aria with vln-Storace and Fischer Fischer-sym with Russian and Tartar melodies Sardi (Sarti)-vocal rondo-Storace sym WB 18 Mar 84:55; WZ 20 Mar 84:586
20 Mar	TR	Richter Mozart-fp con?-Mozart ML 2:870
20 Mar	B	Mozart (postponed) ML 2:870, 872
22 Mar	B	Herr Marchesi d.A.—singer WB 22 Mar 84:100; WZ 24 Mar 84:617

23 Mar   B   Herr Stadler, d.A.—clarinettist
       Mozart-wind music (K. 361?)
       WB 23 Mar 84:111; WZ 24 Mar 84:617;
       Schink/FRAGMENTE, 286

24 Mar   TR   Mozart
       Mozart-fp con (K. 450?)-Mozart
       ML 2:869

27 Mar   TR   Richter
       Mozart played
       ML 2:870

28 Mar   B   Tonkünstler Societät
       Joseph Haydn-*Il ritorno di Tobia*-Anna Storace,
         Mlle Cavalieri, Mlle Teyber, Karl Friberth, Herr
         Mandini
       Fischer-vln con-Herr Fischer
       Haydn directed
       Pohl/TS, 61

29 Mar   B   Regina Strinasacchi—violinist
       WB 29 Mar 84:24; WZ 31 Mar 84:678

30 Mar   B   Tonkünstler Societät
       oratorio as on 28 Mar
       Kreyser-fl con-Herr Freyhold
       Pohl/TS, 61

31 Mar   TR   Mozart
       Mozart-fp con (K. 451?)-Mozart
       ML 2:869

1 Apr   B   Mozart
       Mozart-sym with trumpets and timpani (K. 385)
       aria-Herr Adamberger
       Mozart-fp con (K. 450)-Mozart
       Mozart-new sym (K. 425?)
       aria-Mlle Cavalieri
       Mozart-Quintet (K. 452)-Mozart
       aria-Herr Marchesi d.A.
       Mozart-fp fantasy-Mozart
       Mozart-sym
       WB 1 Apr 84:56; WZ 7 Apr 84:738

3 Apr	TR	Richter Mozart played ML 2:870
4 Apr	B	Ludwig Fischer WB 4 Apr 84; WZ 7 Apr 84:738
11 Apr	B	Mlle Bayer Mozart-fp con-Mozart ML 2:874; Eibl/DOCUMENTA, 43
25 Apr	TR	Herr Häckel—"contra violon," viole de gambe, har- monischer Fass player WB 21 Apr 84:119
29 Apr	B	Regina Strinasacchi Mozart-vln son-Mozart and Strinasacchi Mozart-fp con (K. 453)-Mozart Eibl/DOCUMENTA, 43; Schink/FRAGMENTE, 287-88; ML 2:875 This is probably the concert that occurred on March 29
30 May	B	Concert Paisiello-*La Passione di nostra Signor Gesu Cristo* VIENNA-ONB-TS, WB 29 May 84:220; WB 30 May 84
18 Jul	TR	Concert opening a Casino WB 18 Jul 84:186
22 Jul	K	Herr Häckel arias-court theater singers vln con-Herr Groiss WB 21 Jul 84:114
17 Aug	M	Herr Massari VIENNA-GDMF-SONNLEITHNER
21 Dec	O	Christoph Torricella—organizer Ignaz (Ignace) Pleyel-6 quartets WZ 18 Dec 84:2877

22 Dec   B   Tonkünstler Societät
Thaddäus Huber-sym
Thomas Traetta-*Ifigenia in Tauride*-Mlle Laschi,
  Mlle Cavalieri, Herr Viganoni, Herr Mandini
Haydn-grand chorus
Salieri-oboe and fl con-Herr Triebensee and Herr
  Probus
Pohl/TS, 61

23 Dec   B   Tonkünstler Societät
Thaddäus Huber-sym
Haydn-grand chorus
opera as on 22 Dec
Fodor-vln con-Josef Hofmann
Handel-chorus
Pohl/TS, 61

1785

10 Feb   B   Willmann Family
Morgengesang am Schöpfungstage, vocal piece with
an uncommonly large accompaniment on a text of
Klopstock
Krauss/VERZEICHNISS 1786; WB 9 Feb 85:74

11 Feb   M   Mozart
Mozart-symphonies
Mozart-2 arias
Mozart-fp con (K. 466)-Mozart
ML 2:886

13 Feb   B   Mme Laschi
2 arias-Laschi
vlc con
tenor aria
bass aria
Mozart-fp con (K. 466)-Mozart
ML 2:886; VIENNA-ZINZENDORF

13 Feb   L   Herr Bondra
Geiger/VERZEICHNISS

14 Feb	B	Johann Bora Krauss/VERZEICHNISS 1786
14 Feb	TR	Concert WB 14 Feb 85:118
15 Feb	B	Mlle Distler Mozart—fp con (K. 466)—Mozart Krauss/VERZEICHNISS 1786; ML 2:887
16 Feb	B	? Mozart-fp con-Mozart ML 2:886
17 Feb	B	Josepha Hortensia Müller—fortepianist Krauss/VERZEICHNISS 1786; WB 17 Feb 85:150
18 Feb	B	Herr Schlauf—oboist piece on 2 oboes at the same time-Schlauf Krauss/VERZEICHNISS 1786; WB 18 Feb 85:158
18 Feb	M	Mozart vln con—Heinrich Marchand ML 2:885, 888; Eibl/DOCUMENTA, 45
19 Feb	B	Herr Viganoni Krauss/VERZEICHNISS 1786; WB 19 Feb 85:166
20 Feb	B	Herr and Mme Mandini Krauss/VERZEICHNISS 1786; WB 19 Feb 85:166
21 Feb	B	Cäsar Scheidl (8 years—fortepianist) Krauss/VERZEICHNISS 1786
22 Feb	B	Mlle Ringbauer—violinist Krauss/VERZEICHNISS 1786; WB 22 Feb 85:190
23 Feb	B	Herr and Mme Le Brun—oboist and singer Krauss/VERZEICHNISS 1786; WB 22 Feb 85:190
24 Feb	B	Mme Auernhammer—fortepianist Krauss/VERZEICHNISS 1786; WB 23 Feb 85
25 Feb	M	Mozart ML 2:885, 888
26 Feb	B	Herr Janewitz (Janiewicz)—violinist Krauss/VERZEICHNISS 1786; WB 25 Feb 85:192

27 Feb	B	Herr Weigl—cellist Krauss/VERZEICHNISS 1786; WB 26 Feb 85:226
28 Feb	B	Herr and Mme Le Brun Krauss/VERZEICHNISS 1786; WB 27 Feb 85:228
1 Mar	B	Herr Eberl—fortepianist Krauss/VERZEICHNISS 1786; WB 28 Feb 85:240
2 Mar	B	Herr Marchand—violinist Krauss/VERZEICHNISS 1786; WB 1 Mar 85:12 MB 3:378
3 Mar	B	Herr Schinleckner (Schindlöcker?) Krauss/VERZEICHNISS 1786; WB 2 Mar 85:24
4 Mar	M	Mozart ML 2:885, 888
5 Mar	B	Herr Bohdanovich (Bohdanowicz) *Die Eroberung der Festung,* (Singspiel) "Between the halves a symphony in 24 vocal parts, without text and instruments, will be attempted along with a violin sonata, which will be played by 3 people with 3 violin bows on one violin." Krauss/VERZEICHNISS 1786; WB 5 Mar 85:52; RZ 25 Jan 85:64
6 Mar	B	Herr Benucci Krauss/VERZEICHNISS 1786; WB 5 Mar 85:52
7 Mar	B	Herr and Mme Le Brun Krauss/VERZEICHNISS 1786; WB 7 Mar 85:72
8 Mar	B	Mlle Dermer—harpist, flutist, fortepianist Krauss/VERZEICHNISS 1786; WB 7 Mar 85:72
9 Mar	B	Mme Cecilia Cataldi—flutist Krauss/VERZEICHNISS 1786; WB 9 Mar 85:92
10 Mar	B	Mozart Mozart-fp con (K. 467)-Mozart Krauss/VERZEICHNISS 1786; WB 10 Mar 85:100
11 Mar	M	Mozart ML 2:885, 888

12 Mar	B	Musicians of the Emperor Theodor Lotz played contra-bassoon (?) Krauss/VERZEICHNISS 1786; WZ 7 Sep 85:2109
13 Mar	B	Tonkünstler Societät Joseph Haydn-new sym aria-Herr Mandini aria-Mme Le Brun Gassmann-chorus Haydn-chorus oboe con-Herr Le Brun Mozart-*Davidde penitente*-Mlle Cavalieri, Mlle Distler, Herr Adamberger; Mozart directed Pohl/TS, 61
14 Mar	B	Herr Marchand Krauss/VERZEICHNISS 1786
15 Mar	B	Tonkünstler Societät Haydn-sym aria-Herr Mandini aria-Mlle Cavalieri aria-Herr Adamberger Gassmann-chorus Sacchini-chorus Haydn-chorus vln con-Herr Marchand cantata as on 13 Mar Pohl/TS, 61
16 Mar	B	Herr and Mme Caravoglio—bassoonist and singer Krauss/VERZEICHNISS 1786; WB 16 Mar 85:154
17 Mar	B	Herr Stadler, d.A. *Der Tod Jesu* (oratorio) Krauss/VERZEICHNISS 1786; WB 17 Mar 85:166
18 Mar	M	Mozart ML 2:885, 888
19 Mar	B	Herr Willmann Haydn-*L'isola disabitata* (opera) Krauss/VERZEICHNISS 1786; WB 18 Mar 85:174

20 Mar   B   Mlle Storace
(Paisiello?)-"Saper bramante" from *Il barbiere di Siviglia*
vln piece-Schenker
Krauss/VERZEICHNISS 1786; WB 19 Mar 85:180
VIENNA-ZINZENDORF

8 Aug   Bl   Music Lovers' Concert
vln con-Herr Mestrino
WZ 10 Aug 85:1874

Advent   Mozart—3 subscription concerts
Mozart-fp con in E-flat (K. 482)-Mozart
(the Andante was encored)
ML 2:895; MB 3:484

22 Dec   B   Tonkünstler Societät
Dittersdorf-*Ester*-Mlle Cavalieri, Gianinna Nani,
Rosa Molinella, Herr Adamberger, Vincenzo
Calvesi, Herr Mandini
vln con-Joseph Otter
Director: Salieri
Pohl/TS, 61

23 Dec   B   Tonkünstler Societät
oratorio as on 22 Dec
Mozart-fp con-Mozart
Pohl/TS, 61

1786

9 Mar   M   Peter and Katharine Karnoli
WZ 8 Mar 86:510

11 Mar   K   Concert
Orfee
VIENNA-ZINZENDORF

22 Mar   K   Herr Giarnovichi (Giornovichi)—violinist
VIENNA-ZINZENDORF

7 Apr	B	Mozart Mozart-fp con (K. 491)-Mozart Deutsch/DOKUMENTE, 237; WZ 8 Apr 86:785
b8 Apr	B	Mme Dušek Deutsch/DOKUMENTE, 237
8 Apr	B	Tonkünstler Societät Joseph Haydn-sym Dittersdorf-*Giobbe*, part 1-Mlle Cavalieri, Maria Anna Orsler, Katharina Gsur, Herr Adamberger, Herr Calvesi, Herr Mandini vln con-Herr Fränzl (Fränzel), d.A. Pohl/TS, 61
9 Apr	B	Tonkünstler Societät Thaddäus Huber-sym vln con-Herr Fränzl (Fränzel), d.J. Dittersdorf-*Giobbe*, part 2—as on 8 Apr Dittersdorf—chorus from part 1 of *Giobbe* Pohl/TS, 61
4 Jun	B?	Concert spirituel Sarti-"Miserere"-Mlle Storace, Mlle Laschi, Mlle Cavalieri, Mme Molinelli, Herr Mandini, Herr Benucci, Herr Mombelli, Herr Calvesi VIENNA-ZINZENDORF
15 Jun	B?	Mme Giorgi Banti and Herr Mombelli VIENNA-ZINZENDORF
Summer	A	Concert Dittersdorf-sym Forkel/ALMANACH 89, 128-29
24 Aug	Bl	Music Lovers' Concert WZ 23 Aug 86:2006-07
Advent	TR	Mozart series of 4 concerts MB 3:618

22 Dec   B   Tonkünstler Societät
Anton Teyber-*Gioas*-Thekla Podleska, Anna
Storace, Franz Benucci, Michael O'Kelly (Kelly);
Teyber directed
fp con-Cäsar Scheidel (Scheidl)
Pohl/TS, 62

23 Dec   B   Tonkünstler Societät
oratorio as on 22 Dec
vln con-Joseph Zistler
Pohl/TS, 62

1787

23 Feb   K   Nancy Storace
(Martin y Soler)-Duet from *Una cosa rara*-
Storace
VIENNA-ZINZENDORF; Deutsch/DOKUMENTE,
251

24 Feb   K   Kapellmeister Kloffter
battle symphony with an orchestra of 60
(For the complete text of the program, see Appendix 5.)
WZ 17 Feb 87:378

2 Mar   K   Musicians of the Emperor
Dittersdorf—sym with trumpets and drums
Martin/Went—pieces from *Una cosa rara*-
arranged for 8 winds
sym
Martin/Went-pieces from *Una cosa rara*
Dittersdorf-sym from the first act of *Der
Apotheker und der Doktor*
Dittersdorf/Went-pieces from *Apotheker*
sym
VIENNA-ONB-TS

3 Mar   K   Cäsar Scheidl (11 years)
            Joseph Eybler-new sym with trumpets and
               drums
            Carusio-aria-Herr Adamberger
            Joseph Preindl-fp con-Scheidl
            Sarti-aria-Mlle Cavalieri
            Joseph Sperger-contrabass con-Sperger
            Ludwig Alessandri-duet-Adamberger and
               Cavalieri
            Scheidl-fp fantasy on duet from *Una cosa
               rara*-Scheidl
            VIENNA-ONB-TS

7 Mar   K   Willmann brothers and sisters
            Winter-sym
            Cherubini-recit and scene-Mlle Willmann d.J.
            Kirzinger-leyer con-Mme de -—
            Polish rondo-Mlle de -—
            Mozart-pf con (K. 503?)-Mlle Willmann d.A.
            (Martín y Soler)-aria from *Una cosa rara*-Mlle
               Willmann d.J.
            vlc con with var-Herr Willmann
            Sarti-duet from *Giulio Sabino*-Mlle Willmann
               d.J. and Mlle de -—
            Haydn-sym
            VIENNA-ONB-TS; WZ 28 Mar 87:709

9 Mar   K   Klara Lausch
            Wranitzky-sym
            Anfossi-aria-Mlle Podleska
            Dautrive-vln con-Lausch
            Martín (y Soler)-sym from *Una cosa rara*
            Friedrich Rhein-fl con-Rhein
            Bianchi-vocal rondo-Podleska
            Giornovichi-vln con-Lausch
            Riegl-sym
            VIENNA-ONB-TS

10 Mar   K   Herr Concialini—soprano
                  Haydn-sym
                  Traetta-aria-Concialini
                  Joseph Preindl-fp con-Cäsar Scheidl
                  Sarti-vocal rondo-Concialini
                  Huber-sym with obbligato fl
                  Orazio Mei-aria-Concialini
                  sym
                  Bertoni-scene and aria-Concialini
                  sym
                  VIENNA-ONB-TS

14 Mar   K   Herr Ramm
                  Mozart-sym
                  Paisiello-new aria-Giovanna Nanj
                  oboe con-Ramm
                  Mozart-aria-Mme Lang (Lange)
                  oboe con-Ramm
                  Wranitzky-scene-Nanj
                  sym
                  VIENNA-ONB-TS

16 Mar   K   Christian Fischer
                  Haydn-sym
                  Sacchini-aria-Mlle Cavalieri
                  Christian Fischer-oboe con-Fischer
                  sym movement
                  new rondo-Cavalieri
                  C. Fischer-oboe con-C. Fischer
                  sym movement
                  C. Fischer-French air with var, then, on de-
                      mand, var on his minuet-C. Fischer
                  sym
                  VIENNA-ONB-TS

17 Mar   K   Vincent Martin (y Soler)
                  sym
                  cantata-Mlle Cavalieri, Mlle Willmann d.J., Mlle
                      Podleska
                  sym
                  Martin-"Perche Mai," trio from *Una cosa rara*
                  "a short allegro"

Martin-rondo from *Una cosa rara*-Cavalieri
"a short allegro"
Martin-"Diro che perfida," trio from *Una Cosa*
rara-(probably above soloists)
VIENNA-ONB-TS

21 Mar   K   Ludwig Fischer
Mozart-sym
Piccini-aria-L. Fischer
bassoon con-Herr Kauzner (Kautzner)
Righini-aria-L. Fischer
new sym movement
Mozart-new aria (K. 512)-L. Fischer
Sarti-vocal rondo-Mme Lang (Aloysia Lange)
Umlauf-"Zu Stephan sprach im Traum"-L.
Fischer
Mozart-sym
VIENNA-ONB-TS

23 Mar   K   Vittorino Colombazzo
Kirzinger-cantata with symphony "Debora"-
Herr Adamberger, Herr and Mme Bussani
Kirzinger-aria with obbligato oboe-Colombazzo
and Mme Mandini
Kirzinger-new oboe con-Kirzinger
Martin (y Soler)-pieces from *Una cosa rara* ar-
ranged for 8 winds—Schwarzenberg wind
band (including Went)
sym
VIENNA-ONB-TS; WZ 28 Mar 87:709

24 Mar   K   Joseph Christian Smrezka
Koželuch-new sym
aria-Mlle Podleska
Smrezka-vlc con-Smrezka
Joseph Haydn-sym movement
aria-Mlle Podleska
Peter Fux-vln con-Peter Fux
Wranitzky-sym movement
Reicha-duet for vlc and vln-Smrezka and Fux
sym
VIENNA-ONB-TS

24 Mar   L   Herr Bondra
VIENNA-MUELLER

28 Mar   K   Mlle Distler
Haydn-sym
Cimarosa-aria-Distler
Fux-vln con-Fux
Righini-new recit with rondo composed for
  Mlle Distler-Distler
sym
Hofmeister-fl con-Rhein
Martín (y Soler)-aria from *Una cosa rara*-Distler
sym
VIENNA-ONB-TS

30 Mar   L   Anton and Friedrich Baumann
VIENNA-MUELLER

30 Mar   B   Tonkünstler Societät
Dittersdorf-new sym
Wagenseil-new cantata with chorus-Mlle
  Cavalieri, Mme Mandini, Herr Calvesi
vln and vlc con-Zeno Menzel and Philipp
  Schindlöcker
Joseph Gazzaniga-*I Profeti al Calvario*-Mlle
  Cavalieri, Mme Mandini, Herr Calvesi, Herr
  Saal
Umlauf-director
Pohl/TS, 62

1 Apr   B   Tonkünstler Societät
sym and cantatas from 30 Mar
fl con-Nikolaus Scholl
Martín (y Soler)-pieces from *Una cosa rara* arranged for wind band-musicians of the
  Emperor
Pohl/TS, 62

2 Jun   K   Brigida Giorgi Banti
sym
Paisiello-aria-Banti
Sarti-vocal rondo-Pietro Sartorini (soprano)
viola con-Herr Fayard

		Anfossi-aria-Banti sym Prati-aria allegro-Sartorini Paisiello-aria allegro-Banti sym VIENNA-ONB-TS; WB 8 Jun 87:96
9 Jun	K	Brigida Giorgi Banti WB 8 Jun 87:96
15 Jun	K?	Brigida Giorgi Banti aria-Herr Mombelli VIENNA-ZINZENDORF
Jul-Aug	Bl	Music lovers' concerts WZ 14 Jul 87:1685; WZ 11 Aug 87:1945
8 Sep	?	Mlle Catoni—singer (Cimarosa?)-"Piango parti" from *L'Olympiade*- Mme Morichelli VIENNA-ZINZENDORF
13 Oct	K	Böck (Bök) Brothers Pleyel-new sym aria-Mme Morichelli Rosetti-double horn con-Böck brothers Haydn-new sym completed for the "Concerts Spirituels" in Paris rondo with recit-Morichelli Schlick-vlc con-Herr Geschwendner horn duets with echo, unaccompanied-Böck brothers Dittersdorf-sym with trumpets and drums VIENNA-ONB-TS; WZ 10 Oct 87:2460
22 Dec	B	Tonkünstler Societät Leopold Koželuch-*Moise in Egitto*-Mme Morichelli, Mme Mandini, Herr Calvesi, Herr Mandini; Koželuch directed Koželuch-fp con-Therese Paradies Pohl/TS, 62
23 Dec	B	Tonkünstler Societät program as on 22 Dec Pohl/TS, 62

1788

8 Feb   B   Mme Morichelli
               various composers-*Il convito di Baldassare*-
                   Morichelli, Herr Mandini, Herr Calvesi
               VIENNA-ONB-TS; PROV NACH 23 Feb 88:256

9 Feb   B   Mme Morichelli
               program as on 8 Feb
               VIENNA ONB-TS

13 Feb   B   Mme Morichelli
               program as on 8 Feb
               VIENNA-ONB-TS

15 Feb   B   Herr Mandini
               Mozart-sym
               Albertini-recit and aria-Mandini
               Cimarosa-scene and aria from *L'Olympiade*-Mme
                   Morichelli
               Paisiello-aria-Herr Calvesi
               Sarti(?)-"Che vi par Dorina" from *Due litiganti*-
                   Morichelli, Mandini, Calvesi
               vln con-Josepha Ringbauer
               Haydn-sym
               Martini-three voice a capella canon
               Cimarosa-aria, "L'Impressario"-Mandini
               Bianchi-scene with rondo-Morichelli
               (Salieri?)-exit aria from *Axur*-Mandini
               Guglielmi-trio-Mandini, Morichelli, Calvesi
               sym
               VIENNA-ONB-TS

15 Feb   L   Herr Bondra
               VIENNA-MUELLER

16 Feb   B   Mme Morichelli
               program as on 8 Feb
               VIENNA-ONB-TS

20 Feb   B   Herr Stadler d.A.
               Haydn-sym
               bass clar con-Stadler

Anfossi-aria-Mlle Xur
Stadler-bass clar var-Stadler
Reichardt-"Ariadne auf Naxos," (cantata)-Mme
    Lange, Xur
VIENNA-ONB-TS

20 Feb L Herr Bondra and Herr Schaffmann
VIENNA-MUELLER

22 Feb B Musicians of the Emperor
Martin (y Soler)-*L'arbore di Diana* arranged for 8
    winds by Herr Went-musicians of the
    Emperor-"At the beginning, in the intermis-
    sion and at the end, there will be choruses of
    trumpets and drums."
VIENNA-ONB-TS

22 Feb L Herr Kauer
VIENNA-MUELLER

23 Feb B Josepha Müllner
Salieri-overture from *Die Danaiden*
Salieri-chorus from *Die Danaiden*
Weigl-vocal rondo-Mlle Cavalieri
Schenk (Schenck)-harp con-Müllner
Johann Paisiello-"Perche se tante fiete"- Mme
    Morichelli
Martini-sym from *Heinrich der Vierte* (*Henri IV*)
Salieri-chorus from *Die Danaiden*
Felix Alessandri-"La destra ti chiedo"-
    Morichelli and Cavalieri
Gluck-overture from *Armide*
Gluck-chorus from *Armide*
sym
VIENNA-ONB-TS

27 Feb B Elisabeth and Franziska Distler
Haydn-sym
Piticchio-"Tirsis und Chloris," (cantata)-E. and
    F. Distler
Hoffmeister-vln con-Herr Zistler
Salieri-vocal rondo-E. Distler
(Salieri?)-cavatina from *Axur*-F. Distler

271

sym
VIENNA-ONB-TS

29 Feb   L   Mme Müller
VIENNA-MUELLER

29 Feb   B   Cäsar Scheidl (11 years)
Joseph Haydn-sym with trumpets and drums
aria-Mlle Cavalieri
Joseph Preindl-fp con-Scheidl
Joseph Haydn-sym
Martin (y Soler)-pieces from *L'arbore di Diana*
    arranged for wind band-Schwarzenberg
    wind band (including Went)
aria-Herr Adamberger
Scheidl-fantasy on an aria from *L'arbore di*
    Diana-Scheidl
sym
VIENNA-ONB-TS

7 Mar   B   Sponsored by Baron van Swieten
    C.P.E. Bach-*Die Auferstehung und Himmelfahrt*
    Christi-Mme Lang (Aloysia Lange), Herr Saal,
    Herr Adamberger
    Mozart-keyboard; Umlauf-director
Forkel/ALMANACH 1789, 122

7 Mar   L   Friedrich Baumann
    Mozart-"Ein deutsches Kriegslied"-Baumann
VIENNA-MUELLER; Deutsch/DOKUMENTE, 274

12 Mar   L   Anton Baumann
VIENNA-MUELLER

15 Mar   B   Tonkünstler Societät
    Dominicus Mombelli-*La morte, e la deposizione*
    dalla croce di Gesu Cristo-Mme Mombelli, Mme
    Lange, Herr Mombelli
    Johann Hofmann-concertino-Menzel and Fux
    (vln), Rein (Rhein) (fl), Schindlöcker (vlc)
    Georg Albrechtsberger-new chorus
    director-Salieri
Pohl/TS, 62

16 Mar B   Tonkünstler Societät
            program as on 15 Mar
            Pohl/TS, 62

11 Apr TR Franz Clement (7 years—violinist)
            WZ 9 Apr 88:864

June   TR Mozart series?
            ML 2:915

Nov   J   Mozart
            Handel-*Acis et Galathea* with Mozart's in-
              strumentation (K. 572)
            Pohl/HAYDN 2:136

22 Dec B   Tonkünstler Societät
            Joseph Haydn-2 sym
            Handel-aria with chorus-Mme Ferraresi
            Sacchini-chorus
            vocal rondo-Ferraresi
            Handel-chorus
            vln con-Josef Hofmann
            contrabass con-Johann Sperger
            aria-Herr Morella
            Salieri directed
            Pohl/TS, 62

23 Dec B   Tonkünstler Societät
            program as on 22 Dec with new concertos
            fp con-Mlle Auernhammer
            vln son-Josef Hofmann
            vlc con-Joseph Schindlöcker
            Salieri-director
            Pohl/TS, 62

1789

21 Mar L   Herr Bondra
            Stabat Mater
            VIENNA-MUELLER

273

25 Mar   B   Concert
VIENNA-ZINZENDORF; JOURNAL DES
LUXUS, 244

27 Mar   B   Franz Joseph Clement (8 years—violinist)
WZ 21 Mar 89:681; WZ 22 Apr 89:1003; WZ 13
May 89:1209-10; JOURNAL DES LUXUS,244

28 Mar   B   Concert
JOURNAL DES LUXUS, 244

1 Apr   B   Court theater musicians
VIENNA-ZINZENDORF; JOURNAL DES
LUXUS, 244

1 Apr   B   Tonkünstler Societät
Dittersdorf-best numbers from *Giobbe*-Mlle
Cavalieri, Mme Lange, Herr Adamberger,
Herr Saal
Albrechtsberger-chorus "Alleluja"
vlc con-Max Willmann
Salieri directed
Pohl/TS, 62-63

5 Apr   B   Tonkünstler Societät
Dittersdorf as on 4 Apr
vln con-Heinrich Eppinger
Pohl/TS, 62-63

23 Apr   M   Franz Joseph Clement—violinist
WZ 13 May 89:1209; WZ 22 Apr 89:1003

22 Dec   B   Tonkünstler Societät
Vincenz Righini-*Il natal d'Apollo*-Mlle Cavalieri,
Mme Hofer, Herr Calvesi, Herr Saal
Mozart-quintet (premiere)-Stadler (clar), Zistler
(1st vln)
Pohl/TS, 63

23 Dec   B   Tonkünstler Societät
cantata as on 22 Dec
Devienne-concertino-Stadler (clar), Probus (fl),
Kautzner (bassoon)
Pohl/TS, 63

1790

There were no Tonkünstler Societät concerts in Lent because of the death of Joseph II.

22 Dec B   Tonkünstler Societät
Leopold Koželuch-*Moise in Egitto*-Mme
Ferraresi, Mme Bussani, Herr Calvesi, Herr
Saal; director-Koželuch
Koželuch-fp con-Therese v. Paradies
Pohl/TS, 63

23 Dec B   Tonkünstler Societät
oratorio as on 22 Dec
Anton Wranitzky-vln con-Anton Wranitzky
Pohl/TS, 63

1791

4 Mar J   Herr Bähr (clarinet)
arias-Mme Lange
Mozart-fp con (K. 595?)-Mozart
Deutsch/DOKUMENTE, 339; WZ 12 Mar 91:627

11 Mar B?   Mme Ferrarese
Le roi David (oratorio)
JOURNAL DES LUXUS, 273

12 Mar B?   Concert as on 11 Mar
JOURNAL DES LUXUS, 273

16 Mar B?   Concert as on 11 Mar
JOURNAL DES LUXUS, 273;
VIENNA-ZINZENDORF

18 Mar B?   Concert as on 11 Mar
JOURNAL DES LUXUS, 273

26 Mar B   Herr Dulon
Schenk (Schenck)-new sym with trumpets and
timpani

fl con-Dulon
Sacchini-aria-Mme Lange née Weber
fl fantasy (over 1/4 hour alone)-Dulon
Haydn-the newest sym with trumpets and
    drums, still completely unknown here
Quantz-fl con-Dulon
Paisiello-recit and rondo-Lange
var on theme from audience-Dulon
Dittersdorf-sym with trumpets and timpani still
    unknown here
VIENNA-ONB-TS; JOURNAL DES LUXUS, 274;
WZ 19 Mar 91:707

1 Apr   L   Herr Bondra and Mme Martinau
               Music of Paul Wranitzky
               VIENNA-MUELLER

2 Apr   L   Herr Bondra and Mme Martinau
               Music of Paul Wranitzky
               VIENNA-MUELLER

2 Apr   B   Herr Röllig
               Koželuch-sym with trumpets and timpani
               aria-Mlle Cavalieri
               solo on glass harmonica-Röllig
               Haydn-sym
               bassoon con-Herr Kautzner
               Borghi-vocal rondo-Cavalieri
               solo on glass harmonica
               Haydn-sym with trumpets and timpani
               VIENNA-ONB-TS; WZ 26 Mar 91:785

6 Apr   L   Friedrich Baumann
               VIENNA-MUELLER

8 Apr   L   Mme Müller
               VIENNA-MUELLER

13 Apr B   Joseph Weigl
               Adolph Hasse-sym
               aria-Herr Calvesi
               vlc con-Weigl
               Florian Gassmann-sym

Weigl-"Flora und Minerva" (cantata)-Mme Ferrarese, Mme Bussani
VIENNA-ONB-TS

13 Apr W Joseph Suche
Schenck-sym
aria-Herr Gerl
Viotti-vln con-Suche
Richini (Righini?)-aria-Mme Hofer
Koželuch-fp con-Herr Henneberg
duet from *Oberon*-Mlle Gottlieb, Herr Schack
Joseph Haydn-"Berchtesgadner" sym "in
which Herr Suche will play a trio near the
frog instead of the bridge of the violin"
Koželuch-trio-Hofer, Schack, Gerl
"Gesang der Derwische in der Moschee" and
"Gesang der Sonnenjungfern in ihren
Tempel"
vln solo-Suche
sym
VIENNA-GDMF

13 Apr L Anton Baumann
VIENNA-MUELLER

15 Apr L Herr Baumann and Herr Bondra
VIENNA-MUELLER

15 Apr W Herr Dulon
Joseph Haydn-newest sym played on 26 Mar in
the Burgtheater
fl con-Dulon
Bugnani (Pugnani)-aria-Mme Hofer
Bleyel (Pleyel)-vln con-Herr Reinstein
(brother-in-law of Herr Dulon)
Schenck-bass aria-Herr Gerl
Giarnovich (Giornovichi)-fl con-Dulon
Pleyel-2 movements of a sym
theme and var on fl-Dulon
Pichel (Pleyel?)-concluding movement from
above symphony
VIENNA-GDMF; WZ 13 Apr 91:971

16 Apr B Tonkünstler Societät
           Mozart-sym (K. 550?)
           Paisiello-excerpts from the opera *Phädra* (*Fedra*)-
             Mme Lange, Herr Calvesi, Herr Nenzini
           Mozart-aria-Mme Lange
           Pleyel-vlc con-Cajetan Gottlieb
           Albrechtsberger-chorus "Alleluja"
           Druschetzky-music for 21 wind instruments,
             composed for the coronation in Prague-
             members of the orchestras of Princes
             Esterházy and Grassalkovich
           director-Salieri
           Pohl/TS, 63; Deutsch/DOKUMENTE, p. 344

16 Apr L Theater company
           VIENNA-MUELLER

17 Apr B Tonkünstler Societät
           program as on 16 Apr with new con
             Friedrich Dürand-vln con-Dürand
           Pohl/TS, 63

29 Apr J Luigi Zandonetti—cellist
           WZ 4 May 91:1187

21 Mar B Herr and Mme Maschek—glass harmonica player
             and fortepianist
           WZ 18 May 91:1332; WZ 25 May 91:1401
           PZ 28 May 91:411

10 Jun B Marianne Kirchgessner—glass harmonica
           WZ 13 Aug 91:2109-10; JOURNAL DES LUXUS
           1791:489

19 Aug K Marianne Kirchgessner
           Mozart-quintet for winds and glass harmonica
             (K. 617)
           var on Vanhal's "Nel cor piu non me sento"
             from *Die Molinara*-Kirchgessner
           WZ 13 Aug 91:2109-10

 8 Sep J Marianne Kirchgessner
           WZ 3 Sep 91:2299

23 Dec B   Constanze Mozart (?)
             PZ 31 Dec 91:1116

No Tonkünstler Societät concerts in Advent because of the illness of one of the singers. Pohl/TS, 63

1792

14 Jan B   Francesco Vicaro von Navara
             "After the end of the play, Hr. Francesco
             Vicaro, a blind artist, will have the honor of
             playing the *Flauto dolce*, and other in-
             struments of his own invention, such as a
             flat moss pipe, a small pumpkin rind, and a
             small double flute. He will play various
             pieces and concertos, both alone and with
             the accompaniment of two violins, the small
             flutes one and two, the bass and the bas-
             soon; in addition, he will speak by means of
             the music and imitate a natural English horn
             with the pipe."
             VIENNA-ONB-TS; (see appendix 5 for the Ger-
             man text)

28 Feb K   Herr Döschi—violinist
             vln con-Döschi
             quintet on viola d'amour-Döschi
             WZ 25 Feb 92:502

11 Mar W   Joseph Suche
             Mozart-sym
             Sacchini-aria-Mme Hofer
             Schlick-mandolin con-Herr Sartori
             Stengel-aria with obbligato bassoon-Stengel
             Giornovichi-vln con-Suche
             Cimarosa-duet-Herr Schack and Herr Gerl
             Johann Hofmann-mandolin trio-Sartori
             sym
             VIENNA-GDMF

279

15 Apr B   Tonkünstler Societät
             Joseph Haydn-sym "which is one of the last
               completed in Paris" (perhaps one of the
               Paris Symphonies, Nos. 82-87)
             oboe con-Josef Triebensee d.J.
             Anton Kraft d.A.-vlc con-Anton Kraft d.J.
             Pleyel-aria-Mlle Cavalieri
             Bianchi-aria-Herr Maffoli
             Sacchini-duet-Cavalieri, Maffoli
             Albrechtsberger-quintet *in pieno*
             Handel-chorus
             Haydn-chorus
             Albrechtsberger-chorus
             director-Salieri
             Pohl/TS, 63

16 Apr B   Tonkünstler Societät
             Haydn-sym on prog of 15 Apr
             oboe con-Joseph Triebensee d.J.
             Krumpholz-harp con-Josefa Müllner
             Borghi-aria-Mlle Cavalieri
             Prati-aria-Vinz. Maffoli
             Sacchini-duet-Cavalieri and Maffoli
             Albrechtsberger-quintett *in pieno*
             choruses as on 16 Apr
             director-Salieri
             Pohl/TS, 63

22 Oct K   Luigi Tonelli
             VIENNA-ONB-TS

14 Nov K   Herr Wunder—bass
             WZ 7 Nov 92:3015; WTA 1794

22 Dec B   Tonkünstler Societät
             Joseph Weigl-"Venere, e Adone" (cantata)-Mlle
               Cavalieri, Mme Bussani, Herr Calvesi, Herr
               Saal
             Josef Preindl-fp con-Cäsar Scheidl
             director-Josef Weigl
             Pohl/TS, 63

23 Dec B Tonkünstler Societät concert cancelled because of
the illness of Mlle Cavalieri
Pohl/TS, 63

28 Dec M Franz Joseph Clement
vln con-Clement
quartet on the vln-Clement
vln var-Clement
English duet-Clement and Mme Clement
Weisgärber-basset d'amour con-Weisgärber
WZ 19 Dec 92:3424; WZ 26 Dec 92:3495

1793

2 Jan J Sponsored by Baron van Swieten
Mozart-*Requiem*
VIENNA-ZINZENDORF;
Deutsch/DOKUMENTE, 409

13 Feb B? Johann Nepomuk Zehentner
contrabass con-Zehentner
2 arias
oboe con *a trè*-Teimer brothers
WZ 9 Feb 93:362; WTA 1794

15 Feb B? Herr and Mlle Fladt
WTA 1794

22 Feb B? Mlle T. Höffelmayer
WTA 1794

23 Feb B? Mme Tomeoni and Herr Benucci
(Paisiello?)-*La serva padrona*
WTA 1794

27 Feb B? Mme Tomeoni and Herr Benucci
(Paisiello?)-*La serva padrona*
WTA 1794

2 Mar B? Herr Maffoli
WTA 1794

8 Mar B? Mlle Christiani
WTA 1794

9 Mar   B   Francesco and Mme Bussani
                 Cimarosa-excerpts from the opera *Heimliche*
                 Heirat (*Il matrimonio segreto*) "without sym-
                 phonies mixed in"-Mme Tomeoni, Mme
                 Bussani, Mlle Therese Gassmann, Herr Saal,
                 Herr Maffoli, Herr Calvesi, Herr Bussani
                 WZ 6 Mar 93:591; WTA 1794

13 Mar   B   Mlle Fr. Distler
                 WTA 1794

15 Mar   KR   Joseph Haydn
                 Herr Maffoli and Mme Tomeoni sang
                 VIENNA-ZINZENDORF

16 Mar   B   Mme Josepha Auernhammer
                 WTA 1794

20 Mar   B   Franz Joseph Clement
                 Viotti-vln con-Clement
                 WZ 6 Mar 93:591; WTA 1794

22 Mar   B   Franz Thurner—flutist on flute with 9 keys
                 WZ 20 Mar 93:750; WTA 1794

23 Mar   B   Tonkünstler Societät
                 Weigl-"Venere, e Adone" (cantata)-Therese
                 and Anna Gassmann, Herr Calvesi, Herr
                 Saal
                 director-Joseph Weigl
                 Josef Hofmann-vln con-Hofmann
                 Pohl/TS, 64

24 Mar   B   Tonkünstler Societät
                 cantata as on 23 Mar
                 Preindl-fp con-Johanna Sonnleithner
                 Pohl/TS, 64

21 Mar   J   Herr Lasser
                 VIENNA-ZINZENDORF

25 Mar   O   Taubstummen Institut (organized by L.
                 Koželuch)
                 Koželuch-cantata-Mlle Fillelois
                 VIENNA-ZINZENDORF; WZ 6 Apr 93:953

26 Mar O   Johann Tugend—harpist
                WZ 23 Mar 93:790-91

27 Mar O   Taubstummen Institut
                program as on 25 Mar
                WZ 6 Apr 93:953

2 Jul K   Mme Adriana Ferraresi
                WTA 1794

2 Oct K   Lolly (Lolli) family
                WTA 1795; WZ 28 Sep 93:2862

28 Oct K   Lolly (Lolli) family
                WTA 1795

25 Nov K   Herr Conti
                WTA 1795

22 Dec B   Tonkünstler Societät
                Joseph Haydn-sym
                aria-Therese Gassmann
                Haydn-chorus with German text
                Haydn-sym
                vln con-Heinrich Eppinger
                Haydn-chorus with Italian text
                Haydn-sym
                "The symphonies and the choruses were com-
                  pleted in England by Herr Haydn, who has
                  graciously assumed the direction of the or-
                  chestra."
                director-Salieri
                Pohl/TS, 64

23 Dec B   Tonkünstler Societät
                sym and choruses as on 22 Dec
                aria-Herr Maffoli
                Went-trio for 2 oboes and English horn-Johann,
                  Franz and Philipp Teimer
                director-Salieri
                Pohl/TS, 64

1794

21 Jan   KR   Benefit-war widows and orphans
                   Haydn-new sym
                   Mozart-aria-Mme Lange
                   Koželuch-fp con-Mlle Paradies
                   Marie Therese von Paradies-"Deutsches Monument: Ludwig des Unglücklichen"-Mme Lange, Herr Georg Spangler, Mlle Gassmann, Mlle Celestini, Herr Panschab, Herr Saal
                   VIENNA-ONB-TS; PZ 21 Jan 94:54; PZ 24 Jan 94:67; PZ 31 Jan 94:90; WTA 1795

24 Jan   K   Benefit-war widows and orphans
                   cantata as above
                   Distler-vln con-Herr Clement
                   VIENNA-ONB-TS; OM Mar 94:305; WTA 1795 PZ 31 Jan 94:90

7 Mar   B   Herr and Mme Bussani
                   WTA 1795

12 Mar   B   Herr Hummel "on his English grand Piano-Forte"
                   WTA 1795; WZ 12 Mar 94:744-45

14 Mar   B   Herr Clement (13 years-violinist)
                   WTA 1795; WZ 12 Mar 94:745
                   WZ 26 Mar 94:912

15 Mar   B   Herr Went
                   WTA 1795

19 Mar   B   Herr Saal
                   WTA 1795

22 Mar   B   Luigi Tomasini
                   Mestrino-vln con-Tomasini
                   Tomasini d.A.-vln con-L. Tomasini
                   WTA 1795; WZ 15 Mar 94:786; WZ 9 Apr 94:1053

25 Mar   B   Mme Duschek (Dušek)
                   WTA 1795

28 Mar   B   Herr Lasser and son
                   WTA 1795

6 Apr K Benefit-war widows
WTA 1795

10 Apr J Giuseppi Ferlendis—oboist
WZ 16 Apr 94:1139

11 Apr B Irene Tomeoni and Vincenzo Maffoli
"Demofoonte e Fillide" (cantata)
WTA 1795; WZ 16 Apr 94:1139

12 Apr B Tonkünstler Societät
Joseph Haydn-sym with the beloved andante
(with the drumstroke) (No. 94, "Surprise")
aria with obbligato fl-Therese Gassmann, Franz
Thurner
Joseph Preindl-chorus
aria-Michael Kress
Vincenzo Righini-new vocal quartet
double horn con-Gabriel Lendway and Matthäus Nickel
Johann Paisiello-"Hymnus" for 4 parts with
two orchestras and two choruses
director-Salieri
Pohl/TS, 64

13 Apr B Tonkünstler Societät
Haydn-sym as on 12 Apr
aria-Gassmann and Thurner
Joseph Preindl-chorus
aria-Ignaz Saal
Vincenzo Righini-new vocal quartet
vln con-Franz Clement
Johann Paisiello-"Hymnus"
director-Salieri
Pohl/TS, 64

13 Apr W Kaspar Weiss
Mozart-"Abreise des Fürsten" (cantata)
Maximilian Ulbrich-2 sym
Joseph Michel-oratorio
VIENNA-GDMF

17 Oct K Anton (Antonio) Lolli
WZ 30 Aug 94:2555; WTA 1796

22 Dec   K   Tonkünstler Societät
            Joseph Eybler-*Die Hirten bei der Krippe zu*
               Bethlehem-Mme Lange, Mlle Flamm, Herr
               Saal, Herr Spangler
            Josef Triebensee-oboe con-Triebensee
               director-Salieri
            Pohl/TS, 64

23 Dec   B   Tonkünstler Societät
            program as on 22 Dec plus
            vlc con-Hauschka "in which he will vary the
               much loved theme from *Die Zauberflöte*
            director-Salieri
            Pohl/TS, 64

29 Dec   K   Constanze Mozart
            Mozart-*La Clemenza di Tito*
            Mozart-fp con-Herr Eberl
            WZ 18 Mar 95:740; WTA 1796

1795

25 Mar   B   Josepha Auernhammer
               Gyrowetz-sym
               Christian Bach-vocal rondo-Therese Gassmann
               Mozart-fp con-Auernhammer
               Paisiello-aria-Herr Viganoni
               Haydn-sym "with the beloved Andante"
               vln con-August Dürand
               Giordani-aria-Therese Gassmann
               Auernhammer-var on "Mama mia no mi
                  gridate"-Auernhammer
               Gyrowetz-sym
            VIENNA-ONB-TS

25 Mar   W   Joseph Suche
            VIENNA-GDMF

26 Mar   J   Johann Renner (8 years—fortepianist)
               Mozart-fp con (K. 537)-Renner
            WZ 18 Mar 95:740-41

29 Mar B Tonkünstler Societät
           Cartellieri-*Gioas, re de Giuda*, part 1-Mlle Sessi,
           Mlle Mareschalchi, Herr Viganoni, Herr Saal,
           Herr Vogel (Vogl), Herr Spangler
           Cartellieri-sym
           Ludwig von Beethoven-fp con-(No. 1)-Beethoven
           director-Salieri
           Pohl/TS, 64

30 Mar B Tonkünstler Societät
           part 2 of oratorio
           Cartellieri-sym
           Cartellieri-bassoon con-Herr Matuschek
           director-Salieri
           Pohl/TS, 64

31 Mar B Constanze Mozart
           Mozart-*La Clemenza di Tito*
           Beethoven-fp con (Op. 19?)-Beethoven
           WZ 18 Mar 95:740; VIENNA-ZINZENDORF;
           WTA 1796; Forbes/BEETHOVEN, 175

23 May J Mme and Mlle Lusini, Herr Bartolini
           sym
           Andreozzi-recit and aria-Bartolini
           Gazzaniga-recit and aria-Mme Lusini
           Cimarosa-comic duet-Bartolini and Mme Lusini
           sym
           Paisiello-recit and rondo-Bartolini
           Caruso-serious duet-Bertolini and Mme Lusini
           sym
           VIENNA-GDMF

20 Jun K Mme Plomer
           Paul Wranitztky-sym
           Zingarelli-aria-Mme Peine
           Hoffmeister-fl con-Herr Turner
           sym
           Zingarelli-vocal rondo-Plomer
           Joseph Haydn-sym
           aria with recit-Plomer
           sym
           VIENNA-ONB-TS

8 Sep   L   Bohdanowicz family—given by more than 70 musicians

sym

Sarti-aria from *Olimpiade*-Catharina B.

Anfossi-aria from *Antigono*-Theresia B.

Bertoni-24 voice chorus from *Orfeo*

"Here the family will perform without any outside accompaniment, thereby, my youngest fourth daughter Josepha, 5 years old, will distinguish themselves musically in a special way."

Cimarosa-trio from *Il matrimonio segreto*-Catharina, Theresia and Anna B., accompanied by an orchestra made up of the family

My oldest daughter will sing an entirely new original shepherd's song entitled "Lycydyna." She will by accompanied by the entire family, then by a 24 voice vocal chorus, cellos, basses and a fortepiano without orchestra

Cimarosa-quintet from *Le trame deluse*- "performed only by the family in a remarkable manner"

Guglielmi-trio-three oldest daughters accompanied by the family

Vocal sym already heard in the Burgtheater

Bianchi-aria from *Orfano Cinese*-Anna B.

"Marantula," a shepherd's song-second daughter and second son, Michael

German song with and without text-family

Cimarosa-"Cara non dubitar" from *Il matrimonio segreto*-Catharina and Theresia B.

vln son played by 3 people with 12 fingers and 3 vln bows on one normal violin

"Filomena, Die Nachtigal," here my second daughter will attempt to imitate this forest singer

"Tytyrus" and "Damötas," 2 vocal numbers especially intended as comic entertainment

"Non plus ultra," a duet, and at the same time a quartet with seven var. The first will be sung by my 3 oldest daughters; the last (at the same time as the first) will be played

288

by 4 people with 16 fingers and 4 vln bows
on one normal violin
"Addio, der Abschied," a song with three
divided choruses. The first chorus can be
seen, the second and third make an unseen
echo. NB The second echo is especially intended as a surprise so that we beg most
respectfully the utmost silence from our
honorable listeners.
"A noisy concluding chorus by the family,
joined by the entire orchestra, will conclude
the academy."
VIENNA-STB; VIENNA-MUELLER

18 Dec KR Haydn
Haydn-3 sym written on his last visit to London
Beethoven-fp con-Beethoven
arias-Mme Tomeoni and Herr Mombelli
WZ 16 Dec 95:3623

22 Dec B Tonkünstler Societät
Paul Wranitzky-sym
Righini-aria with chorus
Stengel-aria with obbligato oboe and English
horn-Teimer brothers
Sarti-aria
Salieri-vocal rondo-Mlle Sessi
Pugnani-cavatina-Mlle Sessi accompanying
herself on the guitar
Paisiello-vocal trio-Mlle Sessi, Mlle Willmann,
Herr Viganoni
Viotti-double vln con-Herr Fux, Herr Menzel
Zingarelli-quintet-Sessi, Willmann, Gassmann
sisters, Viganoni
Handel-chorus
Sacchini-chorus
Haydn-chorus
director-Salieri
Pohl/TS, 65

23 Dec   B   Tonkünstler Societät
             Paul Wranitzky-sym
             Salieri-aria with oboe-Mlle Gassmann and Herr
                 Czerwenka
             Stengel-aria as on 22 Dec
             Zingarelli-vocal rondo-Mlle Willmann
             Salieri-rondo as on 22 Dec
             Pugnani-cavatina as on 22 Dec
             Paisiello-trio as on 22 Dec
             Schindlöcker-vlc con-Joseph Kremer
             Zingarelli-quintet as on 22 Dec
             choruses as on 22 Dec plus one of Albrechtsberger
             director-Salieri
             Pohl/TS, 65

1796

8 Jan   KR   Maria Bolla
              Haydn-sym-Haydn directed
              Beethoven-fp con (Op. 19)-Beethoven
              arias-Bolla, Mme Tomeoni, Herr Mombelli
                  (Zinzendorf says Mme Willmann instead of
                  Tomeoni)
              VIENNA-GDMF; VIENNA-ZINZENDORF

20 Mar   W   Joseph Suche
              Haydn-sym
              Süssmayer-*Moses, oder der Auszug aus Egypten*
              VIENNA-SEYFRIED; Landon/C & W, 4:32

20 Mar   B   Tonkünstler Societät
              Salieri-"La Riconoscenza"-Therese Gassmann
              L. Tomasini d.A.-vln con-Tomasini d.J.
              Winter-"Timotheus, oder die Gewalt der
                  Musik'-Mlle Willmann, Therese and Anna
                  Gassmann, Herr Saal, Herr Pondra (Bondra)
              director-Salieri
              Pohl/TS, 65

21 Mar B Tonkünstler Societät
cantatas as on 20 Mar
harp con-Mlle Müllner
Pohl/TS, 65

22 Mar B Concert
Joseph Haydn-sym
aria-Mlle Willmann
aria-Herr Saal
fl con-Herr Gehring
duet-Willmann and Saal
Pugnani-*Werther*, a novel set to music
VIENNA-ONB-TS

4 Apr B Josepha Auernhammer
sym
aria-Herr Simoni
Joseph Wölfel-fp con-Auernhammer
sym
aria-Mlle Willmann
bassoon con-Herr Matuschek
var on the minuet by Mlle
Venturini-Auernhammer
sym
VIENNA-ONB-TS

3 May A Concert
VIENNA-ZINZENDORF

18 May K Josepha Müllner
J. La Motte-vln con-Herr Clement
Clement-vln con ''on the G string on a reversed
violin''-Clement
WZ 14 May 96:1410

July A Concerts every Saturday
Friedrich Witt-sym
Friedrich Witt-clar con-Joseph Bähr
Landon/C & W, 4:34

8 Sep W Herr Rust
VIENNA-SEYFRIED

19 Sep GR Benefit-"Korps der Wiener Freywilligen"
            Haydn-sym
            vln con-Heinrich Eppinger
            Süssmayer-"Der Retter in Gefahr" (cantata)-
            Mlle Gassmann, Mlle Willmann, Mlle Tepfer,
            Herr Saal, Herr Schulz; Joseph Scheidl
            (Scheidl) directed orchestra
            WZ 14 Sep 96:2646-47; WZ 21 Sep 96: 2714;
            WZ 24 Sep 96:2747-48; WZ 28 Sep 96:2792;
            VIENNA-ZINZENDORF

21 Sep GR Benefit-"Korps der Wiener Freywilligen"
            sym and cantata as on 19 Sep
            clar con-Herr Stadler, d.A.
            Sources as for 19 Sep

27 Sep K   Benefit-"Korps der Wiener Freywilligen"
            Joseph Haydn-sym
            Wölfel-clar con-Herr Stadler d.A.
            Süssmayer-"Gemalde mit Musik, Die
            Freywilligen"
            VIENNA-ONB-TS

 4 Oct GR Benefit-"Korps der Wiener Freywilligen"
            Haydn-sym
            Süssmayer-cantata as on 19 Sep
            WZ 1 Oct 96:2820; WZ 26 Oct 96:3071; WZ 29
            Oct 96:3097-98

14 Oct L   "Korps der Wiener Freywilligen"
            Wenzel Müller-"Oesterreich über alles"
            VIENNA-MUELLER

15 Oct L   "Korps der Wiener Freywilligen"
            program as on 14 Oct
            VIENNA-MUELLER

16 Oct L   "Korps der Wiener Freywilligen"
            program as on 14 Oct
            VIENNA-MUELLER

17 Oct L   "Korps der Wiener Freywilligen"
            program as on 14 Oct
            VIENNA-MUELLER

15 Nov GR "Korps der Wiener Freywilligen"?
Haydn-sym?
Süssmayer-cantata as on 19 Sep with Herr
  Krebner substituting for Herr Schulz
WZ 9 Nov 96:3197; WZ 26 Nov 96:3371; WZ 30
  Nov 96:3405

22 Dec B Tonkünstler Societät
Paul Wranitzky-new sym
Süssmayer-"Der Retter in Gefahr"-soloists as
  on 15 Nov
Haydn-chorus
Haydn-"the beloved Andante with the
  drumstroke" (No. 94 "Surprise)
fp con-Wölfel
director-Salieri (?)
Pohl/TS, 65

23 Dec B Tonkünstler Societät
program as on 22 Dec with new con
vlc con-Herr Schindlöcker
Pohl/TS, 65

25 Dec GR Benefit-"Theaterarmen"
Süssmayer-"Der Retter in Gefahr"-court
  theater singers and members of both theater
  orchestras
WZ 21 Dec 96:3646; WZ 24 Dec 96:3671-72

1797

25 Mar GR Benefit-"Theaterarmen"
(Mozart)-overture to *Die Zauberflöte*
oboe con-Herr Czerwenka
(Haydn)-"Gott erhalte den Kaiser"
Süssmayer-"Der Retter in Gefahr"
VIENNA-ONB-TS

5 Apr B Josepha Auernhammer
Mozart-sym
aria-Mlle Gassmann

Mozart-fp con-Auernhammer
aria-Herr Cordecasa
vln con-Herr Kyhm
aria-Mlle Vestris
Auernhammer-var-Auernhammer
Mozart-sym
VIENNA-ONB-TS

6 Apr   J   Ignaz Schuppanzigh
            Mozart-sym
            Ludwig van Beethoven-aria-Mme Willmann
            vln con-Schuppanzigh
            Sarti-aria-Herr Codecasa (Cordecasa)
            Beethoven-quintet (Op 16)-Beethoven
            Schuppanzigh-vln var-Schuppanzigh
            sym
            VIENNA-GDMF

9 Apr   W   Joseph Suche
            VIENNA-GDMF; VIENNA-SEYFRIED

9 Apr   B   Tonkünstler Societät
            Winter-"Timotheus, oder die Gewalt der
                Musik"-Mme Anna Willmann, Therese
                Gassmann, Herr Simoni, Herr Saal
            Triebensee-con for oboe and vln-Herr
                Triebensee and Herr Breymann
            director-Salieri
            Pohl/TS, 65

10 Apr B   Tonkünstler Societät
            cantata as on 9 Apr
            Cartellieri-clar con-Stadler brothers
            Pohl/TS, 65

11 Apr B? Constanze Mozart
            Mozart-*La Clemenza di Tito*
            WZ 1 Apr 97:1006

1 Jun   A   Concert
            VIENNA-ZINZENDORF

25 Nov J   Lorenz Renner—fortepianist
            WZ 4 Nov 97:3302

22 Dec B   Tonkünstler Societät
               Paul Wranitzky-sym
               Handel-chorus
               Süssmayer-"the beloved Andante from "Der
                  Retter in Gefahr,"-Herr Schulz with Herr
                  Stadler (clar)
               Krammer-oboe con-Herr Czerwenka
               Albrechtsberger-"Allelujah"
               Cimarosa-aria-Therese Gassman
               Righini-aria-Herr Saal
               Sacchini-chorus
               Righini-vocal quartet with chorus
               director-Salieri
               Pohl/TS, 65-66

23 Dec B   Tonkünstler Societät
               Paul Wranitzky-sym
               Handel-chorus
               Süssmayer-aria as on 22 Dec
               Anton Wranitzky-con for vln and vlc-Wranitzky
                  and Herr Kraft
               Albrechtsberger-"Allelujah"
               Cimarosa-aria-Therese Gassmann
               Righini-aria-Saal
               Beethoven-trio with var from the opera *Don*
                  Juan for 2 oboes and English horn-Herr
                  Czerwenka, Herr Reuter, Herr Teimer
               Righini-vocal quartet with chorus
               director-Salieri
               Pohl/TS, 65-66

1798

29 Jan K   Eck brothers—violinists
               WZ 27 Jan 98:252; AMZ 10 Jun 01:626

16 Feb K   Bohdanowicz family
               VIENNA-SONNLEITHNER

25 Mar L   Ferdinand Kauer
               "Die Begebenheiten des Wiener Aufgeboths,
                  bis zu dem in Campo Formido geschlossenen
                  Frieden"

VIENNA-STB; WZ 28 Mar 98:886; PZ 30 Mar
98:258

25 Mar W Herr Pischelberger
VIENNA-SEYFRIED

25 Mar ? Concert
aria-Therese Gassmann
VIENNA-ROSENBAUM

29 Mar J Mme Dušek
Anton Wranitzky-sym
Danzi-scene-Dušek
vln con-Schuppanzigh
Mozart-overture to *La Clemenza di Tito*
Mozart-rondo obbligato with basset horn
  ("Non piu di fiori" from *La Clemenza di
  Tito*?)-Herr Stadler and Mme Dušek
Ludwig van Beethoven-fp son with accompani-
  ment (Op. 12?) Beethoven
sym
VIENNA-GDMF

30 Mar B Joseph Weigl
music from acts 1-3 of the ballet *Richard
  Löwenberg*
Weigl-"Die Gefühle meines Herzens"-Mme To-
  meoni, Mme Willmann-Calvani, Mlle Therese
  Gassmann, Herr Angrisani, Herr Saal. "Mme
  Tomeoni and Herr Angrisani will sing not
  only Italian, but also German."
music from acts 1-5 of *Richard Löwenberg*
VIENNA-ONB-TS; WZ 28 Mar 98:888; VIENNA-
ROSENBAUM (Rosenbaum says Vogl sang,
not Saal)

1 Apr B Tonkünstler Societät
Eybler-sym
clar con-Herr Bähr
Joseph Haydn-*Die sieben Worte*-Therese
  Gassmann, Antonia Flamm, Herr Weinmüller
  and Sigismund Hüller; director-Haydn
Pohl/TS, 66

2 Apr B Tonkünstler Societät
sym and cantata as on 1 Apr (Herr Saal sang
instead of Herr Weinmüller)
Beethoven quintet (Op. 16)-Beethoven, Herr
Triebensee (oboe), Herr Bähr (clarinet), Herr
Matuschek (bassoon), Herr Nickel (waldhorn)
Pohl/TS, 66

8 Apr W Constanze Mozart
Mozart-*La Clemenza di Tito*
VIENNA-SEYFRIED; VIENNA-ZINZENDORF

13 Apr J Mlle Caldarini
Haydn-sym
Zingarelli-recit and aria-Louise Caldarini
Mlle de Paradies-fp con-Paradies
Nicolini-"Poloness" Caldarini
Paul Wranitzky-sym
Nasolini-vocal rondo-Caldarini
Stadler d.A.-clar con-Stadler d.A.
Cimarosa-duet with recit-Caldarini and Herr
Vogel (Vogl)
Haydn-Allegro
VIENNA-GDMF

18 Apr B? Concert
VIENNA-INDENDENZ

27 Apr ? Constanze Mozart
Mozart-*La Clemenza di Tito*-Constanze Mozart,
Therese Gassmann, Bescher, Umlauf,
Stengel, Herr Rathmayer
vln con-Herr Clement
VIENNA-ROSENBAUM; Deutsch/DOKUMENTE,
422

28 Apr B Concert
Paul Wranitzky-sym
Mainberger-timpani con-Johann Georg Roth
(Zingarelli?)-pieces from *Juliet et Romeo* arranged
for wind band
24 cadences ("Regimentsschläge") on 16
timpanis

sym
"4 Posten von Regimentsmarschen" on 8 and
16 timpanis with the accompaniment of 8
trumpets
vln con-Herr Clement
Süssmayer-University Corps March on timpani
Intrata on 16 timpanis accompanied by trumpets
VIENNA-ONB-TS; VIENNA-ROSENBAUM

4 May   GR   Benefit for burned-down city of Cilly
Paul Wranitzky-new sym
Joseph Eybler-oboe con-Herr Grohmann
Süssmayer-cantata set to music of "Der Retter
in Gefahr"-Therese Gassmann and Herr
Mendl
VIENNA-ONB-TS; VIENNA-ROSENBAUM;
WZ 2 May 98:1298

31 May   A   Concert
VIENNA-ROSENBAUM

28 Jun   A   Concert
Haydn-"Dove sei mio bel tesoro" from the
cantata "Ariadne"-Anna Ascher with Ignaz
Wenzel Raffel on fp
VIENNA-ROSENBAUM

7 Jul   A   Concert
VIENNA-ROSENBAUM

12 Jul   A   Concert
VIENNA-ROSENBAUM

Summer   A   Benefit-Constanze Mozart
Eibl/DOCUMENTA, 88

8 Sep   W   Concert
Mozart-*La Clemenza di Tito*-Josepha Hofer-Mayer
and Sebastian Meier
Deutsch/DOKUMENTE, p. 423

8 Sep   L   Joseph Heidenreich
"Das Kriegslager, oder der Schlacht"
WZ 25 Aug 98:2593; VIENNA-MUELLER

27 Oct   W   Emanuel Schikaneder—director
             Ritter Edler von Seyfried-new sym
             Righini-aria-Herr Fischer
             Anfossi-vocal rondo-Mme Willmann
             Righini-aria-Fischer
             Mozart-overture to *Die Zauberflöte*
             Mozart-"In diesen heil'gen Hallen" from *Die
             Zauberflöte*-Fischer
             Beethoven-fp con (Op. 15?)-Beethoven
             (Umlauf?)-"Zu Stephan sprach im Traume"-
             Fischer (Johann Ignaz Ludwig?)
             Haydn-"the beloved symphony"
             VIENNA-GDMF

5 Nov   W   Emanuel Schikaneder
             Ritter von Seyfried-sym
             Righini-aria-Fischer
             Wolfgang Amade Mozart-aria-Herr Hüller
             Paisiello-dream aria from *König Theodor* (*Il Re
             Teodoro*)-Fischer
             Paul Wranitzky-overture to *Das Marokkanische
             Reich*
             Mozart-"In diesen heil'gen Hallen" from *Die
             Zauberflöte*-Fischer
             Viotti-vln con-Schuppanzigh
             Beethoven-Adagio on the violin-Schuppanzigh
             (Umlauf?) "Zu Stephan sprach im Traume"
             from *Das Irrlicht*-Fischer
             Haydn-"the beloved symphony"
             VIENNA-GDMF; either the date or the day of
             the week given on the program is incorrect

21 Dec   J   Herr Formaizko and Herr Grohmann
               Salieri-aria-Therese Gassmann
               Cimarosa-vocal rondo-Therese Gassmann
             VIENNA-ROSENBAUM

22 Dec   B   Tonkünstler Societät
               Eybler-sym
               Joseph Haydn-aria-Mlle Flamm
               Haydn-"military sym"-Haydn directed

299

Koželuch-con-Anton Teyber (fp), Herr Zahrad-
nizek (mandolin), Herr Weidinger (trumpet),
Herr Pischelberger (contrabass)
Romagnoli-cantata with choruses-Therese
Gassmann, Antonie Flamm, Ignaz Saal,
Sigismund Hüller
director-Salieri
Pohl/TS, 66

23 Dec B Tonkünstler Societät
program as on 22 Dec
Pohl/TS, 66

23 Dec L Herr Kauer
"Nelson's Schlacht"
VIENNA-MUELLER

28 Dec J Antonio Camera and Angelo Ferlendis—violinist
and oboist
arias-Therese Gassmann
VIENNA-ROSENBAUM

1799

6 Mar J Angiolo Galliani
arias-Therese Gassmann
arias-Herr Pasqua
VIENNA-ROSENBAUM

11 Mar J Concert
arias-Therese Gassmann, Mme Willmann, Herr
Saal, Herr Haunold (?)
VIENNA-ROSENBAUM

17 Mar B Tonkünstler Societät
von Gluck-sym
Haydn-*Die sieben Worte*-Therese Gassmann, An-
tonie Flamm, Herr Weinmüller, Sigismund
Hüller, Haydn directed
Triebensee-oboe con-Herr Triebensee
Pohl/TS, 66

18 Mar	B	Tonkünstler Societät sym and cantata as on 17 Mar Peter Fux-vln con-Fux Pohl/TS, 66
19 Mar	B	Haydn Haydn-*Die Schöpfung*—Mlle Saal, Herr Saal, Herr Rathmayer AMZ 10 Apr 99: 446; VIENNA-ROSENBAUM
25 Mar	B	Mme Auernhammer Auernhammer-var on Salieri's "La Stessa, la Stessissima"-Auernhammer harp piece-Josepha Müllner WZ 27 Mar 99:913; VIENNA-ROSENBAUM
25 Mar	W	Constanze Mozart Mozart-*La Clemenza di Tito*-Josepha and Sebas- tian Mayer (Meier) Hoffmeister-fp con-Josepha Hofer (8 years) VIENNA-SEYFRIED; Eibl/DOCUMENTA, 88
28 Apr	A	Benefit-citizens of Lower Austria sym Hummel-fp con-Hummel? Hummel-melodrama-Mme Koch Schuppanzigh directed Orchestra of the Theater auf der Wieden WZ 24 Apr 99:1257; WZ 1 May 99:1338-39, 1350; AMZ 22 May 99:542-44
30 Apr	?	Herr Berwald and son WZ 3 Apr 99:989
1 May	O	Benefit-"Verunglückten Tyroler" Anton Harr-cantata WZ 15 May 99:1530
3 May	J	Herr Berwald and son aria and vocal rondo-Therese Gassmann WZ 1 May 99:1350; VIENNA-ROSENBAUM

23 May GR Benefit-"Verunglückten Tyroler"
            Joseph Haydn-sym
            harp con-Mlle Müllner
            Salieri-"Der Tyroler Landsturm" (cantata)-
               Therese Gassmann, Therese Saal, Herr
               Rathmayer, Herr Saal
            Joseph Scheidl directed
            Hofkapelle and 2 theater orchestras
            VIENNA-ONB-TS; VIENNA-ROSENBAUM;
            WZ 11 May 99: 1490; WZ 25 May 99:1670

25 May GR Concert
            probably program of 23 May
            VIENNA-ROSENBAUM

30 May A   Schuppanzigh series
            WZ 22 May 99:1636

 7 Jun A   Schuppanzigh series
            WZ 22 May 99:1636

14 Jun A   Schuppanzigh series
            WZ 22 May 99:1636

16 Jun A   Benefit-"verunglückten Familie" (postponed
            from 9 June)
            Haydn-2 sym (premieres)
            various concertos
            WZ 1 Jun 99:1772; WZ 12 Jun 99:1899

21 Jun A   Schuppanzigh series
            WZ 22 May 99:1636

27 Aug R   War widows and orphans
            Hummel-"Siegesfeyer" (cantata)-Therese
               Gassmann
            WZ 21 Aug 99:2815; VIENNA-ROSENBAUM

 8 Sep R   War widows and orphans
            program of 27 August
            WZ 31 Aug 99:2937; WZ 25 Sep 99:3210

15 Nov GR Benefit-"Verunglückten Tyroler"
            Salieri-"Tyroler Landsturm"—Therese
               Gassmann
            WZ 26 Oct 99:3609-10; VIENNA-ROSENBAUM

15 Nov	L	Herr Rotter VIENNA-MUELLER
18 Nov	K	Herr Simoni—oboist Weigl-vocal rondo-Therese Gassmann WZ 13 Nov 99:3838; VIENNA-ROSENBAUM
16 Dec	J	Joseph Bergancini—singer WZ 14 Dec 99:4242
22 Dec	B	Tonkünstler Societät Joseph Haydn-*Die Schöpfung*-Therese Saal, Herr Rathmayer, Herr Saal; Haydn directed Pohl/TS, 66
23 Dec	B	Tonkünstler Societät program as on 22 Dec Pohl/TS, 66

1800

3 Jan	J	Local musicians-benefit for a poor family WZ 1 Jan 00:18
7 Mar	J	Catherina Plomer-Salvini Polonaise-Plomer Haydn-syms VIENNA-ZINZENDORF; AMZ 15 Oct 00:48
25 Mar	L	Bohdanowicz family VIENNA-MUELLER
25 Mar	W	Concert Süssmayer-*Moses, oder der Auszug aus Egypt* VIENNA-SEYFRIED

28 Mar	B	Anton Weidinger
		Joseph Haydn-new sym
		Haydn-trumpet con-Weidinger
		Mozart-aria-Mlle T. Gassmann
		Haydn-sym
		Mozart-duet-Gassmann and
		    Herr Weinmüller
		Süssmayer aria with trumpet-Gassmann and
		    Weidinger

303

Haydn-sym
Kauer-sextet-Joseph Weidinger (trumpet), Franz
   Weidinger (4 timpani), Herr Haberl (clar),
   Herr Mesch (clar), Herr Sedlatscheck (bas-
   soon), Anton Weidinger, (trumpet)
sym
VIENNA-ONB-TS; WZ 22 Mar 00:916

2 Apr B   Ludwig van Beethoven
           Mozart-sym
           Haydn-aria
           from *Die Schöpfung*-Mlle Saal
           Beethoven-fp con-Beethoven
           Beethoven-septet (Op. 20)-Herr Schuppanzigh,
              Schreiber, Schindlöcker, Bähr, Nickel,
              Matuschek, and Dietzel
           Haydn-duet from *Die Schöpfung*-Mlle Saal, Herr
              Saal
           Beethoven-fp fantasy-Beethoven
           Beethoven-sym
           VIENNA-ONB-TS; AMZ 15 Oct 00:49; WZ 26
           Mar 00:965

4 Apr J   Herr Grohmann and Herr Formaizko
           Krommer-sym (premiere)
           Krommer-fl con-Formaizko
           Mozart-quintet for fp, oboe, clar, bassoon, and
              horn (K. 452)-Mlle Krommer
           Haydn-sym
           Krommer-oboe con-Grohmann
           (Pär)-arias from *Camilla* arranged for 13 winds
           sym
           VIENNA-ONB-TS; WZ 26 Mar 00:965

6 Apr B   Tonkünstler Societät
           Haydn-*Die Schöpfung*-Mlle Saal, Herr Saal, Herr
              Rathmayer
           director-Haydn?
           Pohl/TS, 66

7 Apr B   Tonkünstler Societät
           program as on 6 Apr
           Pohl/TS, 66

8 Apr   B   Benefit-"Theaterarmen"
               Guglielmi-*La Morte di Oloferne*-Mme Riccardi
               Pär, Therese and Nannette (Maria Anna)
               Gassmann, Herr Pasqua, Herr Weinmüller
               Joseph Winter-oboe con-Herr Czerwenka
               VIENNA-ROSENBAUM; VIENNA-ONB-TS

18 Apr   K   Herr Punto
               Haydn-sym
               Pär-scene-Mme Riccardi Pär
               horn con-Punto
               Méhul-new overture
               Cartellieri-clar con-Herr Kirstein
               Pär-aria-Mme Riccardi Pär
               Beethoven-horn son (Op. 17)-Punto and
                 Beethoven
               sym
               VIENNA-ONB-TS; WZ 16 Apr 00:1228; AMZ 2
               Jul 00:704; AMZ 15 Oct 00:48

24 May   A   Schuppanzigh series opening concert
               WZ 7 May 00:1485

Summer   A   Steibelt
               Steibelt-"rondo mit dem
                 Donnerwetter"-Steibelt
               Steibelt-fantasy and var-Steibelt
               AMZ 15 Oct 00:50

29 Jun   A   Concert (Schuppanzigh series?)
               VIENNA-ZINZENDORF

24 Jul   A   Concert (Schuppanzigh series?)
               Joseph Mayseder public debut
               VIENNA-GDMF-MAYSEDER

14 Aug   A   Schuppanzigh series
               Martin y Soler-aria from *L'arbore di Diana*-Mlle
                 Perschl
               VIENNA-ROSENBAUM

21 Aug   A   Schuppanzigh series
               Haydn-sym

Mozart-vocal quartet-Therese Gassman, Herr
  Mayer (Meier), Herr Teimer, Herr Seyfried
Cimarosa-aria from *Die Sonnenjungfrau* (*La
  virgine del sole*)-Therese Gassmann
VIENNA-ROSENBAUM

28 Aug A   Schuppanzigh series
  Mozart-vocal rondo-Therese Gassmann
  vocal quartet-Therese and Nanette Gassmann,
    Herr Rathmayer, Herr Mayer (Meier), Herr
    Teimer
  VIENNA-ROSENBAUM

4 Sep A   Schuppanzigh series
  Pär-aria-Therese Gassmann
  Weigl-vocal rondo-Therese Gassmann
  VIENNA-ROSENBAUM

11 Sep A   Schuppanzigh series
  (Zingarelli?)-"Bombia adorata" from *Juliet et
    Romeo*-Mme Hutschenreiter
  VIENNA-ROSENBAUM

18 Sep A   Schuppanzigh series
  aria-Therese Gassmann
  VIENNA-ROSENBAUM

15 Nov L   Theater orchestra
  Haydn-*Die Schöpfung*
  VIENNA-GDMF; WZ 15 Nov 00:3707-08

18 Dec GR Benefit-"Nieder-österreishiche Scharf-
    schützerkorps"
  Mozart-sym
  Franz Xaver Süssmayer-"Der
    Kampf für den Frieden"-Mme Rosenbaum,
    Mlle Saal, Herr Saal, Herr Vogel (Vogl), Herr
    Weinmüller, Herr Bondra
  VIENNA-GDMF; VIENNA-ROSENBAUM;
  Kellner/KREMSMUENSTER, 566

21 Dec GR Benefit-"Nieder-österreichische
    Scharfschützerkorps"
  program of 18 Dec
  VIENNA-GDMF

22 Dec B Tonkünstler Societät
           Haydn-*Die Schöpfung*-Mlle Saal, Herr Saal, Herr
           Rathmayer, Haydn directed?
           Pohl/TS, 66

23 Dec B Tonkünstler Societät
           program as 22 Dec
           Pohl/TS, 66

25 Dec GR Concert
           program of 18 Dec
           VIENNA-ROSENBAUM

1801

16 Jan GR Benefit-wounded soldiers
           Haydn-*Die Schöpfung*-Mlle Saal, Herr Saal, Herr
           Rathmayer
           director-Haydn
           VIENNA-ONB-TS; VIENNA-ROSENBAUM;
           WZ 4 Jan 01:119
           Kellner/KREMSMUENSTER, 567

30 Jan GR Benefit-wounded soldiers
           Joseph Haydn-sym-Haydn directed
           Nasolini-scene and aria from *Merope*-Mme
           Frank
           Beethoven-horn son (Op. 17)-Beethoven and
           Punto
           Nasolini-scene and duet from *Merope*-Frank and
           Herr Simoni
           Joseph Haydn-sym
           Cimarosa-trio with chorus from *Gli Orazi ed i
           Curiazi*-Mme Galvani, Frank, Simoni
           Rispoli-aria with obbligato horn-Simoni and
           Punto
           Cimarosa-scene and finale from *Gli Orazi ed i
           Curiazi*-Galvani, Frank, Simoni and chorus
           VIENNA-GDMF; VIENNA-ROSENBAUM; WZ
           21 Jan 01:194; WZ 7 Feb 01:398; BL 1:49
           AMZ 18 Feb 01:367; Kellner/KREMSMUENSTER,
           568-69

25 Mar B Mme Auernhammer
Gyrowetz-sym from *Semiramis*
Joseph Weigl-aria from *La Principessa d'Amalfi*-
Mlle Saal
Beethoven-fp con-Auernhammer
Viotti-vln con-Clement
Mozart-fp quintet-Auernhammer and winds
Süssmayer-duet from *Die drey Sultaninnen*-Mlle
Saal, Herr Saal
Auernhammer-var on a theme from the ballet
Alceste-Auernhammer
(Haydn)-sym
VIENNA-ONB-TS; Kellner/KREMSMUENSTER,
570-571 (says Mozart instead of Gyrowetz sym)

25 Mar W Emanuel Schikaneder—director
Joseph Haydn-new sym
Sarti-aria-Mme Willmann
horn con-Punto
vlc var-Herr Willmann
Vogl (Vogel)-overture to *Démophon*
Paisiello-duet-Willmann, Herr Hüller
horn quintet-Punto
Haydn-sym
VIENNA-STB

25 Mar L Theater orchestra
Haydn-*Die Schöpfung*
VIENNA-ROSENBAUM; VIENNA-MUELLER

29 Mar B Tonkünstler Societät
Eybler-sym
Haydn-*Die sieben Worte*-Mme Rosenbaum née
Gassmann, Josepha Hammer, Herr Wein-
müller, Sigismund Hüller; Haydn directed
vln con-Alois Tomasini
Pohl/TS, 66

30 Mar B Tonkünstler Societät
sym and cantata as on 29 Mar
Schindlöcker-vlc con-Schindlöcker
Pohl/TS, 66

31 Mar B   Benefit-"Theaterarmen"
              Mozart-*La Clemenza di Tito*-Herr Pasqua, Mme
              Rosenbaum, Mme Calvani-Willmann, Mme
              Schüller, Herr Saal
              Casimir Cartellieri-oboe con-Herr Czerwenka
              VIENNA-ONB-TS; VIENNA-ROSENBAUM

31 Mar W   Herr Punto
              WZ 28 Mar 01:1057; VIENNA-SEYFRIED

5 Apr R   Concert
              Haydn-sym
              clar con-Anton Stadler
              Weigl-"Das beste Geschenk" (cantata)
              VIENNA-ROSENBAUM

3 May A   Concert
              VIENNA-ZINZENDORF

29 May GR Joseph Haydn
              Haydn-*Die Jahreszeiten*
              VIENNA-ROSENBAUM; WZ 20 May 01:1838

6 Jun A   Schuppanzigh series opening concert
              Winter-aria-Mme Willmann
              Beethoven-fp con-Mme Auernhammer
              Mozart-vocal quartet
              VIENNA-ROSENBAUM; WZ 27 May 01:1946

11 Jun A   Schuppanzigh series
              Mozart-arias from *La Clemenza di Tito*-Mme
                Rosenbaum
              Weigl-vocal rondo-Mme Rosenbaum
              vln con-Herr Mayseder
              VIENNA-ROSENBAUM; VIENNA-GDMF

18 Jun A   Schuppanzigh series
              aria-Mme Willmann
               VIENNA-ROSENBAUM

25 Jun A   Schuppanzigh series
               aria-Mme Rosenbaum
               VIENNA-ROSENBAUM

8 Aug	A	Schuppanzigh series

8 Aug A Schuppanzigh series
vln con-Herr Mayseder
VIENNA-ROSENBAUM:
VIENNA-GDMF-MAYSEDER

20 Aug A Schuppanzigh series
"Ombre Adorato"-Mme Willmann
VIENNA-ROSENBAUM

27 Aug A Schuppanzigh series
vln con-Herr Mayseder
(Peter Winter)-aria from *Das Opferfest*
-Mlle Brückl
VIENNA-ROSENBAUM;
VIENNA-GDMF-MAYSEDER

3 Sep A Schuppanzigh series
arias-Mme Rosenbaum
VIENNA-ROSENBAUM

8 Sep W Concert
VIENNA-ROSENBAUM; VIENNA-SEYFRIED

10 Sep A Schuppanzigh series
arias-Mme Rosenbaum
VIENNA-ROSENBAUM

17 Sep A Schuppanzigh series
arias-Mme Rosenbaum
VIENNA-ROSENBAUM

24 Sep A Schuppanzigh series
arias-Mme Rosenbaum
concert cancelled because of rain
VIENNA-ROSENBAUM

15 Nov L Joseph Rotter
Wenzel Müller-new sym with double chorus of
trumpets and timpani
Martini-new aria-Mlle Perschl
Joseph Schmid-fantasy-Joseph Schmid
Cimarosa-aria-Joseph Rotter
Feyer-vln con-Herr Katschinzki
Campi-new aria-Mme Stephanie

Mozart-"In diesen heiligen Hallen"-Herr
Pfeiffer
Pfeiffer-vln con-Pfeiffer
Righini-aria-Rotter
Kauer-new military sym
VIENNA-STB

22 Dec B Tonkünstler Societät
Joseph Haydn-*Die Jahreszeiten*-Therese Saal,
Herr Saal, Herr Rathmayer
director-Haydn
Pohl/TS, 66

23 Dec B Tonkünstler Societät
program as on 22 Dec
Pohl/TS, 66

27 Dec GR Benefit for St. Marx Bürgerspital
Haydn-*Die Schöpfung*-Haydn directed
VIENNA-ROSENBAUM; WZ 19 Dec 01:4520

28 Dec J Herr Capeller—flutist
WZ 23 Dec 01:4566

1802

25 Mar B Mme Auernhammer
Mozart-sym from *La Clemenza di Tito*
aria with recit-Mlle Saal
Ludwig van Beethoven-fp con-Auernhammer
Cimarosa-aria-Herr Brizzi
Abbé Gelinek-fp trio-Auernhammer
Müllner-harp fantasy-Müllner
Salieri-duet from *Axur*-Mlle Salieri and Brizzi
Auernhammer-var on the second march from
(Pär's) *Achille*-Auernhammer
sym
VIENNA-ONB-TS; MT, 205-07

25 Mar W   Benefit-"Fondes für das Kinder-Kranken Institut"
Haydn-*Die Schöpfung*-Mme Willmann, Herr
Teimer, chorus from the Hofkapelle, Schot-
tenstift, and Barnabiten-Kollegiums zum
heiligen Michael
director-Haydn
VIENNA-SEYFRIED; PZ 20 Apr 02

2 Apr B   Herr and Mme Pär
Pär-new overture
Pär-polonaise-Mme Riccardi Pär
Pär-trio "Una campana antica" from *Camilla*
Pär-"Luci Crideli" from *Camilla*-Herr Saal
Pär-recit and trio "Sotto mentita faccia" from
Achille-Herr Brizzi, Herr Saal, Herr Vogel
(Vogl)
Pär-first finale from *Camilla*
Pär-new aria to *Achille*-Vogel
Pär-"No crudel" from *Camilla*-Mme Pär, Saal
Trento-scene and aria-Brizzi
Pär-new aria to *Achille*-Mme Pär, Vogel
Pär-rondo "Clemente ciel" from *Camilla*-Mme
Pär
Pär-second finale with chorus from *Camilla*
Herr Angrisani d.A and d.J., Herr Massa, and
Herr Lotti also sang
VIENNA-ONB-TS; AMZ 21 Apr 02:493-94

8 Apr J   Bohdanowicz family
Martini-overture from *Heinrich IV*
Cimarosa-"Giovane sventurato" from
L'Olympiade-Catharina B.
Paisiello-"Madame pour vous plaire" from
Deux Comtesses (Le due contesse)-Therese B.
Cimarosa-"Che tremore nelle vene," quintet
from *Le trame deluse*
vln son "called:Les premices du monde, which
will be played by 3 people with 12 fingers
and 3 violin bows on a single normal violin"
Giordanello-"Toi que j'adore"-Josepha B.

Giordanello-same aria with Italian text, ''Caro
mio bene'' ''with very complicated variations
and passages that will draw astonishment
from the audience that is inclined to listen''
''newest original (work), entitled *Rareté
extraordinare de la Musique*. An Andantino
with 4 variations set for 4 people on a fortepiano, that is, for 8 hands or 40 fingers
which will be played by the 4 natural sisters
of the Bohdanowicz family''
Caruso-''Partir degg'io amato bene,'' rondo
from *Scipione in Carthagena*-Anna B.
Europas Erstling. ''an original trio concerto,
which will be performed on 3 natural instruments that have second place; singing
has the first, and whistling the third. This
serious, grand trio concerto consists of 265
4/4 notes accompanied by the entire orchestra
with trumpets and drums, has 6 large and
small solos, in which my three oldest sons
have the principle voices. Their solos consist
of all manner of passages, ligatures, stac-
catos, trills, ornaments, etc. The cadence is
especially distinguished by a three-voiced
trill.
''A double original, *a quadro*, which consists of
120 measures, entitled ''Non plus ultra,'' will
be sung by my 4 daughters; I, together with
my three oldest sons—4 violin bows and 16
fingers on a single violin neck''
Cimarosa-''Que cette main blanchette, me batte
et me souflette''-Catharina and Anna B.
''Between the first and second halves of the
academy there will be a vocal symphony
without text with 9 voices and as many
speaking pipes of various sizes with an extraordinarily good and special effect. It consists of an allegro, which will be sung very
noisily by an 18-voice choir, one visible, one
off stage, which often divide themselves into

313

3 choirs, 1 visible, two off stage. Also characteristic of this Andante is the comic cry of the hens, that-at the sight of their enemy-run together and then disperse, therein, the cuckoo and the "Baumhacker", a forest bird, will be imitated. Finally, a presto, entitled "The hunt," this expresses, along with a beautiful melody, the cries and howls of the hunting hounds, the middle and strongest murmer of the bears in a very comical composition; after the cries of the hunters, however, occur the collective shots of the latter at the bears."

VIENNA-GDMF, AMZ 21 Apr 02:494-96

(The latter reprinted the entire program without comment. For the entire German program, see Appendix 5.)

9 Apr	B	Ph. Dornaus—horn harp con with horn-Dornaus and Josepha Müllner (Mozart?)-"Sott're Pini del boschetto," from *Le Nozze di Figaro* VIENNA-ZINZENDORF; WZ 3 Apr 02:1177
11 Apr	B	Tonkünstler Societät Haydn-*Die Jahreszeiten*-Therese Saal, Herr Rathmayer, Herr Saal director-Haydn Pohl/TS, 67
12 Apr	B	Tonkünstler Societät program as on 11 Apr Pohl/TS, 66
12 Apr	J	Georg Bayr—flutist Cimarosa-aria-Mme Rosenbaum VIENNA-ROSENBAUM; WZ 3 Apr 02:1177
13 Apr	B	Benefit "Theaterarmen" Haydn-sym Zingarelli-vocal quartet-Mme Rosenbaum, Mlle Saal, Herr Vogel (Vogl), Herr Weinmüller

Righini-aria-Weinmüller
Tarchi-duet-Rosenbaum, Herr Brizzi
harp fantasy-Mlle Müllner
Sarti-aria-Mlle Saal
Mayer-vocal quartet-Rosenbaum, Saal, Brizzi,
    Weinmüller
aria-Rosenbaum
Tarchi-duet-Saal and Brizzi
Eybler-clar con-Joseph Stadler
Cimarosa-aria-Brizzi
Mayer-vocal quartet-Rosenbaum, Saal, Brizzi,
    Vogel
VIENNA-ONB-TS

21 Apr J Jolien Beau (13 years—violinist)
           aria-Mme Rosenbaum
           vocal rondo-Mme Rosenbaum
           VIENNA-ROSENBAUM

24 Apr J Herr Ruffati and Herr Bartelozzi
           aria-Mme Rosenbaum
           VIENNA-ROSENBAUM

27 May A Concert
           VIENNA-ZINZENDORF

3 Jun   A Schuppanzigh series-opening concert
           aria-Mlle Gloy
           VIENNA-ROSENBAUM; WZ 26 May 02:1947

10 Jun A Schuppanzigh series
           aria from *Mortovina*-Mlle Gloy
           Polacca-Gloy
           vln con-Herr Loginow Labanow
           VIENNA-ROSENBAUM

19 Jun A Schuppanzigh series
           Cimarosa-aria and rondo-Mme Rosenbaum
           VIENNA-ROSENBAUM

24 Jun A Schuppanzigh series
           aria-Mme Campi
           VIENNA-ROSENBAUM

1 Jul A Schuppanzigh series
     Pär-aria "Sa Griselda"-Mlle Gloy
     duet from *Ciabattino ingentilito*-Gloy and Herr
      Mayer (Meier)
     VIENNA-ROSENBAUM

Summer A Schuppanzigh series-various concerts
     Mozart-piece
     Haydn-syms
     Seyfried-sym
     Beethoven-ballet overture (*Die Geschöpfe des Prometheus*, Op. 43)
     MT, 205-07; Fischer, 76

12 Aug A Schuppanzigh series
     aria-Mme Campi
     vln con-German violinist
     VIENNA-ROSENBAUM

19 Aug A Schuppanzigh series
     aria-Mme Willmann
     VIENNA-ROSENBAUM

26 Aug A Schuppanzigh series
     aria-Mme Willmann
     VIENNA-ROSENBAUM

2 Sep A Schuppanzigh series
     Pleyel-aria-Mme Rosenbaum
     Weigl-aria-Mme Rosenbaum
     Beethoven-fp con-Miss Stummer
     Cherubini-overture to *Les deux journée*s
     VIENNA-ROSENBAUM

9 Sep A Schuppanzigh series
     aria-Mme Willmann
     VIENNA-ROSENBAUM

16 Sep A Schuppanzigh series
     aria-Mme Campi
     VIENNA-ROSENBAUM

30 Sep A Ignaz Schuppanzigh
     Haydn-*Die Schöpfung*
     WZ 25 Sep 02:3471

15 Nov J   Bohdanowicz family
                  VIENNA-ROSENBAUM; WZ 10 Nov 02:4029

15 Nov L   Herr Rotter
                  VIENNA-MUELLER

15 Nov W   Concert
                  VIENNA-SEYFRIED

Advent KR   Ferdinand Fränzel—violinist
                  VIENNA-INDENDENZ

5 Dec GR   Ignaz and Anton Böck (Bök)—horn players
                  WZ 1 Dec 02:4332

19 Dec KR   Ferdinand Frönil—violinist
                  WZ 18 Dec 02:4557

22 Dec B   Tonkünstler Societät
                  Haydn-*Die Jahreszeiten*-Therese Saal, Herr Saal,
                     Herr Rathmayer
                  director-Haydn
                  Pohl/TS, 67

23 Dec B   Tonkünstler Societät
                  program as on 22 December
                  Pohl/TS, 66

26 Dec GR   Benefit-"St Marx Bürgerspital"
                  Haydn-*Die Schöpfung*
                  director-Haydn
                  VIENNA-ZINZENDORF; VIENNA-
                  ROSENBAUM; WZ 18 Dec 02:4557

1803

20 Mar ?   Herr Dulon
                  Beethoven-horn son (Op. 17)-Herr Meyerbeer
                  Forbes/BEETHOVEN, 361

25 Mar B   Mme Auernhammer
                  Beethoven-overture (*Prometheus?*)
                  Righini-aria-Mlle Schmalz

Anton Eberl-fp con with trumpets and
timpani-Auernhammer
(Pär?)-aria from *Il Principe di Taranto*-Herr Brizzi
Eberl-new caprice for 2 fp-Auernhammer and
Eberl
Cannabich-vln con-"jünger Böhm"
Hummel-duet-Schmalz and Brizzi
Auernhammer-var on the march from *Die Tage
der Gefahr (Les deux journées)*
(Cherubini)-Auernhammer
sym
VIENNA-ONB-TS; FM 12 Apr 03; ZEW 16 Apr
03:362; AMZ 25 May 03:589

25 Mar   L   Ferdinand Kauer
Kauer-"Die Geschichte des Wiener-
Aufgeboths" (battle sym)
VIENNA-STB; AMZ 25 May 03:590; MT, 213-14;
FM 12 Apr 03:230

25 Mar   W   Concert
Süssmayer-*Moses, oder der Auszug aus Egypten*
VIENNA-SEYFRIED; FM 12 Apr 03:230

1 Apr   J   Herr Mayseder
Mozart-"Parto, parto" from *La Clemenza di Tito*-
Mme Rosenbaum
VIENNA-ROSENBAUM

2 Apr   J   Herr Hradetzky (Hradezky)—horn player
Weigl aria-Mme Rosenbaum
VIENNA-ROSENBAUM

3 Apr   B   Tonkünstler Societät
Joseph Haydn-sym
Ferdinand Pär-*Das heilige Grab*-Therese Saal,
Ludwig Marchesi, Ignaz Saal, Joseph Simoni;
Pär directed
Anton Wranitzky and Martin Schlesinger-
double con for 2 vln-Wranitzky and
Schlesinger
Pohl/TS, 67

4 Apr B Tonkünstler Societät
            cantata and sym as on 3 Apr
            Witt-clar con-Joseph Bähr
            Pohl/TS, 67

5 Apr B Benefit-''Theaterarmen''
            Haydn-*Die Schöpfung*-Mlle Saal, Herr Saal, Herr
              Rathmayer
            VIENNA-ONB-TS

5 Apr W Ludwig van Beethoven
            Beethoven-*Christus am Oelberge*
            Beethoven-sym (No. 1)
            Beethoven-sym (No. 2)
            Beethoven-fp con (Op. 37)-Beethoven
            BL 1:87; VIENNA-ROSENBAUM; AMZ 25 May
            03:590; FM 17 May 03:310; MT, 211; Wegeler &
            Ries/NOTIZEN, 91-92; ZEW 16 Apr 03:363-64

20 Apr K Franz (François) Naderman-harpist
            var on the march from Figaro
            var on the march ''played at the execution of
              the king (of France)''
            VIENNA-ROSENBAUM; AMZ 25 May 03:589;
            WTA

27 Apr GR Mme Mara
            Paisiello-duet-Mara and Herr Brizzi
            Cartellieri-oboe con-Grohmann
            VIENNA-ROSENBAUM; PZ 17 May 03; WTA

17 May A George Polgreen Bridgetower
            Forbes/BEETHOVEN, 332

18 May J Herr Bartelozzi—mandolin player
            arias-Mlle Hackel, Herr Massa
            VIENNA-ROSENBAUM

24 May A George Polgreen Bridgetower
            Beethoven-vln son (Op. 47)-Bridgetower
            aria-Mme Willmann
            VIENNA-ROSENBAUM; FM 1 Aug 03:484;
            Forbes/BEETHOVEN, 332

29 Jun   A   Benefit "Handlungs Institut"
                Kramer-sym-Kramer directed
                fp con-Mlle Stenzel
                Pär-aria from *Camilla*-Mlle Schmalz
                Hummel-melodrama-Mme Roose
                aria-Herr Brizzi, Herr Angrisani, Herr Massa
                   and chorus
                VIENNA-ROSENBAUM

Summer   A   Dorner brothers
                FM 1 Aug 03:484

Summer   A   Schuppanzigh series-various concerts
                Haydn-sym
                Cherubini-overtures to *Die Tagen der Gefahr* (*Les*
                   deux journées), *Medea* (*Médée*), *Lodoïska*, *Das*
                   Portugesische Gasthaus (*L'Hôtellerie portugaise*)
                Righini-overture
                Eberl-aria with obbligato English horn-Anna
                   Milder
                Eberl-fp con-Mlle Hohenadel
                Mozart-sym in C major (K. 551)
                arias-Mme Willmann
                arias-Mlle Hakel (Hackel)
                FM 1 Aug 03:483; ZEW 10 Nov 03:1074-75

28 Jul   A   Schuppanzigh series
                arias-Mlle Hackel and Herr Fröhlich
                VIENNA-ROSENBAUM

22 Sep   A   Schuppanzigh series-final concert
                Haydn-aria-Mlle Milder
                Mozart-fp con-Miss Stummer
                VIENNA-ROSENBAUM; ZEW 10 Nov 03:1074-75

15 Dec   KR   Herr Kalmus and Herr Mitsch—cellist and
                   waldhorn player
                Naumann-aria-Mme Willmann
                "chitarre" pieces-Mitsch
                WZ 7 Dec 03:4630; ZEW 26
                Jan 04:85-86; FM 20 Jan 04:54

22 Dec B Tonkünstler Societät
Abbé Vogler-*Kastor und Pollux* (*Castore e Polluce*)-Mme von Frank née Gerhardi, Mlle Schmalz, Herr Brizzi, Herr Massa, Herr Saal
director-Vogler
Pohl/TS, 67

23 Dec B Tonkünstler Societät
program as on 22 Dec
Pohl/TS, 67

26 Dec GR Benefit-"St Marx Bürgerspital"
Haydn-*Die sieben Worte*-Mlle Schmalz, Mlle Flamm, Herr Weinmüller, Herr Bondra; Haydn directed
vln con-Herr Mayseder
WZ 21 Dec 03:4817; WZ 7 Jan 04:47; AMZ 11 Jan 04:251; FM 20 Jan 04:54; ZEW 26 Jan 04:86

1804

6 Jan J Herr Eberl—fortepianist with Herr Kalmus and Herr Lieber—cellists
Eberl-overture in D minor
Eberl fp con-Eberl
Pleyel-cello duet-Kalmus and Lieber
Eberl-sym in E flat major
Eberl-double fp con-Eberl and Mlle Hohenadel
AMZ 1 Feb 04:294; AMZ 11 Apr 04:468-70; FM 20 Jan 04:55; ZEW 28 Jan 04:93-94
WZ 4 Jan 04:44

Spring J Herr Kalmus
Eberl-duet for cello and fp-Kalmus and Eberl
AMZ 9 May 04:545-46

Spring J Herr Kalkbrenner and Herr Klengel—fortepianists
double fp con in C major-Kalkbrenner and Klengel
AMZ 13 Jun 04:621

2 Mar B   Mme Auernhammer
Anton Eberl-overture from *Die Königen der schwarzen Inseln*
Pär-aria with recit "O la virtu al cimento" from *Griselda*-Mlle Auernhammer
Eberl-fp con in E flat major with trumpets and timpani-Auernhammer
Cimarosa-aria with chorus-Herr Brizzi
Adalbert Gyrowetz-son for fp, clar, vlc-Auernhammer, Herr Stadler d.A., Herr Gennsbacher
Dornaus-duet con for horns-2 students of Joseph Leitgab
(Simon Mayer)-duet from *Ginevra*-Mlle Auernhammer and Herr Brizzi
Auernhammer-var on a theme from Gallet's ballet *Die verliebten Thorheiten*-Auernhammer
Franz Klemp-"Polonaise" played on "ein brauner Krug"-Leitgab students
VIENNA-ONB-TS; AMZ 11 Apr 04:471; ZEW 24 Mar 04:284

23 Mar B   Mlle Müllner
Silver Müller-sym
harp con-Müllner
Paisiello-aria from *Il Re Teodoro*-Herr Brizzi
Anton Cartellieri-vlc con-Herr Kraft d.J.
Naumann-vocal quartet from the oratorio *I Peligrini*-Mlle Saal, Mlle Gassmann, Herr Brizzi, Herr Weinmüller, with the accompaniment of harp, 2 clar, 2 bassoons, 2 horns
harp fantasy with var-Müllner
Méhul-new overture
VIENNA-ONB-TS; VIENNA-ROSENBAUM; WZ 14 Mar 04:919: AMZ 13 Jun 04:621; FM 3 May 04:351

Lent   ?   Herr Kraft d.J.
FM 3 May 04:351

Lent   ?   Herr Metzger and Herr Flat
FM 3 May 04:351; AMZ 13 Jun 04:621

25 Mar   B   Tonkünstler Societät
              Haydn-*Die Schöpfung*-Mlle Saal, Herr
                  Rathmayer, Herr Saal
              Pohl/TS, 67

26 Mar   B   Tonkünstler Societät
              program as on 25 Mar
              Pohl/TS, 67

26 Mar   W   Abbé Vogler
              sym
              "Die Anrufung der Sonne um Mitternacht in
                  Lappland," a capella trio
              "Impromtü des sterbenden Metastasio"
                  arranged as a hymn, sung by a voice, then
                  repeated by the chorus
              "Lob der Harmonie," "from Prof. Meisner,
                  named 'Trichordium' after the melodie of J.J.
                  Rousseau's *Zu drei Tönen*, presented by a
                  chorus and accompanied by var in an in-
                  strumental chorus"
              "Overture to Kotzebue's 'Kreuzfahren,' in
                  which is to be encountered the march of Karl
                  the 12th by Narva and an authentic barbar-
                  esque notated in Africa by the Abbé himself;
                  also, the agreement of the Ritter Balduin and
                  Emus is portrayed"
              "Das Benedictus" from the mass of Abbé
                  Vogler, as an a capella vocal quartet
              "Israels Gebet zu Jehova," "from Moses
                  Mendelssohn's translation of Psalm 84; a
                  small cantata that closes with a bravura aria
                  in which other solos and the chorus enter"
              "Ein nordisches Lied" with var and a pedal
                  fugue on the fp-Vogler
              VIENNA-ROSENBAUM; VIENNA-SEYFRIED;
              WZ 17 Mar 04:971; AMZ 13 Jun 04:621-22; FM 3
              May 04:351; ZEW 5 Apr 04:325-26 (See appendix
              5 for the German text.)

27 Mar   B   Benefit-"Theaterarmen"
             Winter-cantata-Herr Brizzi, Mme Natorp, Mme
                Rosenbaum, Mme Campi, Herr Weinmüller
             oboe con-Herr Flat
             fl con-Herr Metzger
             VIENNA-ROSENBAUM; FM 3 May 04:351

27 Mar   W   Sebastian Meier
             Beethoven-*Christus am Oelberge*
             Cherubini-aria-Mlle Milder
             VIENNA-SEYFRIED; FM 3 May 04:351

1 Apr   GR   Benefit-"Wohlthätigkeitsanstalten"
             Rode-vln con-Herr Mayseder
             singers-Baroness Beatrice Natorp, Herr
                Krebner, Prof. Sonnleithner, Herr Brizzi
             VIENNA-ZINZENDORF; WZ 11 Apr 04:1333-34;
             FM 3 May 04:351

a12 Apr   W   Anna Maria Willmann
             VIENNA-ROSENBAUM; AMZ 13 Jun 04:622

13 Apr   J   Herr Thieriot—violinist
             WZ 7 Apr 04:1290; 13 Jun 04:621

30 Apr   K   Anton Brizzi
             Pär-"Eloise ed Abelard agli elisi" (cantata)
             Brenta, Terziani, Cordelieri-"L'alleanza degli
                sul istro" (cantata)
             WHTA 1805; AMZ 9 May 04:545; AMZ 13 Jun
             04:622

20 May   GR   Benefit-"Wohlthätigkeitsanstalten"
             Pär-*Il trionfo della Chiesa* (oratorio)-Herr
                Crescentini, Herr Simoni, Herr Saal, Herr
                Weinmüller; Hofkapelle
             director-Pär
             Mlle Müllner played harp
             VIENNA-ZINZENDORF; WZ 16 May 04:1921;
             AMZ 13 Jun 04:620

24 May   A   Schuppanzigh series-opening concert
             Beethoven-sym in D major

Beethoven-fp con (Op. 37?)-Herr Ries
Mozart-overture to *Die Zauberflöte*
Arnold-vln con-Herr Schindlöcker d.J.
Mozart-sym in G minor (K. 550)
WZ 16 May 04:1921; AMZ 15 Aug 04: 776-77

5 Jun   KR   Vincenzo Righini
Righini-*Alcide al Bivio* (opera)-Mlle Fischer, Herr
Fischer, Herr Brizzi; Righini directed
WZ 30 May 04:2139; AMZ 13 Jun 04:619-20; FM
29 May 04:428

Summer A   Schuppanzigh series-various concerts
Haydn-sym
Mozart-sym in G minor (K. 550)
Eberl-sym in E-flat Major
Beethoven-fp con (Op. 37?)-Herr Ries
Eberl-fp con in E-flat Major-Mlle Hohenadel
Kreutzer-fp con in E Major-Herr Kreutzer
fl con-Herr Schuster
vln con-Herr Böhm
Blumenthal brothers-trio con for 2 vlns and
viole-Blumenthal brothers
Mozart-overtures to *Die Zauberflöte* and *La
Clemenza di Tito*
Cherubini-overtures to *Medea* (*Médée*), *Lodoïska*,
Die Tagen der Gefahr (*Les deux journées*)
Righini-overture to *Tigranes*
Beethoven-overture to *Prometheus*
AMZ 5 Sep 04:823-24

21 Jun A   Schuppanzigh series
Rode-vln con-Herr Thieriot
Nasolini-aria-Mlle Sattmann
VIENNA-ROSENBAUM; AMZ 5 Sep 04:823-24

5 Jul A   Schuppanzigh series
Mozart-clar con (K. 622)-Herr Stadler
Pär-aria from *Camilla*-Mlle Hackel
VIENNA-ROSENBAUM; AMZ 5 Sep 04:823-24

Sep A   Schuppanzigh series
           Gluck-overture to *Iphigenie*
           Viotti-vln con-Herr Schuppanzigh
           Cannabich-vln duet-Schuppanzigh and Herr
             Mayseder
           Righini-overture to *Tigranes*
           AMZ 17 Oct 04:42

15 Nov GR   Benefit-"Wohlthätigkeitsanstalten"
           Abbé Vogler-*Atalie* (oratorio)-Victoria Sessi,
             Mlle Laucher d.A., Herr Weinmüller; Ludwig
             Brizzi
           director-Vogler
           VIENNA-ROSENBAUM; WZ 7 Nov 04:4531; WZ
           2 Feb 05:433; AMZ 12 Dec 04:174; FM 18 Dec
           04:488

15 Nov W   Theater orchestra
           VIENNA-SEYFRIED

15 Nov L   Ignaz Schuster
           Mozart-overture to *La Clemenza di Tito*
           Pär-aria-Mlle Schmierer
           Kramer-oboe con-Herr Grohmann
           Süssmayer-aria from "Die Freywilligen"-Anton
             Schuster
           Joseph Eybler-overture to *Das Zauberschwerdt*
           "Das erste Quodlibit aus der unrühigen
             Nachbarschaft"-Ignaz Schuster
           Cimarosa-comic duet-I. and A. Schuster
           Henneberg-"Noturno von 8 Singstimmen mit
             Echo und deutschem Text"
           Ignaz Schuster-"neues deutsches
             Gelegenheitslied"-Ignaz Schuster
           VIENNA-STB

6 Dec J   Louis Wolf—guitarist
           guitar con-Wolf
           Mozart-fp con in D minor (K. 466)-Mme Wolf
           WZ 1 Dec 04:4930; AMZ 9 Jan 04:242

13 Dec   R   Therese Blangini—violinist and singer
Viotti-vln con-Blangini
vocal duet-Blangini and Mlle Laucher
WZ 5 Dec 04:4948; AMZ 9 Jan 05:242

b16 Dec   J   Mme Bigot de Morogues
Mozart-fp con in C major (K. 467 or K. 503)-
Bigot de Morogues
AMZ 9 Jan 04:242

22 Dec   B   Tonkünstler Societät
Haydn-*Die Jahreszeiten*-Mlle Saal, Herr
Rathmayer, Herr Saal
Pohl/TS, 67

23 Dec   B   Tonkünstler Societät
program as on 22 Dec
Pohl/TS, 67

25 Dec   GR   Benefit-"St Marx Bürgerspital"
Saul (oratorio)-Mlle Saal, Herr Saal, Herr
Krebner, Herr Weinmüller, Herr Vogel
(Vogl), Herr Bondra;
director-Joseph Weigl
orchestra director-Paul Wranitzky
Herr Umlauff at the keyboard
Mlle Müllner played harp
WZ 15 Dec 04:5097; WZ 5 Jan 05:46; AMZ 13 Feb
05:320-21

1805

25 Jan   J   Eberl
Eberl-overture to the cantata composed in St.
Petersburg
Eberl-double fp con in B-flat-Eberl and Mlle
Hohenadel
Eberl-sym in D major
Eberl-var on the march from Grétry's *Blaubart*-
Eberl and Hohenadel

vln var-Mlle Blangini
chorus set for instruments
WZ 19 Jan 05:280; AMZ 13 Feb 05:322; FM 7
Feb 05:108

Lent   J?   Herr Hradezky
arias-Mlle Milder
AMZ 17 Apr 05:468; FM 19 Apr 05:212

Lent   J?   Herr Hamburger
Steibelt-fp con-Hamburger
Hummel-trio in E flat major
vln con-Herr Möglich
AMZ 17 Apr 05:468; FM 19 Apr 05:212

Lent   J?   Herr Bartelozzi—mandolin player
con with guitar accompaniment-Herr Bartelozzi
and son
Pleyel-sym
aria-Abbé Bevilaqua
AMZ 1 May 05:500

Lent   R   Mme Brizzi
Hummel-con for fp and vln-Hummel and Anton Wranitzky
fantasy
AMZ 12 Jun 05:592

Lent   J   Herr Mayseder
Fränzel-vln con in D major-Mayseder
AMZ 12 Jun 05:593; FM 19 Apr 05:212

25 Mar   B   Mme Auernhammer
Gluck-overture to *Iphigenie*
Mussiny (Mussini)-aria-Mlle Laucher
Mozart-fp con (K. 466)-Auernhammer
Mayer-aria-Herr Brizzi d.A.
Steibelt-duet for harp and fp-Mlle Müllner and
Auernhammer
Mozart-horn con-Giuseppi Pancioli
Pär-duet-Laucher and Brizzi
Auernhammer-var on "In des Tyrannen Eisen-
macht" from (Méhul's) *Die beyden*
Füchse-Auernhammer

sym
VIENNA-ONB-TS;WZ 20 Mar 05:1188
AMZ 17 Apr 05:469; FM 19 Apr 05:212;
BMZ 1:32 (1805):128

25 Mar　L　Bartholomäus Bondra
Haydn-4 voice echo "Gesang"
Haydn-4 voice "Gesang" with fp accompani-
ment, "Die Beredsamkeit"-Herr Pfeiffer, Ig-
naz and Anton Schuster, Bondra
Haydn-3 voice "Gesang," "Die Naturgaben"-
Pfeiffer, Ignaz Schuster, Bondra
Mozart-4 hand fp son-Josepha Hensler and
Theresia Bondra
Haydn-4 voice "Gesang," "Die Harmonie in
der Ehe"-Pfeiffer, 2 Schusters, Bondra
Haydn-3 voice "Gesang"
Haydn-3 voice "Gesang," "Daphnes einziger
Fehler"
Haydn-4 voice "Gesang," "Alles hat seine
Zeit"
Haydn-"Frühling, Sommer und Herbst" from
Die Jahreszeiten-Mme Doberauer, Pfeiffer,
Bondra
VIENNA-STB

25 Mar　W　Franz Teyber
Teyber-Der sterbende Jesu
VIENNA-SEYFRIED; AMZ 17 Apr 05:469; FM 19
Apr 05:212

31 Mar　R　Herr Weidinger—keyed trumpet player
Handel-aria with trumpet from an oratorio
Weidinger
WZ 23 Mar 05:1255-56; FM 19 Apr 05:212

7 Apr　B　Tonkünstler Societät
Haydn-Die Schöpfung-Antonie Laucher, Abbé
Bevilaqua, Carl Weinmüller
Pohl/TS, 67

7 Apr W   Franz Clement
                Cherubini-overture to *Anacréon*
                Nasolini-scene from *Cleopatra*-Mlle Müller
                Clement-vln con (D major)-Clement
                Haydn-chorus, "Der Sturm"
                Beethoven-new sym in D-sharp major-
                  Beethoven directed
                Cherubini-trio from *Anacréon*-Mlle Milder,
                  Müller, Herr Demmer
                vln fantasy-Clement
                Cherubini-quartet from *Anacréon*-Milder,
                  Müller, Demmer, Herr Meier
                Clement-new overture
                WZ 30 Mar 05:1384; AMZ 1 May 05:500-501;
                FM 26 Apr 05:332; BMZ 1:44 (1805):174; WIEN
                FESTSCHRIFT

8 Apr B   Tonkünstler Societät
                program as on 7 Apr
                Pohl/TS, 67

8 Apr W   Constanze Mozart
                Mozart-sym in G minor (K. 550)
                Mozart-fp con in C major (K. 503)-Franz
                  Mozart
                cantata-Franz Mozart
                Idomeneo
                Mozart-var on minuet from *Don Giovanni*-Franz
                  Mozart
                VIENNA-GDMF; VIENNA-ROSENBAUM;
                WZ 23 Mar 05:1255; AMZ 1 May 05:502-503;
                FM 30 Apr 05:344;
                BMZ 1:44 (1805):174

9 Apr B   Benefit-"Theaterarmen"
                Winter-*Tamerlan* (oratorio)-Mlle Milder, Herr
                  Saal, Herr Weinmüller, Herr Vogel (Vogl)
                 VIENNA-ROSENBAUM; AMZ 1 May 05:504;
                FM 30 Apr 05:344

9 Apr W   Benefit-"Theaterarmen"
                Mozart-*Requiem*
                VIENNA-SEYFRIED; FM 30 Apr 05:344

14 Apr GR Benefit "Wohlthätigkeitsanstalten"
              Cherubini-*Anacréon* (opera)-Mlle Laucher d.A.,
              Mlle Müller, Herr Vogel (Vogl), Herr
              Neumann, Mlle Menner; orchestra director-
              Joseph Weigl; director-Salieri
              VIENNA-ROSENBAUM; WZ 6 Apr 05:1514; WZ
              18 May 05:2265-66; PZ 12 Apr 05; PZ 21 May 05;
              AMZ 15 May 05:532-34; FM 11 May 04:376

15 Apr R Herr Müller-Xänorphika player
              VIENNA-ROSENBAUM; AMZ 15 May 05:536-37

19 Apr J Conradin Kreutzer—fortepianist and
              clarinettist
              Kreutzer-overture to *Friedensfest*
              Kreutzer-fp con in E major-Kreutzer
              Kreutzer-clar con-Kreutzer
              WZ 13 Apr 05:1641-42; AMZ 15 May 05:535-36

1 May A Mme Bigot de Morogues
              Cherubini-overture to *Médée*
              aria-Mme Schmidt
              Mozart-fp con-Bigot de Morogues
              Eberl-new sym in D major
              con on Xänorphika-Herr Müller
              fp fantasy-Bigot de Morogues
              (Mozart?)-overture to *Don Juan*
              VIENNA-ROSENBAUM.; WZ 27 Apr 05:1936,
              AMZ 15 May 05:536; ZEW 11 May 05:451-54;
              FM 13 May 04:380; BMZ 1:44 (1805):174

9 May A Herr Zeuner
              Haydn-sym (in B-flat, written in London)
              Cimarosa-aria-Mme von Schmidt
              Zeuner-fp con (A minor)-Zeuner
              Méhul-overture to *Adrian*
              Zeuner-rondo and allegro-Zeuner
              Scottish ballad-Herr Elmenreich
              Zeuner-fp var-Zeuner
              WZ 4 May 05:2014: AMZ 29 May 05:570-71;
              BMZ 1:48 (1805):187-88

16 May A   Schuppanzigh series-opening concert
                Mozart-sym
                Beethoven-fp con (Op. 37)-Herr Ries
                Pär-aria-Mlle Milder
                WZ 1 May 05:1953; AMZ 19 Jun 05:613

23 May A   Schuppanzigh series
                Haydn-sym
                Beethoven-overture to *Prometheus*
                aria-Mlle Hackel
                clar con-Herr Firnak
                AMZ 19 Jun 05:613

28 May A   Johann Posch (on Xänorphika and a pyramid
             shaped fortepiano)
                pieces on Xänorphika
                Haydn-"Kaiserlied" with Xänorphika
                VIENNA-ROSENBAUM; WZ 22 May 05:2347
                AMZ 19 Jun 05:612-13

Summer A   Schuppanzigh series-various concerts
                Steibelt-fp con-Herr Hamburger
                fl con-Herr Bernardi
                Beethoven-fp con-Herr Stein
                Triebensee-clar con-Herr Zenker
                Haydn-sym in E flat major
                (Mozart?)-overture to *Don Juan*
                Viotti-vln con-Herr Raischel
                vln con-Pehatschek-(Pechacek)
                Dussek-fp con-Herr Mölzel
                Clement-vln con-Herr Sieber
                Kreutzer-fp son with vln accompaniment-Herr
                    Schuppanzigh
                AMZ 26 Jun 05:630; AMZ 24 Jul 05:689; AMZ 28
                Aug 05:767; AMZ 18 Sep 05:810-12

2 Jun B   Benefit-"Wohlthätigkeitsanstalten"
                W.A. Mozart-sym
                 Mayer-chorus
                Nasolini-aria-Mlle Laucher d.A. and chorus
                Cimarosa-aria-Abbé Bevilaqua
                Mayer-vocal quartet-Laucher, Anton Brizzi,
                    Bevilaqua, Herr Saal and chorus

Nasolini-duet-Brizzi and Bevilaqua
Müllner-harp fantasy-Müllner
Mayer-aria-Anton Brizzi and chorus
Mayer-finale-Laucher, Brizzi, Bevilaqua, Saal
and chorus
Paul Wranitzky directed orchestra; Joseph
Weigl directed
VIENNA-ONB-TS; WZ 29 May 05:2474; AMZ 19
Jun 05:613-14

b12 Jun ? Josef (Giuseppi) Siboni—singer
AMZ 26 Jun 05:629

12 Jun GR Marianna (Marie Anna) Sessi
Karnavich-sym
Farinelli-duet-Victoria and Marianna Sessi
Pär-aria-Victoria Sessi
Guglielmi-finale-Herr Bianchi, Herr Saal, Vic-
toria and Marianna Sessi
Joseph Weigl-vocal trio-Bianchi, Saal, Marianna
Sessi
Mayer-aria with chorus-Bianchi
Farinelli-aria with chorus-Marianna Sessi
Joseph Weigl-recit and canon-Victoria, Anna
Maria and Marianna Sessi
Mayer-finale with chorus-Brizzi, Victoria and
Marianna Sessi
VIENNA-ONB-MS; AMZ 26 Jun 05:629

13 Jun GR Benefit-"Wohlthätigkeitsanstalten"
program as on 12 Jun without the Weigl recit
and canon
VIENNA-ONB-MS; AMZ 26 Jun 05:629

8 Sep L Herr Schuster
VIENNA-ROSENBAUM

22 Sep J Herr Ferlendis
WZ Sep 05:4760; WTZ 23 Sep 06:167

10 Oct R Mme Bouchred née Thilmet
VIENNA-ROSENBAUM

22 Dec B Tonkünstler Societät
           Cherubini-grand overture
           Mussini-aria-Antonie Laucher
           Cherubini-chorus with solos-Laucher, Herr
             Ehlers, Herr Pfeiffer
           Pär-aria with clar-Mme Campi and Herr Stadler
           Cherubini-chorus
           Pär-aria-Herr Bianchi
           Cherubini-chorus with solos-Laucher, Herr
             Gerlitz, Ehlers, Pfeiffer
           Clement-new vln con-Clement
           Sarti-vocal trio-Campi, Laucher, Bianchi
           Cherubini-chorus
           director-Cherubini
           Pohl/TS, 67

23 Dec B Tonkünstler Societät
           program as on 22 Dec
           Pohl/TS, 67

24 Dec GR Benefit-"Theaterarmen"?
            Haydn-*Die Schöpfung*-Antonie Laucher, Herr
              Neumann, Herr Weinmüller
            VIENNA-ONB-TS; VIENNA-ROSENBAUM

25 Dec GR Benefit-"Theaterarmen"?
            Performers probably as on 24 Dec
            VIENNA-ROSENBAUM

1806

18 Jan O Abbé Vogler—organist
           March
           "Cantabile with the accompaniment of a glass
             harmonica"
           "Terassenlied der Afrikaner, wenn sie ihre
             platten Dä mit Kalch befestigen," in which
             two choruses alternate singing and stomping
           "Die Hirtenwonne vom Donnerwetter
             unterbrochen"

fl con: Allegro-Andante-Allegro
"Gesang der Hottentotten, der aus 3 Takten
und 3 Worten besteht: Mayema, Mayema,
Mayema, Huh, Huh, Huh"
"Die Belagerung von Jericho: a) Israels Gebet
zu Jehova; b) Trompetenschall; c) Umstürzen
der Mauern; d) Einzug der Sieger"
VIENNA-GDMF

23 Feb   R   Marianne Kirchgessner
Cherubini-overture to *Lodoïska*
Pär-aria from *Camilla*-Mlle Müller
"A short fantasy, as introduction to . . "
Mozart-quintet con (K. 617) for glass har-
monica, fl, oboe, viola and vlc-Kirchgessner,
Herr Czerwenka, Herr Gehring, Herr Rut-
zizka, Herr Deabis
Haydn-allegro
Wilms-clar con-Herr Springer
Weber-monologue from Schiller's Jungfrau von
Orleans-declaimed by Mme Roose with glass
harmonica accompaniment
Kirchgessner-theme with var-Kirchgessner
director-Clement
VIENNA-ONB-MS; PZ 25 Feb 06; AMZ 12 Mar
06:377; WJ 1 Mar 06:141-44

b15 Mar   J   Herr Leidesdorfer
Beethoven-fp con (Op. 37)-Leidesdorfer
Leidesdorfer-overture
WJ 15 Mar 06:189-90

16 Mar   J   Concert
Xänorphika piece-Anton Bidell
Clementi directed
PZ 25 Mar 06

25 Mar   B   Mme Auernhammer
Rösner-sym
Mayer-aria from *Alonzo und Coro* (*Alonso e
Cora*)-Mlle Auernhammer
(Pär?)-duet from *Sargines* (*Sargino*?)-Mlle Auern-
hammer and Ludwig Brizzi

335

Beethoven-fp con (Op. 37?)-Auernhammer
Steibelt-fp duet-Mme and Mlle Auernhammer
Auernhammer-var on theme from Beethoven's
Prometheus-Auernhammer
aria-Herr Verri
Clement-vln con-Clement
WZ 19 Mar 06:1106; AMZ 16 Apr 06:459; ZEW 3
May 06:432; WJ 15 Apr 06:241-46

25 Mar W   Herr Teimer
Cherubini-overture to *Bernhardsberg* (Eliza)
Winter-aria-Mme Campi
Xänorphika piece-Mlle Orofino
10-part wind band piece-Teimer on oboe
Mozart-vocal trio from *Don Giovanni*
Clement-overture
Clement-vln con-Clement
Fischer-"Dankgedichte an das Publikum"-
Teimer and two daughters
AMZ 16 Apr 06:459-60; WJ 15 Apr 06:246-47

25 Mar L   Leopold Pfeiffer
Clement-overture
"Anempfehlungs-Chor"-Herr Bondra, Herr
Blacho, Ignaz Schuster, Herr Pfeiffer
C. Kreutzer-aria with bassethorn-Mlle Hackel
Mestrino-vln con-student of Clement
Kreutzer-"Concertant-Chor"
Pfeiffer-"Instrumental Quartet" "which he will
accompany on the "Violon"
Mozart-Italian bass aria-Pfeiffer
Dussek-fp con-C. Kreutzer
C. Kreutzer-vocal duet-Hackel and Bondra
aria-"Mein Dank"
March from *Bacchus und Ariadne*
VIENNA-STB; AMZ 16 Apr 06:459-60; WJ 15 Apr
06:248-49

28 Mar J   Herr Mayseder
Haydn-sym
Pär-aria-Therese Kaiser
Mayseder-vln con in D major-Mayseder

var on the march from (Berton's?) *Aline* with
orchestral accompaniment-Mayseder
Mozart-fp con-Mlle Sieber
Cherubini-overture to *Lodoïska*
AMZ 16 Apr 06:460-61; WJ 15 Apr 06:249-51

30 Mar   B   Tonkünstler Societät
Kanne-sym
Preindl-chorus
Nasolini-aria-Mlle Laucher
Sarti-vocal trio-Antonia and Cäcelie Laucher,
Carl Weinmüller
Sacchini-chorus
Mozart-fp con-Josef Platzer
Salieri-cantata-Weinmüller and Ehlers
director-Salieri
Pohl/TS, 67

31 Mar   B   Tonkünstler Societät
program as on 10 Mar substituting for the
Nasolini aria and the fp con:
Pär-aria with clar-Mme Campi and Herr Stadler
Rode-vln con-Herr Urbany
Pohl/TS, 67

31 Mar   W   Herr Meier
Handel-*Der Messias* with Mozart's instrumenta-
tion (K. 572)-Mlle Milder, Mlle Marconi, Herr
Röckel, Herr Weinkopf
VIENNA-GDMF; VIENNA-SEYFRIED; AMZ 16
Apr 06:461-62; WJ 1 May 06:279-84

1 Apr   B   Benefit-"Theaterarmen"
Joseph Haydn-*Die sieben Worte*-Mlle Flamm,
Mme Rosenbaum, Herr Saal, Herr Ehlers
oboe con-Herr Grohmann (substituting for
Marianne Kirchgessner and Mme Roose due
to Kirchgessner's illness)
VIENNA-ONB-TS; VIENNA-ROSENBAUM
WJ 1 May 06:284-85

6 Apr GR Benefit "St Marx Bürgerspital"
Koželuch-"Galathea" (cantata)-Mme Campi,
Mlle Gerty, Mlle Umlauf; orchestra director-
Paul Wranitzky
WZ 2 Apr 06:1391-92; WZ 28 Jun 06:3204; AMZ
14 May 06:527-28; WJ 1 May 06:285

21 Apr KR Franz Bernardi
Holbein-songs
Lasueur (La Sueur)-arias from *Die Barden*-Mlle
Milder
fl con-"in the Adagio Herr Bernardi will im-
itate the tone of a glass harmonica"
"Herr Heberle will play a wind intrument not
known here. The name is being withheld as
a surprise."
Herr von Holbein, Herr Clement, Herr Ehlers,
Herr Meier, and Herr Neumann also
performed
VIENNA-ONB-MS; WZ 16 Apr 06:1671-72

11 May GR Marianne Kirchgessner
Reicha-quintet for glass harmonica and
strings-Kirchgessner
Zumsteeg-"Romanza"-Mlle Milder,
Kirchgessner
Salieri-aria-Mlle Marconi
Hofmeister-sym
Reicha-monologue from Schiller's Jungfrau von
Orleans-Mme Roose, Kirchgessner
VIENNA-ONB-MS; WJ 1 Jun 06:338-39

20 May KR Franciska Pär
Righini-overture to *Tigrane*
Pär-aria with chorus-Mme Pär
Pär-duet-Mme Pär and Anton Brizzi
Pär-trio from *Sargino*-Mme Pär, Brizzi, and Herr
Verri (father)
Cherubini-overture to *Graf Armand* (*Les deux
journées*)
rondo with chorus-Mme Pär
potpourri for two cellos-Kraft d.A. and d.J.

Pär-duet and aria from *Achille*-Mme Pär and
Brizzi
VIENNA-ONB-MS

25 May GR Benefit-"Wohlthätigkeitsanstalten"
Pär-*Sofonisba* (opera)-Mme Pär and Anton Brizzi
WZ 21 May 06:2420

5 Jun GR Theodor von Schacht "to benefit the wounded
soldiers"
Schacht-sym
Schacht-"4 voice Notturni accompanied by a
wind band instead of a fp because of the size
of the hall"
Schacht-fp con-Joseph Freund
Schacht-soprano scene with chorus and English
horn-Mlle Auernhammer
Schacht-"Sinphonia allegro"
Schacht-No. 2 of the 6 Notturni
Schacht-tenor scene with chorus-Herr Verri
(son)
orchestra director-Paul Wranitzky accompanist
for the vocal pieces-Schacht
VIENNA-ONB-MS; WZ 31 May 06:2651
AMZ 9 Jul 06:655

29 Jun A Benefit-"Handlungs Institute"
Haydn-sym
vln con-Luigi Tomasini
Hummel-"Das Fest des Dankes und der
Freude" (cantata)-Mlle Antonia Laucher d.A.,
Mlle Schill, Ignaz Sonnleithner, Herr Ehlers
WZ 12 Jul 06:3458; PZ 4 Jul 06; AMZ 30 Jul
06:701; WJ 15 Jul 06:437-39

Summer A Schuppanzigh series-various concerts
Mozart-fp con-Mlle Sieber
aria-Mlle Jonas
vln con-Herr Urbany
fl con-Herr Heberle
Rode-vln con-Herr Jehatschek (Pechacek)
Beethoven-fp con (Op. 15)-Herr Czerni
(Czerny)

339

Mozart-fp con in D minor-Herr Stein
Tomášek-sym
Beethoven-overture to *Fidelio*
Andreas Romberg-overture
AMZ 30 Jul 06:701; AMZ 13 Aug 06:729-30; AMZ
29 Oct 06:75; FM 11 Sep 06:212

8 Sep L Ferdinand Kauer
Kauer-*Die Sündfluth* (oratorio)
VIENNA-STB; WZ 30 Aug 06:4407; PZ 9 Sep 06;
WJ 1 Oct 06:593-98

26 Oct GR Fundraiser for war widows and orphans
Fischer-"Feyer der Frauenmilde" (cantata)-
Mlle Milder, Mlle Tomaselli, Herr
Weinmüller
orchestra director-Paul Wranitzky
director-Herr Fischer
VIENNA-ONB-MS; WZ 22 Oct 06:5279; AMZ 19
Nov 06:123

15 Nov GR Benefit "Wohlthätigkeitsanstalten"
Winter-*Castor und Pollux* (opera)
WZ 12 Nov 06:5611; AMZ 7 Jan 07:233

22 Dec B Tonkünstler Societät
Handel-*Judas Maccabäus* with Mozart's
instrumentation-Antonia Laucher, Mlle Marconi, Herr Gottdank, Herr Saal
director-Salieri
Pohl/TS, 67

23 Dec B Tonkünstler Societät
program as on 22 Dec
Pohl/TS, 67

23 Dec W Franz Joseph Clement
Méhul-overture
Beethoven-vln con (Op. 61 premiere)-Clement
Mozart-aria-Mme Campi
Cherubini-overture
Cherubini-vocal quartet-Campi, Herr Ehlers,
Herr Meier, Herr Weinkopf

Clement-vln fantasy and sonata on a single
string with a reversed violin-Clement
Handel-overture and choruses from *Ode to St.
Cäcelia* with Mozart's instrumentation
VIENNA-STB; VIENNA-SEYFRIED; WZ 10 Dec
06:6064; WTZ 8 Jan 07:27; Forbes/BEETHOVEN,
410; IB Apr 07:175-76; Gill/VIOLIN, 166

25 Dec GR Benefit-"St. Marx Bürgerspital"
Handel-*Der Messias*-Mme Campi, Mlle Marconi,
   Herr Weinmüller, Herr Gottdank
orchestra director-Paul Wranitzky
director-Salieri
WZ 20 Dec 06:6215; WZ 24 Jan 07:301
(says Weinkopf sang instead of Weinmüller); PZ
30 Dec 06; AMZ 18 Feb 07:336; WTZ 8 Jan
07:23-24

1807

Jan-Feb ? Mme Gerbini—violinist
AMZ 18 Mar 07:399

23 Jan KR Pixis brothers—violinist and fortepianist
Rode-vln con in D minor-Pixis
Steibelt-fp con-Pixis
WZ 14 Jan 07:167; AMZ 18 Feb 07:337; IB Apr
07:176

25 Jan KR Herr Seidler—violinist
aria-Mlle Häser
Karl Zeuner-rondo in A major-Zeuner
WZ 21 Jan 07:271; AMZ 18 Feb 07:337; IB Apr
07:176; WTZ 16 Feb 07:101-02; WTZ 4 Mar 07:141

15 Feb KR Herr Bamberger (horn), Herr Capeller (fl)
Herr Hanmüller (horn), Herr Roth (horn)
WZ 4 Feb 07:493; PZ 27 Feb 07

22 Feb R Herr Kraft d.J.
Kraft d.A.-vlc con-Kraft d.J.
Romberg-vlc duet-Kraft d.A. and d.J.

341

Pär-vocal quartet with horn from *Leonora*
WZ 18 Feb 07:700; AMZ 18 Mar 07:399-400; PZ
27 Feb 07

Lent ? Herr Metzger and Herr Legrand-flutist and cellist
AMZ 22 Apr 07:482

6 Mar R Louis Wolf
sym
guitar con-Wolf
aria-Mme Campi
Mozart-fp con-Mme Wolf née Mrasek
Wolf-guitar var-Wolf
Hummel-double son for 2 fp-Mme Wolf and
Mlle Karoline Mrasek
sym
VIENNA-ONB-MS; WZ 28 Feb 07:871

22 Mar B Tonkünstler Societät
Cherubini-overture to *Anacréon*
Haydn-chorus written on his last London trip
Johann Nepomuk Hummel-"Endimione e
Diana" (cantata)-Antonia and Cäcelie
Laucher, Herr Verri, Herr Weinmüller
director-Hummel
Mozart-fp con-Mlle Sieber
Handel-"Alleluja" from *Der Messias*
Pohl/TS, 68

22 Mar W Sebastian Meier
Handel-*Alexandersfest* with Mozart's
instrumentation-Mlle Müller, Herr Weinkopf,
Herr Gottdank
VIENNA-STB; VIENNA-ROSENBAUM; AMZ 22
Apr 07:481-82; WTZ 31 Mar 07:187-88

22 Mar L Theater chorus
Haydn-*Die Schöpfung*-Mlle Eigenwahl, Herr
Blacho, Herr Pfeiffer
VIENNA-STB; WTZ 31 Mar 07:189-90

23 Mar B Tonkünstler Societät
program as on 22 Mar substituting for the
Mozart con:

Danzi-vlc con-Herr Legrand
Fürstenau-fl var-Herr Metzger
Pohl/TS, 68

23 Mar   W   Herr Teimer
Hummel-"Das Lob der Freundschaft" (cantata)"- Herr Teimer, Henriette and Caroline Teimer (daughters of Herr Teimer)
Fischer-overture after Grétry
Fischer-aria with obbligato English horn- Mlle Milder and Herr Teimer
vln con-Herr Clement
Fischer-vocal trio with wind instruments
VIENNA-ROSENBAUM; WTZ 31 Mar 07:188-89

24 Mar   B   Benefit-"Theaterarmen"
Haydn-*Die Schöpfung*-Mlle Häser, Herr Weinmüller, Herr Ehlers
VIENNA-ROSENBAUM; WTZ 31 Mar 07:190

29 Mar   GR   Benefit-"Wohlthätigkeitsanstalten"
Ignaz Seyfried and Anton Fischer-"Die Rückkehr des Vaters" (cantata)-Mlle Milder, Herr Weinmüller, Herr Ehlers; Paul Wranitzky directed orchestra
VIENNA-ONB-MS; VIENNA-ROSENBAUM;
AMZ 22 Apr 07:482

19 Apr   KR   Carolina Pinton
arias-Giuseppi Todi and Diego Sommariva
WZ 11 Apr 07:1636

24 Apr   KR   Joseph Mayseder
WZ 22 Apr 07:1829

26 Apr   KR   Mme Carolina Pinton
Cherubini-sym
Portogallo-cavatina-Herr Diego Sommariva
Bonsichi-duet-Giuseppi Todi and Pinton
Leidesdorf-fp con-Leidesdorf (Leidesdorfer?)
Leidesdorf-overture for whole orchestra
Generali-aria-Pinton
Pavesi-duet-Todi and Sommariva
sym
VIENNA-ONB-MS; WZ 22 Apr 07:1829

1 May   A   Klara Sigl (13 years) and Ignaz Sigl (5 years)
Cherubini-overture to *Lodoïska*
Zingarelli-aria-Herr Röckel
Kreutzer-vln con-Klara Sigl
Clement-overture
(Mayer)-duet from *Ginevra di Scovia*-Mlle Müller
and Röckel
Roth-vlc var-I. and K. Sigl
VIENNA-ONB-MS

10 May KR Mme Bolla
Pär-overture to *Sargino*
Mayer-recit and aria-Bolla
Mayer-vocal duet-Bolla and Mlle Auernhammer
vlc rondo with orchestra-Herr Kraft d.J.
Righini-overture
Nasolini-aria-Herr Sommariva
vocal trio-Bolla, Auernhammer, Herr Verri d.J.
orchestra director-Paul Wranitzky
VIENNA-ONB-MS

17 May B Benefit-"Wohlthätigkeitsanstalten"
Joseph Haydn-*Die Jahreszeiten*-Mlle Häser, Herr
Weinmüller, Herr Ehlers; Herr Umlauf at the
keyboard
orchestra director-Paul Wranitzky
director-Salieri
VIENNA-ONB-TS; WZ 13 May 07:2214

12 Jun KR Diego Sommariva
VIENNA-ROSENBAUM

15 Nov L Ferdinand Kauer
Kauer-*Die Sündfluth*-Herr Pfeiffer, Herr Blacho,
Herr Kunert, Herr Handl d.A., Mlle Eigen-
wahl, Mme Preisberger, Mlle Kiker, Mlle
Weidner, Nannette La Roche
VIENNA-STB

15 Nov B Benefit-"Wohlthätigkeitsanstalten"
Cartellieri-overture
Naumann-aria from *Unsere Brüder* (oratorio)-
Herr Weinmüller

B. Romberg-potpourri for 2 vlc-Herr Kraft d.A.
and Herr Kraft d.J.
Ludwig van Beethoven-new sym (No. 4)
Righini-aria-Mlle Fischer
clar con-Herr Purebl
Feichtner-vocal trio-Fischer, Mlle Marconi, Herr
Vogel
Feichtner-chorus
VIENNA-ONB-TS; WZ 11 Nov 07:5251; AMZ 16
Dec 07:184

b25 Nov   M   Liebhaber Concerten
Mozart-overture to *Figaro*
Gluck-overture to *Iphigenie in Aulis*
Beethoven-sym in D major
Cramer-fp con-Mlle Spielmann
director-Hering
AMZ 25 Nov 07:140; Biba/LIEBHABER, 84

b1 Dec   U   Liebhaber Concerten-various concerts
Haydn-sym in G major "with the military
andante"
Mozart-sym in C major (K. 551)
Himmel-overture to *Sylphen*
Beethoven-overture to *Prometheus* (on 29 Nov
07)
Cherubini-overture to *Anacréon*
Rode-vln con-Baron Cerini
Müller-fl con-Herr Kessler
PZ 8 Dec 07; AMZ 16 Dec 07:184-85;
Biba/LIEBHABER, 84

6 Dec   U   Liebhaber Concerten
Beethoven-sym in E-flat major-Beethoven
directed
Biba/LIEBHABER,85; AMZ 6 Jan 08:238-39

13 Dec   U   Liebhaber Concerten
Beethoven-overture to *Coriolan*
fl con-Count Hrzan
Biba/LIEBHABER, 85; AMZ 6 Jan 08:238-39

22 Dec   B   Tonkünstler Societät
Haydn-*Die Schöpfung*-Antonie Laucher, Herr
Weinmüller, Herr Gottdank
director-Salieri
Pohl/TS, 68

22 Dec   W   Benefit-"Theaterarmen"
Handel-*Alexandersfest* with Mozart's instrumen-
tation (K. 591)
VIENNA-SEYFRIED

23 Dec   B   Tonkünstler Societät
program as on 22 Dec
Pohl/TS, 68

23 Dec   W   Franz Joseph Clement
Beethoven-vln con (Op. 61)-Clement
VIENNA-SEYFRIED; AMZ 6 Jan 08:239

23 Dec   L   Benefit-Regina La Roche
VIENNA-STB

25 Dec   K   Benefit-"St Marx Bürgerspital"
F.A. Feichtner-"Die erste Feyer der Him-
melfahrt Jesu" (cantata)-Mlle Fischer, Mlle
Bessenig, Herr Professor Rathmayer
Anton Eberl-fp con (C major)-Mlle Hohenadel
Kunzen-"Das Halleluja der Schöpfung" (can-
tata)-Fischer, Marconi, Rathmayer, Herr Saal
VIENNA-ONB-MS; WZ 16 Dec 07:5830-31; WZ
23 Apr 08:2040; PZ 29 Dec 07 (says 21, not 25
Dec); AMZ 6 Jan 08:239-40

b26 Dec   ?   Josef Beer
Beer-clar con-Beer
Andreas Romberg-vln con-Herr Foyta (Foita)
AMZ 6 Jan 08:238

b26 Dec   U   Liebhaber Concerten-various concerts
Haydn-sym in D major
Beethoven-vln con-Clement
Clement directed
AMZ 6 Jan 08:238-39; Biba/LIEBHABER, 85

27 Dec U Liebhaber Concerten
Beethoven-sym in B-flat
AMZ 27 Jan 08:286-87; Biba/LIEBHABER, 85

1808

b16 Jan ? Anton Flat
Radikati-oboe con-Flat
AMZ 27 Jan 08:287-88

14 Jan KR Bernhard Romberg
"Rondo fandango"-Romberg
Romberg-vlc con in D minor-Romberg
Romberg-vlc con in E minor-Romberg
WZ 6 Jan 08:83; WZ 20 Jan 08:295; AMZ 27 Jan
08:287

17 Jan U Liebhaber Concerten
Beethoven-sym in C major
Biba/LIEBHABER, 85

26 Jan KR Bohrer brothers
WZ 23 Jan 08:372

28 Jan KR Herr Seidler
WZ 23 Jan 08:372

31 Jan U Liebhaber Concerten
Beethoven-fp con (Op. 15)-Herr V. Felsenberg
Biba/LIEBHABER, 85

2 Feb U Liebhaber Concerten
Beethoven-sym in E-flat
Beethoven-overture to *Coriolan*
Biba/LIEBHABER, 85

22 Feb U Liebhaber Concerten
Beethoven-sym in D major
Biba/LIEBHABER, 85

8 Mar KR Bernhard Romberg (part of a series)
"Rondo fandango"-Romberg
Romberg-vlc con in F sharp minor-Romberg
WZ 5 Mar 08:1100; WZ 10 Mar 08:1285-86

12 Mar   L   Herr Mayer
                  "A grand artistic concert in which he will,
                    without using an instrument, only his
                    mouth, imitate quite naturally the tones of
                    waldhorn, the serpent, the trumpet, with the
                    accompaniment of the entire orchestra"
                (Paisiello?)-aria with var from *La Molinara*
                (Paisiello)-horn solo from *Nina*
                Müllet-waltzes
                Martín (y Soler)-overture to *Una cosa rara*
                Fränzel-"Bird song symphony" (imitation of
                    various bird calls without instruments)
                VIENNA-STB

20 Mar   U   Liebhaber Concerten
                Beethoven-sym in C major
                Biba/LIEBHABER, 85

25 Mar   L   Theater chorus
                F.X. Süssmayer-Moses, oder der Auszug aus
                    Egypten-Herr Pfeiffer, Herr Bondra, Mlle
                    Eigenwahl, Mlle Kiker, Herr Roch, Herr Rot-
                    ter, Ignaz Schuster, Herr Blacho, Herr Handl
                    d.A., Mlle Weidner, Herr Groschopf
                VIENNA-STB; VIENNA-ROSENBAUM

25 Mar   B   Herr Weinmüller, Herr Vogel, Herr Saal
                (Peter Winter)-"Timoteus, oder die Gewalt der
                    Musik" (cantata)-Weinmüller, Vogel (Vogl),
                    Mme Campi, Mlle Fischer
                VIENNA-ROSENBAUM; IB May 08:213

27 Mar   U   Liebhaber Concerten
                Haydn-*Die Schöpfung*-Herr Radicchi, Herr Wein-
                    müller, Mlle Fischer; Herr Kreutzer at the
                    keyboard
                    director-Salieri
                VIENNA-ROSENBAUM; WZ 30 Mar 08:1555-56;
                AMZ 20 Apr 08:479-80

 3 Apr   KR   Herr Giuliani
                Giuliani-guitar con-Giuliani
                Giuliani-var with orchestra-Giuliani
                PZ 5 Apr 08; AMZ 18 May 08:538

8 Apr   KR   Mlle Müllner
             harp con-Müllner
             harp fantasy-Müllner
             Paresi-"Traum des Fingels" with chorus from
                Comala e Fingalo-Mme Imperatrice Sessi
             WZ 30 Mar 08:1570; AMZ 18 May 08:539-40 (says
             7 Apr)

10 Apr   L   Herr Tuczek (Tuček)
              Tuczek-*Lanassa oder die Eroberung von Malabar*
                 (opera)
              IB Jun 08:253

10 Apr   B   Tonkünstler Societät
              Haydn-*Die Jahreszeiten*-Antonie Laucher, Herr
                 Weinmüller, Herr Gottdank
              director-Salieri
              Pohl/TS, 68

11 Apr   W   Sebastian Meier
              Mozart-*Davidde penitente* (K. 469)
              Beethoven-sym in E-flat
              C. Kreutzer-fp con in E major-C. Kreutzer
              VIENNA-STB; VIENNA-SEYFRIED; AMZ 18 May
              08:540; IB Jun 08:250

11 Apr   B   Tonkünstler Societät
              program as on 10 Apr
              Pohl/TS, 68

12 Apr   W   Concert
              Mozart-*Davidde penitente*
              Beethoven-sym in D major
              Clement-vln con-Clement
              VIENNA-SEYFRIED, IB Jun 08:250

13 Apr   B   Benefit-"Wohlthätigkeitsanstalten"
              Beethoven-sym in B-flat major
              Giuliani-guitar con-Giuliani
              Paresi-"Traum Fingals"-Mme Sessi
              harp fantasy-Mlle Müllner
              Beethoven-fp con (Op. 37?)-Herr Stein
              Beethoven-overture to *Coriolan*
              director-Beethoven
              AMZ 18 May 08:540-41

17 Apr B Benefit-"Wohlthätigkeitsanstalten
           Haydn-*Die Schöpfung*-Mlle Fischer, Herr Wein-
           müller, Herr Radicchi
           Herr Umlauf at the keyboard
           orchestra director-Paul Wranitzky
           director-Salieri
           200 performers
           VIENNA-ONB-TS; WZ 16 Apr 08:1907

8 May   A Carolina Pinton
           Liverati-*Aeneae in Carthage* (*Enea in Cartagine*)-
           Herr Todi
           VIENNA-ROSENBAUM; WZ 4 May 08:2273

4 Jun   KR Herr Lafont-violinist
           WZ 8 Jun 08:2945-46

b23 Jun A Various virtuoso concerts
           Spohr-vln con-Herr Mayseder
           Mayseder-vln con-Herr Mayseder
           Beethoven-concertino (Op. 56 premiere)
           AMZ 23 Jun 08:623-24

25 Aug A Ball, concert and illumination
           VIENNA-ROSENBAUM

30 Aug A Ball, concert and illumination
           VIENNA-ROSENBAUM

8 Sep   L Herr Kargl
           VIENNA-MUELLER

22 Sep A Fireworks, illumination, concert, ball
           Herr Iffland and Mme Roose declaimed
           arias-Mme Campi, Mlle Milder, Herr Röckel
           VIENNA-ROSENBAUM

15 Nov L Ferdinand Kauer
           Kauer-"Leopolds Jagd, oder der
               wiedergefundene Schleyer" (cantata)
           VIENNA-STB

15 Nov B Benefit-"Wohlthätigkeitsanstalten"
           Beethoven-sym-Beethoven directed
           Zingarelli-vocal rondo-Mlle Fischer

Beethoven-fp con-Herr Stein
Pavesi-aria-Herr Radicchi
Pär-duet from Sargines-Mme Campi and Mlle
  Fischer
Müllner-harp var-Mlle Müllner
Guglielmi-aria with recit-Campi
Beethoven-overture-Beethoven directed
Simon Mayer-vocal quartet with chorus- Cam-
  pi, Fischer, Herr Saal, Radicchi
Herr Gyrowetz at the keyboard; J. Scheidl
  directed
VIENNA-ONB-TS; WZ 12 Nov 08:5675; BL
  1:201-202

15 Nov   W   Franz Joseph Clement
              WZ 9 Nov 08:5625

4 Dec   KR   Alessandro Scaramelli—violinist
              WZ 30 Nov 08:5974

b10 Dec   ?   Concert
              Beethoven-overture to *Coriolan*
              Romberg-vlc piece
              Pär-aria
              Italian guitarist played
              French romance "La Sentinelle"
              Reichardt/VERTRAUTE, 1:218-21

b16 Dec   KR Mme Bigot
              Beethoven-sym
              Beethoven-fp var "on an unusual theme of
                eight measures"-Bigot
              Beethoven-aria (Op. 65?)-(Mlle Killizky)
              Beethoven-duet-Killizky and Herr Radicchi
              Beethoven-overture to *Coriolan*
              Reichardt/VERTRAUTE, 1:234-36

18 Dec   KR   Mlle Longhi
              "Arabisches Konzert"
              aria-Therese Fischer
              aria-Herr Radicchi
              WZ 17 Dec 08:6261., AMZ 25 Jan 09:270;
              Reichardt/VERTRAUTE, 1:243

22 Dec W   Beethoven
                  Beethoven-sym in F major (premiere)
                  Beethoven-"Ah perfido" (Op. 65)-Mlle Killizky
                  Beethoven-Gloria from the C major mass
                  Beethoven-fp con in G major (Op. 56)
                  Beethoven-sym in C minor (premiere)
                  Beethoven-Sanctus from the C major mass
                  Beethoven-fp fantasy with chorus (Op. 80)
                  director-Mayseder
                  BL 1:211-13; WZ 7 Dec 08:6092; WZ 17 Dec
                  08:6261-62; PZ 13 Dec 08; AMZ 25 Jan 09:267-69;
                  Reichardt/VERTRAUTE, 1:254-58

22 Dec B   Tonkünstler Societät
                  Sigismund Neukomm-fantasy for orchestra
                  Haydn-*Il ritorno di Tobia* (part 1)- Mlle Marconi,
                    Mlle Fischer, Mme Campi, Herr Radicchi,
                    Herr Saal
                  director-Neukomm
                  Pohl/TS, 68

23 Dec B   Tonkünstler Societät
                  part 2 of oratorio
                  Beethoven-fp con
                  Pohl/TS, 68; Forbes/BEETHOVEN, 450

23 Dec W   Franz Joseph Clement
                  Beethoven-sym in C minor
                  Beethoven-"Sanctus"
                  Beethoven-choral fantasy (Op. 80)
                  WZ 17 Dec 08:6262; Bauer, A./WIEN, 286

25 Dec GR Benefit-"St Marx Bürgerspital"
                  Ignaz von Seyfried and Anton Fischer-"Die
                    Rückkehr des Vaters"-Mlle Milder, Herr
                    Radicchi, Herr Weinmüller
                  orchestra director-Herr Scheidl
                  B. Buchweiser at the keyboard
                  director-Herr Seyfried
                  Hofkapelle singers and 2 theater orchestras
                  VIENNA-ONB-TS; WZ 10 Dec 08:6151-52; PZ 13
                  Dec 08; AMZ 25 Jan 09:269-70

1809

25 Jan KR Mlle Fischer
Righini-arias-Fischer
Pär-arias-Fischer
arias-Mlle Marconi
harp pieces-Mlle Müllner
vlc con-Herr Kraft d.J.
AMZ 15 Mar 09:384; Reichardt/VERTRAUTE,
1:338-40

28 Jan KR Herr Seidler
Lafont-vln con-Seidler
R. Kreutzer-Spanish rondo-Seidler
R. Kreutzer-double vln con-Seidler and Herr
Schuppanzigh
aria-Herr Grell
fp fantasy-Herr C. Kreutzer
AMZ 15 Mar 09:384; Reichardt/VERTRAUTE
1:445

16 Feb O Herr Gyrowetz
Spohr-vln con-Herr Foita
AMZ 15 Mar 09:384; AMZ 19 Jul 09:669-70;
SAMMLER 18 Feb 09:84

5 Mar KR Herr Kraft d.J. and Mlle Fischer
Kraft-vlc pieces-Kraft
(B.) Romberg-vlc pieces-Kraft
arias-Fischer
BL 1:216; AMZ 12 Jul 09:650;
Reichardt/VERTRAUTE, 2:9

12 Mar KR Ignaz Moscheles
Moscheles-sym
Mozart-fp con-Moscheles
AMZ 12 Jul 09:650; Reichardt/VERTRAUTE,
2:87-88

18 Mar KR Anton Heberle
Cartellieri-fl con-Heberle
AMZ 12 Jul 09:650

25 Mar L Theater chorus
Joseph Haydn-*Die sieben Worte*-Mlle Eigenwahl
(on program, but Mme Bondra sang), Mlle
Laroche (La Roche), Herr Bondra, Herr
Pfeiffer
Gebel-fp quintet with fl, clar, horn, and
bassoon-Mme Rosina Schuster
VIENNA-STB; AMZ 12 Jul 09:651-52;
Reichardt/VERTRAUTE, 2:86-87

25 Mar B Herr Saal, Herr Vogel and Herr Weinmüller
Joseph Haydn-military sym
Joseph Weigl-"Der Kriegs Eid"-Vogel (Vogl),
Weinmüller, chorus
Gyrowetz-"Das Gebeth"-Herr Grell, Saal,
Vogl, Weinmüller; Josephine Müller (Josepha
Müllner) on harp
Pösinger-clar con-Herr Purebl
Gyrowetz-"Der Greis"-Saal
Weigl-"Der Marsch"-chorus
Romberg-Spanish rondo-Herr Kraft d.J.
Weigl-"Der Bräutigam"-Vogel
Süssmayer-"Der Genius Oestreichs" (sic)-Mlle
Milder
Weigl-"Der Abschied eines Wehrmannes von
seinen Eltern"-Milder, Vogel, Weinmüller
Weigl "Oestreich (sic) über Alles"-chorus
VIENNA-ONB-TS; VIENNA-ROSENBAUM;
AMZ 12 Jul 09:651; SAMMLER 28 Mar 09:148

26 Mar B Tonkünstler Societät
Haydn-*Die Schöpfung*-Mlle Fischer, Herr Radicchi, Herr Weinmüller
director-Salieri
Pohl/TS, 68

27 Mar B Tonkünstler Societät
program as on 26 Mar
Pohl/TS, 68

27 Mar W Benefit "Theaterarmen"
Handel/Mozart *Der Messias* (K. 572)-Mme Cam-
pi, Mlle Marconi, Herr Weinkopf, Herr
Gottdank

VIENNA-STB; AMZ 3 May 04:492; SAMMLER 1
Apr 09:156 (says Herr Röckel instead of Herr
Gottdank)

28 Mar B   Benefit-"Theaterarmen"
Joseph Haydn-military sym
Joseph Weigl-"Der Kriegs Eid"-Herr Vogel
(Vogl), Herr Weinmüller, chorus
Gyrowetz-"Das Gebeth"-Herr Grell, Herr Saal,
Herr Vogel, Herr Weinmüller, with Mlle
Müllner (harp)
Conradin Kreutzer-fp con in E major-Kreutzer
Weigl-"Der Marsch"-chorus
Weigl-"Des Volkes Wunsch"-chorus
clar con-Zenker
Gyrowetz-"Der Greis"-Saal
Süssmayer-"Der Genius Oestreichs"-Mlle
Milder
Weigl-"Der Abschied eines Wehrmannes von
seinen Eltern"-Milder, Vogel, Weinmüller
Weigl-"Oestreich über Alles"-chorus
VIENNA-ONB-TS; AMZ 12 Jul 09:651;
SAMMLER 1 Apr 09:156

2 Apr GR   Benefit-"Wohlthätigkeitsanstalten"
program of 25 Mar with new con
Lafont vln con-Herr Seidler
VIENNA-ROSENBAUM; WZ 29 Mar 09:1146;
AMZ 12 Jul 09:651; SAMMLER 6 Apr 09:164

9 Apr KR   Mlle Longhi—fortepianist
VIENNA-ROSENBAUM; AMZ 12 Jul 09:652-53

11 Apr KR   Johann (Iwan) Müller
Paul Struck-sym in E flat major
bassethorn pieces-Müller
Hummel-fp con-Herr Schobenlechner (boy)
WZ 1 Apr 09:1506; AMZ 12 Jul 09:652-53

16 Apr GR   Benefit "Wohlthätigkeitsanstalten"
program of 25 Mar in Burgtheater
VIENNA-ROSENBAUM; AMZ 12 Jul 09:651;
SAMMLER 20 Apr 09:188

18 Apr W   Herr Mälzel
"This artistic figure . . . appears as a trumpeter
of the Imperial Austrian Cuirassier Regiment
of the Archduke Albert and will play without
orchestral accompaniment."
Austrian Cavalry March, with the signals of
the cavalry
The March of the Archduke Albert's Regiment
with orchestra
Moscheles-allegro with orchestra
Salieri-March with orchestra
The figure will appear as a trumpeter of the
Citizen's Cavalry of Vienna and will play a
Regiment's March with orchestra
Dussek-allegro with orchestra
Pleyel-allegro-orchestra
VIENNA-ONB-MS

21 Apr W   Herr Mälzel
program as on 18 Apr
VIENNA-ONB-MS

23 Apr KR   Anton Romberg
AMZ 12 Jul 09:652; AMZ 19 Jul 09:668

30 Apr KR   Herr Went and Herr Foita
Krommer-oboe con in F major-Went
Spohr-vln con in D minor-Herr Foita
Beethoven-overture to *Prometheus*
Beethoven-horn son (Op. 17)-Herr Czerny and
Herr Hradezky
AMZ 12 Jul 09:652; AMZ 19 Jul 09:668-69

4 May A   Herr Gyrowetz (concert cancelled)
VIENNA-PROTOKOL; VIENNA-ROSENBAUM;
AMZ 19 Jul 09:669-70

19 May B   Herr Mälzel
march and all the signals of the Austrian
Cavalry
march of the Archduke Albert's regiment with
orchestra

Moscheles-allegro with orchestra
Salieri-march with orchestra
march and all the signals of the French cavalry
Rica-grand march with orchestra
Frédéric-allegro with orchestra
Pleyel-march with orchestra
VIENNA-ONB-TS

8 Aug   B   Mlle Longhi—harpist and fortepianist
overture
Generali-cavatina-Mlle Fischer
Steibelt-fp con (E major)-Longhi
Pär-aria with recit-Herr Radicchi
overture
Boieldieu-duet for harp and fp-Longhi and Ig-
naz Moscheles
Righini-recit and rondo-Fischer
sym
VIENNA-ROSENBAUM; VIENNA-ONB-TS;
AMZ 18 Oct 09:42 (the first concert in 3 months)

8 Sep   W   Benefit-"Theaterarmen"
L. van Beethoven-sym in E-flat
Mozart-vocal trio from *La villanella rapita*-Mlle
Milder, Herr Grell, Herr Meier
Clement-vln con-Clement
Cherubini-overture to *Anacréon*
Nasolini-aria-Mme Campi
Mozart-vocal quartet from *La villanella rapita*-
Milder, Grell, Meier, Weinkopf
Handel-"Alleluja" from *Der Messias*
VIENNA-ONB-TS; AMZ 7 Feb 10:295-96

22 Oct   O   Ivan Müller
Philipp Jakob Riotte-clar con in C minor-Müller
Portogallo-vocal duet-Mlle Buchweiser and Herr
Grell
Moscheles-clar var-Müller
AMZ 7 Feb 10:298-99

15 Nov   B   Benefit-"Wohlthätigkeitsanstalten"
Haydn-*Die Schöpfung*-Mlle Fischer, Herr
Weinmüller, Herr Radicchi,

357

Herr Umlauf at the keyboard
orchestra director-Herr Scheidl
director-Salieri
Hofkapelle participated
VIENNA-ONB-TS; VIENNA-ROSENBAUM;
AMZ 3 Jan 10:219

22 Dec B   Tonkünstler Societät
Haydn-*Die Jahreszeiten*-Mlle Fischer, Herr Radicchi, Herr Weinmüller
director-Salieri
Pohl/TS, 68

23 Dec B   Tonkünstler Societät
program as on 22 Dec
Pohl/TS, 68

24 Dec W   Franz Joseph Clement
Clement-vln con-Clement
Clement-vln fantasy-Clement
Beethoven-*Christus am Oelberge*-"with a
strengthened orchestra"
VIENNA-STB; AMZ 24 Jan 10:266

24 Dec L   Ferdinand Kauer
Kauer-*Die Sündfluth*-Herr Pfeiffer, Herr Blacho,
Herr Wild, Herr Ramhärter, Mlle Bondra,
Mme Preisberger, Mlle Weiss, Mlle Weidner,
Mlle Nannette Laroche (La Roche)
VIENNA-STB; AMZ 24 Jan 10:266-67

25 Dec GR Benefit-"St Marx Bürgerspital"
Ignaz von Seyfried and Anton Fischer-"Die
Rückkehr des Vaters"
J.G. Arnold-vlc con-Herr Santi-Hüber
VIENNA-ROSENBAUM; WZ 20 Dec 09:3604;
AMZ 24 Jan 10:266-67; SAMMLER 2 Jan 10:4

The AMZ remarked on 7 Feb 20:295 that the few new operas and concerts that had been heard during the period of the French occupation proved how much music ·had suffered during the general hard times.

1810

15 Mar KR Louis Wolf (double guitar)
Triebensee-guitar con-Wolf
Triebensee-rondo alla Polacca-Wolf
WZ 10 Mar 10:np; AMZ 25 Apr 10:476

18 Mar KR Anton Romberg
A. Romberg-bassoon con in F major-Romberg
Schneider-quartet for four bassoons-Romberg
Pär-scene-Herr Grell
Pär-vocal duet-Fischer sisters
AMZ 25 Apr 10:476

25 Mar B Benefit-"Theaterarmen"
Joseph Rösler-sym (first movement)
Mozart-"Parto" from *La Clemenza di Tito*- Mme
Campi
Anton Romberg-bassoon con-Romberg
Nasolini-vocal duet-Herr Fischer and Mlle ?
(the program announcement is torn)
L. v. Beethoven-sym (first movement)
Pär-aria-Mlle Fischer
Lafont-vln con-Emanuel Foita
Pär-vocal quartet-Mlle Fischer, Herr Radicchi,
Herr Vogel (Vogl), Herr Verri
VIENNA-ONB-TS; AMZ 25 Apr 10:477 (Mlle
Fischer substituted for Mme Campi.)

25 Mar L Herr Bondra
Haydn-*Die sieben Worte*
VIENNA-MUELLER

29 Mar KR Herr Leppich and Conradin Kreutzer
Kreutzer-"Eine Idylle: Die Entstehung der Har-
monie" with obbligato panmelodicon-Mlle
Killizky and Herr Grell
AMZ 2 May 10:488-89

1 Apr KR Ivan Müller
Johann Fuss-overture to *Watwort*
Riotte-clar con-Müller
Riotte-clar potpourri with orchestra-Müller

359

Mozart-"Non piu di fiori" (from La Clemenza
di Tito)-Mlle Fischer with Herr Fridlowsky
(bassethorn)
AMZ 30 May 10:556

8 Apr KR Herr Mayseder
Mayseder-vln con-Mayseder
Mayseder-vln var-Mayseder
AMZ 30 May 10:556-57

15 Apr KR Mauro Giuliani—guitarist
WZ 11 Apr 10:n.p.

15 Apr B Tonkünstler Societät
Joseph Eybler-*Die vier letzten Dinge* (oratorio)-
Mlle Milder, Josef Simoni, Herr Weinmüller
director-Salieri
Pohl/TS, 68

16 Apr B Tonkünstler Societät
program as on 15 Apr
Pohl/TS, 68

17 Apr B Benefit-"Theaterarmen"
L. van Beethoven-overture to *Coriolan*
Dussek-fp con (F major)-Mlle Fratti
Mayer-aria from *Alonzo e Cora* (*Alonso e Cora*)-
Mlle Fischer
potpourri on panmelodicon-C. Kreutzer
Nasolini-vocal duet-Mlle Fischer and Herr
Radicchi
Mayseder-vln con (E minor)-Mayseder
sym
VIENNA-ONB-TS; AMZ 6 Jun 10:573

22 Apr GR Benefit-"Wohlthätigkeitsanstalten"
Eybler-*Die vier letzten Dinge*-probably Mlle
Fischer, Herr Simoni, Herr Weinmüller
AMZ 6 Jun 10:573

23 Apr KR Mauro Giuliani
AMZ 6 Jun 10:573

1 May A Joseph Anspacher
Viotti-vln con-Anspacher
AMZ 20 Jun 10:606

6 May A Ignaz Schuppanzigh
Beethoven-sym
Matthäi-vln con-Schuppanzigh
Beethoven-aria-Mlle Killizky
Beethoven-overture
Spanish Bolero-(R.) Kreutzer
WZ 28 Apr 10:n.p.; AMZ 20 Jun 20:607;
SAMMLER 12 May 10:234

10 May A? Josef Gebauer
E. Müller-fl con in C major-Gebauer
Mozart-"Deh per questo istante solo" from *La
Clemenza di Tito*-Mlle Auernheim
Eberl-fp con in C major-Henriette Paris
Gebauer-romance with var on a theme from
(Cherubini's) *Faniska* "Habt Dank für die
Beschwerden"-Gebauer (on the Hungarian
Csakany)
AMZ 20 Jun 10:607-08

5 Jun A Franz Leppich
C. Kreutzer-Idylle for Panmelodicon-Herr and
Mme Ehlers
WZ 2 Jun 10:1072; AMZ 18 Jul 10:675

7 Jun A Schuppanzigh series opening concert
WZ 30 May 10:1006

2 Aug A Schuppanzigh series
B. Romberg-vlc con in E minor-Herr Linke
AMZ 17 Oct 10:879; SAMMLER 16 Aug 10:402

3 Aug L Herr Gleich
Süssmayer-*Moses in Egypten (Moses oder der
Auszug aus Aegypten)*
VIENNA-MUELLER; THALIA 18 Aug 10:58

31 Aug L Herr Gleich
program as on 3 Aug
THALIA 8 Sep 10:80

8 Sep L   Theater chorus
                Mozart-*Titus der gütige*
                VIENNA-MUELLER; AMZ 17 Oct 10:879;
                THALIA 15 Sep 10:88

15 Nov B   Benefit-"Wohlthätigkeitsanstalten"
                Mozart-overture to *La Clemenza di Tito*
                Winter-aria-Mme Campi
                Spohr-vln con-Herr Mayseder
                Cannabich-aria-Herr Siboni
                Haydn-sym
                Krommer-rondo for bassoon-Herr Romberg
                Cimarosa-trio from *Gli Orazi ed i Curiazi*- Herr
                    and Mme Campi, Herr Siboni
                sym
                Herr Scheidl directed; Herr Gyrowetz at the
                    keyboard; Hofkapelle
                VIENNA-ONB-TS; AMZ 26 Dec 10:1058

18 Nov KR   H. Christian Wunder—bass
                AMZ 26 Dec 10:1058

25 Nov ?   Anton Heberle (fl) and Vincenz Schuster (guitar)
                    overture for wind band
                    trio for fl, guitar and viola
                    2 Italian cavatinas with guitar
                    accompaniment-Schuster
                    potpourri for guitar-Schuster
                    vlc var with guitar accompaniment
                    duet from *Giulietta e Romeo*-Mlle Kriehuber and
                      Herr Haunold
                    son for Czackan and guitar-Heberle and
                      Schuster
                  VIENNA-GDMF

30 Nov ?   Anton Heberle and Vincenz Schuster
                    overture for the entire orchestra
                    trio for fl, guitar and viola
                    2 Italian cavatinas-Schuster
                    sym for entire orchestra
                    potpourri for guitar-Schuster
                    Adagio with accompaniment of orchestra

son for Czackan and guitar-Heberle and
Schuster
VIENNA-GDMF

1 Dec   O   Anton Heberle and Vincenz Schuster
overture for wind band
trio with fl, guitar, and viola
German aria-a friend of music
overture for entire orchestra
French aria and duet from *Giulietta e Romeo*
son for Czackan and guitar-Heberle and
Schuster
VIENNA-GDMF

15 Dec   ?   Anton Heberle and Vincenz Schuster
overture
fl con
Mayer-Italian aria-Mme Angiolini
Schuster-vlc var with orchestra-Schuster
concertino for fl, clar, vln with orchestra-
various amateur musicians
Cimarosa-"Sei morelli e quatro baja"-Herr
Desiro
son for Czakan and guitar-Heberle and
Schuster
VIENNA-GDMF

22 Dec   B   Tonkünstler Societät
Haydn-*Die Schöpfung*-Therese Klieber, Herr
Simoni, Herr Weinmüller
director-Salieri
Pohl/TS, 68

23 Dec   B   Tonkünstler Societät
program as on 22 Dec
Pohl/TS, 68

23 Dec   L   Anton Kargel (Kargl)
Cherubini-overture to *Lodoïska*
Clement-vln con-Kargel
Mayer-aria-Mlle Weiss
Cherubini-overture to *Les deux journées* (not
played)

Krommer-nonette for vln, oboe, fl-Herr Neul-
ing, Herr Rutzizka, Herr Kaiser
Maurer-aria-Herr Michalesi
Mozart-fp con in C minor (K. 491?)-(Josef?)
Platzer
AMZ 30 Jan 11:85-86

25 Dec   GR   Benefit-"St Marx Bürgerspital"
Beethoven-overture to *Prometheus*
Mayseder-vln con-Mayseder
Weigl-"Der Sieg der Eintracht"-Mme Campi,
Mlle Mayer, Mlle Teimer, Herr Weinmüller,
Herr Gottdank; Mlle Müllner and Herr Kraft
d.A. and d.J. assisted
WZ 19 Dec 10:2499; AMZ 30 Jan 11:86-87;
SAMMLER 29 Dec 10:634; THALIA 2 Jan 11:4

30 Dec   KR   Herr Bayr
Bayr-fl con-Bayr
Bayr-Polonaise and Andante for solo fl-Bayr
aria-Mlle Buchweiser
AMZ 30 JAN 11:87

APPENDIX TWO

Private Concert Calendar

The format followed here is similar to that of Appendix 1. The name appearing after the date is the concert patron; the program, if available, follows. Sources are given according to their abbreviations in the Bibliography, other abbreviations can be found in the key for Appendix 1. An asterisk before the patron's name indicates the performance actually falls into the category of Social Music, but is included here because a professional musician participated. Two asterisks signify After-Dinner Music. For more exact identification, see Appendix 3 or 4.

1761

4 Mar Count Perlas
    Mansoli sang
VIENNA-ZINZENDORF

29 Mar Prince Esterházy
VIENNA-ZINZENDORF

14 Jun Prince Kaunitz
VIENNA-ZINZENDORF

2 Aug Abbé C. Thurn
VIENNA-ZINZENDORF

25 Sep Count Perlas
    lute piece accompanied by cello and double bass
VIENNA-ZINZENDORF

9 Oct	Count Perlas
	vln piece-Mlle Allavi
	kybd piece-Herr v. Barhof
	kybd piece-Countess Perlas
	VIENNA-ZINZENDORF
10 Oct	Colalto
	VIENNA-ZINZENDORF
23 Oct	Count Perlas
	VIENNA-ZINZENDORF
26 Oct	Colalto
	VIENNA-ZINZENDORF
31 Oct	?
	flute music
	VIENNA-ZINZENDORF
25 Nov	Colalto
	VIENNA-ZINZENDORF
28 Nov	Palm
	vln piece-Collonitsche (?)
	fl piece-Vani (?)
	VIENNA-ZINZENDORF
30 Nov	Colalto
	VIENNA-ZINZENDORF
9 Dec	Colalto
	VIENNA-ZINZENDORF
21 Dec	Colalto
	VIENNA-ZINZENDORF
22 Dec	Herr von Thauernathy
	lute pieces-Kohot (Kohaut?)
	Mme Taeuberin (Teiberin?) sang
	Herr von Kees directed
	VIENNA-ZINZENDORF

1762

3 Jan	Mme de Thurn VIENNA-ZINZENDORF
9 Jan	Herr von Thauernathy VIENNA-ZINZENDORF
24 Jan	Thurn VIENNA-ZINZENDORF
3 Feb	Colalto VIENNA-ZINZENDORF
10 Feb	Colalto VIENNA-ZINZENDORF
20 Feb	Colalto VIENNA-ZINZENDORF
26 Feb	Thauernathy Mme Teiberin sang Holzbauer-sym VIENNA-ZINZENDORF
10 Mar	*Duke of Bragance vlc pieces-Hofmann (Hoffmann) new son from Portugal-Scarlatti VIENNA-ZINZENDORF
12 Mar	Thauernathy Mme Teiberin sang VIENNA-ZINZENDORF
23 Mar	Thurn VIENNA-ZINZENDORF
18 Apr	Thurn VIENNA-ZINZENDORF
30 Jun	Colalto VIENNA-ZINZENDORF
24 Jul	Colalto Nicolini sang VIENNA-ZINZENDORF

4 Aug	Duke of Bragance Scarlatti played and sang VIENNA-ZINZENDORF
18 Sep	Colalto VIENNA-ZINZENDORF
5 Oct	Colalto Mme Bianchi sang 4 year old (Mozart?) played kybd VIENNA-ZINZENDORF
9 Nov	Parhers (?) little Salzburger played Nicolini sang VIENNA-ZINZENDORF
12 Nov	Ambassador ballet *Don Juan* VIENNA-ZINZENDORF
1 Dec	Colalto VIENNA-ZINZENDORF
18 Dec	Durazzo VIENNA-ZINZENDORF

1763

10 Jan	Colalto VIENNA-ZINZENDORF
16 Jan	**Kaunitz Compassi sang VIENNA-ZINZENDORF
19 Feb	Prince Esterházy VIENNA-ZINZENDORF
22 Mar	**Mme de Tarocca *Le Ballet Turc* played on kybd by Mme de Tarocca and ladies of the court VIENNA-ZINZENDORF

30 Apr	Colalto Compressi sang VIENNA-ZINZENDORF
9 May	Ambassador VIENNA-ZINZENDORF
21 Dec	Prince Hildburgshausen VIENNA-ZINZENDORF

22 Dec	Mme de Clary
	  Mme de Poniatowsky, Mme de Thun, and
	    Mlle de Colalto played
	  Mlle de Dietrichstein sang
	VIENNA-ZINZENDORF

25 Dec	French Ambassador VIENNA-ZINZENDORF

1764

11 Jan	Prince Hildburgshausen Guadagni sang VIENNA-ZINZENDORF
18 Jan	Prince Hildburgshausen VIENNA-ZINZENDORF
1 Feb	Prince Hildburgshausen VIENNA-ZINZENDORF
12 Mar	Mme de Schönborn arias from French comic opera on clar and oboe VIENNA-ZINZENDORF
19 Mar	Prince Hildburgshausen Tebaldi sang VIENNA-ZINZENDORF

1773

8 Jan	Mme de Canal—afternoon concert VIENNA-ZINZENDORF

369

5 Apr   Mme de Wallenstein
            Haydn-Farewell sym
            VIENNA-ZINZENDORF

1774

19 Feb   Mme de Wallenstein
            VIENNA-ZINZENDORF

21 Feb   Princess Auersperg
            ''symphonies concertées''
            Mme Franchi sang
            Starzer played vln
            VIENNA-ZINZENDORF

22 Feb   Mme de Zierotin
            Countess Hortense sang
            Mme Weigelin sang
            Scarlatti accompanied
            VIENNA-ZINZENDORF

28 Feb   Auersperg
            VIENNA-ZINZENDORF

5 Mar   Countess Wallenstein (concert ''de la Haute
            Noblesse'')
            Mme Zerotin and Mme de Goes sang
            Vogarti played fl
            con for 2 kybd
            VIENNA-ZINZENDORF

7 Mar   Princess Auersperg
            VIENNA-ZINZENDORF

12 Mar   Mme de Wallenstein
            Mlle Wrbna, Mlle Keventz, and Mlle de
               Zerotin sang
            VIENNA-ZINZENDORF

16 Mar   Princess Schwarzenberg
            Princesses Ernestine and Auersperg sang
            Stamitz played
            VIENNA-ZINZENDORF

20 Mar	Princess Auersperg VIENNA-ZINZENDORF
26 Mar	Spanish Ambassador VIENNA-ZINZENDORF

1776

26 Feb	Prince Golitzin VIENNA-ZINZENDORF
5 Mar	French Ambassador VIENNA-ZINZENDORF

1777

18 Dec	Concert Spirituel VIENNA-ZINZENDORF

1778

14 Mar	Prince Paar Mme de Hatfeld (Hatzfeld?) and Therese Clary sang Mlle de Hartenstein played kybd VIENNA-ZINZENDORF
31 Mar	Prince Paar VIENNA-ZINZENDORF

1781

2 Feb	*Prince Adam Auersperg Mme Gennoglio sang VIENNA-ZINZENDORF
3 Feb	Mme de Esterházy Countess Therese played kybd Herr and Mme Gennoglio sang VIENNA-ZINZENDORF

6 Feb   Prince Golitzin
            VIENNA-ZINZENDORF

28 Feb   Prince Golitzin
            Raun (Ramm?) played oboe
            Gluck-sym
            VIENNA-ZINZENDORF

2 Mar   *Prince Kaunitz
            Naumann-music from *Kora* played on kybd
            VIENNA-ZINZENDORF

15 Mar   *Countess Thun
            Ramm played oboe
            VIENNA-ZINZENDORF

16 Mar   Archbishop of Salzburg
            Mozart played kybd
            ML 2:714

17 Mar   Archbishop of Salzburg
            Mozart played kybd
            Herr Ceccarelli sang
            ML 2:714

23 Mar   Archbishop of Salzburg
            Mozart played vln, Ceccarelli sang
            VIENNA-ZINZENDORF

24 Mar   Herr von Braun
            Mozart played?
            ML 2:714

24 Mar   *French Ambassador
            Mme Varenne played harp
            VIENNA-ZINZENDORF

27 Mar   French Ambassador
            VIENNA-ZINZENDORF

28 Mar   *French Ambassador
            Mme Varenne played harp
            VIENNA-ZINZENDORF

4 Apr	Prince Paar Mme Mara and Herr Adamberger sang Mme Varenne played harp VIENNA-ZINZENDORF
7 Apr	French Ambassador Mme Varenne played harp Herr Varenne played vln VIENNA-ZINZENDORF
8 Apr	Archbishop of Salzburg Mozart-rondo for vln and orchestra (K.373)- Herr Brunetti Mozart-son with vln accompaniment (Kv. 380)-Mozart Mozart-aria with recit (K. 374)-Herr Ceccarelli ML 2:722-23; Eibl/DOCUMENTA, 38
8 Apr	Countess Thun Mme Weigl and Herr Adamberger sang ML 2:723
10 Apr	French Ambassador VIENNA-ZINZENDORF
27 Apr	Archbishop of Salzburg Mozart played ML 2:726
3 May	Count Rosenberg Mme Bernasconi sang VIENNA-ZINZENDORF
5 May	French Ambassador Mme Varenne played VIENNA-ZINZENDORF
16 Nov	Archduke Maximilian ML 2:779

1782

12 Jan	Countess Rumbeck Mozart played ML 2:791
21 Feb	Prince Golitzin VIENNA-ZINZENDORF
9 Mar	Prince Golitzin VIENNA-ZINZENDORF
Spring	Baron van Swieten pieces by J.S. Bach and G.F. Handel Herr Starzer, Hofsekretär Karl von Kohaut played ML 2:801; Bernhardt/VAN SWIETEN, 146
6 Dec	*Prince Oeynhausen Mozart-kybd pieces Bach-kybd pieces VIENNA-ZINZENDORF
14 Dec	*Countess Wilhelmine Thun Mozart played VIENNA-ZINZENDORF
Winter 82-83	Prince Golitzin Mozart engaged for series ML 2:831-32

1783

4 Jan	Hofrath von Spielmann Mozart played ML 2:834
12 Mar	Esterházy Mozart played ML 2:842
20 Mar	*French Ambassador Mme de Buquoy played VIENNA-ZINZENDORF

374

3 Apr	Prince Golitzin
	VIENNA-ZINZENDORF

25 Apr   General Wallmoden
      Mme de Buquoy played
   VIENNA-ZINZENDORF

7 May   ?
      Mozart played
   ML 2:847

1 Jul   Herr von Keith
      Sarti-aria from *Giulio Sabino*-Mlle Storace
      Herr Benucci played kybd
      Sarti-aria from *Pittor Parigino* (?) "Ma il pittor"
      Cimarosa-"Bella, bella, gioja, gioja" from
        L'amor costante-Mlle Storace, Herr Benucci
   VIENNA-ZINZENDORF

14 Oct   *Prince Golitzin
      Mme de Hatzfeld sang "imitating Mlle
      Storace"
   VIENNA-ZINZENDORF

1784

1 Jan   Prince Oeynhausen
      "Never till now"
   VIENNA-ZINZENDORF

26 Feb   Prince Golitzin
      Mozart played
   ML 2:869

1 Mar   Count Johann Esterházy
      Mozart played
   ML 2:869

3 Mar   Prince Golitzin
   VIENNA-ZINZENDORF

4 Mar   Prince Golitzin
      Mozart played
   ML 2:869

5 Mar   Johann Esterházy
            ML 2:869

8 Mar   Johann Esterházy
            ML 2:869

11 Mar   Prince Golitzin
            ML 2:869

12 Mar   Johann Esterházy
            ML 2:869

15 Mar   Johann Esterházy
            ML 2:869

17 Mar   Prince Golitzin
            Herr Marchesi sang
            VIENNA-ZINZENDORF

18 Mar   Prince Golitzin
            Mozart played
            ML 2:869

19 Mar   Johann Esterházy
            Mozart played
            ML 2:869

20 Mar   Count Zichy
            Mozart played
            ML 2:872

22 Mar   Johann Esterházy
            Mozart played
            ML 2:874

25 Mar   Prince Golitzin
            Mozart played
            ML 2:874

26 Mar   Johann Esterházy
            Mozart played
            ML 2:870

29 Mar   Johann Esterházy
            Mozart played
            ML 2:870

31 Mar   Prince Golitzin
         Miss Petty sang
         VIENNA-ZINZENDORF

9 Apr   Prince Pallfy
         Mozart played
         ML 2:870

10 Apr   Prince Kaunitz
         Mozart played
         ML 2:870

15 Apr   Prince Kaunitz
         Mlle Strinasacchi played vln
         Mme de Bassen (?) played kybd
         VIENNA-ZINZENDORF

8 May   Mme de Trattner
         Mozart played
         ML 2:876

6 Jul   *Count Rosenberg
         Paisiello sang
         VIENNA-ZINZENDORF

22 Jul   Mozart
         ML 2:881

18 Sep   *Prince Golitzin
         Salieri played kybd and sang
         VIENNA-ZINZENDORF

25 Dec   Prince Golitzin
         Princess Gagarin sang
         Mme Lang (Lange) sang
         VIENNA-ZINZENDORF

1785

3 Feb   *Mme de Buquoy
         Mme Auernhammer played
         (Paisiello?)-aria from *Il Barbier di Siviglia*-Mlle
         Altamont
         VIENNA-ZINZENDORF

16 Feb   Prince Golitzin
                (Paisiello?)-arias from *Il Re Teodoro and Il Barbier di Siviglia*-Therese Clary
                VIENNA-ZINZENDORF

16 Feb   Herr von Ployer
                Mozart played?
                ML 2:887

21 Feb   Count Zichy
                Herr and Mme Le Brun performed
                Mozart played
                ML 2:887

21 Feb   Herr von Ployer
                ML 2:887

2 Mar   *Prince Golitzin
                Princess Gagarin, Therese Clary, Herr Benucci, Herr Mandini sang
                VIENNA-ZINZENDORF

16 Mar   *Prince Golitzin
                Isabella Wallenstein, Therese Clary and Barbe Gagarin sang
                VIENNA-ZINZENDORF

17 Mar   Mme Trattner
                Mme Trattner played kybd
                VIENNA-ZINZENDORF

23 Mar   Herr von Ployer
                Mlle Ployer played kybd
                VIENNA-ZINZENDORF

27 Apr   Mme de Buquoy
                (Paisiello?)-music from *Il Barbier di Siviglia*
                VIENNA-ZINZENDORF

1786

19 Jan   Prince Golitzin
                VIENNA-ZINZENDORF

9 Feb	Prince Golitzin VIENNA-ZINZENDORF
23 Feb	Prince Golitzin VIENNA-ZINZENDORF
7 Mar	Mme de Buquoy var on Fischer's minuet-Mme Auernhammer VIENNA-ZINZENDORF
9 Mar	Prince Golitzin Nancy Storace sang VIENNA-ZINZENDORF
23 Mar	Prince Paar Paisiello-"Come lasciar potrei" and "Non vi tubate" from *Il Re Teodoro*-Mme Dušek VIENNA-ZINZENDORF
24 Mar	*Mme de Buquoy Mme Dušek sang VIENNA-ZINZENDORF
27 Mar	Prince Paar Mme Dušek sang VIENNA-ZINZENDORF
6 Apr	Prince Paar Paisiello-"Come lasciar potrei"-Mme Dušek "Amor la face"-Mme Dušek Sanhini-aria-Mme Dušek VIENNA-ZINZENDORF
6 Apr	Prince Golitzin VIENNA-ZINZENDORF
30 Apr	Herr von Born VIENNA-ZINZENDORF
Lent	Baron van Swieten Handel-*Judas Maccabäus*-Herr Starzer directed Bernhardt/VAN SWIETEN, 149
29 Nov	Saxon Ambassador (Paisiello)-trio from *Il Barbier di Siviglia*-Mme de Harrach, Mme de Tarocca, French bass VIENNA-ZINZENDORF

1787

27 Jan	Mme de Buquoy VIENNA-ZINZENDORF
22 Feb	Prince Golitzin VIENNA-ZINZENDORF
5 Mar	*Fürstenberg Mme de Fürstenberg played kybd Prince and Count Oettingen played VIENNA-ZINZENDORF
26 Mar	Prince Auersperg Haydn-*Die sieben Worte* VIENNA-ZINZENDORF
29 Mar	**Martin y Soler-*Una cosa rara* on wind instruments VIENNA-ZINZENDORF
5 Apr	**Prince Paar Herr Callenberg sang and played kybd VIENNA-ZINZENDORF
10 Apr	**Count Carl Zinzendorf Herr Callenberg sang and played kybd VIENNA-ZINZENDORF
11 Apr	**Herr von Manzi Herr Callenberg sang and played kybd VIENNA-ZINZENDORF
12 Apr	**Prince Golitzin Herr Comaschini sang VIENNA-ZINZENDORF
15 Apr	**Prince Schwarzenberg Martin y Soler-*Una cosa rara* on wind instruments VIENNA-ZINZENDORF
Lent	Baron van Swieten Hasse-*La conversione di S. Agostino* Bernhardt/VAN SWIETEN, 149

28 Apr   Venetian Ambassador
        duet from *Sarola de Gelosi*-Mme Morichelli,
        Mlle Victoria de Fries
        Mlle Schewel played harp
        VIENNA-ZINZENDORF

5 May   **Prince Schwarzenberg
        Martín y Soler-*Una cosa rara* on wind
        instruments
        VIENNA-ZINZENDORF

1788

4 Feb   *Mme de Buquoy
        Toni Paar played kybd
        German and Italian songs-Mlle ?
        Mme Auernhammer played kybd
        VIENNA-ZINZENDORF

10 Feb   Venetian Ambassador
        Herr Mandini and Mme Morichelli sang
        Mozart played fp
        Mlle Müllner played harp
        VIENNA-ZINZENDORF

11 Feb   **Prince Schwarzenberg
        Martín y Soler-*L'arbore di Diana* played on
        wind instruments
        VIENNA-ZINZENDORF

14 Feb   Prince Golitzin
        Mlle de Czernichen played kybd
        Victoria Fries and Marguerite Cliffton sang
        VIENNA-ZINZENDORF

26 Feb   Johann Esterházy and Baron van Swieten
        C.P.E. Bach-*Die Auferstehung und Himmelfahrt*
        Christi-Mme Lange, Herr Adamberger, Herr
        Saal; Mozart directed; Herr Umlauf at the
        kybd
        Forkel/ALMANACH 1789, 121-22

28 Feb	Prince Golitzin VIENNA-ZINZENDORF
4 Mar	Johann Esterházy and Baron van Swieten program of 26 Feb Forkel/ALMANACH, 1789, 121-22
6 Mar	Prince Golitzin VIENNA-ZINZENDORF
13 Mar	Prince Golitzin VIENNA-ZINZENDORF
29 Mar	Esterházy VIENNA-ZINZENDORF
30 Mar	Venetian Ambassador Mme Morichelli, Herr Adamberger, Herr and Mlle Saal sang VIENNA-ZINZENDORF
15 Nov	Prince Golitzin VIENNA-ZINZENDORF
30 Dec	Johann Esterházy and Baron van Swieten Handel-*Acis et Galatea*-Swieten directed VIENNA-ZINZENDORF

1789

26 Feb	Prince Golitzin VIENNA-ZINZENDORF
6 Mar	Johann Esterházy and Baron van Swieten Handel-*Der Messias*-Herr Adamberger, Herr Saal, Mme Lange, Katharina Altamont; Mozart directed orchestra; Umlauf at the kybd 12 choristers Deutsch/DOKUMENTE, 294
14 Mar	Hofrath von Spiegelfeld "Mozart at his old place" VIENNA-ZINZENDORF

7 Apr   Johann Esterházy and Baron van Swieten
             Handel-*Der Messias*
             VIENNA-ZINZENDORF

1790

22 May   *Mozart
             Mozart-string quartet in B flat major K. 589
             Deutsch/DOKUMENTE, 316

Lent   Baron van Swieten
             Handel-*Der Messias*-Mozart directed?
             Bernhardt/VAN SWIETEN, 149

24 Dec   Prince Golitzin
             VIENNA-ZINZENDORF

1791

12 Jan   Prince Kinsky
             concert and cantata
             VIENNA-ZINZENDORF

17 Jan   Prince Auersperg
             PZ 19 Jan 91:51

5 Mar   *Mme de Buquoy
             Herman Callenberg sang and played kybd
             VIENNA-ZINZENDORF

10 Mar   Prince Golitzin
             VIENNA-ZINZENDORF

9 Apr   *Herr Hadik .
             Mozart-Quintet K. 581-Mozart
             Mozart-Trio K. 563-Mozart
             ML 2:937

13 Apr   Prince Auersperg
             Joseph Weigl-"Flora e Minerva" (cantata)
             VIENNA-ONB-WEIGL

14 Apr   Prince Golitzin
             VIENNA-ZINZENDORF

Lent   Baron van Swieten
Handel-*Alexandersfest* and *Ode auf den Tage der heiligen Cäcilia*
Bernhardt/VAN SWIETEN, 149

Winter   ?
Concert in honor of Haydn
Haydn-sym No. 95 and 96
Landon/C & W, 3:124

1792

23 Feb   Prince Golitzin
Mme de Schönfeld sang
vocal quartet-Mme Bussani, Mme Tomeoni,
Herr Maffoli, Herr Benucci
VIENNA-ZINZENDORF

17 Mar   Spanish Ambassador (Gallo)
Cimarosa played for the improvisor Gaspard
Mollo
VIENNA-ZINZENDORF

21 Mar   Herr von Kees
VIENNA-ZINZENDORF

23 Mar   Don Martius Mastrilly Gallo
Cimarosa played for the improvisor Gaspard
Mollo
VIENNA-ZINZENDORF

29 Mar   *Prince Schwarzenberg
VIENNA-ZINZENDORF

Lent   Baron van Swieten
Mozart-Requiem
Bernhardt/VAN SWIETEN, 149

1793

14 Feb	Prince Golitzin Mme Tomeoni, Mme de Schönfeld, Mme de Hatzfeld sang VIENNA-ZINZENDORF
19 Feb	**Prince Schwarzenberg Mozart-*Die Zauberflöte* played on wind instruments VIENNA-ZINZENDORF
19 Feb	Prince Lobkowitz (young) VIENNA-ZINZENDORF
21 Feb	Prince Golitzin Mme de Hatzfeld and Mme de Schönfeld sang VIENNA-ZINZENDORF
28 Feb	Prince Golitzin VIENNA-ZINZENDORF
? Mar	Prince Dietrichstein Handel/Mozart-Alexandersfest Eibl/DOCUMENTA, 79
5 Mar	Prince Lobkowitz Herr Bekée played VIENNA-ZINZENDORF
7 Mar	Prince Golitzin Mme de Schönfeld and Mme de Menzikof sang VIENNA-ZINZENDORF
12 Mar	Prince Lobkowitz Haydn played VIENNA-ZINZENDORF
14 Mar	Prince Golitzin Mme de Schönfeld and Mme de Menzikof sang VIENNA-ZINZENDORF
21 Mar	Prince Golitzin VIENNA-ZINZENDORF

30 Apr **Prince Schwarzenberg
(Sarti?)-(*Fra i due*) *Litiganti* played on wind
instruments
VIENNA-ZINZENDORF

15 Jul *Princess Caroline Lobkowitz
Princess Therese Lobkowitz sang, accom-
panied by Princess Lobkowitz and Herr
Bekée on kybd
VIENNA-ZINZENDORF

24 Dec Prince Lichnowsky
Handel-*Ode auf den Tage der heiligen Cäcilia* and
Die Wahl Herkules-Mme Lange, Herr Saal,
Joseph Weigl directed; Herr Röllig at the
glass harmonica (because the organ wasn't
in tune); full orchestra
OM 1794:199-200

25 Dec **Prince Schwarzenberg
Cimarosa-*Il matrimonio segreto* played on wind
instruments
VIENNA-ZINZENDORF

28 Dec Prince Schwarzenberg
Handel-Alexandersfest
"Der Sturm"
Olleson/GRIESINGER, 38

1794

16 Feb **Prince Schwarzenberg
Mozart-*Die Zauberflöte* played on wind
instruments
VIENNA-ZINZENDORF

2 Mar **Prince Schwarzenberg
(Sarti?)-(*Fra i due*) *Litiganti* on wind
instruments
VIENNA-ZINZENDORF

8 Apr	Count Callenberg Therese and Sophie Schönfeld sang VIENNA-ZINZENDORF
8 Apr	Prince Lobkowitz "*La Sposerete*"-Mme de Woyna and Prince Lobkowitz Therese Schwarzenberg sang VIENNA-ZINZENDORF
15 Apr	Prince Lichnowsky Handel-*Judas Maccabäus*-Herr Spangler VIENNA-ZINZENDORF
31 Dec	Prince Paar Handel-*Athalia*-Herr Spangler VIENNA-ZINZENDORF

1795

6 Feb	*Herr von Grosschlag aria from *La Sposerete*-Mlle Grosschlag and Princess Auersperg VIENNA-ZINZENDORF
2 Mar	Prince Lobkowitz Beethoven played VIENNA-ZINZENDORF
5 Mar	Prince Lobkowitz VIENNA-ZINZENDORF
12 Mar	Prince Lobkowitz vocal quartet-Mlle de Zichy, Mlle d'Ursil, Prince Lobkowitz, Prince Erneste Schwarzenberg VIENNA-ZINZENDORF
19 Mar	Prince Lobkowitz Herr Teimer, Mlle de Zichy, Mlle d'Ursil, Princess Therese and Prince Erneste Schwarzenberg, Prince Lobkowitz (young) sang VIENNA-ZINZENDORF

27 Mar   Prince Lobkowitz
         Mlle d'Ursil, Mlle de Zichy, Prince Erneste
         Schwarzenberg, Prince Lobkowitz, Mme de
         Woyna, Herr Deymer sang
         VIENNA-ZINZENDORF

5 Apr   Prince Paar
         Handel-*Der Messias*
         VIENNA-ZINZENDORF

20 Apr   *Mme de Ferraris
         Sacchini-aria from *Oedipe*-Louise d'Ursil
         Piccini-aria from *Didon*-Louise d'Ursil
         Gluck-aria from *Alceste*-Louise d'Ursil
         VIENNA-ZINZENDORF

23 Apr   Prince Rasumofsky
         Beethoven played
         VIENNA-ZINZENDORF

11 Nov   *Mme de Schönfeld
         Mme de Schönfeld and Mme de Woyna sang
         with Herr Koželuch accompanying on kybd
         VIENNA-ZINZENDORF

1796

4 Jan   Prince Esterházy
         VIENNA-ZINZENDORF

19 Feb   Prince Lobkowitz
         con-Herr Wranitzky
         VIENNA-ZINZENDORF

26 Feb   Prince Lobkowitz
         Prince Lobkowitz sang
         VIENNA-ZINZENDORF

10 Mar   *Count Windisch-Grätz
         "Liebe mindert alle Plagen" from *Die*
             Zauberflöte-Emilie and Louise d'Ursil
         Mozart-finale from *Le Nozze di Figaro*
         VIENNA-ZINZENDORF

11 Mar	Prince Lobkowitz VIENNA-ZINZENDORF
18 Mar	Prince Lobkowitz Princess Auersperg sang Herr Seigreux played fl VIENNA-ZINZENDORF
19 Mar	Windisch-Grätz aria from *Trofonio*-Louise d'Ursil VIENNA-ZINZENDORF
23 Mar	Prince Auersperg Princess Auersperg sang VIENNA-ZINZENDORF
26 Mar	Prince Schwarzenberg Haydn-*Die sieben Worte* VIENNA-ZINZENDORF
27 Mar	Prince Schwarzenberg program as on 26 Mar VIENNA-ZINZENDORF
30 Mar	*Windisch-Grätz Haydn-sym "coup de canon" VIENNA-ZINZENDORF
2 Apr	Eger VIENNA-ZINZENDORF
7 Apr	**Windisch-Grätz arias from *Renard et Armide*-Emilie and Louise d'Ursil arias from *Spiegel in Arkadien*-above VIENNA-ZINZENDORF
28 Apr	**Windisch-Grätz VIENNA-ZINZENDORF
9 May	**Windisch-Grätz Paisiello-"Come lasciar potrei" from *Il Re Teodoro*-Louise d'Ursil VIENNA-ZINZENDORF

1797

8 Mar   Prince Paar
         Countess Therese played kybd
         Mme Auernhammer played kybd
         VIENNA-ZINZENDORF

24 Mar   Prince Schwarzenberg
         Handel-*Acis et Galatea*-Mlle Gerhardi and Herr
           Spangler
         VIENNA-ZINZENDORF

7 Apr   Prince Schwarzenberg
         Haydn-*Die sieben Worte*
         (performance planned but cancelled)
         Landon/C & W, 4:253

16 Apr   *Mme de Buquoy
         Mme Auernhammer played
         VIENNA-ZINZENDORF

10 Nov   Mme de Boisser
         Mlle de Lilien played kybd
         Mme de Boissier played harp with kybd
           accompaniment
         VIENNA-ZINZENDORF

22 Nov   Baron von Felz
         Mlle de Felz d.A. played kybd and d.J. sang
         Mlle de Lilien d.A. played kybd
         Guglielmi-vocal trio-Mlle Crunpipen, Mlle de
           Felz d.J. and their teacher
         VIENNA-ZINZENDORF

1798

23 Mar   Prince Lobkowitz
         Mozart-quartet from *Le Nozze di Figaro*-
           Prince Lobkowitz, Herr Bridi, Mme
           Breuner, Mlle de Walterskirchen
         VIENNA-ZINZENDORF

31 Mar   Prince Lobkowitz
         VIENNA-ZINZENDORF

5 Apr	Prince Lobkowitz Beethoven-vln son-Herr Kreutzer and Beethoven VIENNA-ZINZENDORF
29 Apr	Prince Schwarzenberg Haydn-*Die Schöpfung* (premiere)-Mlle Christina Gerhardi, Herr Rathmayer, Ignaz Saal; Haydn directed; Salieri at the kybd VIENNA-ZINZENDORF; Croll/SCHWARZENBERG, 85-92
30 Apr	Prince Schwarzenberg program as on 29 Apr sources as above
7 May	Prince Schwarzenberg program as on 29 Apr sources as above
10 May	Prince Schwarzenberg program as on 29 Apr sources as above
12 Jun	*Rosenbaum VIENNA-ROSENBAUM

1799

15 Feb	Prince Lobkowitz Haydn-"messe bruyant" VIENNA-ZINZENDORF
22 Feb	Prince Lobkowitz Mme de Schönfeld, Mme de Haugwitz, Mme de Mailath sang VIENNA-ZINZENDORF
2 Mar	Prince Schwarzenberg Haydn-*Die Schöpfung* VIENNA-ZINZENDORF
4 Mar	Prince Schwarzenberg Haydn-*Die Schöpfung* VIENNA-ZINZENDORF

6 Mar   Spanish Ambassador?—concert of Mme Mailath
           Weigl-aria-Mme Mailath
           Princess d'Amalfi, Herr Pär, Dr. Malfatti sang
           Mlle de Keglevich played kybd
           (Paisiello?)-trio from *Nina*-Mailath, Mme de
              Zois, Herr Pär
           VIENNA-ZINZENDORF

8 Mar   Prince Lobkowitz
           Haydn-"le Tempete"
           VIENNA-ZINZENDORF

16 Mar   Prince Lobkowitz
           (Salieri?)-*Axur*-Herr Pär, Herr Bridi, Dr.
              Malfatti, Mme de Frank, Princess Therese
              Schwarzenberg
           VIENNA-ZINZENDORF

23 Mar   Prince Schwarzenberg
           Handel/Mozart-*Der Messias* (part 1)
           VIENNA-ZINZENDORF

24 Mar   Prince Schwarzenberg
           Handel/Mozart-*Der Messias* (part 2)
           VIENNA-ZINZENDORF

5 Apr   Count Fries
           Haydn-sym
           Doppelhof-couplets-Mlle Saal, Herr Saal, Herr
              Vogel, Mlle de ...
           Giornovichi-vln con-young Swede (Berwald)
           Paisiello-duet from *Elfrida*-Mme de Schönfeld,
              Herr Pär; Pär accompanied on kybd
           (Beethoven-wind quintet?)
           VIENNA-ZINZENDORF

1800

11 Mar   Prince Trautmannsdorf
           Haydn-*Die Schöpfung* performed on 2 vln,
              viola, bassettel and "Flute de zinck"-M de
              Schönborn and Prince Lobkowitz on vln
           VIENNA-ZINZENDORF

27 Mar   Lord Minto
          Steibelt played fp
          Mme Steibelt accompanied on tambourine
          JOURNAL, 37-38

31 Mar   Count Fries
          Paisiello-duet "Nei giomi tuor felice"-Mme de
          Schönfeld and Herr Pär
          VIENNA-ZINZENDORF

3 Apr   Prince Lobkowitz
          Cartellieri-*Angarda, regina de Boemia*-Mlle de
          Walterskirchen, Princess Therese
          Schwarzenberg, Herr Bridi
          VIENNA-ZINZENDORF

4 Apr   Count Fries
          Haydn-*Die Schöpfung* on 9 wind instruments-
          Mme de Schönfeld, Herr Reitmayer
          (Rathmayer), Prince Lobkowitz
          VIENNA-ZINZENDORF

11 Apr?   Prince Schwarzenberg
          Haydn-*Die Schöpfung*-Joseph Weigl directed
          Pohl/HAYDN, 161; Croll/SCHWARZENBERG

12 Apr   Prince Schwarzenberg
          Haydn-*Die Schöpfung*
          Pohl/HAYDN, 161; Croll/SCHWARZENBERG

13 Apr   Prince Schwarzenberg
          Haydn-*Die Schöpfung*
          Croll/SCHWARZENBERG

16 Apr   Prince Lobkowitz
          Wranitzky-septet
          Mme de Schönfeld and Herr Pär sang
          Mme de Frank sang
          Punto played horn
          Steibelt played kybd
          (Piccini?)-finale from *Griselda*-Mme de Schön-
          feld, Princess Therese Schwarzenberg, Mlle
          Francois de Zichy, Mme Frank, Prince
          Lobkowitz and 2 men
          VIENNA-ZINZENDORF

Spring   Count Fries
         Improvisational duels between Beethoven and
            Steibelt
         Forbes/BEETHOVEN, 257

15 Oct   Count Fries (wedding party)
         Pär-cantata-Countess Schönfeld and Countess
            Haugwitz (sisters of Fries) and Herr Pär
            sang
         AMZ 17 Dec 00:200

8 Dec   *Rosenbaums
         Mozart-aria from *La Clemenza di Tito*-Therese
            Rosenbaum
         (Peter Winter)-aria from *Das unterbrochene*
            Opferfest-Rosenbaum
         VIENNA-ROSENBAUM

10 Dec   Countess Josephine Deym
         Beethoven-fp son with vlc-Beethoven and
            Kraft
         Beethoven-son with vln accompaniment (Op.
            12, No. 3)-Josephine Deym and Herr
            Schuppanzigh
         Beethoven-string quartets-Schuppanzigh,
            Kraft, ??
         Forbes/BEETHOVEN, 236-37

1801

27 Jan   Herr Asher
         Herr Asher sang and Herr Cartellieri accom-
            panied on kybd
         Herr Kirchstein played fl
         VIENNA-ROSENBAUM

4 Apr   Prince Lobkowitz
         Haydn-*Die Schöpfung* in Italian-Haydn directed?
         VIENNA-ZINZENDORF

14 Apr   Widow Thurn
         VIENNA-ZINZENDORF

24 Apr	Prince Schwarzenberg Haydn-*Die Jahreszeiten* (premiere)-Mlle Saal, Herr Saal, Herr Rathmayer VIENNA-ZINZENDORF; Pohl/HAYDN, 3:170; Croll/SCHWARZENBERG
27 Apr	Prince Schwarzenberg program as on 24 Apr Sources as above
30 Apr	Herr Schmierer Franz (Franciszek) Lessel-trio for fp, horn and clar VIENNA-ROSENBAUM
1 May	Prince Schwarzenberg program of 24 Apr Sources as above
21 May	Herr Schmierer (the last concert) Mirtakovsky played guitar and sang Herr Lessel played fp VIENNA-ROSENBAUM
28 Sep	Schmierer Schuster-cantata-Schuster, Jeanette and Call (?) aria from *Griselda*-Therese Rosenbaum duet from *Soliman*-Rosenbaum and Schuster VIENNA-ROSENBAUM
16 Nov	Herr Schmierer Haydn-*Die Schöpfung* VIENNA-ROSENBAUM
6 Dec	Mme Eisenkohl Pleyel-quartets aria from *Griselda*-Therese Rosenbaum "later we danced"-29 people there VIENNA-ROSENBAUM
19 Dec	Herr von Keller Mme de Frank, Herr Liberati (Liverati?), Mme de Schönfeld, Herr von Finkenstein and Herr Pär sang VIENNA-ZINZENDORF

1801   Prince Odesalchi
           Beethoven-septet (Op. 20)-Nikalaus Zmeskall,
           Herr Eppinger
           BL 2:69-70

1802

10 Mar   Hofrath Schupp
           Keller "played vln in a quintet"
           fp son with clar-Mlle Gilberg and Russian
             officer
           Tomasini "played vln in a quartet"
           Cimarosa-"Ah torna la bell amora"-Therese
             Rosenbaum
           (lasted from 7:00 to 10:30 P.M.)
           VIENNA-ROSENBAUM

11 Mar   Count Haugwitz
           Mme Poüthon née Litgen played kybd
           Mlle Perschl sang
           VIENNA-ZINZENDORF

16 Mar   Baron Spielmann
           Mlle Spielmann (12 years) played kybd
           Herr Kraft played vlc
           Herr Leibnitz "Jew from Prague" played vln
           VIENNA-ZINZENDORF

17 Mar   Hofrath Schupp
           Mozart-"Parto" from *La Clemenza di Tito*-
             Therese Rosenbaum, Herr Bähr (clar) accom-
             panied by Herr Kruft on kybd
           VIENNA-ROSENBAUM

18 Mar   Baron Braun
           VIENNA-ZINZENDORF

26 Mar   Baron Braun
           Guglielmi-"Debora e Sisara"-Herr Brizzi and
             Mme Pär sang, Herr Wranitzky at the kybd;
           Mlle Müllner played harp in intermission
           VIENNA-ZINZENDORF

29 Mar   Count Fries
             Pär-"Der Teufel, Jungfer belle" from
             Camilla-Herr and Mme Pär, Mme de
             Schönfeld
             (Mayer)-aria from *Ginevra*-Mme Pär and
             Mme de Schönfeld
             (Piccini?)-aria from *Griselda*-L'Iano
             Mlle Müllner played harp
             VIENNA-ZINZENDORF

31 Mar   Hofrath Schupp
             Fuchs-serenate
             (Mozart?)-introduction to *Don Juan*
             con-Mme Jacobi
             (Pär?)-trio from *Achille*
             VIENNA-ROSENBAUM

1 Apr   Baron Braun
             oratorio (or opera as oratorio?)
             Weigl-finale-Herr Marchesi
             VIENNA-ZINZENDORF

7 Apr   Hofrath Schupp
             Haydn-aria from *Die Jahreszeiten*-Herr Jonat
             fp son-Mlle Paulitsch
             VIENNA-ROSENBAUM

8 Apr   Baron Braun
             Czerwenka-oboe con-Czerwenka ('but his con-
             certo put Swieten to sleep')
             Nasolini-aria
             Mlle Müllner played harp
             Paisiello-duet
             Wranitzky-wind band piece
             Cimarosa-finale from *Horace*
             VIENNA-ZINZENDORF

12 Apr   Count Fries
             harp con-Mlle Müllner
             oboe con (Herr Czerwenka?)
             finale from *Polymyra*
             vocal trio from *Trofonio*

vocal trio from *Cesare in famacusa*-Mme de
Schönfeld
VIENNA-ZINZENDORF

14 Apr   Hofrath Schupp
           VIENNA-ROSENBAUM

4 May   Hofrath Schupp
           Pleyel-duet played by "smallest Romano and
           Schupp d.J."
           "afterwards we danced"
           VIENNA-ROSENBAUM

10 May   Rosenbaums
           Mozart-fp con-Mlle Gyulas (with orchestra)
           VIENNA-ROSENBAUM

14 Nov   *Beethoven
           BL 2:80

29 Dec   *Mme de Hoyos
           Herr O'donel sang "l'air du Volontaire a
           l'armee la Bourbonnaise et la parodie des
           Horace"
           VIENNA-ZINZENDORF

1803

19 Feb   *Mme de Hoyos
           Herr O'donel sang
           VIENNA-ZINZENDORF

19 Feb   Herr Quarin
           arias-Italian Abbate (Abbé Bevilqua?)
           Crescentini-duet-Therese Rosenbaum and
           Abbé
           Zingarelli-"Giusto Cielo" from *Giulietta e
           Romeo*
           VIENNA-ROSENBAUM

23 Feb   Hofrath Schupp
           (Pär?)-tenor aria from *Griselda*
           VIENNA-ROSENBAUM

27 Feb	Prince Lobkowitz VIENNA-ZINZENDORF
2 Mar	Hofrath Schupp VIENNA-ROSENBAUM
6 Mar	Prince Lobkowitz Beethoven-fp con-Beethoven Mme de Frank sang VIENNA-ZINZENDORF
9 Mar	Hofrath Schupp quartet-Dod. Rudolph fl var-Herr Bernardi Pär-aria from *Camilla*-Mlle Sattmann quintet with Baron Gruft (Kruft) on fp Buffo bass aria-Herr Sander, Herr Scheidlein VIENNA-ROSENBAUM
11 Mar	Prince Lichnowsky VIENNA-ZINZENDORF
12 Mar	Prince Lobkowitz Herr Brizzi and Mme de Frank sang VIENNA-ZINZENDORF
16 Mar	Sacrati Cimarosa-music to *Horace*-Herr Bellotto, Mlle Costa, ''Angrisani frere et bassa'' VIENNA-ZINZENDORF
16 Mar	Hofrath Schupp Cimarosa-finale from *Armand* VIENNA-ROSENBAUM
23 Mar	Hofrath Schupp Gyrowetz-aria-Herr Scheidlein Pär-trio from *Camilla*-Kirchwetter, Jonah, Sander Weigl-aria-Therese Gassmann VIENNA-ROSENBAUM
30 Mar	Baron Braun Weigl-music of *I solitari* VIENNA-ZINZENDORF; FM 17 May 03:310

3 Apr Gillenberg
       (Pär?)-"Sa Griselda"-Therese Rosenbaum
       accompanied by Herr Kraft
       Haydn-*Die Jahreszeiten* "in quartets"
       VIENNA-ROSENBAUM

6 Apr Hofrath Schupp
       quartet-Herr Tomasini
       Mozart-"Deh per questo istante"-Therese
       Rosenbaum
       Eberl-caprice for 2 fp-Eberl and Baron Gruft
       (Kruft)
       vocal trio-2 Scheidleins and brother
       VIENNA-ROSENBAUM

10 Apr Baron Braun
       Cimarosa-*Gli Orazi ed i Curiazi*
       VIENNA-ZINZENDORF; FM 17 May 03:310

15 Apr Prince Lobkowitz
       Herr Nadermann played harp
       Sophia-Herr Pär, Herr Brizzi, Prince Lobkowitz
       VIENNA-ZINZENDORF

19 Apr Quarin
       duet-Mme Rosenbaum and Abbé Bevilaqua
       VIENNA-ZINZENDORF

26 Apr Prince Lobkowitz
       Möser played vln
       Pär-overture
       Caprice for harp and fp-Herr Nadermann and
       Herr Pär
       VIENNA-ZINZENDORF

13 May Schmierer
       Haydn-*Die Jahreszeiten*-Jeanette and 2
       Schusters; Herr Liparsky directed at fp
       vlns doubled; 16 in chorus including Herr
       Pfeiffer
       VIENNA-ROSENBAUM

6 Jun Prince Lobkowitz
       Vogler-*Castor und Pollux*
       VIENNA-ZINZENDORF

8 Dec	Rosenbaums fl var with orchestra-Herr Bernardi Umlauf-cantata-Mme Sattmann Umlauf-new aria-Therese Rosenbaum orchestra of 28 VIENNA-ROSENBAUM
18 Dec	Prince Lobkowitz Sister and wife of Herr Brizzi performed VIENNA-ZINZENDORF

1804

Lent	Baron Braun Beethoven-sym in D major Eberl-sym in E flat major FM 3 May 04:352

Lent	Herr von Würth-various concerts
	Mozart-overtures to *Die Zauberflöte, Don Juan,*
	  Figaro, Idomeneo, Entführung, La Clemenza di
	  Tito
	Cherubini-overtures to *Der Wasserträger,*
	  Lodoïska
	Peter Winter-overture to *Tamerlan*
	Eberl-overture in D major
	Count Gallenberg-pieces
	Mozart-sym in C major and G minor
	Hofmann-vln con-Baron Cerini
	Herr Metzger, Herr Flat, Herr Kalmus, Herr
	  Pou, Herr Kalkbrenner, Herr Thieriot,
	  Mlle Kurzböck, Baron Kruft, Herr Brehm,
	  Herr Clement directed
	AMZ 11 Apr 04:267-68; AMZ 9 May 04:545-46

18 Mar	Herr Stegmayer Stegmayer-cantata with quartet, fl, and bassoon accompaniment VIENNA-ROSENBAUM

401

24 Apr   Prince Lobkowitz
Clementi played kybd
duet-Mlle de Woyna and Herr Brizzi
VIENNA-ZINZENDORF

7 Aug   Herr Kühnel
Cherubini-*Die Tage der Gefahr* in quartets-
Hummel, 2 Tomasinis, Herr Clamoth
VIENNA-ROSENBAUM

3 Dec   Herr Rottruff
Mayer-aria-Therese Rosenbaum
Weigl-vocal trio from *Herrnhuthern*
VIENNA-ROSENBAUM

Advent   Herr von Würth-various concerts –1
Mozart-sym in C major
Rode-vln con-Herr Clement
Clement-overture in E minor
Cherubini-overture to *Medea* (*Médée*)
AMZ 9 Jan 05:242-43

Advent   Herr von Würth-various concerts –2
Haydn-sym in E-flat major
Cannabich-oboe con in F major-Herr Damm
Vogel-overture to *Démophon*
Cherubini-overture to *Lodoïska*
AMZ 9 Jan 05:243-44

Dec   Prince Lobkowitz
Beethoven-sym in E-flat major-Beethoven
directed
Beethoven-quintet (Op. 16) Beethoven, Herr
Ramm
Forbes/BEETHOVEN, 350

Winter
04-05   Herr von Würth-various concerts
Beethoven-sym in C major
Eberl-sym in E-flat major
Mozart-sym in G minor, E-flat major, D major
Kanne-sym
Beethoven-fp con in C minor-Herr Ries
Mozart-fp quartet in G minor-Mlle Kurzböck,
Herr Clement, Herr Mayseder, Herr Kraft

Dussek-quintet-Mlle Leitersdorfer
Cherubini-overture to *Anacréon*
Gluck-overture to *Alceste*
Mozart-overture to *Don Juan* and *Idomeneo*
Méhul-overture to *Stratonice*
AMZ 13 Feb 05:321; AMZ 26 Feb 05:351-52

1805

7 Jan Aspremont
Herr Brizzi and Mlle Aspremont sang
Mlle Schlesinger played kybd
VIENNA-ZINZENDORF

12 Mar Prince Esterházy
fp competition between Herr Hummel and
Herr Zeuner
BMZ 1:34 (1805):136

Lent Herr von Würth--various concerts
Haydn-several sym
Mozart-fp con in B-flat major-Mme Bigot de
Morogues
horn con-Herr Hradezky
Mozart-fp con in C major-Mlle Kurzböck
(with cadenzas by Eberl)
Koželuch-fp con in C major-Mlle Koželuch
Winter-sym with obbligato vln, clar, horn,
and bassoon
Cherubini-overtures to *Die Gefangenen* and
Das portugesische Gasthaus
Winter-overture to *Das unterbrochene Opferfest*
Righini-overture to *Tigrane*
Mozart-overture to *Die Entführung aus
dem Serail*
Hummel-church music
Hummel-var for orchestra
Haydn-*Die sieben Worte*
AMZ 17 Apr 05:469-70

6 Apr Baron Braun
        Paisiello-*I Giuochi d'Agrigento*-Herr
        Crescentini and Mme Campi
        VIENNA-ZINZENDORF

Winter Schuppanzigh quartet series *where*
        Mozart-string quartets
        Haydn-string quartets
        Beethoven-string quartets
        Eberl-string quartets
        Romberg-string quartets
        Beethoven-sextet (Op. 71)-with Herr Bähr
          Herr Schuppanzigh, Herr Mayseder, Herr
          Schreiber and Herr Kraft d.A.
        AMZ 15 May 05:534-35

1806

9 Feb Count Johann Esterházy
        VIENNA-ROSENBAUM

28 Mar Prince Lobkowitz
        VIENNA-ZINZENDORF

13 Aug Rivolla (?)
        Mozart-aria from *Die Zauberflöte*-
        Therese Rosenbaum
        VIENNA-ROSENBAUM

1807

27 Feb Count Haugwitz
        Naumann-Psalm 103
        Naumann-final chorus of Lutheran cantata
        Naumann-excerpts from "Unsere Brüder"
        (Lutheran cantata)
        Naumann-"Gottes Wege" (Lutheran cantata)
        Sung by Mlle Marconi, Herr Vogel, Herr
        Weinmüller
        VIENNA-ZINZENDORF

b18 Mar   Prince Lobkowitz-various concerts
Beethoven-sym nos. 1-4
Beethoven-overture to *Coriolan*
Beethoven-fp con
Beethoven arias from *Fidelio*
AMZ 18 Mar 07:400; Forbes/BEETHOVEN, 416

28 Mar   Count Haugwitz
Mozart-fp con
Kunzen-"Das Halleluja der Schöpfung"-Herr
Vogel, Herr Weinmüller, Mlle Marconi
Mme Puthon née Lilien and Mme ? née
Puthon played kybd
VIENNA-ZINZENDORF

4 Apr   Prince Lobkowitz
VIENNA-ZINZENDORF

15 Aug   Mme de Buquoy
Beethoven-septet (Op. 20)-Herr Schuppanzigh
played
Princess Salm sang
VIENNA-ZINZENDORF

1808

b16 Jan   ?
Eberl-quintet in E major for fp, vln, viola
oboe and vlc-Herr Flat played oboe
AMZ 27 Jan 08:287-88

8 Mar   Count Callenberg
VIENNA-ZINZENDORF

15 Mar   Count Haugwitz
Naumann-"Zeit und Ewigkeit"
Schutz-"Das Lob Gottes"
VIENNA-ZINZENDORF

19 Mar   Herr Nagy (birthday celebration)
Therese Rosenbaum, Herr Wallaschek, Herr
Möglich sang
Buffo aria-Wallaschek
Müllner-harp fantasy-Mlle Müllner
VIENNA-ROSENBAUM

4 Jun Herr Nitschner (birthday celebration)
Mozart-overture to *Die Zauberflöte*
Mozart-"In diesem heiligen Halle," with new
words-Herr Nitschner d.J.
Triebensee-cantata-Therese Rosenbaum
vocal trio-Josef Goldmann, Herr Werben,
Therese Rosenbaum
comic trios
VIENNA-ROSENBAUM

19 Jul Starhemberg
Count George played kybd
Herr Dragonetti played vlc
VIENNA-ZINZENDORF

19 Sep Starhemberg
Princess Starhemberg and Dragonetti played
VIENNA-ZINZENDORF

b5 Dec Prince Lobkowitz
Reichardt-*Brabante*-Mlle Fischer, Herr Simoni,
Herr Vogel, Prince Lobkowitz; Herr Wranit-
zky directed; Herr Kraft d.J. and d.A in the
orchestra
Reichardt/VERTRAUTE, 1:182-86

b10 Dec Schuppanzigh series at Prince Rasumovsky's
Haydn-string quartet
Mozart-string quartet
Beethoven-septet
Reichardt/VERTRAUTE, 1:208

b10 Dec Countess Erdödy
Beethoven-new piano trio (Op. 70)
Beethoven-string quartet-Schuppanzigh quartet
Reichardt/VERTRAUTE, 1:209

b16 Dec *Herr Arensteiner
Steibelt-double fp son-Mlle Kurzböck and
Mme de Pereira
Reichardt/VERTRAUTE, 2:233

b16 Dec   Schuppanzigh series at Prince Rasumovsky's
          Haydn-string quartet
          Mozart-string quartet
          Beethoven-string quartet
          Ries-string quartet
          Reichardt/VERTRAUTE, 1:231

b21 Dec   Prince Lobkowitz
          Countess Lunin sang
          Reichardt/VERTRAUTE, 1:245

22 Dec   Schuppanzigh series at Prince Rasumovsky's
          Haydn-string quartet
          Mozart-string quartet
          Beethoven-string quartet
          Reichardt/VERTRAUTE, 1:258

b25 Dec   Prince Lobkowitz
          Mlle Goubeau and Countess Potocki sang
          Reichardt/VERTRAUTE,1:266-67

b25 Dec   *Herr von Henikstein
          arias from Italian comic opera
          Mlle Henikstein accompanied on fp; Herr
          Seligmann sang
          Reichardt/VERTRAUTE, 1:268-69

b25 Dec   *Prince Lobkowitz
          Ries-fp trio
          Reichardt/VERTRAUTE, 1:270

b31 Dec   *Prince Lobkowitz
          quartet concert-Herr Seidler played
          Reichardt/VERTRAUTE, 1:279-80

b31 Dec   Countess Erdödy
          Beethoven-fp trio (from Op. 70)
          Reichardt/VERTRAUTE, 1:285-86

b31 Dec   *Goubeau
          Mlle Goubeau-2 fp son-Mlle Goubeau
          J.S. Bach-kybd pieces-Mlle Goubeau
          Beethoven-fp fantasy-Mlle Goubeau
          Reichardt/VERTRAUTE, 1:285

1809

b8 Jan   Prince Esterházy
          Kreutzer-new opera
          Gluck-aria from *Iphigenie*-Herr Grell
          Mlle Marconi sang
          Reichardt/VERTRAUTE 1:291-93

b8 Jan   Schuppanzigh series at Prince Rasumovsky's
          Mozart-string quartet
          Romberg-string quartet
          Beethoven-string quartet
          Herr Seidler played
          Reichardt/VERTRAUTE 1:294

b8 Jan   Prince Lobkowitz
          Prince Louis Ferdinand-fp pieces-Archduke
              Maximilian
          Beethoven-fp pieces-Archduke Maximilian
          Reichardt/VERTRAUTE, 1:294

21 Jan   Mme de Rittersberg
          Kraft quartet played
          VIENNA-ROSENBAUM

b26 Jan   Countess Apponyi
          Handel aria-Countess Apponyi
          Reichardt/VERTRAUTE, 1:344-45

b26 Jan   Mme Bigot
          Beethoven-horn trio
          Beethoven-vln son-Herr Schuppanzigh
          Reichardt/VERTRAUTE, 1:333-34

b26 Jan   *Streicher
          Prince Louis Ferdinand-quartet in F minor ar-
              ranged for 2 fp-Mlle Kurzböck and Mme de
              Pereira
          Reichardt/VERTRAUTE, 1:345-46

b30 Jan   Prince Lobkowitz
          Beethoven-fp con-Archduke Maximilian
          Prince Louis Ferdinand-fp son-Archduke
              Maximilian

       Zingarelli-3rd act from *Giuliette e Romeo*-
       Princess Kinsky and Mlle de Goubeau
       Reichardt/VERTRAUTE, 1:357-38

b15 Feb Prince Kinsky
       Prince Louis Ferdinand-trios-Count Amadei,
       Herr Seidler, Herr Kraft
       Reichardt/VERTRAUTE, 1:409

b20 Feb Nikolaus von Zmeskall-quartet concert
       Beethoven quartet-Baroness von Ertmann (fp),
       Herr Seidler accompanied on vln
       Reichardt/VERTRAUTE, 1:428

27 Feb Prince Starhemberg
       Princess Starhemberg played kybd with bas-
       soon accompaniment by Herr Dragonetti
       VIENNA-ZINZENDORF

b1 Mar Mme de Rittersburg
       Mlle de Zois, Mme Frank, Herr Brizzi, Herr
       Kiesewetter, Herr von Henikstein, Prince
       Lobkowitz sang
       Herr Giuliani played guitar
       Reichardt/VERTRAUTE, 1:465-67

b1 Mar Prince Lobkowitz
       vln con-Herr Germalow
       Beethoven-piece-Herr Seidler, Herr Kraft
       Prince Louis Ferdinand-piece-Seidler, Kraft
       Reichardt/VERTRAUTE, 1:467-68

3 Mar Prince Lobkowitz
       Reichardt-*Bradamante*-Mlle Milder, Mlle
       Laucher, Mlle Marconi
       Reichardt/VERTRAUTE, 2:5-6

b6 Mar Prince Lobkowitz-afternoon quartet
       Count Amadei played fp
       Reichardt/VERTRAUTE, 2:4

b6 Mar Prince Lobkowitz
       Beethoven-"a new gigantic piece"
       duet-Mlle Goubeau and Countess Lunin
       Reichardt/VERTRAUTE, 2:5-6

b27 Mar　Baroness Ertmann
　　　　　J.S. Bach-pieces
　　　　　G.F. Handel-pieces
　　　　　W.A. Mozart-pieces
　　　　　Reichardt/VERTRAUTE, 2:74-75

　b5 Apr　Nikolaus von Zmeskall-quartet afternoon
　　　　　Haydn-quartets-Ertmann accompanied by Herr
　　　　　　von Hering on vln
　　　　　Reichardt/VERTRAUTE, 2:119-20

　13 Apr　Baron Sala
　　　　　Mozart-fp con-Mlle Werthheimstein
　　　　　Italian aria-Italian Abbé
　　　　　Haydn-farewell sym
　　　　　VIENNA-ROSENBAUM

　24 Apr　Herr Stöger
　　　　　Mayer-duet from *Adalesia und Alesiano*-
　　　　　　Therese Rosenbaum and Henriette
　　　　　VIENNA-ROSENBAUM

　17 Aug　*Prince Starhemberg
　　　　　Herr Siboni sang
　　　　　"Aide de campe" of Prince de Hesse sang
　　　　　VIENNA-ZINZENDORF

　　5 Oct　*Prince Starhemberg
　　　　　Mlle Balsamira and Mlle de Goubeau sang
　　　　　VIENNA-ZINZENDORF

　15 Oct　Starhemberg-concert for Therese Buquoy
　　　　　Herr von Hering played vln
　　　　　"Le Comte George" played kybd
　　　　　Princess Starhemberg played kybd with Herr
　　　　　　Dragonetti on his double bass
　　　　　VIENNA-ZINZENDORF

　30 Oct　Prince Starhemberg
　　　　　Herr Moscheles played kybd
　　　　　VIENNA-ZINZENDORF

　15 Nov　Prince Starhemberg
　　　　　Boieldieu-songs
　　　　　VIENNA-ZINZENDORF

Nov-Dec   Mlle de Paradies
          Prince Louis Ferdinand-pieces
          Henriette Paris (12 years) played fp
          Schuster pieces
          AMZ 25 Apr 10:473-74

1810

Lent   Baroness Sala
          Haydn-*Die Schöpfung*-Mlle Hippe, Ignaz Sonn-
          leithner, Herr Anders; Herr von Decret at
          the kybd; Dr. von Ohmeyer directed
          orchestra; Herr Preindl directed;
          orchestra of 60, all amateurs except for the
          first tenor, the horns, trumpets and drums
          SAMMLER 21 Apr 10:192

1 Apr   Count Otto
          Hummel-cantata-Herr Sonnleithner, Mlle
          Fischer, Herr Radicchi, Mlle Ambros
          fp con-Schobenlechner (9 years)
          VIENNA-ZINZENDORF; AMZ 6 Jun 10:573;
          SAMMLER 12 Apr 10:176

21 Apr   Prince Lobkowitz
          Joseph Weigl-*La passione di Giesu cristo*-Princess
          Therese Fürstenberg, Mme d'Apponyi, Mlle
          Wranitzky, Herr Vogel, Herr Simoni, Prince
          Lobkowitz
          VIENNA-ZINZENDORF; SAMMLER 28 Apr
          10:206

23 Dec   Prince Lobkowitz
          VIENNA-ZINZENDORF

411

Concert Calendar Index

The dates in this index refer to performances listed in the two Concert Calenders (Appendices 1 and 2). The following symbols have been used:

* = Person hosted the concert
x = Private concert
b = Before the date given
a = After the date given
z = "Zwischenakt," or intermission feature at a theater (not listed on the Concert Calendar)
B = Burgtheater
K = Kärtnerthortheater
W = Theater an der Wien
L = Theater in der Leopoldstadt

Most of the sources give only last names. When it was possible to identify the person I have given first names and dates. Uncertain attributions are in parentheses with a question mark. If a date is listed twice, the person's name is to be found on two concerts on the same day.

Adamberger, Joseph Valentine (1743-1804). Tenor at the court theaters. Sang various Mozart roles, including Belmonte in *Die Entführung aus dem Serail*. 11 Mar 81, 13 Mar 81, 15 Mar 81, 1 Apr 81, 3 Apr 81, x4 Apr 81, x8 Apr 81, 28 Dec 81, 22 Dec 82, 23 Dec 82, 23 Mar 83, 22 Dec 83, 23 Dec 83, 7 Mar 84, 1 Apr 84, 15 Mar 85, 22 Dec 85, 23 Dec 85, 8 Apr 86, 9 Apr 86, x26 Feb 88, 29 Feb 88, x4 Mar 88, 7 Mar 88, x30 Mar 88, x6 Mar 89, 4 Apr 89, 5 Apr 89, x7 Apr 89.

Albertini, (Joachim?). 15 Feb 88.

Albrechtsberger, Johann Georg (1736-1809). Composer. 1 Apr 81, 3 Apr 81, 15 Mar 88, 16 Mar 88, 4 Apr 89, 16 Apr 91, 17 Apr 91 , 15 Apr 92, 16 Apr 92.

Alessandri, Felice (1747-1798). 23 Feb 88.

Alessandri, Ludwig. 3 Mar 87.

Allavi, Mlle. Violinist. x9 Oct 61.

Altamont, Katharina. x3 Feb 85, x6 Mar 89, x7 Apr 89?.

Amadei, Count. xb15 Feb 09, xb6 Mar 09.

Amalfi, Princess. x6 Mar 99.

Ambros, Mlle. Singer at the court theaters. x1 Apr 10.

Anders, Herr. Singer. xLent 10.

Andreozzi, Gaetano (1755-1826). 23 May 95.

Anfossi, Pasquale (1727-1797). 16 Nov 81, 9 Mar 87, 2 Jun 87, 20 Feb 88, 8 Sep 95, 27 Oct 98.

Angrisani, Carlo. Singer. 30 Mar 98, 2 Apr 02, x16 Mar 03, 29 Jun 03.

Anspacher, Herr. Violinist. 1 May 10.

Apponyi, Countess. xb26 Jan 09, x21 Apr 10.

Arnobaldi, Christof. Singer. 17 Mar 77.

Arnold (Johann Gottfried? 1773-1806). 24 May 04, 25 Dec 09.

Ascher, Anna. Singer. 28 Jun 98, *27 Jan 01.

Asher, Herr. Singer. x4 Apr 01.

Asplmayr, Franz (1728-1786). Composer. 29 Mar 72, 5 Apr 72.

Aspremont, Mlle. Singer. x7 Jan 05.

Auernhammer, Josepha Barbara von (1758-1820). Fortepianist. 26 May 82, 3 Nov 82, x3 Feb 85, 24 Feb 85, x7 Mar 86, x4 Feb 88, 23 Dec 88, 16 Mar 93, 25 Mar 95, 4 Apr 96, x8 Mar 97, 5 Apr 97, 25 Mar 99, 25 Mar 01, 6 Jun 01, 25 Mar 02, 25 Mar 03, 2 Mar 04, 25 Mar 05, 25 Mar 06.

Auernhammer, Marianna. Singer. 2 Mar 04, 25 Mar 06, 5 Jun 06, 10 May 07.

Auernheim, Mlle (Marianna Auernhammer?). Singer at the court theaters. 10 May 10.

Auersperg, Princess. Singer. x16 Mar 74, *26 Mar 87, *17 Jan 91, x18 Mar 96, *23 Mar 96.

Bach, Carl Philipp Emanuel (1714-1788). x26 Feb 88, x4 Mar 88, 7 Mar 88.

Bach, Johann Christian (1735-1782). 30 Oct 72?, 12 Mar 80, 17 Nov 80?, 25 Mar 95.

Bach, Johann Sebastian (1685-1750). Composer. xSpring 82, xb31 Dec 08, xb27 Mar 09.

Bähr (Bär), Franz Josef (1770-1819). Clarinettist with Prince Lichtenstein. 4 Mar 91, Jul 96, 1 Apr 98, 2 Apr 98, 2 Apr 00, x17 Mar 02, 4 Apr 03.

Bagge, Baron. Violinist (?) from Munich. x31 Oct 84.

Baglioni, Costanza. Singer. 17 Dec 72, 20 Dec 72, 21 Mar 73, 25 Mar 73, 18 Dec 74, 21 Dec 74.

Baglioni, Rosina. Singer. 30 Oct 72, 8 Jan 73, 18 Dec 74, 21 Dec 74.

Balsamira, Mlle. Singer. x5 Oct 09.

Bamberger, Herr. Composer. 15 Feb 07.

Banti, Brigida Giorgi (c1756-1806). Soprano. 9 May 81, 2 Jun 87, 9 Jun 87, 15 Jun 87.

Barhof, Herr von. Keyboard player. x9 Oct 61.

Bartelozzi, B. Mandolin player. 24 Apr 02, 18 May 03, Lent 05.

Bartolini (Vincenzo). Contralto. 23 May 95.

Bartta, (Joseph). Composer. 26 Jan 81.

Bassen, Mme de. x15 Apr 84.

Baumann, Anton. 30 Mar 87, 12 Mar 88, 13 Apr 91, 15 Apr 91.

Baumann, Friedrich. Singer and comedian at the Theater in der Leopoldstadt. 30 Mar 87, 7 Mar 88, 6 Apr 91, 15 Apr 91.

Bayer, Mlle. 11 Apr 84.

Bayr, Georg. Flutist. 12 Apr 02, 30 Dec 10.

Beau, Jolien. Violinist. 21 Apr 02.

Beer, Johann Joseph (1744-1812). Clarinettist. b26 Dec 07.

Beethoven, Ludwig van (1770-1827). Composer. x2 Mar 95, 29 Mar 95, 31 Mar 95, x23 Apr 95, 18 Dec 95, 8 Jan 96, 6 Apr 97, 23 Dec 97, 29 Mar 98, 2 Apr 98, x5 Apr 98, 27 Oct 98, 5 Nov 98, 2 Apr 00, 18 Apr 00, x10 Dec 00, 30 Jan 01, 25 Mar 01, 6 Jun 01, 25 Mar 02, Summer 02, 2 Sep 02, *14 Nov 02, x6 Mar 03, 20 Mar 03, 25 Mar 03, 5 Apr 03, xLent 04, 27 Mar 04, 24 May 04, Summer 04, xWinter 04-05, 7 Apr 05, 16 May 05, 23 May 05, Summer 05, b15 Mar 06, 25 Mar 06, Summer 06, 23 Dec 06, xa18 Mar 07, x15 Aug 07, 15 Nov 07, b25 Nov 07, b1 Dec 07, 6 Dec 07, 13 Dec 07, 23 Dec 07, b26 Dec 07, 27 Dec 07, 17 Jan 08, 31 Jan 08, 2 Feb 08, 22 Feb 08, 20 Mar 08, 11 Apr 08, 12 Apr 08, 13 Apr 08, b23 Jun 08, 15 Nov 08, xb10 Dec 08, xb16 Dec 08, b16 Dec 08, 22 Dec 08, 23 Dec 08, xb31 Dec 08, xb8 Jan 09, xb30 Jan 09, xb20 Feb 09, xb6 Mar 09, 30 Apr 09, 8 Sep 09, 25 Mar 10, 17 Apr 10, 25 Dec 10.

Bekée, Herr. x5 Mar 93, x15 Jul 93.

Bellotto, Herr. x16 Mar 03.

Benucci, Francesco (c1745-1824). Bass at the court theaters. Sang various Mozart roles, including Figaro in *Le Nozze di Figaro*, Guglielmo in *Cosi fan tutte* and Leporello in *Don Giovanni*. x1 Jul 83, x16 Feb 85, x2 Mar 85, 6 Mar 85, 22 Dec 86, 23 Dec 86, x14 Feb 88, x23 Feb 92, 23 Feb 93, 27 Feb 93.

Bergancini, Joseph. Composer. 16 Dec 99.

Berger, Mlle. Singer. 26 May 82.

Bernardi, (Franz). Flutist. x9 Mar 03, x8 Dec 03, zK 28 Nov 04, Summer 05, 21 Apr 06.

Berton, Henri Montan (1767-1844). Composer. 28 Mar 06?.

Bertoni, Ferdinando (1725-1813). Composer. 17 Dec 75, 19 Dec 75, 23 Jan 80, 10 Mar 87, 8 Sep 95.

Bidell, Anton. Xänorphica player. 16 Mar 06.

Berwald, Johann Fredrik (1787-1861). Violinist. 30 Apr 99, x5 Apr 99, 3 May 99, zB 6 May 99.

Bescher, Herr. 27 Apr 98.

Bessenig, Mlle. Singer (probably Marianna Auernhammer). 25 Dec 07.

Bevilaqua, Abbé. Tenor with Prince Esterházy von Galantha. x19 Feb 03?, x19 Apr 03, 7 Apr 05, 8 Apr 05, Lent 05, 2 Jun 05.

Bianchi, Herr. Singer at the court theaters. 15 Apr 92, 12 Jun 05, 13 Jun 05, 22 Dec 05, 23 Dec 05.

Bianchi, Mme. Singer. x5 Oct 62.

Bianchi (Antonio or Francesco?). Composer. 9 Mar 87, 15 Feb 88, 8 Sep 95.

Bigot de Morogues (née Kiene), Marie (1786-1820). Fortepianist. b16 Dec 04, xLent 05, 1 May 05, b16 Dec 08, *xb26 Jan 09.

Blacho, Herr. Singer at the Theater in der Leopoldstadt. 25 Mar 06, 22 Mar 07, 15 Nov 07, 25 Mar 08, 24 Dec 09.

Blangini, Therese. Violinist and singer at the court of Pfalz-Bayern. 13 Dec 04, 25 Jan 05.

Blumenthal, Leopold. Violinist at the Theater an der Wien. Summer 04, zW 27 Aug 06.

Böhm, Alexander. Fortepianist. zB 1 Oct 03.

Böhm, Franz. Violinist. zL 16 Sep 97, zL 23 Aug 99, zL 24 Aug 99, zL 25 Aug 99, zL 26 Oct 99, zL 27 Oct 99, zK 14 Mar 01, 25 Mar 03, Summer 04.

Bök, Anton (1754-c1815). Waldhornist. 13 Oct 87, 5 Dec 02.

Bök, Ignaz (1758-c1815). Waldhornist. 13 Oct 87, 5 Dec 02.

Bohdanowicz, Bazyli (1740-1817) and family. Violinist at the Theater in der Leopoldstadt. 5 Mar 85, 8 Sep 95, 16 Feb 98, 25 Mar 00, 8 Apr 02, 15 Nov 02.

Bohrer Brothers. Violinist and cellist. 26 Jan 08.

Boieldieu, François-Adrien (1775-1834). Composer. 8 Aug 09, x15 Nov 09.

Boissier, Mme. *10 Nov 97.

Bolla, Mme. Singer at the court theaters. 10 May 07.

Bolla, Maria. Singer. 8 Jan 96.

Bologna (Luigi?). Composer. 16 Nov 81.

Bondra, (Bartholomäus). Tenor at the Theater in der Leopoldstadt. 13 Feb 85, 24 Mar 87, 15 Feb 88, 20 Feb 88, 21 Mar 89, 1 Apr 91, 2 Apr 91, 15 Apr 91, 20 Mar 96, 21 Mar 96, 18 Dec 00, 21 Dec 00, 26 Dec 03, 25 Dec 04, 25 Mar 05, 25 Mar 06, 25 Mar 08, 25 Mar 09, 25 Mar 10.

Bondra, Theresia. Fortepianist. 25 Mar 05.

Bondra, Mme. Singer. 25 Mar 09.

Bondra, Mlle. Singer. 24 Dec 09.

Bonno, Giuseppe (1711-1788). Composer. 20 Mar 74.

Bonsichi, Herr. Composer. 26 Apr 07.

Bora, Johann. 14 Feb 85.

Borghi, (Giovanni Battista? 1738-1796). Composer. 2 Apr 91, 16 Apr 92.

Bouchred née Thilmet, Mme. 10 Oct 05.

Branizky. See Wranitzky.

Brenta, Herr. 30 Apr 04.

Breuner, Mme de. x23 Mar 98.

Breymann, Anton. Musician with Prince Lichtenstein. 9 Apr 97.

Brichta, Adalbert. Singer. 17 Mar 76; 20 Mar 76.

Bridgetower, George Polgreen (?1779-1860). 17 May 03, 24 May 03.

Bridi, (Antonio Giacomi?). Tenor. x23 Mar 98, x16 Mar 99, x3 Apr 00.

Brizzi, Mme. Singer. x18 Dec 03, Lent 05.

Brizzi, Herr. Tenor at the court theaters. 25 Mar 02, x26 Mar 02, 13 Apr 02, x12 Mar 03, 25 Mar 03, x15 Apr 03, 27 Apr 03, 29 Jun 03, 22 Dec 03, 23 Dec 03, 2 Mar 04, 23 Mar 04, 27 Mar 04, 1 Apr 04, x24 Apr 04, x7 Jan 05, 25 Mar 05, xb1 Mar 09.

Brizzi, Anton. Singer from Munich. 30 Apr 04, 20 May 06, 25 May 06.

Brizzi, Ludwig. Singer at the court theaters. 15 Nov 04, 25 Mar 06.

Brückl, Mme. Soprano. 27 Aug 01.

Brunetti, (Antonio? c1735 or 1745-1786). x8 Apr 81.

Buchweiser, Mlle. Singer. 22 Oct 09, 30 Dec 10.

Buchweiser, B. 25 Dec 08.

Bussani, Dorothea (1763-a1810). Mezzo soprano at the court theaters. Sang Cherubino in Mozart's *Le Nozze di Figaro* and Despina in *Cosi fan tutte*. 23 Mar 87, 22 Dec 90, 23 Dec 90, 13 Apr 91, x23 Feb 92, 22 Dec 92, 9 Mar 93, 7 Mar 94.

Bussani, Francesco (1743-1807). Bass at the court theaters. Sang various Mozart roles, including Bartolo and Antonio in *Le Nozze di Figaro*, Don Alfonso in *Cosi fan tutte*, the Commendatore and Masetto in *Don Giovanni*. 23 Mar 87, 9 Mar 93, 7 Mar 94.

Buquoy, Mme de. Fortepianist. x20 Mar 83.

Caldarini, Luisa. Singer. 13 Apr 98.

Callenberg (Count Georg Alexander Heinrich Hermann?). x5 Apr 87, x10 Apr 87, x11 Apr 87, x5 Mar 91 , *8 Apr 94, *8 Mar 08.

Calvani, Mme. See Willmann-Galvani.

Calvesi, Vincenzo. Tenor at the court theaters. Sang Ferrando in Mozart's *Cosi fan tutte*. 22 Dec 85, 23 Dec 85, 8 Apr 86, 9 Apr 86, 4 Jun 86, 30 Mar 87, 1 Apr 87, 22 Dec 87, 23 Dec 87, 8 Feb 88, 22 Dec 89, 23 Dec 89, 22 Dec 90, 23 Dec 90, 13 Apr 91, 22 Dec 92, 9 Mar 93, 23 Mar 93, 24 Mar 93.

Cambini, (Giuseppe Maria? 1746-1825). 22 Dec 82, 23 Dec 82.

Camera, Antonio. Violinist. zB 19 Sep 98, 28 Dec 98.

Campi, Herr. Composer. 15 Nov 01.

Campi, (Gaetano). Bass. Sang 1st Publius in Mozart's *La Clemenza di Tito*. 15 Nov 10.

Campi, Antonia. Singer at the Theater an der Wien. 24 Jun 02, 12 Aug 02, 16 Sep 02, 27 Mar 04, x6 Apr 05, 22 Dec 05, 23 Dec 05, 25 Mar 06, 31 Mar 06, 6 Apr 06, 23 Dec 06, 25 Dec 06, 6 Mar 07, 25 Mar 08, 22 Sep 08, 15 Nov 08, 22 Dec 08, 23 Dec 08, 27 Mar 09, 8 Sep 09, 25 Mar 10 (scheduled but did not sing), 15 Nov 10.

Cannabich, Carl (1771-1806). 25 Mar 03, Sep 04, xAdvent 04, 15 Nov 10.

Capazzi, Antonio. zB 19 Sep 98.

Capeller, Herr. From Churbayern. 28 Dec 01.

419

Caravoglio, Herr and Mme. 16 Mar 85.

Cartellieri, Herr. 29 Mar 95, 30 Mar 95, 10 Apr 97, x3 Apr 00, 18 Apr 00, x27 Jan 01, 27 Apr 03, 30 Apr 04, 15 Nov 07, 18 Mar 09.

Cartellieri, Anton. Composer with Prince Lobkowitz. zK 5 Mar 02, 23 Mar 04.

Cartellieri, Casimir. Composer with Prince Lobkowitz. 31 Mar 01.

Carusio, Herr. Composer. 3 Mar 87.

Caruso, Herr (Luigi? 1754-1822). Composer. 23 May 95, 8 Apr 02.

Cataldi (Catalde), Cecilia. From Rumania. 9 Mar 85.

Catoni, Mlle. Singer. 8 Sep 87.

Cavalieri, Caterina (1760-1801). Singer at the court theaters. Sang various Mozart roles, including Costanze in *Die Entführung aus dem Serail* and Donna Elvira in *Don Giovanni*. 17 Mar 76, 20 Mar 76, 17 Mar 77, 18 Dec 77, 21 Dec 77, 16 Mar 78, 23 Mar 78, 27 Mar 78, 20 Dec 78, 19 Dec 79, 21 Dec 79, 12 Mar 80, 14 Mar 80, 11 Mar 81, 13 Mar 81, 1 Apr 81, 3 Apr 81, 18 Jan 82, 17 Mar 82, 19 Mar 82, 22 Dec 82, 23 Dec 82, 1 Apr 83, 6 Apr 83, 8 Apr 83, 22 Dec 83, 23 Dec 83, 7 Mar 84, 28 Mar 84, 30 Mar 84, 22 Dec 84, 23 Dec 84, 15 Mar 85, 22 Dec 85, 23 Dec 85, 8 Apr 86, 9 Apr 86, 4 Jun 86, 3 Mar 87, 16 Mar 87, 17 Mar 87, 30 Mar 87, 1 Apr 87, 23 Feb 88, 29 Feb 88, 4 Apr 89, 5 Apr 89, 22 Dec 89, 23 Dec 89, 2 Apr 91, 15 Apr 92, 16 Apr 92, 22 Dec 92.

Ceccarelli, Franz (1762-1814). Castrato with the Archbishop of Salzburg. x17 Mar 81, x23 Mar 81, x8 Apr 81.

Celestini, Mlle. Singer. 21 Jan 94, 24 Jan 94.

Cerini, Baron. Violinist. xLent 04, b1 Dec 07.

Cesarini [Nicolosi], Mme. 18 Mar 83.

Cherubini, Luigi (1760-1842). Composer. 7 Mar 87, 2 Sep 02, 25 Mar 03, Summer 03, xLent 04, 27 Mar 04, Summer 04, x7 Aug 04, xWinter 04-05, xLent 05, 7 Apr 05, 14 Apr 05, 22 Dec 05, 23 Dec 05, 23 Feb 06, 25 Mar 06, 28 Mar 06, 20 May 06, 22 Mar 07, 23 Mar 07, 26 Apr 07, 1 May 07, b1 Dec 07, 8 Sep 09, 10 May 10, 23 Dec 10.

Christiani, Mlle. 8 Mar 93.

Cimarosa, Domenico (1749-1801). Composer. 18 Mar 83, x1 Jul 83, 28 Mar 87, 15 Feb 88, 11 Mar 92, x17 Mar 92, x23 Mar 92, 23 May 95, 8 Sep 95, 22 Dec 97, 23 Dec 97, 13 Apr 98, 21 Dec 98, 21 Aug 00, 30 Jan 01, 15 Nov 01, x10 Mar 02, 8 Apr 02, 12 Apr 02, 13 Apr 02, 19 Jun 02, xWinter 03, x16 Mar 03, 2 Mar 04, 15 Nov 04, 9 May 05, 2 Jun 05, 15 Nov 10, 15 Dec 10.

Clamoth, Herr. x7 Aug 04.

Clary, Therese. Singer. x14 Mar 78, x16 Feb 85, x2 Mar 85, x16 Mar 85, x6 Apr 86.

Clement, Franz (1780-1842). Violinist and concert master at the Theater an der Wien. 11 Apr 88, 27 Mar 89, 23 Apr 89, 28 Dec 92, 20 Mar 93, 24 Jan 94, 14 Mar 94, 13 Apr 94, 18 May 96, 27 Apr 98, 28 Apr 98, 25 Mar 01, xLent 04, xWinter 04-05, 7 Apr 05, Summer 05, 22 Dec 05, 23 Dec 05, 23 Feb 06, 25 Mar 06, 25 Mar 06, 21 Apr 06, zW 24 May 06, 23 Dec 06, 1 May 07, 23 Dec 07, b26 Dec 07, 12 Apr 08, 15 Nov 08 (cancelled), 23 Dec 08, 8 Sep 09, 24 Dec 09, 23 Dec 10.

Clementi, Muzio (1752-1832). Fortepianist and composer. x24 Apr 04, xb27 Mar 09.

Cliffton, Marguerite. Singer. x14 Feb 88.

Colalto, Mlle de. x22 Dec 63.

Colla brothers. Calassioncine players. 30 Nov 70.

Collonitsche, Herr. Violinist. x28 Nov 61.

Cordecasa, Herr. Singer. 5 Apr 97, 6 Apr 97.

Colombazzo, Vittorino. Oboist. 25 Mar 73, 7 Mar 84, 23 Mar 87.

Comaschini, Herr. Singer for the Russian emperor. x12 Apr 87.

Compassi (Compressi), Herr. Singer. x16 Jan 63, 3 Mar 63, 6 Mar 63, x30 Apr 63.

Concialini, Giovanni Carlo. Soprano. 10 Mar 87.

Conti, (Giacomo 1754-1805?). 25 Nov 93.

Costa, Mlle. Singer. x16 Mar 03.

Cramer, (Johann Baptist? 1771-1858). Composer. b25 Nov 07.

Crescentini, Girolamo (1762-1846). Mezzo-soprano. 20 May 04, x6 Apr 05.

Crunpipen, Mlle. Singer. x22 Nov 97.

Czernichen, Mlle de. Fortepianist. x14 Feb 88.

Czerini, Herr. See Cerini.

Czerny, Karl (1791-1857). Fortepianist and composer. Summer 06, 30 Apr 09.

Czerwenka, Josef. Oboist. 23 Dec 95, 25 Mar 97, 22 Dec 97, 23 Dec 97, 8 Apr 00, 31 Mar 01, x8Apr 02, x12 Apr 02, 23 Feb 06.

Dalayrac, C. zW 10 Aug 03, zW 9 Nov 03, zW 21 Nov 03.

Damm, Herr. Oboist at the court of Churbayern. xAdvent 04.

Danzi, Franz (1763-1826). 29 Mar 98, 23 Mar 07.

Dautrive, (Richard?). Composer. 9 Mar 87.

Deabis, Franz. Cellist. 23 Feb 06.

Decret, Herr von. Keyboard player. xLent 10.

de Luka. See Luka.

Demmer, Herr. Singer. 7 Apr 05.

Dermer, Josepha. Harpist, flutist, fortepianist. 4 Mar 84, 8 Mar 85.

Desiro, Herr. 15 Dec 10.

Deym von Stritetz, Countess Josephine. *10 Dec 00.

Devienne, (François? 1759-1803). French flutist, bassoonist and composer. 23 Dec 89.

Deymer, Herr. (Probably Teimer). x27 Mar 95.

Diabelli, Anton. (1781-1858). xW 23 Jan 04.

Dietrichstein, Mlle de. Singer. x22 Dec 63.

Dietzel, Johann. Contrabassist. 2 Apr 00.

Distler, (Johann Georg 1760-1799?). Composer for the Duke of Würtemberg. 24 Jan 94.

Distler, Mlle. Singer. 28 Mar 87.

Distler, Elisabeth. Singer at the court theaters. 15 Feb 85, 27 Feb 88.

Distler, Franziska. Singer. 27 Feb 88, 13 Mar 93.

Dittersdorf, Karl Ditters von (1739-1799). Composer and violinist. 30 Oct 72, 19 Dec 73, 21 Dec 73, 17 Mar 76, 20 Mar 76, 20 Dec 78, 22 Dec 83, 23 Dec 83, 22 Dec 85, 23 Dec 85, 8 Apr 86, 9 Apr 86, Summer 86, 2 Mar 87, 30 Mar 87, 1 Apr 87, 13 Oct 87, 4 Apr 89, 5 Apr 89, 26 Mar 91.

Doberauer, Mme. Singer. 25 Mar 05.

Döschi, Herr. 28 Feb 92.

Doppelhof, Herr. x5 Apr 98.

Dornaus, (Philipp?). 9 Apr 02, 2 Mar 04.

Dorner, Brothers. Summer 03.

Dragonetti, Domenico (1763-1846). Contrabassist. x19 Jul 08, x19 Sep 08, x27 Feb 09, x15 Oct 09, x21 Nov 09.

Drechsler, Herr. Singer. 8 Jan 73.

Druschetzky, Herr. 16 Apr 91, 17 Apr 91.

Dulon, Friedrich Ludwig (1769-1826). Flutist. 26 Mar 91, 15 Apr 91, 20 Mar 03.

Dürand, Friedrich. Violinist from Poland. 17 Apr 91.

Durand, August. Violinist. 25 Mar 95.

Dušek (née Weiser), Josefa (1754-1824). Soprano. x23 Mar 86, x24 Mar 86, x27 Mar 86, x6 Apr 86, b8 Apr 86, 25 Mar 94, 29 Mar 98.

Dussek, Jan Ladislav (1760-1812). xWinter 04-05, Summer 05, 25 Mar 06, 18 Apr 09, 21 Apr 09, 17 Apr 10.

Eberl, Anton (1765-1807). Composer. 9 Mar 84, 1 Mar 85, 29 Dec 94, 25 Mar 03, x6 Apr 03, Summer 03, 6 Jan 04, xLent 04, 2 Mar 04, Summer 04, xWinter 04-05, 25 Jan 05, xLent 05, 1 May 05, 25 Dec 07, xb16 Jan 08, 10 May 10.

Eck, Johann Friedrich (1767-1838). Violinist. Lent 80, 14 Mar 80, 29 Jan 98.

Eck, Franz (1774-1804). Violinist. 29 Jan 98.

Ehlers, Wilhelm. Singer at the court theaters. 22 Dec 05, 23 Dec 05, 30 Mar 06, 31 Mar 06, 1 Apr 06, 21 Apr 06, 29 Jun 06, 23 Dec 06, 24 Mar 07, 29 Mar 07, 17 May 07, 5 Jun 10.

Ehlers, Mme. 5 Jun 10.

Eigenwahl, Mlle. Singer. 22 Mar 07, 15 Nov 07, 25 Mar 08, 25 Mar 09 (scheduled but did not sing).

Eisen, Franz. Waldhornist. zB 21 May 96.

Elmenreich, Johann Baptist. Baritone. 9 May 05.

Eppinger, Heinrich. Violinist. 5 Apr 89, 22 Dec 93, 19 Sep 96.

Ertmann, Baroness. xb20 Feb 09, *b27 Mar 09, xb5 Apr 09.

Esser, Karl Michael Ritter von (1737-c1795). Violinist. 13 Oct 80, 17 Nov 80.

Eybler, Joseph (1765-1846). Composer. 3 Mar 87, 22 Dec 94, 23 Dec 94, 1 Apr 98, 2 Apr 98, 4 May 98, 22 Dec 98, 23 Dec 98, 29 Mar 01, 30 Mar 01, 13 Apr 02, 15 Apr 10, 16 Apr 10, 22 Apr 10.

Farinelli, Giuseppi (1769-1836). Composer. 12 Jun 05, 13 Jun 05.

Fauner, Herr. Baryton player. 1 May 72.

Fayard, Herr. Violist for the King of Prussia. 2 Jun 87.

Feichtner, Herr. Composer. 15 Nov 07, 25 Dec 07.

Felsenberg, Herr von. Fortepianist. 31 Jan 08.

Felz, Mlle. x22 Nov 97.

Ferlendis, Herr. (There are four possibilities—Giuseppi (1755-1802), Antonio, Angelo (b. 1781), and Alessandro (b. 1783). Oboist. zB 16 May 94, zB 26 May 94, 22 Sep 05, zL 1 Oct 06.

Ferlendis, Angelo. Oboist. zB 19 Sep 98, 28 Dec 98.

Ferlendis, Giuseppi. Oboist. 10 Apr 94.

Ferraresi del Bene, Adriana (c1755-a1799). Soprano. Sang in Martin y Soler's *L'arbore di Diana* and Fiordiligi in Mozart's *Cosi fan tutte*. 22 Dec 88, 23 Dec 88, 22 Dec 90, 23 Dec 90, 11 Mar 91, 12 Mar 91, 18 Mar 91, 13 Apr 91, 2 Jul 93.

Feurich, Herr. Glass harmonica player. zB 1 Jul 95.

Feyer, Herr. Composer. 15 Nov 01.

Fiby, Herr. zL 29 Oct 02.

Fillelois, Mlle. Singer. 25 Mar 93, 27 Mar 93.

Finkenstein, Herr von. Singer. x19 Dec 01.

Firnak, Herr. Clarinettist. 23 May 05.

Fischer, Mme. Singer. 17 Mar 82, 19 Mar 82.

Fischer, Mlle (sister of Therese Fischer). Singer. 18 Mar 10.

Fischer, Anton (1778-1808). Composer. 25 Mar 06, 26 Oct 06, 29 Mar 07, 25 Dec 03, 25 Dec 09.

Fischer, Johann Christian (1733-1800). Oboist. x7 Mar 86, 16 Mar 87.

Fischer, Johann Ignaz Ludwig. (1745-1825) Bass. Sang Osmin in Mozart's *Die Entführung aus dem Serail*. 14 Mar 80, 1 Apr 81, 3 Apr 81, 17 Mar 82, 19 Mar 82, 4 Apr 84, 21 Mar 87, 27 Oct 98?, 5 Nov 98?.

Fischer, Therese. Soprano at the court theaters. 5 Jun 04?, 15 Nov 07, 25 Dec 07, 25 Mar 08, 27 Mar 08, 17 Apr 08, 15 Nov 08, xb5 Dec 08, 18 Dec 08, 22 Dec 08, 23 Dec 08, 25 Jan 09, 5 Mar 09, 26 Mar 09, 27 Mar 09, 8 Aug 09, 15 Nov 09, 22 Dec 09, 23 Dec 09, 18 Mar 10, 25 Mar 10, 1 Apr 10, x1 Apr 10, 17 Apr 10, 22 Apr 10.

Fisher, John Abraham (1744-1806). English violinist and composer; husband of Nancy Storace. 10 Jan 84, 18 Mar 84, 28 Mar 84.

Fladt, Herr and Mlle. From Pfalzbayern. 15 Feb 93.

Flamm, Antonia. Singer. 22 Dec 94, 23 Dec 94, 1 Apr 98, 2 Apr 98, 22 Dec 98, 23 Dec 98, 17 Mar 99, 18 Mar 99, 26 Dec 03, 1 Apr 06.

Flat, Anton. Oboist at the court of Churbayern. Lent 04, xLent 04, 27 Mar 04, b16 Jan 08, xb16 Jan 08.

Fodor, Herr. Composer. 23 Dec 84.

Foita, Emanuel. Violinist with Prince Lobkowitz. b26 Dec 07, 16 Feb 09, 30 Apr 09, 25 Mar 10.

Formaizko, Karl. Flutist. 21 Dec 98, zB 14 Jun 99, 4 Apr 00.

Fränzel, d.A., Herr. Violinist with the Kurfürst von Bayern. 8 Apr 86.

Fränzel, Ferdinand (d.J.) (1767-1833). 9 Apr 86, Advent 02, Lent 05, 12 Mar 08.

Franchi, Mme. Singer. x21 Feb 74.

Frank, Mlle. x12 Mar 03.

Frank (née Gerhardi), Christina. Singer. x24 Mar 97, x29 Apr 98, x30 Apr 98, x7 May 98, x10 May 98, x16 Mar 99, x16 Apr 00, 30 Jan 01, x19 Dec 01, 22 Dec 03, 23 Dec 03, xb1 Mar 09.

Fratti, Mlle. 17 Apr 10.

Frédéric, Herr. 19 May 09.

Freund, Joseph. 5 Jun 06.

Freyhold, Herr. Flutist with the Kurfürst von Pfalz-bayern. 30 Mar 84.

Friberth, Karl. Singer. 2 Apr 75, 4 Apr 75, 17 Mar 76, 20 Mar 76, 28 Mar 84, 30 Mar 84.

Friberth, Magdalena. Singer. 2 Apr 75, 4 Apr 75.

Frick, Herr. Court organist at Baden. 1 May 72, 5 May 72.

Fridlowsky, Herr. Bassethorn player at the Theater an der Wien. 1 Apr 10.

Fries, Victoria de. Singer. x28 Apr 87, x14 Feb 88.

Fröhlich, Herr. Tenor. 28 Jul 03.

Frönil, Ferdinand. Violinist from Offenbach. 19 Dec 02.

Fuchs, Herr. (Probably Peter Fux). x31 Mar 02.

Fürstenau, Herr. Composer. 23 Mar 07.

Fürstenberg, Princess Therese. Singer. x21 Apr 10.

Fuss, Johann (Janos Fusz? 1777-1819). Composer. 1 Apr 10.

Fux, Peter (1753-1831). Violinist. 24 Mar 87, 28 Mar 87, 15 Mar 88, 16 Mar 88, 22 Dec 95, 18 Mar 99.

Gagarin, Princess. Singer. x25 Dec 84, x16 Feb 85, x2 Mar 85, x16 Mar 85.

Gallenberg, Count Robert (1783-1839). Composer. zW 11 Oct 03, zW 17 Oct 03, xLent 04.

Galliani, Angiolo. 6 Mar 99.

Galvani, Mme. See Willman-Galvani.

Gassmann, Florian (1729-1774). Composer. 29 Mar 72, 1 Apr 72, 5 Apr 72, 8 Jan 73, 18 Dec 76, 13 Mar 85, 15 Mar 85, 13 Apr 91.

Gassmann, Marie Anna. Singer. 23 Mar 93, 24 Mar 93, 22 Dec 95, 23 Dec 95, 20 Mar 96, 21 Mar 96, 8 Apr 00, 28 Aug 00, 23 Mar 04.

Gassmann-Rosenbaum, Therese (1774-1837). Soprano at the court
theaters. 9 Mar 93, 23 Mar 93, 24 Mar 93, 22 Dec 93, [21 Jan 94, 24 Jan
94—possibly Marie Anna?], 12 Apr 94, 13 Apr 94, 25 Mar 95, 22 Dec
95, 23 Dec 95, 20 Mar 96, 21 Mar 96, [19 Sep 96, 21 Sep 96—possibly
Marie Anna?] 22 Dec 96, 23 Dec 96, [5 Apr 97—possibly Marie Anna?],
9 Apr 97, 10 Apr 97, 22 Dec 97, 23 Dec 97, 25 Mar 98, 30 Mar 98, 1
Apr 98, 2 Apr 98, 27 Apr 98, 4 May 98, 21 Dec 98, 22 Dec 98, 23 Dec
98, 6 Mar 99, 11 Mar 99, 17 Mar 99, 18 Mar 99, 3 May 99, 23 May 99,
27 Aug 99, 15 Nov 99, 18 Nov 99, 28 Mar 00, 8 Apr 00, 21 Aug 00,
28 Aug 00, 4 Sep 00, 18 Sep 00, 18 Dec 00, 29 Mar 01, 30 Mar 01, 30
Mar 01, 11 Jun 01, 25 Jun 01, 3 Sep 01, 10 Sep 01, 17 Sep 01, 24 Sep
01, x28 Sep 01, x6 Dec 01, x17 Mar 02, 12 Apr 02, 13 Apr 02, 19 Jun
02, 2 Sep 02, x19 Feb 03, x23 Mar 03, 1 Apr 03, 2 Apr 03, x6 Apr 03,
x19 Apr 03, *8 Dec 03, 27 Mar 04, x3 Dec 04, 1 Apr 06, x13 Aug 06,
x19 Mar 08, x24 Apr 09.

Gazzaniga, Giuseppe (1743-1818.) 30 Mar 87, 1 Apr 87, 23 May 95.

Gebauer, Josef. Flutist. 10 May 10.

Gebel, Franz Xaver (1787-1843). Composer. 25 Mar 09.

Gehring, Ludwig. Flutist. 12 Mar 80, 8 Apr 83, 22 Mar 96, 23 Feb 06.

Gelinek, Abbé Josef (1758-1825). 25 Mar 02.

Generali, Pietro (1773-1832). Composer. 26 Apr 07, 8 Aug 09.

Gennoglio, Herr. Singer. x3 Feb 81.

Gennoglio, Mme. Singer. x2 Feb 81, x3 Feb 81.

Gennsbacher, Herr. 2 Mar 04.

Gerardi, Christine. See Frank, Christina.

Gerbini, Mlle. Violinist. Jan-Feb 07.

Gerhardi, Mlle. See Frank, Christina.

Gerl, Franz Xaver (1764-1827). Bass at the Wiedner Theater. Sang Sarastro
in Mozart's *Die Zauberflöte*. 13 Apr 91, 15 Apr 91, 11 Mar 92.

Gerlitz, Herr. Singer. 22 Dec 05, 23 Dec 05.

Germalow, Herr. Violinist. xb1 Mar 09.

Gerty, Mlle. Singer. 6 Apr 06.

Geschwendner, Herr. Cellist. 13 Oct 87.

Gilberg, Mlle. Singer. x10 Mar 02.

Giornovichi, Giovanni Mane (c1740-1804). Violinist. 22 Mar 86, zB 26 Mar 86, 9 Mar 87, 15 Apr 91, 11 Mar 92, x5 Apr 99.

Giordanello, (Giuseppi Giordani) (c1753-1798). Composer. 8 Apr 02.

Giordani, Tomasso (1733-1806). Composer. 12 Mar 80.

Giordani, (Giuseppi? or Tomasso?). Composer. 20 Dec 78, 25 Mar 95.

Giuliani, Mauro (1781-1829). Guitarist. 3 Apr 08, 13 Apr 08, xb1 Mar 09, 15 Apr 10, 23 Apr 10.

Gleich, Herr. 3 Aug 10, 31 Aug 10.

Gloy, Mme. Singer. 3 Jun 02, 10 Jun 02, 1 Jul 02.

Gluck, Christoph Willibald (1714-1787). Composer. 30 Oct 72, x28 Feb 81, 22 Dec 82, 23 Dec 82, 23 Feb 88, 17 Mar 99, 18 Mar 99, Sep 04, xWinter 04-05, 25 Mar 05, b25 Nov 07, xb8 Jan 09.

Goes, Mme de. Singer. x5 Mar 74.

Goldmann, Josef. Singer. x4 Jun 08.

Gottdank, Josef. Tenor. 22 Dec 06, 23 Dec 06, 25 Dec 06, 22 Dec 07, 23 Dec 07, 10 Apr 08, 11 Apr 08, 27 Mar 09.

Gottlieb, Cajetan. Cellist from Florence. 16 Apr 91.

Gottlieb, Maria Anna (1774-1856). Soprano. Sang various Mozart roles including Barberina in *Le Nozze di Figaro* and Pamina in *Die Zauberflöte*. 13 Apr 91.

Goubeau, Mlle. xb25 Dec 08, *b31 Dec 08, xb30 Jan 09, xb6 Mar 09.

Graf, Friedrich Hartmann (1727-1795). Composer from Augsburg. 12 Mar 80, 14 Mar 80, 8 Apr 83.

Grell, Herr. Tenor. xb8 Jan 09, 28 Jan 09, 25 Mar 09, 28 Mar 09, 8 Sep 09, 22 Oct 09, 18 Mar 10, 29 Mar 10.

Griesbacher, Joseph. Bassoonist with Count Carl von Palm. 12 Mar 80.

Grohman, Mlle. Fortepianist. zW 21 Mar 02, zW 14 Apr 03.

Grohmann, Sebastian. Oboist. 4 May 98, 21 Dec 98, 4 Apr 00, 27 Apr 03, 15 Nov 04, 1 Apr 06.

Groiss, Herr. Violinist. 22 Jul 84.

Groschopf, Herr. Singer. 25 Mar 08.

Grosschlag, Mlle. Singer. x6 Feb 95.

Grubner, Herr. zB 4 Oct 82.

Gruft, Baron. See Kruft, Baron.

Gsur, Katharina. Singer. 8 Apr 86, 9 Apr 86.

Guadagni, Herr. Singer. x11 Jan 64.

Guardasoni, Dom. Singer. 17 Dec 72, 20 Dec 72, 21 Mar 73, 25 Mar 73.

Guglielmi, (Pietro Alessandro 1728-1804?, or his sons Pietro Carlo 1763-1817 and Giacomo 1782-1820?). Composer. 15 Feb 88, 8 Sep 95, x22 Nov 97, 8 Apr 00, x26 Mar 02, 12 Jun 05, 13 Jun 05, 15 Nov 08.

Gyrowetz, Adalbert (1763-1850). Composer. 25 Mar 95, 25 Mar 01, x23 Mar 03, 2 Mar 04, 15 Nov 08, 16 Feb 09, 25 Mar 09, 28 Mar 09, 4 May 09 (cancelled), 15 Nov 10.

Gyulas, Therese. Fortepianist. x10 May 02.

Haberl, Herr (Possibly Heberl). Clarinettist. 28 Mar 00.

Hackel, Mlle. Singer. 18 May 03, Summer 03, 28 Jul 03, 5 Jul 04, 23 May 05, 25 Mar 06.

Häckel, Herr. Contra-bassist (contra-violon). 25 Apr 84, 22 Jul 84.

Häser, Charlotte Henriette (b. 1784). Singer. 25 Jan 07, 24 Mar 07, 17 May 07.

Hambüchler, Mlle (b. 1780). zL 13 Apr 91, zL 15 Apr 91.

Hamburger, Herr. Fortepianist. Lent 05, Summer 05.

Hammer, Josepha. Singer. 29 Mar 01, 30 Mar 01.

Handel, George Frideric (1685-1759). Composer. 20 Dec 78, 21 Mar 79, 23 Mar 79, 12 Mar 80, 14 Mar 80, xSpring 82, 22 Dec 82, 23 Dec 82, 23 Dec 84, xLent 86, Nov 88, 22 Dec 88, 23 Dec 88, x30 Dec 88, x6 Mar 89, x7 Apr 89, xLent 90, xLent 91, 15 Apr 92, 16 Apr 92, xMar 93, x24 Dec 93, *28 Dec 93, x15 Apr 94, x31 Dec 94, x5 Apr 95, 22 Dec 95, 23 Dec 95, x24 Mar 97, 22 Dec 97, 23 Dec 97, x23 Mar 99, x24 Mar 99, 31 Mar 05, 31 Mar 06, 22 Dec 06, 23 Dec 06, 25 Dec 06, 22 Mar 07, 22 Mar 07, 23 Mar 07, 22 Dec 07, xb26 Jan 09, xb27 Mar 09, 27 Mar 09, 8 Sep 09.

Handl, d.A., Herr. Singer. 15 Nov 07, 25 Mar 08.

Hanmüller, Herr. 15 Feb 07.

Harr, Anton. Composer. 1 May 99.

Harrach, Mme de. Singer. x29 Nov 86.

Hartenstein, Mlle de. Keyboard player. x14 Mar 78.

Hasse, Adolph (1699-1783). Composer. 17 Dec 72, 20 Dec 72, 21 Mar 73, 25 Mar 73, 18 Dec 74, 21 Dec 74, 11 Mar 81, 13 Mar 81, 22 Dec 81, 23 Dec 81, 22 Dec 83, 23 Dec 83, xLent 87, 13 Apr 91.

Hatzfeld, Mme de. x14 Mar 78, x14 Feb 93, x21 Feb 93.

Hauck, Mlle. Singer. 16 Nov 81.

Haugwitz, Mme de. Singer. x22 Feb 99, x15 Oct 00.

Haunold, Herr. Singer. 11 Mar 99, 25 Nov 10.

Hauschka, Vincenz. Cellist. 23 Dec 94.

Haydn, Franz Joseph (1732-1809). Composer. x5 Apr 73, 2 Apr 75, 4 Apr 75, 17 Mar 77, 14 Mar 80, 22 Sep 80, 17 Nov 80, 16 Nov 81, 22 Dec 83, 23 Dec 83, 28 Mar 84, 30 Mar 84, 22 Dec 84, 23 Dec 84, 13 Mar 85, 15 Mar 85, 8 Apr 86, 7 Mar 87, 10 Mar 87, 16 Mar 87, 24 Mar 87, 28 Mar 87, 13 Oct 87, 15 Feb 88, 20 Feb 88, 27 Feb 88, 29 Feb 88, 22 Dec 88, 23 Dec 88, zB 14 Oct 89, 26 Mar 91, 2 Apr 91, 13 Apr 91, 15 Apr 91, 15 Apr 92, 16 Apr 92, x12 Mar 93, 15 Mar 93, 22 Dec 93, 23 Dec 93, x28 Dec 93, 21 Jan 94, 24 Jan 94, 12 Apr 94, 13 Apr 94, 25 Mar 95, 20 Jun 95, zB 21 Sep 95, 18 Dec 95, 22 Dec 95, 23 Dec 95, 8 Jan 96, 20 Mar 96, 22 Mar 96, x26 Mar 96, x27 Mar 96, x30 Mar 96, 19 Sep 96, 21 Sep 96, 27 Sep 96, 4 Oct 96, 15 Nov 96, 25 Mar 97, zW 25 Feb 98, 1 Apr 98, 2 Apr 98, 13 Apr 98, x29 Apr 98, x30 Apr 98, x7 May 98, x10 May 98, 28 Jun 98, 27 Oct 98, 5 Nov 98, 22 Dec 98, 23 Dec 98, x15 Feb 99, x2 Mar 99, x4 Mar 99, x8 Mar 99, 17 Mar 99, 18 Mar 99, 19 Mar 99, x5 Apr 99, 23 May 99, 16 Jun 99, 22 Dec 99, 23 Dec 99, 7 Mar 00, x11 Mar 00, 28 Mar 00, 2 Apr 00, x4 Apr 00, 4 Apr 00, 6 Apr 00, 7 Apr 00, x12 Apr 00, x13 Apr 00, 18 Apr 00, 15 Nov 00, zL 20 Nov 00, 22 Dec 00, 23 Dec 00, 16 Jan 01, 30 Jan 01, 25 Mar 01, 25 Mar 01, 29 Mar 01, 30 Mar 01, 5 Apr 01, x24 Apr 01, x27 Apr 01, x1 May 01, 29 May 01, x16 Nov 01, 22 Dec 01, 23 Dec 01, 27 Dec 01, x19 Mar 02, 25 Mar 02, x7 Apr 02, 11 Apr 02, 12 Apr 02, 13 Apr 02, Summer 02, 30 Sep 02, 22 Dec 02, 23 Dec 02, 26 Dec 02, x3 Apr 03, 3 Apr 03, 4 Apr 03, 5 Apr 03, x13 May 03, Summer 03, 22 Sep 03, 26 Dec 03, xLent 04, 25 Mar 04, 26 Mar 04, Summer 04, xAdvent 04, 22 Dec 04, 23 Dec 04,

25 Mar 05, 7 Apr 05, 7 Apr 05, 8 Apr 05, 9 May 05, 23 May 05, 28 May 05, Summer 05, 24 Dec 05, 25 Dec 05?, 23 Feb 06, 28 Mar 06, 1 Apr 06, 29 Jun 06, 22 Mar 07, 22 Mar 07, 23 Mar 07, 24 Mar 07, 17 May 07, b1 Dec 07, 22 Dec 07, 23 Dec 07, b26 Dec 07, 27 Mar 08, 10 Apr 08, 11 Apr 08, 17 Apr 08, xb10 Dec 08, b16 Dec 08, 22 Dec 08, 23 Dec 08, x31 Dec 08, 25 Mar 09, 25 Mar 09, 26 Mar 09, 27 Mar 09, 28 Mar 09, xb5 Apr 09, x13 Apr 09, 15 Nov 09, 22 Dec 09, 23 Dec 09, 25 Mar 10, 15 Nov 10, 22 Dec 10, 23 Dec 10.

Heberle, Anton. Flutist. 21 Apr 06, Summer 06, 18 Mar 09, 25 Nov 10, 30 Nov 10, 1 Dec 10, 15 Dec 10.

Heidenreich, Joseph. 8 Sep 98.

Heiss (née de Luca), Regina. Salterio player. 23 Jan 80.

Henikstein, Joseph von. Bass. *b25 Dec 08, xb1 Mar 09.

Henneberg, Johann Baptist (1768-1822). Composer. 13 Apr 91, zW 7 Jul 92, zW 26 Feb 98, 15 Nov 04.

Hensler, Josepha. Fortepianist. 25 Mar 05, zL 8 Sep 10.

Hering, Herr von (Johann Baptist von Häring). Violinist. b25 Nov 07, xb5 Apr 09, x15 Oct 09.

Himmel, Friedrich Heinrich (1765-1814). Composer. b1 Dec 07.

Hippe, Mlle. Singer. xLent 10.

Hirsch, Zacharias. Flutist. zB 5 Apr 91, zB 6 Apr 91.

Höffelmayer, Mlle. 22 Feb 93.

Hofen (née Puthon), Mme de. Fortepianist. x28 Mar 07.

Hofer (Hofer-Meier née Weber), Josepha (c1758-1819). Soprano. Sang the Queen of the Night in Mozart's *Die Zauberflöte*. 22 Dec 89, 23 Dec 89, 13 Apr 91, 15 Apr 91, 11 Mar 92, 8 Sep 98, 25 Mar 99.

Hofer, Josepha (b. 1791). Fortepianist. 25 Mar 99.

Hoffmann, Anton. Violinist. 18 Dec 74.

Hoffmann, Johann. Cellist. x10 Mar 62, 18 Dec 74.

Hoffmann, Josef. Singer. 23 Mar 78, 27 Mar 78, 21 Mar 79, 23 Mar 79, 19 Dec 79, 21 Dec 79.

Hofmann, Johann. Composer. 15 Mar 88, 16 Mar 88, 11 Mar 92.

Hofmann, Josef. Violinist. 19 Mar 82, 23 Dec 84, 22 Dec 88, 23 Dec 88, 23 Mar 93.

Hofmann, (Josef?). Violinist. xLent 04.

Hofmann, Joseph. Singer at the court theaters. 12 Mar 80, 14 Mar 80, 6 Apr 83, 8 Apr 83.

Hoffmeister (Hofmeister), Franz Anton (1754-1812). Composer. 28 Mar 87, 27 Feb 88, 20 Jun 95, 25 Mar 99, zB 14 Jun 99, 11 May 06.

Hohenadel, Mlle. Fortepianist. Summer 03, 6 Jan 04, Summer 04, 25 Jan 05, 25 Dec 07.

Holbein, Herr. Composer. 21 Apr 06.

Holzbauer, Ignaz (1711-1783). Composer. x26 Feb 62, 27 Feb 63, 14 Mar 80, 18 Mar 84.

Hradezky, Friedrich. Waldhornist. 2 Apr 03, Lent 05, xLent 05, 30 Apr 09.

Hrzan, Count. Flutist. 13 Dec 07.

Huber, Thaddäus (d. b1812). Composer. 11 Mar 81, 13 Mar 81, 22 Dec 84, 23 Dec 84, 9 Apr 86, 10 Mar 87.

Hüller, Sigismund. Singer. 1 Apr 98, 2 Apr 98, 5 Nov 98, 22 Dec 98, 23 Dec 98, 25 Mar 01, 29 Mar 01, 30 Mar 01.

Hummel, Johann Nepomuk (1778-1837). Composer. 12 Mar 94, 28 Apr 99, 27 Aug 99, 8 Sep 99, 25 Mar 03, 29 Jun 03, x7 Aug 04, xLent 05, Lent 05, x12 Mar 05, 29 Jun 06, 6 Mar 07, 22 Mar 07, 23 Mar 07, 23 Mar 07, x1 Apr 10.

Hutschenreiter, Mme. Singer. 11 Sep 00.

Iffland, Herr. Dramatic reciter. 22 Sep 08.

Insanguine (Giacomo 1728-1795—also known as Monopoli). Composer. 14 Mar 80.

Jacobi, Mme. x31 Mar 02.

Janiewicz, Feliks (1762-1848). Composer and violinist. 26 Feb 85.

Janisch, Herr. 16 Mar 78, 23 Mar 78.

Janitsch. See Janisch.

Janson, Charles. Violinist. 21 Dec 79.

Jonas, Mlle. Singer. Summer 06.

Jonat, Herr. Singer. x7 Apr 02.

Kaiser, Herr. Flutist. 23 Dec 10.

Kaiser, Therese. Singer. 28 Mar 06.

Kalkbrenner, Frédéric. (1785-1849). Pianist. xLent 04, Spring 04.

Kalmus, Herr. Cellist. 15 Dec 03, 6 Jan 04, xLent 04, Spring 04.

Kanne, Friedrich August (1778-1833). xWinter 04-05, 30 Mar 06, 31 Mar 06.

Kargl, Herr. 8 Sep 08, 23 Dec 10.

Karnavich, Herr. Composer. 12 Jun 05, 13 Jun 05.

Karnoli, Katharine (daughter of Peter). Singer. 9 Mar 86.

Karnoli, Peter. Singer. 9 Mar 86.

Katschinzki, Herr. Violinist. 15 Nov 01.

Kauer, Ferdinand (1751-1831). Composer. 22 Feb 88, 25 Mar 98, 23 Dec 98, 28 Mar 00, 15 Nov 01, zB 5 Mar 02, 25 Mar 03, 8 Sep 06, 15 Nov 07, 15 Nov 08, 24 Dec 09.

Kautzner, Herr. Bassoonist. 17 Mar 82, 21 Mar 87, 23 Dec 89, 2 Apr 91.

Kees, Herr von. Concert director. x22 Dec 61.

Keglevich, Mlle de. Fortepianist. x6 Mar 99.

Keller, Herr. *19 Dec 01, x10 Mar 02.

Kelly, Michael (1762-1826). Irish tenor. Sang Don Basilio and Don Curzio in Mozart's *Le Nozze di Figaro*. 18 Mar 84, 22 Dec 86, 23 Dec 86.

Kerber, Herr. zW 29 Jul 95.

Kessler, Herr. Flutist. b1 Dec 07.

Keventz, Mlle. Singer. x12 Mar 74.

Kiesewetter, Raphael Georg (1773-1850). xb1 Mar 09.

Kiker, Mlle. Singer. 15 Nov 07, 25 Mar 08.

Killizky, Mlle. Singer. 22 Dec 08, 29 Mar 10.

Kinsky, Princess. Singer. xb30 Jan 09.

Kirchgessner (Kirchgässner), Marianne (1769-1808). Glass harmonica player. 10 Jun 91, 19 Aug 91, 8 Sep 91, 23 Feb 06, 11 May 06.

Kirchstein, Herr. Flutist. x27 Jan 01.

Kirchwetter, Herr. Singer. x23 Mar 03.

Kirstein, Herr. Clarinettist. 18 Apr 00.

Kirzinger, (Paul Ignaz Kürzinger 1750-1820). Composer at the Thürn und Taxis court. 23 Mar 87.

Klemp, Franz. 2 Mar 04.

Klengel, (August Alexander? 1783-1852). Pianist. Spring 04.

Klieber, Therese. Soprano. 22 Dec 10, 23 Dec 10.

Klöffler, Johann Friedrich (1725-1790). Composer. 24 Feb 87.

Kohaut, Karl von. x22 Dec 61, 17 Mar 77, xSpring 82.

Koželuch, Leopold (1747-1818). Composer. 22 Sep 80, 22 Dec 83, 23 Dec 83, 24 Mar 87, 22 Dec 87, 23 Dec 87, 22 Dec 90, 23 Dec 90, 2 Apr 91, 13 Apr 91, 25 Mar 93, 27 Mar 93, 21 Jan 94, x11 Nov 95, 22 Dec 98, 23 Dec 98, xLent 05, 6 Apr 06.

Koželuch, Catharina (1785-1858). Fortepianist. xLent 05.

Kraft, Herr (either Anton or Nicolas). Cellist. x16 Mar 02, xWinter 04-05, x21 Jan 09, bx15 Feb 09.

Kraft, Anton (d.A.) (1749-1820). Cellist. 15 Apr 92, 23 Dec 97, 20 May 06, 22 Feb 07, 15 Nov 07, xb5 Dec 08, x10 Dec 10.

Kraft, Anton (d.J.). 15 Apr 92 (Probably Nikolaus).

Kraft, Nikolaus (d.J.) (1778-1853). Cellist. 23 Mar 04, 20 May 06, 22 Feb 07, 10 May 07, 15 Nov 07, xb5 Dec 08, 25 Jan 09, 5 Mar 09, 25 Mar 09.

Kramer, Herr. 29 Jun 03, 15 Nov 04.

Krammer, Herr. Composer. 22 Dec 97.

Krebner, Georg von. 22 Dec 96, 23 Dec 96, 1 Apr 04, 25 Dec 04.

Kremer, Joseph. Cellist. 23 Dec 95.

Kress, Michael. 12 Apr 94.

Kreutzer, Conradin (1780-1849). Fortepianist. Summer 04, 19 Apr 05, Summer 05, 25 Mar 06, 1 May 07, 27 Mar 08, 11 Apr 08, xb8 Jan 09, 28 Jan 09, 28 Mar 09, 29 Mar 10, 17 Apr 10, 5 Jun 10.

Kreutzer, Rodolphe (1766-1831). Violinist. x5 Apr 98, 28 Jan 09, 6 May 10.

Kreyser, Herr. Composer 30 Mar 84.

Kriehuber, Mme de. Singer. 25 Nov 10.

Krommer, Mlle. 4 Apr 00.

Krommer (Franz 1759-1831?). Composer. 4 Apr 00, 15 Nov 10, 23 Dec 10.

Kruft, Baron. x17 Mar 02, x9 Mar 03, x6 Apr 03, xLent 04.

Krumpholz, (Jean-Baptiste 1742-1790). 30 Oct 72, 16 Apr 92.

Küffel, Ignaz. Cellist. 17 Dec 72, 2 May 82.

Kunert, Herr. 15 Nov 07.

Kunzen, (Friedrich Ludwig Aemilius 1761-1817?). Composer. 25 Dec 07, x28 Mar 07.

Kurzböck, Magdalene. Fortepianist. xLent 04, xWinter 04-05, xLent 05, xb16 Dec 08, x26 Jan 09.

Kurzen, Mme. Singer. 30 Oct 72, 8 Jan 73.

Kyhm, Herr. Violinist. 5 Apr 97.

Lafont, Charles Philippe (1781-1839). Violinist. 4 Jun 08, zK 17 Jun 08, 28 Jan 09, 2 Apr 09, 25 Mar 10.

La Motte, J. 18 May 96.

La Motte, Franz. 29 Dec 66, 29 Mar 72, 5 Apr 72.

Lange (née Weber), Aloysia (c1759-1839). Soprano at the court theaters. Sang various Mozart roles including Donna Anna in Don Giovanni. 12 Mar 80, 14 Mar 80, 11 Jan 83, 11 Mar 83, 23 Mar 83, x25 Dec 84, 14 Mar 87, 21 Mar 87, 20 Feb 88, x26 Feb 88, x4 Mar 88, 7 Mar 88, 15 Mar 88, 16 Mar 88, x6 Mar 89, 4 Apr 89, 5 Apr 89, x7 Apr 89?, 4 Mar 91, 26 Mar 91, 16 Apr 91, 17 Apr 91, x24 Dec 93, 21 Jan 94, 24 Jan 94, 22 Dec 94, 23 Dec 94.

La Roche, Nannette. Singer. 15 Nov 07, 25 Mar 09, 24 Dec 09.

La Roche, Regina. 23 Dec 07.

Laschi (Laschi-Mombelli), Luisa (c1760-c1790). Soprano at the court theaters. Sang the Countess in Mozart's *Le Nozze di Figaro* and Zerlina in *Don Giovanni*. 22 Dec 84, 23 Dec 84, 13 Feb 85, 4 Jun 86.

Lasser, Emanuel (b. 1784). 24 Mar 93, 28 Mar 94.

Lasser, Johann Baptist (1751-1805). 24 Mar 93, 28 Mar 94.

Lausch, Klara. Violinist. 9 Mar 87.

Laucher, Mlle. 13 Dec 04, 25 Mar 05, 24 Dec 05, 25 Dec 05?.

Laucher, Antonie (d.A.). Court opera singer. 15 Nov 04, 7 Apr 05, 8 Apr 05, 14 Apr 05, 2 Jun 05, 22 Dec 05, 23 Dec 05, 30 Mar 06, 31 Mar 06, 29 Jun 06, 22 Dec 06, 23 Dec 06, 22 Mar 07, 23 Mar 07, 22 Dec 07, 23 Dec 07, 10 Apr 08, 11 Apr 08.

Laucher, Cäcelie. Singer. 30 Mar 06, 31 Mar 06, 22 Dec 07, 23 Dec 07.

Le Brun (née Danzi), Franciska (1756-1791). Soprano. x21 Feb 85, 23 Feb 85, 28 Feb 85, 7 Mar 85, 13 Mar 85.

Le Brun, Louis August (1752-1790). Oboist. x21 Feb 85, 23 Feb 85, 28 Feb 85, 7 Mar 85, 13 Mar 85.

Legrand, Peter (d.J.). Cellist from Munich. Lent 07, 23 Mar 07.

Leibnitz, Herr. From Prague. x16 Mar 02.

Leidesdorfer, M. J. b15 Mar 06, 26 Apr 07.

Leitersdorfer, Mlle. xWinter 04-05.

Lendway, Gabriel. Waldhorn player. 12 April 94.

Leppich, Franz. 29 Mar 10, 5 Jun 10.

Lessel, Franciszek (c1780-1838). x30 Apr 01, x21 May 01.

Le Sueur, Jean-François (1760-1837). Composer. 21 Apr 06.

Lieber, Herr. 6 Jan 04.

Lilien, Mlle (Baroness Antoinette or Baroness Josephine?). Fortepianist. x10 Nov 97, x22 Nov 97, x28 Mar 07 (Puthon née Lilien).

Linke, Herr. Cellist with Count Rasumofsky. 2 Aug 10.

Liparsky, Joseph (1772-1810). x13 May 03.

Lippert, Friedrich Carl. Tenor from Pfalz-Bayern. Sang Belmonte in Mozart's *Die Entführung aus dem Serail*. 2 May 82.

Liverati, (Giovanni 1772-1846?). x19 Dec 01, 8 May 08.

L'lano, Herr. From Spain. x29 Mar 02.

Lobkowitz, Prince Joseph Franz Maximilian (1772-1816). x11 Mar 00, x4 Apr 00, xb1 Mar 09. (See Appendix 4 for his activities as patron.)

Loginow, Labanow. Violinist. 10 Jun 02.

Lolli, Antonio (1725-1802). Violinist. zB 12 Sep 93, 2 Oct 93, 28 Oct 93, 17 Oct 94.

Longhi, Carolina. Fortepianist and harpist. 18 Dec 08, 9 Apr 09, 8 Aug 09.

Lotti, Herr. Singer. 2 Apr 02.

Lotz, Herr. Clarinettist. 17 Dec 72.

Lotz, Theodor. Contrabassoon player. 12 Mar 85.

Louis Ferdinand, Prince (1772-1806). Composer. xb8 Jan 09, xb26 Jan 09, xb30 Jan 09, xb15 Feb 09, xb1 Mar 09, xNov-Dec 09.

Luka, Regina de. Salterio player. Nov 82.

Lunin, Mlle. From Russia. xb21 Dec 08, xb6 Mar 09.

Lusini, Mlle. Singer. 23 May 95.

Mälzel, Johann Nepomuk (1772-1838). Inventor. 18 Apr 09, 21 Apr 09, 19 May 09.

Maffoli, Vincenzo. Tenor. x23 Feb 92, 15 Apr 92, 16 Apr 92, 9 Mar 93, 15 Mar 93, 23 Dec 93, 11 Apr 94.

Mailath, Mme. x22 Feb 99, x6 Mar 99.

Mainberger, (J. C. b. 1750?). 28 Apr 98.

Majo, Francesco (1732-1770). Composer. 22 Sep 80.

Malfatti, Dr. Singer. x6 Mar 99, x16 Mar 99.

Malzat, Ignaz (1757-1804). Oboist from Passau. zB 7 Oct 97, zB 13 Aug 03.

Mandini, Maria. Soprano at the court theaters. Sang Marcellina in Mozart's *Le Nozze di Figaro*. 29 Feb 84, 20 Feb 85, 23 Mar 87, 30 Mar 87, 1 Apr 87, 22 Dec 87, 23 Dec 87.

Mandini, Herr (Stefano 1750-c1810—baritone, or Paolo 1757-1842—tenor). Singer at the court theaters. 22 Dec 83 ,23 Dec 83, 29 Feb 84, 7 Mar 84, 28 Mar 84, 30 Mar 84, 22 Dec 84, 23 Dec 84, x16 Feb 85, 20 Feb 85, x2 Mar 85, 13 Mar 85, 15 Mar 85, 8 Apr 86, 9 Apr 86, 4 Jun 86, 22 Dec 87, 23 Dec 87, 8 Feb 88, 9 Feb 88, x10 Feb 88, 13 Feb 88, 15 Feb 88, 16 Feb 88.

Mansoli, Herr. Singer. 12 Feb 61, 24 Feb 61, x4 Mar 61, 10 Mar 61.

Mara, Gertrude Elisabeth (1749-1833). Soprano. 22 Sep 80, 20 Mar 81, x4 Apr 81, xWinter 03, x10 Apr 03, 27 Apr 03.

Mara, Johann (1746-1808). Cellist. 22 Sep 80.

Marchand, Heinrich. Violinist. 18 Feb 85, 2 Mar 85, 14 Mar 85, 15 Mar 85.

Marchesi, d. A. (Luigi 1755-1829?). Singer. x17 Mar 84, 22 Mar 84, 1 Apr 84.

Marchesi, Luigi (1755-1829). Castrato. x1 Apr 02, 3 Apr 03, 4 Apr 03.

Marconi, Marianna. Alto. 31 Mar 06, 11 May 06, 22 Dec 06, 23 Dec 06, 25 Dec 06, x27 Feb 07, x28 Mar 07, 15 Nov 07, 25 Dec 07, 22 Dec 08, 23 Dec 08, xb8 Jan 09, 25 Jan 09, 27 Mar 09.

Mareschalchi, Herr. Singer at the court theaters. 29 Mar 95, 30 Mar 95.

Marteau, Xaverio. Cellist. 4 Apr 75.

Martin, Philipp Jakob. Concert entrepreneur. 26 Mar 82, 11 Aug 82, 18 Aug 82.

Martín y Soler, Vincent (1754-1806). Composer. 23 Feb 87, 2 Mar 87, 3 Mar 87, 7 Mar 87, 9 Mar 87, 17 Mar 87, 23 Mar 87, 28 Mar 87, x29 Mar 87, x5 Mar 87, 1 Apr 87, x11 Feb 88, 22 Feb 88, 29 Feb 88, 14 Aug 00, 12 Mar 08.

Martinau, Mme. 1 Apr 91, 2 Apr 91.

Martines, Marianne. Composer. 17 Mar 82, 19 Mar 82.

Martini, Herr. Composer. 17 Dec 75, 20 Mar 76, 15 Feb 88, 23 Feb 88, 15 Nov 01, 8 Apr 02.

Maschek, Herr (Vincenc Mavsek 1755-1831? or Pavel Lambert 1761-1826?). Glass harmonica player and fortepianist. 21 May 91.

Maschek, Mme. Glass harmonica player and fortepianist. 21 May 91.

Massa, Herr. 2 Apr 02, 18 May 03, 29 Jun 03, 22 Dec 03, 23 Dec 03.

Massari, Herr. 17 Aug 84.

Matthäi, Herr. Composer. 6 May 10.

Matuschek, Vinzenz. Bassoonist with the Herzogliche Würtembergische Kapelle. 30 Mar 95, 4 Apr 96, 2 Apr 98, 2 Apr 00.

Maurer, Ludwig Wilhelm (1789-1878). Violinist. 23 Dec 10.

Mayer, Herr. Chalmaux player. 26 Apr 76.

Mayer, Herr. Bassoonist from Passau. zB 7 Oct 97.

Mayer, Herr. Brass player from Mannheim. 12 Mar 08.

Mayer, (Simon 1763-1845?). Composer. x29 Mar 02, 13 Apr 02, 2 Mar 04, x3 Dec 04, 25 Mar 05, 2 Jun 05, 12 Jun 05, 13 Jun 05, 25 Mar 06, 1 May 07, 10 May 07, 15 Nov 08, x24 Apr 09, 17 Apr 10, 23 Dec 10.

Mayseder, Joseph (1789-1863). Violinist. 24 Jul 00, 11 Jun 01, 8 Aug 01, 27 Aug 01, 1 Apr 03, 26 Dec 03, 1 Apr 04, Sep 04, xWinter 04-05, Lent 05, 28 Mar 06, 24 Apr 07, b23 Jun 08, 22 Dec 08, 8 Apr 10, 17 Apr 10, 15 Nov 10, 25 Dec 10.

Méhul, Étienne-Nicolas (1763-1817). Composer. 18 Apr 00, 23 Mar 04, xLent 04, xWinter 04-05, 25 Mar 05, 9 May 05.

Mei, Orazio (1731-1788). Composer. 10 Mar 87.

Meier, (née Weber) Josepha. 8 Sep 98, 25 Mar 99.

Meier, Sebastian. Bass at the court theaters. 8 Sep 98, 25 Mar 99, 21 Aug 00, 28 Aug 00, 1 Jul 02, 27 Mar 04, 31 Mar 06, 21 Apr 06, 23 Dec 06, 22 Mar 07, 10 Apr 08, 8 Sep 09.

Mendl, Herr. Singer. 4 May 98.

Menner, Mlle. Singer. 14 Apr 05.

Menzel, Zeno. Violinist. 30 Mar 87, 15 Mar 88, 16 Mar 88, 22 Dec 95.

Menzikof, Mme de. Singer. x7 Mar 93, x14 Mar 93.

Mesch, Herr (Mösch?). Clarinettist. 28 Mar 00.

Messerer, Herr. Trombone player. 26 Apr 76.

Mestrino, Nicolo (1748-1789). 8 Aug 85, 22 Mar 94, zK 14 Mar 01, 25 Mar 06.

Metter, Mlle. Fortepianist. zL 21 Oct 99.

Metzger, Carl Theodore. Musician at the court of Chur- Bayern. xLent 04, Lent 04, 27 Mar 04, Lent 07, 23 Mar 07.

Meyerbeer, Herr. 20 Mar 03.

Michalesi, Herr. Bass. 23 Dec 10.

Michel, Joseph. Composer. 13 Apr 94.

Milder, Anna. Singer at the court theaters and the Theater an der Wien. Summer 03, 22 Sep 03, 27 Mar 04, Lent 05, 9 Apr 05, 16 May 05, 31 Mar 06, 21 Apr 06, 11 May 06, 26 Oct 06, 29 Mar 07, 22 Sep 08, 25 Dec 08, 25 Mar 09, 28 Mar 09, 8 Sep 09, 15 Apr 10, 16 Apr 10.

Milliko, Joseph. Singer and member of the Italian opera company. 30 Nov 70.

Minito, Herr. Composer. 18 Mar 83.

Mirtakovsky, Herr. Guitarist. x21 May 01.

Mischel, Herr. zK 3 Oct 04.

Mitsch, Herr. Waldhorn player. 15 Dec 03.

Möglich, Herr. Violinist. Lent 05, x19 Mar 08.

Mölzel, Herr. Fortepianist. Summer 05.

Möser, (Karl 1774-1851?). Violinist. x26 Apr 03.

Molinelli, Rosa. Singer. 22 Dec 85, 23 Dec 85, 4 Jun 86.

Mollo, Gaspard. x23 Mar 92.

Mombelli, Mme. 15 Mar 88, 16 Mar 88.

Mombelli, Domenico. Singer at the court theaters. 4 Jun 86, 15 Jun 86, 15 Mar 88, 16 Mar 88, 18 Dec 95, 8 Jan 96.

Monsoli. See Mansoli.

Monza, Herr. 12 Mar 80, 14 Mar 80.

Morella, Herr. Singer at the court theaters. 22 Dec 88.

Morichelli, Anna (d. 1800). Singer at the court theaters. x28 Apr 87, 8 Sep 87, 13 Oct 87, 22 Dec 87, 23 Dec 87, 8 Feb 88, 9 Feb 88, x10 Feb 88, 13 Feb 88, xl4 Feb 88, 16 Feb 88, 23 Feb 88, x30 Mar 88.

Morigi, Margarethe. Singer. 17 Mar 76, 20 Mar 76.

Moscheles, Ignaz (1794-1870). 12 Mar 09, 18 Apr 09, 21 Apr 09, 19 May 09, 8 Aug 09, 22 Oct 09, x30 Oct 09.

Mozart, Wolfgang Amadeus (1756-1791). Fortepianist and composer. x5 Oct 62?, x9 Nov 62, x16 Mar 81, x17 Mar 81, x23 Mar 81, x24 Mar 81, 3 Apr 81, x8 Apr 81, x27 Apr 81, x16 Nov 81, x23 Nov 81, x12 Jan 82, 3 Mar 82, xSpring 82, 26 May 82, 18 Aug 82, 3 Nov 82, x14 Dec 82, xGolitzin concerts 82-83, x4 Jan 83, 11 Jan 83, 11 Mar 83, x12 Mar 83, 23 Mar 83, 30 Mar 83, x7 May 83, 22 Dec 83, 23 Dec 83, x26 Feb 84, x1 Mar 84, x4 Mar 84, x5 Mar 84, x8 Mar 84, x11 Mar 84, x12 Mar 84, x15 Mar 84, 17 Mar 84, x18 Mar 84, x19 Mar 84, 20 Mar 84, 21 Mar 84, x22 Mar 84, 23 Mar 84, 24 Mar 84, x25 Mar 84, x26 Mar 84, 27 Mar 84, x29 Mar 84, 31 Mar 84, 1 Apr 84, 3 Apr 84, x9 Apr 84, x10 Apr 84, 11 Apr 84, 29 Apr 84, *22 Jul 84, *31 Oct 84, 11 Feb 85, 13 Feb 85, 15 Feb 85, x16 Feb 85, 18 Feb 85, x21 Feb 85, 25 Feb 85, 4 Mar 85, 10 Mar 85, 11 Mar 85, 13 Mar 85, 15 Mar 85, 18 Mar 85, 23 Dec 85, 7 Apr 86, 7 Mar 87, 14 Mar 87, 21 Mar 87, x10 Feb 88, 15 Feb 88, x26 Feb 88, x4 Mar 88, 7 Mar 88, (June 88 series?), November 88, x6 Mar 89, 22 Dec 89, x14 Mar 89, xLent 90, *22 May 90, 4 Mar 91, x9 Apr 91, 16 Apr 91, 17 Apr 91, 19 Aug 91, 23 Dec 91, 11 Mar 92, xLent 92, 21 Jan 94, 24 Jan 94, x16 Feb 94, 13 Apr 94, 29 Dec 94, 25 Mar 95, 26 Mar 95, 31 Mar 95, x10 Mar 96, zW 25 Mar 97, 25 Mar 97, 5 Apr 97, 6 Apr 97, 11 Apr 97, x23 Mar 98, 29 Mar 98, 1 Apr 98, 2 Apr 98, 8 Apr 98, 27 Apr 98, 8 Sep 98, 27 Oct 98, 5 Nov 98, 25 Mar 99, zW 13 Nov 99, 28 Mar 00, 2 Apr 00, 4 Apr 00, 21 Aug 00, 18 Dec 00, 25 Mar 01, 31 Mar 01, 6 Jun 01, 11 Jun 01, 15 Nov 01, zW 21 Mar 02, 25 Mar 02, x31 Mar 02, 9 Apr 02, x10 May 02, Summer 02, 1 Apr 03, zK 2 Apr 03, x6 Apr 03, zK 14 Apr 03, Summer 03, 22 Sep 03, xLent 04, 24 May 04, Summer 04, 5 Jul 04, 15 Nov 04, xAdvent 04, xWinter 04-05, xLent 05, 25 Mar 05, 25 Mar 05, 8 Apr 05, 9 Apr 05, 1 May 05, 16 May 05, 2 Jun 05, Summer 05, 23 Feb 06, 25 Mar 06, 25 Mar 06, 28 Mar 06, 30 Mar 06, 31 Mar 06, Summer 06, x13 Aug 06, 22 Dec 06, 23 Dec 06, 6 Mar 07, 22 Mar 07, x28 Mar 07, b25 Nov 07, b1 Dec 07, 22 Dec 07, 11 Apr 08, 12 Apr 08, x4 Jun 08, xb10 Dec 08, xb16 Dec 08, xb31 Dec 08, xb8 Jan 09, 12 Mar 09, xb27 Mar 09, x13 Apr 09, 8 Sep 09, 1 Apr 10, 10 May 10, 8 Sep 10, 15 Nov 10, 23 Dec 10.

Mozart, Franz Xaver (1791-1844). Composer. 8 Apr 05.

Mrasek, Karoline. Fortepianist. 6 Mar 07.

Müller, Herr. Xänorphika player. 15 Apr 05, 1 May 05.

Müller, (August Eberhard 1767-1818?). b1 Dec 07, 10 May 10.

Müller, Ivan (1786-1854). Bassethorn player. 11 Apr 09, 22 Oct 09, 1 Apr 10.

Müller, Josepha Hortense. Fortepianist. 17 Feb 85.

Müller, Louise. Soprano at the Theater an der Wien. 14 Apr 05, 23 Feb 06, 1 May 07.

Müller (née Reinigsthal), Magdalena (c1770-1794). Singer. 29 Feb 88, 8 Apr 91.

Müller, Silverius (1745-1812). Composer. 23 Mar 04.

Müller, Wenzel (1767-1835). Kapellmeister at the Theater in der Leopoldstadt. 14 Oct 96, 15 Oct 96, 16 Oct 96, 17 Oct 96, 15 Nov 01.

Müllet, Herr. From Amsterdam. 12 Mar 08.

Müllner, Mme. Fortepianist. zK 23 Jun 08.

Müllner, Josepha. Harpist. 14 Mar 84, x10 Feb 88, 23 Feb 88, 16 Apr 92, 21 Mar 96, 18 May 96, 25 Mar 99, 23 May 99, 25 Mar 02, x26 Mar 02, x29 Mar 02, x8 Apr 02, 9 Apr 02, x12 Apr 02, 13 Apr 02, zB 27 Mar 03, 23 Mar 04, 20 May 04, 25 Dec 04, 25 Mar 05, 2 Jun 05, x19 Mar 08, 8 Apr 08, 13 Apr 08, 15 Nov 08, 25 Jan 09, 25 Mar 09, 28 Mar 09.

Muschietti, Herr. Soprano with the King of Sardinia. 8 Jul 83.

Mussini, Herr. Composer. 25 Mar 05, 22 Dec 05, 23 Dec 05.

Naderman, François-Joseph (1781-1835). Harpist. x15 Apr 03, 20 Apr 03, x26 Apr 03.

Nagel, Herr. Waldhorn player with Count Carl Palm. 12 Mar 80.

Nanj, Giovanna. Singer. 14 Mar 87.

Nani, Gianinna. Singer. 22 Dec 85, 23 Dec 85.

Nasolini, Sebastiano (c1768-c1806). Composer. 13 Apr 98, 30 Jan 01, x8 Apr 02, 21 Jun 04, 7 Apr 05, 2 Jun 05, 30 Mar 06, 10 May 07, 8 Sep 09, 25 Mar 10, 17 Apr 10.

Natorp (née Sessi). See Sessi-Natorp.

Naumann, Johann Gottlieb (1741-1801). 22 Dec 82, 23 Dec 82, 15 Dec 03, 23 Mar 04, x27 Feb 07, 15 Nov 07, x15 Mar 08.

Neukomm, Herr. Harpist. 2 Mar 83.

Neukomm, Herr. 22 Dec 08, 23 Dec 08.

Neuling, Herr. Violinist. 23 Dec 10.

Neumann, Herr. Singer. 14 Apr 05, 24 Dec 05, 25 Dec 05, 21 Apr 06.

Nickel, Matthäus. Waldhorn player. 12 Apr 94, 2 Apr 98, 2 Apr 00.

Nicolini, Herr. Singer. 3 Mar 63, x24 Jul 62, x9 Nov 62.

Nicolini, Giuseppi (1762-1842). Composer. 13 Apr 98.

Nicolosi. See Cesarini.

O'donel, Herr. Singer. x29 Dec 02, x19 Feb 03.

Oettingen, Count. Violinist. x5 Mar 87.

Ohmeyer, Dr. von. Violinist. xLent 10.

Ordonez, Carlo d' (1734-1786). Composer. 17 Mar 77, 18 Dec 77.

Orofino, Mlle. Xänorphika player. 25 Mar 06.

Orsler, Maria Anna. Singer. 8 Apr 86, 9 Apr 86.

Otter, Joseph. Violinist. 22 Dec 85.

Paar, Toni (Mme de). Keyboard player. x4 Feb 88.

Pär, Herr. See Bär.

Pär, (née Riccardi), Francesca. Singer. 8 Apr 00, 18 Apr 00, x26 Mar 02, x29 Mar 02, 2 Apr 02, 20 May 06, 25 May 06.

Pär, Ferdinando (1771-1839). Composer. x6 Mar 99, x16 Mar 99, x5 Apr 99, x31 Mar 00, x16 Apr 00, 18 Apr 00, 4 Sep 00, x15 Oct 00, x19 Dec 01, 25 Mar 02, x29 Mar 02, x31 Mar 02, 2 Apr 02, 1 Jul 02, x23 Mar 03, 25 Mar 03?, x3 Apr 03, 3 Apr 03, 4 Apr 03, x15 Apr 03, x26 Apr 03, 29 Jun 03, 2 Mar 04, 30 Apr 04, 20 May 04, 5 Jul 04, 15 Nov 04, 25 Mar 05, 16 May 05, 12 Jun 05, 13 Jun 05, 22 Dec 05, 23 Dec 05, 23 Feb 06, 25 Mar 06?, 28 Mar 06, 31 Mar 06, 20 May 06, 25 May 06, 22 Feb 07, 10 May 07, 15 Nov 08, b10 Dec 08, 25 Jan 09, 8 Aug 09, 18 Mar 10, 25 Mar 10.

Paisible, Herr. Violinist. 17 Mar 77.

Paisiello, Giovanni (1740-1816). Composer. 23 Mar 83, 30 May 84, x6 Jul 84, x16 Feb 85, 20 Mar 85, x27 Apr 85?, x23 Mar 86, x6 Apr 86, x29 Nov 86, 14 Mar 87, 2 Jun 87, 15 Feb 88, 23 Feb 88, 26 Mar 91, 23 Feb 93?, 27 Feb 93?, 13 Apr 94, 25 Mar 95, 23 May 95, 22 Dec 95, 23 Dec 95, 5 Nov 98, x6 Mar 99, x5 Apr 99, x31 Mar 00, 25 Mar 01, x8 Apr 02, 8 Apr 02, 27 Apr 03, 23 Mar 04, x6 Apr 05.

Pancioli, Giuseppi (b. 1795). Waldhorn player. 25 Mar 05.

Panschab, Leopold. Singer at the court theaters. 11 Mar 81, 13 Mar 81, 17 Mar 82, 19 Mar 82, 22 Dec 82, 23 Dec 82, 6 Apr 83, 8 Apr 83, 21 Jan 94, 24 Jan 94.

Papendik, Herr. Flutist. 23 Mar 79.

Paradies, Marie Therese von (1759-1824). Fortepianist. 22 Dec 87, 23 Dec 87, 22 Dec 90, 21 Jan 94, 24 Jan 94, 13 Apr 98.

Paris, Henriette (b. 1797). Fortepianist. xNov-Dec 09, 10 May 10.

Paresi, Herr. 8 Apr 08, 13 Apr 08.

Pasqua, Herr. 6 Mar 99, 8 Apr 00, 31 Mar 01.

Paulitsch, Mlle. x7 Apr 02.

Pavesi, (Stefano 1779-1850?). 26 Apr 07, 15 Nov 08.

Payer, Anna. Violinist. 21 Dec 77.

Pechacek, d.J. (Franz Xaver 1793-1840). Summer 05, Summer 06.

Peine, Mme. 20 Jun 95.

Pereira, Mme de. xb 16 Dec 08, xb 26 Jan 09.

Perlas, Countess. Keyboard player. x9 Oct 61.

Perotti (Augustin?). From Venice. 23 Jan 80.

Perschl, Mlle. Singer. 14 Aug 00, 15 Nov 01, x11 Mar 02.

Pesci, Antonio. Singer. 18 Dec 77, 21 Dec 77.

Petty, Miss. From England. x31 Mar 84.

Pfeiffer, Leopold. Bass at the Theater in der Leopoldstadt, later at the Theater an der Wien. zL 15 Feb 91, 15 Nov 01, 25 Mar 05 , 22 Dec 05, 23 Dec 05, 25 Mar 06, 22 Mar 07, 15 Nov 07, 25 Mar 08, 25 Mar 09, 24 Dec 09.

Piccini, Luigi (1728-1800). 8 Jan 73, 21 Mar 87.

Pichel, (Vaclav 1741-1805?). 15 Apr 91.

Pichl, Herr. Violinist. 30 Oct 72.

Pinton, Carolina. Singer. 19 Apr 07, 26 Apr 07, 8 May 08.

Pischelberger, Herr. 25 Mar 98, 22 Dec 98, 23 Dec 98.

Piticchio, (Francesco?). From Palermo. 27 Feb 88.

Pixis, Friedrich Wilhelm (1785-1842). Violinist. 23 Jan 07.

Pixis, Johann Peter (1788-1874). Fortepianist. 23 Jan 07.

Plaske, Herr. Clarinettist. zW 22 Feb 98.

Platzer, Josef. Fortepianist. zK 14 Apr 03, 30 Mar 06, 23 Dec 10.

Pleyel, Ignace Joseph (1757-1831). Composer. 21 Dec 84, 13 Oct 87, 15 Apr 91, 16 Apr 91, 15 Apr 92, x6 Dec 01, x4 May 02, 2 Sep 02, 6 Jan 04, Lent 05, 18 Apr 09, 21 Apr 09, 19 May 09.

Plomer-Salvini, Catherina. Singer from England. 20 Jun 95, 7 Mar 00.

Ployer, Mlle (Barbara von). Keyboard player. x23 Mar 85.

Podleska, Thekla. Singer. 22 Dec 86, 23 Dec 86, 9 Mar 87, 17 Mar 87, 24 Mar 87.

Pösinger, Franz Alexander. 25 Mar 09.

Poggi, Clementine. Singer. 17 Dec 72, 20 Dec 72, 21 Mar 73, 25 Mar 73.

Poggi, Domenico. Singer. 30 Oct 72, 17 Dec 72, 20 Dec 72, 21 Mar 73, 25 Mar 73, 18 Dec 74, 21 Dec 74.

Poniatowsky, Mme de. x22 Dec 63.

Pondra, Herr. See Bondra.

Ponschab, Herr. Singer. 17 Mar 77.

Portogallo (Marcos Antonio da Fonseca 1762-1830). Composer. 26 Apr 07, 22 Oct 09.

Posch, Johann. Violinist and fortepianist. 28 May 05.

Postpischel, Herr. z Landstrasse 11 Sep 93.

Potocki, Mlle. Singer. xb25 Dec 08.

Pou, Herr. xLent 04.

Poüthon (née Litgen), Mme. Fortepianist. x11 Mar 02.

Prati, Herr. Composer. 2 Jun 87, 16 Apr 92.

Preindl, Joseph (1756-1823). Fortepianist. 3 Mar 87, 10 Mar 87, 29 Feb 88, 22 Dec 92, 24 Mar 93, 12 Apr 94, 13 Apr 94, 30 Mar 06, 31 Mar 06, xLent 10.

Preisberger, Mme. Singer. 15 Nov 07, 24 Dec 09.

Probus, Herr. Flutist at the court theaters. 22 Dec 84, 23 Dec 89.

Pugnani, Gaetano (1731-1798). Composer. 22 Sep 80, 15 Apr 91, 22 Dec 95, 23 Dec 95, 22 Mar 96.

Punto, Giovanni (Johann Wenzel Stich 1746-1803). Waldhorn player. x16 Apr 00, 18 Apr 00, 30 Jan 01, 25 Mar 01, 31 Mar 01.

Purebl, Herr. Clarinettist with the Hofkapelle. 15 Nov 07, 25 Mar 09.

Quantz, Johann Joachim (1697-1773). 26 Mar 91.

Radicchi, Julius. Tenor. 27 Mar 08, 17 Apr 08, 15 Nov 08, b16 Dec 08, 18 Dec 08, 22 Dec 08, 23 Dec 08, 25 Dec 08, 26 Mar 09, 27 Mar 09, 8 Aug 09, 15 Nov 09, 22 Dec 09, 23 Dec 09, 25 Mar 10, x1 Apr 10, 17 Apr 10.

Radikati, Felice Alessandro (1775-1820). Composer. b16 Jan 08.

Raffel (Raphael), Ignaz Wenzel (d. 1799). Tenor. 28 Jun 98.

Raischel, Herr. Violinist. Summer 05.

Ramhärter, Herr. Singer. 24 Dec 09.

Ramm, Friedrich. Oboist. 18 Dec 76, 21 Mar 79, 13 Mar 81, x28 Feb 81, x15 Mar 81, 14 Mar 87.

Rathmayer, Mathias. Tenor. 27 Apr 98, x29 Apr 98, x30 Apr 98, x7 May 98?, x10 May 98?, 19 Mar 99, 23 May 99, 22 Dec 99, 23 Dec 99, x4 Apr 00, 6 Apr 00, 7 Apr 00, 28 Aug 00, 22 Dec 00, 23 Dec 00, x24 Apr 01, 22 Dec 01, 23 Dec 01, 11 Apr 02, 12 Apr 02, 22 Dec 02, 23 Dec 02, 5 Apr 03, 25 Mar 04, 26 Mar 04, 22 Dec 04, 23 Dec 04, 25 Dec 07.

Raumann, Herr. 22 Sep 80.

Redlich, Herr. Flutist. zK 29 Aug 99.

Reicha, Josef (1752-1795). Composer and cellist. 16 Mar 78?, 27 Mar 78, 24 Mar 87.

Reicha, Antoine (1770-1836). Composer. 11 May 06.

Reichardt, Johann Friedrich (1752-1814). Composer. 20 Feb 88, xb5 Dec 08.

Reinstein, Herr. Violinist. 15 Apr 91.

Renner, Johann. 26 Mar 95.

Renner, Lorenz. Fortepianist. 25 Nov 97, zL 20 Sep 99.

Reuter, Herr. Oboist with Prince Schwarzenberg. 23 Dec 97.

Rhein, Friedrich (d. b1799). Flutist. 9 Mar 87, 15 Mar 88, 16 Mar 88.

Rica, Herr. 19 May 09.

Richini (Righini?), Herr. 13 Apr 91.

Richter, Franz Xaver (1709-1789). 19 Mar 02.

Richter, Georg Friedrich. 20 Mar 84, 27 Mar 84, 3 Apr 84.

Riegl, (Heinrich Joseph 1741-1799?). 9 Mar 87.

Ries, Ferdinand (1784-1838). Fortepianist. xWinter 04-05, 24 May 04, 16 May 05, xb16 Dec 08, xb25 Dec 08.

Righini, Vincenzo (1756-1812). Composer. 18 Dec 77, 21 Dec 77, 21 Mar 87, 28 Mar 87, 22 Dec 89, 23 Dec 89, 16 Apr 91, 17 Apr 91, 12 Apr 94, 13 Apr 94, 22 Dec 95, 22 Dec 97, 23 Dec 97, 27 Oct 98, 5 Nov 98, 15 Nov 01, 13 Apr 02, 25 Mar 03, Summer 03, 5 Jun 04, Sep 04, xLent 05, 20 May 06, 10 May 07, 15 Nov 07, 25 Jan 09, 8 Aug 09.

Ringbauer, Josepha (b. 1773). Violinist. 16 Mar 84, 22 Feb 85, 15 Feb 88, x8 Dec 03.

Riotte, Philipp Jakob (1776-1856). Clarinettist. 22 Oct 09, 1 Apr 10.

Rispoli, (Salvatore? c1736-1812). Composer. 30 Jan 01.

Roch, Herr. Singer. 25 Mar 08.

Rode, Pierre (1774-1830). Composer. 1 Apr 04, 21 Jun 04, xAdvent 04, 31 Mar 06, zW 9 Jun 06, zW 21 Jun 06, Summer 06, 23 Jan 07, b1 Dec 07.

Röckel, Joseph August (1783-1870). Tenor. 31 Mar 06, 1 May 07, 22 Sep 08.

Röllig, Karl Leopold (d. 1804). Glass harmonica player. 2 Apr 91, x24 Dec 93.

Rösler, Joseph (1771-1813). zB 20 Jan 07, 25 Mar 10.

Rösner, Herr. Composer. 25 Mar 06.

Röth, Herr. 15 Feb 07.

Rolla, Alessandro (1757-1841). zW 3 Nov 03, zW 26 Nov 03, zW 1 Dec 03.

Romagnoli, Herr. Composer. 22 Dec 98, 23 Dec 98.

Romberg, Andreas Jakob (1767-1821). Violinist. Summer 06, b26 Dec 07.

Romberg, Anton (1771-1842). Bassoonist. 23 Apr 09, 18 Mar 10, 25 Mar 10, 15 Nov 10.

Romberg, Bernhard Heinrich (1757-1841). Cellist. 22 Feb 07, 15 Nov 07, 14 Jan 08, 8 Mar 08, b10 Dec 08, xb8 Jan 09, 5 Mar 09, 25 Mar 09.

Roose, Mme. Dramatic reciter. 29 Jun 03, 23 Feb 06, 1 Apr 06.

Rosenbaum, Mme. See Gassmann-Rosenbaum, Therese.

Rosetti, (Franz Anton Rösler (c1750-1792). 1 Apr 83, 13 Oct 87.

Roth, Herr. 1 May 07.

Roth, Johann Georg. Timpanist. 28 Apr 98,

Rotter, Joseph. Singer. 15 Nov 99, 15 Nov 01, 15 Nov 02, 25 Mar 08.

Rudolph, Archduke (1788-1831). Fortepianist. xb8 Jan 09, xb30 Jan 09, xb1 Mar 09.

Ruffati, Herr. Violinist. 24 Apr 02.

Rust, (Wilhelm Karl 1787-1855?). 8 Sep 96.

Rutzizka, (Wenzel?). Oboist. 23 Feb 06, 23 Dec 10.

Saal, Ignaz. Bass with the court theaters. 30 Mar 87, 1 Apr 87, x26 Feb 88, x4 Mar 88, 7 Mar 88, x30 Mar 88, x6 Mar 89, 4 Apr 89, 5 Apr 89, x7 Apr 89?, 22 Dec 89, 23 Dec 89, 22 Dec 90, 23 Dec 90, 22 Dec 92, 9 Mar 93, 23 Mar 93, 24 Mar 93, x24 Dec 93, 21 Jan 94, 24 Jan 94, 19 Mar 94, 13 Apr 94, 22 Dec 94, 23 Dec 94, 29 Mar 95, 30 Mar 95, 20 Mar 96, 21 Mar 96, 22 Mar 96, 19 Sep 96, 21 Sep 96, 22 Dec 96, 23 Dec 96, 9 Apr 97, 10 Apr 97, 22 Dec 97, 23 Dec 97, 30 Mar 98, 2 Apr 98, x29 Apr 98, x30 Apr 98, x7 May 98, x10 May 98, 22 Dec 98, 23 Dec 98, 11 Mar 99, 19 Mar 99, x5 Apr 99, 23 May 99, 22 Dec 99, 23 Dec 99, 2 Apr 00, 6 Apr 00, 7 Apr 00, 18 Dec 00, 21 Dec 00, 22 Dec 00, 23 Dec 00, 25 Dec 00, 25 Mar 01, 31 Mar 01, x24 Apr 01, 22 Dec 01, 23 Dec 01, 11 Apr

02, 12 Apr 02, 22 Dec 02, 23 Dec 02, 3 Apr 03, 4 Apr 03, 5 Apr 03, 22 Dec 03, 23 Dec 03, 25 Mar 04, 26 Mar 04, 20 May 04, 22 Dec 04, 23 Dec 04, 25 Dec 04, 9 Apr 05, 2 Jun 05, 12 Jun 05, 13 Jun 05, 1 Apr 06, 22 Dec 06, 23 Dec 06, 25 Dec 07, 25 Mar 08, 15 Nov 08, 22 Dec 08, 23 Dec 08, 25 Mar 09, 28 Mar 09.

Saal, Therese. Soprano at the court theaters. 19 Mar 99, x5 Apr 99, 23 May 99, 22 Dec 99, 23 Dec 99, 2 Apr 00, 6 Apr 00, 7 Apr 00, 18 Dec 00, 21 Dec 00, 22 Dec 00, 23 Dec 00, 25 Dec 00, 25 Mar 01, x24 Apr 01, 22 Dec 01, 23 Dec 01, 25 Mar 02, 11 Apr 02, 12 Apr 02, 13 Apr 02, 22 Dec 02, 23 Dec 02, 3 Apr 03, 4 Apr 03, 5 Apr 03, 23 Mar 04, 25 Mar 04, 26 Mar 04, 22 Dec 04, 23 Dec 04, 25 Dec 04.

Sacchini, Antonio (1730-1786). Composer. 20 Dec 78, 14 Mar 80, 16 Nov 81, 22 Dec 82, 23 Dec 82, 22 Dec 83, 23 Dec 83, 15 Mar 85, 16 Mar 87, 22 Dec 88, 23 Dec 88, 26 Mar 91, 11 Mar 92, 15 Apr 92, 16 Apr 92, x20 Apr 95, 22 Dec 95, 23 Dec 95, 22 Dec 97, 30 Mar 06, 31 Mar 06.

Salieri, Antonio (1750-1825). Composer. 18 Dec 77, 21 Dec 77, 22 Dec 82, 23 Dec 82, 1 Apr 83, x18 Sep 84, 22 Dec 84, 22 Dec 85, 23 Dec 85, 15 Feb 88, 23 Feb 88, 27 Feb 88, 15 Mar 88, 16 Mar 88, 22 Dec 88, 23 Dec 88, 4 Apr 89, 5 Apr 89, 16 Apr 91, 17 Apr 91, 15 Apr 92, 16 Apr 92, 12 Apr 94, 13 Apr 94, 22 Dec 94, 23 Dec 94, 29 Mar 95, 30 Mar 95, 22 Dec 95, 23 Dec 95, 20 Mar 96, 21 Mar 96, 22 Dec 96, 23 Dec 96, 9 Apr 97, 10 Apr 97, 22 Dec 97, 23 Dec 97, x29 Apr 98, x30 Apr 98, x7 May 98?, x10 May 98?, 21 Dec 98, 22 Dec 98, 23 Dec 98, 23 May 99, 15 Nov 99, 25 Mar 02, *12 Apr 02, 14 Apr 05, 30 Mar 06, 31 Mar 06, 11 May 06, 22 Dec 06, 23 Dec 06, 25 Dec 06, 17 May 07, 22 Dec 07, 23 Dec 07, 10 Apr 08, 11 Apr 08, 17 Apr 08, 26 Mar 09, 27 Mar 09, 18 Apr 09, 21 Apr 09, 19 May 09, 15 Nov 09, 22 Dec 09, 23 Dec 09, 15 Apr 10, 16 Apr 10, 22 Dec 10, 23 Dec 10.

Salm, Princess. Singer. x15 Aug 07.

Sander, Herr. Singer. x9 Mar 03, x23 Mar 03.

Santi Hüber, Herr. Cellist. 25 Dec 09.

Sarti, Giuseppe (1729-1802). 20 Dec 78, x1 Jul 83, 22 Dec 83, 23 Dec 83, 18 Mar 84, 4 Jun 86, 3 Mar 87, 7 Mar 87, 10 Mar 87, 2 Jun 87, x30 Apr 93?, 8 Sep 95, 22 Dec 95, 6 Apr 97, 25 Mar 01, 13 Apr 02, 22 Dec 05, 23 Dec 05, 30 Mar 06, 31 Mar 06.

Sartori, Herr. Mandolin player. 11 Mar 92.

Sartorini, Pietro. Soprano. 2 Jun 87.

Sattmann, Mlle. Singer. x9 Mar 03, x8 Dec 03, 21 Jun 04.

Scaramelli, Alessandro. Violinist. 4 Dec 08.

Scarlatti, Herr. Composer and keyboard player. x10 Mar 62, x4 Aug 62, x22 Feb 74.

Schacht, Theodore von (1748-1823). Composer. 5 Jun 06.

Schack (Benedikt 1758-1826?). Tenor. Sang Tamino in Mozart's *Die Zauberflöte*. 11 Mar 92.

Schaffmann, Herr. 20 Feb 88.

Schcerd, Herr. Cellist. zL 23 Jul 98.

Scheidl, Cäsar. Fortepianist. 21 Feb 85, 22 Dec 86, 3 Mar 87, 10 Mar 87, 29 Feb 88, 22 Dec 92.

Scheidl, Joseph. Violinist. 19 Sep 96, 21 Sep 96, 23 May 99, 15 Nov 08, 25 Dec 08, 15 Nov 09, 15 Nov 10.

Scheidlein, Herr. Singer. x9 Mar 03, x23 Mar 03, x6 Apr 03.

Schenck, Johann Baptist (1753-1836). Composer. 23 Feb 88, 26 Mar 91, 13 Apr 91, 15 Apr 91.

Schenker, Herr. Violinist. 20 Mar 85.

Schewel, Mlle. Harpist. x28 Apr 87.

Schikaneder, Emanuel (1751-1812). 27 Oct 98, 5 Nov 98, 25 Mar 01.

Schill, Mlle. 29 Jun 06.

Schindler, (Catharina d. 1788?). 11 Mar 84.

Schindlöcker, Philipp. Cellist. 16 Nov 81, 20 Mar 83, 3 Mar 85, 30 Mar 87, 15 Mar 88, 16 Mar 88, 23 Dec 88, 23 Dec 95, 23 Dec 96, 2 Apr 00, 30 Mar 01, 24 May 04.

Schlauf, Wenzeslaus. 18 Feb 85.

Schlesinger, Martin. Concert master with Prince Grassalkowich, then with Count Josef Erdödy. 23 Dec 83, 3 Apr 03.

Schlesinger, Mlle. Fortepianist. x7 Jan 05.

Schlick, Johann Conrad. 13 Oct 87, 11 Mar 92.

Schmalz, Amalie. Singer at the court theaters. 25 Mar 03, 29 Jun 03, 22 Dec 03, 23 Dec 03, 26 Dec 03.

Schmid, Joseph. Fortepianist. zW 13 Nov 99, 15 Nov 01.

Schmid, Ludwig. Violinist. 21 Dec 79.

Schmidt, Mme de. Singer. 1 May 05, 9 May 05.

Schmierer, Johanna. Singer. 15 Nov 04.

Schneider, Herr. Bassoonist. 18 Mar 10.

Schobenlechner, Franz (1797-1843). x1 Apr 10.

Schönborn, Mme de. Singer. x31 Mar 00.

Schönfeld, Therese. Singer. x23 Feb 92, x14 Feb 93, x21 Feb 93, x7 Mar 93, x14 Mar 93, x8 Apr 94, *11 Nov 95, x22 Feb 99, x5 Apr 99, x31 Mar 00, x4 Apr 00, x16 Apr 00, x15 Oct 00, x19 Dec 01, x29 Mar 02, x12 Apr 02.

Scholl, Nikolaus. Flutist with Prince Grassalkovich. 1 Apr 87.

Scholl, 2 children. zL 2 May 00.

Schreiber, Herr. 2 Apr 00.

Schüler, (née Bonasegla), Mme. Singer. 31 Mar 01.

Schutz, (Heinrich Schütz? 1585-1672). x15 Mar 08.

Schulz, Anton. Flutist. 1 Apr 72, 21 Dec 73.

Schulz, Herr. Singer. 19 Sep 96, 21 Sep 96, 22 Dec 97, 23 Dec 97.

Schuppanzigh, Ignaz (1776-1830). Violinist. 6 Apr 97, 29 Mar 98, 5 Nov 98, 28 Apr 99, 30 May 99, 7 Jun 99, 14 Jun 99, 21 Jun 99, 2 Apr 00, Summer 00 including: 24 May 00, 29 Jun 00, 24 Jul 00, 14 Aug 00, 21 Aug 00, 28 Aug 00, 4 Sep 00, 11 Sep 00, 18 Sep 00; x10 Dec 00; Summer 01 including: 6 Jun 01, 11 Jun 01, 18 Jun 01, 25 Jun 01, 8 Aug 01, 20 Aug 01, 27 Aug 01, 3 Sep 01, 17 Sep 01, 24 Sep 01; Summer 02 including: 3 Jun 02, 10 Jun 02, 19 Jun 02, 24 Jun 02, 1 Jul 02, 12 Aug 02, 19 Aug 02, 26 Aug 02, 2 Sep 02, 9 Sep 02, 16 Sep 02, 30 Sep 02; Summer 03 including: 28 Jul 03, 22 Sep 03; Summer 04 including: 24 May 04, 21 Jun 04, 5 Jul 04; Sep 04; Summer 05 including: 16 May 05, 23 May 05; Winter 05, Summer 06, x15 Aug 07, xb10 Dec 08, xb16 Dec 08, xb31 Dec 08, xb8 Jan 09, xb26 Jan 09, 28 Jan 09, 6 May 10; Summer 10 including 2 Aug 10.

Schuster, Herr. Composer. xNov-Dec 09.

Schuster, Anton. Singer. x13 May 03, 15 Nov 04, 25 Mar 05.

Schuster, Ignaz (1779-1835). Bass. x28 Sep 01, x13 May 03, 15 Nov 04, 25 Mar 05, 8 Sep 05, 25 Mar 06, 25 Mar 08.

Schuster (Joseph Anton?). Flutist. Summer 04.

Schuster, Rosina. Fortepianist. 25 Mar 09.

Schuster, Vincenz. Guitarist. 25 Nov 10, 30 Nov 10, 1 Dec 10, 15 Dec 10.

Schwarz, Herr. Bassoonist. 19 Apr 76.

Schwarzenberg, Princess Ernestine. Singer. x16 Mar 74, x12 Mar 95, x19 Mar 95, x27 Mar 95.

Schwarzenberg, Princess Therese. Singer. x8 Apr 94, x19 Mar 95, x16 Mar 99, x3 Apr 00, x16 Apr 00.

Sedlatscheck, Herr. Bassoonist at the court theaters. 28 Mar 00.

Seidler, Ferdinand August (b. 1778). Violinist from Berlin. 25 Jan 07, 28 Jan 08, xb31 Dec 08, xb8 Jan 09, 28 Jan 09, xb15 Feb 09, xb20 Feb 09, xb1 Mar 09, 2 Apr 09.

Seligmann, Herr. Tenor from Munich. xb25 Dec 08.

Sessi-Natorp, Imperatrice (d. 1808). Singer. 27 Mar 04, 1 Apr 04, 8 Apr 08, 13 Apr 08.

Sessi, Anna Maria. Singer. 12 Jun 05, 13 Jun 05.

Sessi, Marianna. Singer. 12 Jun 05, 13 Jun 05.

Sessi, Mathilde?. Singer. 29 Mar 95, 30 Mar 95, 22 Dec 95, 23 Dec 95.

Sessi, Victoria. Singer. 15 Nov 04, 12 Jun 05, 13 Jun 05.

Seyfried, Ignaz Ritter von (1776-1841). 27 Oct 98, 5 Nov 98, 21 Aug 00, 29 Mar 07, 25 Dec 08, 25 Dec 09.

Siboni, Giuseppi (1780-1839). Tenor. b12 Jun 05, x17 Aug 09.

Sieber, Herr. Violinist. Summer 05.

Sieber, Mlle. Fortepianist. 22 Mar 07.

Sieber, Mlle. Singer. 28 Mar 06.

Sigl, Ignaz (b. 1802). 1 May 07.

Sigl, Klara (b. 1794). 1 May 07.

Sigmuntowsky, Herr (b. 1771). Cellist. Lent 80.

Simoni, Herr. Oboist from Salzburg. 18 Nov 99.

Simoni, Josef. Tenor. 4 Apr 96, 9 Apr 97, 10 Apr 97, 30 Jan 01, 3 Apr 03, 4 Apr 03, 20 May 04, xb5 Dec 08, 15 Apr 10, 16 Apr 10, x21 Apr 10, 22 Apr 10, 22 Dec 10, 23 Dec 10.

Smrezka, Christian. Cellist. 24 Mar 87.

Sommariva, Diego. Singer. 19 Apr 07, 26 Apr 07, 10 May 07, 12 Jun 07.

Sonnleithner, Johanna. 24 Mar 93.

Sonnleithner, Ignaz (1770-1831). Bass. 1 Apr 04, 29 Jun 06, xLent 10, x1 Apr 10.

Souter, Matthäus. Singer at the court theaters. 20 Dec 78, 21 Mar 79, 23 Mar 79, 19 Dec 79, 21 Dec 79, 12 Mar 80, 14 Mar 80.

Spangler, Herr or Mlle? Singer. 18 Dec 77, 21 Dec 77.

Spangler, Johann Georg (1752-1802). Tenor. 21 Mar 79, 23 Mar 79, 21 Apr 94, 24 Apr 94, x15 Apr 94, 22 Dec 94, 23 Dec 94, x31 Dec 94, 29 Mar 95, 30 Mar 95, x24 Mar 97.

Spangler, Margaretha. Singer. 18 Dec 74, 21 Dec 74, 2 Apr 75, 4 Apr 75.

Specht, Christian. Singer. 2 Apr 75, 4 Apr 75.

Sperger, Johann. Contrabass player. 20 Dec 78, 22 Dec 88.

Sperger, Joseph. Contrabass player. 3 Mar 87.

Spielmann, Mlle. Fortepianist. x16 Mar 02, b25 Nov 07.

Spohr, Louis (1784-1859). Composer. b23 Jun 08, 16 Feb 09, 15 Nov 10.

Springer, (Vincent?). Clarinettist. 23 Feb 06.

Stadler, Anton Paul (d.A.) (1753-1812). Clarinettist. 21 Mar 73, 19 Dec 75, 12 Mar 80, 23 Mar 84, 17 Mar 85, 20 Feb 88, 22 Dec 89, 23 Dec 89, 21 Sep 96, 27 Sep 96, 10 Apr 97, 22 Dec 97, 23 Dec 97, 29 Mar 98, 13 Apr 98, 2 Mar 04?, 5 Jul 04?.

Stadler, Johann Nepomuk Franz (1755-1804). Clarinettist. 21 Mar 73, 19 Dec 75, 12 Mar 80, 10 Apr 97, 22 Dec 05, 23 Dec 05, 31 Mar 06.

Stadler, Joseph. Clarinettist. 13 Apr 02.

Starhemberg, Princess. x19 Sep 08, xb27 Feb 09, x15 Oct 09.

Stamitz, Carl (1745-1801). Violist. 20 Dec 72, x16 Mar 74, 20 Mar 74.

Starzer, Joseph. Composer. 29 Mar 72, 1 Apr 72, 5 Apr 72, x21 Feb 74, 23 Mar 78, 27 Mar 78, 23 Mar 79, 12 Mar 80, xSpring 82, 22 Dec 83, 23 Dec 83, xLent 86.

Stegmayer, Matthäus (1771-1820). Composer. x18 Mar 04.

Steibelt, Daniel (1765-1823). Fortepianist. x27 Mar 00, x16 Apr 00, Summer 00, Lent 05, 25 Mar 05, Summer 05, 25 Mar 06, 23 Jan 07, xb16 Dec 08, 8 Aug 09.

Stein, Friedrich (1784-1809). Fortepianist. Summer 05, Summer 06, 13 Apr 08, 15 Nov 08.

Stengel, G. Baritone. 11 Mar 92, 22 Dec 95, 23 Dec 95, 27 Apr 98.

Stenzel, Mlle. Fortepianist. 29 Jun 03.

Stephanie, Mme. Singer. 15 Nov 01.

Storace, Nancy (1765-1817). Soprano. Sang Suzanna in Mozart's *Le Nozze di Figaro*. x1 Jul 83, 18 Mar 84, 28 Mar 84, 30 Mar 84, 20 Mar 85, x9 Mar 86, 4 Jun 86, 22 Dec 86, 23 Dec 86, 23 Feb 87.

Strauss, Joseph. Violinist. zW 21 Jun 03.

Strinasacchi, Regina (1764-1839). Violinist. 29 Mar 84, x15 Apr 84, 29 Apr 84.

Struck, Paul (1776-1820). Pupil of Haydn. 11 Apr 09.

Stummer, Miss. Fortepianist. 2 Sep 02, 22 Sep 03.

Suche, Joseph. 13 Apr 91, 11 Mar 92, 25 Mar 95, 20 Mar 96, 9 Apr 97.

Süssmayer, Franz Xaver (1766-1803). Composer. 20 Mar 96, x7 Apr 96?, 19 Sep 96, 21 Sep 96, 4 Oct 96, 15 Nov 96, 22 Dec 96, 23 Dec 96, 25 Dec 96, 22 Dec 97, 23 Dec 97, 28 Apr 98, 4 May 98, 25 Mar 00, 28 Mar 00, 18 Dec 00, 21 Dec 00, 25 Dec 00, 25 Mar 03, 15 Nov 04, 25 Mar 08, 25 Mar 09, 28 Mar 09, 2 Apr 09.

Swieten, Baron Gottfried van (1733-1803). Composer. 20 Dec 78?, 26 May 82.

Tarchi, Angelo (c1760-1814). Composer. 13 Apr 02.

Tarocca, Mme de. Keyboard player. x22 Mar 63.

Tarocca, Mme de. Singer. x29 Nov 86.

Tauber, Maria Anna. Singer. 23 Mar 78, 27 Mar 78.

Tebaldi, Herr. Singer. x19 Mar 64.

Teiberin, Mme. Singer. x22 Dec 61, x26 Feb 62, x12 Mar 62.

Teimer, Herr. Singer at the Theater an der Wien. x19 Mar 95, 21 Aug 00, 28 Aug 00, 25 Mar 02.

Teimer, Herr. Oboist. zB 21 Feb 95, 25 Mar 06, 23 Mar 07.

Teimer, Brothers (Johann, Franz, Philipp). Oboists. 13 Feb 93, 23 Dec 93, zB 22 Sep 95, 22 Dec 95, 23 Dec 95.

Teimer, Caroline. Singer. 25 Mar 06, 23 Mar 07.

Teimer. Henriette. Singer. 25 Mar 06, 23 Mar 07.

Teimer, Philipp. Oboist. 23 Dec 97.

Tepfer, Mlle. Singer. 19 Sep 96, 21 Sep 96, 22 Dec 96, 23 Dec 96.

Terziani, Herr. 30 Apr 04.

Teyber, Anton. Composer. 22 Dec 86, 23 Dec 86, 22 Dec 98, 23 Dec 98.

Teyber, Barbara. Singer. 2 Apr 75, 4 Apr 75.

Teyber, Franz (1758-1810). Composer. 20 Dec 78, 23 Mar 05.

Teyber, Therese. (1760-1830) Soprano at the court theaters. Sang various Mozart roles, including Blonde in *Die Entführung aus dem Serail*. 20 Dec 78, 19 Dec 79, 21 Dec 79, 12 Mar 80, 14 Mar 80, 11 Mar 81, 13 Mar 81, 1 Apr 81, 3 Apr 81, 17 Mar 82, 19 Mar 82, 23 Mar 83?, 30 Mar 83?, 6 Apr 83, 8 Apr 83, 28 Mar 84, 30 Mar 84.

Thieriot, Paul. Violinist from Leipzig. xLent 04, 13 Apr 04, 21 Jun 04.

Thun, Mme de. x22 Dec 63.

Thurner, Franz. Flutist. 22 Mar 93, 12 Apr 94, 13 Apr 94.

Töschi, Johann. Concert master with the Kurfürst von Pfalzbayern. 12 Mar 80.

Todi, Giuseppi. Soprano. 19 Apr 07, 26 Apr 07, 8 May 08.

Tody, Luisa Rosa (1753-1833). Mezzo soprano. 28 Dec 81, 18 Jan 82.

Tomášek, Jan Křtitel (1774-1850). Composer. Summer 06.

Tomaselli, Herr. Baritone. 26 Oct 06.

Tomasini, Alois Luigi (d.A.) (1741-1808). 2 Apr 75, 22 Mar 94, 20 Mar 96.

Tomasini, Alois Basil Nikolaus (1779-1858). Violinist. 22 Mar 94, 20 Mar 96, 29 Mar 01, x6 Apr 03, x7 Aug 04, 29 Jun 06.

Tomeoni, Irene (1763-1830). Singer. x23 Feb 92, 9 Mar 93, 15 Mar 93, 11 Apr 94, 18 Dec 95, 8 Jan 96, 30 Mar 98.

Tonelli, Luigi. Singer. 22 Oct 92.

Toricella, Christoph (c1715-1798). 21 Dec 84.

Traetta, Tommaso (1727-1779). Composer. 3 Mar 76, 17 Mar 77, 22 Dec 84, 23 Dec 84, 10 Mar 87.

Trattner, Mme (Therese 1758-1793). Keyboard player. x17 Mar 85.

Trento, Vittorio (c1761-1833). Composer. 2 Apr 02.

Tretter, Herr. Harpist. 20 Mar 64.

Triebensee, Herr. Oboist at the court theaters. 17 Mar 82, 22 Dec 84.

Triebensee, Josef (d.J.) (1772-1846). Composer and oboist. 15 Apr 92, 16 Apr 92, 22 Dec 94, 23 Dec 94, 9 Apr 97, 2 Apr 98, 17 Mar 99, Summer 05, x4 Jun 08, 15 Mar 10.

Tuček, Vincenc (Franz) (1773-a1821). Composer. 10 Apr 08.

Türk, Herr. Child violinist. 26 May 82.

Tugend, Johann. Harpist. 26 Mar 93.

Turner, Herr. Flutist with the Herzogliche Würtenbergische Kapelle. 20 Jun 95.

Ulbrich, Maximilian (?1741-1814). Composer. 19 Dec 79, 21 Dec 79, 6 Apr 83, 8 Apr 83, 13 Apr 94.

Ulrich, Herr. Oboist. 8 Jan 73.

Umlauf, Mlle. Singer. 27 Apr 98, 6 Apr 06.

Umlauf, Liese. Singer. x8 Dec 03.

Umlauf, Ignaz (1746-1796). Composer. 1 Apr 83, 21 Mar 87, 30 Mar 87, 1 Apr 87, x26 Feb 88, x4 Mar 88, 7 Mar 88, x6 Mar 89, 27 Oct 98, 5 Nov 98.

Umlauf, Michael (1781-1842). x8 Dec 03, 25 Dec 04, 17 May 07, 17 Apr 08, 15 Nov 09.

Urbany, Herr. Violinist. 31 Mar 06, Summer 06.

d'Ursil, Emilie. Singer. x10 Mar 96.

d'Ursil, Louise. Singer. x12 Mar 95, x19 Mar 95, x27 Mar 95, x20 Apr 95, x10 Mar 96, x19 Mar 96, x9 May 96.

Vani, Herr. Flutist. x28 Nov 61.

Vanhal, Johann Baptist (1739-1813). 19 Aug 91, zB 1 Oct 03.

Varenne, Mme. Harpist. x28 Mar 81, 29 Mar 81, x4 Apr 81, x7 Apr 81, x5 May 81.

Ventovini, Herr. Oboist. 16 Oct 72, 16 Nov 81.

Venturini, Herr. See Ventovini.

Venturini, Mlle. Composer. 4 Apr 96.

Verri, Herr. Bass. 25 Mar 06, 20 May 06 (father), 5 Jun 06 (son), 22 Mar 07, 23 Mar 07, 10 May 07 (son), 25 Mar 10.

Vestris, Mlle. Singer. 5 Apr 97.

Vicaro, Francesco. Flutist. 14 Jan 92.

Viganoni, Herr. Singer. 22 Dec 84, 23 Dec 84, 19 Feb 85, zB 16 Mar 94, zB 26 Mar 94, 25 Mar 95, 29 Mar 95, 30 Mar 95, 22 Dec 95, 23 Dec 95.

Viotti, Giovanni Battista (1755-1824). 13 Apr 91, 20 Mar 93, 22 Dec 95, 5 Nov 98, 25 Mar 01, Sep 04, Summer 05, 1 May 10.

Vitadeo (Vittadeo), Marianne. Singer. 17 Mar 76, 20 Mar 76, 17 Mar 77, 21 Mar 79, 23 Mar 79.

Vogarti, Herr. Flutist. x5 Mar 74.

Vogel, Johann Christoph (1756-1788). 25 Mar 01, xAdvent 04.

Vogl (Vogel), Johann Michael (1768-1840). Baritone. 29 Mar 95, 30 Mar 95, 30 Mar 98, 13 Apr 98, x5 Apr 99, 18 Dec 00, 21 Dec 00, 25 Dec 00, 2 Apr 02, 13 Apr 02, 25 Dec 04, 9 Apr 05, 14 Apr 05, x27 Feb 07, x28 Mar 07, 15 Nov 07, 25 Mar 08, xb5 Dec 08, 25 Mar 09, 28 Mar 09, 2 Apr 09, 25 Mar 10, x21 Apr 10.

Vogler, Abbé Georg Joseph (1749-1814). Composer, fortepianist, and organist. zW 11 Mar 02, zW 22 Mar 02, 22 Dec 03, 23 Dec 03, 26 Mar 04, 15 Nov 04, 18 Jan 06.

Volkert, (Franz Joseph? 1778-1845). Fortepianist. zL 8 Sep 10.

Wagenseil, Georg Christoph (1717-1777). 17 Mar 77, 22 Dec 82, 23 Dec 82, 30 Mar 87, 1 Apr 87.

Wallaschek, Herr. Singer. x19 Mar 08.

Wallenstein, Isabella. Singer. x16 Mar 85.

Walterskirchen (Anna Maria? 1773-1855). Singer. x3 Apr 00.

Weber, Herr. Composer. 23 Feb 06.

Weber, Mlle. See Lange, Aloysia.

Weberle, Mlle. Singer. zL 19 Jun 89.

Weidinger, Anton (1767-1852). Court trumpet player. zB 28 Nov 98, 22 Dec 98, 23 Dec 98, 28 Mar 00, zK 5 Mar 02, 31 Mar 05.

Weidinger, Joseph and Franz. Trumpet and Timpani players. 28 Mar 00.

Weidner, Mlle. Singer. 15 Nov 07, 25 Mar 08, 24 Dec 09.

Weigl, Joseph (1766-1846). Composer. 23 Feb 88, 13 Apr 91, 22 Dec 92, 23 Mar 93, 24 Mar 93, x24 Dec 93, 30 Mar 98, x6 Mar 99, 18 Nov 99, x12 Apr 00, x13 Apr 00, 4 Sep 00, 25 Mar 01, 5 Apr 01, 11 Jun 01, x1 Apr 02, 2 Sep 02, xLent 03, x23 Mar 03, x30 Mar 03, 2 Apr 03, x3 Dec 04, 25 Dec 04, 14 Apr 05, 12 Jun 05, 13 Jun 05, 25 Mar 09, 28 Mar 09, 2 Apr 09, 16 Apr 09, x21 Apr 10, 25 Dec 10.

Weigl, Joseph Franz (1740-1820). Cellist. 21 Dec 74, 11 Mar 81, 27 Feb 85.

Weiglin (Weigelin), Mme. Singer. 30 Oct 72, x22 Feb 74.

Weinkopf, Herr. Bass. 31 Mar 06, 23 Dec 06, 25 Dec 06, 27 Mar 09, 8 Sep 09.

Weinmüller, Karl. Bass at the court theaters. 1 Apr 98, 17 Mar 99, 18 Mar 99, 28 Mar 00, 8 Apr 00, 18 Dec 00, 21 Dec 00, 29 Mar 01, 30 Mar 01, 13 Apr 02, 26 Dec 03, 23 Mar 04, 20 May 04, 15 Nov 04, 25 Dec 04, 7 Apr 05, 8 Apr 05, 24 Dec 05, 25 Dec 05?, 30 Mar 06, 31 Mar 06, 26 Oct 06, 25 Dec 06, x27 Feb 07, 22 Mar 07, 23 Mar 07, 24 Mar 07, x28 Mar 07, 29 Mar 07, 17 May 07, 15 Nov 07, 22 Dec 07, 23 Dec 07, 25 Mar 08, 27 Mar 08, 10 Apr 08, 11 Apr 08, 17 Apr 08, 25 Dec 08, 25 Mar 09, 26 Mar 09, 27 Mar 09, 28 Mar 09, 2 Apr 09, 16 Apr 09, 15 Nov 09, 22 Dec 09, 23 Dec 09, 15 Apr 10, 16 Apr 10, 22 Apr 10, 22 Dec 10, 23 Dec 10.

Weisin, Mme. Singer. 30 Oct 72, 8 Jan 73.

Weisgärber, Christoph. Clarinettist. 28 Dec 92, zK 3 Oct 04.

Weiss, Mlle. Singer. 24 Dec 09, 23 Dec 10.

Weiss, Anna Maria. Singer. 17 Dec 72, 20 Dec 72, 21 Mar 73, 25 Mar 73, 18 Dec 74, 21 Dec 74, 23 Mar 78, 27 Mar 78.

Weiss, Kaspar. 13 Apr 94.

Wendling, Johann Baptist. Flutist. 17 Mar 76, 23 Mar 79.

Went, Johann Nepomuk (1745-1801). Oboist and composer. 6 Apr 83, 8 Apr 83, 2 Mar 87, 23 Mar 87, 22 Feb 88, 29 Feb 88, 23 Dec 93, 15 Mar 94, 30 Apr 09.

Wertheimstein, Mlle. x13 Apr 09.

Widerkehr, Herr. zW 4 Feb 04, zW 6 Feb 04.

Wild, Herr. Singer. 24 Dec 09.

Willmann (née Tribolet), Anna Maria Antonetta (1768-1813). Singer at the Theater an der Wien. 8 Jan 96, 6 Apr 97, 27 Oct 98, 11 Mar 99?, 25 Mar 01, 6 Jun 01, 18 Jun 01, 20 Aug 01, 25 Mar 02, 19 Aug 02, 9 Sep 02, Summer 03, 15 Dec 03, a12 Apr 04.

Willmann, Johann Ignaz (1739-1815). 19 Mar 85.

Willmann, Karl Johann (1773-1811). Violinist. zW 23 Feb 98.

Willmann, Maximilian (1767-1813). Cellist. 16 Mar 84, 10 Feb 85, 7 Mar 87, 4 Apr 89, 25 Mar 01.

Willmann, Maximiliana Valentina (1769-1835). Fortepianist. 16 Mar 84, 10 Feb 85, 7 Mar 87.

Willmann-Galvani, Johanna (1771-1801). Soprano at the court theaters. 16 Mar 84, 10 Feb 85, 7 Mar 87, 17 Mar 87, 22 Dec 95, 23 Dec 95, 20 Mar 96, 21 Mar 96, 22 Mar 96, 4 Apr 96, 19 Sep 96, 21 Sep 96, 22 Dec 96, 23 Dec 96, 9 Apr 97, 10 Apr 97, 30 Mar 98, 30 Jan 01, 31 Mar 01.

Wilms, Johann Wilhelm (1772-1847). Composer. 23 Feb 06.

Winter, Joseph. Composer. 8 Apr 00.

Winter, Peter (1754-1825). Composer. 20 Mar 96, 21 Mar 96, 9 Apr 97, 10 Apr 97, xLent 04, xLent 05, 9 Apr 05, 15 Nov 06, 25 Mar 08.

Winter, (Peter?). Composer. 7 Mar 87, zW 24 Feb 98, 6 Jun 01, 27 Mar 04, 25 Mar 06, 15 Nov 10.

Witt, Friedrich. Composer. July 96, 4 Apr 03.

Wölfel, Joseph (1772-1812). Fortepianist and composer. 4 Apr 96, 27 Sep 96, 22 Dec 96, zW 4 Sep 98.

Wolf, Louis. Guitarist. 6 Dec 04, 6 Mar 07, 15 Mar 10.

Wolf (née Mrasek), Anna. Fortepianist. 6 Dec 04, 6 Mar 07.

Woyna, Herr. x8 Apr 94, x11 Nov 95.

Woyna, Mlle de. Singer. x24 Apr 04.

Woyna, Mme de. Singer. x27 Mar 95.

Wranitzky, Anton (1761-1820). Violinist. 23 Dec 90, x19 Feb 96, 23 Dec 97, 29 Mar 98, x16 Apr 00, 3 Apr 03, Lent 05, xb5 Dec 08.

Wranitzky, Karoline Seidler (c1790-1872). x21 Apr 10.

Wranitzky, Paul (1756-1808). Composer. (16 Nov 81, zK 8 Nov 85, 9 Mar 87, 14 Mar 87, 24 Mar 87?—or Anton?), 1 Apr 91, 2 Apr 91, 20 Jun 95, 22 Dec 95, 23 Dec 95, 22 Dec 96, 23 Dec 96, 22 Dec 97, 23 Dec 97, 28 Apr 98, 4 May 98, 5 Nov 98, x26 Mar 02, (x8 Apr 02?), 25 Dec 04, 6 Apr 06, 5 Jun 06, 26 Oct 06, 25 Dec 06, 29 Mar 07, 10 May 07, 17 May 07, 17 Apr 08.

Wrbna, Mlle. Singer. x12 Mar 74.

Wunder, (Hartmann Christian? b. 1754). 14 Nov 92, 18 Nov 10.

Xur, Mlle. Singer. 20 Feb 88.

Zahradnizek, Josef. Mandolin player and court trumpet player. 22 Dec 98, 23 Dec 98.

Zandonetti, Luigi. Cellist. 29 Apr 91.

Zehentner, Johann Nepomuk. Contrabass player for Prince Oetting-Wallerstein. 13 Feb 93.

Zenker, Herr. Clarinettist. Summer 05, 28 Mar 09.

Zerotin, Mme de. Singer. x5 Mar 74, x12 Mar 74.

Zeuner, Karl (1775-1841). Fortepianist. x12 Mar 05, 9 May 05, 25 Jan 07.

Zichy, Mlle de. x12 Mar 95, x19 Mar 95, x27 Mar 95, x16 Apr 00.

Zingarelli, Niccolo (1752-1837). Composer. 20 Jun 95, 23 Dec 95, 13 Apr 98, 13 Apr 02, x19 Feb 03, 1 May 07, 15 Nov 08, xb30 Jan 09.

Zistler, Herr. Violinist with Count Erdödy. 5 May 72.

Zistler, Herr. Violinist with Prince Grassalkowich. 22 Dec 82, 23 Dec 82, 23 Dec 86, 27 Feb 88, 22 Dec 89.

Zistler, Joseph. Violinist. 20 Dec 78.

Zmeskall, Nikolaus. x1801.

Zois, Baroness. Singer. x6 Mar 99.

Zois, Mlle de. Singer. xb1 Mar 09.

Zumsteeg, Johann Rudolf (1760-1802). 11 May 06.

Zwirzina, Herr. Waldhorn player with Count Carl von Palm. 12 Mar 80.

APPENDIX FOUR

Private Concert Patrons

This appendix contains an index of all the patrons found in the Private Concert Calendar (Appendix 2). An asterisk after the name indicates that biographical information is to be found at the end of the listings. In some cases, it was possible to identify the person exactly, in others, there were several possible candidates. The information was taken from Wurzbach/LEXIKON and NEW GROVE.

Archbishop of Salzburg*. 16 Mar 81, 17 Mar 81, 23 Mar 81, 8 Apr 81, 27 Apr 81.

Apponyi, Count and Countess*. b26 Jan 09.

Arensteiner, Baron*. b16 Dec 08.

Asher, Herr. 27 Jan 01.

Aspremont. 7 Jan 05.

Auersperg, Prince and Princess*. 21 Feb 74, 28 Feb 74, 7 Mar 74, 20 Mar 74, 2 Feb 81, 26 Mar 87, 17 Jan 91, 13 Apr 91, 23 Mar 96.

Bigot, Mme*. b26 Jan 09.

Boissier, Mme de. 10 Nov 97.

Born, Herr von*. 30 Apr 86.

Bragance, Duke of. 10 Mar 62, 4 Aug 62.

Braun, Baron*. 24 Mar 81, 18 Mar 02, 26 Mar 02, 1 Apr 02, 8 Apr 02, 30 Mar 03, 10 Apr 03, Winter 03, 6 Apr 05.

Buquoy, Mme de. 3 Feb 85, 27 Apr 85, 7 Mar 86, 24 Mar 86, 27 Jan 87, 4 Feb 88, 5 Mar 91, 16 Apr 97, 15 Aug 07.

Callenberg, Count*. 8 Apr 94, 8 Mar 08.

Canal, Mme. 8 Jan 73.

Clary, Mme. 22 Dec 63.

Colalto, (Prince). 10 Oct 61, 26 Oct 61, 25 Nov 61, 30 Nov 61, 9 Dec 61, 21 Dec 61, 3 Feb 62, 10 Feb 62, 20 Feb 62, 30 Jun 62, 24 Jul 62, 18 Sep 62, 5 Oct 62, 1 Dec 62, 10 Jan 63, 30 Apr 63.

Deym von Stritetz, Countess Josephine von. 10 Dec 00.

Dietrichstein*. Mar 93.

Durazzo, Count. 18 Dec 62.

Eger*. 2 Apr 96.

Eisenkohl, Mme. 6 Dec 01.

Erdödy, Countess*. b10 Dec 08, b31 Dec 08.

Ertmann, Baroness. b27 Mar 09.

Esterházy*. 12 Mar 83, 29 Mar 88.

Esterházy, Mme de*. 3 Feb 81.

Esterházy, Prince*. 29 Mar 61, x19 Feb 63, 4 Jan 96, 12 Mar 05, b8 Jan 09.

Esterházy, Count Johann*. 1 Mar 84, 5 Mar 84, 8 Mar 84, 12 Mar 84, 15 Mar 84, 19 Mar 84, 22 Mar 84, 26 Mar 84, 29 Mar 84, 26 Feb 88, 4 Mar 88, 30 Dec 88, 6 Mar 89, 7 Apr 89, 9 Feb 06.

Felz, Baron. 22 Nov 97.

Ferraris, Mme de*. 20 Apr 95.

French Ambassador. 25 Dec 63, 5 Mar 76, 24 Mar 81, 27 Mar 81, 28 Mar 81, 7 Apr 81, 10 Apr 81, 5 May 81, 20 Mar 83.

Count Fries*. 5 Apr 99, 31 Mar 00, 4 Apr 00, Spring 00, 15 Oct 00, 29 Mar 02, 12 Apr 02.

Fürstenberg, Prince and Princess*. 5 Mar 87.

Golitzin, Prince*. 26 Feb 76, 6 Feb 81, 28 Feb 81, 21 Feb 82, 9 Mar 82, Winter 82-83, 3 Apr 83, 14 Oct 83, 26 Feb 84, 3 Mar 84, 4 Mar 84, 11 Mar 84, 17 Mar 84, 18 Mar 84, 25 Mar 84, 31 Mar 84, 18 Sep 84, 25 Dec 84, 16 Feb 85, 2 Mar 85, 16 Mar 85, 19 Jan 86, 9 Feb 86, 23 Feb 86, 9 Mar 86, 6 Apr 86, 22 Feb 87, 12 Apr 87, 14 Feb 88, 28 Feb 88, 6 Mar 88, 13 Mar 88, 15 Nov 88, 26 Feb 89, 24 Dec 90, 10 Mar 91, 14 Apr 91, 23 Feb 92, 14 Feb 93, 21 Feb 93, 28 Feb 93, 7 Mar 93, 14 Mar 93, 21 Mar 93.

Gallo (Ambassador from Naples)*. 17 Mar 92, 23 Mar 92.

Gillenberg. 3 Apr 03.

Goubeau. b31 Dec 08.

Grosschlag. 6 Feb 95.

Hadik*. 9 Apr 91.

Haugwitz, Count. 11 Mar 02, 27 Feb 07, 28 Mar 07, 15 Mar 08.

Henikstein, Baron Joseph. b25 Dec 08.

Hildburgshausen, Prince. 21 Dec 63, 11 Jan 64, 18 Jan 64, 1 Feb 64, 19 Mar 64

Hoyos, Mme de*. 29 Dec 02, 19 Feb 03.

Kaunitz, Prince*. 14 Jun 61, 16 Jan 63, 2 Mar 81, 10 Apr 84, 15 Apr 84.

Kees, Herr von*. 21 Mar 92.

Keith, Chevalier. 1 Jul 83.

Keller. 19 Dec 01.

Kinsky, Prince*. 12 Jan 91, b15 Feb 09.

Kühnel, Herr. 7 Aug 04.

Lichnowsky, Prince*. 24 Dec 93, 15 Apr 94, 11 Mar 03.

Lobkowitz, Prince*. 19 Feb 93 (young), 5 Mar 93, 12 Mar 93, 8 Apr 94 (young), 2 Mar 95, 12 Mar 95, 19 Mar 95 (old), 27 Mar 95, 19 Feb 96, 26 Feb 96, 11 Mar 96, 18 Mar 96, 23 Mar 98, 31 Mar 98, 5 Apr 98, 15 Feb 99, 22 Feb 99, 8 Mar 99, 16 Mar 99, 3 Apr 00, 16 Apr 00, 4 Apr 01, 27 Feb 03, 6 Mar 03, 12 Mar 03, 15 Apr 03, 26 Apr 03, 6 Jun 03, 18 Dec 03, 24 Apr 04, Dec 04, 28 Mar 06, b18 Mar 07, 4 Apr 07, b5 Dec 08, b21 Dec 08, b25 Dec 08, b31 Dec 08, b8 Jan 09, b30 Jan 09, b1 Mar 09, 3 Mar 09, 6 Mar 09, 21 Apr 10, 23 Dec 10.

Lobkowitz, Princess Caroline*. 15 Jul 93, 5 Mar 95.

Manzi, Herr von. 11 Apr 87.

Maximilian, Archduke*. 16 Nov 81.

Minto, Lord. 27 Mar 00.

Nagy, Herr*. 19 Mar 08.

Nitschner, Herr*. 4 Jun 08.

Odeschalchi, Prince. 1801.

Oeynhausen, Prince. 6 Dec 82, 1 Jan 84.

Otto, Count (French Ambassador). 1 Apr 10.

Paar, Prince*. 14 Mar 78, 31 Mar 78, 4 Apr 81, 23 Mar 86, 27 Mar 86, 6
   Apr 86, 5 Apr 87, 31 Dec 94, 5 Apr 95, 8 Mar 97.

Palffy, Leopold. 9 Apr 84.

Palm. 28 Nov 61.

Paradies, Maria Therese von*. Nov-Dec 09.

Parhers. 9 Nov 62.

Perlas, Count. 4 Mar 61, 25 Sep 61, 9 Oct 61, 23 Oct 61.

Ployer, Herr von*. 16 Feb 85, 21 Feb 85, 23 Feb 85, 23 Mar 85.

Quarin, Herr. 19 Feb 03, 19 Apr 03.

Rasumofsky, Prince*. 23 Apr 95, b10 Dec 08, b16 Dec 08, b31 Dec 08.

Rittersburg, Mme de. 21 Jan 09, b1 Mar 09.

Rivolla. 13 Aug 06.

Rosenbaum, Joseph. 12 Jun 98.

Rosenbaum, Joseph and Therese*. 8 Dec 00, 10 May 02, 8 Dec 03.

Rosenberg, Count*. 3 May 81, 6 Jul 84.

Rottruff, Herr. 3 Dec 04.

Rumbeck, Countess. 12 Jan 82.

Sacrati, Marquise de. 16 Mar 03.

Sala, Baron and Baroness. 13 Apr 09, Lent 10.

Saxon Ambassador. 29 Nov 86.

Schmierer family. 30 Apr 01, 21 May 01, 28 Sep 01, 16 Nov 01, 13 May 03.

Schönborn, Mme. 12 Mar 64.

Schönfeld, Mme de. 11 Nov 95.

Schubb, Hofrath. 10 Mar 02, 17 Mar 02, 31 Mar 02, 7 Apr 02, 14 Apr 02, 4 May 02, 23 Feb 03, 2 Mar 03, 9 Mar 03, 16 Mar 03, 23 Mar 03, 6 Apr 03.

Schwarzenberg, Prince*. 29 Mar 87, 15 Apr 87, 5 May 87, 11 Feb 88, 29 Mar 92, 19 Feb 93, 30 Apr 93, 25 Dec 93, 28 Dec 93, 16 Feb 94, 2 Mar 94, 26 Mar 96, 27 Mar 96, 24 Mar 97, 7 Apr 97, 29 Apr 98, 30 Apr 98, 7 May 98, 10 May 98, 2 Mar 99, 4 Mar 99, 23 Mar 99, 24 Mar 99, 11 Apr 00, 12 Apr 00, 13 Apr 00, 24 Apr 01, 27 Apr 01, 1 May 01.

Schwarzenberg, Princess. 16 Mar 74.

Spanish Ambassador. 26 Mar 74, 6 Mar 99.

Spielmann, Hofrath Baron von*. 4 Jan 83, 16 Mar 02, 23 Mar 02.

Spiegelfeld, Hofrath von*. 14 Mar 89.

Starhemberg, Prince and Princess*. 19 Jul 08, 19 Sep 08, 27 Feb 09, 17 Aug 09, 5 Oct 09, 15 Oct 09, 30 Oct 09, 15 Nov 09, 21 Nov 09.

Stegmayer, Herr*. 18 Mar 04.

Stöger, Herr. 24 Apr 09.

Streicher, Herr*. b26 Jan 09.

Swieten, Baron*. Spring 82, Lent 86, Lent 87, 26 Feb 88, 4 Mar 88, 30 Dec 88, 6 Mar 89, 7 Apr 89, Lent 90, Lent 91, Lent 92.

Tarocca, Mme de. 22 Mar 63.

Thauernathy, Herr von. 22 Dec 61, 9 Jan 62, 26 Feb 62, 12 Mar 62.

Thun, Countess*. 15 Mar 81, 8 Apr 81, 14 Dec 82.

Thurn, Abbe C. 2 Aug 61.

Thurn, Mme de. 3 Jan 62, 24 Jan 62, 23 Mar 62, 18 Apr 62.

Thurn, Widow*. 14 Apr 01.

Trattner, Mme de*. 8 May 84, 17 Mar 85.

Trauttmansdorf, Prince*. 11 Mar 00.

APPENDIX FOUR

Venetian Ambassador. 28 Apr 87, 10 Feb 88, 30 Mar 88.

Walmoden, General. 25 Apr 83.

Wallenstein, Mme. 5 Apr 73, 19 Feb 74, 5 Mar 74, 12 Mar 74.

Windisch-Grätz*. 10 Mar 96, 19 Mar 96, 30 Mar 96, 7 Apr 96, 28 Apr 96, 9 May 96.

Würth, Herr von*. Lent 04, Advent 04, Winter 04-05, Lent 05.

Zichy, Count*. 20 Mar 84, 21 Feb 85.

Zinzendorf, Count Carl. 10 Apr 87.

Zierotin, Mme de. 22 Feb 74.

Zmeskall, Nikolaus. b20 Feb 09, b5 Apr 09.

BIOGRAPHIES

Archbishop of Salzburg. Prince Colloredo-Mansfeld (Hieronymus I) (1732-1812). Archbishop from 1772-1803. Mozart's first employer.

Apponyi, Count Anton Georg? (1751-1817).

Arensteiner, Baron. Probably Baron Nathan Adam (1758-1818) and Baroness Franziska von Arnstein.

Auersperg, Prince Johann Adam (1721-95) and Maria Joseph née Lobkowitz (b. 1776). The 1796 citation is either their son or the Widow Auersperg. Johann Adam held several court positions, including Geheimer Rath and Kämmerer, Obersthof- und Landjägermeister, and Feldmarschall-Leutnant.

Bigot, Mme. Probably Marie Bigot de Morogues, a pianist. See Appendix 3.

Born, Ignaz Edler von (1742-1791). Geologist, minerologist, and Hofrath der Hofkammer im Münz und Bergwesen.

Callenberg, Count. Probably Count Georg Alexander Heinrich Hermann. See Appendix 3.

Dietrichstein, Prince. Either Karl Johann Baptist Walter von Dietrichstein-Proskau-Leslie (1728-1808) or his son Franz Joseph (1767-1854). Also a Count Moritz (b. 1775).

Eger, Herr. Possibly Joseph Egger Edler von Eggstein (1747-1815).

Esterházy. It is not always possible to separate all the Esterházys. Three princes lived during this time: Nikolaus (1714-1790), Paul Anton II (1738-1794), and Nikolaus (1765-1833). Count Johann Esterházy (1774-1829) was the only one to be consistently called by his full name.

Ferraris. Possibly Count Joseph (1726-1814) and Countess Henriette née von Ursel.

Fries, Count Moritz (1777-1825). Son of Johann (elevated to Baron in 1762 and Count in 1783) and Anna née d'Escherny. One of Vienna's most enthusiastic patrons of the arts, he boasted a library of 1600 volumes, an art collection with over 300 paintings, (among them works by Raphael, Rembrandt and Dürer), and fine print, mineral and coin collections. He served as head of the banking firm Fries & Co. until it went bankrupt in 1823. At that time, his collections were auctioned to pay his debts. He married Maria Theresia Josepha Princess von Hohenlohe-Waldenburg-Schillingsfürst on October 15, 1800.

Fürstenberg. Possibly Prince Karl Alois (1760-1799) and Princess Elizabeth née Thurn und Taxis. Other candidates are Count Joachim Egon (1749-1828) or Friedrich Karl Joachim (1774-1856).

Golitzin, Prince Dimitry Michajlowitsch (1721-1793). Russian Ambassador to Vienna.

Gallo, Don Martius Mastrilly (b. 1753). Ambassador from Naples from 1790-1797.

Greiner, Hofrath Franz Ritter von (1732-1798). Court official whose daughter Caroline von Greiner Pichler achieved fame as a poet and salon hostess in the early nineteenth century.

Hadik. Either Count Johann (b. 1755) and Countess Franzisca née von Breuner, Count Karl Joseph (1756-1800) and Countess Maria Therese née von Kolowrat-Krakowsky (1756-1844), or Count Andreas (1764-1840) and Countess Maria née von Gammerschwang (1783-1854).

Hoyos. Probably Count Johann Philipp Joseph (1747-1803) and Marie Christine née Princess von Clary and (1755-1821). Their son was Johann Ernst (1779-1849).

Kaunitz, Prince Wenzel Anton (1711-1794). One of Austria's leading statesmen and chief advisor to the Empress Maria Theresia.

Kees, Hofrath Franz Georg Ritter von (1747-1799), son of the music lover, Franz Bernhard von Kees.

Kinsky, Prince. Possibly Prince Ferdinand Johann Nepomuk Joseph (1781-1812).

Lichnowsky, Prince Karl (d. 1814) and Christine née Countess von Thun.

Lobkowitz, Prince. There were two Prince Lobkowitzes who were enthusiastic supporters of the arts: Joseph Maria Carl (1725-1802) who married Maria Joseph née Countess Harrach in 1752, and Prince Joseph Franz Maximilian (1725-1802), who married Marie Caroline née Princess Schwarzenberg. The younger was Beethoven's patron.

Nitschner, Franz (d. 1819). Hauptmann and Hof Rechnungsführer.

Paar, Prince. Either Wenzel Johann Joseph (1719-1792) and Antonia née Countess Esterházy (1719-1771); Wenzel (1744-1812) and Maria Antonia née Princess Liechtenstein (1749-1813); or Johann Karl (1772-1819) who accompanied Marie Antoinette to Paris. There were also two counts: Wenzel (c1770-1800) and Ludwig (1783-1849).

Paradies, Marie Therese von (1759-1824). Blind pianist who made extensive tours in Europe.

Rasumofsky, Prince Andreas Kyrillowitsch (1752-1806). Russsian Ambassador to Vienna from 1793 to 1799, when he was relieved of his post because his Emperor considered his opinions too pro-Austrian. After the ascension of Alexander I, he resumed his duties until 1809, when he was fired again because his anti-Napoleon sympathies were not in line with current Russian policy. He remained in Vienna and built a luxurious palace, which burned in 1814, destroying his library and collections. He sponsored the string quartet headed by Ignaz Schuppanzigh and was one of Beethoven's patrons. He was married twice, once to the Countess Thun-Klösterle, and again in 1816 to Constantia von Thürheim.

Rosenberg, Prince Franz Xaver Wolf (1723-1796). Son of Count Wolf Sigmund and Countess Maria Elenore née Hohenfeld, he was raised to the rank of prince in 1790. As a statesman, he served in London, Copenhagen and Madrid, before returning to Vienna as Oberstkämmerer and Conferenzminister under Joseph II. His position as Oberstkämmerer gave him control of the court theaters. He never married.

Schönfeld. Possibly Johann Ferdinand Ritter von Schönfeld (1750-1821).

Schwarzenberg, Prince Joseph Johann Nepomuk (1769-1833). Son of Prince Johann Nepomuk and Maria Eleonora née Countess von Oettingen-Wallerstein. Unlike many of the high-ranking nobility, he personally administered his estates. He was also one of the directors of the "Commerzialbank," an institution founded to aid the development of industry. Though he never had an official court position, he held several unofficial posts, including that of Geheimer Rath. In 1794 he married Princess Pauline Karolina Iris von Arenberg-Archot, who burned to death in the fire that broke out at the feast for the marriage of Napoleon to the Austrian princess Maria Louise in Paris in 1810.

Spielmann, Baron Anton von (1738-1813). Hofrath and statesman, raised to a Baron in 1790. He married Mlle de Humlauer, and their children were often featured on the private concerts they gave: Josephine (1780-1837), Franziska and Maria (1789-1857), Clement (1791-1809) and Ignaz (1781-1833).

Spiegelfeld. Possibly Baron Johann Nepomuk or Baron Franz Cajetan.

Stegmayer. Possibly Matthäus (1771-1820), a composer, actor and dramatist who joined the company at the Theater an der Wien in 1796 and later served as chorus and opera director at the court theaters.

Streicher. Johann Andreas (1761-1833) and Nannette Stein-Streicher (1769-1833). Johann was a piano teacher who married the piano builder Nannette Stein and moved with her to Vienna in 1794. Their circle of friends included Beethoven.

Swieten, Baron Gottfried van (1734-1803). Statesman and prefect of the court library.

Thun, Countess. The Countess Thun has mystified historians for decades. There were several who lived in Vienna and were active patrons of music. They include: Maria Wilhelmine née Uhlefeld, Maria Anna née Kolowrat-Liebsteinsky, Maria Therese née Altems, Therese née Wratislaw-Mitrowitz, and Elisabeth née Baroness Henniger von Eberg.

Trattner. Johann Thomas Edler von Trattner (1717-1798) was a publisher whose building on the Graben (Trattnerhof) housed several public concerts in the early 1780s. His second wife, the Mme de Trattner referred to here, was the daughter of Joseph Anton Nagel and an active patron of the arts.

Trauttmannsdorf, Prince Ferdinand (1749-1827). Held the court position of Obersthofmeister from 1807. Married to the Princess Carolina née Colloredo.

Windisch-Grätz, Count Joseph Nikolaus (1744-1802). Political, philosophical author whose house in the suburb of Gumpendorf was a center
of intellectual activity. His son, Alfred Candidus Ferdinand (1787-1862),
was made a prince in 1804.

Würth, Herr von. Banker and patron of the arts.

Zichy, Count. Probably Count Karl von Zichy-Vasonykeö (1753-1826) and
Countess Anna Maria née Khevenhüller-Metsch.

Foreign Language Quotations

This Appendix contains all of the foreign language quotations. Count Zinzendorf's French was exceptionally poor; he rarely used accents (or Umlauts in German) and frequently mixed up verb tenses. When a word or phrase is particularly unclear I have inserted a question mark, otherwise I have given the text without comment. The translations from the Zinzendorf diaries were done by Mr. Lars Larson. The remaining ones are my own.

CHAPTER ONE

1. Es sey nun Erkältung für Kunstliebe, oder Mangel am Geschmacke, oder Häuslichkeit, oder auch andere Ursachen, kurz, zum Schaden der Kunst hat diese löbliche Gewohnheit sich verloren, und eine Kapelle verlosch nach der andern, so, dass ausser der fürstl. Schwarzenbergischen fast gar keine mehr existirt.. . . Fürst Grassalkowitz hat seine Kapelle in eine Harmonie reduzirt, wobei der grosse Klarinetist Griessbacher Direktor ist. Hr. Baron von Braun hält eine eigene Harmonie zur Tafelmusik.

2. Chez Pce Galizin ou nous dinerent avec les Woyna, les Jublonowsky, Mme de Durazzo et de Brenner, M. de St. Sarphoun, Renner, Mme de Bassewitz et Lalotte. Pendant que nous jouions au whist, Lalotte joua du Clavecin et Mme de Woyna chanta comme un ange.

3. In ein Assamblei hat s' mich auch schon ein paar Mahl mit gnommen. O je Herr Vetter, da sieht's curios aus. Da sitz'n d' Herrn und Fraun in

ein Kreis herum, und schaun einander an; oder plaudern ein Lang und ein Breits vom schlimmen Wetter, oder von Moden, oder von dem, was s' gessen oder trunken habn; d' Fraun aber richten gmeiniglich d' Leut aus.

Das dauert ein Weil; dann fangn s' an Maul aufzreissen, als wenns' vier und zwanzig Stund nichts gschlaffn hätten. Aber so bald d' Frau vom Haus merkt, das d' Kompagnie z' gametsen anfangt, so kommen d' Karten aufn Tisch.

Oder wenn ein Fräule im Haus ist, so muss s' ein Weil eins aufn Klavier schlagen, und dazu singen, dass den Herrn und Fraun der Schlaf vergeht.

Da muss sich der Herr Vetter um's Klavier herumstellen, und bravo schreyn, wenn d' Fräule gleich oft heult, wie ein kleiner Hund. Endlich kommts zum Kartenspielen, und da wird die ganze Kompagnie wieder lebendig.

4. In der Liebhaberey der Damen gilt noch immer auf ihrem Lieblingsinstrument, dem Pianoforte, vor andern Kozeluch. Aber, wer ihm doch neuerlich beynahe den Rang abläuft, ist *Pleyel*, dessen Symphonien und Violin-Quadros nun schon in den zweiten Winter allgemein gesucht werden, und der nun auch sonderlich etliche der letztern aufs Clavier übergetragen hat.

5. Diné chez le Pce S. . . La musique du Prince executa l'arbre de Diane.

Diné . . . Chez le Pce Schwarzenberg avec les Furstenberg, les Jean Lichtenstein, Caroline Furstenberg. Nous etions 13. Charmante musique apres le diner de Mozart Die Zauberflöte.

Diné chez la Psse S. avec 2 Lobkowitz, 2 Ferrari, 2 Wilzek et la Psse Oettingen, Chaminisse de Thoren, Mme de Wilzek. On joua apres table la musique de Matrimonie Segreto.

6. Illumination bey Nitschner . . . Nach Tisch gleich in Garten. . . wir arbeiteten bis 9 Uhr. Der Wind hinderte uns sehr und verdarb uns viel . . . Schon began die Gesellschaft in Garten heraus zu schleichen, wir waren noch nicht fertig. Dann der Wind löschte uns immer das Angezundene wieder aus. Die Sinfonie der Zauberflöte wurde zuerst gemacht dann sang Nitschner die Arie "In diesen heil. Hallen," mit auf seinem Vater passenden Text, zum Ende stiege romanische Lichten und es erschien transparent "dem Biedermanne Franz Nitschner." Darauf sang Therese die Cantata von Triebensee, vortrefflich, da erschien "dem Thaliens Priester Franz Nitschner von seinen Brüder." Den Schluss

machten Terzetten von Goldmann Jos., Therese und Werlen gesungen. Endlich wurde auch komische Terzetten gesungen—im Garten wurde auch gleich soupirt . . . Vor 12 Uhr begannen wir auszulöschen.

7. Bey Tisch verabredeten wir von der grossen Musik, welche wir morgen über 8 Tage geben wollen. Die 1st Arie, die Umlauf für seine Schwester Pepi schon vor 3 Jahren zu Th. Namens Feyer schrieb, wird seine Schwester Liesi, und seine neue grosse Arie, die er für Th. schrieb Th. selbst singen. . . . Die Gyulas Th. soll während beyden Arien mit Accompagniment der Violine gespielt von Mad. Pepi Ringbauer, eine Sonate spielen. Wir bestimmten schon das Orchester, welche wir dazu nehmen wollen, um ein Ganzes Grosses zu erhalten.

Am 11 Uhr kam Salieri, Th. passirte mit ihm Umlauffs Arie, die ihm so ganz passabel behagte. . . . Th. und ich berathschlagten das Arrangement wegen Donnerstag zur Musik. Das Spass macht viele Angelegenheit.

Th. und ich verabredeten das Nöthige zum Donnerstag, und schrieben Alles auf.

Zum Scheiyer .. . [um] sie . . . am Donnerstag zu laden. . . . Ich traf Moreau und Schmidt, die ich einlud, und die mir vorschlugen, ein Quodlibet aus verschiedenen Stücke zu machen, welche ich gern accordite. Schmidt trug ich mit Umlauff die Besorgung des Orchesters auf. . . . Nach Tisch wurde schon Verschiedene zum Donnerstag rangirt, und ordonirt. Ich gieng zum Glasere wegen Gläser und Flaschen. Zu Schardlager, Brandl und Nilschner wegen Geflügl.

Vor Tisch war Umlauff da, der uns die von Dönst geschriebenen Musikalien mit der Aeusserung brachte, dass sie schlecht geschrieben sind, und manches neu geschrieben werden muss—Fatal!—dann dass beyde Weidinger erst um 5 Uhr, und eben vielleicht gar nicht kommen kann. . .—Nach Mittag steckte und richtete ich die Lichter. Th. war den Abend zu Hauss und reinigte Porzellain.

Nach Tisch kam Umlauf um die Fehler in den Arien zu verbessern. . . . Ich war meistens auf dem Theater, um mit Umlauff, Schmidt und dem Kothel das Orchester und die Instrumente zu besorgen.

Der Eckhart, den ich gestern in Knittel Versen einlud, nahm sie an in Knittelversen. Th. lud die Tepfer Babet und Bruder. . . . Schmidt und Moreau kamen, halfen mir die Betten hinaus tragen und verschiedenes hinaus raumen und ordnen. Moreau schickte ich zur Sattmann, damit sie anstatt der kranken Liesi Umlauf die kleine Cantate singe. . . . Am

1/2 11 Uhr trafen wir zu Hause zusammen, begannen für 11 Personen, Kärner konnte wegen den Fürsten nicht, so waren nur 10. Woller, Frau, Lisette, Kühnel, Frau, Umlauff, Meyer mit Pepi, Th. und ich. Vom Grafen erhielt ich 3 Bout. Champagne und 2 Bout. Tokayer, welche Mittags sprangen. Am 3 Uhr rückte schon das Orchester an. Wir sassen noch. Man bediente sie gleich mit Aufgeschnittnen, weissen und rothen Wein, Bier. Am 4 Uhr began Bernardi mit Begleitung des ganzen Orchesters Variationen zu blasen an. Er blies sehr schön. Nachher sang die Sattmann die kleine Cantate vom Umlauf, gedichtet vor 3 Jahren vom seel. Lippert, zur Namens Feyers Th. . . . Schmidt theilte unter die Gesellschaft gedruckte Exemplare aus. Nachher sang Th. die neue Arie vom Umlauf, welche wiederholt wurde. Mit dem Orchester von 28 Personen waren zusammen 101 Personen. Nebst der 10 Personen bey Tisch waren Kärner, Salieri, Schreiber, Frau, Benko, Nannl und Peter, Tepfer Babet und Caspar, Schwiger und Frau, Lavola und Frau, Rottruff, Frau und Nanel, Latzl, Gabrieli, 2 Moreau, Storch, Gridl, und Wagner, Mayer, Klimbke und Turnauer, Poltoni, Schmidt, und Tandler, Brandl, sie und Therese, Arzt und Frau, Eckhart, Stegmayer und Frau, Schmierer Jeanette, Vadaky, Sanli und Rosenstingl, Sattmann, Sturioni, Lieber, mein Bruder, Ninna, Rosalie, die Hocheder, Gyulas, 2 Mädeln, Kunz, Klob, Ringbauer, Korn, Rösner und Frau, Goldman Jos., Barony und Tornette, Woller Charles und Hunneker, Bernardi. Diese Zahl war ohne der Bedienung unterhalten, und hinlänglich bedient worden. Nach dem 1ten Stück wurden alle mit Coffee bedient. Das Orchester verlohr sich, nach Genüge erquickt (wobey manche Indiscretion Platz griff) um 1/2 7 Uhr, da waren schon ohne weissen Wein und Bier 40 Bout. Offner geleert. Eine Stunde wurde getanzt. Die Ringbauer spielte Violine, Sattmann pianoforte, abwechselnd spielten und accompagnirten auf der Violine Tandler, Schmidt, Lieber, Stegmayer, Scholl (Flautist) welche 18 Saiten allschlug. Umlauf spielte auch, war aber so begeistert, dass er sich sehr schwer aufrecht erhalten konnte. Rottauf, Sattmann, Tandler, Latzl, Schmidt, und Th. sangen abwechselnd Canons. Sturioni sang einige Arien und accompagnirte sich auf dem Guitarre. Später parodirte er in Stimmen und Manier den Simoni und Halleschek. Am 9 Uhr began Moreau und Korn ihr Intermezzo. *Ein Schelm tut mehr als er kann* vom Franzky. Moreau spielte in 9 Verkleidungen 9 Choradese, manche aber vortreflich. Besonders gefiel er als schöner Carl, als Kutscher, Jesas! Jesas! als Französin, als schnell plaudernder Bedienter. Nachher wurde wieder getanzt und ihne zu pansiren immer mit Aufgeschnittenen, Coffee und und andern Getränken servirt. Am 1 Uhr endete sich diese Unterhaltung, die nach einstimmiger

Versicherung für alle wirkliche Unterhaltung. Mein Wunsch, dass alle unser Haus zufrieden lassen, scheint erreicht zu seyn. Rosalin sang auf ein paar Arietle sehr artig. Sie schlief bey uns. Schmidt und Tandler half uns die Betten hereintragen, Thüren einhängen, u.d.g. Am 2 Uhr legten wir uns. Th und ich hatten Aerger weil zuletzt der Coffee so lange nicht fertig wurde. Th. theilte mit mir die Blumenstrauss unter die Tisch Gesellschaft. . . . Wir schliefen wenig, waren sehr müde und echaufirt.

8. Der Sonntagsvormittag, allenfalls auch der Freitag, ist gewöhnlich der eigentlichen Musik gewidmet, die man hier zu keiner Zeit ganz aus den Augen verliert. Man spielt gewöhnlich Violinquartetten von Haydn, Mozart, Beethoven oder Romberg, zuweilen von Wranitzki. Die leichtere Klaviermusik eines Pleyels, Wanhal, Kozeluch ist ganz aus der Mode. Kompozitionen von Clementi, Cramer, Beethoven, Dussek sind an ihre Stelle getreten.

9. Er giebt alle Jahre einige sehr grosse und prächtige Musiken, wo nur Stücke von alten Meistern aufgeführt werden. Vorzüglich liebt er den Hendelschen Styl, von welchem er meistens grosse Chöre aufführen lässt. Erst am verwichenen Weihnachtsfeste gab er eine solche Akademie beim Fürsten von Paar, wo ein Oratorium von diesem Meister aufgeführt wurde.

10. Wien, am 26sten Febr. 1788. An diesen Tage und am 4ten März wurde Ramlers Cantate, *die Auferstehung und Himmelfahrt Christi* nach der vortreflichen Composition des unvergleichlichen Hamburger Bachs, bey dem Grafen Johann Esterhazy, von einem Orchester von 86 Personen in Gegenwart und unter Leitung des grossen Kenners der Tonkunst, des Freyherrn von Swieten, mit dem allgemeinsten Beyfall aller vornehmen Anwesenden aufgeführt. Der Kaiserl. Königliche Capellmeister, Hr. Mozart taktirte und hatte die Partitur, und der Kaiserl. Königl. Capellmeister Hr. Umlauff spielte den Flügel. . . . Unter den Sängern waren Madam Lang, der Tenorist Adamberger, der Bassist Saale, 30 Choristen. Am 7ten wurde das nemliche Stück im Kais. Königl. Hof-National-Theater aufgeführt.

11. Es gibt hier eine musikalische Gesellschaft, deren Mitglieder 24 der angesehensten und reichsten hiesigen Cavaliers sind, als: die Fürsten Lichtenstein, Esterhazy, Schwarzenberg, Kinsky, Lobkowitz, die Grafen Trautmannsdorf, Harrach, Fries, Esterhazy, u.a. Baron Swieten ist der Stifter und eigentliche Director dieser Gesellschaft. . . . Die Concerte, welche die Gesellschaft gibt, sind an keine Zeit gebunden; gewöhnlich

aber werden in der Fastenzeit im fürstlichen Schwarzenbergischen Pallaste aufgeführt.

12. Wer der Musik wegen reisen will, muss nicht im Sommer, sondern im Winter reisen. Die vorzüglichsten Konzerte und musikalische Schauspiele hört man im Winter. Die grossen Herren, die Kapellen halten, geniessen im Sommer den Landlust und beschäftigen ihre Musik nicht. Die Virtuosen sind alsdann auf Reisen u.s.w.

13. Sie führen grosse Musikstücke, als Symphonien, Concerte und Ouvertüren, mit einer Präcision und Richtigkeit aus, die um so bewunderungswürdiger ist, da diese grössten Theils sehr stark besetzten Orchester, beinahe durchaus aus Dilettanten bestehen, wenn man wenige Blase-Instrumente ausnimmt, auf die man sich hier nicht so häufig legt.

14. Mozart ist nun auch als Kaiserl. Kapellmeister nach Wien gegangen. Er ist ein merkwürdiger Mann für jeden philosophischen Liebhaber der Tonkunst. Er war ein äusserst frühzeitiges Genie und componirte und spielte schon in seinem neunten Jahre, (ja noch früher) als wahrer Virtuos, zu jedermanns Verwunderung. Was aber sehr selten ist, er war nicht nur ungewöhnlich früh ein geschickter Musikus, sondern reiste auch glücklich fort und zeigte sich in bleibender Gedeihlichkeit auch noch als Mann. Man kennt die vorüberblitzenden schnellen Genien aus leideger Erfahrung! Wo sind die Früchte zu rechter Zeit? und Dauer in Solidät? Nicht so bey Mozart! Jetzt nur ein Paar Worte über ein bizarres Phänomen, das er (oder seine Berühmtheit) veranlasst. Es kam vor einiger Zeit von ihm ein einzelnes Quadro (für Clavier, 1. Violin, 1. Viola (Bratsche) und Violoncell) gestochen heraus, welches sehr künstlich gesetzt ist, im Vortrage die äusserste Präcision aller vier Stimmen erfordert, aber auch bey glücklicher Ausführung doch nur, wie es scheint, Kenner der Tonkunst in einer *Musica di Camera* vergnügen kann und soll. Der Ruf: ''Mozart hat ein neues gar besonderes Quadro gesetzt, und die und die Fürstin und Gräfin besitzt es und spielt es!''—verbreitete sich bald, reitzte die Neugier und veranlasste die Unbesonnenheit, diese originelle Composition in grossen lärmenden Concerten zu produciren, und sich damit, *invita Minerva*, zum Prunk hören zu lassen. Manches andre Stück soutenirt sich noch auch bey einem mittelmäsigen Vortrage; dieses Mozartische Produkt aber ist würklich kaum anzuhören, wenn es unter mittelmäsige Dilettanten- Hände fällt, und vernachlässigt vorgetragen wird.— Diess ist nun im vorigen Winter unzähligemal geschehen; beynahe wo ich auf

478

meiner Reise nur hinkam, und in einige Concerte eingeführt wurde, kam ein Fräulein, oder ein stolzirende bürgerliche Demoiselle, oder sonst ein naseweiser Dilettante in rauschender Gesellschaft mit diesem Quadro angestochen, und prätendirte, dass es *goutirt* würde. Es *konnte* nicht gefallen; alles gähnte vor Langerweile über dem unverständlichen Tintamarre von 4 Instrumenten, die nicht in vier Takten zusammen passten, und bey deren widersinnigem *Concentu* an keine Einheit der Empfindung zu denken war; aber es *musste* gefallen, es *musste* gelobt werden! Mit welchem Eigensinn man diess beynahe allerwärts zu erzwingen gesucht hat, kann ich Ihnen kaum beschreiben. Diese Thorheit eine ephemerische *Manie du jour* zu schelten, sagt zu wenig, . . . Denn in der That ist diese unschickliche Vordringlichkeit nicht nur unanständig, und nicht nur ohne Nutzen und Frommen, sondern sie schadet auch der Kunst und Verbreitung des ächten Geschmacks. "Ist nichts weiter als das?" (denkt der halbgelehrte Zuhörer der Musik) "das soll in Vortrefflichkeit an die Extreme der Kunst gränzen? Und ich fühle doch Versuchung, mir öfters die Ohren dabey zuzuhalten? Wie reimt sich das? Weiss ich auch nur zuletzt, was ich aufrichtig in Musik loben oder tadeln darf?"—So verleidet man wahre Musik- Liebhaberey, macht den gesunden Menschenverstand und gesundes Natur-Gefühl irre, und hindert diejenige Geradheit und Gründlichkeit in Cultur, ohne welche doch keine Kunst zu haltbarer Höhe jemals emporsteigt. Welch ein Unterschied, wenn dieses vielbemeldete Kunstwerk von vier geschickten Musikern, die es wohl studirt haben, in einem stillen Zimmer, wo auch die Suspension jeder Note dem lauschenden Ohr nicht entgeht,nur in Gegenwart von zwey oder drey aufmerksamen Personen, höchst präcis vorgetragen wird!

15. A 6 h 1/2 passe dans la maison de Fries sans anti chambre. On entre d'abord dans un Salon a cheminée. . . . Mme de Fries occupoit le Sofa entornée de Dames dans l'autre chambre . . . Le concert dans un beau Salon tres sonores.

16. Le soir a 7 h au Concert de M. de Braun, ou Je me tuis anstantment dans la seconde chambre de peur de mourir de chaud. A 7 h j'allois chez l'Ambassadeur de France . . . J'allois avec Dietrichstein dans la seconde chambre.

17. Die Tonkunst wirkt hier täglich das Wunder, dass man sonst nur der Liebe zuschrieb: Sie macht alle Stände gleich. Adeliche und Bürgerliche, Fürsten und ihre Vasallen, Vorgesetzte und ihre Untergebenen, sitzen an einem Pulte beysammen, und vergessen über der Harmonie der Töne die Disharmonie ihres Standes. Dem ausübenden Musiker öffnen sich

alle Palläste und alle Börsen, und der Komponist von einiger Bedeutung wird mit all der Auszeichnung behandelt, die er sich nur immer wünschen kann, was bey manchem dieser Herren sehr viel sagen will.

18. Die Musik bewirkte diese freie Annäherung in einem Grade,von dem unsere demokratisch doch so vorgeschrittene Zeit keine Ahnung mehr hat. Schon der Umstand dass Reichardt, ein einfacher Capellmeister und keineswegs Berühmtheit ersten Ranges, in diesen vornehmsten Kreisen um die Wette eingeladen und fetirt wurde, spricht für deren Kunstinteresse und Liebenswürdigkeit.

19. Nie aber wurde ich durch eine Unart oder Zurückweisung von Seite der Damen an den Unterschied unseres Standes in der Gesellschaft erinnert.

20. Dann komme ich . . . in den Konzerten von Lobkowitz, die aber schon einer allgemeinen Assemblee ähnlicher sind.

21. wurde am Charsamstage Abends im fürstlichen Lobkowitzischen Theater, vor dem allerhöchsten Hofe und dem ersten Adel aufgeführt.

22. Es ward bei dem an Musik ganz unersättlichen Fürsten wieder von acht bis zwölf Uhr in einem fort gesungen.

23. Dela chez les Lobkowitz, d'on je ne sortis que les 1 h apres minuit passees. Il y avoient pres de 40 Dames, dont les Stemberg et les Buquoy en allerent al'assemblee. D'abord un Sextetto de Wranizky, puis Mme de Schönfeld chanta avec Pär, puis Mme Frank chanta comme un ange. Punto fit entendre son Solo de cor de chasse. Steuebel toucha du clavessin avec une volubilite peu interessante. Mme de Schönfeld, Therese Schwarzenberg, Mlle Francois Zichy, Mme Frank, le Pce Lobkowitz et deux hommes executerent ensemble le final dela Griselda a merveille. Puis les soupers. . . . Apres les souper Mme Steubel joua un jeu d'enfant avec une espere de tambourin qui pourtant doit lui fair une grand mal aux doigts.

24. A 6 3/4 chez le Prince Lobkowitz. . . . Mlle Goubaud chanta un morceau de Coriolan, L'archduc joua une Simphonie de Hummel qui etoit tres belle. La Bsse Kraft l'accompagnoit sur un autre clavessin.

J'allois dela au concert de Lobkowitz. D'abord l'ouverture d'un Opera Comique entitule Johanna, musique de Mehul, ne me de plut pas. Puis un Quintetto du Prince Louis de Presse funt moreuement lang, . . . Puis un Duo de Weinmuller qui suceda a un chant de Vogel le Duo jouoit del'Adrien de Weigl. Un Basson (fagatto) a Börmann de Berlin, . .. Un quatuor d'Axur. Cafin le joueur de harpe Casimir.

25. Avant 7 h au Concert spirituel chez le Comte Haugwitz. Beaucoup de Dames et le Duc Albert. Je me trouvois derniere Mme de Bisringen, entre le Pce Clari et Nani Dietrichstein, devant la Pesse Lobkowitz et Mme de Schönborn. D'abord on donna Zeit und Ewigkeit, musique de Naumann, belle touchant, parfaitemant executee. . . . Le second das Lob Gottes. Musique de Schutz.

26. A 7 h a un concert chez le jeune Fries. Dans la chambre du Billard deux beau Hakert et un Kauchich representant les Vestales fuyent Rome mise en feu par Brenus et ses garrlois. . . . Dans la chambre du concert trois *Wutki* l'un le Vesures, l'autre les Cascatelli priser d'un joli ponct (?) de vue. Apre une Jolie Symphonie Mme de Schonfeld chanta avec Par un duo de Paisiello. *Nei giomi tuor felice.* Le furneux cor de chasse Stich, Bohème de notion joua avec une delicatesse et un justesse admirable.

27. A 7 h passe au Concert du B. Braun . . . La chaleur etoit forte. Je m'erris (?) sur le devant a coté de Hardegkh et de Spielmann. Czervenka joua bien du hautbois, mais son concert endornit Swieten. Dans le second acte la harpe de Mme Muller, le Duo de Paisiello, l'Harmonie de Wranizki, Vair de Nasoline et le final des Horaces de Cimarosa me firent grand plaisir. Le bon Wrbna etoit la un commencement et revuit pour la fin. La Pesse Auersberg etoit triste.

Le soir a 7 h au Concert de M. de Braun, ou je metuis anstament dans la seconde chambre de peur de mourir de chaud. Gli Orazj ed i Eriazi fut l'opera que l'on donna. Mme Mara y chanta d'une voix touchante et sarut (?) crier, comme il fesoit, il y a vuit aus. Je me trouvois longtems a coté de Mme de Metternich. Mlle de Revaj gentille.

28. Die Musiken bei Herrn von Würth nähern sich ihrem Ende. Diese schöne Anstalt, in welcher die Liberalität des Unternehmers die Musik-kenner und Freunde aller gebildeten Stände versammelt, hat auch diesesmal beinahe durchaus nur die grössten musikalischen Meisterwerke eines Mozarts, Haydn, Eberl, Beethoven, u.A. im vollen Glanze einer schönen und gelungenen Ausführung gezeigt.

29. Das Kunstvergnügen wird dort noch durch das humane gefällige Benehmen des Herrn vom Hause, und durch eine sehr gewählte Gesellschaft vermehrt.

30. Am 7 Uhr kam Kühlbach und fuhren in die Musik zum Hofrath Schubb. Keller geigte in einem Quintetto, Fräule Gilberg schlug eine Sonata, welche ein russischer Officier mit dem Clarinett accompagnirte. Tomasini geigte ein Quartett, Th. sang die Arie von Cimarosa "Ah torna la bell aurora'. Am 1/2 11 kamen wir nach Hause.

Nach 7 Uhr mit Th. zum Hofrath Schubb. Sie sang die Arie Parto aus Clemenza di Tito accompagnirt von Gruft, obligat mit dem Clarinet, gespielt von Pär. . . . Nach 10 ging ich.

Abends giengen Th, Naumann, Moreau und ich zum Schupp. Es wurde zum Anfang die Serenate von Fuchs gemacht, dann die Introduction von Don Juan, ein Concert von Mad. Jacobi und Terzett von Achille.

31. Heute sind wir (da wegen Trauer der Kaiserin Louisa keine Theater sind) zum Schmierer abends geladen. Die 4 Jahreszeiten werden gegeben. . . .Th. und ich giengen zu Schmierer um 7 Uhr. Die Jeanette und beyde Schuster sangen. Liparsky dirigirte am Pianoforte sehr prae (?). Da waren die Violinen doppelt besetzt, Violoncello, und Violos. Mit den Knaben mögen 16 Chorsänger, worunter Pfeifer war, gewesen seyn. Die Aufführung gelung. Die Gesellschaft war zahlreich. Lang.. . . der Dichter Weissenbach. . . .die 2 Strak. Wir Unterhielten uns recht angenehm und blieben bis 1/2 12 Uhr.

CHAPTER TWO

1. Wöchentlich wird, nebst andern gestifteten Akademien, als z.B. bey dem Hrn. Grafen von Collaldo, beym Herrn Landschafts-Beysitzer Herr von Kees, beym Herr von Oertel und wenigstens einmal bey des Prinzen von Sachsen Hildburghausen Durchl[aut] unter dem Direction des Herrn Joseph Bono musikalisches Concert gehalten.

2. Aus einer neuerlich bekannt gewordenen Nachricht über *Wiener Theaterwesen* erhellet, wie sehr der dortige Geschmack für musikalische, insonderheit italienische Singschauspiele sey. Innerhalb einem Jahr (vom 15ten November 1791 bis 15. December 1792) hat man italienische Oper . . . 180 mal gegeben. Eine einzige Opera seria ist 24 mal aufgeführt worden. . . . Ballets sahe man . . . 163 mal.

3. Wien. Das hier die bekannte Liebe des Publikums zu den Vergnügungen der Schaubühne auch während der Schrecken des Krieges nicht abgenommen hat; sondern wohl noch gestiegen ist, sieht man täglich an dem Gedränge beym Eingange in die drey beliebtesten Theater.

4. NB. Es wird hiemit dem Publico zu wissen gemacht, dass künftigen Sonntag als den 7ten dies in dem Königlichen privilegirten Theatro nächst der Burg, Nachmittag präcise um halber 7 Uhr die Accademien von verschiedener Vocal und Instrumental Musik zum Erstenmal gehalten, die übrige Täge aber weiterhin behörig kund gemacht werden sollen.

5. Demnach bey vorseyender heiligen Fastenzeit alle Schauspiele und Comödien eingestellet seynd, so werden in dem kaiserl. Theatro nächst an der Burg zur Unterhaltung des hohen Adels, wie auch des Publici alle Wochen dreymalen, als Sonntag, Dienstag, und Donnerstag, Musikalische Academien gehalten.

6. J.J.M.M. . . . erschynen Abends bey den heut zum ersten Mahl auf den Theatre nächst der Burg gehaltenen Concert oder so genannten Academie de musique womit alle Sonn- Diens- und Donnerstag continuiret wurde, dieses Fasten Spectacle daurte von 6 biss 9 Uhr, mann bezahlte die Entree, jedermann kunte darunter spillen, das Theatre ware sehr schön zugerichtet und wohl illuminiret, und um Leuthe zu attiriren, befliessen sich der Conte Durazzo, als welcher nun die Inspection dieses Departements hat, theils fremmde Stimmen, worunter eine sichere Sa. Gabrieli detta la cochetta, bella voce di soprane, sich hören lassen, anhero zu beschreiben, theils verschiedene Variationen von Chori, oratory, salmi, arie, duetti zu produciren, wie sich dann imerdar ein zahlreiches Auditorium eingefunden hat.

7. Sonntags den 28. dieses lauffenden Monats Februarii werden in dem K. K. privilegirten Theater nächst der Burg die musicalischen Academien ihren Anfang nehmen, und die Fasten hindurch wochentlich dreymal, nämlich Sonntag, Dienstag und Donnerstage gehalten werden; die Preise davon sind, wie sie andere Jahr gewesen. Es wird auch ein Platz auf dem Theater seyn, um den sonst gewöhnlichen Preis des zweyten Parterre. Wegen den Abbonirungen sowol der Logen als der Entree auf die Gallerie, ist sich beym Logenmeister anzumelden.

8. La 1re Accademie. Le Theatre a ete orne par une Decoration transparente, representant la Protection que L'Auguste Maison d'Autriche a accorde en tous tems aux beaux Arts. Cinq voix y ont chante, et il y a eu un Concert de Pantaleon joue par le Sr. Helman, avec un Choeur de la Composition du Sr. Gluck.

La 7me Accademie avec une nouvelle Decoration qui representoit un Temple orne des Dornres, et transparents. Au milieu du quel parmi les exclamations du Peuple, la renomee celebre, et Couronne, le Nom de Nos Souverains. On y a chante plusieurs Airs nouveaux, et un Choeur de la

Composition du Sr. Porpora. Et un Concert a plusieurs Instrumens seul de la Composition du Sieur Wagenseil.

La 13me Accademie. Ce jour la Decoration a represente un nouveau grand Tableau transparent, et representoit Telemaque conduit par Minerve, et couvert de son Bouclier s'avancent par un chemin escarpe vers le Temple de l'Immortalite. On luy montre de loin les Marques d'honneur, et la Gloire qui l'attend. On voit le precipiter dans les Abimes l'Orgenil, l'Envie et les autres vices, ou Monstres qui s'opposaienta son Passage. Par ce Symbolesi reconnu on veut rapeller l'Idee de ce quoi on doit attendre d'un jeane Heros lorsqu'il est conduit par la Largesse. Dans cette Decoration on a execute un oratoire a quatre Voix, dont la Musique est de la Composition du Sr. Balthaser Galuppi suonomme Boranello; Et le Titre a etre Adamo et Eva.

9. La 4me Accademie. Le Concert a eu l'ordinaire Decoration. Entra autres qui on chante il y avoit le Sr.Joseph Aprile dit Sciroletto. Le Sr. Francois et Grück tenore pour la 1re fois. Tous les airs ont ete entremele des Symphonies, et il y en a une concertee de plusieurs Instrumens Solo de la composition du Sr. San Martino.

La 5me Accademie. Le Concert a ete encore decore a l'ordinaire. Les memes voix ont chante et il y a eu un Concert d'Hautbois joue par le Sr. Jauzer.

10. La 6me Accademie. Entre autres qui ont chante, Le Sieur Ciroletto n'a chante que des airs qui ont ete demande. Le Sr. Helman a joue un Concert sur le Pantaleon, et il a aussi joue differens Caprices.

11. La. 15me et derniere Accademie. Ornee comme le deux jours suparavant. N. B.: Les differens voix qui on chante dans le Cours de Careme s'ont fait entendu avec des Airs nouvelles. A on a repete quelqu'un de leux qui on paru etre plus de gout du Public. Le Sieur Helman a joue un Concert sur le Pantaleon. On a execute plusieurs Simphonies d'un gout nouveau. Et a la fin on a repete pour la seconde fois le nouveau grand choeur du Sieur Wagenseil. On a commence a 6 heures.

12. 20. Februar. . . . Die Concerts auf dem Theatre fiengen erst die künfftige Wochen an und wurde darmit al solito die Sonn-, Dienst-, und Donnerstäge continuiret.

13. Im Jahr 1769 erhielt die Direktion wiederum Erlaubniss, sowohl Freytags, als auch in der Advent und Fastenzeit Akademien zu geben. Doch sind die letzten Tagen im Advent, und die letzten 14 Tagen in der Fasten ausgenommen.

14. Nächstkommenden Montag als den 29ten Christmonats, wird der unter dem Namen des kleinen Engländers hier bekannte junge Niederländer, Franz la Motte, 13 Jahr alt mit gnädigster Erlaubniss des Hofes die Ehre haben, in dem Theater nächst der kais. Burg ein Musikconcert zu geben. Der Anfang ist Präcise um 6 Uhr, und der Preiss wie gewöhnlich im Theater.

15. Während der Fasten wurden 6 musikalische Akademien im Burgtheater und 3 grosse musikalische Akadamien im Kärnthnerthortheater gegeben, wovon 1 ganze und 2 halbe Einnahmen zum Besten der Wittwen und Waisen hiesiger Tonkünstler bestimmt sind.

16. In der Fasten waren 8 in den Monaten April und [am] May 6, und in den letzten 9 Tagen der Adventzeit 3 musikalische Akademien.

17. Künftigen Freytags, den 30. Winterm. wird in dem Schauspielhause nächst der kais. königl. Burg eine musikalische Akademie gehalten werden, wobey die zween Gebrüdere Colla, berühmte Tonkünstler auf dem seltenen Instrumente Calassioncino genannt, eine Gattung wie die bekannte Mandoline, verschiedene Concerte aufführen werden. Der Herr Joseph Milliko, so wie der meiste Theil der Sängerinnen von der hiesigen italiänischen Schauspielergesellschaft, werden dabey verschiedene Arien, und besonders der erwehnte Herr Milliko eine mit dem Calassioncino obligate absingen, und solcher gestalten wird mit Duetten, Concerten, und Symphonien abgewechselt werden. Niemand wird weder auf das Parterre, noch in die Logen frey eingelassen werden.

18. Den 30. musikalische Akademie. Die Musik fieng mit einer grossen Symphonie von Hrn. Ditters an. Me. Weiglin, Weisen, Kurzin, Mlle. Rosina Baglioni und Hr. Poggi sangen verschiedene Arien. Me. Weisin und Hr. Poggi wiederholten auch einige aus der Oper Armida. Hr. Pichl spielte ein neues Konzert auf der Geige, so wie Hr. Krumpholz ebenfalls eines von neuer Erfindung auf der grossen Harfe. Alle diese Stücke waren mit Simphonien vermengt, worunter eine mit dem englishchen Horn vom Chevalier Gluck war, und eine andere von dem Hrn. Bach, womit die Akademie beschlossen wurde.

19. Den 8. musikalische Akademie. Herr Drechsler liess sich zum erstenmale mit einigen neuen Arien hören, wovon eine mit solo de Haubois begleitet wurde. Hr. Ulrich blies zum erstenmale ein Konzert und ein Solo auf eben diesem instrumente. Beyde grosse Virtuosen sind in anspachischen Diensten. Mlle. Rosa Baglioni, Me. Weisin, und Kurzin sangen einige Arien. Alle diese Stücke waren mit einigen grossen Sim-

phonien vermischt, wovon die erste von Hrn.Piccini, die zweyte von Hrn. Gassman war.

20. Montags den 16. dieses war in dem hiesigen Schauspielhaus nächst dem Kärntnerthore für die Musikliebhaber ein grosses Koncert, wobey sich zwey fremde erst kürzlich hier angelangte in hochfürstl. Oettingen-Wallersteinischen Diensten stehende Virtuosen, nämlich Herr Janisch auf der Violine, und Herr Reicha auf dem Violoncell in ganz nach neuen Geschmacke gesetzten Concerten, und Duetten, mit der ihnen eigenen Stärke und Annehmlichkeit meisterhaft hören liessen. Mademoiselle Cavallieri, eine gebohrne Wienerinn, sang dabey zwey Arien in ihrer bekannten harmonischen Grösse, und das so zahlreich als glänzende Auditorium belohnte die Bemühungen dieser unvergleichlichen Tonkünstler mit wohlverdientem allgemeinen Beyfalle.

21. Er schrieb mir das er in Eyle 3 Subscriptions Accademien gegeben von 120 Subscribenten.

22. Auf allerhöchsten Befehl wird nach Ostern jegliches Monat gegen Bezahlung eine Redoute, wie auch für die Delectanten eine musikalische Akademie gegeben werden, bei welcher jedermann frey stehet, nach vorher ausgehaltener Probe sich hören zu lassen. Die Einnahm dieser Unterhaltung wollen des Armen Institut gewidmet werden.

23. Herr P. J. Martio allhier hat ein grosses Dilettantenkonzert unternommen, welches auf den grossen Saale in der Mehlgrube, Sommers und Winders von halb sieben, bis neun Uhr Abends gehalten wird, und in welchem sich jeder Dilettante beyderley Geschlechts auf seinen Instrument üben und hören lassen kann. Monatlich wird 2 fl 10 kr Beytrag gegeben; in den Nebenzimmern werden Spieltische für alle Arten Kommerzspiele bereit gehalten, und jederman auf Begehren mit allen Arten Erfrischungen bedienet.

24. Oeffentliche Konzerte sind im Sommer nicht, aber viele im Winter. Besonders in der Fastenzeit, wenn die Schauspielhäuser geschlossen sind, und also Mangel an Zeitvertreib ist, werden viele sogenannte Akademien öffentlich und in Privathäusern gehalten, wo denn unter dem Musiciren auch Karten gespielt und Erfrischungen gegessen und getrunken werden. Als ich in Wien war, kündigte einer Namens Philippe Jacques Martin als Unternehmer die Errichtung eines grossen Dilettanten-Konzerts in Wien an, "bey dem viele hiesige Herren Dilettanten sich mit vollständigem Orchester üben wollen, und sich unsere schönen Gesellschaften dabey versammeln, sich sehen, unterhalten, welches für fremde Bemerker der Na-

tional Unterhaltungen einer der herrlichsten Anblicke werden könnte.
...'' Dieses Liebhaberkonzert sollte Freitags von 1/2 7 bis 1/2 9 Uhr Sommers und Winters in der Mehlgrube gehalten werden. Es ist auch wirklich zu Stande gekommen, hat aber den folgenden Sommer aufgehört. Im #VI der Ankündigung hiess es: "In den Nebenzimmern werden Spieltische für alle Arte Kommercespiele bereit gehalten, für deren *à Discretion* Spielgeld erlegt wird, so wie auch die Gesellschaft mit allen Arten von Erfrischungen auf Begehren bedienet werden wird.'' Diess ist wenigstens nicht nach dem Muster des Liebhaberkoncerts zu Berlin eingerichtet. Daselbst ist man mit dem blossen Vergnügen an der Musik zufrieden, ohne das Vergnügen des Kartenspielens und Essens und Trinkens dazu haben zu wollen. Man würde daselbst glauben, sowohl den musikübenden Liebhabern als den Musikern von Profession eine Unhöflichkeit zu bezeigen und die Musik zu entehren, wenn man Spielmarken und Schokolatetassen dazwischen klappern liesse.

Es gibt in Wien viele eifrige Liebhaber der Musik und auch nicht wenige, die Kenner sind, und mehr oder weniger für Virtuosen gelten können. Diese billigen es gewiss nicht, dass man dort die Unterhaltung mit der Musik, welche den Geist dessen, der Musik zu empfinden fähig ist, so ganz erfüllen kann, durch Kartenspielen und Essen hindert. In Privatkoncerten wahrer Liebhaber, denen ich in Wien beygewohnt habe, war es auch nicht so.

25. So hat auch Herr Martin sein unlängst in der Stadt auf der Mehlgrube errichtetes Dilettantenkonzert für diesen Sommer in den Augarten verpflanzt, wo man nun, um billige Preise, alle Sonntage das Vergnügen haben kann, manche Virtuosen beyderley Geschlechts dabey zu bewundern, und sich auf das angenehmste in der schönen Gesellschaft unterhalten.

26. Unterzeichneter hat, nach erhaltener allerhöchsten Erlaubniss, die Ehre einem hohen und gnädigsten Adel, wie auch dem hochschätzbaresten Publikum hiemit gehorsamst anzukündigen, dass er auf wiederholtes Begehren der Hrn. Gönner und Liebhaber der edeln Tonkunst, seine so sehr beliebt und höchst angenehmen grossen Musiken im k. k. Augarten wieder zu erneuern, und sie für Jedermann unentgeltlich, jedoch auf nachstehende Art zu geben, das schmeichelhafteste Vergnügen haben wird. 1) Werden diese seine theils stark vollstimmigen, theils auch bestgewählten Harmoniemusiken im k. k. Augarten, früh von 5 bis 8 Uhr alle Montäge unter freyem Himmel, wobey aber die besten Anstalten gegen die heftige Sonnenhitze getroffen werden; 2) an

487

Dienstägen aber zunächst der Lusthausallee, am Platze des letzten Kaffeehauses, von 5 bis 7 Uhr Nachmittags, 3) an Donnerstägen immer in der Stadt am Hof, nach geendigten Theater, von 10 Uhr bis Mitternacht (als Serenaten betrachtet) den ganzen Sommer hindurch gehalten werden. 4) Nur die Abonnirten allein haben den Eintritt im Cercle; ausser den grossen Kreis aber kann Jedermann nach Belieben diese Musiken unentgeltlich mit anhören. . . . P. I. Martin, Directeur du Concert d'Amateurs.

27. Unterzeichneter hat hiemit die Ehre gehorsamst noch anzuzeigen, dass, weil er bloss zuo mehrerer Bequemlichkeit derjenigen, so theils wegen bevorstehender Abreise aufs land, theils wegen andern Geschäften sich nicht zu abonniren gedenken, sondern bloss nur hie und da einigen von diesen Musiken mit beyzuwohnen Belieben tragen wollen, somit er dieselben auch und zwar gegen einen freywilligen Geldbeytrag mit Billets d'entree zu verstehen die Ehre haben wird. . . . Der Unterzeichneter wegen nicht hinlänglichen Abonnement (weil fast alle Herrschaften, die ihn sonst, wie immer, aufs gnädigst unterstützt haben würden, von hier schon abgereiset, und täglich noch aufs Land sich verreisen) genöthiget ist, seine erste Musik im k. k. Augarten, statt am 6. auf den 14. Juni im Prater zurück zu setzen.

28. Dann sind gewöhnlich zwölf Musiken, im Augarten des Morgens, unter den Nahmen Dilettanten Musiken. Diese entstanden durch Hrn. Vice-Präsidenten von Kees, nach der Zeit, als Kaiser Joseph zu seinem ewigen Ruhm, den Augarten dem öffentlichen Vergnügen geweiht hatte, bestand das Personale, ausser den Blaseinstrumenten und Contrebassen, meistens aus Liebhabern. Selbst von dem höchsten Adel liessen sich Damen hören. Das Auditorium war sehr brillant, und alles ging mit einer Ordnung und mit einem Anstand, dass jedermann nach allen Kräften zur Unterstützung des Instituts gern beytrug. Den Ertrag des geringen Abonnements verwendete man ganz auf die Unkosten. Nachher übernahm Hr. Rudolph die Direktion. Es ging zwar noch immer gut, aber nicht mehr so glanzend: der Adel zog sich zurück, indem im Grunde der grösste Theil desselben dem Kaiser Joseph zu Gefallen hinausgegangen war; doch waren die Aufführungen noch immer sehr angenehm. Jetzt hat sie Hr. Schupanzig und jenes aufmunternde Auditorium ist ganz weg. Kein Liebhaber von *wahrer* Bedeutung mag sich mehr hören lassen; selbst die Musiker spielen nur sehr selten Konzerter. Ueberhaupt ist das Feuer für dies Institut ganz erloschen. Die Konzerte werden selten gut akkompagnirt; die Symphonien aber gehen besser. Da der Zweck des Unternehmers jezt nich sowohl mehr Liebe zur Kunst oder Vergnügen,

als vielmehr sein Nutzen ist: so ist es, bey dem geringen Abonnement gar nicht möglich etwas Namhaftes auf die Musik zu verwenden.

29. Am 30 d. M. May werden die Liebhaber Konzerte im Augarten ihren Anfang nehmen, und durch die folgenden drey Donnerstäge fortgesetzt werden. Die Herren Abonenten belieben ihre Pränumerazionsscheine in der obern Bäckerstrasse Nr. 813 im dritten Stock bey Unterzeichnetem abholen zu lassen. Für jeden Pränumerazionsscheine sind 4 fl 30 kr zu erlegen, wofür zu jedem Konzerte 6 Eintrittsbilleten erfolgt werden.

30. Die gewöhnlichen Akademien haben ihren Fortgang. Man bekommt gute Sinfonien fast immer gut zu hören. Uebrigens treten meistens Liebhaber oder Liebhaberinnen, von denen manche freylich erst ihre Schule zu machen gedenken, mit Spiel oder Gesang auf. Es hat dies für manche Zuhörer ein gar nicht zu tadelndes Interesse, aber für den Musiker wenig oder gar keins.

31. Mir hat dieser Garten . . . oft hohen Genuss gewährt, besonders lebhaft, wenn an einem heitern kühlen Morgan Herr Schuppanzigh seine Concerte im Gartensaale giebt. . . . Die Stücke, welche hier beinahe ganz von Dilettanten gegeben werden, beschränkten sich auf grosse Symphonien, Ouvertüren, Singstücke und Concerte. Die ersteren, besonders Cherubini's herrliche Ouvertüren aus den Tagen der Gefahr, Medea, Lodoiska, werden hier nach dem einstimmigen Urtheile aller Kenner mit einer Genauigkeit, Präcision, und Stärke vorgetragen, die selbst auf unserm Hoftheater, dessen Orchester doch brav ist, selten erreicht wird.

32. Die aufgeführten Stücke waren grösstentheils sehr gewählt, und wurden mit Fleiss, Präzision und Feuer vorgetragen, obgleich die Gesellschaft beynahe ganz aus Dilettanten besteht.

33. Obgleich die ehemaligen Augarten Konzerte, unter Schuppanzigh's Direktion, für diesen Sommer nicht wieder aufzukommen scheinen; so haben wir doch seit dem 1sten May schon mehrere Akademieen gehört, die von andern hiesigen Künstlern daselbst gegeben wurden.

34. Nachdem so viele Freunde der Tonkunst so sehnlichst den Wunsch äussern, dass im k. k. Augarten-Saale wieder die sogenannten Liebhaber-Morgan-Concerte ihren Anfang nehmen sollen, so ist Schuppanzigh Willens, diese Anteprise zu übernehmen. Jeder Freund oder Freundin der Tonkunst, welchem es Vergnügen macht, sich daselbst zu producirien, oder auch im Orchester mitzuspielen, und auch zugleich die dazu erforderlichen Talente besitzt, wird hier öffentlich eingeladen. Jeder

dieser Dilettanten hat sich in der Wohnung des Schuppanzigh, nämlich auf der Landstrasse im gräflich Rasoumofskyschen ersten Seitengebäude im zweyten Stock anzumelden, und auch zu versprechen, bey jeder dieser Concerte, deren 6 an der Zahl gegeben werden, gewiss, und verlässlich jedesmal zu erscheinen. Die dazu erforderlichen Instrumente werden immer schon in der Bereitschaft seyn. Nachdem diese Anteprise doch immer mit vielen Auslagen verbunden ist, so ist doch nothwendig, dass Schuppanzigh für die dazu nöthigen Auslagen im voraus für Schaden gedeckt ist. . . . Jeder Abonnent, im Falle, dass wegen Mangel der Abonnenten kein Concert gegeben würde, sein Geld wieder zurückbekommen kann.

35. Eine Gesellschaft ansehnlicher Musikfreunde und Tonkünstler, giebt seit einigen Wochen zur Unterhaltung des hiesigen Publikums alle Montäge, wenn es die Witterung zulässt, des Morgens im Garten des Belvedere öffentliche musikalische Akademie, wobey jederzeit eine angenehme Gesellschaft der hiesigen Einwohner sich einfindet. Am verwichenen Montage den 8. d. M. hat Hr. Mästrino, Musikus bey dem Grafen Ladislaus Erdödi, zum allgemeinen Vergnügen sich allda in einem vortreflichen Concerte auf der Violine hören lassen.

Eine Gesellschaft von Musikliebhabern ergötze in diesem Jahre, wie im verflossenen, das hiesige Publikum an Donnerstägen oder Montägen des Morgens im Belvedere mit einer vortreflichen Musik, wobey jedesmal eine ansehnliche Menge von Zuhörern sich einfande. Donnerstags den 24 d. M. wird allda für heuer zum letztenmal diese musikalische Unterhaltung gegeben.

Einige Freunde der Tonkunst geben in diesem Jahre wieder allwöchentlich des Morgens einmal, zur Ergötzung des Publikums, Konzerte im Belvedere. Sonst war dieselbe jeden Donnerstag. Von nun an aber ist die Mittwoche dazu bestimmt.

36. Die Produktion der Meisterwerke des In- und Auslandes wird den Geschmack reinigen und ihm eine fest, bleibende Richtung geben;—sie wird die vaterländischen Künstler unter sich zur Nacheiferung aufmuntern;—das Genie vor der Unterdrückung der Kabale sichern;—junge Talente zur Vollkommenheit bringen, und aus sich selbst durch fortwährende gemeinschaftliche Uibung im Orchester vollendete Meister auf den verschiedenen Instrumenten bilden, welche eine gute Methode durch ihre Zöglinge überall verbreiten werden. Und: Jedes Concert muss sich durch Aufführung bedeutender und entschieden vortrefflicher Musik-

stücke auszeichnen, weil das Institut nur auf solche Art seine Würde zu behaupten und eine stets höhere Vollkommenheit zu erreichen im Stande ist.

CHAPTER THREE

1. No. 18. Thurner, Franz bittet im Nationaltheater eine Akademie auf der Flöte geben zu dürfen.

2. Mit den Schauspielen wechseln musikalische Akademien ab, welche verschiedene Virtuosen auf ihre eigene Faust und zu ihrem eigenen Besten geben.

3. Da während dieser Fastenzeit von dem k. k. Nationalhofschauspielern fünf Wochen lang allemal Sonntags, Montags, Dienstags und Donnerstags im k. k. Hoftheater beym Kärntnerthor Schauspiele gegeben werden sollen, so wurde Donnerstag den 2. März der Anfang gemacht. . . . An den übrigen Tagen in jeder Woche werden in demselben Theater musikalische Akadamien gegeben: die erste war zum Vortheil der Sig. Coltellini, und die zweyte für Herrn Calvesi, beide Mitglieder von dem k. k. italienische Singspiele.

4. Wird dem Hr. Vizedirektor auch frei gestellt, unmaskirte Bälle—concerts spirituels, oder andern dergleichen Unterhaltungen nach seinem Wilkuhr zu veranstalten.

5. Bei dieser Gelegenheit kann man billig fragen, warum nicht unsern grossen Meistern, als Beethoven, Eberl, u.a.m.—das Theater nicht verliehen wird, und man es lieber ungenützt verschlossen lässt? Warum das Schicksal so vieler vortreflichen Künstler in mehreren Fächern von den Launen eines Einzigen abhangen soll?

6. Die ersten beyden Orte sind sehr schwer, und ohne besondere hohe Empfehlung gar nicht vom Hrn. Baron Braun zu erlangen. Die Ursache davon kenne ich nicht; denn der verbrauchte Redoutensaal kann wohl schwerlich mehr abgenützt werden, als er es ohnehin schon ist, und ein Theater stehet oft ganz leer—wenn nämlich nur in dem andern gespielt wird und keine Probe vorfällt.

7. Hier muss ich auch des Theaters am Burgthor erwähnen, welches von aussen gar nicht erscheint, aber innen fast zu zierlich und golden geschmückt, und für Wien nicht gross genug ist.

8. In beyden hat das Parterre Sitz! Man theilt es in das gemeine, und das Parterre noble. . . . Beyde werden von Frauenzimmern und Mannespersonen besucht, und in das letztere darf sich kein Mann zu gehen schämen, sein Rang sey, welcher er wolle.

9. Parterre. Das noble Parterre, gleichsam der Schauplatz der Edelleute. Das gemeine Volk aber, welches die französischen Namen hasset, nennet diesen Raum den Ochsengries oder den Ochsenzwinger wegen einer ähnlichen Einschränkung für die Ochsen vor dem Stubenthor.

10. Das Schauspiel in der Leopoldstadt lockt durch Farcen, Travestirungen, Zaubereien und Darstellungen des Niedrigkomischen, worin es mit dem Theater an der Wien rivalisirt und, nach dem Urtheile einiger vorstädtischen Kunstfreunde, ihm bisweilen den Rang abgewinnt.

11. Sein Kunsttemple erhob sich in dem gegen die Schleifmühlgasse gelegenen rückwärtigen Hofe, und sah—nach der Schilderung Castelli's—einer grossen, länglich viereckigen Kiste nicht unähnlich. Das Theater hatte beiläufig die Grosse des Josephstädter-Theaters und nur zwei Stockwerke. Der Zuschauerraum war ganz einfach bemalt; seitwärts des Portals, vor der Buhne, standen die lebensgrossen Figuren eines Ritters mit einem Dolche und einer halb verlarvten Dame.

12. Das Ampitheater hat ein freundliches Ansehen, es ist himmelblau mit Silber. Es hat achtzehn Logen, zwey Parterre, und vier Gallerien über einander. Um für mehr Menschen Platz zu gewinnen, hat man die Sitze allenthalben etwas mehr zusammen gedrängt als bequem ist. Im Ganzen ist dieses Theater besser gebaut als die übrigen hier.

13. Gestern als den 1. May hat Herr Jahn Trakteur in Schönbrunn den Anfang gemacht das hiesige Publikum auch in dem Augarten zu bedienen. . . . In 13 Tafelzimmern, worunter 10 mit besonderen Eingang versehen sind und dem grossen Saal können die Gäste nicht nur mit Mittagtafeln, sondern auch Frühstuck, Jausen, Nachtessen, Gesundheitswässern . . . und in gegenwärtigen Monat mit der gewöhnlichen Kräutersuppe bedient werden. Akademien, Tanzmusik, Hochzeiten, Pique nique, erlaubte Spiele, und andere Erlustigungen können auch gehalten werden.

14. Spaziergänge und Erlustigungsörter: Augarten. Zwei Tanzsäle sind mit schöner Musik besetzt, die sich auch im Garten selbst oft an verschiedenen Orten hören lässt.

15. Ein grosser schattiger Halbzirkel, der ringsum mit Tischen, grünen Stühlen und Bänken besetzt ist, macht den Eingang in den Augarten selbst. In der Fronte ist die mit vielen Bänken besetzte, perspektivische Seufzerallee. Zur rechten ist die sehr einfache Sommerwohnung des Monarchen, und zur linken die den Augarten durchschneidende Seitenalleen, und ein kleines geschlossenes Gärtchen. In diesem grünen Ampitheater wird oft des Morgens Musik gemacht.

16. Um 6 Uhr gieng ich in Augarten. Es waren viele Menschen und auf dem oval Platz Harmonie.

17. Eröffnung des Augartens, und das neu mit sehr viel Geschmack zugerichteten Concert Saales. . . . Mit wahren Vergnügen sahen wir den sehr schön meulblirten Saal.

18. An seinem Eingange sind mehrere grosse Gebäude von Kaiser Joseph gebaut, in einem Viereck. . . .Diese Zimmer hat ein gewisser Jahn gepachtet, bey dem alle mögliche Artikel des Magenluxus, oder der blossen Leibesnothdurft wohlfeil und theuer zu haben sind. Hier ist meistens des Morgens Gesellschaft, die einen Kaffee, oder Chokolade einnimmt, und in den schönen Gängen oft bis Mittag herumwandelt, und in den Sälen, oder unter den hohen Kastanien und Pappeln endlich ein weidliches Mahl hält. Auch des Abends giebt es hier oft einige. In den grössten Sälen werden häufig Akademien gehalten, oder Musiken von Dilettanten aufgeführt, wie jetzt alle Donnerstäge geschieht. Häufig ladet man hierher auch eine ganze Gesellschaft, und Jahn richtet die Bewirthung ein, je nachdem man prächtiger oder frugaler schmausen will. . . . Zu Mittage findet man meistens Musik da, oft das Orchester der Leopoldstädter Bühne. . . . Es ist . . .[das Lieblingsplatz] für die Wiener Schönen, die man hier des Morgens, besonders an Konzerttagen, in grosser Menge auf und ab wandeln sieht, in der liebenswürdigen und schmachtenden Blässe des Morgans—das ist nicht wahr, die meisten beschmieren sich bis an die Ohren mit Roth, wie sie aus dem Bette steigen—und in den holden Négligée, worin Amor seine grössten Schelmereyen ausheckt, und worauf man allen unvorsichtigen Augen und flatternden Herzen mit grossen Buchstaben ein Cavate! schreiben sollte. Hier also geht das grosse Schauspiel eines langen lüstigen Tages an.

19. Bei der Regierung Theresiens, war der Augarten blos vor dem hohen Adel, mit Ausschliessung der andern Stände bestimmt, aber der Kaiser Joseph öfnete solchen, vermöge seiner philantropischen Grundsätze vor alle Menschen, . . . Da der Kaiser Joseph hier ein sehr einfaches Wohnhaus

im Augarten hatte, und sich oft unter die Spaziergänger mischte, so wurde dieser Ort sehr besucht, aber nach seinem Tode hat die Gesellschaft abgenommen. An Sonntägen ist es noch ziemlich zahlreich, in der Woche aber oft leer; der vornehme Adel veranstaltet hier Festins, und gibt grosse Dienes, aber sonst ist es Ton, nach dem Prater zu fahren.

20. Apres 9 h a l'Augarten musique. Beaucoup de bourgeoisie.

21. Mir hat dieser Garten . . . oft hohen Genuss gewährt, besonders lebhaft, wenn an einem heitern kühlen Morgan Herr Schuppanzigh seine Concerte im Gartensaale giebt. . . . Es versammelt sich dabei alles vom Mittelstande, was den Genuss des schönen Morgens im Augarten mit dem grössten Theils gut gewählten und ausgeführten Musik verbinden will.

22. Die Mehlgrube ist ein grosses Gebäude auf dem neuen Markte . . . wobey weitem die grösste Zahl der Anwesenden gut und modisch gekleidet ist. . . . Es ist der eigentliche Belustigungsort der guten bürgerlichen Stände, der wohlhabenden Ladenkrämer, einiger Künstler, Regierungsbedienter, reicher Handwerker und dergleichen. . . . Indessen sind auch die ganz niedern Stände, besonders in der Faschingszeit, nicht ausgeschlossen, wofern sie nur auf eine gewisse Art gekleidet sind. Die Livree und das Corset der Stubenmädchen werden nicht zugelassen, so wenig als ein Frauenzimmer, das allein kommt.

23. Wien den 2. November. Gestern hatten wir einen Auftritt â la Paris in Mignature. Auf der sogenannten Mehlgrube hatte man Musik. Einem der Gäste gefiel die Musik nicht: er schimpfte. Ein Virtuos vom starken taktfesten Orchester gab ihm eine derbe Ohrfeige, beinahe wie Achill dem Thersites in Homer. Hierdurch war das Point d'honneur der gegenwärtigen Noblesse angegriffen. Unsere herkulische Jugend, sammt vielen Schönen schrie: allons! Stürmt die Bastille! Man fiel über den groben Orpheus her. Man schloss einen Kreis um ihn. Er musste niederknien und Abbitte thun. Das fand der übrige Chor der Söhne Apollos für ihre edle Kunst entehrend. Sie rüsteten sich die Schande ihres Kameraden zu rä-chen. Die Kellner und Hausknechte eilten ihnen zum Sukkurse herbei. Nun ward das Scharmützl allgemein. Alle klingenden Instrumenten wurden zertreten und zerschlagen. Die Silberlöffel der Kellner, und Flaschen, Gläser und Stühle flogen allenthalben herum. Endlich wurde diese komische Festung von der Uebermacht der Feinde erobert: die überwältigten Einwohner suchten sich mit der Flucht zu retten, und die Sieger giengen dann auch, nachdem sie die Verwüstung, die ihre Tapferkeit angerichtet, bewundert hatten, lachend auseinander.

24. Ich will Dich nun zum Hof Traiteur Jan führen, der in der sogenannten Himmelpfortgasse ein eignes, ziemliches artiges Haus hat dessen
erstes Geschoss ganz der Bewirthung seiner Gäste bestimmt ist. Es ist
ein langer aber sehr schmaler Saal, der eigentlich aus drey ehmaligen Zim-
mern gemacht ist. Die Bogen, die noch dort gespannt sind, wo einst die
Scheidewände standen, verengern den ohnediess schmalen Raum für die
Tänzer . . . Uebrigens ist der Saal sehr artic meublirt, mit Brillantlüstern
beleuchtet, die eine weit bessere Wirkung machen, als die ehmaligen
vergoldeten hölzernen Armleuchter, von denen ich immer fürchtete, ihre
Centnerlast möchte einmahl von der ziemlich niederen Decke auf die Tänzer herabfallen, und einige Paare todtschlagen. An den Saal stossen zu
beyden Seiten sehr hübsch eingerichtete Spiel und Souperzimmer.

In diesem Saale und den anstossenden Zimmer bewirthet der Hoftracteur
das ganze Jahr hindurch seine Gäste zu Mittag und Abends, und man
kann Dinérs und Soupers zu allen Preisen bestellen und haben.

25. Der Jahnische Saal endlich ist nicht hoch genug und auch zu schmal,
so dass er die Wirkung der Musik beschränkt, überdies fasst er höchstens
bis 400 Zuhörer.

26. Es ist auffallend, wie sie als eine Fremde sich ein Ansehen geben und
Anspruch zuf solche Vorzüge machen will, die man kaum inländischen
Dames von höhern Range zugestehen würde. . . .

Eben so wenig begreife ich, wie die Gräfin Hatzfeld und ihre sämtlichen
Dilletanten auf irgend einer Art herabgewürdiget werden können, wenn
sie sich . . . in einem der Hoftheater im Singen oder auf Instrumenten
hören lassen. Diese Herbeylassung würde vielmehr den allgemeinen
Beyfall erhalten.

Die Einnahme würde auch weit beträchtlicher seyn als in einem Redoutensaal, weil im ersten Falle alle Klassen der hiesigen Einwohner dazu
beytragen könnten; wo im Gegentheil bekannt ist, dass sich mehrere
Leute scheuen, bey einer musikalischen Akademien in dem Redoutensaale zu erscheinen.

27. 18 December 06. An Mlle Fischer in Berlin. Ueber Ihr Schreiben vom
29ten November hat die Hoftheaterdirection beschlossen, Ihnen einen
Jahresgehalt von Viertausand Gulden . . . und das Benefic einer
musikalischen Academie im grossen Redoutensaal gegen dem zu
bewilligen, dass Sie verpflichtet seyen, als prima Donna abwechselnd auf
den dreyen, unter der Leitung der Gesellschafts stehenden Theatern in
deutschen und italienischen Opern zu singen.

28. Die Aufführung war nicht vorzüglich: . . . Man muss aber auch gestehen, dass der ungeheure Redoutensaal der Musik sehr ungünstig ist; die letzteren im Saal können weder die Sänger verstehen, noch die Musik an leisern Stellen vernehmen. Ueberhaupt wird ein passender Konzertsaal für Wien noch lange ein frommer Wunsch bleiben.

29. Indess ist der grosse Redoutensaal mit seinen weiten Ecken der Musik nicht günstig und der Eindruck war ungleich grösser, welchen dies herrliche Meisterwerk im Theater an der Wien hervorbrachte.

30. 4 stimmigen Sing-Notturni, welche obwohl eigentlich nur mit Begleitung des Claviers gesetzt, wegen der Grösse des Platzes mit Harmonie Musik begleitet wird.

31. Doch bemerkt man, dass sich dort vielstimmige Stücke, Konzerten und Symphonien besser als einzelne Stimmen ausnehmen, welche der weite Saal zum Theil verschlingt.

CHAPTER FOUR

1. Herr und Madame Benda aus Ludwigslust sind seit kurzem hier in Wien angekommen und finden unter den Herrschaften viele Gönner und Freunde. Sie haben sich bey dem Fürsten von Kaunitz und bey der Gräfin von Bassewitz mit vielem Beyfall hören lassen, und werden nächtens ein öffentliches Concert geben.

2. Der Ueberbringer dieses Schreibe ist der k. k. Unterthan Anton Griesbacher, der eine Reise durch Deutschland nach London [macht] um sein musikalisches Talent geltend zu machen. Er spielt auf dem sogenannten Paridon mit vieler Fertigkeit und wünscht sich sowohl in öffentlichen Accademien als auch in Privat Concerten hören zu lassen. Ich ersuch demnach Eure ihm zur Erreichung dieser seiner Absicht best möglich behilflich zu seyn.

3. Der seiner besondern Geschicklichkeit wegen auf dem Violoncello zu spielen bekannte kleine Pohl von 9 Jahren hat die Ehre, einem hohen Adel seine mehrmalige Ankunft allhier wissend zu machen, und da er sich seit der Zeit seines letzten Hierseyns auf seinen Reisen durch Frankreich, Holland und das römische Reich weit stärker in seiner Kunst befestigt hat, so hofft er die Gnade zu geniessen, bey hohen Herrschaften sich produciren zu dürfen, und ist diesfalls nur in seine Wohnung im goldenen

Ochsen am neuen Markt Nr. 8 zu schicken, und die Stunde und der Ort zu bestimmen, wo und wann er aufwarten soll.

4. Eine allhier erst angekommene Musikgesellschaft bestehend aus dreyen Frauenzimmern und vier Mannspersonen, welche die hohe Erlaubniss erhalten sich aus Ton- und Instrumentalkunst in verschiedenen Arten, als mit buffischen Arien, Duetten, Terzetten und Finalien, in Particularhäusern hören zu lassen, tragt hiemit dem hohen Adel und einem geehrtesten Publiko seine gehorsamste Dienst an, mit der Versicherung, und in der schmeichelhaften Hoffnung einen allgemeinen Beifall zu erhalten.

Ihre Wohnung ist beym rothen Thurn Nro. 674 im zweyten Stock. Auf an sie geschenkene gnädige Anzeige wird selbe sogleich nach Verlangen erscheinen.

Es wird dem Ermessen der Heren Liebhaber gänzlich überlassen werden, die Belohnung nach Verdienst zu bestimmen.

5. Den 27ten haben wir Gesang und Tanz bey Fürst Auersperg gegeben in Gegenwart des allerhöchsten Hofs-kaiser. könig. Erz. . . . Fürst Auersperg gab der Gesellschaft 50 Ducaten zum vertheilen.

6. Die Erlaubniss zur Abhaltung musikalischer Akademien in öffentlichen Oertern wird einseitig von der Polizey ertheilt.

7. No. 218 Polizei Minister—9 Dez. 1802 zeigt an, dass dem Musiker Ferd. Franzl die Abhaltung einer musikalischen Akademie im Redoutensaale aus dem Grunde verweigert wurde, weil in der Adventzeit eine solche nicht stattfinden dürfe; dass sich über Baron Braun darüber äusserte, derlei Bewilligungen seien ihm contractlich zugesichert und nicht der Polizei anheimgestellet. Schliesslich wird um Weisung an Bar. Braun gebeten.

Expedirt—beantwortet an Polizei Ministerium, dass diese Angelegenheit zur Kenntniss Sr. Majestät gebracht worden ist, und Baron Braun angewiesen wird, kunftig alle derlei Gesuche zur Kenntniss der Polizei zu bringen. Die . . . Akademie darf stattfinden, aber erst nach 1 Uhr beginnen.

8. Mme Mozart a passé a ma porte pour me piver de venir demain a son Concert.

9. Die Bohdanovicz brachte Billet zum montägigen Accademie beym Jahn.

10. Karl brachte ihr einen Part, zum Armens Accademie am Dienstag und bat sie im Namen des Barons zu singen.

11. Zu Fuchs, wo wir von der heutigen sicher mangelhaften Aufführung der Cantate von Bethowen, Christus am Oelberg, sprachen, weil Braun im B. Th. mit beydm Orchester die Schöpfung zum Besten der Theater Armen giebt.

12. Dass Accombanement der übrigen Musicis kostete Me. Duschek 100 Thaler. Theure österreichische Musikanten. Wo es ehe bey unsern doch in Wahrheit höflichen Landsleuthen etwa 12 Dukaten gekostet hätte.

13. Bald nachher machte Th. die Toilette zum Jahn, wo sie ein Concert des Flötisten Bayr eine Arie von Cimarosa sang. . . . Dem Rotruff, Korn, Weibe, Gridl gab ich Billets dahin.

14. Obgleich H. ein braver Flötenspieler ist, so wollte doch sein Missgeschick, dass er nicht einmal die Unkosten herausbrachte,welches sonst Jahre lang keinem Künstler hier in Wien wiederfahren ist.

15. Heute kam Diego Somoriva, nach seiner um 12 Uhr Mittags gegebene Accademie im kleinen Redouten Saal, wegen Schulden ins Gefängniss.

16. 8 December 1800—zum Besten des Fonds vom niederösterreichischem Scharfschützerkorps: Der bestimmte Eintrittspreis ist ein Gulden; die Grossmuth kann nicht beschränkt werden.

CHAPTER FIVE

1. Sie gab durchaus Singstücke von Pär, Farinelli und Mayr. Schon dadurch, dass gar kein Instrumentalstück vorkam, wurde das Konzert eintönig.

2. Meine Neugierde auf das erste Stück, nähmlich auf die Symphonie von Rösner . . . wurde so zu sagen ganz unvermerkt befriedigt. Die Symphonie hat einen sehr sonderbaren Anfang, der aber gar nicht frappirt; denn was soll es für einen Effekt machen, wenn das ganze Haus in einem wohlbehaglichen Gemurmel begriffen ist, und nach dem gewöhnlichen Zeichen zum Anfangen (ich meine von Seiten des Direkteurs) der Anfang selbst in einem leisen Unisono der Violinen besteht. Man wusste nicht recht, ob noch einmahl gestimmt, präludirt, oder wirklich angefangen werde. Der Compositeur wird wissen, was für eine Idee ihm bei diesem Eingange vorschwebte. Mir fielen folgende Gedanken bei: Die Violinen (Viola, Violonzell und Violon mit eingerechnet) sind in Symphonien doch eigentlich die allgemeinen, mehr charakterlosen Bestand-

theile. Es sind die Bausteine, die alles tragen und verbinden. Die Man-
nichfaltigkeit, die Zierde der bestimmten Charakter wird zuvorderst durch
gehörige Benutzung und Vertheilung der Blasinstrumente her-
vorgebracht. Da nun aber die Symphonie bey uns schon eine bestimmte
Form, einen bestimmten Charakter hat, so ist es unbefriedigend, wenn
sie sich mit einem charakterlosen Anfang ankündigt. Meines Wissens hat
noch kein Tonsetzer seine Symphonie mit einem Unisono von Violinen
allein anfangen lassen, und zwar im Adagio.—Der Anfang soll zum Hören
einladen und auffordern. Diess geschieht entweder durch einen vollen
Akkord, oder durch ein reiches Unisono, oder durch eine interessante
aber etwas schnellere Melodie. Hr. Rösner könnte dem allen abhelfen,
wenn er vor seine Symphonie nur eine Note mit einem Ferma, entweder
einen Akkord von was immer für Instrumenten, oder ein Unisono von
allen setzen wollte.

3. Vorerst ein Quartett oder eine Symphonie, welche im Grunde als
nothwendiges Uebel angesehen, (man muss doch mit Etwas anfangen!)
und also verplaudert wird.

4. Das Konzert eröffnete sich mit einer Haydnschen Sinfonie, welche,
wie gewöhnlich die Anfangstücke der Konzerte, halb überhört wurde.

5. Des Orchesters im Theater am Kärnthnerthore habe ich schon erwähnt.
Das im Theater am Burgthore scheint mir fast noch vorzüglicher. Ich bin
sehr aufmerksam gewesen, nicht allein in Singspielen, sondern auch auf
die Symphonien zwischen den Akten, auf welche die Zuhörer
gewöhnlicherweise so wenig Acht zu geben pflegen.

6. Die Accademie der Mad. Margot dauerte ewig lange. Wir fuhren um
3/4 auf 11 Uhr nach Hauss und sie war noch nicht geendet.

7. Uibrigens ist die Einrichtung so getroffen, dass die ganze Akademie
um 2 Uhr geendigt ist.

8. Erste Abtheilung: Symphonie von Hrn. Capellmeister Rössler, davon
wurde nur das erste Stück—zwar gut ausgeführt, doch ohne Beyfall
aufgenommen. . . . Von einer Symphonie des Hrn. Ludwig van
Beethoven, B dur (Nr. 4) wurde nur das erste Stück—und das
schlecht—ausgeführt.

9. Ich schliesse diese Uebersicht . . . mit dem frommen Wunsche, dass
wir doch auch bei Schauspielen etwas anders, als die allerältesten Haydnschen Symphonien zu hören bekommen mögten. Zwar dürfte dies mit
einigen Mozartschen, Beethovenschen und Eberlschen schwer werden,

weil sie eine sehr genaue und studierte Exekution fordern, aber mehreren Proben würde es sich gewiss geben. Zudem könnten wohl die neuesten Haydnschen, die leichtern Mozartschen, Rombergschen u.s.w. auch wohl öfter vorgeführt werden.

10. Leztens aus einem Presto, betitelt die Jagd; dieses drückt, neben einem schönen Gesange, auch das Gebelle und Jauchten der Jagdhunde, das mittelmässige und stärkste Gemurmel der Bären in sehr komischer Komposition aus; nach dem Geschrey der Jäger aber geschehen zum Schlusse die sämmtlichen Schüsse der letzteren auf die Bären.

11. Warum will doch jeder ausübende Tonkünstler zugleich Componist seyn?

CHAPTER SIX

1. Ueberhaupt zwang das Ganze, sowohl, als das Arrangement, da das Orchester am gewöhnlichen Platz war, er aber auf der Bühne das piano forte quer stellt, und en Profil mit den Rucken gegen die Hof Loge sass. Zum Rechten und Linken sassen die Sänger und Chore.

2. Der Flügel dient hauptsächlich zum Accompagniren beim Gesang, zur Zusammenhaltung und Führung einer ganzen Musik, besonders bei Opern, und das eigentliche Tempo zu bestimmen.

3. So oft gesungen wird, hat ein Quer Fortepiano vorne am Orchester zu stehen welches zwey Stunden vor Anfang des Concerts gestimt wird.

4. Am selben Tage war Akademie im Hoftheater. Die Sinfonie von Rosetti aus D dur war eine Imitation von Haydns Sinfonie, die ich in Regensburg gehört hatte. Herr Umlauf dirigirte vom clavecin.

5. Auch spielte er die Chitarre recht artig, freilich kein Instrument, welches sich zu einem grossen Konzert gehört, es müsste denn als Erholung von den grossen Musikstücken angesehen werden.

6. Als Solostimme, und besonders als Konzertinstrument, kann sie nur die Mode rechtfertigen und schön finden.

7. Das Orchester darf seinen dermaligen Personal-Stand nicht überschreiten, denn seine Stärke und Güte hängt nicht von der grössern Zahl, sondern von der Fähigkeit seiner Mitglieder ab.

8. Seine Bewegungen . . . [müssen] noch stärker seyn, so dass er wegen Tempo und Takt oft mit dem Kopf, den Händen und Füssen arbeiten muss, ja, er ist nicht selten genöthigt, die Führung auf dem Flügel ganz zu unterlassen, um mit beiden Armen die Luft zu durchsäbeln. Freilich könnte man es für einen Misbrauch erklären, dass der Kapellmeister so holzhackermässig arbeiten muss; allein es ist nun schon einmal so unter uns eingeführt, und wir sind daran gewöhnt.

9. Hiezu ist ihm aber die einfache Stimme der ersten Violin nicht genug, sondern er muss die Partitur zu Hülfe nehmen, besonders wenn es ein Singstück ist.

10. Zuerst muss er sich auf sein Instrument verlassen können, er muss sicher seyn, dass es die übrigen an Stärke übertrifft. Allein dieses ist noch nicht genug, um 18 andere Violinen und so viele Stimmen mehr überschreien zu können, sondern er muss auch einen Arm haben, der mehr gilt, als die übrigen; das heisst, er muss bei einem deutlichen und kräftigen Vort.:age alle Vortheile seinem Instrumente und sich selbst ablernen, wodurch er seinen Ton, so viel als möglich, verstärken und durchdringen machen kann. Um bei dem Anfange des Stücks den übrigen die Bewegung recht deutlich und vernehmlich zu machen, hatte Pisendel die Angewohnheit, bei den ersten Takten in währendem Spielen die Bewegung mit dem Halse und Kopfe der Violin anzugeben. Waren es vier Viertel, die den Takt ausmachten, so bewegte er die Violine einmal unterwärts, dann hinauf, dann zur Seite, und wieder hinauf; waren es drei Viertel, so bewegte er sie einmal hinunter, dann zur Seite, dann hinauf. Wollte er das Orchester mitten im Stücke anhalten, so strich er nur die ersten Noten jedes Takts an, um diesen desto mehr Kraft und Nachdruck geben zu können, und darinnen hielte er zurück u.s.w. Ein jeder achtsamer Anführer muss beständig aufmerksam seyn, solche Vortheile zu finden, wozu ihm sehr oft verschiedene Vorfälle Gelegenheit geben, wenn er nur acht darauf hat.

11. In den Konzerten aber stehen Sänger und Instrumentisten gleich, und wenn auch die Orchestre nach hinten zu etwas erhöhet sind, und die Sänger vorn den Zuhörern näher stehen, so stehen sie doch auch tiefer, als die Instrumentisten. . . Man hört Arien ohne Gesang, höchstens Gesang ohne Worte.

12. Zu meinem Erstaunen (sagt Wranizky) hörte ich eine Sinfonie von meiner Composition und glaubte, dass die Musik gar nicht im Theater ist oder dass sie sehr schwach besetzt sei. Ich sah hin und sah eine Quan-

tität Menschen arbeiten: Woher mag das kommen? Der breite Platz, wo sonst das Orchester ist, der beste, weil er nahe an die Zuhörer und mehr im Theater ist, befand sich ganz leer, die übrige Maschine befand sich zu tief auf dem Theater, wo sich alles verschlägt und zu hoch, wo der Ton über das ganze Parterre fliegt. Ich fand ferner, dass die Violinen durch alle die Bässe, die alle voran stehen, gar nicht durchdringen konnten." Wranizky schlägt nun Abänderungen vor, worunter namentlich, dass der Raum des gewöhnlichen Theaterorchesters überbrückt werde, worauf dann vorne das Clavier und zu beiden Seiten die Solosänger und alle Choristen je 8 bei jeder Stimme, aufgestellt sein sollen.

13. Nachher wurden Saal und Gallerie zum drücken voll. . . . Dass ein Lichtenputzer vom Orchester herabfiel, Pülten und die Barrere mit sich hinab riess, machte Unterhaltung zum Vorspiel.

14. Der Saal ist sehr gut, aber das Orchester übel gestellt, (gerade in die Mitte ohne die mindeste Erhöhung).

15. Am 11 Uhr hatte Th. Probe von den 2 Arien welche selbe im Augarten morgen singen wird. . . . Am 5 Uhr kam Salieri, sie sang beyde Arien. Am 7 Uhr sang, oder probierte Th. etwas ihre Arien, dann fuhren wir . . . in Augarten. Es war ein schönes Concert. Th. sang mit vieler Kunst und grosserem Beifall.

Um 10 Uhr hatte Th. Probe von den 2 Arien, Schuppanzigh und Umlauf accompagnirten.

Th . . . und ich fuhren ins Augartenconcert.

16. Concert der Madame Mara im Redouten Saal. . . . Am 1/2 12 Uhr gingen wir zusammen zur Probe der Mara. Sie sang im Schlafrock, aber immer meisterhaft, doch ihre Jahre errinert uns sehr deutlich an das Gewesen. . . . Am 1/2 7 ging ich ins Concert.

17. Die Probe fing um acht Uhr Morgens an und von neuen Sachen, nebst dem Oratorium, wurden, ebenfalls zum erstenmal aufgeführt: Beethovens zweite Symphonie in D Dur, das Clavier-Concert in C moll und noch ein neues Stück, dessen ich mich nicht mehr erinnere. Es war eine schreckliche Probe und um halb drei Uhr waren Alle erschöpft und mehr oder weniger unzufrieden.

Fürst Karl Lichnowsky, der von Anfang der Probe beiwohnte, hatte Butterbrot, kaltes Fleisch und Wein in grossen Körben holen lassen. . . . Die Probe fing also wieder an. Das Concert begann um sechs Uhr, war aber so lang, dass ein Paar Stücke nicht gegeben wurden.

18. Die Musik wurde erst, ehe und während sich die übrige Gesellschaft versammelte durchprobiert.

19. Nachdem Klement beinahe bei jeder Passage beklatscht worden war, brachte er in die Fermate des letzten Stückes die Melodie aus Faniska an: "So glücklich ist auf Erden, Nun ausser mir kein Mann." Ein originell witzige musikalische Art dem Publikum zu danken.

20. In der ersten Symphonie wurde ein Stück da Capo gerufen und vom Orchester wiederholt. Nach dem Variazionen mit der Pedalfuge hielt das Publikum mit einem feurigen Handeklatschen so lang an, bis sich der Abt Vogler noch ein Mal ans Fortepiano sezte. Er wählte das hiesige Lieblingsstück aus seiner Oper 'Kastor und Pollux.'

21. Eine Sonate für Fortepiano und Waldhorn, komponirt von Beethoven, und gespielt von diesem und Punto so auszeichnete und so gefiel, dass, trotz der neuen Theaterordnung, welche das *Da Capo* und laute Applaudiren im Hoftheater untersagt, die Virtuosen dennoch durch lauten Beyfall bewogen wurden, sie, als sie am Ende war, wieder von vorn anzufangen und nochmals durchzuspielen.

CHAPTER SEVEN

1. Er gestand, dass er keinen zu nennen wisse, der einen guten Aufsatz machen könne, und er selbst habe den Grundsatz, so viel als möglich zu thun, und nichts davon zu reden.

2. Donnerstag den 20 März wird Herr Schindlöker die Ehre haben in dem k. k. Nationaltheater eine musikalische Akademie zu seinen Vortheil zu geben; wobey er sich auch mit seinem gewesten Scolaren, einem Delettanten, mit einem ganz neu dazu verfertigten Concerten auf dem Violoncello wird hören lassen. Er schmeichelt sich, den sowohl von einem hohen Adel, als auch verehrungswürdigen Publikum, ihme schon öfters gelegenheitlich ertheilten Beyfall, nicht nur allein zu erhalten, sondern auch aufgemuntert, durch Anlage, und fortgesetzten Fleiss, ihn wohl gar noch zu verdoppeln.

3. Konzert Anzeige. Herr Anton Eberl wird Freytag Abends den 6. Jäner im Saale des k. k. Hof-Traiteurs Jahn, ein grosses Konzert zu seinem Vortheile zu geben, und darin verschiedene ganz neue Stücke von seiner Komposizion aufzuführen die Ehre haben. Herr Calmus wird durch sein rühmlich bekanntes Talent zum Vergnügen des Publikums mitwirken,

und Fräulein v. Hohenadl, Herrn Eberl's Schülerinn, aus besonderer Gefälligkeit für den Unternehmer, mit Demselben ein ganz neues Doppel Konzert auf zwey Forte Piano spielen.

Das Nähere wird der Anschlagszettel am Tage des Konzertes selbst bestimmen.

Die Eintritts-Billete sind in Herrn Eberls Wohnung im Eisgrübel, nächst dem Peters-Platze Nro. 645 im vierten Stock von 8 bis 11 Uhr Morgens zu haben.

4. Musikalische Akademien. Gaben im k. k. Nationalhoftheater am 1. d. M. Hr. Mozart und am 4. Hrn. Ludwig Fischer, vormalige Sänger bei dem deutschen Singspiel des k. k. Nationaltheaters.

5. Die jüngst angekündigte musikalische Akademie zum Bessten der Verwundeten bey der k. k. Armee, wurde am 30 Januar d. J. zum grössten Vergnügen aller Zuhörer abgehalten; sie zeichnete sich eben so sehr durch geschmackvolle Wahl der Gegenstände, als durch die vollendetste Kunst in der Ausführung aus. Die edle Unternehmerin, Frau Christiana v. Frank, gebohrne Gerhardi, ärntete durch den so seltenen Vorzug ihres Gesanges die allgemeine Bewunderung ein. Herr v. Bethoven spielte auf den Piano Forte eine von ihm verfertigte Sonate, die vom Herrn Punto auf dem Waldhorn begleitet wurde. Beyde entsprachen ganz der Erwartung, welche das Publikum von diesen Meistern in ihrer Kunst hegte. Frau Galvani und Herr Simoni trugen ebenfalls durch ihren Gesang, so wie Herr Kapellmeister Pär und Herr Conti durch die Leitung des Orchesters zur Verherrlichung dieser Akademie bey. Endlich übernahm der grosse Hayden die Direkzion zweyer von ihm verfertigten Symphonien. Der Beyfall war allgemein. Die Einnahme betrug die ansehnliche Summe von 9463 Guld. 11 Kr., wobey Ihre Majestäten der Kaiser und die Kaiserin, dann die Königen von Neapel, so wie I.I. k. k. H. H. die Erzherzoge, dann der Herzog Albert die gewohnten Beweise Ihre Grossmuth wiederhohlten.

6. Besonders ist der Fagotist Hr. Schwarz ein ausserordentlicher Mann, wenigstens hat er mich entzückt und ich gestehe es gern, ich habe noch nichts Gleiches je von dem Fagot gehört.

7. Festgesezte Akademien giebt es keine, ausser jene vier, welche jährlich für den Wittwenfond der Musiker bestimmt sind. Diese waren vordem oft sehr schlecht; doch jezt, da P. Wranizky Sekretair dabey ist, hört man doch z. B. die *sieben Worte*, und die *Schöpfung* von Haydn. . . .

Dann sind gewöhnlich zwolf Musiken, im Augarten des Morgens, unter dem Nahmen Dilettanten-Musiken. . . . Jezt hat sie Hr. Schupanzig und jenes aufmunternde Auditorium ist ganz weg. Kein Liebhaber von *wahrer* Bedeutung mag sich mehr hören lassen; selbst die Musiker spielen nur sehr selten Konzerts. Ueberhaupt ist das Feuer für dies Institut ganz erloschen. Die Konzert werden selten gut akkompagnirt; die Symphonien aber gehen besser. Da der Zweck des Unternehmers jezt nicht sowohl mehr Liebe zur Kunst oder Vergnügen, als vielmehr sein Nutzen ist: so ist es, bey dem geringen Abonnement gar nicht möglich, etwas Namhaftes auf die Musik zu verwenden. Das Auditorium, wie es jezt gemeiniglich zusammen kömmt, ist zu wenig aufmunternd, zu wenig einladend. . .

Zufällige Akademien von reisenden Künstlern giebt es verhältnissmässig wenig, weil die Theater-Direktion selten, ohne grosse Verwendung, das Theater herleiht. Auch ist nicht eben viel dabey zu gewinnen. . . .

Im allgemeinen liebt man die Akademien hier nicht sehr, weil man schon zu oft getäuscht wurde, sowohl von fremden als einheimischen Spekulanten, worunter mancher brave Künstler leiden muss, wenn er nicht viel Protektion hat. Man erschwert ihm schon die Erlaubniss genug und dann sind noch die Kosten sehr bedeutend.

Festgesezte Privat-Akademien von Bedeutung giebt es keine mehr. . . .

Das Glück reisender Künstler liegt in den Händen dieser Dilettanten, die wahrlich zu wenig Kenntniss, aber oft viel Partheylichkeit besitzen. Erscheint der Fremde nicht bey jeder Einladung, schmeichelt nicht, findet lobpreisend überall Talent u.s.w., so muss er ein Mann von *grösstem* Ruf seyn, um *allenfalls* durchzudringen. Sollte es ihm einfallen hier bleiben zu wollen, so ist das ganze *Corpus musicum* sein Feind.

8. Ich weis nicht, ob in irgend einem Lande die Urtheile der Einwohner das einen Theils über die des andern, so verschiedenartig sind, als die Urtheile der südlichen und nördlichen Deutschen über einander. Es ist hier der Ort nicht diese Urtheile, wodurch beyde einander so oft Unrecht thun, im Einzelnen zu verfolgen: irre ich aber nicht, so nimmt der nördliche Deutsche von seinem südlichen Bruder als Grundlage seines Thuns und Treibens in der Regel an: er will bequem geniessen; und der südliche Deutsche vom nördlichen: er will mühsam grämeln. Was Musik betrifft, so gestehet das *gemeine* Vorurtheil des südlichen Deutschen dem nördlichen die Kritik zu, spricht ihm aber gern alles Uebrige, das entschiede, ab; das *gemeine* Vorurtheile des nördlichen Deutschen gestehet dagegen dem südlichen, regsamern Sinn für Musik und nicht unfeinen Takt besonders für das Singen zu, spricht ihm aber gern alles Uebrige, das

entschiede, ab. Dass diesen Urtheilen, wie allem Nationalen, *etwas* Wahres zum Grunde liegt, ist wohl eben so einleuchtend, als dass, wenn beyde diesen Urtheilen im *Einzelnen* folgen oder sie zum Prinzip *tiefer* gehender Beurtheilung machen wollten—beyde einander sehr oft Unrecht thun würden. Beyde sind Gemeinsprüche, und Gemeinsprüche sind nie über—höchstens bis an die grössere Hälfte wahr. Aber, irre ich mich nicht, so haben diese angeführten Gemeinsprüche in das Urtheil auch der gebildeten nördlichen und südlichen Deutschen nicht wenig Einfluss. Die nördlichen Deutschen führen ihre Sache schon selbst; ich will aber wenigstens einen Anfang machen zum Versuch, die Sache der südlichen Deutschen, und besonders der Wiener (da diese über das südliche Deutschland in Sachen der Kunst und des Geschmacks entscheiden) zu führen. Andere mögen dann fortfahren.

9. Uebersicht des gegenwärtigen Zustandes der Tonkunst in Wien.

Wenn man annehmen könnte, dass die Cultur der Tonkunst mit der Geistesbildung gleichen Schritt halte, so hätte man sehr Ursache, den Einwohnern dieser Hauptstadt Glück zu wünschen: denn wohl nirgends wird diese göttliche Kunst so ausgebreitet betrieben, so sehr geliebt, und so eifrig ausgeübt, wie hier; nirgends wird man unter den Liebhabern (Dilettanten) auf fast allen Instrumenten so viele vollendete Ausübende finden, deren manche sich den Professoren dieser Kunst an die Seite setzten dürfen, ja wohl einige sie sogar noch übertreffen. Die Tonkunst wirkt hier täglich das Wunder, das man sonst nur der Liebe zuschrieb: Sie macht alle Stände gleich. Adeliche und Bürgerliche, Fürsten und ihre Vasallen, Vorgesetzte und ihre Untergebenen, sitzen an einem Pulte beysammen, und vergessen über der Harmonie der Töne die Disharmonie ihres Standes. Dem ausübenden Musiker öffnen sich alle Palläste und alle Börsen, und der Komponist von einiger Bedeutung wird mit all der Auszeichnung behandelt, die er sich nur immer wünschen kann, was bey manchem dieser Herren sehr viel sagen will. Ausübung der Tonkunst ist hier zu einem stehenden und unentbehrlichen Artikel in der Reihe der Kenntnisse geworden, welche nur einigermassen vermögliche Eltern ihren Kindern lehren lassen. Man würde ersteren das Gegentheil als eine unverzeichliche Vernachlässigung in der Erziehung ihrer Familie anrechnen, und wirklich ist es eine Art von Seltenheit geworden, einen Jüngling oder ein Mädchen aus einem Hause des gebildeten Mittelstandes zu sehen, welchem diese Kunst fremd geblieben wäre. Das Geburtsfest der Eltern wird mit Musik gefeyert, und wenn diese ihren Kindern einen angenehmen Abend bereiten wollen, so geschieht es durch Musik. Keine

feyerliche Gelegenheit geht vorüber, die nicht durch diese Kunst verherr-
licht würde; und nur durch sie glaubt man seine Freunde und Verwand-
te ehren und vergnügen zu können.

In dieser grossen Residenz wird man wenige Häuser finden, in denen
nicht an jedem Abende diese oder jene Familie sich mit einem Violin-
Quartet, oder einer Klaviersonate unterhielte, und, Dank sey dem Apollo,
die einst so despotisch herrschenden Spielkarten darüber aus der Hand
gelegt hätte.

So viel jedoch für diese sogenannte Kammermusik gethan wird, so wenig
Gelegenheit biethet sich für das volle Orchester, für Simfonien, Conzerte,
Oratorien u. dar. Seit dem Tode des, um diese letztere Gattung Musik
so sehr verdienten Vice-Präsidenten v. Kees, ist in diesem Fache nichts
Solides, wenigstens nichts Dauerhaftes stabilirt worden. Zwar hat im
vorigen Jahre des Grosshändler von Würth grosse Conzerte gegeben, die
sowohl in Hinsicht der Auswahl als der Ausführung sich sehr vortheilhaft
auszeichneten; allein sie sind, man weiss nicht, aus welcher Ursache, nicht
weiter fortgesetzt worden. Ein paar spirituelle Conzerte, womit Herr Graf
v. Haugwitz im vorigen Jahre einer gewahlten Anzahl von Musik Ken-
nern und Liebhabern ein herrliches Fest bereitete, waren gleichsam nur
schnell vorübergehende Meteore. Die grossen Conzerte, die unter der
Direction und zum Vortheile des Herrn Schuppanzig, den Sommer hindurch wöchentlich des Morgens im Augartensaale aufgeführt werden,
kann man mit jenen des verstorbenen Hrn. v. Kees und des Grafen v.
Haugwitz nicht ganz in Vergleichung bringen, da hierbey weniger die
Beförderung des Geschmacks, als bloss des Vergnügens beabsichtet zu
seyn scheinet. Endlich glaubt man für die Aufnahme der Simphonie
wieder hoffen zu dürfen, als eine Gesellschaft angesehener und ver-
möglicher Musikfreunde zu Anfange dieses Winters, eine Anstalt unter
dem bescheidenen Titel Liebhaber-Conzert, bildete, die jeden Wunsch,
den man für die gute Sache hegen konnte, erfüllt zu sehen, hoffen liess.

. . . Ausser dieser Gelegenheit, die Musik im Grossen zu geniessen,
ereignet sich auch noch manchmal eine ähnliche Gelegenheit dadurch,
dass die Pächter der k. k. Hoftheater, mit der hier allgemein herrschenden
Humanität und Achtung gegen fremde durchreisende Künstler,
denselben den k. k. kleinen Redoutensaal überlassen, um das Publicum
mit ihrem Talente zu vergnügen. Endlich giebt, mit Erlaubniss Sr. Majestät, die Pensionsgesellschaft der Musiker-Wittwen alle Jahre im Advent und in der Fasten, jedesmahl zwey Conzerte zum Vortheile ihres
Fonds, welche von einem aus 200 Tonkünstlern bestehenden Orchester

aufgeführt werden, und deren Effect die Gesellschaft durch eine neu angebrachte kostspielige Resonanzkuppel, beträchtlich verstärkt hat; obschon diese Musiken übrigens durch eine minder glückliche Wahl der aufgeführten Compositionen, seit einiger Zeit am Werthe abzunehmen scheinen.

10. Sein Bruder der Fortepianist hat Schnelligkeit und in beyden Handen Kraft, es fehlt ihm aber noch jene Sicherheit und Präzision, auf welcher erst die vollendete Schönheit ruhen kann, und welche ihre wesentliche Grundbedingung bey jeder Kunst ist.

11. Es würde dem Publikum wenig Vergnügen bringen, wenn wir jedes unbedeutende Gekreisch mancher eingebildeten Virtuosen hier recensiren würden. Wir beschränken uns daher nur auf vorzügliche Produktionen, um bessern Gegenständen nicht den Platz zu rauben.

12. Die Chöre haben mitunter entsetzlich geschrien.

13. Madame Auernhammer spielte das Konzert von Beethoven im Ganzen nicht übel. Hie und da mehr Präzision, und besonders im Adagio mehr Ausdruck und Empfindung wäre sehr zu wünschen gewesen. An dem grossen Duo, von Stiebelt, das sie mit Demoiselle Auernhammer spielte, fand man ein besonderes Behagen. Bey den von ihr komponirte Variationen über ein Thema aus dem Prometheus von Beethoven, war zu bedauern, dass das Thema wenig Gesang hatte, also das Ganze, aus Mangel an klarer Einheit, mehr eine Fantasie glich. Man fand diese Arbeit gar nicht interessant. Hr. Veri, der Bassist, hat mich keineswegs bezaubert.—Eine ungeschlachte Tiefe, gezwungene Höhe, wenig Manieren machen seine Charakteristik aus. Vielleicht nimmt er sich alla camera besser aus.

14. Alle parteilosen Musikkenner und Freunde waren darüber vollkommen einig, dass so etwas Unzusammenhängendes, Grelles, Verworrenes, das Ohr Empörendes schlechterdings noch nie in der Musik geschrieben worden sey.

15. Mad. Auernhammer erhielt auch diessmal, wie alle Jahre, das k. auch k. k. Hoftheater zur der Produkzion ihres Konzertes von dem ihr besonders geneigten Herrn Theaterdirektor. Sie wählte unglücklicherweise van Beethovens grosses Konzert aus C moll, wovon sie die Partie mit der rechten Hand ziemlich geläufig herunter-hackte, mit der linken Hand aber stumm über die Tasten hin und her gleitete, ohne sie zu beruhren, und so hörten wir das erste Mal ein einhändiges Konzert auf dem Pianoforte.

16. Man fand . . . einzelne Stellen sehr schön, doch das Ganze zu gedehnt, zu kunstreich im Satz und ohne gehörigen Ausdruck, vorzüglich in den Singstimmen. Der Text von F. X. Huber schien eben so flüchtig gearbeitet, als die Musik.

17. B's Musik war im Ganzen gut, und hat einige vorzügliche Stellen, besonders that eine Arie des Seraphs mit Posaunen begleitung vortrefliche Wirkung, und in dem oben angeführten Chore [des Kriegsknechte . . . Wir haben ihn gesehn] hat Hr. v. B. gezeigt, dass ein Tonsetzer von Genie selbst aus dem schlechtesten Stoffe etwas Grosses zu machen im Stande ist.

18. Ich bemerke nur jene Stücke, die noch nicht gegeben wurden oder wo ein Fortschreiten des Talents sichtbar ist.

19. Fräulein Kurzbök spielte ein Mozartsches Klavierkonzert aus C dur mit jener Delikatesse, Anmuth und Zierlichkeit, die man an ihrem Vorträge so sehr liebt, welchen etwas mehr Schatten, Sicherheit und Kraft zum Vortrefflichen erhöhen könnten.

20. Den Geschmack in der Musik beherrschen hier die Italiäner. . . . So gelang es Marchesi, durch ewige Schnörkel und Triller den herzergreifenden Vortrag seine grossen Vorgängers Crescenti vergessen zu machen. Brizzi thut es Marchesi so viel möglich in Schnörkeln nach: bei ihm bleibt keine Note ungehudelt; und das ist denn der wahre Gesang!

21. Madam Campi, die im Messias die Sopranstimme sang, hat wenig Sinn und Verstand dadurch verrathen, dass sie Hendels hohe Simplicität und feinen edlen ernsten Ausdruck durch Schnörkeln und Rouladen verbessern wollte. Es war nicht gut, das sie dafür beklatscht wurde, man hätte ihr vielmehr seinen Unwillen zeigen sollen.

22. Eine Arie von Mozart sollte von Mad. Campi gesungen werden: wegen plötzlicher Unpässlichkeit übernahm dieselbe Dem. Fischer. Es war die schöne Arie aus *Clemenza di Tito*: Parto! mit obligater Clarinette. Dass man es nicht lassen kann, ein Kleid von ächtem Goldstoff noch mit Flittern zu bebrämen! Dem. Fischer, diese mit Recht geschätzte, brave Künstlerin, nehme doch ja nie bey einer solchen Mozartschen Arie die gewöhnlichen italienischen Schnörkeleyen zu Hülfe; denn es ist für den Kenner sehr unangenehm, so ein Kunstwerk nicht in seiner gediegenen Klarheit geniessen zu können.

23. Die Sängerinn der Altstimme hat unstreitig mit dem grossen Sinn und Verstand gesungen, der dem erhabenen Gegenstande angemessen war.

Die andern drey haben wohl gefühlt, dass hier keine Theaterkadenzen und Arabesken am Ort sind; diese vernünftige Enthaltsamkeit hat sie aber vielleicht veranlasst, die übrigen Mittel des Nachdrucks, die Schattirungen des Forte und Piano, die deutlichere Aussprache der Worte u.s.w. etwas zu vernachlässigen.

24. *Leopoldstadt*. Hier treibt Herr Wenzel Müller sein Unwesen nach wie vor. Wie Pilze schiessen ihm die neuen Opern auf. Ist und bleibt irgend ein Komponist unerschöpflich, so bleibt er es; denn jeder neue Ländler bietet ihm ja ein Thema zu einer neuen Arie an. Er giebt der Sache nun das gehorige Wasser—einige verbrauchte Figuren u. dgl. jezt noch Trompeten und Pauken dazu, und der Satz ist fertig, mag ihn der Held oder der Trossbube vorzutragen bekommen.

25. Nie ist wohl ein erhabener, und poetischer Stoff so gemein und prosaisch in einem Oratorium weggekommen, als hier der Fall ist.

26. Auch in der Leopoldstadt wurde Haydns Schöpfung zum Vortheil der Choristen gegeben. Dlle. Eigenwahl, Herr Pfeiffer und Herr Blacho (!) hatten die Hauptstimmen übernommen, und sangen sehr gemein.

27. Mad. Auernhammer war des Konzertes nicht mächtig genug, sie spielte mit zu wenig Sicherheit und Präcizion.

28. Aber auch hier fehlte es an Ausdruck, Schnelligkeit, und vornehmlich an jenem Geiste im Vortrag, der durch kein ausgeschriebenes forte und piano bezeichnet wird, und der dem Virtuosen (in seinem Innern vorausgesetzt, was vorauszusetzen ist) nur durch klare und tief empfundene Ansicht des auszuführenden Kunstwerks zukommen kann.

29. Madame Auernhammer hatte ein volles Haus, wenn gleich ihr Klavierspiel sehr gegen die jetzige Stufe der Kunst zurückgeblieben ist.

30. Mad. Auernhammer spielte ein Mozartsches Klavierkonzert auf ihre gewöhnliche Weise— nicht ohne Geschwindigkeit, aber ohne Ausdruck und Präcision.

31. Mad. Auernhammer gab im Hoftheater ein Concert bei vollem Hause. Sie spielte das Mozartsche Clavierconcert aus D Moll, aber wer den Geist dieser Composition kennt (Referent hört es von Mozart selbst vortragen) konnte unmöglich mit Mad. Auernhammers Ausführung zufrieden seyn. Sie nahm alle Tempos zu langsam, oder rallentirte gerade die brillanten und feurigen Stellen, weil sie nicht Präcision und Sicherheit genug hat. Möchten doch alle Virtuosen, die sich hören lassen wollen, vorher Gö-

thes Spruch wohl überdenken: Nur aus vollendeter Kraft strahlet die Anmuth hervor.

32. So war ich . . . Zeuge des ausserordentlichen Effekts, den das . . . Klavierquartett von Eberl hervorbrachte, welches jetzt beinahe von allen unsern guten Klavierspielerinnen studiert wird, unter denen Fräulein Hohenadel durch Stärke, Präcision, Feuer und Richtigkeit einen der ersten Plätze behauptet.

33. Fräulein Hohenadel . . . gehört jetzt unstreitig unter unsre besten Klavierspielerinnen, und wird an Geschwindigkeit, Leichtigkeit, Stärke und Feinheit wohl sehr wenig Nebenbuhlerinnen, selbst in Wien finden, wo doch ein Beethoven, Eberl, Hummel, eine Kurzbök und Spielmann leben, die gewiss eine sehr hohe Stufe der Kunst erreicht haben.

34. Sie [gehört] unter die stärksten Violinisten (Männer mit eingerechnet) . . . und [besitzt] eine Kraft des Bogens, eine Sicherheit und Stärke selbst in den höchsten Tönen und eine Präzision des Vortrags, welche sie des allgemeinsten Beyfalles vollkommen würdig machen.

35. Mad. Gerbini, . . . deren ausserordentliche Kraft des Bogens, deren Stärke in Passagen und Schwierigkeiten für ein Frauenzimmer beynahe bis zum Unglaublichen geht.

36. Heute gab der berühmte Herr Chevalier Mozart eine musikalische Academie zu seinem Antheil im Nationaltheater, in welcher Stücke von seiner ohnehin sehr beliebten Compositionen aufgeführt wurden. Die Academie war mit ausserordentlich starken Zuspruch beehret, und die zween neuen Concerte und übrigen Fantasien, die Hr. Mozart auf dem Forte Piano spielete, wurden mit dem lautesten Beyfall aufgenommen. Unser Monarch, der die ganze Academie, gegen seine Gewohnheit, mit seiner Gegenwart beehrte, und das ganze Publicum ertheilten denselben so einstimmig Beyfall, dass man hier kein Beyspiel davon weiss. Die Einnahme der Academie wird im Ganzen auf 1600 Gulden geschätzt.

37. Das Merkwürdigste, was sich mit dem Theater zutrug, ist die Anstellung des grössten Genies, das unser Jahrhundert in der Tonkunst aufzuweisen hat, Herrn Wolfgang Mozart in kaiserliche Dienste.

38. Die vorkommenden Stücke bestande dann aus zwey Symphonien, von denen aber die erstere aus dem Grunde mehr Werth als die letztere hat, weil sie mit ungezwungener Leichtigkeit durchgeführt ist, während in der zweiten das Streben nach dem neuen und Auffallendern schon mehr sichtbar ist. Uebrigens versteht es sich von selbst, dass es beiden

an auffallenden und brillianten Schönheiten nicht mangelte. Weniger gelungen war das folgende Konzert aus C Moll, das auch Hr. v. B. der sonst als ein vorzüglicher Klavierspieler bekannt ist, nicht zur vollen Zufriedenheit des Publikums vortrug.

39. Den ersten Theil eröffnete die grosse heroische Symphonie von L. van Beethoven No. 3. Etwas über den Werth dieses kunstreichen und colossalen Werkes zu sagen, wäre hier überflussig.

40. Indessen kann man, wie bekannt, über Beethovensche Kompositionen selten beym Erstenmale ein bestimmtes Urtheil fällen, deshalb verspare ich auch, etwas weiteres über dies Concertino zu sagen, bis wir es mehrmals gehört haben.

41. Man spielt gewöhnliche Violin-quartetten von Haydn, Mozart, Beethoven, oder Romberg, zuweilen auch von Wranitzky.

42. im Ganzen unbedeutend; besonders musste es hier also erscheinen, wo man Mozartische, Eberlische und Beethovensche Klavierkonzerte gewohnt ist.

43. Die Sinfonieen waren von Haydn, Mozart, Beethoven und Eberl.

44. Seit den Mozartschen, Haydnschen und Beethovenschen Sinfonieen ist wol nichts in dieser Gattung erschienen, das sich so ehrenvoll jenen zur Seite stellen könnte.

45. Bis jetzt sind Quartetten von Mozart, Haydn, Beethoven, Eberl und Romberg gegeben worden.

46. Nebst diesen Kompositionen und mehreren Beethovischen, erhalten sich Mozarts, Haydns, Clementis Meisterstücke noch immer in ihren Rechten.

47. Sie [dastand] in Gesellschaft der übrigen Meisterstück eines Mozart, Haydn, Eberl, Beethoven, Righini, Cherubini u.a. die man sonst hier hörte, wie die Krähen unter den Pfauen.

48. Man . . . hört die berühmtesten Musikwerke grosser Meister, eines Haydn, Mozart, Beethoven, Righini, Cherubini, u.a. sehr gut aufführen.

49. Die Musiken bei Herrn von Würth . . . haben . . . durchaus nur die grössten musikalischen Meisterwerke eines Mozart, Haydn, Eberl, Beethoven u.a. . . . im vollen Glanze einer schönen und gelungenen Ausführung gezeigt.

50. Der unsterbliche Mozart, ein Haydn, Beethoven, Cherubini, alle diese Männer durchdachten seine Werke, und schöpften Kraft und Leben aus ihnen.

CHAPTER EIGHT

1. Merkwürdig ist die Tagesordnung der Stadt, merkwürdig, wie die verschiedenen Menschenklassen ihre Geschäfte betreiben, den Mässiggang fröhnen, und von früh Morgens, bis spät in die Nacht die Zeit tödten.— Von sechs bis sieben Uhr früh, sieht man die männlichen und weiblichen Domestiken in die Kirchen zur Messe wandern, und ihr Frühstück in den Caffeehäusern einnehmen. . . . Um sieben und acht Uhr kommen die Landleute mit ihren Produkten, und die Kreuter- Geflügel- Obst- und Milchweiber breiten ihre Waaren auf den Märkten aus, wo die Einkäufer, Köche, Köchinnen, die Weiber der Geringen Bürger und niedern Canzleibeamten, sich zu ganzen Schaaren einfinden; hier hört man, wie in der Halle zu Paris, die kreitschenden widrigen Accente der Marktweiber, die eine ganze Tonleiter von Schimpfwörtern im österreichischen groben Dialekt herschworen, um diese Zeit sind die Strassen mit Korn, Holz, Fleisch, und andern Fuhrwerken angefüllt, die vom Lande, oder aus den Vorstädten vor die Bedürfnisse des Stadters, der nach der Ruhe pflegt, sorgen. Nach acht Uhr kommen aus den Vorstädten, theils die Krämer, Fabrikanten, Künstler und Handwerker, die Buden und Gewölber in der Stadt haben, theils die niedern Canzleibeamten, das grosse Heer der Accesisten, Protokollisten, Ingrossisten, Concipisten und andern — isten, und — anten Protokollanten, Registranten, Auscultanten, und wandern erst im Vorbeigehn in die Caffee und Weinhäuser, und dann in die Canzleien auf das Rathhaus, und die Mauth.—Nach neun Uhr rollen die Carossen mit den Präsidenten und Räthen nach den Canzeleien, Justizstellen und andern Collegiis.—Die bürgerliche andächtige Matrone geht, oder führt mit ihren Töchtern in die Messen zum heilige Stephan, St. Peter und zu den Schotten, anstatt die vornehmen Damen sich erst allmählig gegen 10 und 11 Uhr aus den Betten erheben. Die Caffeehäuser sind um diese Zeit, mit Leuten aus allen Ständen angefüllt, welche die Zeitungen lesen, Handel und Wandel treiben. Von 1/2 12 Uhr bis 12 geht die schöne und galante Welt in die stille Messe zum heil. Michäl, Stephan u.a.: Die Stuzzer halten ihre Parade auf dem Graben und Michälerplaz, machen ihre Toiletsvisiten und halten verstohlne Rendezvous in den heiligen Hallen. Zwischen 12 und 1 Uhr,

macht die hohe Noblesse mit allen die ihr angehören, dazu auch die Stuzzer und Schooshunde gehören, eine Spazierfarth im Prater, ein anderer Theil vom Mittelstande spaziert bei schönem Wetter im Frühlinge und Herbst auf der Bastei, und ein grosser Theil eilt zu den Garküchen, die so lieblich entgegen dampfen.— Der Bürger und Handwerksmann speiset um 12 Uhr, der Mittelstand, so wie der Geschäftsmann um 1 Uhr, der Adel um 2, ja der höchste, erst um 3 Uhr, und der Staatskänzler Fürst Kauniz, erst um 5 Uhr. Ganz stille wird es daher auf den Strassen nicht, denn wenn ein grosser Theil in den Speisehäusern sich befindet, so sucht ein anderer Theil sich erst durch Bewegung den Appetit zu verschaffen, den er durch ein gutes Frühstück gestillt hat, und wiederum ein anderer Theil sucht die Verdauung durch schwarzen Caffee zu befördern. Manche aus dem Geschlecht der Nimmersatten, eilen in verschiedene Speisehäuser, versuchen ein Gericht nach dem andern, und es ist nicht selten, dass jemand um 12 Uhr in einer Garküche die erste, und um 2 Uhr mit eben so starken Appetit, die zwote Mahlzeit zu sich nimmt. Um drei Uhr gehen die Dicasterianten inferioris Ordinis, an ihre Geschäfte, denn die Herren der obern Ordnung, ruhen von der Bürde des Tages bei der vollen Tafel aus. Nach vier Uhr rollen die Wagen im Sommer, nach Baden, Schönbrunn, u.—um fünf Uhr ist die grosse Praterallee mit den Carossen des Adels angefüllt, der nach dem Lusthause sich erhebt, die Fussgänger aus allen Ständen, sitzen in den Buden und Zeltern, die im Prater in grosser Zahl stehen, und geniessen gebackene Händel, Würste u. Wein, Bier, Caffee, Punsch, Limonade, Eis u. a. Zwischen sechs und sieben Uhr ist das Getöse in den Strassen am grössten.—Die Herrschaften kommen zum Theil von den Spazierfarthen zurück, zum theil eilen sie in die Theater, Concerte, Assambleen und Bällen.—Die Canzleibeamten suchen Erholung, die Kaufleute, Krämer und Handwerker schliessen ihre Läden, ein grosser Theil von ihnen, so wie von der arbeitenden Volksklasse eilt nach seinen Wohnungen, in die Vorstädte zurück, ein Theil der Andächtigen in verschiedener Bedeutung holet sich den Seegen der zwischen 4 bis 6 in allen Kirchen ertheilt wird, ein anderer Theil der Lüsternden sucht Azung, postirt sich am Graben, und schleicht den Nimpfen nach, welche die Pantomine ihres Gewerbes geschickt zu spielen wissen. Nach sieben Uhr, bis gegen neun, ist es in den Strassen am ruhigsten. Die Wagen fahren einzeln, die Theater sind voll, die Wein- Bier- und Caffeehäuser fassen das Heer der Durstigen, Spielenden und Mässigen; liebende Paare wandeln im Mondschein, in einsamen Gassen, statt auf den Plätzen, der bekannte Gott in der Gesellschaft der Faunen und Bachantinnen sein Umwesen theoretisch und praktisch treibt. Um neun Uhr erhebt sich das Getöse von Wagen, und Fussgängern von neuen, die Theater schliessen sich, die Zuschauer eilen in die Speisehäuser, und Tabagien, im Winter sind um 10 Uhr die Häuser geschlossen, der Sommer macht eine Ausnahme, doch sind um 11 Uhr die Strassen einsam, und es herrscht eine Stille in dieser kleinen Welt, ausgenommen im Fasching, denn da daurt das Fahren die ganze Nacht durch, und die Fussgänger kommen erst gegen Morgen aus der Redoute, und den Tanzsälen, und man sieht schlafende Gruppen in den Caffeehäusern. Dieses wäre ein Gemälde der Tagesordnung und welchen Stoff liefert dasselbe, dem Menschenbeobachter, der alle Dinge nicht nach dem äussern Schein, sondern nach ihrer wahren Gestalt beurtheilt, der weise Britte hatte dahero wohl Recht. Ueberall herrscht Zeitvertreib, des Menschen höchster Wunsch; Spielen ist leben—und ist es dann noch ein Spielwerk zu sterben?

2. Der Mann von dieser Beschreibung und in dieser Lage wird einen Theil seines Vormittags auf dem Zimmer mit Lesen zubringen. Er erholt sich dann durch den Anblick einer heitern und freyen Scene ausserhalb seines Hauses, athmet frische Luft auf den Wällen der Stadt, oder macht gelegentlich einen grössern Spaziergang in den Prater, den Augarten, oder weiter in die freye, schöne Natur, die Wien umgibt. Die schöne Aussicht und die trockenen Kiesgänge von Belvedere stehen ihm immer offen, so wie die Gemähldesammlung, die einen ewigen Schatz von Unterhaltung anbiethet. Zur Abwechselung durchwandert er einige Gärten, oder macht eine Fahrt auf ein nahe gelegenes Dorf. Bald werden ihn die Fahrzeuge auf der Donau, bald ein geschäftiges Heer von Menschen auf den Ausladungsplätzen anziehen. Hier verweilt er bey einem neuen Baue, dort bey den Anlagen, die man in einem der Gärten macht, die jedermann offen stehen. Ist er Liebhaber der Literatur und Kunst, so wird ihn bald ein neues Product in den Buchläden, bald ein Werk der verschiedenen Künstler unterhalten, das er unter ihren Händen hervor gehen sieht. Hier wird eine neu angekommene Kunstsammlung aufgestellt, dort hat man kürzlich einige Gemählde erhalten. Dieser ladet ihn ein, die schönen Ausgaben zu sehen, die er eben aus London und Paris bekommen hat, jener kündiget ihm eine Vermehrung seiner Kupferstiche an. Zur Abwechselung geht er gelegentlich auf die Kaiserliche Bibliothek, liest eine Stunde in irgend einem Werke, das er sonst nirgends findet, oder lässt sich eine Seltenheit geben, die er lang nicht gesehen hat. Nebenher hat er irgend einen Freund zu besuchen, mit diesem oder jenem Frauenzimmer eine halbe Stunde zu verplaudern.—Schon naht die Stunde der Mahlzeit heran; er eilt sich zu

kleiden, und noch wird er in den Gassen aufgehalten, wo diese oder jene neue Erfindung, irgend ein vorzüglich gut gearbeitetes Stück, oder ein geschmackvolle Tändelely an den Fenstern der Kaufmannsläden ihn anzieht. In seinem Speisehause findet er eine wohl zubereitete Mahlzeit und eine Gesellschaft, von der einige durch langen Umgang seine nähere Bekannte geworden sind. Er hört die Neuigkeiten des Tages, und daneben liegen, zur Abwechselung, einige Zeitungen.—Oder er ist in eine Familie versprochen, wo ihn eine reicher besetzte Tafel und das freundliche Gesicht der Eigenthümer zu Genuss und Freude einladen.

Allmählich kommt der Abend heran! Aber er hat noch einige Besuche in Familien zu machen, wovon der weibliche Theil immer um diese Stunde zu Hause ist.—Nun hat er die Wahl, ob er im Schauspiele das neue Stück sehen, eine neue Oper hören, oder in eins der Concerte gehen will, die in so vielen Häusern häufig gegeben werden, und wohin der Zutritt so leicht ist.—Oder soll er den ganzen Abend bey einer Thee- und Spielpartie zubringen, oder vorher auf eine Stunde in jene Assembleen gehen, wo man bey Zeiten sich versammelt und wo man nicht zu bleiben gehalten ist?—Gelegentlich geht er in ein Haus, wo wenig oder gar nicht gespielt wird, und findet eine angenehme Unterhaltung, die eben darum geistreich ist, weil sie ohne Ansprüche geführt wird, und weil man sie verlässt, so bald man sich ermüdet fühlt.

3. Eine von den willkommensten Vergnügungen dieser Stadt sind die Abendgesellschaften. Sie werden vom höchsten Adel an, durch alle Classen herunter, bis zum wohlhabenden Bürger gegeben. Sie sind hauptsächlich in den Wintermonathen gewöhnlich, vom November an bis zu Ende der Fasten. . . Im Winter fangen sie um 7, im Sommer um 8 Uhr an, und dauern bis um 10 Uhr. In einigen Häuser gibt man sie dreymahl die Woche, in andern zweymahl, auch wohl nur alle 14 Tage einmahl; in sehr wenigen alle Tage. Die Unterhaltung dabey ist verschieden: in einigen muss alles spielen; in andern spielt wer will; in einigen wird Musik gemacht; in andern getanzt; wieder in anderen vertreibt man den Abend bloss mit freundschaftlichem Gespräche. Alle diese Gesellschaft sind gemischt; es erscheinen Witwen, Frauen und Mädchen dabey, und von Männern aus allen Ständen: Beamte, Geistliche, Gelehrte, Soldaten, Künstler, Bürger u.s.w.; die Gesellschaften von höherem Adel ausgenommen, wo man bloss mit seines Gleichen umgeht.

4. Einige Familien des zweyten Adels zu Wien leben auf einen Fuss, der manchen des ersten wenig nachgibt und andere übertrifft. Mehrere derselben haben, so wie jene, öffentliche Tage, an denen ein Jeder, der

ein Mahl eingeführt ist, uneingeladen erscheinen kann. Ja est ist eine Höf-
ichkeit und ein Zeichen von Achtung, nicht mehrere dieser öffentlichen
Abende hingehen zu lassen, ohne sich wenigstens zu zeigen. Auch sie
geben gelegentlich Mittagsmahlzeiten, wozu denn auch die Fremden
geladen werden, die entweder bey ihnen eingeführt, oder besonders emp-
fohlen worden sind.

5. 27 Jan. Dela au Concert de Me de Buquoy. Il y fesoit chaud, je puis
du froid en mertant l'escalier et tous sois horriblement.

22 Feb. Puis au Concert du Pce Galizin, ou je vis Me du Buquoy.

23 Feb. Le soir a 7 h au Concert de la Storace. No. 11. du Theatre de la
porte de Carinthie, premiere etage a gauche. Bonne loge, mes tapis firent
bon effet. Le Pce Lobkowitz jouit aussi moi paye. Le Duo dela Cosa rara
fut repetee trois fois, un air de bravourie qu'elle chant a un peu emmyeux.
Son compliment allemand tisé des equvoci feroit un joli air. Donne le bas
a Me d'Auersburg.

2 Mar. Le soir au Concert ou la musiciens de l'Empereur jouerent toute
la Cosa rara, dans la musique fit un effet charmant.

5 Mar. Diné chez les Furstenberg avec le Prince de Weilburg, le B. Dunger,
le Pce Oettingen, le Cte Oettingen et Sekendorf. Petit concert apres le
diner. Me de Furst. joua du clavecin et la B. D. et les deux Oettingen
du violon.

10 Mar. Le soir au Theatre dela porte Carinthie ou j'entendis chanter Con-
cioline et jouer du clavecin le jeune Schudel.

14 Mar. Le Soir au Theater dela porte Carinthie. Concert de Ramm. Son
hautbois me plut, dans un morceau il imitoit le chalimeau. La voix de
Mlle Nani ni celle de Me Lang ne me plurent gueres.

16 Mar. Le soir au Concert de Christian Fischer l'auteur du fameux
menuet, se hautbois au servis du roi d'angleterre. Il tire des sous biens
doux, bien pars, bien souterns, bien difficiles de cet instrument, mais le
choix de la musique, toute angloise et francoise ne plut pas. Me de la
Lippe ne fut toute affligée. . . .Me d. A. au Theatre avec le Prince Lobk.

26 Mar. Le soir chez le Pce Adam Auersperg au Concert de Hayden sur
les 7 paroles de notre Signeur sur la croix. La seconde du Paradis la der-
nière du Fevrier soupir me punct bien experimee. J'etois dans la loge avec
Me de Kinsky, de Rothenhahn, et de Buquoy et ne vis pouit ma belle
qui etoit un parterre.

29 Mar. Diné chez le Pce Schwarzenberg avec les Chotek, les Clary, Me

de Hoyos, Me de Trautmannsdorf et sa fille, Cobenzl. Joli diner Me de Clary jolie musique dela Cosa rara divinement rendire par les instruments a vent.

5 Apr. Diné chez le Prince de Paar avec Me de la Lippe et son frere et le Comte Auersberg. . . .Apres diner Callenberg jouer du clavecin et chanta des airs franzois comme un ange.

10 Apr. Me de Hoyo eut la bouté de m'envoyer son piano forte pour que Me de Callenberg put se faire intendre apres le diner. Il dine chez moi les Clary, les Hoyos, Me de Buquoy, les Lippe, ma belle soeur, Marschall et Callenberg, qui souffroit du sa migraine . . . demandu un sal a pie et nous chanta apres le diner la chanson de *hortense,* ma paisible indifference est elle un mal, est elle un bien. *Elle est un bien*! Et puis de Zelie amour je ne veux plus. Et une allemande. die Schuen welche gleichgültig blieb.

11 Apr. Diné chez les Manzi avec les Lippe, Callenberg et les Khevenhuller. Callenberg y joua du clavecin et chanta en allemand. Hilf mir geliebte zu werden. die leichte Kunst zu linden weis ich schon.

12 Apr. Diné, chez le Pce Galizin avec les Hoyos, les Clary, Me de Thun et Caroline, le Baron Pellegrini, Lamberg, M. Littleton, les generaus Braun, Renner, Clerfayt, Comaschini, chantre de colhambre del Im. de Russie, et Righini, le maitre de chapelle. Comaschini chanta d'abord apres le diner.

15 Apr. Diné chez les Schwarzenberg avec les Lippe, Callenberg, les Kalb, on joua la musique dela Cosa rara.

28 Apr. Dela a la Comedie Allemande. Fini la soirée chez l'amb. de Venise, ou il y avoit de jolies dames et de la musique. Mlle Schewel pinca la harpe. La Morichelli chanta seule, puis Mlle Victoria de Fries. Ensuite elles chanterent ensemble le joli duo dela Sarola de Gelosi.

5 May. Diné, chez la Psee Schwarzenberg avec la marquise et Joseph Colloredo. On joua la Cosa rara.

7 May. Le soir chez Me de Starhemberg. . . . Elle [Me de Clary] me chanterant de jolies chansons francoises. La *bouve foiest ma chimere* avec une musique de Callenberg. *Plaisirs d'amour* ne durent q'un instant, chagrin d'amour durent tout la vie avec une musique de Me d'Ursil.

8 Sep. Dela au Concert d'une demoiselle *Catoni* qui est jolie et chanta fort mal. La *Morichelli* chanta en perfection un air del'olympiade. *Piangendo parti.*

23 Dec. Le soir au Concert des veuves.

APPENDIX ONE

1. 24 Feb 87. Kapellmeister Kloffter. 1) eine zweychörige Overture, bestehend aus einem Allegro, Andante, Flauto, Solo und Presto, macht den Prolog zur Battaille, dann folgt, 2) der Eingang, oder die ernsthafte u. schreckbare Musik vor dem Marsch beider Armeen. 3) die Avantgarde rückt vor, und die Husaren flankiren, man hört auch einige Musketen und Kanonenschüsse. 4) verschiedene Märsche der beiden Armeen, zwischen welchen einige Musketen und Kanonenschüsse abwechseln. 5): a) die Bewegung der beiden Armeen zum anmarschiren, begleitet von der Kanonade auf beiden Seiten. b) das Pelotonfeuer der Infanterie von beiden Seiten; c) der Sturm und Vernichtung der feindlichen Armee; d) der letzte Angrif mit Musketenfeuer auf die erste feindliche Linie; e) die Eroberung der Redoute 6) ein Ungewitter, das zwischen beiden Armeen einen Stillstand macht, endet die erste Abtheilung. Zweite Abtheilung: 7) der Kriegsrath der einen Armee: ein begleitetes Recitativ, Violino Solo. 8) Zeichen zum Angriff für die Kaballerie. 9) der Angriff selbst: a) der Trapp der Pferde; b) der Galopp; c) Geschrey der Kavallerie; d) das Gerausch der Waffen. 10) die Flucht der Feinde. 11) die überwundene Armee blässt zum Rückzug, und setzt sich wieder. 12) Zeichen zum abermaligen Angriff für die Kavallerie der siegenden Armee. 13): a) der Trapp der Pferde; b) der Galopp; c) das Geschrey der Kavallerie; d) unordentlicher Lärm beider Armeen. 14) die siegende Armee bläst zum Rückzug, nachdem das feindliche Battaillon sich wohl vertheidigt hat. 15) die Husaren flankiren noch, und man hört noch einige Nachschüsse. 16) der Vorgang und die Einleitung zum Verbinden der Verwundeten. 17) die Empfindung vor der Verbindung. 18) das Klagen und Seufzen der Verwundeten bei der Verbindung, Oboe Solo. 19) Victoria! ein dreimal wiederholtes lebhaftes Allegro, zwischen welchem ein Siegesfeuer von Musketen und Artillerie gemacht wird. 20) verschiedene Märsche machen den Beschluss der Battaille und das End der zweiten Abtheilung. Nach einer kleinen Pause werden alsdann noch einige Flötenkonzerte für eine Principalflöte und für zwey Concertantflöten von der Komposition des Kapelldirektor Kloffter gemacht; zuletzt folgt eine Sinphonie in zwey Chören mit Paucken und Trompetten, in welcher im ersten Stück das Echo angebracht ist. (WZ 17 Feb 87:378)

2. 14 Jan 92. Francesco Vicaro von Navara. Nach geendigten Stücke wird Hr. Francesco Vicaro von Navara, ein Blinder Künstler, auf dem Flauto dolce, und andern von ihm selbst erfundeten blasenden Instrumenten,

... einem glatten Moosrohr, einer kleinen Kürbisschaale, und einer kleinen doppelten Flaute, sich hören zu lassen die Ehre haben. Er wird verschiedene Stücke und Konzerte sowohl allein, als mit Begleitung zweyer Violinen, und mit der ... kleinen Flaute Prim, Sekond, den Bass und den Fagott spielen; nebst dem wird er mittels die Musik sprechen, und durch das Rohr ein wirkliches, und natürliches englishes Horn vorstellen. (VIENNA-ONB-TS)

3. 8 Apr 02, Bohdanowicz family. Zur Beförderung der ausserordentlichen Musik über die Hermanns-Schlacht von Klopstock bestehend aus dreyen abgesönderten Orchestern, und eben solchen dreyen Vocal-choren. Erste Hauptfrage. Wer hat wohl je in Deutschland, ja selbst in Europa solch' ein ausserordentliche Musik gehört?

Zur Beförderung der vorhabenden Reise der musikalischen Familie Bohdanowicz durch Deutschland und Italien, wo der schöne Zweck des Familien-Vaters einzig dahin gehet, seine 8 Kinder zu guten musikalischen Weltgliedern auszubilden, und als solche dann ihrem deutschen Vaterlande, oder vielmehr ihrer geliebten Mutterstadt Wien zum Opfer zurückzuführen. Zweyte Hauptfrage. Ist nicht solch' eine grosse seltene Reise von so einer so zahlreichen Familie anerhört? . . . *Le trame deluse*

Dritte Frage. Wer hat jemals ein solches Meisterstück von 8 leiblichen Geschwistern irgendwo gehört?

Eine Violin Sonate, genannt: Les premices du monde, welche nur auf einer einzigen gewöhnlichen Violine von 3 Personen mit 12 Fingern, und 3 Violin-Bögen gespielt wird.

Vierte Frage. Wer hat solch' eine sinnreiche musikalische Composition (ausser in Wien) jemals in Europa gehört? . . . . "Caro mio bene" mit sehr starken Variationen und Passagen, die dem geneigt horchenden Publico sein Staunen entlocken werden. . . .

Neuestes Original, betitelt, Rarité extraordinaire de la Musique. Ein Andantino mit 4 Variationen auf ein Fortepiano für 4 Personen gesezt, das ist, für 8 Hände oder 40 Finger, welches durch die 4 leiblichen Schwestern der Familie Bohdanowicz ausgeführt wird.

Sechste Frage. Hat man wohl jemals 4 Personen, und zwar 4 leibliche Schwestern irgendwo (ausser in Wien) auf einem Forte piano spielen gehört? . . . Anna Bohdanowicz

Siebente Frage. Wer hat wohl je eine seltnere, schönere, und stärkere Contra-Alt-Stimme gehört?

Europas Erstling, ein Original-Terzett-Konzert, welches mit Naturinstru-

menten ausgeführt wird, die in der musikalischen natürlichen Spaäre den
2ten Range einnehmen, wovon das Singen im 1sten und das Pfeifen im
2ten Range sich verhält. Dieses ernsthafte grosse Terzettkonzert bestehet
aus 265 vier-Viertal-Noten begleitet von ganzen Orchester mit Trompeten
und Pauken, hat 6 grössere und kleine Solo's, davon führen meine drey
ältern Söhne die Prinzipalstimmen. Ihre soli bestehen fast aus allen Arten
Passagen, Ligaturen, Stocatto, Trillern, Manieren, u.s.w. Besonders
zeichnet sich die Kadenz davon mit 3-stimmigen Trillern aus.

Achte Frage. Wo hat man jemals eine solche Seltenheit von drey
Gebrüdern (ausser in Wien) ausführen gehört?

Ein doppeltes Original a Quadro, welches aus 120 Takten bestehet, betitelt
Non plus ultra, wird von meinen 4 Töchtern gesungen und von mir selbst,
sammt meinen 3 ältern Söhnen, folglich von 4 Personen mit 4 Violinbögen
und 16 Fingern auf einem einzigen Violin-Griffblatte gespielet werden.

Neunte Frage. Welcher Musik-Kenner muss nicht den Titel dieser aussero
deutlichen sinnreichen Erfindung bekräftigen? . . . Rondo

Zwischen dem ersten und zweyten Abtheilung der Akademie wird eine
Vocal-Sinfonie ohne Text von neun Singstimmen, ohne und eben so
vielen mit Sprachröhren von verschiedner Grösse mit ausnehmet gutem
und besonderm Effekte ausgeführt werden. Sie bestehet aus einem
Allegro, welches sehr lärmend von dem 18 stimmigen Chore abgesungen
wird; dann aus einem Andante, welches sich öfters in 3 Chöre, als einen
sichtbaren und 2 unsichtbare, die ein doppeltes Echo vorstellen, theilet.
Auch charakterisirt dieses Andante sehr lustig das Geschrey der
erschrockenen Hähner, die beym Erblicken ihres Feindes, Habichts, bald
zusammenlaufen und bald sich wieder zerstreuen, ingleichen werden die
Guguke und Baumhacker (Waldvögel) möglichst nachgeahmt. Leztens
aus einem Presto, betitelt die Jagd; dieses drückt, nebst einem schönen
Gesange, auch das Gebelle und Jauchzen der Jagdhunde, das mittelmässige und stärkste Gemurmel der Bären in sehr komischer Komposition aus; nach dem Geschrey der Jäger aber geschehen zum Schlusse
die sämmtlichen Schüsse der leztern auf die Bären. Fünfte Frage. Wer
hat eine solche Vokal—NB nicht Instrumental-Sinfonie ohne Text, von
solcher Laune, solcher Charakteristik, und solcher im höchsten Grade
lustig unterhaltenden, sinnreichen Komposition u.s.w. in Europa jemals
gehört, die auch dem tiefsinnigsten Pedanten sein lächeln anzuzwingen
vermag? (AMZ 21 Apr 02:494-96)

4. 26 Mar 04. Abbé Vogler. Die Anrufung der Sonne um Mitternacht in
Lappland, von Ascerbi, e Terzettohne Begleitung.

521

Impromtü des sterbenden Metastasio, als Hymne bearbeitet, vorgesungen von einer Stimme, wiederholt vom Chor.

Lob der Harmonie, vom Prof. Meisner, nach der Melodie vorgetragen vom Singchor und von Variazionen des Instrumentalchors begleitet. Overtüre zu Kozebues 'Kreuzfahren,'' wo der Marsch Karls des 12ten bei Narva und ein ächtes barbareskes, von dem Abt selber in Afrika notirtes Lieblingsstück zusammen treffen, und die Uebereinstummung des Ritter Balduin und des Emus zu schildern. Das Benedictus, aus der Messe von A. Vogler, als Quartett von 4 Singstimmen ohne Begleitung.

Israels Gebet zu Jehova, aus dem 84ten Psalm Davids nach Moses Mendelssohns Uebersetzung, eine kleine Kantate, die mit einer vom englishen Horn begleiteten Bravourarie, wo nach andre Solo's und der Chor eintraten, schloss.

Ein nordisches Lied, mit Variazionen, vom Fortepiano und einer Pedal Fuge, gespielt vom A. Vogler.

Bibliography

ALLMANACH 1782
Allgemeiner Theater Allmanach vom Jahre 1782. [Vienna]: Joseph Gerold, 1782.

ALMANACH 1774
Almanach des Theaters in Wien. Vienna: Joseph Kurzböck, 1774.

AMZ
Allgemeine Musikalische Zeitung (Leipzig), 1798-1811.

Antonicek/FESTSAAL
Antonicek, Theophil. *Musik im Festsaal der österreichischen Akademie der Wissenschaften.* Veröffentlichungen der Kommission für Musikforschung. Edited by Erich Schenk, no. 14. Vienna: Herman Böhlaus Nachf., 1972.

Arndt/BRUCKSTUECKE
Arndt, Ernst Moritz. *Bruckstücke aus einer Reise von Baireuth bis Wien im Sommer 1798.* Leipzig: Heinrich Gräff, 1801.

Arndt/REISEN
_____. *Reisen durch einen Theil Teutschlands, Ungarns, Italiens und Frankreichs.* 4 vols. Leipzig: Heinrich Gräff, 1804.

Bauer/WIRTH
Bauer, Carl. "Er war . . . kein guter Wirth." *Acta Mozartiana* 25 (April 1978): 30-53.

Bauer, A./WIEN
Bauer, Anton. *150 Jahre Theater an der Wien.* Zurich, Leipzig, and Vienna: Amalthea Verlag, 1952.

Bauer, W./BRIEFE
Bauer, Wilhelm, ed. *Briefe aus Wien.* Oestereichische Bibliothek, no. 20. Leipzig: Insel-Verlag, [1900].

Becker/KRITIKER
Becker, Carl Ferdinand. "Mozart und die Kritiker seiner Zeit." *Acta Mozartiana* 27 (February 1980): 15-19.

Bernhardt/VAN SWIETEN
Bernhardt, Reinhold. "Aus der Umwelt der Wiener Klassiker: Freiherr van Swieten (1734-1803)." *Der Bär* (1929-30): 74-164.

Bertuch/BEMERKUNGEN
Bertuch, Carl. *Bemerkungen auf einer Reise aus Thüringen nach Wien im Winter 1805 bis 1806.* 2 vols. Weimar: Im Verlage des Landes-Industrie Comptoirs, 1808.

BESCHREIBUNG 1808
Neueste Beschreibung der kais. kön. Haupt- und Residenzstadt Wien. Vienna: Binzischen Buchhandlung, 1808.

Biba/CONCERT LIFE
Biba, Otto. "Concert Life in Beethoven's Vienna." In *Beethoven Performers and Critics: The International Beethoven Congress, Detroit, 1977.* Edited by Robert Winter and Bruce Carr. Detroit: Wayne State University Press, 1980.

Biba/HAYDN ORATORIEN
_____ ."Beispiele für die Besetzungsverhältnisse bei Aufführungen von Haydns Oratorien in Wien zwischen 1784 und 1808." *Haydn Studien* 4 (May 1978): 94-104.

Biba/KONZERTWESEN
_____ . "Grundzüge des Konzertwesens in Wien zu Mozarts Zeit." *Mozart-Jahrbuch* (1978/79): 132-43.

Biba/LIEBHABER
_____ . "Beethoven und die 'Liebhaber Concerte' in Wien im Winter 1807/08." *Beiträge '76-78: Beethoven-Kolloquium 1977: Dokumentation und Aufführungspraxis.* Edited by Rudolf Klein. Kassel: Bärenreiter, 1978, pp. 82-93.

Biba/MUSIZIEREN
_____ . "Geselliges Musizieren rund um Wien." *Wiener Figaro* 43 (January 1976): 8-18.

BL
Beethoven, Ludwig van. *The Letters of Beethoven.* 3 vols. Collected, translated, and edited by Emily Anderson. London: Macmillan Co.; New York: St. Martin's Press, 1961.

BMZ-REICHARDT
Berlinische Musikalische Zeitung. Edited by Johann Friedrich Reichardt, 1805-06.

BMZ-SPAZIER
Berlinische Musikalische Zeitung. Edited by Carl Spazier, 1794.

Böck/KHEVENHUELLER
Böck, Ludwig, ed. *Zur Geschichte des Theaters am Wiener Hofe. Aus den Tagebüchern des Fürsten Joseph Khevenhüller-Metsch.* Vienna: Moritz Perles, 1896.

Brosche & Maier/BURGTHEATER
[Brosche, Günter and Maier, Elisabeth.] *Musik im Burgtheater.* Vienna: Oesterreichische Nationalbibliothek, 1976.

Burney/PRESENT STATE
Burney, Charles. *The Present State of Music in Germany, the Netherlands and United Provinces.* London, 1775; facsimile ed., New York: Broude Bros., 1969.

Burney/TOUR
_____ . *Dr. Burney's Musical Tours in Europe.* Vol. 2: *An Eighteenth-Century Musical Tour in Central Europe and the Netherlands.* Edited by Percy H. Scholes. London: Oxford University Press, 1959.

CHARACTERISTIK
Vertraute Briefe zur Characteristik von Wien. Vienna: Heimsdorf und Anton, 1793.

Cloeter/TRATTNER
Cloeter, Hermine. *Johann Thomas Trattner.* [Vienna]: Wiener Bibliophile Gesellschaft, 1952.

COLLOQUIUM
"Colloquium des Zentralinstitutes für Mozartforschung über Probleme der instrumentalen Aufführungspraxis Mozarts und seiner Zeit (1968): II. Fragen der Besetzung und der Direktion des Orchesters." *Mozart-Jahrbuch* (1968-70): 35-37.

Cramer/MAGAZIN
Cramer, Carl Friedrich. *Magazin der Musik.* Hamburg: In der musikalischen Niederlage I (Jan-June 1783); II/2 (1786).

Croll/QUELLEN
Croll, Gerhard. "Neue Quellen zu Musik und Theater in Wien 1758-1763," in *Festschrift Walter Senn zum 70. Geburtstag*. Edited by Erwald Fässler. Munich and Salzburg: Emil Katzbichler, 1975.

Croll/SCHWARZENBERG
_____ . "Mitteilungen über die 'Schöpfung' und die 'Jahreszeiten' aus dem Schwarzenberg-Archiv." *Haydn-Studien* 3 (April 1974): 85-92.

Czerke/WIEDEN
Czerke, Felix. *Wieden*. Wiener Bezirksführer, no. 4. Vienna: Jugend und Volks Verlags, 1981.

Deutsch/CURRENCY
Deutsch, Otto Erich. "Austrian Currency Values and Their Purchasing Power." *Music & Letters* (July 1934), pp. 236-38.

Deutsch/DOKUMENTE
_____ , ed. *Mozart: Die Dokumente seines Lebens*. Kassel: Bärenreiter, 1961.

Dittersdorf/AUTOBIOGRAPHY
Dittersdorf, Karl Ditters von. *The Autobiography of Karl von Dittersdorf dictated to his son*. Translated by A. D. Coleridge. N.p., 1896; reprint ed., New York: Da Capo, 1970.

Eibl/DOCUMENTA
Eibl, Joseph Heinz, ed. *Mozart Documenta: Addenda und Corrigenda*. Kassel: Bärenreiter, 1978.

Engerth/MOZART
Engerth, Rüdiger. *Hier hat Mozart gespielt*. Salzburg: Salzburger Nachrichten Verlags, 1968.

Fellerer/MOZART-KRITIK
Fellerer, Karl Gustav. "Zur Mozart-Kritik im 18./19. Jahrhundert." *Mozart-Jahrbuch* (1959): 80-94.

Fétis/BIOGRAPHIE
Fétis, [François] J[oseph]. *Biographie Universelle des Musiciens*. 10 vols. Paris: Librairie de Firmen Didot Frères, Fils et Cie., 1860-80.

Fischer/REISEN
Fischer, Jul. Wil. *Reisen durch Oesterreich, Ungarn, Steyermark, Venedig, Böhmen und Mähren in den Jahren 1801 und 1802*. 3 vols. Vienna: Anton Doll, 1803.

Flotzinger & Gruber/MUSIKGESCHICHTE
Flotzinger, Rudolf and Gruber, Gernot. *Musikgeschichte Oesterreichs.* 2 vols. Graz: Verlag Styria, 1979.

FM
Der Freimüthige (Berlin), 1803-06, 1808-09.

Forbes/BEETHOVEN
Forbes, Elliot, rev. and ed. *Thayer's Life of Beethoven.* Princeton, N.J.: Princeton Univ. Press, 1969.

Forkel/ALMANACH
[Forkel, Johann Nikolaus.] *Musikalischer Almanach für Deutschland.* Leipzig: Schwickertschen Verlag, 1782, 1783, 1784, 1789.

Forster/TAGEBUECHER
Forster, Georg. *Georg Forsters Tagebücher.* Edited by Paul Zincke and Albert Leitzmann. Deutsche Literaturdenkmäle des 18. und 19. Jahrhunderts, no. 149. Berlin: B. Behr's Verlag (Friedrich Feddersen), 1914.

Friedel/BRIEFE
Friedel, Johann. *Briefe aus Wien verschiedenen Inhalts an einen Freund in Berlin.* 2nd ed. in 2 vols. Leipzig and Berlin: n.p., 1784.

Geiger/TASCHENBUCH
Geiger, Franz. *Taschenbuch des Leopoldstädtertheaters, oder genaues Verzeichniss der in dem k. k. privil. Marinellischen Schauspielhause vom 1ten Christmonats 1784 bis Ende des Wintermonats 1785, gegebenen Schauspiele.* Vienna: Mathias Andreas Schmidt, [1785].

Geiger/VERZEICHNISS
_____ . *Richtiges Verzeichniss der gegebenen Schauspiele in dem kais. königl. privil. Marinellischen Schauspielhause in der Leopoldstadt vom ersten Jänner bis Ende November des 1784sten Jahres.* Vienna: Mathias Andreas Schmidt, [1785].

Gerber/ALTES LEXIKON
Gerber, Ernst Ludwig. *Historisch-Biographisches Lexikon der Tonkünstler.* Leipzig: Breitkopf & Härtel, 1790-92; reprint ed. edited by Othmar Wessely. Graz: Akademische Druck- u. Verlagsanstalt, 1977.

Gerber/NEUES LEXIKON
_____ . *Neues Historisch-Biographisches Lexikon der Tonkünstler.* Leipzig: A. Kühnel, 1812-14; reprint ed. edited by Othmar Wessely. Graz: Akademische Druck- u. Verlagsanstalt, 1966-69.

Gill/VIOLIN
Gill, Dominic, ed. *The Book of the Violin*. New York: Rizzoli, 1984.

Gleich/WTA
Gleich, Joseph Alois. *Wiener Theater Almanach auf das Jahr 1807, 1809*. Vienna: Jos[eph] Riedl, [1808, 1810].

Gluck/CORRESPONDENCE
Gluck, Christoph Willibald. *The Collected Correspondence and Papers*. Edited by Hedwig and E. H. Müller von Asow. Translated by Stewart Thomson. London: Barrie Rockliff, 1962.

GM
Grätzer Merkur, 1780.

Gugitz/BIBLIOGRAPHIE
[Gugitz, Gustav.] *Bibliographie zur Geschichte und Stadtkunde von Wien*. 5 vols. Vienna: Touristik Verlag, 1947.

GYROWETZ BIOGRAPHIE
Biographie des Adalbert Gyrowetz. Vienna: Mechitharisten-Buchdruckerei, 1848.

Hadamowsky/AKADEMIEN
Hadamowsky, Fr[anz]. "Leitung, Verwaltung und ausübende Künstler des deutschen und französischen Schauspiels, der italienischen ernsten und heiteren Oper, des Ballets und der musikalischen Akademien am Burgtheater (Französischen Theater) und am Kärntnerthortheater (Deutschen Theater) in Wien 1754-1764." *Jahrbuch der Gesellschaft für Wiener Theaterforschung* 12 (1960):113-33.

Hadamovsky/HOFTHEATER
_____ . *Die Wiener Hoftheater (Staatstheater) 1776-1966. Teil 1: 1776-1810*. Veröffentlichung der österreichischen Nationalbibliothek. Neue Folge, 1:4. Vienna: Georg Prachner Verlag, 1966.

Hadamowsky/LEOPOLDSTADT
Kataloge der Theatersammlung der Nationalbibliothek in Wien. 3 vols. Vienna: O. Höfels Wwe, 1934. Vol. 3: *Das Theater in der Wiener Leopoldstadt 1781-1860*, by Franz Hadamowsky.

Hanslick/CONCERTWESEN
Hanslick, Eduard. *Geschichte des Concertwesens in Wien*. Vienna: Wilhelm Braumüller, 1869.

Hanson/BIEDERMEIER
Hanson, Alice M. *Musical Life in Biedermeier Vienna*. Cambridge Studies in Music. Cambridge, London and New York: Cambridge University Press, 1985.

Hanson/INCOMES
_____. "Incomes and Outgoings in the Vienna of Beethoven and Schubert." *Music & Letters* 64 (July-October 1983): 173-82.

Harich/HAYDN-ORCHESTRA
Harich, Janos. "Das Haydn-Orchester im Jahr 1780."*Haydn Yearbook* 8 (1971): 5-52.

Harpner & Landon/ADELSSITZEN
Harpner, Stefan and Landon, H. C. Robbins, ed. "Die Musik auf den Adelssitzen rund um Wien." *Haydn Yearbook* 10 (1978).

HARVARD-GUMPENHUEBER
Harvard University Library. Boston, Massachusetts. Manuscript. Gumpenhüber, Philippe. [Repertoire de tous les spectacles qui ont ete donnes au Theatre de la Ville.] 4 vols. 1758, 1759, 1761, 1763.

Haydn/CCLN
Haydn, Joseph. *The Collected Correspondence and London Notebooks*. Translated and edited by H. C. Robbins Landon. London: Barrie & Rockcliff, 1959.

HAYDN ZEIT
Joseph Haydn in seiner Zeit: Eisenstadt 20. Mai - 26. Oktober. Edited by Gerda Mraz, Gottfried Mraz, Gerald Schlag. Eisenstadt: Amt der Burgenländischen Landesregierung, [1982].

Heartz/JADOT
Heartz, Daniel. "Nicolas Jadot and the Building of the Burgtheater." *The Musical Quarterly* 68 (January 1982): 1-31.

Hennings/BURGTHEATER
Hennings, Fred. *Zweimal Burgtheater*. Vienna: Kremayr & Scheriau, 1955.

Hiller/NACHRICHTEN
Wöchentliche Nachrichten und Anmerkung die Musik betreffend. Edited by Ferdinand Hiller. Leipzig, 1766-70.

Hofbauer/WIEDEN

Hofbauer, Karl. *Die Wieden mit den Edelsitzen Conradswerd, Mühlfeld, Schaumbergerhof und dem Freigrunde Hungerbrunn.* Vienna: Karl Gorischek's k. k. Universitäts-Buchhandlung, 1864.

Holschneider/BACH

Holschneider, Andreas. "C. Ph. E. Bachs Kantate 'Auferstehung und Himmelfahrt Jesu' und Mozarts Aufführung des Jahres 1788." *Mozart-Jahrbuch* (1968-70): 264-80.

IB

Intelligenzblatt der Annalen der Literatur und Kunst in den österreichischen Staaten (Vienna), 1803-05, 1807-11.

Jahn/MOZART

Jahn, Otto. *W. A. Mozart.* 4 vols. Leipzig: Breitkopf & Härtel, 1856-59.

Jahn-Abert/MOZART

Jahn, Otto, rev. and ed. *W. A. Mozart by Hermann Abert.* 6th ed. in 2 vols. Leipzig: Breitkopf & Härtel, 1923-24.

JOURNAL

Journal Kept During a Visit to Germany in 1799, 1800. Edited by the Dean of Westminster. London: Savell & Edwards, [1861].

JOURNAL DER MODEN

Journal des Luxus und der Moden (Weimar), 1788-92.

Kellner/KREMSMUENSTER

Kellner, Altman. *Musikgeschichte des Stiftes Kremsmünster.* Kassel: Bärenreiter, 1956.

Kelly/REMINISCENCES

Kelly, Michael. *Reminiscences.* London: Colburn, 1826; reprint ed. edited by Roger Fiske. London: Oxford University Press, 1975.

Khevenhüller-Metsch/TAGEBUCH

Khevenhüller-Metsch, Johann Josef. *Aus der Zeit Maria Theresias. Tagebuch des Fürsten Johann Josef Khevenhüller-Metsch,* vol. VIII (1774-80). Edited by Maria Breunlich-Pawlik and Hans Wagner. Vienna: Adolf Holzhausens Nfg., 1972.

Kirchner/ZEITSCHRIFTEN

Kirchner, Joachim, ed. *Bibliographie der Zeitschriften des deutschen Sprachgebiets bis 1900.* Stuttgart: Anton Hiersemann, 1969.

Klein/AUGARTEN
Klein, Rudolf. "Musik im Augarten." *Oesterreichische Musikzeitschrift* 26 (May-June 1973): 239-48; 28 (September 1973): 397.

Klein/BEETHOVEN
———. *Beethovenstätten in Oesterreich.* Vienna: Verlag Elisabeth Lafite, [1970].

Klein/JAHN I
———. "Der Saal des Ignaz Jahn." *Acta Mozartiana* 3 (November 1970): 51-57.

Klein/JAHN II
———. "Ein Alt-Wiener Konzertsaal: Das Etablissement Jahn in der Himmelpfortgasse." *Oesterreichische Musikzeitschrift* 28 (January 1973): 12-18.

Klemm & Heufeld/THEATRALKALENDAR
[Klemm, Christian Gottlob and Heufeld, Franz.] *Theatralkalender von Wien.* 3 vols. Vienna: n.p., 1772-74.

KOMMERZIALSCHEMA 1780
Der kaiser. königlichen Residenzstadt Wien Kommerzialschema. Vienna: Joseph Gerold, 1780.

KOMMERZIALSCHEMA 1789
Wienerisches Kommerzialschema oder Bürger-Allmanach. Vienna: Joseph Gerold, 1789.

KOMMERZIALSCHEMA 1798
Wienerisches Kommerzialschema oder Auskunfts- und Geschäfts-buch für Inländer und Fremde. Vienna: Joseph Gerold, 1798.

Komorzynski/FREIHAUSTHEATER
Komorzynski, Egon. "Sänger und Orchester des Freihaustheaters." *Mozart-Jahrbuch* (1951): 138-50.

Kramer/MOZART
Kramer, Uwe. "Wer hat Mozart verhungern lassen?" *Musica* 30 (1976): 203-11.

Krauss/VERZEICHNISS 1786
Krauss, Joseph. *Vollständiges Verzeichniss der National-Schauspiele und Besetzung . . . welche in beiden k. k. Hoftheatern . . . im Jahr 1785 aufgeführt worden sind. Nebst einen Anhang von musikalischen Akademien.* Vienna: n.p., 1786.

Krauss/VERZEICHNISS 1787
Krauss, Joseph. *Vollständiges Verzeichniss der National Schauspiele und Besetzung, auch italienischer und deutscher Singspiele, welche in beiden k. k. Hof-Theatern . . . im Jahre 1786 aufgeführt worden sind. Nebst einem Anhang.* Vienna: n.p., 1787.

Küttner/REISE
Küttner, Carl Gottlob. *Reise durch Deutschland, Dänemark, Schweden, Norwegen und einen Theil von Italien, in den Jahren 1797, 1798, 1799.* 2nd revised ed. 4 vols. Leipzig: Georg Joachim Göschen, 1804.

Küttner/WANDERUNGEN
[Küttner, Carl Gottlob.] *Wanderungen durch die Niederlande, Deutschland, die Schweiz und Italien in den Jahren 1793 und 1794.* 2 vols. Leipzig: Voss und Kompagnie, 1796.

Kunz/ALMANACH
Kunz, F. C. *Almanach der k. k. National-Schaubühne in Wien auf das Jahr 1788.* Vienna: Joseph Gerold, [1789].

Landon/BEETHOVEN
Landon, H. C. Robbins, comp. and ed. *Beethoven: A Documentary Study.* London: Thames & Hudson, 1970.

LANDON/C & W
_____ . *Haydn: Chronicle and Works.* 5 vols. Bloomington and London: Indiana University Press, 1976-80.

LANGE BIOGRAPHIE
Biographie des Joseph Lange. Vienna: Peter Rehms sel. Witwe, 1808.

Leux-Henschen/KRAUS
Leux-Henschen, Irmgard. *Joseph Martin Kraus in seinen Briefen.* Stockholm: Svenskt Musikhistoriskt Arkiv, 1978.

Matthew/CONCERTS
Matthew, James E. "The Antient Concerts, 1776-1848." *Proceedings of the Royal Music Association* 33 (1906-07): 55-79.

MB
Mozart, Wolfgang Amadeus. *Briefe und Aufzeichnungen.* 7 vols. Collected and edited by Wilhelm A. Bauer and Otto Erich Deutsch. 4 vols. Kassel: Bärenreiter, 1962-75.

MEINUNGEN
Die Meinungen der Babet. Eine Wochenschrift (Vienna), 1774.

Messner/WIEDEN
Messner, Robert. *Die Wieden im Vormärz.* Vienna: Verlag der wissenschaftlichen Gesellschaften Oesterreichs, 1975.

Michtner/BURGTHEATER
Michtner, Otto. *Das alte Burgtheater als Opernbühne.* Theatergeschichte Oesterreichs 3:1. Vienna: Hermann Böhlaus Nachf., 1970.

ML
Mozart, Wolfgang Amadeus. *The Letters of Mozart and His Family.* Translated and edited by Emily Anderson. 2nd ed. by A. Hyatt King and Monica Carolan. London: Macmillan; New York: St. Martin's Press, 1966. Used by permission.

Mörner/SILVERSTOLPE
Mörner, C. G. Stellan. *Johann Wikmanson und die Brüder Silverstolpe.* Stockholm: n.p., 1952.

MT
Musikalisches Taschenbuch auf das Jahr 1805. Edited by Friedr[ich] Theodor Mann. Penig: F. Dienemann & Co., [1806].

Müller/GESCHICHTE
Müller, Johann Heinrich Friedrich. *Geschichte und Tagebuch der Wiener Schaubühne.* Vienna: Johann Thomas Edler von Trattner, 1776.

Müller/NACHRICHTEN
_____ . *Genaue Nachrichten von beydn kaiserlich. königlichen Schaubühnen und andern öffentlichen Ergötzlichkeiten in Wien.* Vienna: von Ghelenschen Schriften, 1772.

Müller/NEUIGKEITEN
_____ . *Theatral Neuigkeiten.* Vienna: von Ghelenschen Buchhandlung, 1773.

MUENCHNER
Münchner Wochenblatt (Munich), 1801.

Murray/ROESLER-ROSETTI
Murray, Sterling E. "The Rösler-Rosetti Problem: A Confusion of Pseudonym and Mistaken Identity." *Music & Letters* 57 (April 1976): 130-43.

MW
Musikalisches Wochenblatt. Studien für Tonkünstler und Musikfreunde fürs Jahr 1792. Edited by F. Ae. Kunzen and F. Reichardt. Berlin, 1793.

NACHRICHTEN
Kurzgefasste Nachrichten von den bekanntesten deutschen Nationalbühnen überhaupt, und von dem k. k. Nationaltheater zu Wien, und der damit verbundenen Operette insbesondere. Vienna: Johann Thomas Edler von Trattner, 1779.

NEW GROVE
The New Grove Dictionary of Music and Musicians. 20 vols. Edited by Stanley Sadie. London: Macmillan Publishers Limited, 1980.

Nicolai/BESCHREIBUNG
Nicolai, Friedrich. *Beschreibung einer Reise durch Deutschland und die Schweiz, im Jahre 1781.* Berlin and Stettin: n.p., 1785.

Niemtschek/MOZART
Niemtschek, Franz. *Leben des k. k. Kapellmeisters Wolfgang Gottlieb Mozart.* Prague: In der Herrlischen Buchhandlung, 1798.

Obzyna/BURGTHEATER
Obzyna, Gertrude,ed. *Burgtheater 1776-1976.* 2 vols. Oesterreichischer Theater Band. Vienna: n.p., n.d.

Olleson/GRIESINGER
Olleson, Edward. "Georg August Griesinger's Correspondence with Breitkopf & Härtel." *Haydn Yearbook* 3 (1965): 5-53.

Olleson/SWIETEN
_____ . "Gottfried van Swieten: Patron of Haydn and Mozart." *Proceedings of the Royal Music Association* 89 (1962-63): 63-74.

Olleson/ZINZENDORF
_____ . "Haydn in the Diaries of Count Karl von Zinzendorf." *Haydn Yearbook* 2 (1963-64): 45-83.

OM
Oesterreichische Monatsschrift (Prague and Vienna), 1793-94.

Orel/MUSIKERBRIEFE
Orel, Alfred, ed. *Wiener Musikerbriefe aus zwei Jahrhunderten.* Oesterreichische Bücherei, no. 14. Edited by Friedrich Walter. Vienna and Leipzig: A. Hartleben's Verlag, n.d.

Pandi & Schmidt/PRESSBURGER
Pandi, Marianne and Schmidt, Fritz. "Musik zur Zeit Haydns und Beethovens in der Pressburger Zeitung." *Haydn Yearbook* 8 (1971): 165-266.

PARIS

Paris, Wien und London. Ein fortgehendes Panorama dieser drei Hauptstädte. Vol. 1. Rudolfstadt: Hof Buch- und Kunsthandlung, 1811.

Payer/BURGTHEATER

Payer von Thurn, Rudolf. *Joseph II als Theaterdirektor: Ungedruckte Briefe und Aktenstücke aus den Kinderjahren des Burgtheaters.* Vienna and Leipzig: Leopold Heidrich, 1920.

Pemmer/ALT-WIENER

Pemmer, Hans. "Alt-Wiener Gast- und Vergnügungsstatten." Typescript in the Wiener Stadt- und Landesarchiv.

Perinet/WTA

Perinet, Joachim. *Wiener Theater Almanach.* Vienna: Jos. Riedel, 1803, 1804, 1806.

Pezzl/BESCHREIBUNG

Pezzl, Joh[ann]. *Beschreibung und Grundriss der Haupt- und Residenzstadt Wien.* Vienna: J. V. Degen, 1809.

Pezzl/SKIZZE

[Pezzl, Johann]. *Neue Skizze von Wien.* 2 vols. Vienna: J. V. Degen, 1805.

PFEFFER

Pfeffer und Salz (Salzburg), 1786.

Pichler/DENKWUERDIGKEITEN

Pichler, Caroline. *Denkwürdigkeiten aus meinem Leben.* 4 vols. Vienna: A. Pichler's sel. Wittwe, 1844.

Pisarowitz/BAER

Pisarowitz, Karl Maria. "Der Bär den man uns aufband: Differenzierung ewig Verwechselter." *Acta Mozartiana* 20 (November 1963): 62-68.

Pohl/HAYDN

Pohl, C. F. *Joseph Haydn.* Completed by Hugo Botstiber. 3 vols. Leipzig: Breitkopf & Härtel, 1875-1927; facsimile ed., Wiesbaden: Dr. Martin Sündig oHG, 1970-71.

Pohl/TS

_____ . *Denkschrift aus Anlass des hundertjährigen Bestehens der Tonkünstler-Societät.* Vienna: Carl Gerold's Sohn, 1871.

PRAGER NZ

Prager Neue Zeitung und ihr Begleiter der Böhmische Wandersmann, 1802.

Preussner/MUSIKKULTUR
　　Preussner, Eberhard. *Die Bürgerliche Musikkultur: Ein Beitrag zur deutschen Musikgeschichte des 18. Jahrhunderts.* Hamburg: Hanseatischer Verlag, 1935.

Pribram/PREISE
　　Pribram, Alfred Francis. *Materialen zur Geschichte der Preise und Löhne in Oesterreich.* Vol. 1. Vienna: Carl Ueberreuters Verlag, 1938.

Protkhe/LEOPOLDSTADT
　　Protkhe, Joseph Ernst. *Das Leopoldstädter Theater von seiner Entstehung an skizzirt.* Vienna: Josef Stöckholzer von Hirschfeld, 1847.

PROV NACH
　　Provinzialnachrichten (Vienna), 1782-84.

PZ
　　Pressburger Zeitung, 1790-95, 1797-98, 1800, 1810.

RAPPORT
　　Rapport von Wien, 1788-89.

Reichardt/VERTRAUTE
　　Reichardt, Johann Friedrich. *Vertraute Briefe geschrieben auf einer Reise nach Wien und den österreichischen Staaten zu Ende des Jahres 1808 und zu Anfang 1809.* 2 vols. Amsterdam: Kunst- und Industrie-Comtoir, 1810.

REISEN
　　Reisen durch das südliche Teutschland. Vol. 1. Leipzig and Klagenfurth: S. L. Crusius und Friedrich Carl Walliser, 1789.

Richter/EIPELDAUER I
　　[Richter, Joseph.] *Briefe eines Eipeldauers an seinen Herrn Vetter in Krakau, über d'Wienstadt.* Vienna: Christoph Peter Rehm, 1794-97.

Richter/EIPELDAUER II
　　_____ . *Der wiederaufgelebte Eipeldauer.* Vienna: Christoph Peter Rehm, 1799-1800.

Richter/EIPELDAUER III
　　_____ . *Briefe des jungen Eipeldauers an seinen Herrn Vettern in Krakau.* Vienna: Christoph Peter Rehm, 1802-1810.

Ridendo/PLUNDER
　　Ridendo, Magister [Friedrich Hegrad]. *Wiener Plunder.* 2 vols. Vienna: Sebastian Hartl, 1784.

Rosenbaum/DIARIES
  Rosenbaum, Joseph Carl. *The Diaries of Joseph Carl Rosenbaum, 1770-1829.* Edited and translated by Else Radant. Haydn Yearbook 5.

RZ
  Realzeitung (Vienna), 1771-86.

SAMMLER
  Der Sammler (Vienna), 1809-10.

Scheib/WD
  Scheib, Wilfried. "Die Entwicklung der Musikberichterstattung im Wienerischen Diarium von 1703-1780 mit besonderer Berücksichtigung der Wiener Oper." Ph.D. dissertation. University of Vienna, 1950.

Schindler/BURGTHEATER
  Schindler, Otto G. "Der Zuschauerraum des Burgtheaters im 18. Jahrhundert: Eine baugeschichtliche Skizze." *Maske und Kothurn* 22 (1976): 20-53.

Schink/FRAGMENTE
  Schink, Johann Friedrich. *Literarische Fragmente.* Graz: n.p., 1785.

Schönfeld/JTWP
  [Schönfeld, Johann Ferdinand]. *Jahrbuch der Tonkunst von Wien und Prag.* [Vienna]: Schönfeldischer Verlag, 1796.

Schwarz/DILEKTANTEN
  Schwarz, Herr. *Ueber das Wiener Dilektanten-Konzert.* Vienna: Sebastian Hartl, 1782.

SITTENGEMAEHLDE
  Neuestes Sittengemählde von Wien. Vienna: Anton Pichler, 1801.

SONNTAGSBLATT
  Das Sonntagsblatt oder Unterhaltungen von Thomas West (Vienna), 1807-08.

Southgate/GARDENS
  Southgate, T. Lea. "Music at the Public Gardens of the 18th Century." *Proceedings of the Royal Music Association* 38 (1911-12): 141-59.

Stein/BEMERKUNGEN
  Kurze Bemerkungen über das Spielen, Stimmen und Erhalten der Fortepiano welche von den Geschwistern Stein in Wien verfertigt werden. Vienna: Albertischen Schriften, 1801.

Steptoe/MOZART
Steptoe, Andrew. "Mozart and Poverty." *The Musical Times* 125 (April 1984): 196-201.

TA 1773
Theatralalmanach von Wien, für das Jahr 1773. Vienna: Joseph Kurzböck, [1774].

TA 1774
Theatralalmanach von Wien für das Jahr 1774. Vienna: Schulzischen Schriften, [1775].

TASCHENBUCH 1777
Taschenbuch des Wiener Theaters. Vienna: Johann Thomas Edler v. Trattner, 1777.

THALIA
Thalia (Vienna), 1810-11.

THEATERKALENDER
Wiener Theaterkalender auf das Jahr 1787. Vienna: Joseph Gerold, [1788].

TJ 1808
Theater Journal . . . aller im k. k. priv. Theater an der Wien im Jahr 1808 aufgeführten Schauspiele und Opern. Vienna: n.p., 1809.

TJ 1810
Theater-Journal oder vollständige Ueberblick aller in den beyden k. k. Hoftheatern, und dem k. k. privileg. Theater an der Wien im Jahre 1810 aufgeführten Schauspiele, Opern u. Ballete. Vienna: n.p., 1811.

TK 1772
Theatralkalender von Wien, für das Jahr 1772. Vienna: Joseph Kurzböck, [1773].

Ullrich/ZMESKALL
Ullrich, Hermann. "Nikolaus Zmeskall von Domanowetz." *Wiener Figaro* 43 (January 1976): 19-25.

Vassbach/JOSEPHSTADT
Vassbach, Franz. *Theater-Almanach, der Franz Scherzerischen deutschen Schauspieler-Gesellschaft sonst genannten Bauernfeindish. Saale in der Josephst.* Vienna: Johann Joseph Jahn, 1779.

VB
Vaterländische Blätter für den oesterreichischen Kaiserstaat. (Vienna) 1808, 1810.

538

VERZEICHNISS
Vollständiges Verzeichniss der in dem k. k. privil. Theater an der Wien aufgeführten Schauspiele und Opern vom 1ten Januar bis 31ten December 1804. Vienna: n.p., 1805.

VIENNA-CAMERALE
Vienna. Hof-Kammer Archiv. Camerale, Faszikel 67: Theatral Auslage 1762-1800.

VIENNA-GDMF
Vienna. Archiv der Gesellschaft der Musikfreunde. Konzert Zettel.

VIENNA-GDMF-MAYSEDER
Vienna. Archiv der Gesellschaft der Musikfreunde. "Biography of Josef Mayseder."

VIENNA-GDMF-SONNLEITHNER
Vienna. Archiv der Gesellschaft der Musikfreunde. Leopold Sonnleithner Papiere. "Materialien zur Geschichte der Oper und des Ballets (sic) in Wien. 1te Abtheilung: Die k. k. Hoftheater; 3te Abtheilung: Das Theater in der Leopoldstadt und das Theater am Franz-Josephs Quai; 4te Abtheilung: Das Theater in der Josephstadt."

VIENNA-INTENDENZ
Vienna. Haus- Hof- und Staatsarchiv. General Intendenz der Hoftheater.

VIENNA-KABINETT
Vienna. Haus- Hof- und Staatsarchiv. Kabinettskanzlei. Wissenschaft und Kunst.

VIENNA-KOMMERZ
Vienna. Hof-Kammer Archiv. Kommerz: Litor RN 550, Nr. 55, 1753-96.

VIENNA-MUELLER
Vienna. Stadt- und Landesbibliothek; Handschriften Sammlung. "Wenzel Müllers Tagebuch."

VIENNA-ONB-MS
Vienna. Oesterreichische Nationalbibliothek; Musik Sammlung. Hoftheater Zettel, 1805-1810.

VIENNA-ONB-TS
Vienna. Oesterreichische Nationalbibliothek; Theater Sammlung. Hoftheater Zettel, 1776-1810.

VIENNA-PROTOKOL
Vienna. Haus- Hof- und Staatsarchiv. Hofparthienprotokol, 1794, 1796, 1809, 1810.

VIENNA-ROSENBAUM
Vienna. Oesterreichische Nationalbibliothek; Handschriften Sammlung. "Carl Rosenbaums Tagebücher, 1797-1810." Cod. Ser. n. 194-204.

VIENNA-SEYFRIED
Vienna. Stadt- und Landesbibliothek; Handschriften Sammlung. "Ignaz Ritter von Seyfrieds Journal des Theaters an der Wien."

VIENNA-STB
Vienna. Stadt- und Landesbibliothek. Konzert und Theater Zettel.

VIENNA-WEIGL
Vienna. Oesterreichische Nationalbibliothek; Handschriften Sammlung. "Autobiographie Joseph Weigl."

VIENNA-ZINZENDORF
Vienna. Haus- Hof- und Staatsarchiv. "Graf Karl von Zinzendorf Tagebücher, 1760-1813."

Voll/VERZEICHNISS
[Voll, Matthaeus.] *Chronologisches Verzeichniss aller Schauspiele, deutschen und italienischen Opern . . . die . . . seit dem Monath April 1794 bis wieder dahin 1807 . . . aufgeführt worden sind.* Vienna: Johann Baptist Wallishauser, 1807.

Wallace/BEETHOVEN
Wallace, Robin. *Beethoven's Critics: Aesthetic Dilemmas and Resolutions during the Composer's Lifetime.* Cambridge and New York: Cambridge University Press, 1986.

WB
Das Wienerblättchen (Vienna), 1783-91.

Weber/CONTEMPORANEITY
Weber, William. "The Contemporaneity of Eighteenth-Century Musical Taste." *The Musical Quarterly* 70 (Spring 1984): 175-94.

Weber/SOCIAL
_____ . *Music and the Middle Class: The Social Structure of Concert Life in London, Paris and Vienna.* New York: Holmes & Meier, 1975.

Wertheimer/GESCHICHTE
   Wertheimer, Eduard. "Zur Geschichte Wiens im Jahre 1809." *Archiv für österreichische Geschichte* 74 (1889): 161-202.

Weschel/LEOPOLDSTADT
   Weschel, Leopold Matthias. *Die Leopoldstadt bey Wien*. Vienna: Anton Strauss, 1824.

Wegeler & Ries/NOTIZEN
   Wegeler, F. C. and Ries, Ferdinand. *Biographische Notizen über Ludwig van Beethoven*. New edition with additions and comments by Alfr. Chr. Kalischer. Berlin and Leipzig: Schuster & Löffler, 1906.

WHTA
   Wiener Hof-Theater Almanach [Wiener Hof-Theater Taschenbuch 1805-11]. Vienna: Ph. J. Schalbacher and Joh. Bapt. Wallishausser, 1804-11.

WIEN FESTSCHRIFT
   Das Theater an der Wien. Festschrift zum 28. Mai 1962. Vienna: n.p., 1962.

WJ
   Wiener Journal für Theater, Musik und Mode, 1806.

WTA
   Wiener Theater Almanach. Vols. 1794-96. Vienna: Kurzbeckische Buchhandlung (1794), Jos. Camesina & Co., (1795-96).

WTZ
   Wiener Theater Zeitung, 1806-08. [*Zeitung für Theater, Musik und Poesie*, 1808].

Wurzbach/LEXIKON
   Wurzbach, Constant von. *Biographisches Lexikon des Kaiserthums Oesterreich*. Vienna: k. k. Hof- und Staatsdruckerei, 1856-86.

WZ
   Wiener Zeitung, 1745-1811. [*Wienerisches Diarium* 1745-80].

Zaslaw/ORCHESTRA
   Zaslaw, Neal. "Toward the Revival of the Classical Orchestra." *Proceedings of the Royal Music Association* 103 (1976-77): 158-87.

Zechmeister/THEATER
   Zechmeister, Gustav. *Die Wiener Theater nächst der Burg und nächst dem Kärntnerthor von 1747-1776*. Theatergeschichte Oesterreichs 3:2. Vienna: Hermann Böhlaus Nachf., 1971.

ZEW
Zeitung für die elegante Welt (Leipzig), 1803-10.

Zinsendorf/DIARIES
Zinsendorf, Karl. *Wien von Maria Theresia bis zur Franzosenzeit: Aus den Tagebücher des Grafen Karl von Zinsendorf.* Edited by Hans Wagner. Vienna: n.p., 1972.

Zobel & Warner/STRUCTURAL
Zobel, Konrad and Warner, Fredrich E. ''The Old Burgtheater: A Structural History, 1741-1788.'' *Theater Studies* 19 (1972-73): 19-53.

Index

Adamberger, Frau, 113
Adamberger, Joseph Valentine, 12,
    113, 122
Adolfati, Andrea, Psalm No. 6, 40
Adolfati-Wagenseil, *rovetto di Mose, Il*,
    40
Advent, 13, 39, 46, 49, 125, 204
Allgemeine Musikalische Zeitung, xvi,
    xviii, xix, 60–61, 70, 101, 120,
    135, 159, 166, 171–72, 184,
    193, 194, 200, 211, 213
amateur performance. *See* dilettante
    performance
Antonicek, Theophil, xix
Apponyi, Count Anton Georg?, 10, 16
Apponyi, Mme de, 18
Aprile, Joseph, 42, 44
Arndt, Ernst Moritz, xx, 59, 96–97, 114
Arnstein, Baron Nathan Adam von,
    17
audience
    attitude of, 22–25, 32–33, 54, 63, 78
    deportment of, 100–1, 188–89
    size of, 51, 63, 85, 89, 90, 102, 106–7,
Auernhammer, Josefa, 50, 55, 70, 159,
    166, 206, 207, 209–10, 216
Auersperg, Prince Adam von, 14, 16,
    122, 230
Auersberg, Princess, 30
Augarten, xvi, 56–59, 61, 93–98, 107,
    123, 127, 129, 134, 144, 146,
    170, 185, 186, 187, 200, 211,
    213, 226, 232

Bach, Carl Philipp Emanuel,
    *Auferstehung und
    Himmelfahrt Christi, Die*, 11,
    180
Bach, Johann Christian, 47
Bach, Johann Sebastian, 8
Baglioni, Clementina, 42
Baglioni, Rosina, 47
Bähr, Joseph, 59, 101, 172
Ballassa, Count von, 16
Bareggi, Paolo, 42
Bartelozzi, Herr, 171
Bassewitz, Countess, 3, 118
Bassewitz, Lalotte, 3
Batthyana, Count, 10
Bayr, Georg, 126, 161
Beer, Josef, 172
Beethoven, Carl, 70
Beethoven, Ludwig van, xvi, xviii,
    xix, xxii, 9, 27, 31, 70, 89, 124,
    127, 135–36, 144, 162–63, 168,
    181, 187–88, 206, 207–9, 217,
    218–20, 233, 235–36
    Christus am Oelberge, 127, 149, 219
    concertos: 159–60, 209–10; Violin
        (Op. 61), 205
    Missa Solemnis, 149
    as performer, 166
    quintets: Piano (Op. 16), 162
    Septet (Op. 20), 162
    sonatas: 189, 198; horn (Op. 17),
        162; violin (Op. 12?), 162
    symphonies: 156; No. 3, 210; No. 4,
        154

Belli, Giuseppe, 42
Belvedere Palace, 59, 62, 90, 93, 198, 226
Benda, Herr and Mme, 118
Beneventi, Maria, 42
Benucci, Herr., 113
Berger, Mlle, 55
Berlin, 200
Berlinische Musikalische Zeitung, 182, 193, 199, 205
Bernardi, Franz, 7, 134
Bernasconi, Andrea, *Betulia Liberata, La*, 40
Berwald, Franz, 133, 169
Berwald, Johann, 186
Biba, Otto, xviii, xix
Bigot de Morogues, Marie, 134, 146
Blacho, Herr, 215
Blangini, Therese, 170
Boccherini, Herr, 42
Bohdanowicz, Bazyli, 84–85, 125, 133, 157–58, 215
Boieldieu, Adrien, Duet for harp and fortepiano, 162
Bök, Anton, 146, 172
Bök, Ignaz, 146, 172
Bono, Joseph, 36
Bon-Ruvinetti, Rosa, 42
Börmann, Herr, 28
Bortoletti, Herr, 42
Braun, Baron Peter von, 1, 17, 22, 29, 30, 50, 67, 85, 103, 125, 127
Brenner, Mme, 3
Brizzi, Herr, 214
Brockmann, Herr, 113
Brunetti, Antonio, 26
Buffendorf, Baroness von, 16
Buquoy, Mme de, 14, 16, 17, 28, 229, 231
Bürgerspital, 138
Burgtheater, xvi, 11, 38, 39, 40, 46–50, 66, 68–70, 71–78, 81, 85, 90, 103, 114, 127, 131, 133, 135, 143, 153, 157, 169, 175, 185, 186, 196, 197, 216, 218, 231
Burney, Charles, xx
Bussani, Herr., 113

Caldarini, Luisa, 133
Callenberg, Count Georg Alexander Heinrich Hermann, 230–31
Calmus, Herr, 196
Calvesi, Vincenzo, 68, 113
Campi, Antonia, 214
Carlani, Carlo, 42
Casimer, Herr, 28
Catoni, Mlle, 231
Cavalieri, Caterina, 48, 113
Ceccarelli, Franz, 26, 128
chamber music, 3, 160–62
Cherubini, Luigi, 60, 106, 150, 156, 221
Cimarosa, Domenico, 5, 30, 31, 149, 150, 163
Clary family, 230–31
Clement, Franz Josef, 15, 89, 156, 159, 170, 188, 207
Clementi, Muzio, 9, 221
Colalto, Prince von, 16
Colla brothers, 47
Collaldo, Count, 36
Collona, Sgra., 42
Colloredo, Count Franz, 67
Colloredo, Joseph, 122, 231
Coltellini, Herr, 68
Comaschini, Herr, 231
concert locations, xvii, 41–45, 50
    acoustics, 106–7
    ambiance, 54, 71, 73, 75, 85, 89–90, 93, 96, 97–98, 100–4
    capacity, 75, 81, 89, 90, 102, 106
    size, 73, 75–81, 85, 89, 90, 98, 102
concerts, private
    after-dinner music, 3, 5
    ambiance, 4, 8, 20, 31
    gala occasions, 3, 10–13
    musical salons, xvii, xviii, xx, 13–20, 22–33, 36
    chamber music, participatory, 3, 8–9
    parties and celebrations, 3, 5–8
    social music, 3, 4, 19, 179
concerts, public
    advertising and publicity, 118, 120, 125, 195–99, 212–13

concerts, public (cont.)
 criticism, 49, 51, 59, 60, 84, 141,
   143–44, 158–59, 171–72,
   199–201
  reviews, critical, 197–98, 204–14
  reviews, non-critical, 196–198
  reviews, number of, 192, 199
  sexism, 217–18
  slant, 200–4, 207–10, 213
 expenses, 123, 126–30
 receipts and profits, 41–43, 47,
   51–52, 120–22, 131–39,
   198, 219
 regulations, 47, 124–25
 rehearsals, 55, 186–88
 relation to other events, xvii, 37,
   49–50, 107, 226–29
 series and societies, xv, xvii, 35–43,
   49–51, 53–61, 232–33
 sponsors
  charity fundraisers, 46, 49,
   51–53, 71, 103, 126,
   137–38, 148–49, 178–79,
   197–98
  entrepreneur, 53–61
  Friends of Music, xvii, xix, 35,
   37, 49, 61–64, 233
  virtuoso benefits, xvi, 46–52, 68,
   104, 133–37, 151, 187, 213
 ticket prices, 41, 53, 55–59, 131–35
Concerts Spirituels, 38
Conciolone, Herr, 230
Conti, Giacomo (?), 181
Conti, Herr, 198
Cramer, Johann Baptist?, 9
Crescentini, Girolamo, 214
Czerny, Karl, 166
Czerwenka, Josef, 30

d'Affliso, Giuseppe, 45–46
Dauer, Frau, 113
Deym, Countess Josephine von, 17
Dietrichstein, Prince, 10, 22
dilettante performance, 2–4, 15, 19,
   26–27, 30–31, 35, 37, 52–55,
   57–62, 96, 103–4, 127, 166,
   173, 177, 188, 200–3

Dimezzo, Pietro, 42
Distler, Herr, 113
Dittersdorf, Karl Ditters von, 42, 47,
  235
Dönst, Herr, 7,
Drechsler, Herr, 47
Dulon, Friedrich Ludwig, 153, 161
Dunger, Baron, 230
Durazzo, Count Giacomo, 39–41, 120
Durrazzo, Mme, 3
Dušek, Josefa, 127–28, 130, 133
Dussek, Jan Ladislav, 9

Eberl, Anton, 31, 70, 156, 159–60, 166,
  196, 205, 207, 210, 216, 221
 Caprice for 2 pianos, 162
Eck, Friedrich Johann (?), 127, 136
Eckhart, Herr, 7
Eigenwahl, Mlle, 215
Eipeldauer Briefe, xxi, 4
Eppinger, Heinrich, 9
Esser, Michael, 161, 171, 198
Esterházy, Count Franz, 16, 67
Esterházy, Count Franz Nikolaus, 39,
  67, 71
Esterházy, Count Johann, 7, 11–13,
  16, 180
Esterházy, Prince Nikolaus von, xxi,
  11–13, 67, 71, 112, 122

Farinelli, Giuseppi, 141
Farinelli, Maria, 42
Fayard, Herr, 171
Ferrari family, 5
financial matters
 currency, 109–111
 income, 111–14
 living expenses, 111, 114–18
Fischer, Herr and Frau, 137
Fischer, Johann Christian, 230
Fischer, John Abraham, 50–51
Fischer, Ludwig, 197
Fischer, Therese, 214
Foita, Emanuel, 159
Förster, Emanuel, 9
Francois, Herr, 44

Frank, Christina (née Gerhardi), 137, 198
Frank, Mme, 28
Franklin, Benjamin, 173
Franz Joseph I (Emperor), 103, 124
Fränzl, Ferdinand, 124–25
Freimüthige, Der, 97–98, 166, 193, 206–9, 210, 213, 219
French Ambassador, 16, 22
Friedl, Johann, 85
Fries, Count Moritz von, 13, 17, 20, 29
Fries, Mlle Victoria, 231
Fuchs, Herr, 32
Fumagalli, Mme, 48
Fürstenberg, Caroline, 5
Fürstenberg, Prince and Princess, 5, 18, 230

Gabriel, Katharina, 40, 42
Gabrielli, Franzisca, 42
Galliani, Angiolo, 132, 133
Gallieni, Giuseppe, 42
Galuppi, Balthasar, 44
Galvani. *See* Willmann-Galvani
Gassmann, Florian, xvi, 13, 47, 49
Gassmann, Marie Anna?, 113
Gassmann-Rosenbaum, Therese, xxi, 6–8, 18, 25, 31–32, 113, 122, 126, 129, 130, 168, 184, 187, 188
Gebel, Piano quintet with flute, clarinet, horn, and bassoon, 162
Gerbini, Mlle, 170, 217–18
Gesellschaft der Associierten Cavaliere, 10–11
Gesellschaft der Musikfreunde, xvii, xix, xxi–xxii, 62, 152
Gesellschaft von Kavaliere, 71, 85, 103
Gewandhaus Concerte, 35
Giacommazzi, Antonia, 42
Giacommazzi, Theresia, 42
Giardini, Giovanni Dom, 42
Gilberg, Mlle, 31
Giuliani, Mauro, 171
Gluck, Christoph Willibald, 42, 43, 47
Psalm No. 8, 40

Goldmann, Joseph, 6
Golitzin, Prince Dimitry Michajlowitsch, 3, 16, 25, 27, 229, 231
Goubeau (Goubaud), Mlle, 28
Grassalkowitz, Prince, 1
Greiner, Hofrath Franz Ritter von, 16
Griesbacher, Anton, 120
Griesinger, Georg August, 194, 211
Griessbacher, Joseph, 1
Grüch, Felice, 43
Grüch, Herr, 44
Guarducci, Tommaso, 43
Gumpenhüber, Philipp, 41, 43–45
Gyrowetz, Adalbert, 59, 168
Sonata for fortepiano, clarinet and cello, 162
Gyulas, Mlle, 6

Häckel, Herr, 171
Handel, George Frideric, 10, 12
Acis et Galathea, 12
Alexander's Feast, 11, 12, 221
Athalie, 12
Judas Maccabäus, 11, 12
Messias, Der, 11, 106, 180, 214
Ode auf den Tag der heiligen Cäcilia, 11, 12
oratorios, 11, 148, 179
Wahl Herkules, Die, 12
Hanslick, Eduard, xviii, 23–25, 158
Hantz, Frau, 113
Hardegkh, Herr, 30
Harrach, Count, 13
Hartl, Joseph, 71
Hasse, Johann Adolf, *conversione di S. Agostino, La*, 11
Hatzfeld, Countess Hortense, 103, 104
Haugwitz, Count, 17, 25, 28–29, 203
Haydn, Franz Joseph, xviii, xix, xxii, 9, 12, 31, 59, 136, 151, 163, 199, 218, 220, 221, 233, 235, 236
Isola, desabitata, L', 149
Jahreszeiten, Die, 32, 148, 169, 180
ritorno di Tobia, Il, 178–79, 183

Haydn, Franz Joseph (cont.)
  Schöpfung, Die, 12, 32, 63, 106,
    127–28, 135, 147–48, 169,
    177, 180, 186, 198, 200
  sieben Worte, Die, 12, 122, 200, 230
  Sturm, Der, 12
  symphonies, 143, 153–55
Heberle, Anton, 134, 137
Heidenreich, *Kriegslager, Das,* 157
Heiss, Regina, 161
Helman, Herr, 43, 45
Henikstein, Baron Joseph von, 16
Hensler, Karl Friedrich, 84
Hildburgshausen, Prince, 2, 16, 36
Hilverding van Wewens, Franz, 45
Hirsch, Herr, 44
Hofbauer, Karl, 89
Hoffmeister, Franz Anton, 160
Hohenadel, Mlle, 160, 166, 196, 216–17
Holleschek, Herr, 8
Hoyos family, 231
Hoyos, Mme, 230
Hummel, Johann Nepomuk, 9, 217
  Sonata for 2 fortepianos, 162
  Trio in E-flat, 162

Intelligenzblatt der Annalen der
    Literatur und Kunst in den
    österreichischen Staaten, 193,
    204–5

Jacob, K., 206, 213
Jacobi, Mme, 32
Jahn, Ignaz, 11, 93, 96, 98, 101–2, 106,
    107, 123, 125, 129, 132, 133,
    135, 139, 196
Janisch, Herr, 48
Jauzer, Herr, 44
Jomelli, Niccolo, *Sacrificio d'Abramo, Il,*
    40
Joseph II (Emperor), 58, 68, 93, 96, 97,
    218
Jublonowsky family, 3

Kalb family, 231
Kalkbrenner, Frédéric, 166, 220
Kannabich, Christian, Violin duet, 162

Karner, Herr, 7, 130
Kärntnerthortheater, 38, 46–50, 53, 66,
    68–71, 78–82, 84, 85, 90, 104,
    114, 131, 143, 174–75, 216, 230
Kauer, Ferdinand, 84, 215
  Begebenheiten des Wiener
    Aufgeboths, Die, 157
  Geschichte des Wiener Aufgeboths,
    Die, 157
  Nelson's Schlact, 157
  Wind sextet, 162
Kaunitz, Prince Wenzel Anton, 118,
    231
Kees, Franz Georg Ritter von, xvi, 16,
    30, 36, 57–59, 179, 203
Kees, Hofrath von, 16
Keller, Herr, 31
Kellerin, Carolina, 43
Kelly, Michael, 120
Khevenhüller-Metsch, Johann Josef,
    45, 67
Kienmayer, Baron Johann Michael, 67
Kinsky, Prince, 12
Kirchgessner, Marianne, 146, 173
Klein, Rudolph, 219
Kleinhardt, Johann Thomas, 127–28
Klengel, Herr, 220
Klöffler, Johann Friedrich, 157, 175,
    177, 196
Koch, Heinrich Christoph, 169–70
Kohary, Count Johann, 45–46
Korn, Herr, 8
Kotzebue, August von, 206
Koželuch, Leopold, 4, 9, 52, 153, 235
Kraft, Anton, 171–72
Kraft, Baroness, 28
Kraft, Nicolas, 171–72
Kraus, Joseph Martin, 114, 169
Kreutzer, Conradin, 133, 134, 216
  Piano sonata with violin
    accompaniment, 162
Kruft (Gruft), Baron, 31
Krumpholz, Herr, 47
Küfstein, Count Johann Ferdinand,
    67
Kühnel, Herr, 7
Kurzböck, Mlle, 212, 217

Kurzen, Mme, 47
Küttner, Carl Gottlob, xx, 13, 115

La Motte, Franz, 46
Lafont, Charles Philippe, 198
Lamberg, Herr, 231
Lang, Herr, 32, 113
Lange (née Weber), Aloysia, 12, 113, 230
Latzl, Herr, 8
Lausch, Klara, 170
Lebruns, 136
Leipzig, 200
Lent, xx, 13, 38–41, 43–46, 49, 51, 54–55, 68–69, 194, 197, 198, 204, 228, 232, 234
Leppich, Franz, 134
Lichnowsky, Prince Karl, 9, 188
Lichtenstein, Prince, 12
Lieber, Herr, 8
Liebhaber Concerte, xix, 62–63, 100, 107, 127, 169, 170, 73 202, 204, 221, 233
Liechtenstein, Jean, 5
Liechtenstein, Prince Louis, 126–27
Linke, J., 9
Liparsky, Herr, 32, 169
Lippe, Mme de la, 230
Lippe family, 231
Liszt, Franz, 167
Lobkowitz, Prince Franz Maximilian von, 16, 17
Lobkowitz, Prince Joseph, 5, 10, 12, 15, 16, 20–21, 23, 26–28, 67, 71, 171, 179, 188, 229, 230
Lodron, Count Hieronymus, 67, 71
Longhi, Carolina, 134
Lotz, Theodor, 172
Louis of Prussia, Prince, 28
Lucchi, Tommaso, 43
Lusini, 133

Maffoli, Herr, 113
Magazin der Musik, 192, 218
Mälzel, Johann Nepomuk, 173
Manzi family, 231

Mara, Gertrude Elisabeth, 134, 136, 187
Marchand, Heinrich, 129, 136
Marchesi, Luigi, 214
Marconi, Marianna, 165, 215
Maria Theresia (Empress), xxi, 39–40, 97
Marinelli, Carl, 81
Marinelli, Franz, 85
Marschal, Herr, 231
Martin, Philipp Jacques, xvi, 53–58, 98, 233
Martines, Marianna von, 17
Martín y Soler, Vincent, 5, 150, 230
Masi, Violante, 43
Maximilian, Archduke, 168
Mayer, Herr, 174
Mayer, Pepi, 7
Mayer (Mayr), Simon, 141, 150
Mayern, Hofrath Baron von, 17
Mayseder, Joseph, 9, 101, 170
Mazzanti, Ferdinando, 43
Mehlgrube, 48, 50–51, 53, 55, 63, 98, 101, 106, 107, 123, 136
Méhul, Étienne-Nicolas, 28, 156
Merkel, Gottlieb, 206
Mestrino, Herr, 62
Metternich, Mme de, 30
Meyer, Hofrath von, 17
Milliko, Joseph, 47
Mitsch, Herr, 171
Moreau, Herr, 7, 8
Morichelli, Anna?, 231
Morning Chronicle, 36, 199
Moscheles, Ignaz, 166
Mozart, Constanze, 124–25, 136, 149
Mozart, Leopold, 51, 128–130, 136, 235
Mozart, Maria Anna, (Nannerl), 51
Mozart, Wolfgang Amadeus, xvi, xviii, xix, xxii, 8–9, 11, 18–20, 26, 30, 50–51, 55–56, 101, 115, 121–23, 126–28, 135–36, 149, 150, 153, 161–63, 168, 197–98, 210, 218–21, 233–36
Clemenza di Tito, La, 149, 214
concertos: 158–60; piano in C, 212; piano in d, 216

Mozart, W.A. (cont.)
  as performer, 166
  quintets: winds (K.452), 161, 162;
    winds and glass
    harmonica (K.617), 161–62
  Requiem, 11, 149
  sonatas: piano (four hands), 162;
    violin (K.454), 161
  symphonies, 156
Müller, Iwan, 134, 172
Müller, Wenzel, 84, 215
Müllner, Josepha, 30, 172
Musikalisches Taschenbuch, 193, 200
Musikalisches Wochenblatt, 200
Muzzarelli, Herr and Frau, 114

Naderman, François Joseph, 172
Nani, Mlle, 230
Napoleon Bonaparte, 122
Nasolini, Sebastiano, 30, 150
Naumann, Johann Gottlieb, 29
Navara, Francesco Vicaro von, 174
Nicolai, Friedrich, 13, 53, 56, 100–1,
    143–44, 200
Nitschner, Franz, 6
Norma days, 39, 66, 68, 84

Oettingen, Countess, 230
Oettingen, Prince, 230
Oettingen, Princess, 5
orchestra
  direction of, 11, 169–70, 180–83, 198
  placement of, 183–86
  private concerts, 1, 6–8, 11–12, 15,
    31–32
  size and composition, 11–13,
    32–33, 179–80
  public concerts, xvi, 127–28, 174–79
  use of, 96, 126–27, 141–42, 168
Orsini-Rosenberg, Count Franz
    Xaver, 67
Österreichische Monatsschrift, 193, 199,
    213

Paar, Prince, 10, 14, 16, 17
Paisiello, Giovanni, 30, 150, 235
Palffy, Count Ferdinand, 67, 71

Pär, Ferdinando, 28, 141, 150, 211
Pär, Francesca Ricardi, 150
Paradies, Marie Therese, 17, 103
Paradies, Regierungsrath von, 17
Pellegrini, Baron, 231
performance customs
  accompaniment of pieces, 28, 31,
    167–68
  continuo, use of, 12, 168–70
  encores, 188–89
  harpsichord, use of, 12, 166–70
  ornamentation, 214–15
  partial performance, 152–54, 158
  piano, use of, 4, 28, 51, 166–69
  winds, 15, 55, 58
Pezzl, Johann, xx–xxi, 115–16
Pfeiffer, Herr, 32, 162, 215
Piccini, Luigi, 47
Pichl, Herr, 47
Pichler, Caroline, 23
Pilaja, Catharina, 43
Pixis, Friedrich Wilhelm, 134, 146
Pixis, Johann Peter, 134, 146, 166, 205
Pleyel, Ignace Joseph, 4, 9, 153
  Cello duet, 162
Ployer, Gottfried Ignaz von, 16
Poggi, Herr, 47
Pohl, Herr, 120–21
Porpora, Nicolas, 43
  choruses, 40
Posch, Johann, 134
Prager Neue Zeitung, 192, 193, 199
Prener, Fräulein, 113
Pressburger Zeitung, 192, 193, 199, 212
Provinzialnachrichten, 193
programs, xix–xx
  length, 27–28, 53–54, 59, 144–47
  order of pieces, 142–44
  type of pieces, 15, 28–33, 40, 49,
    52–53, 60, 141–44
    chamber, 8–9, 160–62
    symphonic, 30–31, 142–44,
      151–60
    vocal, 4–5, 10, 148–51
Pugnani, Herr, 43
Punto (Johann Wenzel Stich), 9, 172,
    189, 198

Quarin, Herr, 17

Ramm, Friedrich, 230
Rasumofsky, Prince Andreas
        Kyrillowitsch, 9–10, 59, 170
Rautenstrauch, Herr Lizentiat von, 52
Realzeitung, 47, 193, 194, 198–99, 212
Redoutensaal (Grosser and Kleiner),
        53, 70, 102–7, 124, 129, 132,
        133, 136, 137, 146, 183, 185,
        187, 204, 229, 232
Reicha, Antoine, 48
    Quintet for harmonica with
            strings, 162
Reichardt, Johann Friedrich, xx, 10,
        23–24, 27–28, 127, 144, 187
Renuer, Herr, 3
Revaj, Mme de, 30
Rhem, Barbara, 43
Richter, Georg Friedrich, 50–51
Richter, Joseph, xxi
Ries, Ferdinand, 166, 187
Riesbeck, Kaspar, xvi
Righini, Vincenzo, 221, 235
Ringbauer, Josepha (Pepi), 6, 8, 170
Rittersburg, Mme de, 15, 17
Rochus de la Presti, Baron, 39
Rode, Pierre, 160
Röllig, Karl Leopold, 173
Romberg, Anton, Bernard, or
            Andreas, 9, 132, 136
Romberg, Bernhard, 120, 171, 198,
        220, 221
    Duet for 2 cellos, 162
Roselli, Franc., 43
Rosenbaum, Joseph Carl, xxi, 5–8,
        13–14, 24–25, 101, 106, 122,
        126, 127, 129, 144, 146, 168,
        180, 184–85, 188
Rosetti, Herr. *See* Rösler, Franz Anton
Rösler, Franz Anton, 154
Rösner, Herr, 142–43
Rossbach, Christian, 85, 89
Roth, Johann Georg, 173
    Variations for cello with
            fortepiano
            accompaniment, 162

Rotlauf, Herr, 8
Rudolph, Herr, xvi, 58, 59

Saal, Ignaz, 12, 113
Saint Marx Bürgerspital, 52
Sais, Mlle, 44
Saiz, Sigra., 43
Sala, Baroness, 180
Salieri, Antonio, xvi, 6, 28, 113, 114,
        183, 185, 187
Salzburg, Archbishop of, 122
Sammartini (?), Giuseppi or
        Giovanni, 40, 44
Sammler, Der, 27, 193, 199, 213
Sarphoun, Saint M de, 3
Sarti, Giuseppi, 150
Sattmann, Herr, 8
Sattmann, Mme, 7–8
Scaramelli, Alessandro, 134
Schewel, Mlle, 231
Schikaneder, Elenore, 85
Schikaneder, Emanuel, 85
Schindlöcker, Herr, 196
Schmidt, Herr, 7–8
Schmierer family, 14, 18, 25, 31, 32, 169
Schmierer, Herr, 17, 180
Schneider, Quartet for 4 bassoons, 162
Scholl, Herr, 8
Schönfeld, Johann Ferdinand Ritter
        von, 14, 170
Schönfeld, Mme, 28
Schreyer family, 7
Schubb, Hofrath von, 17, 18, 31
Schudel, Herr, 230
Schuppanzigh, Ignaz, 9, 53, 58–61, 97,
        133, 134, 146, 170, 181, 200,
        203, 221, 232
Schuster family, 31, 32
Schuster, Vincenz, 134
Schütz, Heinrich, 29
Schwarzenberg, Prince Joseph
        Johann Nepomuk, 1, 5,
        10–14, 16, 17, 25, 67, 71, 180,
        230
Schwarzenberg, Princess Therese
        von, 5, 28, 231

Seidler, Ferdinand August, 134
Sekendorf, Herr, 230
Selliers, Joseph, 38–39
Sessi, Marianna, 113, 134, 141
Simoni, Josef, 8, 18, 198
Smrezka, Joseph Christian, 153
social class, 223–28
    mixing of, xvii–xviii, 22–27, 32–33,
        202–3, 228–29, 232
    patrons, 6, 14–17, 123, 228
    private concert audiences, 2,
        22–25, 229
    public concert audiences, 75, 78,
        85, 97–98, 100, 103–4, 111,
        229, 232
Sommariva, Diego, 137
Spazier, Carl, 182
Sperger, Joseph, 171
Spielmann, Baron Anton von, 17, 30
Spielmann, Mlle, 217
Spork, Count Wenzel, 45
Stäbel, Herr, 28
Stadler, Anton, 172
Stamitz, Carl, 171
Starhemberg, Count, 120
Starhemberg, Mme de, 231
Starhemberg, Prince Adam Georg, 25,
        89, 103
Starhemberg, Princess Luise von, 17
Starzer, Joseph, 11
Stegmayer, Herr, 8
Steibelt, Daniel, 206
    Duet for harp and fortepiano, 162
    Piano duet, 162
Stemberg family, 28
Stephani, Herr, 113
Sternberg, Count Franz, 127
Steubel, Mme, 28
Storace, Nancy, 113, 136, 198, 229
Strak family, 32
Strassoldo, Count Vinzenz, 67
Streicher, Johann, 184
Strinasacchi, Regina, 170
Stritetz, Countess Josephine Deym
        von, 9
Sturioni, Herr, 8
Süssmayer, Franz Xaver, 52–53, 147

Swieten, Baron Gottfried van, 8,
        10–11, 13, 17, 30, 55, 149, 194

Tandler, Herr, 8
Tepfer, Babet, 7
Thalia, 193, 204
Thauernathy, Herr von, 16, 30
Thayer, Alexander Wheelock, xvi
Theater an der Wien, 84–85, 90–92,
        124, 127, 132, 149, 156, 167,
        170, 174, 176, 216
Theater auf der Wieden, 85, 89, 90
Theater in der Josephstadt, 81
Theater in der Leopoldstadt, 53, 81,
        84–90, 127, 132, 133, 151,
        156–57, 174, 176, 215
Thoren, Chaminesse de, 5
Thun, Caroline, 231
Thun, Countess, 122, 231
Thurn, Mme de, 16
Thurner, Franz, 66, 68
Tibaldi, Pietro, 43
Tomasini, Alois Basil Nikolaus, 31
Tomášek, Jan Křtitel, 221
Tomeoni, Irene, 113
Tonkünstler Societät, 46, 48–49, 51,
        69, 127, 131, 137, 138, 178,
        183–84, 200, 204, 231, 234
Torre, Teresa, 43
Torti, 43
Trattnerhof, 50, 123
Trautmansdorf, Count, 12–13
Türk, Herr, 55

Ugarte, Count Johann Wenzel, 67
Ulrich, Herr, 47
Umlauf, Ignaz, 6–8, 12, 113, 169, 183,
        187
Umlauf, Liese, 7
Umlauf, Pepi, 6
University Aula, 63, 107, 177
Ursel, Mme, 231

Vanhal, Johann Baptist, 9
Varenne, Mme, 172

INDEX

*Vaterländische Blätter für den
österreichischen Kaiserstaat,*
xix, 22, 193, 202–4
Venetian Ambassador, 16, 231
Verri, Herr, 206
Viotti, Giovanni Battista, 160
Vogel. *See* Vogl
Vogl, Johann Michael, 18
Vogler, Abbé Georg Joseph, 89, 147,
149, 156, 167, 189, 211
Vulcani, Herr, 114

Wagenseil, Georg Christoph, 43, 45
Gioas, 40
Redenzione, La, 40
Wallenstein, Mme de, 16
Wanhal. *See* Vanhal
Weidinger, Anton, 146, 173
Weidinger brothers, 7
Weigl, Joseph Franz, 18, 27, 114, 186
Weigl, Mme, 122
Weiglin, Mme, 47
Weilburg, Prince, 230
Weilen, Herr, 6
Weinmüller, Karl, 28
Weisin, Mme, 47
Weiskerns, Friedrich Wilhelm, 71
Weiss, Franz, 9
Weissenbach, Herr, 32
Went, Johann Neopmuk, 159
Widows and Orphans Society. *See*
Tonkünstler Societät
*Wiener Journal für Theater, Musik und
Mode,* 193, 194, 206, 213
Wiener Theater Zeitung, 193, 194, 205–6
Wiener Zeitung (Wienerisches Diarium),
38, 47, 48, 53, 62, 68, 101, 118,
129, 135, 154, 177, 191, 193,
195–99, 212, 234

Wienerblättchen, Das, 68, 118, 193, 198,
212, 234
Willmann-Galvani, Johanna, 198
Wilzek family, 5
Windischgrätz, Count, 25
Witt, Friedrich, 59
*Wöchentliche Nachrichten die Musik
betreffend,* 36, 199
Wohlthätigkeitsanstalten, 52, 138,
178, 183
Wolf, Louis, 134, 171
Woller, Herr and Mme, 7
Woscicka, Herr, 44
Woyna, Mme de, 3
Wranitzky, Anton, 186
Wranitzky, Anton or Paul, 9, 28, 30,
59, 153, 183, 220, 234
Wranitzky, Karoline Seidler, 18
Wranitzky, Paul, 30, 181, 185, 186, 200
Wrbna-Freudenthal, Count Rudolf,
30, 67
Würth, Herr von, 15, 17, 30–31, 170,
179, 207, 221

Zeitung für die elegante Welt, 60, 171,
193, 209–11, 219
Zeuner, Karl, 134, 136, 205
Zichy, Count Stephan, 67, 71
Zichy, Francoise, 28
Zinzendorf, Count Karl von, xxi, 3, 5,
14–15, 20, 24–27, 30–31, 97,
103, 167, 168, 228–29
Zmeskall, Nikolaus, 9
Zois, Baroness von, 17
Zumsteeg, Johann Rudolf, 151